Farwell's Rules
of the
Nautical Road

Farwell's Rules of the Nautical Road

Originally known as
The Rules of the Nautical Road
by Captain Raymond F. Farwell

Fifth Edition prepared by
Frank E. Bassett, Commander, U.S. Navy
Richard A. Smith, Commander, Royal Navy

Naval Institute Press   Annapolis, Maryland

Library of Congress Catalog Card Number: 77-74417
ISBN: 0-87021-182-X
Fifth Edition

The opinions and assertions of the authors of this
book are personal ones and do not necessarily
reflect the views of either the Navy or the naval
service as a whole.

Contents

Illustrations

Preface to the Fifth Edition

This book was first published in 1941 as *The Rules of the Nautical Road*, by the late Captain Raymond F. Farwell, U. S. Naval Reserve. Since its first publication, numerous statutory and regulatory changes have been made in both local and international nautical rules. Such changes automatically necessitate revisions of any authoritative texts pertaining to this subject, and hence the book has been revised whenever occasion demanded.

Over the years, common usage has made Captain Farwell's name synonymous with the book itself; accordingly, since the Fourth Edition it has been titled *Farwell's Rules of the Nautical Road*.

Among the specific statutory and regulatory actions resulting in changes may be listed the following:

Executive Order 9083, effective 1 March 1942, which transferred the functions of the former Bureau of Marine Inspection and Navigation to the U. S. Coast Guard. The authority reposing in the Board of Supervising Inspectors, Bureau of Marine Inspection and Navigation, to promulgate Pilot Rules to supplement and have co-jurisdiction with the local statutory rules was thereby temporarily given to the Commandant, U. S. Coast Guard.

Reorganization Plan No. 3 of 1946, effective 16 July 1946, which made the transfer of the functions of the former Bureau of Marine Inspection and Navigation to the U. S. Coast Guard permanent.

The renumbering and reorganization of the Code of Federal Regulations, effective 30 November 1948, which resulted in the renumbering of the respective Pilot Rules.

Public Law 544, 80th Congress, i.e., Act of May 21, 1948, effective 1 January 1949, relating to and revising the statutory rules for the prevention of collisions on certain inland waters of the United States and on the western rivers.

The 1948 International Conference on Safety of Life at Sea at London, which, in addition to revising the 1929 International Convention for the Safety of Life at Sea, revised the International Rules drawn up in 1889 at a

Conference of twenty-six maritime nations, adopted by this country in 1890, and put into effect in 1897.

Public Law 172, 82nd Congress, i.e., Act of October 11, 1951, adopting the 1948 revision of the International Rules and authorizing the President to fix their effective date by Presidential Proclamation.

The announcement by the United Kingdom on 19 December 1952, in accordance with the provisions of the Final Act of the 1948 International Conference on Safety of Life at Sea, *of the effective date of the revised International Rules as 1 January 1954.*

Public Law 232, 83rd Congress, i.e., Act of August 8, 1953, extending the applicability of the Inland Rules and the Pilot Rules published pursuant thereto to the Mobile River and its tributaries above Choctaw Point.

Public Law 552, 84th Congress, i.e., Act of June 4, 1956, revising the lights required to be carried by motorboats when in inland waters, the western rivers, or the Great Lakes.

Public Law 350, 85th Congress, i.e., Act of March 28, 1958, extending Great Lakes Rules to foreign vessels and increasing penalties for violation of Great Lakes Rules.

Public Law 635, 85th Congress, i.e., Act of August 14, 1958, amending rules regarding towing lights and stern lights in inland waters and western rivers.

Public Law 658, 85th Congress, i.e., Act of August 14, 1958, clarifying authority to establish pilot rules in inland waters and western rivers and increasing penalties for violation of Inland Rules.

The 1960 International Conference on Safety of Life at Sea, at London, which proposed numerous changes to International Rules revised by the 1948 Conference, as well as making various recommendations as to how to use radar as an aid in avoiding collisions.

Public Law 84, 88th Congress, i.e., Act of August 5, 1963, revising anchorage regulations for vessels at anchor in inland waters.

Public Law 131, 88th Congress, i.e., Act of September 24, 1963, adopting the 1960 revision of the International Rules, and authorizing the President to proclaim same effective at a subsequent date.

Public Law 163, 88th Congress, i.e., Act of October 30, 1963, providing for special regulations for vessels passing under low bridges built on navigable waters of the United States.

Proclamation 3632 by the President on 29 December 1964, that the 1948 International Rules would be rescinded and the 1960 International Rules made effective on 1 September 1965.

Public Law 670, 89th Congress, i.e., Act of October 15, 1966, transferring functions, powers, and duties of the Secretary of the Army re water vessel anchorage in *special anchorage areas* to the Secretary of Transportation.

Public Law 764, 89th Congress, effective 3 February 1967, requiring small sail vessels and power boats under 65 feet to keep clear of larger vessels when in narrow channels.

The transfer of the Coast Guard on 1 April 1967 from the Department of the Treasury *to the Department of Transportation.*

Miscellaneous revisions and amendments to the Pilot Rules since the first edition, dated February 1941.

The 1972 International Convention on Revision of the International Regulations for Preventing Collisions at Sea, at London, that proposed numerous changes, including a major editorial reorganization, to the International Rules revised by the 1960 Conference.

The IMCO Recommendation on Navigational Watchkeeping, which gives guidance on standards pertinent to the rules of the road, particularly on the subject of lookout.

Public Law 340, 92nd Congress, i.e., Act of July 10, 1972, known as the Ports and Waterways Safety Act of 1972, which authorizes the establishment of vessel traffic services in the navigable waters of the United States.

The Vessel Bridge-to-Bridge Radiotelephone Act, effective 1 January 1973, requiring certain vessels to maintain watch on a radiotelephone while underway on the navigable waters of the United States.

The International Maritime Consultative Organization (IMCO) Resolution of 20 November 1973 adopting Routing Systems on the high seas, in harmony with the International Regulations for Preventing Collisions at Sea, 1972.

The announcement by IMCO in June 1976 in accordance with the provisions of Article IV of the 1972 Convention on the International Regulations for Preventing Collisions at Sea, of the effective date of the revised International Rules as 15 July 1977.

The acceptance by the President of the United States on 12 December 1975 of the 1972 Convention on the International Regulations for Preventing Collisions at Sea, and the *deposit of this acceptance with IMCO,* effective 23 November 1976.

The major impetus for the publication of this edition was due to the significant changes to the International Rules of the Road as contained in the International Regulations for Preventing Collisions at Sea, 1972, that went into effect world wide on 15 July 1977. Much legislative and regulatory work remains to be accomplished to fully implement the revised International Rules into United States law. Many references in this edition are concerned with the existing law, which has yet to be amended in legislative due course. It is not expected that the intent of these references will be significantly changed.

Special thanks are due to William H. Tate, Lieutenant, U. S. Naval Reserve, for his significant work in the revision of Part II of this edition and to M. W. Oehler, Lieutenant, U. S. Navy, for his contribution to portions of Part I.

This book is dedicated to the proposition that obedience to the rules is the surest way to avoid collision. As long as differences in the rules for the high seas and the inland waters are allowed to persist, an accurate knowledge of these differences must continue to be one of the mariner's most important items of professional equipment.

Frank E. Bassett
Commander, U. S. Navy

Richard A. Smith
Commander, Royal Navy

Preface to the First Edition

Marine Collision Law has too long been a specialty of judges on the admiralty bench and of a very limited number of admiralty lawyers at the bar. It should, of course, be instead a specialty of the mariner on the bridge. The present book is planned to satisfy the needs of classes in seamanship such as those at the Naval Academy and at Naval R.O.T.C. colleges, and at the same time to serve as a useful handbook on the subject for the officers at sea in the actual practice of navigation. To this two-fold end an adequate amount of case material has been included, and in addition an index sufficiently comprehensive so that ready references may be made to any desired rule.

To the man on the bridge it may be superfluous to say that a collision situation is neither the time nor the place for him to look up the law that determines his proper action. But it must be pointed out that the alternative is such a thorough understanding of his duty in every situation that his action will almost instinctively be the proper one from the standpoint of both law and seamanship. It is said that Admiral Knight required his officers to read through the rules of the road each time before getting underway. Certain it is that the complexity of rules effective under American law makes frequent study of them both desirable and necessary.

As teacher and practical mariner of some experience, the writer believes that a clear, definite, positive knowledge of the principles here presented should be an essential part of the professional equipment of every man on the bridge engaging in the practice of navigation. Court decisions in an overwhelming number prove that nearly all marine collisions follow violations of the rules of the road. The inference is that the rules, if implicitly obeyed, are practically collision-proof. It is the writer's opinion that most of this seeming disregard of the law is due to misunderstanding of the rules as interpreted by the courts. The rules will not be better obeyed until they are better understood. Such a better understanding by the mariner is the primary purpose of this book.

Raymond F. Farwell
Captain, U. S. Naval Reserve

University of Washington
December 15, 1940

Part I

The Rules of the Nautical Road

1
Summary of Changes in International Rules*

On 15 July 1977, all mariners will sail under the revised International Rules of the Road, technically known as the International Regulations for Preventing Collisions at Sea, 1972. These rules apply to all international waters and to local waters of those countries having adopted them which do not have different local rules of their own. They supersede the International Rules revised in 1960 and placed in effect in 1965, thereby making it necessary for mariners to familiarize themselves with all the changes brought about by the provisions of the revised rules. It is the purpose of these pages to draw attention to the principal changes in order that those familiar with the 1960 International Rules may quickly and readily determine the nature and the extent of the changes. For the detailed consideration of any point in question it is suggested the reader refer to the index.

In addition to substantive alterations to the rules, major editorial changes have been made. The Steering and Sailing Rules now appear before the rules prescribing lights and shapes. The 1960 Radar Annex has been incorporated into the main body of the 1972 Rules. Technical material, of more interest to the shipbuilder than to the mariner, has been extracted from the rules and placed in Annexes. Provision is made for amendments to the rules to be introduced without recourse to a full-scale revision

---

*The reader will note variations in spelling and usage throughout this book. For instance, certain words are spelled in different ways: sidelights and side lights, colored and coloured, all round and all around, draught and draft. These differences are due in part to the British style in which the International Rules were written, and the American style in which the U. S. rules are phrased. There are also differences among the various U.S. rules, reflecting the exact form in which they were established by Acts of Congress. It is not permissible to alter spelling and usage to bring the style of the various Rules into common agreement.

conference. However, despite these changes in the 1972 Regulations, a comparison with the 1960 Regulations reveals that to a very large extent they remain comparable. In other words, the changes are of an evolutionary nature.

PART A—GENERAL

Application

RULE 1 1. The 1960 Rules exemption for lights and shapes to military vessels of special construction has been extended to all vessels and has been expanded to include sound signaling apparatus. Since seaplanes are now considered vessels within the meaning of the rules they no longer warrant mention because of their special construction.

2. The 1960 Rules giving governments the right to make special rules for the additional lights or whistle signals of warships, convoys, and vessels fishing as a fleet are now included in this rule. Again, reference to the seaplane as a unique case has been deleted.

3. Special rules made by an appropriate authority are now authorized, rather than a "special rule duly made by local authority." In addition, there is an admonition for such special rules to conform as closely as possible to the 1972 Rules.

4. A new provision is that the Intergovernmental Maritime Consultative Organization (IMCO) is authorized to adopt traffic separation schemes.

Responsibility

RULE 2 This rule takes in both the old "Rule of Good Seamanship" and the "General Prudential Rule." The former has been expanded to include failure to comply with all of the rules rather than the simple neglect to carry lights or signals. The latter is almost identical to the old rule, replacing "limitations of the craft" with "limitations of the vessels." Excluded is the requirement to keep a proper lookout, which is now covered in 1972 Rule 5.

General Definitions

RULE 3 1. The word "vessel" now includes nondisplacement craft and seaplanes. Thus surface effect ships, hovercraft, hydrofoils, and seaplanes are considered as ordinary vessels within the rules.

2. The definition of "sailing vessel" is now expressed in more positive terms, stressing the nonuse of propelling machinery.

3. The term "engaged in fishing" has been expanded to include any fishing apparatus that restricts maneuverability. Trolling lines remain excluded.

4. The term "vessel not under command" is defined for the first time. The reason why a vessel may be considered not under command is clarified.

5. A new definition is a "vessel restricted in her ability to manoeuvre," which encompasses the activities of cable and pipe layers, dredgers, and ships engaged in replenishing underway, flight operations, or minesweeping. Included is a new category of vessels engaged in difficult towing operations.

6. A new provision is the term "vessel constrained by her draught." It recognizes the maneuvering limitations of large vessels operating in shallow seas or channels. However, phrased as it is, this rule applies not only to deep-draft vessels but to any vessel similarly constrained.

7. Instead of repeating the conditions that constitute restricted visibility as a preamble to each relevant rule, the term has been placed in Rule 3 concerning definitions. Sandstorms are now added to the list of conditions.

PART B—STEERING AND SAILING RULES

Section 1—Conduct of Vessels in any Condition of Visibility

Application

RULE 1 A new rule that states that the rules in this section apply in both clear and restricted visibility. This rule in fact recognizes that ships do navigate in conditions of restricted visibility.

Lookout

RULE 5 A new rule that goes much further than the 1960 Rule 29 that made reference to "any neglect to keep a proper lookout." The term "lookout" now includes the use of sight and hearing as well as any other available means appropriate. This is mandatory on all vessels and at all times.

Safe Speed

RULE 6 On the whole a new rule, but based on the concept of "moderate speed" found in the 1960 Rules and Radar Annex. The term "safe speed" replaces "moderate speed" and, unlike the latter, must be maintained at all times and in all visibilities. A list of factors to be taken into account in determining a safe speed is given.

Risk of Collision

RULE 7 An amalgam of the old preliminary to the 1960 Steering and Sailing Rules and the Radar Annex. New features are that all available means appropriate must be used to determine risk of collision and that proper use of operational radar, including plotting, is mandatory. In discussing change of bearing, warning is given that risk of collision can still exist with vessels at close range, even though an appreciable bearing change is evident. This rule applies in all visibilities.

Action to Avoid Collision

RULE 8 1. Basically unchanged from various 1960 Rules but with more positive wording. Action taken "to avoid collision shall . . . be positive" rather than "should" as in the 1960 Rules. Mariners are required to check "until . . . finally past and clear" that their actions taken to avoid collision "shall . . . result in passing at a safe distance."

2. Alterations of course and/or speed now have to be large enough to be readily apparent to another vessel, whether she be observing visually or by radar.

3. The 1960 rule requiring a vessel to "slacken her speed or stop or reverse" has been reworded and made more explicit. It now applies to all vessels, not just those in sight of each other, and not merely to avoid collision, but also to "allow more time to assess the situation."

Narrow Channels

RULE 9 1. All vessels, not just power-driven vessels, are now required to keep not merely to the starboard side of a channel, but "as near to the outer limit . . . as is safe and practicable."

2. Small vessels and sailing vessels are enjoined in stronger language not to impede the passage of vessels restricted to a narrow channel or fairway.

3. A vessel engaged in fishing is similarly instructed not to impede the passage of vessels restricted to a channel. The 1960 Rules stated a vessel fishing must not obstruct a fairway, which implied a total ban on activities, such as drift nets, across a channel. The new rule, however, implies that such type of fishing could be undertaken if the channel was not being used by other vessels.

4. A new rule prohibits vessels crossing narrow channels or fairways from impeding the passage of vessels confined to the channel. If such a meeting inadvertently takes place, and both vessels are in sight of each other, then the rules for the crossing situation apply.

5. A new rule adopts the principle of signals of proposal and agreement, at present used under U.S. Inland Rules, for vessels overtaking in narrow channels when the privileged vessel must move over to permit passing. Despite this rule coming under Section 1, conduct of vessels in any visibility, the appropriate signals referred to are found under new Rule 34 which applies only to vessels in sight of one another. Thus, overtaking which requires the lead vessel to take assisting action, can only take place when the two vessels are in sight. Notwithstanding any agreement reached, the overtaking vessel is still strictly bound by new Rule 13, i.e., she remains burdened.

6. All vessels, not just power-driven vessels, are now required to exer-

cise caution and sound the appropriate signal on approaching a blind bend.

7. A new rule prohibits, "if the circumstances of the case admit," anchoring in a narrow channel.

Traffic Separation Schemes

RULE 10 1. A totally new rule that provides guidance for vessels using traffic separation schemes, but only those schemes adopted by IMCO. The qualification is important, as there are, in various parts of the world, traffic separation schemes introduced by governments without consulting IMCO. In these schemes are found variations in principles and wording from those used by IMCO.

2. The rule basically requires vessels using the schemes to keep to lanes flowing in the same direction. Provisions are made for local and crossing traffic and their relation to the scheme, as well as for emergencies and fishing vessels. The use, by through traffic, of inshore traffic zones is discouraged but not prohibited. Indeed, the use of traffic separation schemes themselves is not mandatory, but a number of governments have introduced legislation to make it an offense for ships of their flag to proceed against the established direction of traffic flow.

Section 11—Conduct of Vessels in Sight of One Another

Application

RULE 11 This rule specifies the applicability of all rules in this section.

Sailing Vessels

RULE 12 Virtually no change from the 1960 Rules except for the third provision, where a vessel, with the wind on the port side, that cannot determine on which side another vessel has the wind, shall assume she is to give way. This conforms more closely to the International Yacht Racing Rules.

Overtaking

RULE 13 Although rearranged, this rule is similar to the 1960 Rules.

Head-on Situation

RULE 14 This rule is virtually the same as the 1960 Rules for power-driven vessels, except for the third provision, which is a new rule. This rule obliges a vessel, when in doubt, to consider the situation a head-on one and act accordingly. This, therefore, requires an alteration to starboard and eliminates the possibility of conflicting maneuvers when two vessels are meeting almost end on.

Crossing Situation

RULE 15 This rule is similar to the 1960 Rule 19 requiring a vessel to port of another to give way, but with emphasis on the need to avoid crossing ahead of the stand-on vessel. However, it now applies strictly only to power-driven vessels and not to all vessels as in 1960 Rule 22.

Action by Give-way Vessel

RULE 16 Very little change in this rule to take "early and substantial action" to keep clear.

Action by the Stand-on Vessel

RULE 17 1. A vessel that is privileged—now defined as the stand-on vessel—is directed, as in the 1960 Rules, to keep her course and speed.

2. As before, a stand-on vessel finding herself in extremis is required to take "such action as will best aid to avoid collision."

3. A new provision is that the stand-on vessel is given freedom to take action prior to extremis "as soon as it becomes apparent that the vessel required to keep out of the way is not taking appropriate action." This is a major change. The reasoning is that a stand-on vessel cannot know the alertness prevailing in the give-way vessel, nor her capabilities, and, as a result, may have in the past unnecessarily stood on until a dangerous situation had arisen. Now she can take action to avoid collision by her maneuvers alone, providing, if the circumstances permit, she does not alter to port for a vessel on her own port side. Notwithstanding this, the give-way vessel is not relieved of her responsibilities.

Responsibilities Between Vessels

RULE 18 1. This is a new rule that gathers together all those vessels who are restricted in their ability to maneuver for various reasons. Clear details are given of those vessels required to keep clear of certain other types of vessels. Particular emphasis is given to a vessel constrained by her draft. This is designed to take into account the fact that in shallow seas, deep-draft vessels are less maneuverable than other vessels. Despite this proviso, vessels constrained by their draft are reminded that, although granted a privilege, they must take into account their lack of maneuverability.

2. The rule for seaplanes on the water remains effectively the same.

Section 111—Conduct of Vessels in Restricted Visibility

Conduct of Vessels in Restricted Visibility

RULE 19 1. This new rule takes much of the material from the 1960 Rule 16 and the Radar Annex, making it more comprehensive and expressing it in a more positive manner. The 1972 rule clearly applies to all vessels out of sight of one another, not only in an area of restricted visibility, but also to any near such an area.

2. The mariner is strictly reminded of the importance of maintaining a safe speed in all visibilities, with specific emphasis on the need to take into account the circumstances of restricted visibility. In addition, a new requirement is that a power-driven vessel must have her engines ready for immediate maneuver.

3. Clear advice is offered on avoiding action when a developing close-quarters situation is detected by radar alone; i.e., before the other vessel is visual or her fog signal heard. The wording is more positive than the 1960 Rule 16(c) though it contains an escape clause of "so far as possible the following shall be avoided. . . ." To be able to take the necessary action under this rule it is axiomatic that systematic radar observation and plotting, whether manual or automatic, is required. If such plotting reveals that a close-quarters situation is developing, then avoiding action is mandatory, as opposed to the permissive requirements of the 1960 Rules.

4. The action to be taken by a vessel on hearing a fog signal apparently forward of her beam has been changed. If risk of collision or a close-quarters situation has been deemed not to exist, presumably through the medium of radar, there is no requirement to "stop engines" as under the 1960 Rules. More flexibility is therefore given to a vessel capable of making efficient use of radar. However, if this exception proviso does not apply, then a vessel must reduce her speed to the minimum at which she can effectively steer. If this action is insufficient then the vessel must take all way off and navigate with extreme caution. This applies to all vessels and not just power-driven vessels as in the past. In effect, the new rule requires all vessels to reduce speed, and maintain a much lower speed than the previous requirement for vessels so fitted to merely "stop engines" for an unspecified period of time.

PART C—LIGHTS AND SHAPES

Application

RULE 20 1. Although basically similar to 1960 Rule 1(b), the new rule requires, rather than permits, vessels to show lights in restricted visibility between sunrise and sunset.

2. Technical details of lights and shapes are omitted in this section. The requirements for their size, color, and shape are now consolidated in Annex I of the Rules.

Definitions

RULE 21 1. The repetition in various 1960 Rules of describing the arcs, ranges, and position of various lights is avoided in the new rules. This particular rule defines the meaning, color, and arcs of lights. Technical details of positioning such lights are relegated to Annex I. Only the information essential to the mariner is contained here.

2. In this rule the use of the metric system for linear measurement is first mentioned.

3. The peculiar difficulties of certain types of vessels, such as tugs, supply ships, stern trawlers, or LASH vessels with open sterns, is recognized in the placement of the sternlight. It no longer must be on the stern but "as nearly as is practicable at the stern."

4. A new color has been added to the spectrum in the towing light for vessels being towed to steer by. It is a yellow light shown in addition to, and having the same characteristics as, a sternlight.

5. For the first time a flashing light for use on vessels is introduced and defined.

Visibility of Lights

RULE 22 This rule lists the range of visibility of lights for vessels depending upon their length measured in meters. In general, for large vessels, ranges have been increased by one mile. For smaller vessels the minimum visibility ranges generally remain the same, except for the sidelights in one class and the masthead light in another.

Power-driven Vessels Underway

RULE 23 1. This rule neatly gathers together the requirements for lights to be shown by a power-driven vessel. It is far less cumbersome to read and understand than the 1960 Rule 2. The requirements are basically the same as before.

2. A new, all-round flashing yellow light is prescribed for air-cushion vessels operating in the nondisplacement mode.

3. Small power-driven vessels not having the capability for, or experiencing difficulty in showing, the usual lights are accommodated in part (c) of this rule.

Towing and Pushing

RULE 24 1. For a vessel towing astern the new rules are much the same as the 1960 Rules, except for the introduction of a yellow towing light and the fact that the length of tow is measured in meters. The optional "small white light abaft the funnel . . . for the tow to steer by" no longer exists and a white sternlight is now mandatory. The yellow towing light is directly above the sternlight and covers the same arc.

2. A vessel pushing ahead that is rigidly connected to the vessel being pushed is regarded as a composite unit with the same maneuverability as

a power-driven vessel and is therefore required to be lighted as a power-driven vessel.

3. A vessel pushing ahead that is not a composite unit shows the same lights as in the 1960 Rules. It does not show the new, distinctive yellow light required for a vessel towing astern. For the first time in the International Rules, towing alongside is recognized and a vessel so engaged shows the same lights as a vessel pushing ahead.

4. The requirement for a towing or pushing vessel, 50 meters or more in length, to display a second masthead light (i.e., range light) is now explicit. Previously it had been inferred from old Rule 2(a)(ii). A range light remains optional for a towing vessel of under 50 meters in length.

5. The lights, and where applicable the shape, for a vessel or object being towed remain basically the same as in the 1960 Rules. However, sternlights must always be shown on each vessel as opposed to the optional steering light of the previous rules.

6. Vessels being towed alongside or being pushed in a group are to be lighted as one vessel. This is an extension of the 1960 Rule 5(c) which referred only to vessels being pushed ahead.

7. A new provision recognizes that some tows are difficult to light and constitute a navigational hazard—e.g., timber. This rule applies only to vessels being towed and not to vessels being pushed ahead. The yellow towing light required of the tug by new Rule 24 (a)(iv) will assist other vessels in identifying those cases where the tow is not lighted.

Sailing Vessels Underway and Vessels Under Oars

RULE 25 1. This rule is essentially identical to the 1960 Rules with the following exceptions:

(a) in vessels under 12 meters in length the sternlight may also be incorporated into a combined lantern, which may be displayed near the top of the mast.

(b) the optional red over green masthead lights for a sailing vessel now have their arc extended from 20 points to all-round lights, but are not permitted in a sailing vessel showing the combined lantern in (a) above.

2. Small vessels are encouraged to exhibit normal navigation lights but if they cannot, are required to show a white light in sufficient time to prevent collision.

3. The same day shape remains for a sailing vessel proceeding under power.

Fishing Vessels

RULE 26 1. The lights for fishing vessels engaged in trawling remain unchanged, except for a vessel of 50 meters or more which is now required to show a second masthead light (range light) abaft and above the green and white all-round lights. Previously the range light had been voluntary, abaft but lower. This should assist more clearly in determining the aspect of trawlers.

2. The lights for vessels engaged in fishing, other than trawlers, remain unchanged, except that lengths are expressed in meters.

3. Vessels engaged in fishing frequently operate in close proximity to each other. A new provision is additional signals, laid down in Annex II, to enable vessels, not necessarily only fishing vessels, to identify vessels engaged in special fishing operations; e.g., pair trawling or purse seining.

Vessels Not Under Command or Restricted In Their Ability to Manouvre

RULE 27 1. The lights and shapes for a vessel not under command are unchanged.

2. The special identification lights for vessels restricted in their ability to maneuver that were commonly known previously as "special operations" remain unchanged. However, when underway and making way, masthead lights are now shown as well as sternlights and sidelights. This should assist mariners in more easily determining the aspect of an approaching vessel. The shapes remain the same but the color is now black. In the event that such a vessel should anchor, she continues to show the lights or shapes for a vessel restricted in her ability to maneuver plus the normal anchor lights or shape.

3. A new provision is that a vessel engaged in a towing operation that renders her unable to deviate from her course shows, in addition to her normal towing lights, the lights or shapes of a vessel restricted in her ability to maneuver.

4. Vessels engaged in dredging are included in the rules for the first time. They are grouped with vessels engaged in underwater operations, and when underway, show the same lights and shapes as a vessel restricted in her ability to maneuver. In addition they must, when an obstruction exists, indicate the clear and foul side by use of special lights and shapes. When at anchor, however, vessels engaged in dredging or underwater operations only display their special identification, and when appropriate, obstruction lights and no anchor lights.

5. For small vessels engaged in diving operations where it is impracticable to show the proper lights and shapes, an alternate signal, adopted from the International Code of Signals, is provided.

6. Minesweepers are now required to carry all three green lights or black balls regardless of the side on which operations are being conducted.

Vessels Constrained by Their Draught

RULE 28 A new rule giving a vessel constrained by her draft an additional special identification signal by day and night.

Pilot Vessels

RULE 29 There is now no difference between a sailing pilot vessel and a power-driven pilot vessel. The requirement for a flare-up light no longer exists.

Anchored Vessels and Vessels Aground

RULE 30 1. A vessel less than 50 meters in length may now show her all-round white light "where it can best be seen" and not in the fore part of the vessel as in the 1960 Rule.

2. Vessels at anchor, over 100 meters in length, are required to illuminate their decks. Although a new provision in the rules, the practice of exhibiting deck lights is common. It aids considerably in identifying vessels at anchor.

3. Recognition is given to small vessels under 7 meters in length that have difficulty in carrying the lights and shapes in this rule. Notwithstanding this, if such a vessel does anchor or ground "in or near a narrow channel, fairway or anchorage, or where other vessels normally navigate" she must show the required lights and shapes.

Seaplanes

RULE 31 This rule sets forth the requirement for seaplanes to comply as closely as possible in their exhibition of lights and shapes. The verbose requirements of the 1960 Rules are condensed into one sentence.

PART D—SOUND AND LIGHT SIGNALS

Definitions

RULE 32 The definition of "whistle" has been revised to take into account the new technical requirements laid down in Annex III to the Rules.

Equipment for Sound Signals

RULE 33 1. All vessels over 12 meters, not merely power-driven ones, are now required to carry a whistle and a bell. If the vessel is over 100 meters a gong is also required. The term "foghorn" has been removed. Automatic sounding equipment is permitted, but must always be capable of manual operation. Technical specifications are relegated to Annex III.

2. Vessels under 12 meters must be able, through other means, to make efficient sound signals if they cannot carry the equipment above. This new provision excludes the specific exemptions for seaplanes and small vessels that were contained in the 1960 Rules.

Manoeuvring and Warning Signals

RULE 34 1. The meaning of one, two, and three short blasts remains unchanged, though the latter is defined "operating astern propulsion" to cover those vessels with engines that continue in the same direction when going astern; e.g., ships fitted with variable pitch propellers.

2. Light signals are permitted to supplement maneuvering whistle signals. They no longer need to be synchronized. The light signals may be repeated without repeating the sound signal.

3. The new signals of intent to be used in overtaking in narrow channels (1972 Rule 9(e)) are included. To distinguish an overtaking vessel's signal of intent from normal maneuvering signal, they are preceded by two prolonged blasts. The signal for agreement is the International Morse Code letter "C".

4. The application of the so-called "in doubt" signal, previously authorized only for the stand on power-driven vessel is extended. Now either vessel approaching each other may sound the signal if she is in doubt as to the intentions or actions of the other vessel. The use of the all-inclusive term "vessels" means that the signal is no longer restricted to power-driven vessels but to any types of vessels in sight of one another. The signal may also be repeated on the maneuvering light.

5. The requirement to sound a whistle signal on approaching a "blind bend" remains very similar to the 1960 Rules, except for the elimination of the distance criterion of one-half mile.

6. Vessels fitted with two or more whistles that are more than 100 meters apart are to use only one whistle for giving maneuvering and warning signals. This is to prevent misunderstanding which might result from reception of the same signal at differing times.

Sound Signals in Restricted Visibility

RULE 35 1. All vessels underway sound signals at intervals of not more than two minutes. This is to avoid the distinct possibility of lookouts not hearing other sound signals due to temporary deafness caused by their own whistle signals if given at the one-minute intervals as required in some parts of the 1960 Rules.

2. There is only one small change for a power-driven vessel underway: the increased length of the interval between two prolonged blasts when stopped and not making way. A composite unit, pushing ahead, sounds the signals for a power-driven vessel.

3. Vessels hampered in some way, i.e., not under command, restricted in their ability to maneuver, constrained by their draft, engaged in towing or pushing, engaged in fishing and sailing vessels, all sound the same signals of one prolonged blast followed by two short blasts. Sailing vessels no longer sound a specific signal indicating their point of sail, which could have been confused with maneuvering signals for vessels in sight of one another.

4. The signal for a manned vessel being towed, or the last of a series of vessels towed, remains the same but at intervals of two minutes instead of one minute.

5. All vessels anchored or aground sound required fog signals at intervals of not more than one minute. Apart from expressing lengths in meters and requiring the gong, where needed, to be sounded immediately after the bell, there is virtually no change.

6. Optional signals, with no required interval, are permitted for vessels at anchor, aground, or engaged in pilotage duties.

7. Vessels of less than 12 meters, whether underway or not, are released from the obligation to sound the previous signals, but must, instead, make an efficient sound signal at not more than two-minute intervals.

Signals to Attract Attention

RULE 36 This is essentially the same as the 1960 Rules, with the use of a searchlight to indicate the direction of danger authorized for all vessels.

Distress Signals

RULE 37 A brief reference to use the signals in Annex IV of the Rules if in distress and requiring assistance. The distress signals were not placed in the main body of the Rules because they are not directly connected with preventing collisions at sea.

PART E—EXEMPTIONS

Exemptions

RULE 38 1. This new rule allows exemptions for vessels built, or whose keels had been laid, prior to the entry into force of the Regulations. The change of units from feet to meters for the placing of lights and the new technical requirements for lights, shapes, and sound-signaling apparatus could result in costly alterations for existing vessels.

2. Permanent exemption is granted for the repositioning of:

(a) lights due to the conversion of measure, and

(b) masthead lights, in vessels under 150 meters in length, for the purpose of more accurately indicating the length of a vessel.

3. Nine years' exemption is granted for:

(a) the repositioning of masthead lights in vessels 150 meters and over for purposes of more accurately indicating length;

(b) the repositioning of masthead lights taking into account all normal conditions of trim;

(c) the repositioning of sidelights; and

(d) the requirements for sound-signal apparatus.

4. Four years' exemption is granted for the installation of lights with color and range specifications.

ANNEX I

Positioning and Technical Details of Lights and Shapes

1. This annex is concerned with the structural positioning of lights and the color and size of shapes, all of which used to appear in the body of the 1960 Rules. Many of the details are the same as before with minor variations due to the conversion from imperial to metric measurement. In addition, technical specifications for navigation lights, of primary interest to the shipbuilder or manufacturer, are laid down to ensure conformity in construction, color, and intensity, and thus range.

2. New items of interest to the mariner are:

(a) allowance must be made for all normal conditions of trim in the vertical separation of masthead lights. On a long voyage it is possible for the after (range) light not to be visible above, or separately from, the forward (masthead) light.

(b) masthead lights must be placed above and clear of all other lights.

(c) horizontal spacing of lights for power-driven vessels must be such as to give a more accurate indication of the approximate length of the vessel.

(d) for vessels 20 meters or more in length, the sidelights must not be placed in front of the forward masthead light.

(e) screens for sidelights must be painted matt black.

(f) all shapes are now black.

(g) notwithstanding Item 2(b) above, the maneuvering light should be placed on the same fore and aft vertical plane as the masthead lights, and where practicable, at a minimum height of 2 meters above the forward masthead light, provided that it is not placed less than 2 meters above or below the after masthead light.

ANNEX II

Additional Signals for Fishing Vessels Fishing in Close Proximity

1. This new annex provides additional signals for vessels fishing in the proximity of each other. The signals are optional but, as fishing vessels do frequently operate at close quarters, they afford the opportunity to apprise other vessels of the particular stage of fishing operations that is in progress. This will provide standardized signals for fishing vessels on a worldwide basis and, hopefully, remove much of the conflict, confusion, and entanglement of nets that occur when fishing vessels of different types or nationalities are fishing the same grounds.

2. While of primary interest to the fishing industry and those agencies that enforce the regulations, it behooves every mariner to know these signals. In the event of an inadvertent or necessary approach to a fleet of fishing vessels, he will be better placed to extract himself with minimum damage to all.

ANNEX III

Technical Details of Sound Signal Appliances

Details of primary interest to manufacturers of the equipment are found in this annex. They include frequencies, audible ranges, signal intensity, directional properties, and positioning. The object is to ensure minimum standards among all vessels. Even though fitted with automatic sound signal apparatus, the mariner is required to be able to operate them in a manual mode.

ANNEX IV

Distress Signals

1. The majority of signals are as before, with the exception of signals transmitted by emergency position—indicating radio beacons, e.g., IFF.
2. The relevance of the International Code of Signals and the Merchant Ship Search and Rescue Manual is brought to the attention of the mariner.

NOTES

The 1972 Regulations were written to be readily usable by the mariner and shipbuilder alike. Although many of the changes in the regulations are only evolutionary, the rules as a whole have been presented in a new form that is considered more easily read and understood than before. Future advances in technology, that could lead to changes in the rules, can now be accommodated through amendment procedures. It is no longer necessary to assemble a conference to change the rules.

The new rules also aimed for a truly uniform set of worldwide regulations, especially in the areas of traffic separation schemes and "special rules." The latter, while still allowed, ". . . shall conform as close as possible to . . ." the 1972 Rules. Most maritime countries do follow the basic International Rules in their local waters as well as on the high seas, only adding special rules to supplement the International Rules when local conditions so demand. Regrettably, the existing divergence between the 1964 International Rules and the U. S. local Rules for Inland Waters, the Great Lakes, and the Western Rivers, is further increased by the ratification of the 1972 International Rules. The multiplicities and occasional conflicts between the various U. S. sets of rules, and also with the new International Rules, have been recognized by the cognizant authority in the Coast Guard. Draft proposals for a new "U.S. Waters Rules" have been formulated for discussion with interested parties. Committees have met to discuss the problems. Despite early optimism, it is considered unlikely that changes to existing U.S. Rules will come into effect in the immediate future.

Unless revision and unification of the U. S. Rules to conform, where practicable, with the 1972 Regulations are achieved, the interest of maritime safety is affected. To the mariner, there is a risk of confusion in differentiating between the requirements placed upon him by two different sets of rules, especially when operating near the boundaries of those rules. Until the U. S. removes the unnecessary differences between the various rules, she remains at fault in this respect.

2
Applicability, Scope, and Definitions

International Rules

APPLICATION OF INTERNATIONAL REGULATIONS FOR PREVENTING COLLISIONS AT SEA (33 U.S.C. 1051)[1]

The President is authorized to proclaim the regulations set forth in sections 1061–1094 of this title for preventing collisions involving waterborne craft upon the high seas, and in all waters connected therewith. The effective date of such proclamation shall be not earlier than the date fixed by the Inter-Governmental Maritime Consultative Organization[2] for application of such regulations by Governments which have agreed to accept them. Such proclamation, together

Inland and Pilot Rules

APPLICATION OF INLAND RULES OF THE ROAD (33 U.S.C. 154)

The following regulations for preventing collisions shall be followed by all vessels upon the harbors, rivers, and other inland waters of the United States, except the Great Lakes and their connecting and tributary waters as far east as Montreal, and the waters of the Mississippi River between its source and the Huey P. Long Bridge and all of its tributaries emptying thereinto and their tributaries, and that part of the Atchafalaya River above its junction with the Plaquemine-Morgan City alternate waterway, and the Red River of the North;

---

[1] *These U.S. Codes are for the 1960 Rules. Executive order 11964 ratified the 1972 Rules for the U.S. They are published in Title 33 of the Code of Federal Regulations as App. A to Part 87 in the absence of enabling legislation.*

[2] *See Notes at end of chapter.*

with the regulations, shall be published in the Federal Register and after the effective date specified in such proclamation such regulations shall have effect as if enacted by statute and shall be followed by all public and private vessels of the United States and by all aircraft of United States registry to the extent therein made applicable. Such regulations shall not apply to the harbors, rivers, and other inland waters of the United States; to the Great Lakes of North America and their connecting and tributary waters as far east as the lower exit of the Saint Lambert Lock at Montreal in the Province of Quebec, Canada; to the Red River of the North and the rivers emptying into the Gulf of Mexico and their tributaries; nor with respect to aircraft in any territorial waters of the United States.

and are hereby declared special rules duly made by local authority.

NAVY AND COAST GUARD VESSEL EXCEPTIONS
(33 U.S.C. 1052) (See Fn. 1, p. 17)

Any requirement of such regulations in respect of the number, position, range of visibility, or arc of visibility of the lights required to be displayed by vessels shall not apply to any vessel of the Navy or of the Coast Guard whenever the Secretary of the Navy or the Secretary of Transportation in the case of Coast Guard vessels operating under the Department of Transportation, or such official as either may designate, shall find or certify that, by reason of special construction, it is

NAVY AND COAST GUARD VESSEL EXCEPTIONS
(33 U.S.C. 360)

Any requirement as to the number, position, range of visibility, or arc of visibility of lights required to be displayed by vessels under . . . sections 154-231 of this title . . . and all laws amendatory thereto, shall not apply to any vessel of the Navy or of the Coast Guard, where the Secretary of the Navy, or the Secretary of Transportation in the case of Coast Guard vessels operating under the Department of Transportation, or such official or officials as either may designate,

not possible for such vessel or class of vessels to comply with such regulations. The lights of any such exempted vessel or class of vessels, however, shall conform as closely to the requirements of the applicable regulations as the Secretary or such official shall find or certify to be feasible. Notice of such findings or certification and of the character and position of the lights prescribed to be displayed on such exempted vessel or class of vessels shall be published in the Federal Register and in the Notice to Mariners and, after the effective date specified in such notice, shall have effect as part of such regulations.

shall find or certify that, by reason of special construction, it is not possible with respect to such vessel or class of vessels to comply with the statutory provisions as to the number, position, range of visibility, or arc of visibility of lights. The lights of any such exempted vessel or class of vessels shall, however, comply as closely to the requirements of the applicable sections as the Secretary shall find to be feasible.

PUBLICATION OF NAVY AND COAST GUARD VESSEL EXCEPTIONS (33 U.S.C. 360a)

When the Secretary of the Navy or the Secretary of Transportation, or such official or officials as either may designate, shall make any finding or certification as prescribed in section 360 of this title, notice of such finding or certification and the character and position of the lights to be displayed on such vessel shall be published in "Notice to Mariners."

AUTHORITY FOR PILOT RULES (33 U.S.C. 157)

(a) The Secretary of the Department in which the Coast Guard is operating shall establish such rules to be observed, on the waters described in section 154 of this title by steam vessels in passing each other and as to the lights and day signals to be carried on such waters by ferryboats, by vessels and craft of all types when in tow of steam vessels or operating by hand power or horsepower or drifting with the current, and by any other vessels not otherwise provided for, not inconsistent with the provisions of this Act, as he from time to time may deem necessary for safety, which rules are hereby declared special rules duly made by local authority. A pamphlet containing such Act and regulations shall be furnished to all vessels and craft subject to this Act. On vessels and craft over sixty-five feet in length the pamphlet shall, where practicable, be kept on board and available for ready reference.

(b) Except in an emergency, before any rules or any alteration, amendment, or repeal thereof are established by the Secretary under the provisions of this section, the said Secretary shall publish the proposed rules, alterations, amendments, or repeals, and public hearings shall be held with respect thereto on such notice as the Secretary deems reasonable under the circumstances.

AUTHORITY FOR SPECIAL
REGULATIONS
NEAR LOW BRIDGES
(33 U.S.C. 157a)

(a) The Secretary of the Department in which the Coast Guard is operating may permit vessels desiring to navigate or operate under bridges constructed over navigable waters of the United States to temporarily lower any lights, day signals, or other navigational means and appliances prescribed or required pursuant to law, rule, or regulation, and, if necessary, may authorize vessels so navigating or operating to depart from the rules to prevent collisions as prescribed by law, rule, or regulation. The Secretary of the Department in which the Coast Guard is operating may also prescribe such special regulations to be observed by vessels so navigating or operating as in his judgment the public safety may require for prevention of collisions.

(b) Notice of the regulations to accomplish the purposes of this section shall be published in the Federal Register and in the Notice to Mariners, and after the effective date specified in such notices, such regulations shall have the force of law.

(c) Any person who navigates or operates a vessel in violation of the regulations established pursuant to this section shall be liable to a penalty not exceeding $500. In addition, any vessel navigated or operated in violation of the regulations established pursuant to this section shall be liable to a penalty of $500, for which sum such vessel may be seized and proceeded against, by way of libel, in the district court of the United States for any district within which such vessel may be found.

AUTHORITY FOR INLAND/ INTERNATIONAL LINE OF DEMARCATION (33 U.S.C. 151)

The Commandant of the Coast Guard is authorized, empowered, and directed from time to time to designate and define by suitable bearings or ranges with lighthouses, light vessels, buoys, or coast objects, the lines dividing the high seas from rivers, harbors, and inland waters.

PENALTY FOR VIOLATIONS BY PILOT, ENGINEER, MATE OR MASTER (33 U.S.C. 158)

Every licensed and unlicensed pilot, engineer, mate, or master of any vessel[3] who violates the provisions of this Act or the regulations established pursuant hereto shall be liable to a penalty of not exceeding $500, and for all damages sustained by any passenger, in his person or baggage, as a result of such violation: Provided, That nothing herein shall relieve any vessel, owner, or corporation from any liability incurred by reason of such violation.

PENALTY FOR VIOLATIONS BY VESSEL (33 U.S.C. 159)

Every vessel which is navigated in violation of any of the provisions of this Act or the regulations estab-

[3] *For a definition of the word "vessel," see Rule 3(a), International Rules.*

lished pursuant hereto shall be liable to a penalty of $500, one-half to go to the informer, for which sum such vessel may be seized and proceeded against by action in any district court of the United States having jurisdiction of the offense.

APPLICATION

RULE 1 (a) These rules shall apply to all vessels upon the high seas and in all waters connected therewith navigable by seagoing vessels.

APPLICATION OF INLAND RULES OF THE ROAD
(33 U.S.C. 154)

The following regulations for preventing collisions shall be followed by all vessels upon the harbors, rivers and other inland waters of the United States, except the Great Lakes and their connecting tributary waters as far east as Montreal, and the waters of the Mississippi River between its source and the Huey P. Long Bridge and all of its tributaries emptying thereinto and their tributaries, and that part of the Atchafalaya River above its junction with the Plaquemine-Morgan City alternate waterway, and the Red River of the North; and are hereby declared special rules duly made by local authority.

(b) Nothing in these rules shall interfere with the operation of special rules made by an appropriate authority for roadsteads, harbours, rivers, lakes or inland waterways connected with the high seas and navigable by seagoing vessels. Such special rules shall conform as closely as possible to these rules.

(c) Nothing in these rules shall interfere with the operation of any special rules made by the Government of any State with respect to additional station or signal lights or whistle signals for ships of war and vessels proceeding under convoy, or with respect to additional station or signal lights for fishing vessels engaged in fishing as a fleet.

Art. 13. Nothing in these rules shall interfere with the operation of any special rules made by the Government of any nation with respect to additional station and signal lights for two or more ships of war or for vessels sailing under convoy, or with the exhibition of recognition signals adopted by shipowners, which have been authorized

These additional station or signal lights or whistle signals shall, so far as possible, be such that they cannot be mistaken for any light or signal authorized elsewhere under these rules.

(d) Traffic separation schemes may be adopted by the Organization for the purpose of these rules.

(e) Whenever the Government concerned shall have determined that a vessel of special construction or purpose cannot comply fully with the provisions of any of these rules with respect to the number, position, range or arc of visibility of lights or shapes, as well as to the disposition and characteristics of sound-signalling appliances, without interfering with the special function of the vessel, such vessel shall comply with such other provisions in regard to the number, position, range or arc of visibility of lights or shapes, as well as to the disposition and characteristics of sound-signalling appliances, as her Government shall have determined to be the closest possible compliance with these rules in respect to that vessel.

by their respective Governments, and duly registered and published.

Art. 30. The exhibition of any light on board of a vessel of war of the United States or a Coast Guard cutter may be suspended whenever, in the opinion of the Secretary of the Navy, the commander in chief of a squadron, or the commander of a vessel acting singly, the special character of the service may require it.

EXEMPTIONS—NAVY AND COAST GUARD VESSELS
(Sec. 1, 59, Stat. 590, 33 U.S.C. 360)

Any requirement as to the number, position, range of visibility, or arc of visibility of lights required to be displayed by vessels under . . . sections 154-231 of this title . . . and all laws amendatory thereto, shall not apply to any vessel of the Navy or of the Coast Guard, where the Secretary of the Navy, or the Secretary of the Treasury in the case of Coast Guard vessels operating under the Treasury Department, or such official or officials as either may designate, shall find or certify that, by reason of special construction, it is not possible with respect to such vessel or class of vessels to comply with the statutory provisions as to the number, position, range of visibility, or arc of visibility of lights. The lights of any such

International Rules	Inland and Pilot Rules

International Rules

Inland and Pilot Rules

exempted vessel or class of vessels shall, however, comply as closely to the requirements of the applicable sections as the Secretary shall find to be feasible.

RESPONSIBILITY

RULE 2. (a) Nothing in these rules shall exonerate any vessel, or the owner, master or crew thereof, from the consequences of any neglect to comply with these rules or of the neglect of any precaution which may be required by the ordinary practice of seamen, or by the special circumstances of the case.

Art. 29. Nothing in these rules shall exonerate any vessel, or the owner or master or crew thereof, from the consequences of any neglect to carry lights or signals, or of any neglect to keep a proper lookout, or of the neglect of any precaution which may be required by the ordinary practice of seamen, or by the special circumstances of the case.

(b) In construing and complying with these rules due regard shall be had to all dangers of navigation and collision and to any special circumstances, including the limitations of the vessels involved, which may make a departure from these rules necessary to avoid immediate danger.

Art. 27. In obeying and construing these rules due regard shall be had to all dangers of navigation and collision, and to any special circumstances which may render a departure from the above rules necessary in order to avoid immediate danger.

GENERAL DEFINITIONS

RULE 3. For the purpose of these rules, except where the context otherwise requires:

(a) The word "vessel" includes every description of water craft, including nondisplacement craft and seaplanes, used or capable of being used as a means of transportation on water.

International Rules

(b) The term "power-driven vessel" means any vessel propelled by machinery.

(c) The term "sailing vessel" means any vessel under sail provided that propelling machinery, if fitted, is not being used.

(d) The term "vessel engaged in fishing" means any vessel fishing with nets, lines, trawls or other fishing apparatus which restrict manoeuvrability, but does not include a vessel fishing with trolling lines or other fishing apparatus which do not restrict manoeuvrability.

(e) The word "seaplane" includes any aircraft designed to manoeuvre on the water.

(f) The term "vessel not under command" means a vessel which through some exceptional circumstance is unable to manoeuvre as required by these rules and is therefore unable to keep out of the way of another vessel.

(g) The term "vessel restricted in her ability to manoeuvre" means a vessel which from the nature of her work is restricted in her ability to manoeuvre is required by these rules and is therefore unable to keep out of the way of another vessel.

The following vessels shall be regarded as vessels restricted in their ability to manoeuvre:

Inland and Pilot Rules

Art. 1. The words "steam vessel" shall include any vessel propelled by machinery.

In the following rules every steam vessel which is under sail and not under steam is to be considered a sailing vessel, and every vessel under steam, whether under sail or not, is to be considered a steam vessel.

Art. 9. (c) All vessels, when fishing, dredging, or fishing with any kind of drag nets or lines, shall . . . .

(i) a vessel engaged in laying, servicing or picking up a navigation mark, submarine cable or pipeline;

(ii) a vessel engaged in dredging, surveying or underwater operations;

(iii) a vessel engaged in replenishment or transferring persons, provisions or cargo while underway;

(iv) a vessel engaged in the launching or recovery of aircraft;

(v) a vessel engaged in minesweeping operations;

(vi) a vessel engaged in a towing operation such as severely restricts the towing vessel and her tow in their ability to deviate from their course.

(h) The term "vessel constrained by her draught" means a power-driven vessel which because of her draught in relation to the available depth of water is severely restricted in her ability to deviate from the course she is following.

(i) The word "underway" means that a vessel is not at anchor, or made fast to the shore, or aground.

Art. 1. A vessel is "underway," within the meaning of these rules, when she is not at anchor, or made fast to the shore, or aground.

(j) The words "length" and "breadth" of a vessel means her length overall and greatest breadth.

(k) Vessels shall be deemed to be in sight of one another only when one can be observed visually from the other.

Art. 15. In fog, mist, falling snow, or heavy rain storms, whether by day or night, . . .

Art. 16. Every vessel shall, in a fog, mist, falling snow, or heavy rainstorms, . . .

(l) The term "restricted visibility" means any condition in which visibility is restricted by fog, mist, falling snow, heavy rainstorms, sandstorms or any other similar causes.

SAFE SPEED

RULE 6. Every vessel shall at all times proceed at a safe speed so that she can take proper and effective action to avoid collision and be stopped within a distance appropriate to the prevailing circumstances and conditions.

In determining a safe speed the following factors shall be among those taken into account:

(a) By all vessels:

(i) the state of visibility;

(ii) the traffic density including concentrations of fishing vessels or any other vessels;

(iii) the maneuverability of the vessel with special reference to stopping distance and turning ability in the prevailing conditions;

(iv) at night the presence of background light such as from shore lights or from back scatter of her own lights;

(v) the state of wind, sea and current, and the proximity of navigational hazards;

(vi) the draught in relation to water.

(b) Additionally, by vessels with operational radar:

(i) the characteristics, efficiency and limitations of the radar equipment;

(ii) any constraints imposed by the radar range scale in use;

(iii) the effect on radar detection of the sea state, weather and other sources of interference:

(iv) the possibility that small ves-

Art. 16. Every vessel shall, in a fog, mist, falling snow, or heavy rainstorms, go at a moderate speed, having careful regard to the existing circumstances and conditions.

sels, ice and other floating objects may not be detected by radar at an adequate range;

(v) the number, location and movement of vessels detected by radar;

(vi) the more exact assessment of the visibility that may be possible when radar is used to determine the range of vessels or other objects in the vicinity.

RISK OF COLLISION

RULE 7. (a) Every vessel shall use all available means appropriate to the prevailing circumstances and conditions to determine if risk of collision exists. If there is any doubt such risk shall be deemed to exist.

(b) Proper use shall be made of radar equipment if fitted and operational, including long-range scanning to obtain early warning of risk of collision and radar plotting or equivalent systematic observation of detected objects.

(c) Assumptions shall not be made on the basis of scanty information, especially scanty radar information.

(d) In determining if risk of collision exists the following considerations shall be among those taken into account:

(i) such risk shall be deemed to exist if the compass bearing of an approaching vessel does not appreciably change;

(ii) such risk may sometimes exist even when an appreciable bearing

STEERING AND SAILING RULES

PRELIMINARY

Risk of collision can, when circumstances permit, be ascertained by carefully watching the compass bearing of an approaching vessel. If the bearing does not appreciably change, such risk should be deemed to exist.

change is evident, particularly when approaching a very large vessel or a tow or when approaching a vessel at close range.

APPLICATION

RULE 20. (a) Rules in this part shall be complied with in all weathers.

(b) The rules concerning lights shall be complied with from sunset to sunrise, and during such times no other lights shall be exhibited, except such lights as cannot be mistaken for the lights specified in these rules or do not impair their visibility or distinctive character, or interfere with the keeping of a proper look-out.

(c) The lights prescribed by these rules shall, if carried, also be exhibited from sunrise to sunset in restricted visibility and may be exhibited in all other circumstances when it is deemed necessary.

(d) The rules concerning shapes shall be complied with by day.

(e) The lights and shapes specified in these rules shall comply with the provisions of Annex I to these regulations.

Art. 1. The rules concerning lights shall be complied with in all weathers from sunset to sunrise, and during such time no other lights which may be mistaken for the prescribed lights shall be exhibited.

DEFINITIONS

STEAM VESSELS—
MASTHEAD AND RANGE
LIGHTS

RULE 21. (a) "Masthead light" means a white light placed over the fore and aft centreline of the vessel showing an unbroken light over an arc of the horizon of 225 degrees and so fixed as to show the light from right ahead to 22.5 degrees

Art. 2. A steam vessel when underway shall carry—(a) On or in the front of the foremast, or if a vessel without a foremast, then in the fore part of the vessel, a bright white light so constructed as to show an unbroken light over an arc

International Rules

abaft the beam on either side of the vessel.

(b) "Sidelights" means a green light on the starboard side and a red light on the port side each showing an unbroken light over an arc of the horizon of 112.5 degrees and so fixed as to show the light from right ahead to 22.5 degrees abaft the beam on its respective side. In a vessel of less than 20 metres in length the sidelights may be combined in one lantern carried on the fore and aft centreline of the vessel.

Inland and Pilot Rules

of the horizon of twenty points of the compass, so fixed as to throw the light ten points on each side of the vessel, namely, from right ahead to two points abaft the beam on either side, and of such a character as to be visible at a distance of at least five miles.

(f) All steam vessels (except seagoing vessels and ferryboats), shall carry in addition to green and red lights required by article two (b), (c), and screens as required by article two (d), a central range of two white lights; the after light being carried at an elevation at least fifteen feet above the light at the head of the vessel. The headlight shall be so constructed as to show an unbroken light through twenty points of the compass, namely, from right ahead to two points abaft the beam on either side of the vessel, and the after light so as to show all around the horizon.

Art. 2 (b) On the starboard side a green light so constructed as to show an unbroken light over an arc of the horizon of ten points of the compass, so fixed as to throw the light from right ahead to two points abaft the beam on the starboard side, and of such a character as to be visible at a distance of at least two miles.

(c) On the port side a red light so constructed as to show an unbroken light over an arc of the horizon of ten points of the compass, so fixed as to throw the light from right ahead to two points abaft the beam on the port side, and of such a character as to be visible at a distance of at least two miles.

(c) "Sternlight" means a white light placed as nearly as practicable at the stern showing an unbroken light over an arc of the horizon of 135 degrees and so fixed as to show the light 67.5 degrees from right aft on each side of the vessel.

Art. 10. (a) A vessel when underway, if not otherwise required by these rules to carry one or more lights visible from aft, shall carry at her stern a white light, so constructed that it shall show an unbroken light over an arc of the horizon of twelve points of the compass, so fixed as to show the light six points from right aft on each side of the vessel, and of such a character as to be visible at a distance of at least two miles. Such light shall be carried as nearly as practicable on the same level as the side lights.

(d) "Towing light" means a yellow light having the same characteristics as the "sternlight" defined in paragraph (c) of this rule.

(e) "All round light" means a light showing an unbroken light over an arc of the horizon of 360 degrees.

(f) "Flashing light" means a light flashing at regular intervals at a frequency of 120 flashes or more per minute.

Art. 3. (b) A steam vessel carrying towing lights the same as the white light mentioned in article 2 (a), when pushing another vessel or vessels ahead, shall also carry at or near the stern two bright amber lights in a vertical line, one over the other, not less than three feet apart; each of these lights shall be so constructed as to show an unbroken light over an arc of the horizon of twelve points of the compass, so fixed as to show the light six points from right aft on each side of the vessel, and of such a character as to be visible at a distance of at least two miles. A steam vessel carrying towing lights the same as the white light mentioned in article 2 (a) may also carry, irrespective of the position of the tow, the after range light mentioned in article 2 (f); however, if the after range light is carried by such a vessel when pushing another vessel or vessels ahead, the amber lights shall be carried in a vertical line with and at least three feet lower than the after range light. A steam vessel carrying towing lights the same as the white light mentioned in article 2 (a), when towing one or more vessels astern, may also carry, in lieu of the stern light specified in article 10, a small white light abaft the funnel or aftermast for the tow to steer by, but such light shall not be visible forward of the beam.

DEFINITIONS

RULE 32. (a) The word "whistle" means any sound signalling appliance capable of producing the prescribed blasts and which complies with the specifications in Annex III to these regulations.

(b) The term "short blast" means a blast of about one second's duration.

(c) The term "prolonged blast" means a blast of from four to six seconds' duration.

Art. 15. All signals prescribed by this article for vessels underway shall be given:

1. By "steam vessels" on the whistle or siren.

2. By "sailing vessels" and "vessels towed" on the fog horn.

The words "prolonged blast" used in this article shall mean a blast of from four to six seconds' duration.

Sec. 80.03 Signals. (a) The whistle signs provided in the rules in this part shall be sounded on an efficient whistle or siren sounded by steam or by some substitute for steam.

(1) A short blast of the whistle

shall mean a blast of about one second's duration.

(2) A prolonged blast of the whistle shall mean a blast of from 4 to 6 seconds' duration.

PILOT RULES

GENERAL

Sec. 80.01 General instructions. The regulations in this part apply to vessels navigating the harbors, rivers, and inland waters of the United States, except the Great Lakes and their connecting and tributary waters as far east as Montreal, the Red River of the North, the Mississippi River and its tributaries above Huey P. Long Bridge, and that part of the Atchafalaya River above its junction with the Plaquemine-Morgan City alternate waterway.

Sec. 80.02 Definition of steam vessel and vessel under way; risk of collision. In the rules in this part the words "steam vessel" shall include any vessel propelled by machinery. A vessel is underway, within the meaning of the rules in this part, when she is not at anchor, or made fast to the shore, or aground. Risk of collision can, when circumstances permit, be ascertained by carefully watching the compass bearing of an approaching vessel. If the bearing does not appreciably change, such risk should be deemed to exist.

Sec. 80.14 Lights; time for. The following rules in this part concerning light shall be complied with in all weathers from sunset to sunrise.

RULES PAMPHLET

Sec. 80.13 (b) Pamphlet containing pilot rules. All vessels and craft over 65 feet in length upon the waters described in Section 80.01 shall, where practicable, carry on board and maintain for ready reference copies of the current edition of Coast Guard Pamphlet CG-169. Nothing in this section shall require copies of this pamphlet to be carried on board any motorboat as defined by Section 1 of the Act of April 25, 1940, as amended (54 Stat. 163; 46 U.S.C. 526).

UNAUTHORIZED USE OF LIGHTS; UNNECESSARY WHISTLING

Sec. 80.34 Rule relating to the use of searchlights or other blinding lights. Flashing the rays of a searchlight or other blinding light onto the bridge or into the pilot-house of any vessel underway is prohibited. Any person who shall flash or cause to be flashed the rays of a blinding light in violation of the above may be proceeded against in accordance with the provisions of R. S. 4450, as amended, looking to the revocation or suspension of his license or certificate.

Sec. 80.35 Rule prohibiting unnecessary sounding of the whistle. Unnecessary sounding of the whistle is prohibited within any harbor limits of the United States. Whenever any licensed officer in charge of any vessel shall authorize or permit such unnecessary whistling, such officer may be proceeded against in accordance with the provisions of R. S. 4450, as amended, looking to a revocation or suspension of his license.

Sec. 80.36 Rule prohibiting the carrying of unauthorized lights on vessels. Any master, or pilot of any vessel who shall authorize or permit the carrying of any light, electric or otherwise, not required by law, that in any way will interfere with distinguishing the signal lights, may be proceeded against in accordance with the provisions of R. S. 4450, as amended, looking to a suspension or revocation of his license.

UNDER LOW BRIDGE

Sec. 80.40 Exceptions to the statutory and regulatory requirements for lights, day signals, or other navigational means and appliances when operating under bridges. (a) Any vessel while passing under a bridge may temporarily lower any lights, day signals, or other navigational means and appliances when required to do so because of the restricted vertical clearance under the bridge. Immediately when clear of the bridge, all lights, day signals, or other navigational means and appliances shall be exhibited as required by law or regulation.

BOUNDARY LINES

Sec. 82.01 General basis and purpose of demarcation lines (a) The regulations in this part establish the lines of demarcation delineating those waters upon which mariners must comply with the International Regulations for Preventing Collisions at Sea, 1972 (72 COLREGS) and those waters upon which mariners must comply with the Navigation Rules for Harbors, Rivers, and Inland Waters (Inland Rules).

(b) The waters inside of the lines are INLAND RULES WATERS. The waters outside the lines are COL-REGS WATERS.

(c) The regulations in this part do not apply to the Great Lakes or their connecting and tributary waters as described in Part 90 of this Chapter, or the Western Rivers as described in Part 95 of this Chapter.

NOTES

International Rules The International Rules are based on international agreement of maritime nations of the world. They are given force by separate statutes by the maritime countries. The present International Rules are the outgrowth of the International Conference on Safety of Life at Sea in London, England, in 1972. Officially, the rules are known as "The International Regulations for Preventing Collisions at Sea, 1972"; The Senate gave its advice and consent on October 28, 1975, the President approved acceptance on December 12, 1975, and the acceptance was deposited with IMCO effective November 23, 1976. The Secretary General of IMCO declared the 1972 Rules to be in effect from 1200 local time, July 15, 1977. They were proclaimed by the President in January 1977 and put into effect without enabling legislation by Congress.

Inland Rules The Inland Rules are "special rules made by appropriate authority" which have been enacted by Congress pursuant to Rule 1(b), International Rules. Congress, in enacting these rules, has given authority to the Coast Guard to make other rules to supplement and implement the Inland Rules. These other rules are the Pilot Rules, which have the same force and effect as the Inland Rules when not in conflict. The Inland Rules are statutory and the Pilot Rules are regulatory in nature. Both date back to the 1890's.

Codification The Inland Rules may be found in Title 33, United States Code, Sections 154 through 232. The International Rules can be found in Title 33, Code of Federal Regulations, as Appendix A to Part 87. The Pilot Rules for Inland Waters are in Part 80 of Title 33, Code of Federal Regulations.

Applicability Every vessel and every seaplane on the water, regardless of flag, ownership, or service, navigates under International Rules on the high seas and their approaches outside prescribed inland waters. Similarly, every vessel is under Inland and Pilot Rules on the inland waters of the United States, the Great Lakes and certain rivers emptying into the Gulf of Mexico excepted. Other special rules apply to those waters and to the Panama Canal.

Specific boundary lines of inland waters have been established in most of the areas subject to the Inland and Pilot Rules. These may be found in Appendix A. In areas where no specific boundary lines have been established, boundary lines of inland waters are determined by:

(1) The shore line

(2) At buoyed entrances, a line approximately parallel with the general trend of the highwater shoreline across the entrance to small bays and inlets.

Penalty The International Rules do not contain a monetary penalty, as such a penalty would be more or less unenforceable. Compliance with the rules is based on liability in a collision and, in some countries, action against licenses of mariners involved. In Inland Rules, where enforcement is more feasible, various penalties are provided. Generally, these penalties also apply to violations of the Pilot Rules. Certain countries have also made it an offense for vessels of their flag to violate traffic separation schemes, e.g., in the English Channel where both France and the United Kingdom police the straits. The Inland Rules do not mention traffic separation schemes, but they are provided for in the Ports and Waterways Safety Act of 1972 (see Appendix U).

International Definitions British Admiralty courts have held that a vessel using her anchor to assist a turn in a river is *underway* and not at anchor. A vessel is only at anchor so long as the anchor is down and *holding*. A vessel continues to be at anchor until the anchor ceases to hold or is broken out on weighing. Thus vessels dredging with the current, or dragging their anchor or riding to chain without the anchors attached, are not properly at anchor and should be considered underway. However, if the anchor or chain should foul an obstruction, and holds, then the vessel is at anchor. For most purposes a ship moored to a buoy may be treated as a vessel at anchor.

Examples of vessels *not under command*, apart from obvious cases of casualties to propulsion or steering that prevent compliance with the Rules, could well include: a vessel hove to in heavy weather, a vessel dragging her anchor or riding to chain with no anchor attached, or a sailing ship "in irons" or becalmed.

Preliminaries In the preliminary observations regarding Inland Steering and Sailing Rules, special attention is drawn to risk of collision. The preliminary observation regarding risk of collision is not a rule of navigation, but properly used will often give positive information that risk of collision exists; that is, when consecutive bearings taken of the other vessel show no change in bearing or a very slight change in bearing. Such bearings should therefore always be taken. The practical effect is to exclude a radar contact as a visual sighting.

Under International Rules similar observations are required to determine risk of collision, but specifically under all conditions of visibility and using all appropriate means. Whereas the use of compass bearing is stressed, so, too, is the proper use of radar equipment. The International Rules later set down separate courses of action to avoid a close-quarters situation, dependent on whether in sight of the other vessel or not.

Again the Inland Rules are silent as to lights in daytime, the extent of visibility notwithstanding. Under International Rules the prescribed lights are mandatory from sunset to sunrise and during restricted visibility. They are permissive at other times.

The Inland Rules do not mention radar.

Under International Rules the definition of vessels engaged in fishing specifically excludes vessels fishing with trolling lines. The Inland Rules make no such distinction. Strictly, a vessel with trolling lines, under Inland Rules, is engaged in fishing with lines. However, for such a vessel, fishing with trolling lines, to claim a privileged status in Inland Waters, it would be necessary for her to indicate her occupation by displaying the special lights or shape required by the Inland Rules.

Exemptions Navy and Coast Guard vessels of *special construction* are permitted limited modifications in lights prescribed by Inland Rules. The same exemption applies to such vessels in International Rules but is also extended to cover *all vessels of special construction or purpose.* The authority is a restricted authority, limited in intent and coupled with specified procedural steps to give the modifications force. For current exemptions of U. S. Navy and Coast Guard ships, see Appendixes Q and R.

IMCO IMCO, the Intergovernmental Maritime Consultative Organization, is an outgrowth of an international conference in Geneva in 1948, whose purpose was to create an organization to disseminate, coordinate, and modernize shipping matters heretofore dealt with by intermittent international conferences. IMCO was established in 1958. Its membership now includes nearly all maritime countries of the world.

Seaplanes While the Inland and Pilot Rules are silent with respect to seaplanes on the inland waters, as are the rules for the Great Lakes and Western Rivers, seaplanes on the local waters of the United States are governed by Civil Air Regulations in conformance with the rules applicable to vessels. The latter regulations may be found in Title 14, Code of Federal Regulations, Section 60.22, 60.23. They are not reprinted herein in view of their conformance to the nautical rules to prevent collisions, and in view of the rarity of a seaplane being outside a reserved seaplane area while on the local waters of the United States. The revised International Rules, which do provide for seaplanes on the high seas, warn mariners of the relative lack of maneuverability of seaplanes in the act of landing or taking off.

3
Running and Anchor Lights

International Rules

DEFINITIONS

RULE 21. (a) "Masthead light" means a white light placed over the fore and aft centreline of the vessel showing an unbroken light over an arc of the horizon of 225 degrees and so fixed as to show the light from right ahead to 22.5 degrees abaft the beam on either side of the vessel.

(b) "Sidelights" means a green light on the starboard side and a red light on the port side each showing an unbroken light over an arc of the horizon of 112.5 degrees and so fixed as to show the light from right ahead to 22.5 degrees abaft the beam on its respective side. In a vessel of less than 20 metres in length the sidelights may be combined in one lantern carried on the fore and aft centreline of the vessel.

Inland and Pilot Rules

Art. 1. The word "visible" in these rules, when applied to lights, shall mean visible on a dark night with a clear atmosphere.
(33 U.S.C. 156)

Note: Definitions of lights are contained in the articles requiring the lights.

(c) "Sternlight" means a white light placed as nearly as practicable at the stern showing an unbroken light over an arc of the horizon of 135 degrees and so fixed as to show the light 67.5 degrees from right aft on each side of the vessel.

(e) "All round light" means a light showing an unbroken light over an arc of the horizon of 360 degrees.

(f) "Flashing light" means a light flashing at regular intervals at a frequency of 120 flashes or more per minute.

VISIBILITY OF LIGHTS

RULE 22. The lights prescribed in these rules shall have an intensity as specified in Section 8 of Annex I to these regulations so as to be visible at the following minimum ranges:

(a) In vessels of 50 metres or more in length:

—a masthead light, 6 miles;

—a sidelight, 3 miles;

—a sternlight, 3 miles;

—a white, red, green or yellow all-round light, 2 miles.

(b) In vessels of 12 metres or more in length but less than 50 metres in length:

—a masthead light, 5 miles; except that where the length of the vessel is less than 20 metres, 3 miles;

—a sidelight, 2 miles;

—a sternlight, 2 miles;

—a white, red, green or yellow all-round light, 2 miles.

Note: Visibility of lights are contained in the articles requiring the lights.

International Rules

Inland and Pilot Rules

(c) In vessels of less than 12 metres in length:
—a masthead light, 2 miles;
—a sidelight, 1 mile;
—a sternlight, 2 miles;
—a white or yellow all-round light, 2 miles.

POWER-DRIVEN VESSELS UNDERWAY[1]

RULE 23. (a) A power-driven vessel underway shall exhibit: (i) a masthead light forward;

(ii) a second masthead light abaft of and higher than the forward one; except that a vessel of less than 50 metres in length shall not be obliged to exhibit such light but may do so;

(iii) sidelights;[2]

(iv) a sternlight.

STEAM VESSELS UNDERWAY

Art. 2.[2] A steam vessel when underway shall carry—(a) On or in the front of the foremast, or if a vessel without a foremast, then in the fore part of the vessel, a bright white light so constructed as to show an unbroken light over an arc of the horizon of twenty points of the compass, so fixed as to throw the light ten points on each side of the vessel, namely, from right ahead to two points abaft the beam on either side, and of such a character as to be visible at a distance of at least five miles.

(e) A seagoing steam vessel when underway may carry an additional white light similar in construction to the light mentioned in subdivision (a). These two lights shall be so placed in line with the keel that one shall be at least fifteen feet higher than the other, and in such a position with reference to each

---

[1] Heights of lights, including vertical and horizontal separations are found in Annex I to the International Rules.

[2] Construction details of screens are found in Annex I to the International Regulations.

[2] Article 2 amended by the Motorboat Act of April 25, 1940, to exclude certain motorboats not more than 65 feet in length. See subsequent text this chapter or Appendix H for motorboat requirements.

other that the lower light shall be forward of the upper one. The vertical distance between these lights shall be less than the horizontal distance.

(f) All steam vessels (except seagoing vessels and ferryboats), shall carry in addition to green and red lights required by article two (b), (c), and screens as required by article two (d), a central range of two white lights; the after light being carried at an elevation at least fifteen feet above the light at the head of the vessel. The headlight shall be so constructed as to show an unbroken light through twenty points of the compass, namely, from right ahead to two points abaft the beam on either side of the vessel, and the after light so as to show all around the horizon.

Art. 2 (b) On the starboard side a green light so constructed as to show an unbroken light over an arc of the horizon of ten points of the compass, so fixed as to throw the light from right ahead to two points abaft the beam on the starboard side, and of such a character as to be visible at a distance of at least two miles.

(c) On the port side a red light so constructed as to show an unbroken light over an arc of the horizon of ten points of the compass, so fixed as to throw the light from right ahead to two points abaft the beam on the port side, and of such

FIG. 1. Power-driven (or steam) vessel underway, with after range light, high seas or inland waters. International Rule 23(a); Inland Rules, Article 2.

FIG. 2. An air-cushion vessel operating in the non-displacement mode, showing all-round flashing yellow light. International Rule 23(b).

a character as to be visible at a distance of at least two miles.

(d) The said green and red side lights shall be fitted with inboard screens projecting at least three feet forward from the light, so as to prevent these lights from being seen across the bow.

(b) An air-cushion vessel when operating in the non-displacement mode shall, in addition to the lights prescribed in paragraph (a) of this rule, exhibit an all-round flashing yellow light.

(c) A power-driven vessel of less than 7 metres in length and whose maximum speed does not exceed 7 knots may, in lieu of the lights prescribed in paragraph (a) of this Rule, exhibit an all-round white light. Such vessel shall, if practicable, also exhibit sidelights.

Art. 10. (a) A vessel when underway, if not otherwise required by these rules to carry one or more lights visible from aft, shall carry at her stern a white light, so constructed that it shall show an unbroken light over an arc of the horizon of twelve points of the compass, so fixed as to show the light six points from right aft on each side of the vessel, and of such a character as to be visible at a distance of at least two miles. Such light shall be carried as nearly as practicable on the same level as the side lights.

MOTOR BOATS

The Motorboat Act of April 25, 1940 Public Law 484, 76th Congress, as amended, corresponds to Rules 22 (b) (c) and 23 (c), International Rules, by exempting or reducing the requirements for certain small machinery-propelled vessels not over 65 feet from the lighting requirements prescribed in Art. 2, Inland Rules for steam vessels on the Inland Waters of the United States. It provides in part:

FIG. 3. Non-seagoing steam vessel underway, with all around after range light, inland waters only. Inland Rules, Article 2(f).

FIG. 4. Power-driven (i.e., seagoing steam) vessel underway, with fixed stern light, high seas or inland waters. International Rule 23(a); Inland Rules, Article 10.

Be it enacted by the Senate and House of Representatives of the United States of America in Congress assembled, That the word "motorboat" where used in this Act shall include every vessel propelled by machinery and not more than sixty-five feet in length except tugboats and towboats propelled by steam. The length shall be measured from end to end over the deck, excluding sheer: Provided, That the engine, boiler or other operating machinery shall be subject to inspection by the Coast Guard, and to their approval of the design thereof, on all said motorboats, which are more than forty feet in length, and which are propelled by machinery driven by steam.

Sec. 2. Motorboats subject to the provisions of this Act shall be divided into four classes as follows:

Class A. Less than sixteen feet in length.

Class 1. Sixteen feet or over and less than twenty-six feet in length.

Class 2. Twenty-six feet or over and less than forty feet in length.

Class 3. Forty feet or over and not more than sixty-five feet in length.

Sec. 3. Every motorboat in all weathers from sunset to sunrise shall carry and exhibit the following lights when underway, and during such time no other lights which may be mistaken for those prescribed shall be exhibited:

(a) Every motorboat of classes A

FIG. 5. Motorboat Act lights, Class A or 1 motorboat underway, power only (or both sail and power), inland waters only. Motorboat Act, Sections 3(a) and (b).

FIG. 6. Lights, Class A or 1 motorboat underway, power only (or both sail and power), inland waters or high seas. A combined lantern may be shown in lieu of the sidelights. International Rule 23(a); Motorboat Act, Section 3(f).

and 1 shall carry the following lights:

First. A bright white light aft to show all around the horizon.

Second. A combined lantern in the fore part of the vessel and lower than the white light aft, showing green to starboard and red to port, so fixed as to throw the light from right ahead to two points abaft the beam on their respective sides.

(b) Every motorboat of classes 2 and 3 shall carry the following lights:

First. A bright white light in the fore part of the vessel as near the stem as practicable, so constructed as to show an unbroken light over an arc of the horizon of twenty points of the compass, so fixed as to throw the light ten points on each side of the vessel; namely, from right ahead to two points abaft the beam on either side.

Second. A bright white light aft to show all around the horizon and higher than the white light forward.

Third. On the starboard side a green light so constructed as to show an unbroken light over an arc of the horizon of ten points of the compass, so fixed as to throw the light from right ahead to two points abaft the beam on the starboard side. On the port side a red light so constructed as to show an unbroken light over an arc of the horizon of ten points of the compass, so fixed as to throw the light from right ahead to two points

FIG. 7. Motorboat Act lights, Class 2 or 3 motorboat underway, power only (or both sail and power), inland waters only. Motorboat Act, Sections 3(b) and (e).

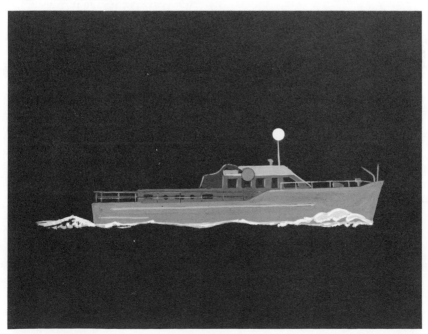

FIG. 8. Lights, Class 2 or 3 motorboat underway, power only (or both sail and power), inland waters or high seas. A combined lantern may be shown in lieu of the sidelights. International Rule 23(a); Motorboat Act, Section 3(f).

abaft the beam on the port side. The said side lights shall be fitted with inboard screens of sufficient height so set as to prevent these lights from being seen across the bow.

(c) Motorboats of classes A and 1 when propelled by sail alone shall carry the combined lantern, but not the white light aft, prescribed by this section. Motorboats of classes 2 and 3, when so propelled, shall carry the colored side lights, suitably screened, but not the white lights, prescribed by this section. Motorboats of all classes, when so propelled, shall carry, ready at hand, a lantern or flashlight showing a white light which shall be exhibited in sufficient time to avert collision.

(d) Every white light prescribed by this section shall be of such character as to be visible at a distance of at least two miles. Every colored light prescribed by this section shall be of such character as to be visible at a distance of at least one mile. The word "visible" in this Act, when applied to lights, shall mean visible on a dark night with clear atmosphere.

(e) When propelled by sail and machinery any motorboat shall carry the lights required by this section for a motorboat propelled by machinery only.

(f) Any motorboat may carry and exhibit the lights required by the Regulations. . . . [This paragraph will be modified to permit motorboats

FIG. 9. Sailing vessel underway, showing optional foremast lights, high seas only. In inland waters vessel shows only side lights and a stern light not visible this view. International Rule 25(c).

FIG. 10. Sailing vessel underway at sea, foremast lights omitted, high seas or inland waters. International Rule 25(a); Inland Rules, Article 5.

to show the lights required by the 1972 International Rules in lieu of the lights required by this section.]

SAILING VESSELS UNDERWAY
AND VESSELS UNDER OARS

RULE 25. (a) A sailing vessel underway shall exhibit:

(i) sidelights;

(ii) a sternlight.

(b) In a sailing vessel of less than 12 metres in length the lights prescribed in paragraph (a) of this rule may be combined in one lantern carried at or near the top of the mast where it can best be seen.

(c) A sailing vessel underway may, in addition to the lights prescribed in paragraph (a) of this rule, exhibit at or near the top of the mast, where they can best be seen, two all-round lights in a vertical line, the upper being red and the lower green, but these lights shall not be exhibited in conjunction with the combined lantern permitted by paragraph (b) of this rule.

(d)(i) A sailing vessel of less than 7 metres in length shall, if practicable, exhibit the lights prescribed in paragraph (a) or (b) of this rule, but if she does not, she shall have ready at hand an electric torch or lighted lantern showing a white light which shall be exhibited in sufficient time to prevent collision.

(ii) A vessel under oars may exhibit the lights prescribed in this rule for sailing vessels, but if she does not, she shall have ready at hand an electric torch or lighted

SAILING VESSELS

Art. 5. A sailing vessel underway and any vessel being towed, except barges, canal boats, scows, and other vessels of nondescript type, when in tow of steam vessels, shall carry the same lights as are prescribed by article 2 for a steam vessel underway, with the exception of the white lights mentioned therein, which they shall never carry.

ROWING BOATS AND
RAFTS

Art. 7. Rowing boats, whether under oars or sail, shall have ready at hand a lantern showing a white light which shall be temporarily exhibited in sufficient time to prevent collision.

Art. 9. (d) Rafts, or other water craft not herein provided for, navigating by hand power, horse power, or by the current of the river, shall carry one or more good white lights, which shall be placed in such manner as shall be prescribed by the Commandant of the Coast Guard.

Sec. 80.32. Lights for rafts and other craft. (a) Any vessel propelled by hand power, horse power, or by the current of the river, except rafts and rowboats, shall carry one white

FIG. 11. Sailing vessel, less than 12 meters in length showing combined lantern at or near top of mast, high seas only. International Rule 25(b).

FIG. 12. Sailing vessel underway, stern view, inland waters or high seas. International Rule 25(a); Inland Rules, Article 10(a).

lantern showing a white light which shall be exhibited in sufficient time to prevent collision.

light forward not less than 8 feet above the surface of the water.

(c) The white lights required by this section shall be carried from sunset to sunrise, in a lantern so fixed and constructed as to show a clear, uniform, and unbroken light, visible all around the horizon, and of such intensity as to be visible on a dark night with a clear atmosphere at a distance of at least one mile. The lights for rafts shall be suspended from poles of such height that the lights shall not be less than 8 feet above the surface of the water.

LIGHTS FOR SMALL VESSELS IN BAD WEATHER

Art. 6. Whenever, as in the case of vessels of less than ten gross tons under way during bad weather, the green and red side lights cannot be fixed, these lights shall be kept at hand, lighted and ready for use; and shall, on the approach of or to other vessels, be exhibited on their respective sides in sufficient time to prevent collision, in such manner as to make them most visible, and so that the green light shall not be seen on the port side nor the red light on the starboard side, nor, if practicable, more than two points abaft the beam on their respective sides. To make the use of these portable lights more certain and easy the lanterns containing them shall each be painted outside with the color of the light they respec-

FIG. 13. Lights, power-driven vessel (or **boat**) of less than 20 meters, showing combined lantern in lieu of sidelights. International Rules 21(b) and 23(a).

FIG. 14. A vessel under oars (or less than 7 meters in length, under sail) with lighted lantern (or torch) showing a white light. International Rule 25(d).

tively contain, and shall be provided with proper screens.

Art. 10 (b) In a small vessel, if it is not possible on account of bad weather or other sufficient cause for this light to be fixed, an electric torch or a lighted lantern showing a white light shall be kept at hand ready for use and shall, on the approach of an overtaking vessel, be shown in sufficient time to prevent collision.

LIGHTS FOR FERRYBOATS

Sec. 80.15 Ferryboats. (a) Ferryboats propelled by machinery and navigating the harbors, rivers, and other inland waters of the United States, except the Great Lakes and their connecting and tributary waters as far east as Montreal, the Red River of the North, the Mississippi River and its tributaries above Huey P. Long Bridge, and that part of the Atchafalaya River above its junction with the Plaquemine-Morgan City alternate waterway, shall carry the range lights and the colored side lights required by law to be carried on steam vessels navigating those waters, except that double-end ferryboats shall carry a central range of clear, bright, white lights, showing all around the horizon, placed at equal altitudes forward and aft, also on the starboard side a green light, and on the port side a red light, of such a character as to be visible on a dark night with

FIG. 15. Small rowing boat under sail, high seas or inland waters. International Rule 25(d), (i); Inland Rules, Article 7.

FIG. 16. Double-ended ferry, with special blue light, inland waters. Pilot Rules, Section 80.15.

a clear atmosphere at a distance of at least 2 miles, and so constructed as to show a uniform and unbroken light over an arc of the horizon of 10 points of the compass, and so fixed as to throw the light from right ahead to 2 points abaft the beam on their respective sides.

(b) The green and red lights shall be fitted with inboard screens projecting at least 3 feet forward from the lights, so as to prevent them from being seen across the bow.

(c) Officers in Charge, Marine Inspection, in districts having ferryboats shall, whenever the safety of navigation may require, designate for each line of such boats a certain light, white or colored, which will show all around the horizon, to designate and distinguish such lines from each other, which light shall be carried on a flagstaff amidships, 15 feet above the white range lights.

LIGHTS FOR SUBMARINES[4]

Sec. 707.1 Display of distinctive lights by submarines. (a) In accordance with Rule I (c) International Rules and Article 13, Inland Rules, the Secretary of the Navy has authorized the display of a distinctive light by U.S. Naval submarines in international waters and in the inland waters of the United States. The light will be exhibited in addition to the presently prescribed navigational lights for submarines.

[4] *Sec. 707.1 applies to both inland waters and high seas.*

(b) The normal navigational lights of submarines have been found to be easily mistaken for those of small vessels when in fact submarines are large deep-draft vessels with limited maneuvering characteristics while they are on the surface. The newly authorized light is expected to promote safety at sea by assisting in the identification of submarines.

(c) United States submarines may therefore display an amber colored rotating light producing 90 flashes per minute visible all round the horizon at a distance of at least 3 miles, the light to be located approximately 6 feet above the masthead light.

INTERPRETIVE RULINGS

Sec. 86.05-1 White lights for motorboats carried on centerline. Every white light required by section 3 of the Act of April 25, 1940, as amended (46 U.S.C. 526b), shall be carried on the centerline of the motorboat, except that the all around white light aft on a motorboat of Class A or 1 may be carried off the centerline.

Sec. 86.05-5 Stern lights for all vessels. Article 10 of section 1 of the Act of June 7, 1897, as amended by the Act of August 14, 1958 (33 U.S.C. 179), requires "A vessel when underway, if not otherwise required by these rules to carry one or more lights visible from aft, shall carry at her stern a white light, . . ." and this requirement shall be applied to all

International Rules

ANCHORED VESSELS AND VESSELS AGROUND

RULE 30. (a) A vessel at anchor shall exhibit where it can best be seen:

(i) in the fore part, an all-round white light or one ball;

(ii) at or near the stern and at a lower level than the light prescribed in subparagraph (i), an all-round white light.

(b) A vessel of less than 50 metres in length may exhibit an all-round white light where it can best be seen instead of the lights prescribed in paragraph (a) of this rule.

(c) A vessel at anchor may, and a vessel of 100 metres and more in length shall, also use the available working or equivalent lights to illuminate her decks.

(d) A vessel aground shall exhibit the lights prescribed in paragraph (a) or (b) of this rule and in addition, where they can best be seen:

(i) two all-round red lights in a vertical line;

(ii) three balls in a vertical line.

(e) A vessel of less than 7 metres in length, when at anchor or aground, not in or near a narrow channel, fairway or anchorage, or

Inland and Pilot Rules

vessels, including but not limited to, tugs, barges, sail vessels, motorboats when propelled by sail alone, etc.

ANCHOR LIGHTS

Art. 11. (b) Except as provided in paragraph (c) of this article, a vessel of one hundred and fifty feet or upward in length, when at anchor, shall carry in the forward part of the vessel, at a height of not less than twenty feet above the hull, one such light, and at or near the stern of the vessel, and at such a height that it shall be not less than fifteen feet lower than the forward light, another such light.

Art. 11. (a) Except as provided in paragraph (c) of this article, a vessel under one hundred and fifty feet in length when at anchor shall carry forward, where it can best be seen, a white light in a lantern so constructed as to show a clear, uniform, and unbroken light visible all around the horizon at a distance of at least two miles.

(c) The Secretary of Transportation may, after investigation, by rule, regulation, or order, designate such areas as he may deem proper as 'special anchorage areas'; such special anchorage areas may from time to time be changed, or abolished, if after investigation the Secretary of Transportation shall deem such change or abolition in the interest of navigation. When anchored within such an area—

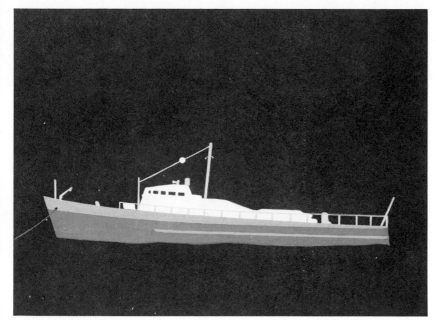

FIG. 17. Vessel less than 150 feet in length at anchor, inland waters. Inland Rules, Article 11(a).

FIG. 18. Vessel 150 feet or more in length at anchor, inland waters. Vessel at anchor, high seas. A vessel less than 50 meters may show only one white light, high seas. International Rules 30(a) and (b); Inland Rules, Article 11(b).

where other vessels normally navigate, shall not be required to exhibit the lights or shapes prescribed in paragraphs (a), (b) or (d) of this rule.

(1) a vessel or not more than sixty-five feet in length shall not be required to carry or exhibit the white light required by this article;

(2) a barge, canal boat, scow, or other nondescript craft of one hundred and fifty feet or upward in length may carry and exhibit the single white light prescribed by paragraph (a) of this article in lieu of the two white lights prescribed by paragraph (b) of this article; and

(3) where two or more barges, canal boats, scows, or other nondescript craft are tied together and anchored as a unit, the anchor light prescribed by this article need be displayed only on the vessel having its anchor down.

LIGHTS FOR MOORED BARGES

Sec. 80.16a Lights for barges, canal boats, scows, and other nondescript vessels on certain inland waters on the Gulf Coast and the Gulf Intracoastal Waterway. (h) Lights for moored barges shall be as described in this paragraph.

(1) The following barges, when moored in or near a fairway, shall display between the hours of sunset and sunrise the barge lights described in subparagraph (2) of this paragraph:

(i) Every barge projecting into a buoyed or restricted channel.

(ii) Every barge so moored that it reduces the available navigable width of any channel to less than 250 feet.

SEAPLANES

RULE 31. Where it is impracticable for a seaplane to exhibit lights and shapes of the characteristics or in the positions prescribed in the rules of this part she shall exhibit lights and shapes as closely similar in characteristics and position as is possible.

FIG. 19. Vessel less than 150 feet in length aground, inland waters. Inland Rules, Article 11(a).

FIG. 20. Vessel aground, high seas. A vessel under 50 meters in length aground may show only one white light. Neither permitted in inland waters. International Rule 30(d).

(iii) Barges moored in fleets more than two barges wide or to a maximum width of over 80 feet, parallel to the bank.

(iv) Every barge moored to the bank in any manner other than parallel thereto.

(2) Barges required to be lighted under subparagraph (1) of this paragraph shall carry two white lights of such character as to be visible on a dark night with a clear atmosphere at a distance of at least 1 mile, so located as to give unobstructed view and arranged as follows:

(i) On a single moored barge, a light on each outboard or channelward corner.

(ii) On barges moored in group formation, a light on the upstream outboard or channelward corner of the outer upstream barge and a light on the downstream outboard or channelward corner of the outer downstream barge. In addition, any barge projecting toward or into the channel in such a group formation shall have two white lights similarly placed on the outboard or channelward corners of the barge.

(3) Barges moored in any slip or slough which is used primarily for mooring purposes are exempt from the lighting requirements of this paragraph.

EXEMPTIONS—NAVY AND
COAST GUARD VESSELS

EXEMPTIONS—NAVY AND
COAST GUARD VESSELS

RULE 1(e) Whenever the Gov-

33 U.S.C. 360. Any requirement

ernment concerned shall have determined that a vessel of special construction or purpose cannot comply fully with the provisions of any of these Rules with respect to the number, position, range or arc of visibility of lights or shapes, without interfering with the special function of the vessel or seaplane, such vessel shall comply with such other provisions in regard to the number, position, range or arc of visibility of lights or shapes as well as to the disposition and characteristics of sound signalling appliances as her Government shall have determined to be the closest possible compliance with these Rules in respect of that vessel.

33 U.S.C. 1052. Any requirement of such regulations in respect of the number, position, range of visibility, or arc of visibility of the lights required to be displayed by vessels shall not apply to any vessel of the Navy or of the Coast Guard whenever the Secretary of the Navy or the Secretary of Transportation, in the case of Coast Guard vessels operating under the Department of Transportation, or such official as either may designate, shall find or certify that, by reason of special construction, it is not possible for such vessel or class of vessels to comply with such regulations. The lights of any such exempted vessel or class of vessels, however, shall conform as closely to the requirements of the applicable regulations as the Secretary or such official

as to the number, position, range of visibility, or arc of visibility of lights required to be displayed by vessels under . . . sections 154-231 of this title . . . and all laws amendatory thereto, shall not apply to any vessel of the Navy or of the Coast Guard, where the Secretary of the Navy, or the Secretary of Transportation in the case of Coast Guard vessels operating under the Department of Transportation, or such official or officials as either may designate, shall find or certify that, by reason of special construction, it is not possible with respect to such vessel or class of vessels to comply with the statutory provisions as to the number, position, range of visibility, or arc of visibility of lights. The lights of any such exempted vessel or class of vessels shall, however, comply as closely to the requirements of the applicable sections as the Secretary shall find to be feasible.

33 U.S.C. 360a. When the Secretary of the Navy or the Secretary of Transportation, or such official or officials as either may designate, shall make any finding or certification as prescribed in section 360 of this title, notice of such finding or certification and the character and position of the lights to be displayed on such vessel shall be published in "Notice to Mariners."

shall find or certify to be feasible. Notice of such findings or certification and of the character and position of the lights prescribed to be displayed on such exempted vessel or class of vessels shall be published in the Federal Register and in the Notice to Mariners and, after the effective date specified in such notice, shall have effect as part of such regulations.

ANNEX I

EXTRACT FROM
POSITIONING AND TECHNICAL
DETAILS OF LIGHTS AND
SHAPES

1. Definition

The term "height above the hull" means height above the uppermost continuous deck.

2. Vertical Positioning and Spacing of Lights

(a) On a power-driven vessel of 20 metres or more in length the masthead lights shall be placed as follows:

(i) the forward masthead light, or if only one masthead light is carried, then that light, at a height above the hull of not less than 6 metres, and, if the breadth of the vessel exceeds 6 metres, then at a height above the hull not less than such breadth, so however that the light need not be placed at a greater height above the hull than 12 metres;

(ii) when two masthead lights are

carried the after one shall be at least 4.5 metres vertically higher than the forward one.

(b) The vertical separation of masthead lights of power-driven vessels shall be such that in all normal conditions of trim the after light will be seen over and separate from the forward light at a distance of 1000 metres from the stem when viewed from sea level.

(c) The masthead light of a power-driven vessel of 12 metres but less than 20 metres in length shall be placed at a height above the gunwale of not less than 2.5 metres.

(d) A power-driven vessel of less than 12 metres in length may carry the uppermost light at a height of less than 2.5 metres above the gunwale. When however a masthead light is carried in addition to sidelights and a sternlight, then such masthead light shall be carried at least 1 metre higher than the sidelights.

(e) One of the two or three masthead lights prescribed for a power-driven vessel when engaged in towing or pushing another vessel shall be placed in the same position as the forward masthead light of a power-driven vessel.

(f) In all circumstances the masthead light or lights shall be so placed as to be above and clear of all other lights and obstructions.

(g) The sidelights of a power-driven vessel shall be placed at a height above the hull not greater than three quarters of that of the forward masthead light. They shall not be so low as to be interfered with by deck lights.

(h) The sidelights, if in a combined lantern and carried on a power-driven vessel of less than 20 metres in length, shall be placed not less than 1 metre below the masthead light.

(i) When the rules prescribe two or three lights to be carried in a vertical line, they shall be spaced as follows:

(i) on a vessel of 20 metres in length or more such lights shall be spaced not less than 2 metres apart, and the lowest of these lights shall, except where a towing light is required, not be less than 4 metres above the hull;

(ii) on a vessel of less than 20 metres in length such lights shall be spaced not less than 1 metre apart and the lowest of these lights shall, except where a towing light is required, not be less than 2 metres above the gunwale;

(iii) when three lights are carried they shall be equally spaced.

(j) The lower of the two all-round lights prescribed for a fishing vessel when engaged in fishing shall be at a height above the sidelights not less than twice the distance between the two vertical lights.

(k) The forward anchor light, when two are carried, shall not be less than 4.5 metres above the after one. On a vessel of 50 metres or more in length this forward anchor light shall not be less than 6 metres above the hull.

3. Horizontal Positioning and Spacing of Lights

(a) When two masthead lights are prescribed for a power-driven vessel, the horizontal distance between them shall not be less than one half of the length of the vessel but need not be more than 100 metres. The forward light shall be placed not more than one quarter of the length of the vessel from the stem.

(b) On a vessel of 20 metres or more in length the sidelights shall not be placed in front of the forward masthead lights. They shall be placed at or near the side of the vessel.

4. Details of Location of Direction-indicating Lights for Fishing Vessels, Dredgers and Vessels Engaged in Underwater Operations— . . . .

5. Screens for Sidelights

The sidelights shall be fitted with inboard screens painted matt black, and meeting the requirements of Section 9 of this Annex. With a combined lantern, using a single vertical filament and a very narrow division between the green and red sections, external screens need not be fitted.

6. Shapes— . . . .

7. Colour Specification of Lights

The chromaticity of all navigation

lights shall conform to the following standards, which lie within the boundaries of the area of the diagram specified for each colour by the International Commission on Illumination (CIE).

The boundaries of the area for each colour are given by indicating the corner co-ordinates, which are as follows:

(i) *White:*

x	0.525	0.525	0.452	0.310
	0.310	0.443		
y	0.382	0.440	0.440	0.348
	0.283	0.382		

(ii) *Green:*

| x | 0.028 | 0.009 | 0.300 | 0.203 |
| y | 0.385 | 0.723 | 0.511 | 0.356 |

(iii) *Red:*

| x | 0.680 | 0.660 | 0.735 | 0.721 |
| y | 0.320 | 0.320 | 0.265 | 0.259 |

(iv) *Yellow:*

| x | 0.612 | 0.618 | 0.575 | 0.575 |
| y | 0.382 | 0.382 | 0.425 | 0.406 |

8. Intensity of Lights

(a) The minimum luminous intensity of lights shall be calculated by using the formula:

$$I = 3.43 \times 10^6 \times T \times D^2 \times K^{-D}$$

where

I is luminous intensity in candelas under service conditions,

T is threshold factor 2×10^{-7} lux,

D is range of visibility (luminous range) of the light in nautical miles,

K is atmospheric transmissivity.

For prescribed lights the value of K shall be 0.8, corresponding to a meteorological visibility of approximately 13 nautical miles.

(b) A selection of figures derived from the formula is given in the following table:

Range of visibility (luminous range) of light in nautical miles D	Luminous intensity of light in candelas for K = 0.8 I
1	0.9
2	4.3
3	12.0
4	27.0
5	52.0
6	94.0

Note: The maximum luminous intensity of navigation lights should be limited to avoid undue glare.

9. Horizontal Sectors

(a)(i) In the forward direction, sidelights as fitted on the vessel must show the minimum required intensities. The intensities must decrease to reach practical cut-off between 1 degree and 3 degrees outside the prescribed sectors.

(ii) For sternlights and masthead lights and at 22.5 degrees abaft the beam for sidelights, the minimum required intensities shall be maintained over the arc of the horizon up to 5 degrees within the limits of the sectors prescribed in Rule 21. From 5 degrees within the prescribed sectors the intensity may decrease by 50 percent up to the prescribed limits; it shall decrease steadily to reach practical cut-off at not more than 5 degrees outside the prescribed limits.

(b) All-round lights shall be so located as not to be obscured by masts, topmasts or structures within angular sectors of more than 6 degrees, except anchor lights, which need not be placed at an impracticable height above the hull.

10. Vertical Sectors

(a) The vertical sectors of electric lights, with the exception of lights on sailing vessels shall ensure that:

(i) at least the required minimum intensity is maintained at all angles from 5 degrees above to 5 degrees below the horizontal;

(ii) at least 60 percent of the required minimum intensity is maintained from 7.5 degrees above to 7.5 degrees below the horizontal.

(b) In the case of sailing vessels the vertical sectors of electric lights shall ensure that:

(i) at least the required minimum intensity is maintained at all angles from 5 degrees above to 5 degrees below the horizontal;

(ii) at least 50 percent of the required minimum intensity is maintained from 25 degrees above to 25 degrees below the horizontal.

(c) In the case of lights other than electric these specifications shall be met as closely as possible.

11. Intensity of Non-Electric Lights

Non-electric lights shall so far as

practicable comply with the mini-
mum intensities, as specified in the
Table given in Section 8 of this
Annex.

NOTES

The definitions of various lights and visibilities required on the high
seas are contained in Rules 21 and 22, International Rules. In inland waters,
the various lights and visibilities required are described within the context
of each requirement. The technical provisions of Annex I, International
Rules, are concerned with the placement and specifications of lights. These
details are provided to ensure uniform construction of navigation lights by
all manufacturers. In the past, operating under definitions such as "visible
on a dark night with a clear atmosphere (still current under the Inland
Rules), it was possible for manufacturers to use different parameters for
calculating ranges and chromaticities, leading to varying color intensities
on board vessels.

RUNNING LIGHTS There are five basic differences in the ordinary
running lights to be displayed by power-driven vessels governed by Rules
21 and 23, International Rules, and by nonseagoing steam vessels governed
by Articles 2 and 10, Inland Rules:

High Seas.

(1) The minimum height of the masthead light is clearly specified in
Annex I.

(2) The after range light is optional for vessels under 50 meters in
length.

(3) The after range light, if carried, is to be a 225° light like the masthead light.

(4) The horizontal distance between the masthead and after range
lights is clearly specified in Annex I.

(5) A vessel underway must show a fixed 12-point sternlight. A vessel
of less than 7 meters may show an all-round white light (power-driven
vessel) or a white lantern/torch (sailing vessel) in lieu of the fixed sternlight.

Inland Waters.

(1) No minimum height is prescribed for the masthead light.

(2) The after range light is mandatory for nonseagoing steam vessels
over 65 feet in length.

(3) The after range light must be visible all around the horizon, but has no minimum visibility specified.

(4) There is no minimum horizontal separation between the masthead and after range lights.

(5) A vessel underway does not show a fixed 12-point sternlight, unless she has no other prescribed light visible from aft.

Naval and Coast Guard vessels of special construction are authorized some variation in the carriage of lights required by the rules, but such vessels are required to be in the *closest possible compliance* with the lighting requirements prescribed. The extent of the exemptions authorized such vessels by the International Rules is clear when Rule 1(e) is taken with 33 U.S.C. 1052. The Inland and Pilot Rules are silent in this respect. However, similar exemptions are authorized these vessels by 33 U.S.C. 360, which applies to the inland waters of the United States. For current exemptions for naval and Coast Guard vessels, see Appendices Q and R respectively.

Submarines are among the exempted vessels. Pursuant to Rule 1(c) International Rules, and Article 13, Inland Rules, submarines are also authorized to display a flashing amber-colored light in addition to the modified navigation lights as a special identifying signal. This signal is published separately in Section 707.1, Title 32, Code of Federal Regulations, and may be found both in this chapter and Appendix Q.

Sailing vessels on the high seas *may* show an all-round red light over an all-round green light in addition to the sidelights and stern light required to be shown by sailing vessels in inland waters and on the high seas. A sailing vessel less than 12 meters in length and on the high seas, may show a combined lantern of sidelights and stern light near the top of the mast, but then is disqualified from using the optional red over green top lights.

Ferryboats operating on the inland waters are subject to the same requirements as other steam vessels, except that double-ended ferry boats must carry a central range of all around white lights as provided in Section 80.15, Pilot Rules.

Power-driven vessels of less than 50 meters and less than 12 meters in length, navigating the high seas, have reduced requirements under Rule 22, International Rules, for visibility of lights. For a power-driven vessel under 7 meters in length and whose *maximum* speed does not exceed 7 knots, an all-round white light may be substituted. Rule 23(c), International Rules, does not define maximum speed but it presumably refers to the maximum speed at which a vessel's machinery is normally capable of propelling her, rather than the best speed she is currently achieving. The Motorboat Act provides for machinery-propelled vessels (other than steam tugs) not more than 65 feet in length navigating the inland waters of the

United States. Under both rules reduced, but not identical, navigation light requirements are prescribed for these small vessels. Rule 25(d) makes similar provision for sailing vessels of less than 7 meters and vessels under oars. The Motorboat Act, however, applies only to sailing auxiliaries not over 65 feet.

Motorboat operators near the coastline of the United States should particularly note and apply Section 3(f) of the Motorboat Act, as it permits all classes of motorboats to carry the lights of Rule 23, International Rules, in inland waters in lieu of the lights prescribed in the Act itself. Thus, a motorboat may carry *legally* the same lights in both inland waters and the high seas, provided the lights are the lights of Rule 23, International Rules. The reverse, carrying Motorboat Act lights into high seas, is not permitted.

There are also specific lighting requirements for air-cushion vessels underway on the high seas and watercraft operating by handpower, horse-power, or current on the inland waters of the United States. In the case of air-cushion vessels, and other similar craft, it must be borne in mind that their heading, as indicated by their lights, may be considerably different from their track over the sea. This is caused by drift, due to strong winds and the unique handling features of the craft. The flashing all-round yellow light required by Rule 23(b), International Rules, should alert mariners of the need for caution when meeting these high-speed craft which have difficulty in indicating their true aspect.

Interpretive rulings   An interpretive ruling that changes a statute may be binding on the interpreting authority but will not necessarily be upheld in litigation.

Anchor lights   Rule 30, International Rules, provides for vessels at anchor or aground in the high seas. Article 11, Inland Rules, merely provides for vessels at anchor on the inland waters. On the high seas a vessel of less than 50 meters in length at anchor may show only one anchor light where best it may be seen. In inland waters a vessel of less than 150 feet in length at anchor must show only one anchor light. The two red lights shown by a vessel aground outside inland waters must, under the International Rules, be shown along with the proper anchor light or lights, but cannot be used by a vessel aground in inland waters. In the latter instance a vessel can show anchor lights. Similarly, on the high seas, the special occupation lights of Rules 27(b) and 29 are shown with the anchor lights of Rule 30 (a) or (b), while in inland waters vessels so occupied show only the lights prescribed by Pilot Rules.

In inland waters special provision is made for barges and other non-descript vessels.

On the high seas Rule 30 (e), International Rules, exempts, in certain circumstances, vessels of less than 7 meters from the necessity to show the anchor and aground lights of Rule 30 (a) (b) or (d). In inland waters any vessel 65 feet or less in length at anchor in a *special anchorage area* established pursuant to Article 11, Inland Rules, need not show any light whatsoever. These anchorages may be found in numerous places along the coasts of the United States. Descriptions of the anchorages are published separately in Title 33, Code of Federal Regulations.

Barges in inland waters may anchor in a *special anchorage* area, irrespective of length, either singly or several together as a single unit. In either case only one anchor light need be shown. Outside of a special anchorage area barges at anchor are required to show the lights of Article 11, except when on the Gulf Coast where special lights are prescribed in Section 80.16a(h), Pilot Rules.

4
Towing Lights

DEFINITIONS

RULE 21. (d) "Towing light" means a yellow light having the same characteristics as the "sternlight" defined in paragraph (c) of this rule.

VISIBILITY OF LIGHTS

RULE 22. (a) In vessels of 50 metres or more in length:

—a towing light, 3 miles;

(b) In vessels of 12 metres or more in length but less than 50 metres in length:

—a towing light, 2 miles;

(c) In vessels of less than 12 metres in length:

—a towing light, 2 miles;

POWER DRIVEN VESSELS WHEN TOWING OR PUSHING

TOWING AND PUSHING

RULE 24. (a) A power-driven vessel when towing shall exhibit:

(i) instead of the light prescribed

STEAM VESSELS WHEN TOWING OR PUSHING

Art. 3. (a) A steam vessel when towing another vessel or vessels alongside or by pushing ahead shall, in addition to her side lights, carry two bright white lights in a vertical line, one over the other, not less than three feet apart, and when towing one or more vessels astern, regardless of the length of the tow, shall carry an additional bright white light three feet above or below such lights. Each of these lights shall be of the same construction and character, and shall be carried in the same position as the white light mentioned in article 2 (a) or the after range light mentioned in article 2 (f).

(b) A steam vessel carrying towing lights the same as the white light mentioned in article 2 (a), when pushing another vessel or vessels ahead, shall also carry at or near the stern two bright amber lights in a vertical line, one over

International Rules

in Rule 23(a)(i), two masthead lights forward in a vertical line. When the length of the tow, measuring from the stern of the towing vessel to the after end of the tow exceeds 200 metres, three such lights in a vertical line;

(ii) sidelights;

(iii) a sternlight;

(iv) a towing light in a vertical line above the sternlight;

(b) When a pushing vessel and a vessel being pushed ahead are rigidly connected in a composite unit they shall be regarded as a power-driven vessel and exhibit the lights prescribed in Rule 23.

(c) A power-driven vessel when pushing ahead or towing alongside, except in the case of a composite unit, shall exhibit:

(i) instead of the light prescribed in Rule 23a()(i), two masthead lights forward in a vertical line;

(ii) sidelights;

(iii) a sternlight.

(d) A power-driven vessel to which paragraphs (a) and (c) of this rule apply shall also comply with Rule 23(a)(ii).

VESSELS BEING TOWED AND VESSELS BEING PUSHED AHEAD

(e) A vessel or object being towed shall exhibit:

(i) sidelights;

(ii) a sternlight;

(f) Provided that any number of vessels being towed alongside or

Inland and Pilot Rules

the other, not less than three feet apart; each of these lights shall be so constructed as to show an unbroken light over an arc of the horizon of twelve points of the compass, so fixed as to show the light six points from right aft on each side of the vessel, and of such a character as to be visible at a distance of at least two miles. A steam vessel carrying towing lights the same as the white light mentioned in article 2 (a) may also carry, irrespective of the position of the tow, the after range light mentioned in article 2 (f); however, if the after range light is carried by such a vessel when pushing another vessel or vessels ahead, the amber lights shall be carried in a vertical line with and at least three feet lower than the after range light. A steam vessel carrying towing lights the same as the white light mentioned in article 2 (a), when towing one or more vessels astern, may also carry, in lieu of the stern light specified in article 10, a small white light abaft the funnel or aftermast for the tow to steer by, but such light shall not be visible forward of the beam.

VESSELS BEING TOWED

Art. 5. A sailing vessel under way and any vessel being towed, except barges, canal boats, scows, and other vessels of nondescript type, when in tow of steam vessels, shall carry the same lights as are prescribed by article 2 for a steam ves-

80   Farwell's Rules of the Nautical Road

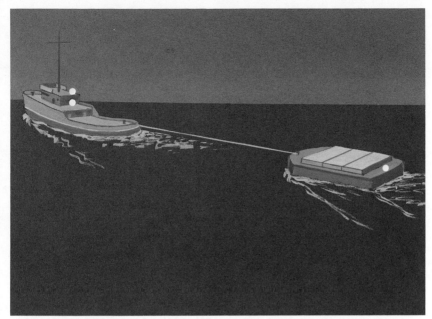

FIG. 21. Tug (any length) with barge in tow (any length of tow), high seas, view from astern. International Rules 24(a) and (e).

FIG. 22. Tug with large power-driven vessel in tow, towing lights forward, high seas or inland waters. At sea, after range may be omitted if towing vessel is under 50 meters. International Rules 24(a) and (e); Inland Rules, Articles 3 and 5.

pushed in a group shall be lighted as one vessel,

(i) a vessel being pushed ahead, not being part of a composite unit, shall exhibit at the forward end, sidelights;

(ii) a vessel being towed alongside shall exhibit a sternlight and at the forward end, sidelights.

sel under way, with the exception of the white lights mentioned therein, which they shall never carry.

Art. 10. (a) A vessel when underway, if not otherwise required by these rules to carry one or more lights visible from aft, shall carry at her stern a white light, . . . of twelve points. . . .

NONDESCRIPT VESSELS BEING TOWED OR PUSHED AHEAD

ATLANTIC AND PACIFIC COASTS

Sec. 80.16 Lights for barges, canal boats, scows and other nondescript vessels on certain inland waters on the Atlantic and Pacific Coasts. (a) On the harbors, rivers, and other inland waters of the United States except the Great Lakes and their connecting and tributary waters as far east as Montreal, the Red River of the North, the Mississippi River and its tributaries above the Huey P. Long Bridge, and that part of the Atchafalaya River above its junction with the Plaquemine-Morgan City alternate waterway, and the waters described in §§ 86.16a and 80.17, barges, canal boats, scows, and other vessels of nondescript type not otherwise provided for, when being towed by steam vessels, shall carry lights as set forth in this section.

(b) Barges and canal boats towing astern of steam vessels, when

FIG. 23. Tug with barges, length of tow not over 200 meters, high seas. After range light may be omitted if tug is under 50 meters. International Rules 24(a) and (e).

FIG. 24. Tug with barges, length of tow over 200 meters, high seas. After range light may be omitted if tug is under 50 meters. International Rules 24(a) and (e).

towing singly, or what is known as tandem towing, shall each carry a green light on the starboard side and a red light on the port side, and a white light on the stern, except that the last vessel of such tow shall carry two lights on her stern, athwartship, horizontal to each other, not less than 5 feet apart, and not less than 4 feet above the deck house, and so placed as to show all around the horizon. A tow of one such vessel shall be lighted as the last vessel of a tow.

(c) When two or more boats are abreast, the colored lights shall be carried at the outer sides of the bows of the outside boats. Each of the outside boats in last tier of a hawser tow shall carry a white light on her stern.

(d) The white light required to be carried on stern of a barge or canal boat carrying red and green side lights except the last vessel in a tow shall be carried in a lantern so constructed that it shall show an unbroken light over an arc of the horizon of 12 points of the compass, namely, for 6 points from right aft on each side of the vessel, and shall be of such a character as to be visible on a dark night with a clear atmosphere at a distance of at least 2 miles.

(e) Barges, canal boats or scows towing alongside a steam vessel shall, if the deck, deck houses, or cargo of the barge, canal boat or scow be so high above water as to obscure the side lights of the tow-

FIG. 25. Tug with tow astern, towing lights forward, inland waters. Inland Rules, Article 3.

FIG. 26. Tug with tow astern, towing lights aft, inland waters. Inland Rules, Article 3.

ing steamer when being towed on the starboard side of the steamer, carry a green light upon the starboard side; and when towed on the port side of the steamer, a red light on the port side of the barge, canal boat, or scow; and if there is more than one barge, canal boat or scow abreast, the colored lights shall be displayed from the outer side of the outside barges, canal boats or scows.

(f) Barges, canal boats or scows shall, when being propelled by pushing ahead of a steam vessel, display a red light on the port bow and a green light on the starboard bow of the head barge, canal boat or scow, carried at a height sufficiently above the superstructure of the barge, canal boat or scow as to permit said side lights to be visible; and if there is more than one barge, canal boat or scow abreast, the colored lights shall be displayed from the outer side of the outside barges, canal boats or scows.

(g) The colored side lights referred to in this section shall be fitted with inboard screens so as to prevent them from being seen across the bow, and of such a character as to be visible on a dark night, with a clear atmosphere, at a distance of at least 2 miles, and so constructed as to show a uniform and unbroken light over an arc of the horizon of 10 points of the compass, and so fixed as to throw the light from right ahead to 2 points abaft the beam on either

FIG. 27. Tug with submerged tow, towing lights forward, inland waters. Pilot Rules, Section 80.18(b).

FIG. 28. Tug with submerged tow, towing lights aft, inland waters. Pilot Rules, Section 80.18(b).

side. The minimum size of glass globes shall not be less than 6 inches in diameter and 5 inches high in the clear.

(h) Scows not otherwise provided for in this section on waters described in paragraph (a) of this section shall carry a white light at each end of each scow, except that when such scows are massed in tiers, two or more abreast, each of the outside scows shall carry a white light on its outer bow, and the outside scows in the last tier shall each carry, in addition, a white light on the outer part of the stern. The white light shall be carried not less than 8 feet above the surface of the water, and shall be so placed as to show an unbroken light all around the horizon, and shall be of such a character as to be visible on a dark night with a clear atmosphere at a distance of at least 5 miles.

(i) Other vessels of nondescript type not otherwise provided for in this section shall exhibit the same lights that are required to be exhibited by scows by this section.

Note: The regulations in §§ 80.16 to 80.17, inclusive, are not applicable to rafts. The requirements regarding lights for rafts are in § 80.32.

GULF COAST AREA

Sec. 80.16a Lights for barges, canal boats, scows, and other nondescript vessels on certain inland waters on the Gulf Coast and the Gulf Intracoastal Waterway. (a) On

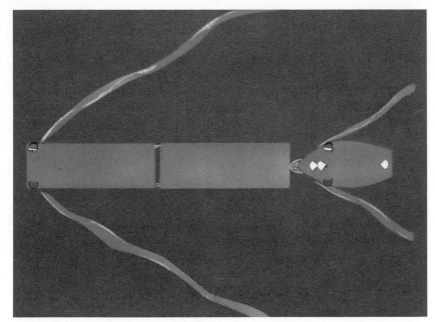

FIG. 29. Towboat under 50 meters pushing barges or other vessels, after range light omitted, high seas. After range must be shown if towboat is 50 meters or longer. International Rules 24(c) and (e)(i).

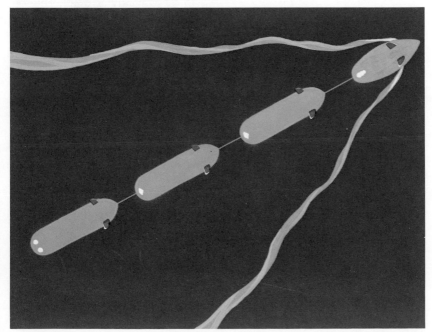

FIG. 30. Tug with barges in tandem, towing lights aft, inland waters. Inland Rules, Article 3; Pilot Rules, Section 80.16(b).

the Gulf Intracoastal Waterway and on other inland waters connected therewith or with the Gulf of Mexico from the Rio Grande, Texas, to Cape Sable (East Cape), Florida, barges, canal boats, scows, and other vessels of nondescript type not otherwise provided for, when being towed by steam vessels shall carry lights as set forth in this section.

(b) When one or more barges, canal boats, scows, or other vessels of nondescript type not otherwise provided for, are being towed by pushing ahead of a steam vessel, or by a combination of pushing ahead and towing alongside of a steam vessel, such tow shall be lighted by a flashing amber light at the extreme forward end of the tow, so placed as to be as nearly as practicable on the centerline of the tow, a green light on the starboard side of the tow, so placed as to mark the maximum projection of the tow to starboard, and a red light on the port side of the tow, so placed as to mark the maximum projection of the tow to port.

(c) When one or more barges, canal boats, scows, or other vessels of nondescript type not otherwise provided for, are being towed alongside a steam vessel, there shall be displayed a white light at each outboard corner of the tow. If the deck, deck house, or cargo of such barge, etc., obscures the sidelight of the towing vessel, such barge, etc., shall also carry a green light upon

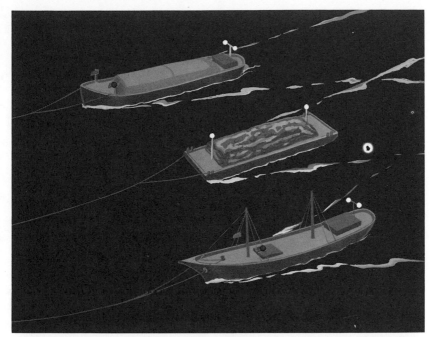

FIG. 31.   Last canal boat, scow, or barge in three separate tandem tows, inland waters. Similar lighting for single canal boat, scow, or barge, in tow. Pilot Rules, Section 80.16.

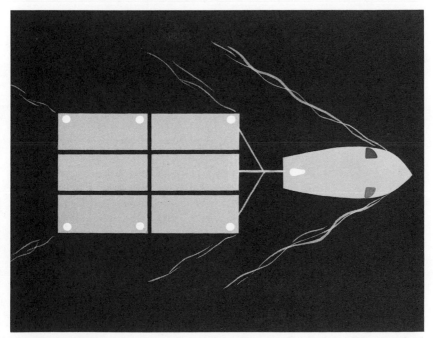

FIG. 32.   Tug with scows astern, in two tiers, three abreast, towing lights aft, inland waters. Inland Rules, Article 3; Pilot Rules, Section 80.16(h).

the starboard side when being towed on the starboard side of a steam vessel or shall carry a red light on the port side of the barge, etc., when being towed on the port side of the steam vessel. If there is more than one such barge, etc., being towed abreast, the appropriate colored sidelight shall be displayed from the outer side of the outside barge.

(d) When one barge, canal boat, scow or other vessel of nondescript type not otherwise provided for, is being towed singly behind a steam vessel, such vessel shall carry four white lights, one on each corner or outermost projection of the bow and one on each corner or outermost projection of the stern.

(e) When two or more barges, canal boats, scows, or other vessels of nondescript type not otherwise provided for, are being towed behind a steam vessel in tandem, with a hawser length, between vessels, of 75 feet or more, such vessels shall carry white lights as follows:

(1) The first vessel in the tow shall carry three white lights, one on each corner or outermost projection of the bow and a white light at the stern amidships.

(2) Each intermediate vessel shall carry two white lights, one at each end amidships.

(3) The last vessel in the tow shall carry three white lights, one on each corner or outermost projection of the stern and a white light at the bow amidships.

FIG. 33. Tug with scows, in two tiers, two abreast, towing lights aft, inland waters. Inland Rules, Article 3; Pilot Rules, Section 80.16(h).

FIG. 34. Tug with loaded barge, canal boat, or scow alongside obscuring tug's side light, towing lights aft, inland waters. Inland Rules, Article 3; Pilot Rules, Section 80.16(e).

(f) When two or more barges, canal boats, scows, or other vessels of nondescript type not otherwise provided for, are being towed behind a steam vessel in tandem, with a hawser length between vessels, of less than 75 feet, such vessels shall carry white lights as follows:

(1) The first vessels in the tow shall carry three white lights, one on each corner or outermost projection of the bow and a white light at the stern amidships.

(2) Each intermediate vessel shall carry a white light at the stern amidships.

(3) The last vessel in the tow shall carry two white lights, one on each corner or outermost projection of the stern.

(g) When two or more barges, canal boats, scows, or other vessels of nondescript type not otherwise provided for, are being towed behind a steam vessel two or more abreast, in one or more tiers, each of the outside vessels in each tier shall carry a white light on the outboard corner of the bow, and each of the outside vessels in the last tier shall carry, in addition, a white light on the outboard corner of the stern.

(i) The colored side lights shall be so constructed as to show a uniform and unbroken light over an arc of the horizon of 10 points of the compass, so fixed as to show the light from right ahead to 2 points abaft the beam on their respective sides, and of such a character as to

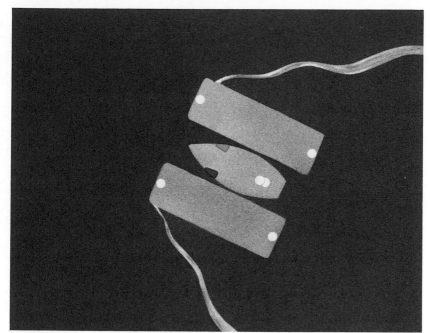

FIG. 35. Tug with barges, canal boats, or scows alongside, tug's side lights not obscured, towing lights aft, inland waters. Inland Rules, Article 3; Pilot Rules, Section 80.16(i).

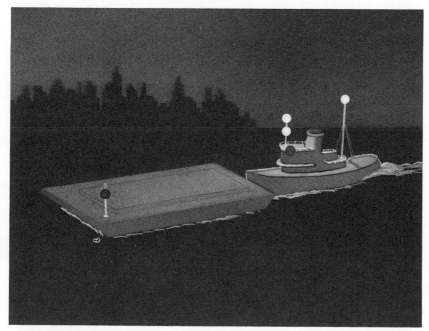

FIG. 36. Towboat pushing barge, canal boat, or scow, towing lights forward, inland waters. Inland Rules, Article 3; Pilot Rules, Section 80.16(f).

be visible at a distance of at least 2 miles, and shall be fitted with inboard screens so as to prevent either light from being seen more than half a point across the centerline of the tow.

(j) The amber light shall flash 50 to 70 times per minute and be so constructed as to show a uniform and unbroken light over an arc of the horizon of 20 points of the compass, so fixed as to show the light 10 points on each side of the tow, namely, from right ahead to two points abaft the beam on either side, and of such a character as to be visible at a distance of at least 2 miles.

(k) The white lights shall be so constructed and so fixed as to show a clear, uniform, and unbroken light all around the horizon, and of such a character as to be visible at a distance of at least 2 miles.

(l) All the lights shall be carried at approximately the same height above the surface of the water and, except as provided in paragraph (h) of this section, shall be so placed with respect thereto as to be clear of and above all obstructions which might tend to interfer with the prescribed arc or distance of visibility.

TRAVERSING WATERS WITH
DIFFERING REQUIREMENTS

Sec. 80.16b. Lights for barges, canal boats, scows, and other nondescript vessels temporarily operating on waters requiring differ-

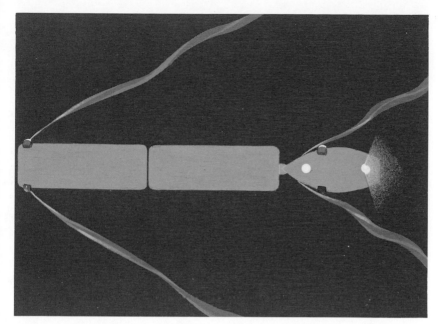

FIG. 37. Towboat pushing barges, canal boats, or scows, towing lights forward, inland waters. Inland Rules, Article 3; Pilot Rules, Section 80.16(f).

FIG. 38. Towboat pushing barge, canal boat, or scow, towing lights forward, optional after range light, Gulf Intracoastal Waterway and vicinity. Inland Rules, Article 3; Pilot Rules, Section 80.16a(b).

ent lights. Nothing in §§ 80.16, 80.16a, or 80.17 shall be construed as compelling barges, canal boats, scows, or other vessels of nondescript type not otherwise provided for, being towed by steam vessels, when passing through any waters coming within the scope of any regulations where lights for such boats are different from those of the waters whereon such boats are usually employed, to change their lights from those required on the waters on which their trip begins or terminates; but should such boats engage in local employment on waters requiring different lights from those where they are customarily employed, they shall comply with the local rules where employed.*

NEW YORK HARBOR AND VICINITY

Sec. 80.17 Lights for barges and canal boats in tow of steam vessels on the Hudson River and adjacent waters and Lake Champlain. (a) All nondescript vessels known as scows, car floats, lighters, and vessels of similar type, navigating the waters referred to in this section, shall carry the lights required to be carried by barges and canal boats in tow of steam vessels, as prescribed in this section.

(b) Barges and canal boats, when being towed by steam vessels on the waters of the Hudson River and

* See also Interpretive Ruling 86.05-10 at end of chapter.

FIG. 39. Tug with barge, canal boat, or scow alongside, towing lights aft, Gulf Intra-coastal Waterway and vicinity. Inland Rules, Article 3; Pilot Rules, Section 80.16a(c).

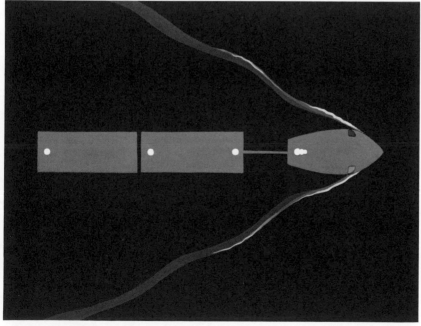

FIG. 40. Tug with two barges, canal boats, or scows in tandem, separating hawser under 75 feet, towing lights aft, Gulf Intracoastal Waterway and vicinity. Inland Rules, Article 3; Pilot Rules, Section 80.16a(f).

its tributaries from Troy to the boundary lines of New York Harbor off Sandy Hook, as defined pursuant to section 2 of the act of Congress of February 19, 1895 (28 Stat. 672; 33 U.S.C. 151), the East River and Long Island Sound (and the waters entering thereon, and to the Atlantic Ocean), to and including Narragansett Bay, R.I., and tributaries, and Lake Champlain, shall carry lights as follows:

(1) Barges and canal boats being towed astern of steam vessels when towing singly shall carry a white light on the bow and a white light on the stern.

SINGLY

(2) When towing in tandem, with a hawser length, between vessels, of less than 75 feet, each boat shall carry a white light on its stern and the first or hawser boat shall, in addition, carry a white light on its bow.

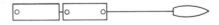

TANDEM (WITH A HAWSER
LENGTH, BETWEEN VESSELS,
OF LESS THAN 75 FEET

(3) When towing in tandem with a hawser length of 75 feet or more between the various boats in the tow, each boat shall carry a white light on the bow and a white light on the stern, except that the last

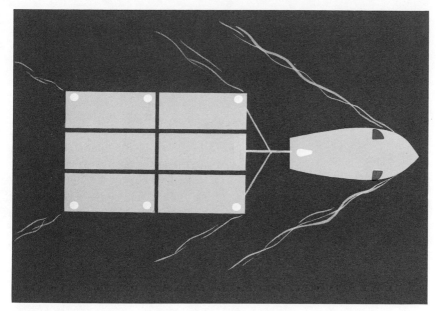

FIG. 41. Tug with barges, canal boats, or scows in two tiers, three abreast, towing lights aft, Gulf Intracoastal Waterway and vicinity. Inland Rules, Article 3; Pilot Rules, Section 80.16a(g).

FIG. 42. Tug with two nondescript vessels in tandem, separating hawser under 75 feet, towing lights aft, New York Harbor and vicinity. Inland Rules, Article 3; Pilot Rules, Section 80.17(b)(2).

vessel in the tow shall carry two white lights on her stern, athwartship, horizontal to each other, not less than 5 feet apart and not less than 4 feet above the deck house, and so placed as to show all around the horizon: Provided, That seagoing barges shall not be required to make any change in their seagoing lights (red and green) on waters coming within the scope of the rules of this section, except that the last vessel of the tow shall carry two white lights on her stern, athwartship, horizontal to each other, not less than 5 feet apart, and not less than 4 feet above the deck house, and so placed as to show all around the horizon.

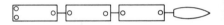

TANDEM (WITH A HAWSER LENGTH, BETWEEN VESSELS, OF 75 FEET OR MORE)

(4) Barges and canal boats when towed at a hawser, two or more abreast, when in one tier, shall each carry a white light on the stern and a white light on the bow of each of the outside boats.

TWO OR MORE ABREAST IN ONE TIER

(5) When in more than one tier, each boat shall carry a white light

FIG. 43. Tug with two nondescript vessels in tandem, separating hawser 75 feet or longer, towing lights aft, New York Harbor and vicinity. Inland Rules, Article 3; Pilot Rules, Section 80.17(b)(3).

FIG. 44. Tug with nondescript vessels astern, three abreast in one tier, towing lights aft, New York Harbor and vicinity. Inland Rules, Article 3; Pilot Rules, Section 80.17(b)(4).

on its stern and the outside boats in the hawser or head tier shall each carry, in addition, a white light on the bow.

TWO OR MORE ABREAST AND IN MORE THAN ONE TIER

(6) The white bow lights for barges and canal boats referred to in the preceding rules shall be carried at least 10 feet and not more than 30 feet abaft the stem or extreme forward end of the vessel. On barges and canal boats required to carry a white bow light, the white light on bow and the white light on stern shall each be so placed above the hull or deck house as to show an unbroken light all around the horizon, and of such a character as to be visible on a dark night with a clear atmosphere at a distance of at least 2 miles.

(7) When nondescript vessels known as scows, car floats, lighters, barges or canal boats, and vessels of similar type, are towed alongside a steam vessel, there shall be displayed a white light at the outboard corners of the tow.

TOWED ALONGSIDE— VARIOUS POSITIONS

(8) When under way between the hours of sunset and sunrise there shall be displayed a red light on the port bow and a green light

FIG. 45. Tug with nondescript vessels in three tiers, three abreast, towing lights aft, New York Harbor and vicinity. Inland Rules, Article 3; Pilot Rules, Section 80.17(b)(5).

FIG. 46. Tug with nondescript vessels alongside, towing lights aft, New York Harbor and vicinity. Inland Rules, Article 3; Pilot Rules, Section 80.17(b)(7).

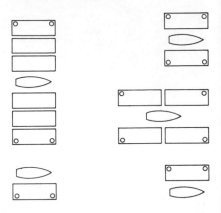

on the starboard bow of the head barge or barges, properly screened and so arranged that they may be visible through an arc of the horizon of 10 points of the compass; that is, from right ahead to 2 points abaft the beam on either side and visible on a dark night with a clear atmosphere at a distance of at least 2 miles, and be carried at a height sufficiently above the superstructure of the barge or barges pushed ahead as to permit said side lights to be visible.

PROPULSION OF BARGE OR BARGES BY PUSHING

(9) Dump scows utilized for transportation and disposal of garbage, street sweepings, ashes, excavated material, dredging, etc., when navigating on the Hudson

FIG. 47. Tug with nondescript vessels alongside, towing lights aft, New York Harbor and vicinity. Inland Rules, Article 3; Pilot Rules, Section 80.17(b)(7).

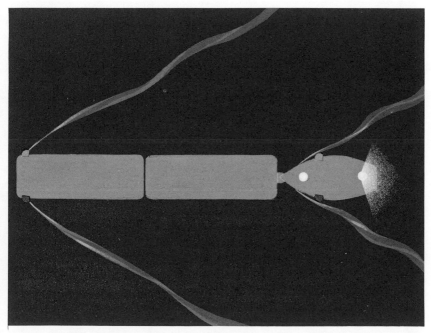

FIG. 48. Towboat pushing nondescript vessels, towing lights forward, New York Harbor and vicinity. Inland Rules, Article 3; Pilot Rules, Section 80.17(b)(8).

River or East River or the waters tributary thereto between loading points on these waters and the dumping grounds established by competent authority outside the line dividing the high seas from the inland waters of New York Harbor, shall, when towing in tandem, carry, instead of the white lights previously required, red and green side lights on the respective and appropriate sides of the scow in addition to the white light required to be shown by an overtaken vessel.

(10) The red and green lights herein prescribed shall be carried at an elevation of not less than 8 feet above the highest deck house, upon substantial uprights, the lights properly screened and so arranged as to show through an arc of the horizon of 10 points of the compass, that is, from right ahead to 2 points abaft the beam on either side and visible on a dark night with a clear atmosphere a distance of at least 2 miles.

Provided, That nothing in the rules of this section shall be construed as compelling barges or canal boats in tow of steam vessels, passing through any waters coming within the scope of said rules where lights for barges or canal boats are different from those of the waters whereon such vessels are usually employed, to change their lights from those required on the waters from which their trip begins or terminates; but should such vessels engage in local employment on waters requiring different lights from those where they are customarily employed, they shall comply with the local rules where employed.

TOWING OBJECT DIFFICULT TO LIGHT

(g) Where from any sufficient cause it is impracticable for a vessel or object being towed to exhibit the lights prescribed in paragraph (e) of this rule, all possible measures shall be taken to light the vessel or object towed or at least to indicate the presence of the unlighted vessel or object.

TOWING SUBMERGED OBJECTS

Sec. 80.18 Signals to be displayed by a towing vessel when towing a submerged or partly submerged object upon a hawser when no signals can be displayed upon the object which is towed.
(b) By night the towing vessel shall display the regular side lights, but in lieu of the regular white tow-

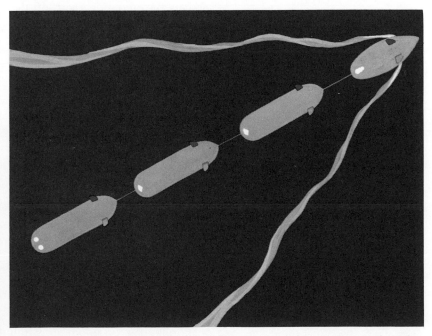

FIG. 49. Tug with seagoing barges in tandem, towing lights aft, New York Harbor and vicinity. Same for scows dumping at sea except that last scow in tandem carries a single 12-point stern light. Inland Rules, Article 3; Pilot Rules, Sections 80.17(b)(3) and (9).

International Rules

Inland and Pilot Rules

ing lights shall display four lights in a vertical position not less than three feet nor more than six feet apart, the upper and lower of such lights to be white and of the same character as the regular towing lights and the middle of such lights to be red and of such character as to be visible on a dark night with a clear atmosphere for a distance of at least 2 miles.

RAFTS IN TOW

Sec. 80.32. Lights for rafts and other craft. (b) Any raft while being propelled by hand power, by horse power, or by the current of the river, while being towed, or while anchored or moored in or near a channel or fairway, shall carry white lights as follows:

(1) A raft of one crib in width shall carry one white light at each end of the raft.

(2) A raft of more than one crib in width shall carry 4 white lights, one on each outside corner.

(3) An unstable log raft of one bag or boom in width shall carry at least 2 but not more than 4 white lights in a fore and aft line, one of which shall be at each end. The lights may be closely grouped clusters of not more than 3 white lights rather than single lights.

(4) An unstable log raft of more than one bag or boom in width shall carry 4 white lights, one on each outside corner. The lights may be closely grouped clusters of not

more than 3 white lights rather than single lights.

(c) The white lights required by this section shall be carried from sunset to sunrise, in a lantern so fixed and constructed as to show a clear, uniform, and unbroken light, visible all around the horizon, and of such intensity as to be visible on a dark night with a clear atmosphere at a distance of at least one mile. The lights for rafts shall be suspended from poles of such height that the lights shall not be less than 8 feet above the surface of the water, except that the lights prescribed for unstable log rafts shall not be less than 4 feet above the water.

INTERPRETIVE RULING

Sec. 86.05-5 Stern lights for all vessels. Article 10 of section 1 of the Act of June 7, 1897, as amended by the Act of August 14, 1958 (33 U.S.C. 179), requires "A vessel when underway, if not otherwise required by these rules to carry one or more lights visible from aft, shall carry at her stern a white light, . . . " and this requirement shall be applied to all vessels, including but not limited to, tugs, barges, sail vessels, motorboats when propelled by sail alone, etc.

Sec. 85.05-10 Navigational lights for barges traveling both international and inland waters. Notwithstanding the provisions of Sec. 80.16b of this chapter, every barge which shall have occasion during its voyage to operate upon waters to which the International Regulations for Preventing of Collisions at Sea pertain, may, for the duration of said voyage, display the navigational lights and shapes required by International Rule 5 (33 U.S.C. 1065).

NOTES

Advances in ship design have resulted in the capability of a pushing vessel being rigidly connected to a vessel she is pushing ahead. This composite unit is usually designed with sufficient power to operate in the open sea. It is regarded as a power-driven vessel and shows, on the high seas, the lights as such (Rule 24(b)).

Differences in towing lights   On the high seas (Rule 24), a power-driven vessel with a tow alongside, pushed ahead or astern, must show, irrespective of the number of vessels in the tow, in addition to the regular sidelights and the required fixed sternlight, two 225° white lights in a vertical line in the forepart of the vessel, and if 50 meters or more in length a 225° white after range light (Rule 23(a)(ii), except when the length of the tow, measured from the stern of the towing vessel to the stern of the last vessel towed, is more than 200 meters. Then it must carry and show three such lights in a vertical line equally spaced. These lights must be of the same construction and character as the masthead light, and one of them must be in the same position as the masthead light. The lower towing light may be below the masthead light.

Under the Inland Rules (Article 3), these differences should be noted: (1) A steam vessel with a tow ahead or alongside must carry, in addition to the regular side lights, two white towing lights in a vertical line at least 3 feet apart, and if the tow is astern, three such lights, regardless of the length of the tow or the number of vessels towed; (2) the towing lights may be of the construction, character, and position of the forward masthead light or the after all around range light; thus, if one of the towing lights is the masthead light, they must be 20-point lights, and if one of the towing lights is the after range light, they must be all around lights; (3) the forward masthead light is not required when towing lights are aft, nor is the after range light required when towing lights are forward, but in the latter case an additional all around after range light, of sufficient height not to be confused with the towing lights from ahead, is proper; (4) if the tow is being pushed ahead and the towing lights are 20-point lights, two amber lights must be shown aft, in lieu of the stern light, and irrespective of whether the all around after range light is shown.

Note that under International Rules the after range light is always a 225° white light and that it is optional for towing vessels under 50 meters in length (Rule 24(d)).

Special stern towing lights are used on both the high seas and inland waters. International Rule 24 (a) requires a yellow 135° towing light, placed above the white sternlight, for a power-driven vessel towing another astern. Inland Rules, Article 3 (b) requires two 12-point amber lights also placed to show over the same arc, but in lieu of, a stern light, for a steam vessel pushing ahead.

The Inland and Pilot Rules are silent as to seaplanes towing, whereas the International Rules considers a seaplane as a power-driven vessel.

Towing vessel with submerged tow By a submerged tow is meant any underwater tow or any tow which is awash or nearly so, upon which it is impossible to display lights. A vessel with such a tow on high seas would show the two or three vertical masthead lights or the red-white-red occupation lights of Rule 27 (b), as appropriate, unless it were a minesweeper, in which case it would show the special lights of Rule 27 (f). When showing two or three vertical masthead lights, the required yellow towing light for a tow astern will assist other vessels in identifying the towing vessel and alerting them to the possibility of an unlighted tow. In inland waters, all vessels with a submerged tow show the white-red-red-white lights of Section 80.18, Pilot Rules. If the four special towing lights are 20-point lights carried forward on the towing vessel, an additional all around after range light is proper. If, as is more common in practice, the special towing lights are carried aft and are all around lights, the usual forward masthead light shall not be carried.

Towed vessels, etc. Rule 24 (e) International Rules, provides for all vessels and objects being towed. Article 5, Inland Rules, on the other hand, is silent as to vessels of nondescript type in tow, although it does provide for sailing vessels underway and common vessels being towed.

On the high seas, all vessels being towed or pushed must carry properly screened red and green sidelights and if towed astern or alongside, a fixed sternlight. A *group* of vessels pushed ahead or towed alongside must be lighted as one vessel. Thus, even an ocean-going crib of logs or a target raft in tow should carry sidelights and a sternlight at sea, though the difficulty in achieving this is recognized in Rule 24 (g) and by the provision of the yellow towing light on the tug.

On the inland waters, a sailing vessel underway is required to carry side lights in accordance with Article 5 and a stern light pursuant to Article 10.

The same is true of common vessels being towed. Barges, scows, canal boats, and other nondescript vessels being towed on the inland waters are required to carry special lights prescribed in the Pilot Rules. In effect, in so far as nondescript craft of this type are concerned, the requirements are grouped into three distinct categories, although each is contained in the Pilot Rules applicable to the inland waters. One set of requirements applies to such vessels on certain inland waters on the Atlantic and Pacific coasts. Another set of requirements applies to such vessels on certain inland waters on the Gulf Coast and the Gulf Intracoastal Waterway. The third set of requirements for such vessels applies to the Hudson River and adjacent waters and Lake Champlain. These requirements are contained in Sections 80.16, 80.16a, and 80.17.

As in the case of small vessels towing or pushing in inland waters, the Inland and Pilot Rules do not make any special provision for small vessels being towed or pushed ahead. On the high seas, however, such vessels apply the appropriate requirements of Rule 22, International Rules.

Log rafts which are towed in inland waters customarily carry the white lights prescribed in Section 80.32, Pilot Rules.

5
Special Lights

International Rules

Inland and Pilot Rules

VISIBILITY OF LIGHTS

RULE 22. The lights prescribed in these rules shall have an intensity as specified in Section 8 of Annex I to these regulations so as to be visible at the following minimum ranges:

(a) In vessels of 50 metres or more in length:

—a white, red, green or yellow all-round light, 3 miles;

(b) In vessels of 12 metres or more in length but less than 50 metres in length:

—a white, red, green or yellow all-round light, 2 miles;

(c) In vessels of less than 12 metres in length:

—a white, red, green or yellow all-round light, 2 miles.

LIGHTS FOR FISHING VESSELS

FISHING VESSELS

RULE 26. (a) A vessel engaged in fishing, whether underway or at

LIGHTS FOR FISHING VESSELS

Art. 9 (c) All vessels, when trawling, dredging, or fishing with any kind of drag nets or lines, shall exanchor, shall exhibit only the lights and shapes prescribed in this rule.

(b) A vessel when engaged in trawling, by which is meant the dragging through the water of a dredge net or other apparatus used as a fishing appliance, shall exhibit:

(i) two all-round lights in a vertical line, the upper being green and the lower white, . . .

(ii) a masthead light abaft of and higher than the all-round green light; a vessel of less than 50 metres in length shall not be obliged to exhibit such a light but may do so;

(iii) when making way through the water, in addition to the lights prescribed in this paragraph, sidelights and a sternlight.

(c) A vessel engaged in fishing, other than trawling, shall exhibit:

(i) two all-round lights in a vertical line, the upper being red and the lower white, . . .

(ii) when there is outlying gear extending more than 150 metres horizontally from the vessel, an all-round white light . . . in the direction of the gear;

(iii) when making way through the water, in addition to the lights prescribed in this paragraph, sidelights and a sternlight.

(d) A vessel engaged in fishing in close proximity to other vessels engaged in fishing may exhibit the additional signals described in Annex II to these regulations.

(e) A vessel when not engaged in fishing shall not exhibit the lights . . . prescribed in this rule, but only

hibit, from some part of the vessel where they can be best seen, two lights. One of these lights shall be red and the other shall be white. The red light shall be above the white light, and shall be at a vertical distance from it of not less than six feet and not more than twelve feet; and the horizontal distance between them, if any, shall not be more than ten feet. These two lights shall be of such a character and contained in lanterns of such construction as to be visible all around the horizon, the white light a distance of not less than three miles and the red light of not less than two miles.

Art. 9. (a) Fishing vessels of less than ten gross tons, when underway and when not having their nets, trawls, dredges, or lines in the water, shall not be obliged to carry the colored side lights; but every such vessel shall, in lieu thereof, have ready at hand a lantern with a green glass on one side and a red glass on the other side, and on approaching to or being approached by another vessel such lantern shall be exhibited in sufficient time to prevent collision, so that the green light shall not be seen on the port side nor the red light on the starboard side.

(b) All fishing vessels and fishing boats of ten gross tons or upward, when underway and when not having their nets, trawls, dredges, or lines in the water, shall carry

those prescribed for a vessel of her length.

and show the same lights as other vessels underway.

ANNEX II
ADDITIONAL SIGNALS FOR
FISHING VESSELS FISHING
IN CLOSE PROXIMITY

1. General

The lights mentioned herein shall, if exhibited in pursuance of Rule 26(d), be placed where they can best be seen. They shall be at least 0.9 metre apart but at a lower level than lights prescribed in Rule 26(b) (i) and (c)(i). The lights shall be visible all round the horizon at a distance of at least 1 mile but at a lesser distance than the lights prescribed by these rules for fishing vessels.

2. Signals for trawlers

(a) Vessels when engaged in trawling, whether using demersal or pelagic gear, may exhibit:

(i) when shooting their nets: two white lights in a vertical line;

(ii) when hauling their nets: one white light over one red light in a vertical line;

(iii) when the net has come fast upon an obstruction: two red lights in a vertical line.

(b) Each vessel engaged in pair trawling may exhibit:

(i) by night, a searchlight directed forward and in the direction of the other vessel of the pair;

(ii) when shooting or hauling their nets or when their nets have come fast upon an obstruction, the lights prescribed in 2(a) above.

3. Signals for purse seiners

Vessels engaged in fishing with purse seine gear may exhibit two yellow lights in a vertical line. These lights shall flash alternately every second and with equal light and occultation duration. These lights may be exhibited only when the vessel is hampered by its fishing gear.

VESSELS NOT UNDER COMMAND OR RESTRICTED IN THEIR ABILITY TO MANOEUVRE

RULE 27. (a) A vessel not under command shall exhibit:

(i) two all-round red lights in a vertical line where they can best be seen;

(iii) when making way through the water, in addition to the lights prescribed in this paragraph, sidelights and a sternlight.

(b) A vessel restricted in her ability to manoeuvre, except a vessel engaged in minesweeping operations, shall exhibit:

(i) three all-round lights in a vertical line where they can best be seen. The highest and lowest of these lights shall be red and the middle light shall be white;

(iii) when making way through the water, masthead lights, sidelights and a sternlight, in addition to the lights prescribed in subparagraph (i);

(iv) when at anchor, in addition

SPECIAL OCCUPATIONAL LIGHTS

Sec. 80.33 Special signals for vessels employed in hydrographic surveying.

(b) It must be distinctly understood that these special signals serve only to indicate the nature of the work upon which the vessel is engaged and in no way give the surveying vessel the right-of-way over other vessels or obviate the necessity for a strict observance of the rules for preventing collisions of vessels.

(c) By night a surveying vessel of the Coast and Geodetic Survey, under way and employed in hydrographic surveying, shall carry the regular lights prescribed by the rules of the road.

Note: There is no article equivalent to Rule 27 in the Inland Rules. The following special lights provided by the Pilot Rules, in part, correspond to the International Rules' prescribed lights for vessels unable to get out of the way due to the nature of their work.

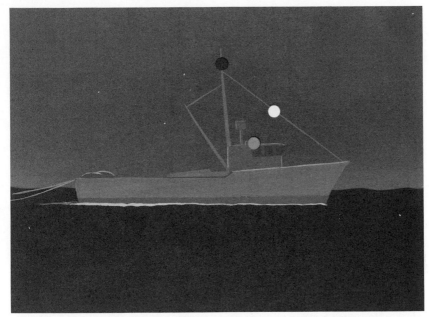

FIG. 50. Fishing vessel trawling, dredging, or fishing with nets or lines, inland waters, underway or at anchor. Inland Rules, Article 9(c).

FIG. 51. Vessel fishing with nets or lines extending more than 150 meters horizontally, trolling lines excepted, underway making way, high seas only. International Rule 26(c).

to the lights . . . prescribed in sub-paragraphs (i) and (ii), the light, lights . . . prescribed in Rule 30.

(c) A vessel engaged in a towing operation such as severely restricts the towing vessel and her tow in their ability to deviate from their course shall, in addition to the lights . . . prescribed in subparagraph (b) (i) and (ii) of this rule, exhibit the lights . . . prescribed in Rule 24(a).

(d) A vessel engaged in dredging or underwater operations, when restricted in her ability to manoeuvre, shall exhibit the lights . . . prescribed in paragraph (b) of this rule and shall in addition, when an obstruction exists, exhibit:

(i) two all-round red lights . . . in a vertical line to indicate the side on which the obstruction exists;

(ii) two all-round green lights . . . in a vertical line to indicate the side on which another vessel may pass;

(iii) when making way through the water, in addition to the lights prescribed in this paragraph, mast-head lights, sidelights and a stern-light;

(iv) a vessel to which this paragraph applies when at anchor shall exhibit the lights . . . prescribed in subparagraphs (i) and (ii) instead of the lights . . . prescribed in Rule 30.

(d) A vessel of the Coast and Geodetic Survey, when at anchor in a fairway on surveying operations, shall display from the mast during the daytime two black balls in a vertical line not less than 6 feet apart. At night two red lights shall be displayed in the same manner. In the case of a small vessel the distance between the balls and between the lights may be reduced to not less than 3 feet if necessary.

(e) Such vessels, when at anchor in a fairway on surveying operations, shall have at hand and show, if necessary, in order to attract attention, a flare-up light in addition to the lights which are, by this section, required to be carried.

Sec. 80.21 Dredges underway and engaged in dredging operations. (a) The term "dredging operations" shall include maneuvering into or out of position at the dredging site but shall not include proceeding to or from the site.

(b) By night self-propelled dredges underway and engaged in dredging operations shall carry, in addition to the regular running lights, two red lights in a vertical line beneath the white masthead light. These red lights shall be not less than three feet nor more than six feet apart and the upper red light shall be not less than three feet nor more than six feet below the masthead light. They shall also carry on or near the stern two red lights in a vertical line not less than three feet nor

FIG. 52.   Vessel trawling, making way, showing after range light, high seas only. Vessels less than 50 meters need not show range light. International Rule 26(b).

FIG. 53.   Vessel fishing with nets or lines extending over 150 meters, underway but not making way, high seas only. International Rule 26(c).

FIG. 54. Vessels engaged in pair trawling, showing searchlights forward and in direction of other vessel, high seas only. International Rule 26(b) and Annex II, 2(b)(i).

FIG. 55. Vessel engaged in trawling, not making way, with net fast upon an obstruction. International Rule 26(b) and Annex II, 2(a)(iii).

FIG. 56. Vessel engaged in purse seining, hampered by its fishing gear, showing optional, flashing, alternate yellow lights. International Rules 26(c), and Annex II, 3.

FIG. 57. Vessel engaged in trawling, underway, making way, and shooting her nets, high seas only. International Rule 26(b) and Annex II, 3.

more than six feet apart, to show through twelve points of the compass; that is, from right astern to six points on each quarter. The forward red lights and after red lights shall be of such character as to be visible on a dark night with a clear atmosphere for a distance of at least 2 miles.

(c) By night, a non-self-propelled dredge which is underway and engaged in dredging operations while being pushed ahead by a towboat shall be considered, with such towboat, for the purpose of compliance with Rules of the Road requirements for lights and shapes, as a single vessel. This vessel shall carry the lights described in paragraph (b) of this section, except that both the dredge and towboat shall carry the sidelights normally required for a barge towed by being pushed ahead and a vessel towing, respectively. When not engaged in dredging operations, this unit shall carry the regular lights for vessels towing and being towed.

Sec. 80.33a. Warning signals for Coast Guard vessels while handling or servicing aids to navigation. (a) Coast Guard vessels while engaged in handling or servicing an aid to navigation during . . . the nighttime may display, in a position where they may best be seen, two red lights in a vertical line not less than three feet nor more than six feet apart.

(b) Vessels, with or without tows, passing Coast Guard vessels dis-

FIG. 58. Vessel engaged in trawling (less than 50 meters), underway but not making way, and hauling her nets, high seas only. International Rule 26(b) and Annex II, 2(a)(ii).

FIG. 59. Vessel not under command, underway but not making way, high seas only. International Rules 27(a).

FIG. 60. Vessel not under command, underway and making way, high seas only. International Rule 27(a).

FIG. 61. Vessel engaged in towing operation, length of tow over 200 meters such as renders her unable to deviate from her course, high seas only. International Rules 24(a) and 27(c).

FIG. 62. Vessel at anchor, restricted in her ability to maneuver. International Rule 27(b)(i) and (iv).

FIG. 63. Vessel engaged in dredging, restricted in her ability to maneuver, underway with way on, high seas only, with no obstruction. International Rule 27(b)(i and iii).

FIG. 64. Vessel engaged in dredging or underwater operations, restricted in her ability to maneuver, at anchor with an obstruction existing. International Rule 27(d).

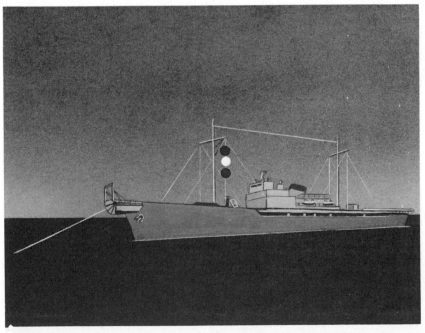

FIG. 65. Cable ship at work, underway but not making way, high seas only. Same for vessel servicing navigation mark, surveying, replenishment, or launching or recovery of aircraft. International Rule 27(b).

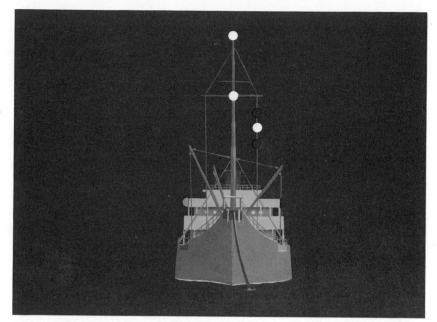

FIG. 66. Cable ship at work, underway and making way, high seas only. After masthead light optional for vessels less than 50 meters. Same for vessel servicing navigation marks, surveying, replenishment, or launching or recovery of aircraft. International Rule 27(b).

FIG. 67. Stringout across navigable channel, inland waters only. Pilot Rules, Section 80.22(c).

playing this signal, shall reduce their speed sufficiently to insure the safety of both vessels, and when passing within 200 feet of the Coast Guard vessel displaying this signal, their speed shall not exceed 5 miles per hour.

Sec. 80.19 Steam vessels, derrick boats, lighters, or other types of vessels made fast alongside a wreck, or moored over a wreck which is on the bottom or partly submerged, or which may be drifting.

(b) By night this situation shall be indicated by the display of a white light from the bow and stern of each outside vessel or lighter not less than six feet above the deck, and in addition thereto there shall be displayed in a position where they can best be seen from all directions two red lights carried in a vertical line not less than three feet nor more than six feet apart, and not less than 15 feet above the deck.

Sec. 80.20 Dredges held in stationary position by moorings or spuds.

(b) By night they shall display a white light at each corner, not less than six feet above the deck, and in addition thereto there shall be displayed in a position where they can best be seen from all directions two red lights carried in a vertical line not less than three feet nor more than six feet apart, and not less than 15 feet above the deck. When scows are moored alongside a dredge in the foregoing situation

FIG. 68. Vessel (un)loading dangerous cargo, fast to dock, inland waters only. Pilot Rules, Section 80.38(a).

FIG. 69. Self-propelling dredge, underway and dredging, inland waters only. Pilot Rules, Section 80.21(b).

FIG. 70. Self-propelling dredge, underway and dredging, inland waters only. Pilot Rules, Section 80.21(b).

FIG. 71. Vessel moored over a wreck, inland waters only. Pilot Rules, Section 80.19(b).

FIG. 72. Stationary dredge with scow alongside, inland waters only. Pilot Rules, Section 80.20(b).

FIG. 73. Vessel engaged in submarine construction or similar activities, inland waters only. Pilot Rules, Section 80.22(b).

they shall display a white light on each outboard corner, not less than six feet above the deck.

Sec. 80.22 Vessels moored or anchored and engaged in laying cables or pipe, submarine construction, excavation, mat sinking, bank grading, dike construction, revetment, or other bank protection operations.

(b) By night they shall display three red lights, carried in a vertical line not less than three feet nor more than six feet apart, in a position where they can best be seen from all directions, with the lowermost light not less than 15 feet above the deck.

(c) Where a stringout of moored vessels or barges is engaged in the operations, three red lights carried as prescribed in paragraph (b) of this section shall be displayed at the channelward end of the stringout. Where the stringout crosses the navigable channel and is to be opened for the passage of vessels, the three red lights shall be displayed at each side of the opening instead of at the outer end of the stringout. There shall also be displayed upon such stringout one horizontal row of amber lights not less than six feet above the deck, or above the deck house where the craft carries a deck house, in a position where they can best be seen from all directions, spaced not more than 50 feet apart so as to mark distinctly the entire length and course of the stringout.

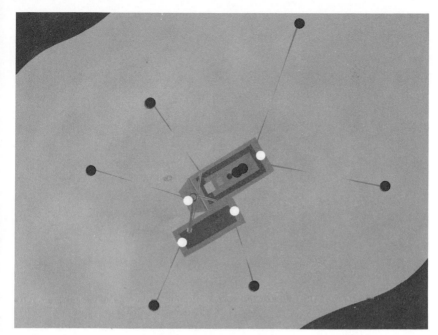

FIG. 74. Floating plant with breast, stern, and bow anchors, inland waters only. Pilot Rules, Section 80.29.

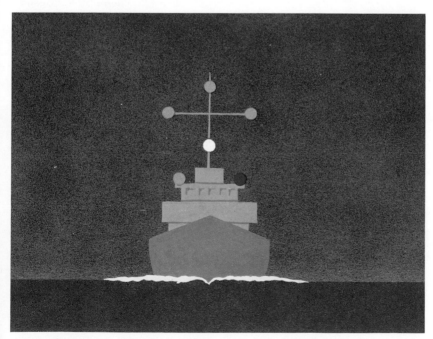

FIG. 75. Minesweeper with gear out, high seas only. International Rule 27(f).

Sec. 80.23 Lights to be displayed on pipe lines. Pipe lines attached to dredges, and either floating or supported on trestles, shall display by night one row of amber lights not less than eight feet nor more than 12 feet above the water, about equally spaced and in such number as to mark distinctly the entire length and course of the line, the intervals between lights where the line crosses navigable channels to be not more than 30 feet. There shall also be displayed on the shore or discharge end of the line two red lights, three feet apart, in a vertical line with the lower light at least eight feet above the water, and if the line is to be opened at night for the passage of vessels, a similar arrangement of lights shall be displayed on each side of the opening.

Sec. 80.24 Lights generally. (a) All the lights required by §§ 80.18 to 80.23, inclusive, except as provided in § 80.18 (b) shall be of such character as to be visible on a dark night with a clear atmosphere for a distance of at least two miles. The white lights provided for in § 80.18 (b) shall be visible for at least 5 miles.

Sec. 80.29 Aids to navigation marking floating plant moorings. Breast, stern, and bow anchors of floating plant working in navigable channels shall be marked by barrel or other suitable buoys. By night approaching vessels shall be shown the location of adjacent buoys by

FIG. 76. Tug with submerged tow, towing lights aft, inland waters only. Pilot Rules, Section 80.18(b).

FIG. 77. Survey vessel surveying at anchor, or Coast Guard vessel servicing a navigation mark, inland waters only. Pilot Rules, Sections 80.33(d) and 80.33a(a).

throwing a suitable beam of light from the plant on the buoys until the approaching vessel has passed, or the buoys may be lighted by red lights, visible in all directions, of the same character as specified in § 80.24 (a): *Provided*, That the foregoing provisions of this section shall not apply to the following waters of New York Harbor and adjacent waters: the East River, the North River (Battery to Spuyten Duyvil), the Harlem River and the New York and New Jersey Channels (from the Upper Bay through Kill Van Kull, Newark Bay, Arthur Kill, and Raritan Bay to the Lower Bay).

(f) A vessel engaged in minesweeping operations shall, in addition to the lights prescribed for a power-driven vessel in Rule 23, exhibit three all-round green lights. . . . One of these lights . . . shall be exhibited at or near the foremast head and one at each end of the fore yard. These lights . . . indicate that it is dangerous for another vessel to approach closer than 1,000 metres astern or 500 metres on either side of the minesweeper.

(g) Vessels of less than 7 metres in length shall not be required to exhibit the lights prescribed in this rule.

(h) The signals prescribed in this rule are not signals of vessels in distress and requiring assistance. Such signals are contained in Annex IV to these regulations.

Sec. 80.18 Signals to be displayed by a towing vessel when towing a submerged or partly submerged object upon a hawser when no signals can be displayed upon the object which is towed. (b) By night the towing vessel shall display the regular side lights, but in lieu of the regular white towing lights shall display four lights in a vertical position not less than three feet nor more than six feet apart, the upper and lower of such lights to be white and of the same character as the regular towing lights and the middle of such lights to be red and of such character as to be visible on a dark night with a clear atmosphere for a distance of at least 2 miles.

VESSELS CONSTRAINED
BY THEIR DRAUGHT

RULE 28. A vessel constrained by

PILOT VESSELS

Art. 8. Pilot vessels when engaged

FIG. 78. Vessel constrained by her draught. International Rule 28.

FIG. 79. Power-driven or steam pilot vessel underway on station (in inland waters only, between flare-up intervals), high seas or inland waters. International Rule 29(a), Inland Rule, Article 8.

her draught may, in addition to the lights prescribed for power-driven vessels in Rule 23, exhibit where they can best be seen three all-round red lights in a vertical line, ...

on their stations on pilotage duty shall not show the lights required for other vessels, but shall carry a white light at the masthead, visible all round the horizon, and shall also exhibit a flare-up light or flare-up lights at short intervals, which shall never exceed fifteen minutes.

On the near approach of or to other vessels they shall have their side lights lighted, ready for use, and shall flash or show them at short intervals, to indicate the direction in which they are heading, but the green light shall not be shown on the port side nor the red light on the starboard side.

A pilot vessel of such a class as to be obliged to go alongside of a vessel to put a pilot on board may show the white light instead of carrying it at the masthead, and may, instead of the colored lights above mentioned, have at hand ready for use, a lantern, with a green glass on the one side and a red glass on the other, to be used as prescribed above.

PILOT VESSELS

RULE 29. (a) A vessel engaged on pilotage duty shall exhibit:

(i) at or near the masthead, two all-round lights in a vertical line, the upper being white and the lower red;

(ii) when underway, in addition, sidelights and a sternlight;

(iii) when at anchor, in addition to the lights prescribed in subparagraph (i), the anchor light, lights. . . .

(b) A pilot vessel when not engaged on pilotage duty shall exhibit

Pilot vessels, when not engaged on their station on pilotage duty, shall carry lights similar to those of other vessels of their tonnage.

A steam pilot vessel, when engaged on her station on pilotage duty and in waters of the United States, and not at anchor, shall in addition to the lights required for all pilot boats, carry at a distance of eight feet below her white masthead light a red light, visible all around the horizon and of such a

International Rules

the lights . . . prescribed for a similar vessel of her length.

SIGNALS TO ATTRACT ATTENTION

RULE 36. If necessary to attract the attention of another vessel, any vessel may make light or sound signals that cannot be mistaken for any signal authorized elsewhere in these rules, or may direct the beam of her searchlight in the direction of the danger, in such a way as not to embarrass any vessel.

STATION AND SIGNAL LIGHTS

1(c) Nothing in these rules shall interfere with the operation of any special rules made by the Government of any State with respect to additional station or signal lights or whistle signals for ships of war and vessels proceeding under convoy, or with respect to additional station or signal lights for fishing vessels engaged in fishing as a fleet. These additional station or signal lights or whistle signals shall, so far as pos-

Inland and Pilot Rules

character as to be visible on a dark night with a clear atmosphere at a distance of at least two miles, and also the colored side lights required to be carried by vessels when underway.

When engaged on her station on pilotage duty and in waters of the United States, and at anchor, she shall carry in addition to the lights required for all pilot boats the red light above mentioned, but not the colored side lights. When not engaged on her station on pilotage duty, she shall carry the same lights as other steam vessels.

SIGNALS TO ATTRACT ATTENTION

Art. 12. Every vessel may, if necessary, in order to attract attention, in addition to the lights which she is by these rules required to carry, show a flare-up light or use any detonating signal that cannot be mistaken for a distress signal.

STATION AND SIGNAL LIGHTS

Art. 13. Nothing in these rules shall interfere with the operation of any special rules made by the Government of any nation with respect to additional station and signal lights for two or more ships of war or for vessels sailing under convoy, or with the exhibition of recognition signals adopted by shipowners, which have been authorized by their respective Governments, and duly registered and published.

sible, be such that they cannot be mistaken for any light or signal authorized elsewhere under these rules.

Art. 30. The exhibition of any light on board of a vessel of war of the United States or a Coast Guard cutter may be suspended whenever, in the opinion of the Secretary of the Navy, the commander in chief of a squadron, or the commander of a vessel acting singly, the special character of the service may require it.

NAVY AND COAST GUARD VESSEL EXCEPTIONS
(33 U.S.C. 1052)

NAVY AND COAST GUARD VESSEL EXCEPTIONS
(Sec. 1, 59 Stat. 590; 33 U.S.C. 360)

Any requirement of such regulations in respect of the number, position, range of visibility, or arc of visibility of the lights required to be displayed by vessels shall not apply to any vessel of the Navy or of the Coast Guard whenever the Secretary of the Navy or the Secretary of Transportation, in the case of Coast Guard vessels operating under the Department of Transportation, or such official as either may designate, shall find or certify that, by reason of special construction, it is not possible for such vessel or class of vessels to comply with such regulations. The lights of any such exempted vessel or class of vessels, however, shall conform as closely to the requirements of the applicable regulations as the Secretary or such official shall find or certify to be feasible. Notice of such findings or certification and of the charac-

(See Title 33, Code of Federal Regulations, Part 135 and Title 32, Code of Federal Regulations, Parts 706 and 707.)

Any requirement as to the number, position, range of visibility, or arc of visibility of lights required to be displayed by vessels under . . . sections 154-231 of this title . . . and all laws amendatory thereto, shall not apply to any vessel of the Navy or of the Coast Guard, where the Secretary of the Navy, or the Secretary of Transportation in the case of Coast Guard vessels operating under the Department of Transportation, or such official or officials as either may designate, shall find or certify that, by reason of special construction, it is not possible with respect to such vessel or class of vessels to comply with the statutory provisions as to the number, position, range of visibility, or arc of visibility of lights. The lights of any such exempted vessel or class of vessels shall, however, comply as closely to the requirements of the applicable sections as the Secretary shall find to be feasible.

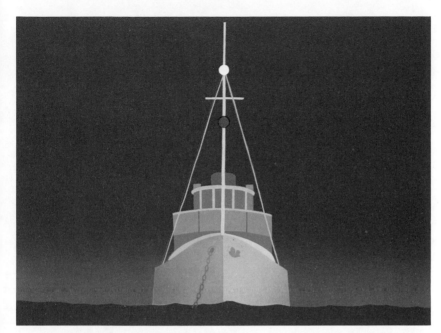

FIG. 80. Steam pilot vessel on station at anchor, between flare-up intervals, inland waters only. At sea, a power-driven pilot vessel would also show anchor lights for her class. Inland Rules, Article 8.

FIG. 81. Trawling.

ter and position of the lights prescribed to be displayed on such
exempted vessel or class of vessels
shall be published in the Federal
Register and in the Notice to Mariners and, after the effective date
specified in such notice, shall have
effect as part of such regulations.

PUBLICATION OF NAVY AND COAST GUARD VESSEL EXCEPTIONS (Sec. 2. 59 Stat. 591: 33 U.S.C. 360a)

When the Secretary of the Navy
or the Secretary of the Treasury, or
such official or officials as either
may designate, shall make any
finding or certification as prescribed in section 360 of this title,
notice of such finding or certification and the character and position
of the lights to be displayed on such
vessel shall be published in "Notice
to Mariners."

VESSEL (UN)LOADING DANGEROUS CARGO

**Sec. 80.38 Warning signal dis-
played while transferring dangerous cargoes.** (a) *At a dock.* While
fast to a dock, a vessel during the
loading or unloading of hazardous
or dangerous cargoes, such as explosives, combustible or inflammable liquids or gases, or certain
chemicals in bulk, is required to
display . . . a red light by night.

(b) *At anchor.* When at anchor,
a vessel during the loading or unloading of such hazardous or dangerous cargoes is required to display a red flag by day. (No special
warning signal is displayed at night.)

Note.—The regulations in 46, Code of
Federal Regulations, 35.30–1(a), 98.05–
50(h), 98.10–45(g), 98.15(h), 98.25–90(f),
and 146.29–25(o) require vessels to display warning signals when loading or
unloading bulk cargoes of inflammable
or combustible liquids or gases, ele-

FIG. 82. Pair trawling.

FIG. 83. Drift net fishing.

mental prosphorus in water, sulfuric acid, hydrochloric acid, liquid chlorine, or anhydrous ammonia, or military explosives.

UNAUTHORIZED LIGHTS PROHIBITED

Sec. 80.34 Rule relating to the use of searchlights or other blinding lights. Flashing the rays of a searchlight or other blinding light onto the bridge or into the pilot-house of any vessel under way is prohibited. Any person who shall flash or cause to be flashed the rays of a blinding light in violation of the above may be proceeded against in accordance with the provisions of R. S. 4450, as amended, looking to the revocation or suspension of his license or certificate.

Sec. 80.36 Rule prohibiting the carrying of unauthorized lights on vessels. Any master, or pilot of any vessel who shall authorize or permit the carrying of any light, electric or otherwise, not required by law, that in any way will interfere with distinguishing the signal lights, may be proceeded against in accordance with the provisions of R. S. 4450, as amended, looking to a suspension or revocation of his license.

Sec. 80.45 Distinctive blue light authorized for use by law enforcement vessels. (Identical to Sec. 90.30 paragraphs *a*, *b*, and *c*, Pilot Rules for the Great Lakes.)

EXTRACT FROM ANNEX I—
POSITIONING AND TECHNICAL
DETAILS OF LIGHTS AND SHAPES
PART C—LIGHTS AND SHAPES

2.(f) In all circumstances the masthead light or lights shall be so placed as to be above and clear of all other lights and obstructions.

2.(j) The lower of the two all-round lights prescribed for a fishing vessel when engaged in fishing shall be at a height above the sidelights not less than twice the distance between the two vertical lights.

4. *Details of location of direction-indicating lights for fishing vessels, dredgers and vessels engaged in underwater operations*

(a) The light indicating the direc-

FIG. 84. Seine net fishing.

tion of the outlying gear from a vessel engaged in fishing as prescribed in Rule 26(c)(ii) shall be placed at a horizontal distance of not less than 2 metres and not more than 6 metres away from the two all-round red and white lights. This light shall be placed not higher than the all-round white light prescribed in Rule 26(c)(i) and not lower than the sidelights.

(b) The lights . . . on a vessel engaged in dredging or underwater operations to indicate the obstructed side and/or the side on which it is safe to pass, as prescribed in Rule 27(d)(i) and (ii), shall be placed at the maximum practical horizontal distance, but in no case less than 2 metres, from the lights . . . prescribed in Rule 27(b)(i) and (ii). In no case shall the upper of these lights . . . be at a greater height than the lower of the three lights or shapes prescribed in Rule 27(b)(i) and (ii).

NOTES

Fishing vessels Inland Rules Article 9 requires *all* vessels engaged in fishing to exhibit a red all around light over a white all around light, though not necessarily in the same vertical line. Unlike the international definition of "engaged in fishing," the Inland Rules do not mention, and therefore do not, *ipso facto*, exclude, trolling lines. Any inland sport fisherman using trolling lines and wishing to assert right of way over a sailing vessel, however, must show the requisite lights. On the high seas, trolling, since it does not restrict maneuverability, is not considered as engaged in fishing.

Fishing vessels on the high seas are divided into two broad categories: trawlers, and vessels fishing by any method other than trawling. Trawlers drag behind them, at varying depths, a dredge net or similar apparatus. Normally, it descends into the sea at a short distance from the trawler.

Trawlers show a green all-round light to indicate the comparative safety with which they may be approached. In addition, except when handling gear or fast to an obstruction, they are normally making way. However, the development of trawlers working together with a single apparatus, *i.e., pair trawling*, requires more caution of the mariner, specifically in not passing between two such vessels. The side-by-side maneuvers of a pair, plus the searchlights authorized by Annex II, should help mariners, and not just fishermen, to recognize the situation. The other lights shown by trawlers, when fishing in company with other vessels also fishing, are primarily of interest to their fellow fishermen. Nevertheless, it behooves the mariner to be knowledgeable of these extra signals in the not too unlikely event of meeting, on approach to land, a fleet of fishermen. By knowing what the trawlers are doing there is less risk of causing damage to nets.

Other methods of fishing are diverse but sometimes involve the use of extensive lengths of lines or nets, which hamper a vessel's maneuverability far more than a trawler's dredge. The gear used in such methods often lies close to the surface, can be several miles in length, is usually unlighted and is vulnerable to the screws of a power-driven vessel. The all-round red light of International Rules 26(c) serves to warn the prudent mariner of the need to give such vessels a wide berth, particularly when they are fishing in close proximity to each other.

In both inland waters and on the high seas, fishing vessels engaged in fishing while at anchor do not show anchor lights. It is not, therefore, possible to distinguish by lights alone if a vessel engaged in fishing is at anchor. However, International Rules 26(b) and (c), unlike Inland Article 9, require vessels engaged in fishing to show sidelights and sternlights if making way through the water.

Should any vessel fishing on the high seas, other than trawlers, have gear out that extends over 150 meters horizontally, she is required by Rule 26(c)(ii) to show an additional white light in the direction of the gear. A trawler does not show such a light, due to the nature of her gear, but does show a white 225° range light higher and abaft the all-round green light, except that for a trawler of less than 50 meters in length such a light is optional.

Not under command or restricted in ability to maneuver   The two-red-light signal in Rule 27(a) cannot be used by a vessel broken down in inland waters in view of the nonapplicability of the International Rules to local waters of the United States. A vessel broken down at night in inland waters must display her regular lights. To attract the attention of an approaching vessel, it is necessary to use the Inland danger signal, a distress signal, or a signal authorized by Article 12.

Vessels not under command on the high seas do not display masthead or range lights but do show sidelights and sternlights when making way. On the other hand, vessels restricted in their ability to maneuver *do* show masthead and range lights as well as sidelights and sternlights when making way. In the event of any of the latter group anchoring, they display anchor lights as well as the red-white-red occupational lights, with the exception of a vessel engaged in dredging or underwater operations, which does not show anchor lights.

Special lights in Pilot Rules It will be noted that the two-red-light signal mentioned in Rule 27(a), International Rules, is an essential part of the required lighting in inland waters, under the Pilot Rules, for vessels at work on wrecks, for stationary and moving dredges and pipe lines connected therewith, for hydrographic survey vessels, and for Coast Guard vessels handling or servicing aids to navigation. The red-white-red light signal in Rule 27(b), International Rules, for similar vessels is not to be found in the Inland and Pilot Rules, nor is it to be used in inland waters.

Minesweepers Rule 27(f), International Rules, should be read with Section 80.18. Pilot Rules for Inland Waters. Rule 27(f) requires one of the three all-round green lights to be shown *at or near the foremast head.* Annex I 2(f), International Rules, states that *in all circumstances* the masthead light shall be placed above and clear of all other lights. The two requirements seem, for the minesweeper, to be contradictory. It is assumed that Rule 27(f) overrides Annex I in this minor matter.

Vessels constrained by their draft There is no equivalent to this International Rule in the Inland or Pilot Rules. Such a vessel in inland waters would need to invoke Article 27, the General Prudential Rule, and use the danger signal or radiotelephone to signify her constraint.

Pilot vessels No mention is made in International Rules of the sailing pilot vessel of Article 8, Inland Rules. It is doubted if any still exist. The differences between a vessel engaged in pilotage duties on the high seas and a steam pilot vessel on inland waters are mostly concerned with anchor and stern lights. On inland waters neither anchor nor stern lights are shown; on the high seas both are shown on the appropriate occasions. Otherwise, the use of the white-over-red identification lights and side lights is identical. There is no equivalent, under International Rules, for the flare-up light shown by an inland pilot vessel.

Naval and Coast Guard vessels Rule 1(c), International Rules, and Article 13, Inland Rules, permit naval and Coast Guard vessels to carry speed lights and other special lights in addition to their prescribed lights. Rule 1(e), as modified by 33 U.S.C. 1052, provides exemptions regarding lights to be carried by naval and Coast Guard vessels of *special construction.* Note that *closest possible compliance* with the rules is required by vessels of special construction. The Inland and Pilot Rules in themselves do not provide similar exemptions, but exemptions are contained in 33 U.S.C. 360 with respect to such vessels on the inland waters of the United States. For current exemptions for naval and Coast Guard vessels, see Appendixes Q and R respectively, and note that, in general, naval and Coast Guard vessels are in no way relieved from the obligation to carry the lights prescribed by the respective rules.

Vessels (un)loading dangerous cargo The red light of Section 80.38, Pilot Rules, is shown only when a vessel is made fast to a dock. The note to Section 80.38 lists applicable cargoes.

6
Day Shapes

PART C—LIGHTS AND SHAPES

APPLICATION

RULE 20. (a) Rules in this part shall be complied with in all weathers.

(d) The rules concerning shapes shall be complied with by day.

(e) The . . . shapes specified in these rules shall comply with the provisions of Annex I to these regulations.

TOWING AND PUSHING

RULE 24. (a) A power-driven vessel when towing shall exhibit:

(v) when the length of the tow exceeds 200 metres, a diamond shape where it can best be seen.

(e) A vessel or object being towed shall exhibit:

(iii) when the length of the tow exceeds 200 metres, a diamond shape where it can best be seen.

TOWING SUBMERGED OBJECTS

Sec. 80.18 Signals to be displayed by a towing vessel when towing a submerged or partly submerged object upon a hawser when no signals can be displayed upon the object which is towed. (a) The vessel having the submerged object in tow shall display by day, where they can best be seen, two shapes, one above the other, not less than six feet apart, the lower shape to be carried not less than 10 feet above the deck house. The shapes shall be in the form of a double frustum of a cone,

International Rules	Inland and Pilot Rules

International Rules

Inland and Pilot Rules

base to base, not less than two feet in diameter at the center nor less than eight inches at the ends of the cones, and to be not less than four feet lengthwise from end to end, the upper shape to be painted in alternate horizontal stripes of black and white, eight inches in width, and the lower shape to be painted a solid bright red.

SAILING VESSELS UNDERWAY

RULE 25. (e) A vessel proceeding under sail when also being propelled by machinery shall exhibit forward where it can best be seen a conical shape, apex downwards.

Art. 14. A steam vessel proceeding under sail only, but having her funnel up, may carry in daytime, forward, where it can best be seen, one black ball or shape two feet in diameter.

FISHING VESSELS

RULE 26. (a) A vessel engaged in fishing, whether underway or at anchor, shall exhibit only the . . . shapes prescribed in this rule.

(b) A vessel when engaged in trawling, by which is meant the dragging through the water of a dredge net or other apparatus used as a fishing appliance, shall exhibit:

. . . a shape consisting of two cones with their apexes together in a vertical line one above the other; a vessel of less than 20 metres in length may instead of this shape exhibit a basket;

(c) A vessel engaged in fishing, other than trawling, shall exhibit:

. . . a shape consisting of two cones with apexes together in a vertical line one above the other; a vessel of less than 20 metres in

Sec. 80.32a Day marks for fishing vessels with gear out. All vessels or boats fishing with nets or lines or trawls, when underway, shall in daytime indicate their occupation to an approaching vessel by displaying a basket where it can best be seen. If vessels or boats at anchor have their gear out, they shall, on the approach of other vessels, show the same signal in the direction from the anchor back towards the nets or gear.

length may instead of this shape exhibit a basket;

(ii) when there is outlying gear extending more than 150 metres horizontally from the vessel, . . . a cone apex upwards in the direction of the gear;

(d) A vessel engaged in fishing in close proximity to other vessels may exhibit the additional signals described in Annex II to these regulations.

(e) A vessel when not engaged in fishing shall not exhibit the . . . shapes prescribed in this rule, but only those prescribed for a vessel of her length.

VESSELS NOT UNDER COMMAND
OR RESTRICTED IN THEIR ABILITY
TO MANOEUVRE

RULE 27. (a) A vessel not under command shall exhibit:

(ii) two balls or similar shapes in a vertical line where they can best be seen;

(b) A vessel restricted in her ability to manoeuvre, except a vessel engaged in minesweeping operations, shall exhibit:

(ii) three shapes in a vertical line where they can best be seen. The highest and lowest of these shapes shall be balls and the middle one a diamond;

(iv) when at anchor, in addition to the . . . shapes prescribed in subparagraphs (i) and (ii), the . . . shape prescribed in Rule 30.

(c) A vessel engaged in a towing operation such as renders her un-

Note: The Inland Rules are silent as to vessels and seaplanes not under command and vessels unable to get out of the way of approaching vessels due to the nature of the work engaged in. However, the Pilot Rules provide special day signals for vessels engaged in certain activities whereby they may be considered as vessels unable to get out of the way due to the nature of work engaged in:

VESSELS WORKING ON
WRECKS

Sec. 80.19 Steam vessels, derrick boats, lighters, or other types of vessels made fast alongside a wreck, or moored over a wreck which is on the bottom or partly submerged,

FIG. 85. Vessel towing, vessel towed, length of tow over 200 meters, high seas only. International Rules 24(a) and (e).

FIG. 86. Vessel fast to dock, (un)loading dangerous cargo, inland waters only. Pilot Rules, Section 80.38a().

able to deviate from her course shall, in addition to the . . . shapes prescribed in subparagraph (b) . . . (ii) of this rule, exhibit the . . . shape prescribed in Rule 24(a).

(d) A vessel engaged in dredging or underwater operations, when restricted in her ability to manoeuvre, shall exhibit the . . . shapes prescribed in paragraph (b) of this rule and shall in addition, when an obstruction exists, exhibit:

(i) . . . two balls in a vertical line to indicate the side on which the obstruction exists;

(ii) . . . two diamonds in a vertical line to indicate the side *on* which another vessel may pass;

(iv) a vessel to which this paragraph applies when at anchor shall exhibit the . . . shapes prescribed in subparagraphs (i) and (ii) instead of the . . . shape prescribed in Rule 30.

(e) Whenever the size of a vessel engaged in diving operations makes it impracticable to exhibit the shapes prescribed in paragraph (d) of this rule, a rigid replica of the International Code flag "A" not less than 1 metre in height shall be exhibited. Measures shall be taken to ensure all-round visibility.

(f) A vessel engaged in minesweeping operations shall exhibit . . . three balls. One of these . . . shall be exhibited at or near the foremast head and one at each end of the fore yard. These . . . shapes indicate that it is dangerous for another vessel to approach closer than 1,000

or which may be drifting. (a) Steam vessels, derrick boats, lighters, or other types of vessels made fast alongside a wreck, or moored over a wreck which is on the bottom or partly submerged, or which may be drifting, shall display by day two shapes of the same character and dimensions and displayed in the same manner as required by § 80.18 (a),[1] except that both shapes shall be painted, a solid bright red; but where more than one vessel is working under the above conditions, the shapes need be displayed only from one vessel on each side of the wreck from which they can best be seen from all directions.

STATIONARY DREDGES

Sec. 80.20. Dredges held in stationary position by moorings or spuds. (a) Dredges which are held in stationary position by moorings or spuds shall display by day two red balls not less than two feet in diameter and carried in a vertical line not less than three feet nor more than six feet apart, and at least 15 feet above the deck house

---

[1] *The shapes shall be in the form of a double frustum of a cone, base to base, not less than two feet in diameter at the center nor less than eight inches at the ends of the cones, and not less than four feet lengthwise from end to end. They shall be displayed where they can best be seen, one over the other, not less than 6 feet apart, in such a manner that the lower shape is carried not less than 10 feet above the deck house.*

FIG. 87. Tug with submerged tow, inland waters only. Pilot Rules, Section 80.18(a).

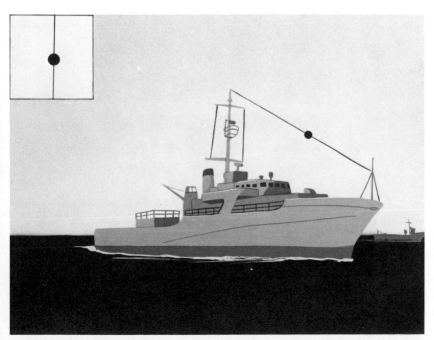

FIG. 88. Vessel aground, inland waters only. Same as at anchor. Pilot Rules, Section 80.25.

Day Shapes   157

FIG. 89. Vessel under sail and power by day, high seas only. International Rule 25(e).

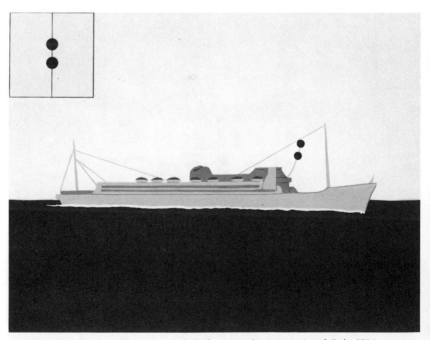

FIG. 90. Vessel not under command, high seas only. International Rule 27(a).

FIG. 91. Vessel restricted in her ability to maneuver, underway, high seas only. When at anchor, one ball would be shown in addition. International Rule 27(b)(ii) and (iv).

FIG. 92. Vessel engaged in towing, unable to deviate from her course and length of tow over 200 meters, high seas only. International Rule 27(c).

metres astern or 500 metres on either side of the minesweeper.

(h) The signals prescribed in this rule are not signals of vessels in distress and requiring assistance. Such signals are contained in Annex IV to these regulations.

and in such a position where they can best be seen from all directions.

DREDGES UNDERWAY

Sec. 80.21 Dredges under way and engaged in dredging operations. (a) Dredges underway and engaged in dredging operations shall display by day two black balls not less than two feet in diameter and carried in a vertical line not less than three feet nor more than six feet apart, and where they can best be seen from all directions. The term "dredging operations" shall include maneuvering into or out of position at the dredging site but shall not include proceeding to or from the site.

UNDERWATER OPERATIONS, ETC.

Sec. 80.22 Vessels moored or anchored and engaged in laying cables or pipe, submarine construction, excavation, mat sinking, bank grading, dike construction, revetment, or other bank protection operations. (a) Vessels which are moored or anchored and engaged in laying cables or pipe, submarine construction, excavation, mat sinking, bank grading, dike construction, revetment, or other bank protection operations, shall display by day, not less than 15 feet above the deck, where they can best be seen from all directions, two balls not less than two feet in diameter, in a vertical line not less than three feet nor more than six feet apart, the upper ball to be painted in al-

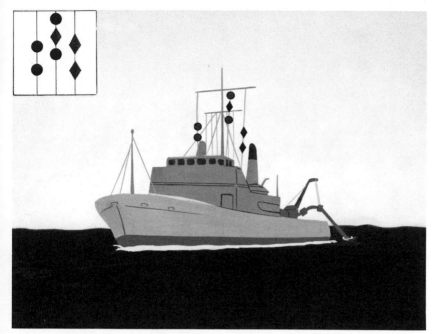

FIG. 93. Vessel engaged in dredging or underwater operations, restricted in her ability to maneuver when underway, or at anchor with an obstruction existing to one side, high seas only. International Rule 27(d).

FIG. 94. Minesweeper at work, high seas only. International Rule 27(f).

FIG. 95. Vessel fishing, gear out more than 150 meters, high seas only. International Rule 26(c).

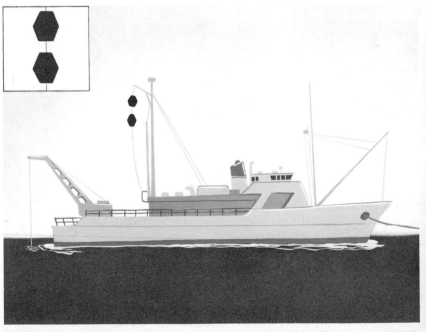

FIG. 96. Vessel moored over a wreck, inland waters only. Pilot Rules, Section 80.19(a).

FIG. 97. Stationary dredge, inland waters only. Pilot Rules, Section 80.20(a).

FIG. 98. Dredge underway dredging, inland waters only. Pilot Rules, Section 80.21(a).

ternate black and white vertical stripes six inches wide, and the lower ball to be painted a solid bright red.

SURVEY VESSELS

Sec. 80.33 Special signals for vessels employed in hydrographic surveying. By day a surveying vessel of the Coast and Geodetic Survey, underway and employed in hydrographic surveying, may carry in a vertical line, one over the other not less than 6 feet apart where they can best be seen, three shapes not less than 2 feet in diameter of which the highest and lowest shall be globular in shape and green in color and the middle one diamond in shape and white.

(a) Vessels of the Coast and Geodetic Survey shall carry the above-prescribed marks while actually engaged in hydrographic surveying and underway, including drag work. Launches and other boats shall carry the prescribed marks when necessary.

(b) It must be distinctly understood that these special signals serve only to indicate the nature of the work upon which the vessel is engaged and in no way give the surveying vessel the right-of-way over other vessels or obviate the necessity for a strict observance of the rules for preventing collisions of vessels.

(d) A vessel of the Coast and Geodetic Survey, when at anchor in a fairway on surveying operations,

FIG. 99. Vessel at work on submarine construction, inland waters only. Pilot Rules, Section 80.22(a).

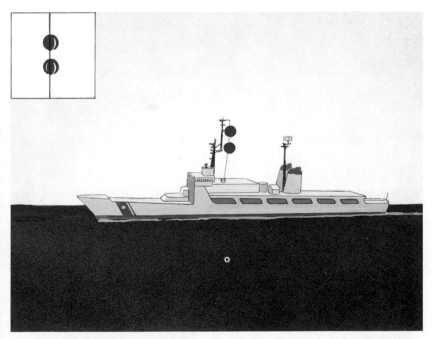

FIG. 100. Coast Guard vessel handling or servicing navigation mark, inland waters only. Pilot Rules, Section 80.33a(a).

shall display from the mast during the daytime two black balls in a vertical line and 6 feet apart. . . . In the case of a small vessel the distance between the balls and between the lights may be reduced to 3 feet if necessary.

COAST GUARD TENDERS

Sec. 80.33a Warning signals for Coast Guard vessels while handling or servicing aids to navigation. (a) Coast Guard vessels while engaged in handling or servicing an aid to navigation during the daytime may display from the yard two orange and white vertically striped balls in a vertical line not less than three feet nor more than six feet apart.

(b) Vessels, with or without tows, passing Coast Guard vessels displaying this signal, shall reduce their speed sufficiently to insure the safety of both vessels, and when passing within 200 feet of the Coast Guard vessel displaying this signal, their speed shall not exceed 5 miles per hour.

VESSELS CONSTRAINED BY THEIR DRAUGHT

RULE 28. A vessel constrained by her draught may, . . . exhibit where they can best be seen . . . a cylinder.

ANCHORED VESSELS AND VESSELS AGROUND

RULE 30. (a) A vessel at anchor shall exhibit where it can best be seen:

(i) in the fore part, . . . one ball;

Sec. 80.25 Vessels moored or at anchor. Vessels of more than 65 feet in length when moored or anchored in a fairway or channel shall display between sunrise and sunset on the forward part of the vessel where it can best be seen from other vessels one black ball not less than two feet in diameter.

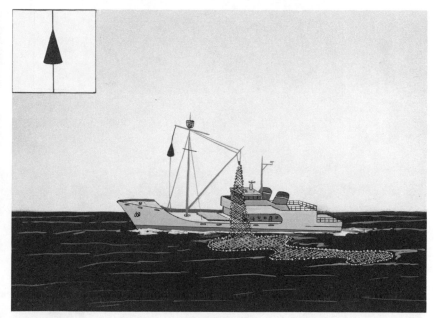

FIG. 101. Fishing vessel with nets, lines, or trawls out, underway, inland waters. At sea, permitted only if fishing vessel is less than 20 meters; also, if gear extends over 150 meters horizontally, must also show a black conical shape, apex upward. International Rule 26(c); Pilot Rules, Section 80.32a.

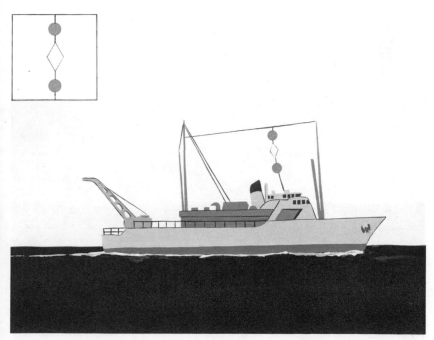

FIG. 102. Large hydrographic surveying vessel underway, inland waters only. Pilot Rules, Section 80.33(a).

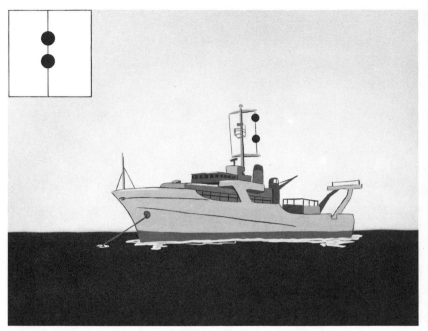

FIG. 103. Hydrographic surveying vessel at anchor, inland waters only. Pilot Rules, Section 80.33(d).

FIG. 104. Vessel constrained by her draught, high seas only. International Rule 28.

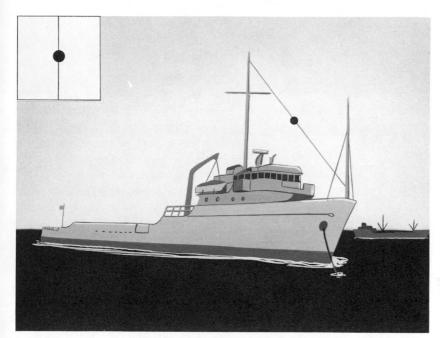

FIG. 105. Vessel at anchor at sea, or vessel over 65 feet in length at anchor in inland waters. International Rule 30(a); Pilot Rules, Section 80.25.

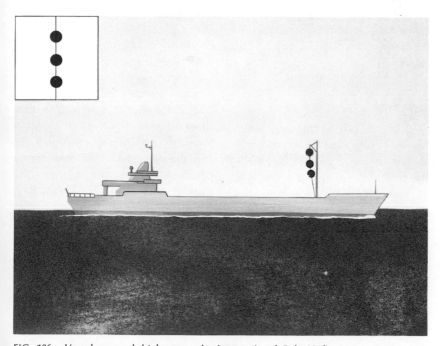

FIG. 106. Vessel aground, high seas only. International Rule 30(d).

VESSEL (UN)LOADING DANGEROUS CARGO

Sec. 80.38 Warning signal displayed while transferring dangerous cargoes. (a) *At a dock*. While fast to a dock, a vessel during the loading or unloading of hazardous or dangerous cargoes, such as explosives, combustible or inflammable liquids or gases, or certain chemicals in bulk, is required to display a red flag by day.

(d) A vessel aground shall exhibit . . . where they can best be seen:

(ii) three balls in a vertical line.

(e) A vessel of less than 7 metres in length, when at anchor or aground, not in or near a narrow channel, fairway or anchorage, or where other vessels normally navigate, shall not be required to exhibit the . . . shapes prescribed in paragraphs (a), . . . or (d) of this rule.

(b) *At anchor*. When at anchor, a vessel during the loading or unloading of such hazardous or dangerous cargoes is required to display a red flag by day.

Sec. 80.29 aids to navigation marking floating-plant moorings. Breast, stern, and bow anchors of floating plants working in navigable channels shall be marked by barrel or other suitable buoys. Provided, That the foregoing provisions of this section shall not apply to the following waters of New York Harbor and adjacent waters: the East River, the North River (Battery to Spuyten Duyvil), the Harlem River and the New York and New Jersey Channels (from the Upper Bay through Kill Van Kull, Newark Bay, Arthur Kill, and Raritan Bay to the Lower Bay).

SEAPLANES

RULE 31. Where it is impracticable for a seaplane to exhibit . . . shapes of the characteristics or in the positions prescribed in the rules of this part she shall exhibit . . . shapes as closely similar in characteristics and position as is possible.

ANNEX I

6. Shapes

(a) Shapes shall be black and of the following sizes:

(i) a ball shall have a diameter of not less than 0.6 metre;

(ii) a cone shall have a base diameter of not less than 0.6 metre and a height equal to its diameter;

(iii) a cylinder shall have a diameter of at least 0.6 metre and a height of twice its diameter;

(iv) a diamond shape shall consist of two cones as defined in (ii) above having a common base.

(b) The vertical distance between shapes shall be at least 1.5 metre.

(c) In a vessel of less than 20 metres in length shapes of lesser dimensions but commensurate with the size of the vessel may be used and the distance apart may be correspondingly reduced.

NOTES

Application　As with lights, the technical details concerning the color, size, and placement of shapes on the high seas are consolidated in Annex I, paragraph 6. Note that all day shapes under International Rules, but not Inland Rules, are black.

Tows over 200 meters　On the high seas, under Rule 24 (a), International Rules, a vessel with a tow extending more than 200 meters astern (measured from the stern of the towing vessel to the stern of the last vessel of the tow) is required to display a diamond shape. Rule 24 (e) requires the vessel or object towed to also show the same signal. This day signal is applicable only to tows astern. In inland waters long tows show no day signals. However, in the case of barges, some effort is made to regulate tow length. A vessel in inland waters which is towing a submerged or partly submerged object upon a hawser under conditions where no signals can be displayed on the object would show the shape described by Section 80.18 Pilot Rules.

Under sail and power　The conical shape required by Rule 25(e), International Rules, is mandatory on the high seas, whereas the black ball or shape provided by Article 14, Inland Rules, is optional on inland waters. Rule 25(e) meets the need for a signal denoting that a vessel under sail and power must obey the rules for a power-driven vessel. Article 14 is obsolete and appears to serve no worthwhile purpose.

Fishing vessels Rule 26 requires vessels engaged in fishing on the high seas to display by day, whether at anchor or underway, a shape consisting of two cones point to point. A vessel less than 20 meters in length may substitute a basket for this special black shape, but any vessel of any size with gear extending more than 150 meters horizontally must also show one cone, point up, in the direction of the gear. Under Section 80.32a, Pilot Rules, all vessels fishing in inland waters show a basket. If the fishing vessel is at anchor, the basket is shown in the direction of the gear. In international waters no difference is made in the shapes, as was done in the lights, of vessels engaged in trawling and vessels engaged in fishing by other means.

Vessels not under command or restricted in ability to maneuver The day signal for a vessel not under command under Rule 27(a), International Rules, is only applicable to vessels on the high seas. The Inland and Pilot Rules are silent concerning this situation. In the International Rules, Rule 27 (b) provides for a special shape for vessels restricted in their ability to maneuver, except minesweeping vessels, consisting of one black ball above a diamond and one black ball below. If such a vessel were to anchor, she would show this shape plus the normal anchor shape. A vessel towing, which for any reason is unable to deviate from its course, would indicate this by the same signal for vessels restricted in their ability to maneuver as prescribed in Rule 27 (c), International Rules, in addition to a diamond shape when the length of tow is greater than 200 meters. Vessels, when dredging or engaged in underwater operations on the high seas, also display the shape for a vessel restricted in its ability to maneuver, as well as special signals to indicate on which side an obstruction may exist. However, when at anchor they do *not* exhibit an anchor shape. Rule 27 (e) requires a day shape consisting of a rigid replica of the International Code Flag "A" for small vessels engaged in diving operations, which are unable to show the shape of International Rule 27 (d).

Minesweepers Minesweepers on the high seas must show a day shape of one black ball at the foremast head and one at each end of the foreyard regardless of the side on which the danger exists. However, such shapes would undoubtedly be impractical on craft such as air-cushion vehicles or rotary-wing aircraft, which are increasingly being used in mine countermeasures operations.

Special daymarks in Pilot Rules The two-black-ball day signal must be carried by a dredge dredging underway and by a hydrographic surveying vessel on surveying operations at anchor. Other specific daymarks are prescribed for a vessel with a submerged tow; a vessel at work on a wreck;

a stationary dredge; an anchored or moored vessel engaged in laying cable or pipe or engaged in submarine construction or excavation or bank protection operations; a hydrographic survey vessel underway; and a Coast Guard tender servicing an aid to navigation. These vessels have characteristics in common in that they are stationary or moving slowly and are to some degree unable to maneuver as required by the rules. When outside the inland waters of the United States they normally would display the signal prescribed by Rule 27, International Rules. However, an Inland or a Pilot Rule does not carry over into the jurisdiction of the International Rules, the latter rules excluding all others on the high seas, any more than does an International Rule carry over to inland waters. Any doubt on this point is dispelled by reference to the Enacting clause of the International Rules.

It will be noted that the Pilot Rules day signals are all mandatory for vessels on the inland waters of the United States, with the exception of the signals for a hydrographic surveying vessel underway on surveying operations and a Coast Guard tender handling or servicing an aid to navigation, which are optional.

Vessels constrained by their draft   Rule 28, International Rules, provides for a situation increasingly seen on the shallow seas and straits of the world—a large deep-draft ship which has such a small clearance between the hull and the seabed that the ability to alter course effectively and in time may be restricted. The vessel may show by day a black cylinder shape. The Inland Rules, not surprisingly, do no mention this recent outgrowth of the modern development of very large crude carriers (VLCCs).

Vessels at anchor or aground   Rule 30 (a), International Rules, requires all vessels at anchor to exhibit one black ball. Section 80.25, Pilot Rules, requires a similar ball for vessels over 65 feet in length moored or anchored in a fairway or channel in the inland waters of the United States. Should a vessel go aground in inland waters, she should display the anchor signal as the Inland and Pilot Rules do not provide for such a situation, unlike International Rule 30 (d).

Seaplanes   Rule 31, International Rules, requires seaplanes to conform as closely as possible to the shapes required for vessels. Seaplanes are not mentioned in Inland or Pilot Rules.

Vessel (un)loading dangerous cargo   The red warning flag of Section 80.38, Pilot Rules, is shown by itself, usually from the foreyard, when the vessel is alongside a dock. If the vessel is at anchor, the red flag is shown in addition to the anchor ball of Section 80.25. The use of this flag is consistent with Flag Bravo, International Code of Signals, and therefore may also be seen on the high seas.

7
Sound and Light Signals for All Vessels

International Rules

Rule 1(c). Nothing in these rules shall interfere with the operation of any special rules made by the Government of any State with respect to additional station or signal lights or whistle signals for ships of war and vessels proceeding under convoy, or with respect to additional station or signal lights for fishing vessels engaged in fishing as a fleet. These additional station or signal lights or whistle signals shall, so far as possible, be such that they cannot be mistaken for any light or signal authorized elsewhere under these rules.

PART D—SOUND AND
LIGHT SIGNALS

DEFINITIONS

RULE 32. (a) The word "whistle" means any sound signalling appliance capable of producing the pre-

Inland and Pilot Rules

Art. 13. Nothing in these rules shall interfere with the operation of any special rules made by the Government of any nation with respect to additional station and signal lights for two or more ships of war or for vessels sailing under convoy, or with the exhibition of recognition signals adopted by shipowners, which have been authorized by their respective Governments, and duly registered and published.

Art. 15. All signals prescribed by this article for vessels underway shall be given:

1. By "steam vessels" on the whistle or siren.

scribed blasts and which complies with the specifications in Annex III to these regulations.

(b) The term "short blast" means a blast of about one second's duration.

(c) The term "prolonged blast" means a blast of from four to six seconds' duration.

EQUIPMENT FOR SOUND SIGNALS

RULE 33. (a) A vessel of 12 metres or more in length shall be provided with a whistle and a bell and a vessel of 100 metres or more in length shall, in addition, be provided with a gong, the tone and sound of which cannot be confused with that of the bell. The whistle, bell and gong shall comply with the specifications in Annex III to these regulations. The bell or gong or both may be replaced by other equipment having the same respective sound characteristics, provided that manual sounding of the required signals shall always be possible.

(b) A vessel of less than 12 metres in length shall not be obliged to carry the sound-signalling appliances prescribed in paragraph (a) of this rule but if she does not, she shall be provided with some other means of making an efficient sound signal.

MANOEUVRING AND WARNING SIGNALS

RULE 34. (a) When vessels are in sight of one another, a power-

2. By "sailing vessels" and "vessels towed" on the fog horn.

The words "prolonged blast" used in this article shall mean a blast of from four to six seconds' duration.

Sec. 80.03 Signals. (a)(1) A short blast of the whistle shall mean a blast of about one second's duration.

Art. 15. A steam vessel shall be provided with an efficient whistle or siren, sounded by steam or by some substitute for steam, so placed that the sound may not be intercepted by any obstruction, and with an efficient fog horn; also with an efficient bell. A sailing vessel of twenty tons gross tonnage or upward shall be provided with a similar fog horn and bell.

Art. 18. Rule IX. The whistle signals provided in the rules under

driven vessel underway, when manoeuvring as authorized or required by these rules, shall indicate that manoeuvre by the following signals on her whistle:

—one short blast to mean "I am altering my course to starboard";

—two short blasts to mean "I am altering my course to port";

this article, for steam vessels meeting, passing, or overtaking, are never to be used except when steamers are in sight of each other, and the course and position of each can be determined in the day time by a sight of the vessel itself, or by night by seeing its signal lights. In fog, mist, falling snow or heavy rain storms, when vessels can not see each other, fog signals only must be given.

Art. 18. Rule I. When steam vessels are approaching each other head and head, that is, end on, or nearly so, it shall be the duty of each to pass on the port side of the other; and either vessel shall give, as a signal of her intention, one short and distinct blast of her whistle, which the other vessel shall answer promptly by a similar blast of her whistle, and thereupon such vessels shall pass on the port side of each other. But if the courses of such vessels are so far on the starboard of each other as not to be considered as meeting head and head, either vessel shall immediately give two short and distinct blasts of her whistle, which the other vessel shall answer promptly by two similar blasts of her whistle, and they shall pass on the starboard side of each other.

The foregoing only applies to cases where vessels are meeting end on, or nearly end on, in such a manner as to involve risk of collision; in other words, to cases in which, by day, each vessel sees the masts of the other in a line, or nearly in a line, with her own, and by night to cases in which each vessel is in such a position as to see both the sidelights of the other.

It does not apply by day to cases in which a vessel sees another ahead crossing her own course, or by night to cases where the red light of one vessel is opposed to the red light of the other, or where the green light of one vessel is opposed to the green light of the other, or where a red light without a green light or a green light without a red light, is seen ahead, or where both green and red lights are seen anywhere but ahead.

(See also Sec. 80.4, Pilot Rules— Appendix E.)

CROSSING STEAMERS

Sec. 80.03 Signals. (a) (3) One short blast of the whistle signifies intention to direct course to own starboard, except when two steam vessels are approaching each other at right angles or obliquely, when it signifies intention of steam vessel which is to starboard of the other to hold course and speed.

Art. 28. When vessels are in sight of one another a steam vessel underway whose engines are going at full speed astern shall indicate that fact by three short blasts on the whistle.

—three short blasts to mean "I am operating astern propulsion."

(b) Any vessel may supplement the whistle signals prescribed in paragraph (a) of this rule by light signals, repeated as appropriate, whilst the manoeuvre is being carried out:

(i) these light signals shall have the following significance:

—one flash to mean "I am altering my course to starboard";

—two flashes to mean "I am altering my course to port";

—three flashes to mean "I am operating astern propulsion";

(ii) the duration of each flash shall be about one second, the interval between flashes shall be about one second, and the interval between successive signals shall be not less than ten seconds;

(iii) the light used for this signal shall, if fitted, be an all-round white light, visible at a minimum range of 5 miles, and shall comply with the provisions of Annex I.

(c) When in sight of one another in a narrow channel or fairway:

(i) a vessel intending to overtake another shall in compliance with Rule 9(e)(i) indicate her intention by the following signals on her whistle:

—two prolonged blasts followed by one short blast to mean "I intend to overtake you on your starboard side";

—two prolonged blasts followed by two short blasts to mean "I intend to overtake you on your port side."

(ii) the vessel about to be over-

Art. 18. Rule VIII. When steam vessels are running in the same direction, and the vessel which is astern shall desire to pass on the right or starboard hand of the vessel ahead, she shall give one short blast of the steam whistle as a signal of such desire, and if the vessel ahead answers with one blast, she shall direct her course to starboard; or if she shall desire to pass on the left or port side of the vessel ahead, she shall give two short blasts of the steam whistle as a signal of such desire, and if the vessel ahead answers with two blasts, shall direct

taken when acting in accordance with Rule 9(e)(i) shall indicate her agreement by the following signal on her whistle:

—one prolonged, one short, one prolonged and one short blast, in that order.

her course to port; or if the vessel ahead does not think it safe for the vessel astern to attempt to pass at that point, she shall immediately signify the same by giving several short and rapid blasts of the steam whistle, not less than four, and under no circumstances shall the vessel astern attempt to pass the vessel ahead until such time as they have reached a point where it can be safely done, when said vessel ahead shall signify her willingness by blowing the proper signals. The vessel ahead shall in no case attempt to cross the bow or crowd upon the course of the passing vessel.

(See also Sec. 80.6, Pilot Rules—Appendix E.)

(d) When vessels in sight of one another are approaching each other and from any cause either vessel fails to understand the intentions or actions of the other, or is in doubt whether sufficient action is being taken by the other to avoid collision, the vessel in doubt shall immediately indicate such doubt by giving at least five short and rapid blasts on the whistle. Such signal may be supplemented by a light signal of at least five short and rapid flashes.

(e) A vessel nearing a bend or an area of a channel or fairway where other vessels may be obscured by an intervening obstruction shall sound one prolonged blast. Such signal shall be answered with a prolonged blast by any approaching

Art. 18. Rule III. If, when steam vessels are approaching each other, either vessel fails to understand the course of intention of the other, from any cause, the vessel so in doubt shall immediately signify the same by giving several short and rapid blasts, not less than four, of the steam whistle.

(See also Sec. 80.1, Pilot Rules, Appendix E, which designates this as the danger signal.)

Art. 18. Rule V. Whenever a steam vessel is nearing a short bend or curve in the channel, where from the height of the banks or other cause, a steam vessel approaching from the opposite direction can not be seen for a distance

vessel that may be within hearing around the bend or behind the intervening obstruction.

of half a mile, such steam vessel, when she shall have arrived within half a mile of such curve or bend, shall give a signal by one long blast of the steam whistle, which signal shall be answered by a similar blast given by any approaching steam vessel that may be within hearing. Should such signal be so answered by a steam vessel upon the farther side of such bend, then the usual signals for meeting and passing shall immediately be given and answered; but, if the first alarm signal of such vessel be not answered, she is to consider the channel clear and govern herself accordingly.

When steam vessels are moved from their docks or berths, and other boats are liable to pass from any direction toward them, they shall give the same signal as in the case of vessels meeting at a bend, but immediately after clearing the berths so as to be fully in sight they shall be governed by the steering and sailing rules.

INTERPRETIVE RULING

Sec. 86.10-1 Bend signal and subsequent meeting situation. Article 18, Rule V, and Article 18, Rule IX, of section 1, of the Act of June 7, 1897, as amended (33 U.S.C. 203), must be read together and followed after a bend signal is answered and the word "immediately" as used in Rule V shall be construed to require the exchange of sound signals

(f) If whistles are fitted on a vessel at a distance apart of more than 100 metres, one whistle only shall be used for giving manoeuvring and warning signals.

for passing immediately upon sighting the other vessel.

Sec. 80.2 Cross signals. Steam vessels are forbidden to use what has become technically known among pilots as "cross signals," that is, answering one whistle with two, and answering two whistles with one. (Former Pilot Rule II.)

Sec. 80.3 Vessels passing each other. (a) The signals for passing, by the blowing of the whistle, shall be given and answered by pilots, in compliance with the rules in this part, not only when meeting "head and head," or nearly so, but at all times when the steam vessels are in sight of each other, when passing or meeting at a distance within half a mile of each other, and whether passing to the starboard or port.

(b) The whistle signals provided in the rules in this part for steam vessels meeting, passing, or overtaking are never to be used except when steam vessels are in sight of each other, and the course and position of each can be determined in the daytime by a sight of the vessel itself, or by night by seeing its signal lights. In fog, mist, falling snow, or heavy rainstorms, when vessels cannot so see each other, fog signals only must be given. (Former Pilot Rule III.)

Sec. 80.26 Passing signals. (a) Vessels intending to pass dredges or other types of floating plant working in navigable channels, when within a reasonable distance therefrom and not in any case over a mile, shall indicate such intention by one long blast of the whistle, and shall be directed to the proper side for passage by the sounding, by the dredge or other floating plant, of the signal prescribed in the local pilot rules for vessels underway and approaching each other from opposite directions, which shall be answered in the usual manner by the approaching vessel. If the channel is not clear, the floating plant shall sound the alarm or danger signal and the approaching vessel shall slow down or stop and await further signal from the plant.

(b) When the pipe line from a dredge crosses the channel in such a way that an approaching vessel cannot pass safely around the pipe line or dredge, there shall be sounded immediately from the dredge the alarm or danger signal and the approaching vessel shall slow down or stop and await further signal from the dredge. The pipe line shall then be opened and the channel cleared as soon as practicable; when the channel is clear for passage the dredge shall so indicate by sounding the usual passing signal as prescribed in paragraph (a) of this section. The approaching vessel shall answer with a corresponding signal and pass promptly.

(c) When any pipe line or swinging dredge shall have given an approaching vessel or tow the signal that the channel is clear, the dredge shall straighten out within the cut for the passage of the vessel or tow.

Note: The term "floating plant" as used in §§ 80.26 to 80.31a, inclusive, includes dredges, derrick boats, snag boats, drill boats, pile drivers, maneuver boats, hydraulic graders, survey boats, working barges, and mat sinking plants.

SOUND SIGNALS IN
RESTRICTED VISIBILITY

RULE 35. In or near an area of restricted visibility, whether by day or night, the signals prescribed in this rule shall be used as follows:

(a) A power-driven vessel making way through the water shall sound at intervals of not more than 2 minutes one prolonged blast.

(b) A power-driven vessel underway but stopped and making no way through the water shall sound at intervals of not more than 2 minutes two prolonged blasts in succession with an interval of about 2 seconds between them.

(c) A vessel not under command, a vessel restricted in her ability to manoeuvre, a vessel constrained by her draught, a sailing vessel, a vessel engaged in fishing and a vessel engaged in towing or pushing another vessel shall, instead of the signals prescribed in paragraphs (a) (b) of this rule, sound at intervals of not more than 2 minutes three blasts in succession, namely one prolonged followed by two short blasts.

(d) A vessel towed or if more than one vessel is towed the last vessel of the tow, if manned, shall at intervals of not more than 2

Art. 18. Rule IX. In fog, mist, falling snow or heavy rain storms, when vessels can not see each other, fog signals only must be given.

Art. 15 In fog, mist, falling snow, or heavy rain storms, whether by day or night, the signals described in this article shall be used as follows, namely:

(a) A steam vessel underway shall sound, at intervals of not more than one minute, a prolonged blast.

(c) A sailing vessel underway shall sound, at intervals of not more than one minute, when on the starboard tack, one blast; when on the port tack, two blasts in succession, and when with the wind abaft the beam, three blasts in succession.

(e) A steam vessel when towing, shall, instead of the signals prescribed in subdivision (a) of this article, at intervals of not more than one minute, sound three blasts in succession, namely, one prolonged blast followed by two short blasts. A vessel towed may give this signal and she shall not give any other.

(d) A vessel when at anchor shall, at intervals of not more than one minute, ring the bell rapidly for

minutes sound four blasts in succession, namely one prolonged followed by three short blasts. When practicable, this signal shall be made immediately after the signal made by the towing vessel.

(e) When a pushing vessel and a vessel being pushed ahead are rigidly connected in a composite unit they shall be regarded as a power-driven vessel and shall give the signals prescribed in paragraphs (a) or (b) of this rule.

(f) A vessel at anchor shall at intervals of not more than one minute ring the bell rapidly for about 5 seconds. In a vessel of 100 metres or more in length the bell shall be sounded in the forepart of the vessel and immediately after the ringing of the bell the gong shall be sounded rapidly for about 5 seconds in the after part of the vessel. A vessel at anchor may in addition sound three blasts in succession, namely one short, one prolonged and one short blast, to give warning of her position and of the possibility of collision to an approaching vessel.

(g) A vessel aground shall give the bell signal and if required the gong signal prescribed in paragraph (f) of this rule and shall, in addition, give three separate and distinct strokes on the bell immediately before and after the rapid ringing of the bell. A vessel aground may in addition sound an appropriate whistle signal.

(h) A vessel of less than 12 metres

about five seconds, except that the following vessels shall not be required to sound this signal when anchored in a special anchorage area established pursuant to paragraph (c) of article 11:

(1) a vessel of not more than sixty-five feet in length; and

(2) a barge, canal boat, scow, or other nondescript craft.

(f) All rafts or other water craft, not herein provided for, navigating by hand power, horse power, or by the current of the river, shall sound a blast of the fog horn, or equivalent signal, at intervals of not more than one minute.

in length shall not be obliged to give the above-mentioned signals but, if she does not, shall make some other efficient sound signal at intervals of not more than 2 minutes.

(i) A pilot vessel when engaged on pilotage duty may in addition to the signals prescribed in paragraphs (a), (b) or (f) of this rule sound an identity signal consisting of four short blasts.

SIGNALS TO ATTRACT
ATTENTION

RULE 36. If necessary to attract the attention of another vessel, any vessel may make light or sound signals that cannot be mistaken for any signal authorized elsewhere in these rules, or may direct the beam of her searchlight in the direction of the danger, in such a way as not to embarrass any vessel.

Art. 12. Every vessel may, if necessary, in order to attract attention, in addition to the lights which she is by these rules required to carry, show a flare-up light or use any detonating signal that cannot be mistaken for a distress signal.

Sec. 80.34 Rule relating to the use of searchlights or other blinding lights. Flashing the rays of a searchlight or other blinding light onto the bridge or into the pilothouse of any vessel underway is prohibited. Any person who shall flash or cause to be flashed the rays of a blinding light in violation of the above may be proceeded against in accordance with the provisions of R. S. 4450, as amended, looking to the revocation or suspension of his license or certificate.

Sec. 80.35 Rule prohibiting unnecessary sounding of the whistle. Unnecessary sounding of the whistle is prohibited within any harbor limits of the United States. When-

ANNEX I—POSITIONING
AND TECHNICAL DETAILS
OF LIGHTS AND SHAPES
12. Manoeuvring Light

Notwithstanding the provisions of paragraph 2(f) of this Annex the manoeuvring light described in Rule 34(b) shall be placed in the same fore and aft vertical plane as the masthead light or lights and, where practicable, at a minimum height of 2 metres vertically above the forward masthead light, provided that it shall be carried not less than 2 metres vertically above or below the after masthead light. On a vessel where only one masthead light is carried the manoeuvring light, if fitted, shall be carried where it can best be seen, not less than 2 metres vertically apart from the masthead light.

ever any licensed officer in charge of any vessel shall authorize or permit such unnecessary whistling, such officer may be proceeded against in accordance with the provisions of R. S. 4450, as amended, looking to a revocation or suspension of his license.

DISTRESS SIGNALS

RULE 37. When a vessel is in distress and requires assistance she shall use or exhibit the signals prescribed in Annex IV to these regulations.

ANNEX IV—DISTRESS
SIGNALS

1. The following signals, used or exhibited either together or separately, indicate distress and need of assistance:

(a) a gun or other explosive signal fired at intervals of about a minute;

Art. 31. When a vessel is in distress and requires assistance from other vessels or from the shore the following shall be the signal to be used or displayed by her, either together or separately, namely:

In the daytime—

A continuous sounding with any fog-signal apparatus, or firing a gun.

At night—

First. Flames on the vessel as from a burning tar barrel, oil barrel, and so forth.

Second. A continuous sounding with any fog-signal apparatus, or firing a gun.

(b) a continuous sounding with any fog-signalling apparatus;

(c) rockets or shells, throwing red stars fired one at a time at short intervals;

(d) a signal made by radiotelegraphy or by any other signalling method consisting of the group . . . - - - . . . (SOS) in the Morse Code;

(e) a signal sent by radiotelephony consisting of the spoken word "Mayday";

(f) the International Code Signal of distress indicated by N.C.;

(g) a signal consisting of a square flag having above or below it a ball or anything resembling a ball;

(h) flames on the vessel (as from a burning tar barrel, oil barrel, etc.)

(i) a rocket parachute flare or a hand flare showing a red light;

(j) a smoke signal giving off orange-coloured smoke;

(k) slowly and repeatedly raising and lowering arms outstretched to each side;

(l) the radiotelegraph alarm signal;

(m) the radiotelephone alarm signal;

(n) signals transmitted by emergency position-indicating radio beacons.

2. The use or exhibition of any of the foregoing signals except for the purpose of indicating distress and need of assistance and the use of other signals which may be confused with any of the above signals is prohibited.

3. Attention is drawn to the rele-

Sec. 80.37 Distress signals. (a) *Daytime.* (1) Slowly and repeatedly raising and lowering arms outstretched to each side.

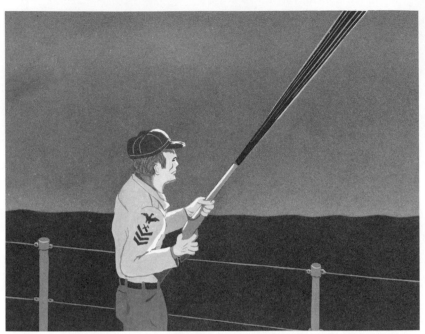

FIG. 107. Firing a gun. (Day or night distress signal.) International Rules, Annex IV; Inland Rules, Article 31.

FIG. 108. Red rockets at night indicate distress, high seas or inland waters. International Rules, Annex IV.

FIG. 109. Distress signal (NC), high seas or inland waters. International Rules, Annex IV.

FIG. 110. Distant distress signal, high seas or inland waters. International Rules, Annex IV.

vant sections of the International
Code of Signals, the Merchant Ship
Search and Rescue Manual and the
following signals:

(a) a piece of orange-coloured
canvas with either a black square
and circle or other appropriate symbol (for identification from the air);

(b) a dye marker.

ANNEX III TECHNICAL
DETAILS OF SOUND
SIGNAL APPLIANCES

1. Whistles

(a) *Frequencies and range of audibility.* The fundamental frequency
of the signal shall lie within the
range of 70-700 Hz.

The range of audibility of the signal from a whistle shall be determined by those frequencies, which
may include the fundamental and/
or one or more higher frequencies,
which lie within the range 180-700
Hz (±1 percent) and which provide the sound pressure levels
specified in paragraph 1(c) below.

(b) *Limits of fundamental frequencies.* To ensure a wide variety of whistle characteristics, the
fundamental frequency of a whistle
shall be between the following limits:

(i) 70-200 Hz, for a vessel 200
metres or more in length,

(ii) 130-350 Hz, for a vessel 75
metres but less than 200 metres in
length;

(iii) 250-700 Hz, for a vessel less
than 75 metres in length.

FIG. 111. Flames at night indicate distress, high seas or inland waters. International Rules, Annex IV; Inland Rules, Article 31.

FIG 112. Distress signal, inverted ensign, high seas or inland waters. There is no applicable rule; this practice is based on custom.

FIG. 113. Distress signal, orange smoke, high seas or inland waters. International Rules, Annex IV.

FIG. 114. Distress signal, person raising and lowering arms outstretched to each side, high seas or inland waters. International Rules, Annex IV; Pilot Rules, Section 80.37.

FIG. 115. Submarine distress signal, high seas or inland waters.

FIG. 116. Airplane with red Very's signal. "Send assistance to save personnel," high seas or inland waters.

(c) *Sound signal intensity and range of audibility.* A whistle fitted in a vessel shall provide, in the direction of maximum intensity of the whistle and at a distance of 1 metre from it, a sound pressure level in at least one ⅓-octave band within the range of frequencies 180-700 Hz (±1 percent) of not less than the appropriate figure given in the table below.

Length of vessel in meters	1/3-octave band level at 1 metre in dB referred to 2×10^{-5} N/m²	Audibility range in nautical miles
200 or more ...	143	2
75 but less than 200	138	1.5
20 but less than 75	130	1
Less than 20 ...	120	0.5

The range of audibility in the table above is for information and is approximately the range at which a whistle may be heard on its forward axis with 90 percent probability in conditions of still air on board a vessel having average background noise level at the listening posts (taken to be 68dB in the octave band centred on 250 Hz and 63 dB in the octave band centred on 500Hz).

In practice the range at which a whistle may be heard is extremely variable and depends critically on weather conditions; the values given can be regarded as typical but under conditions of strong wind or high ambient noise level at the listening post the range may be much reduced.

(d) *Directional properties.* The sound pressure level of a directional whistle shall be not more than 4 dB below the sound pressure level on the axis at any direction in the horizontal plane within ±45 degrees of the axis. The sound pressure level at any other direction in the horizontal plane shall be not more than 10 dB below the sound pressure level on the axis, so that the range in any direction will be at least half the range on the forward axis. The sound pressure level shall be measured in that one-third octave band which determines the audibility range.

(e) *Positioning of whistles.* When a directional whistle is to be used as the only whistle on a vessel, it shall be installed with its maximum intensity directed straight ahead.

A whistle shall be placed as high as practicable on a vessel, in order to reduce interception of the emitted sound by obstructions and also to minimize hearing damage risk to personnel. The sound pressure level of the vessel's own signal at listening posts shall not exceed 110 dB (A) and so far as practicable should not exceed 100 dB (A).

(f) *Fitting of more than one whistle.* If whistles are fitted at a distance apart of more than 100 metres, it shall be so arranged that they are not sounded simultaneously.

(g) *Combined whistle systems.* If due to the presence of obstructions the sound field of a single whistle or of one of the whistles referred to in paragraph 1(f) above is likely to have a zone of greatly reduced signal level, it is recommended that a combined whistle system be fitted so as to overcome this reduction. For the purposes of the rules a combined whistle system is to be regarded as a single whistle. The whistles of a combined system shall be located at a distance apart of not more than 100 metres and arranged to be sounded simultaneously. The frequency of any one whistle shall differ from those of the other by at least 10 Hz.

2. Bell or gong

(a) *Intensity of Signal.* A bell or gong, or other device having similar sound characteristics shall produce a sound pressure level of not less than 110 dB at 1 metre.

(b) *Construction.* Bells and gongs shall be made of corrosion-resistant material and designed to give a clear tone. The diameter of the mouth of the bell shall be not less than 300 mm for vessels of more than 20 metres in length, and shall be not less than 200 mm for vessels of 12 to 20 metres in length. Where practicable, a power-driven bell striker is recommended to ensure constant force but manual operation shall be possible. The mass of the striker shall be not less than 3 percent of the mass of the bell.

3. Approval

The construction of sound signal appliances, their performance and their installation on board the vessel shall be to the satisfaction of the appropriate authority of the State where the vessel is registered.

NOTES

Additional signals Both sets of rules authorize additional light signals for men of war or other vessels proceeding in company. The International Rules extend this to include also vessels fishing as a fleet and, for all categories, to permit the use of additional whistle signals.

Sound signal apparatus The term "whistle" is comprehensively specified in Annex III to the International Rules. There is no longer any mention of a foghorn under International Rules. Vessels 12 meters or more in length on the high seas are required to carry a whistle and a bell whether power-driven or sailing vessels. Under Inland Rules only steam vessels must have a whistle, with sailing vessels using a foghorn, but both must have a bell. Inland Rules, Article 15, by inference, excludes sailing vessels of less than 20 gross tons from carrying sound devices, though not from giving prescribed fog signals. The Motorboat Act of April 25, 1940, Appendix H, regulates sound devices for motorboats without, however, explicitly exempting them from the requirement of Article 15 for *all* power vessels, irrespective of size, to carry a whistle, a foghorn, and a bell. A gong is to be carried under International Rules for a vessel over 100 meters in length.

Signals when vessels are in sight of one another International Rule 34(a) makes the one-and two-blast signals for power-driven vessels purely rudder signals to be given whenever course is changed in accordance with the rules but *not* to be given *unless* course is changed. The proper signal must be given with a change in course whether the other vessel is a power-driven or a sailing vessel. No means of acknowledging such a signal is provided, but if the other vessel makes a change in course she would, if power driven, be required to make the proper signal.

Under Section 80.3, Pilot Rules, the same signals in inland waters must be given *and answered* whenever the vessels approach within half a mile, regardless of a change in course by either or both vessels. This does not mean that vessels should always wait until within one-half mile before signaling, but it does mean that in inland waters they must never approach that close without exchanging one- or two-blast signals. It is becoming common practice to exchange these signals verbally between vessels guarding the VHF channel used for Bridge-to-Bridge Radio Telephone communications. (See Appendix S.) Article 28, Inland Rules, does not mention these signals, but their proper use as signals of intent for steam vessels meeting head-on is given in Article 18, Rule I, and for overtaking and overtaken vessels in Article 18, Rule VIII. The signal section of the Pilot Rules (Section 80.03) provides a one-blast signal for steam vessels crossing in accordance with the Inland Rules, and this signal has been approved by the courts, although that part of the Pilot Rules attempting to make the one- and two-blast signals rudder signals as in the International Rules is invalid. (See pages 275 and 276.)

International Rule 34(c) provides whistle signals for vessels intending to overtake in narrow channels. These signals can only be used when the conditions of Rule 9()e(i) are met, that is, the vessel being overtaken has to take action to permit safe passing. This new rule more closely corresponds with the principles of the sound signals of proposal and agreement in Article 18, Rule VIII, Inland Rules.

Former Pilot Rule II, now Section 80.2, Pilot Rules, has been declared valid by the Supreme Court, and cross signals are, therefore, illegal.

International Rule 34(a) and Article 28, Inland Rules, both require a three-short-blast signal to be given when a vessel's engines are backing and that vessel is in sight of another vessel, sail or power, irrespective of the limiting terminology in Article 28. Rule 34(a) is explicit in its intent. Article 28 has been construed by Court decision to mean "the engines are backing at any speed, or the vessel actually has sternway."

Article 18, Rule IX, Inland Rules, like Rules 34(a), (b), and (c), International Rules, excludes the one-, two-, and three-blast signals in fog before the vessels sight each other and limits their application to cases where each vessel can see the other or her lights.

Whistle light Under International Rule 34(b), vessels operating to seaward of inland waters *may* further supplement the "in sight" whistle signals of Rule 34(a) by means of an all-round white light, such that the number of flashes corresponds to the number of short blasts. The white light does not have to be synchronized and the light signal can be repeated without necessarily repeating the whistle signal. Both the Inland and Pilot Rules and the courts are silent on this point, though there is a similar amber light authorized in the Western Rivers Rules.

Danger signal Article 18, Rule III, contains the well-known "danger signal" of four or more short blasts, which is valid in inland waters only and which is a definite requirement in the case of any disputed passing signal or any evidence of misunderstanding. The second paragraph of Section 80.7, Pilot Rules (former Pilot Rule II), has been declared valid by the Supreme Court and must be obeyed promptly in a crossing situation in the inland waters if there is misunderstanding or objection to signals. The equivalent "in doubt" signal authorized by Rule 34(d), International Rules, is equally mandatory but applies to *all* vessels on the high seas and not merely to steam vessels as do the Inland Rules. A vessel failing to use the proper danger signal when circumstances require is almost certain to be held liable for the collision.

Bend signal   The required long blast of Article 18, Rule V, Inland Rules, should be interpreted as being longer than the "prolonged" blast of four to six seconds required by Rule 34(e), International Rules. In the light of Article 18, Rule IX, Inland Rules, the mandate for steam vessels to exchange signals for meeting and passing *immediately* after hearing an answer to the bend signal must be understood to mean *immediately after sighting each other*.

Rule 34(e), International Rules, requires a prolonged blast on the part of *any* vessel nearing a bend where another vessel approaching from the other direction may not be seen. It is similar to the Inland bend signal but without the distance stipulation and, in addition, does not apply to a vessel leaving her berth, as does the signal required by Article 18, Rule V.

It will be noted that a vessel using the bend signal in the manner required in the inland waters of the United States when leaving her berth must, if backing, also sound the three-short-blast signal as soon as she sights another vessel.

Sound signals in restricted visibility are required under Rule 35, International Rules, in or near an area of restricted visibility whether by day or night. Article 18, Rule IX, Inland Rules, requires fog signals when vessels cannot see each other *in fog, mist, falling snow or heavy rain storms*. Both International and Inland Rules exempt small craft from the obligation to make precisely the laid-down signals, but if they do not or cannot, they must make some other equally effective sound at the required interval.

Intervals between required sound signals in restricted visibility should be regarded as maximum intervals only. In conditions of heavy traffic, or more probably when another vessel is known to be near, it may well be prudent that the signals be given more frequently. All required signals under the Inland Rules are given at intervals of not more than one minute. The International Rules differentiate between vessels underway, which make required signals at intervals of not more than two minutes, and certain vessels not underway that make required signals at intervals of not more than one minute.

Power vessel underway in restricted visibility The Inland Rules do not provide a signal to distinguish between a power vessel underway, making way, and one underway, not making way. International Rules 35 (a) and (b) do make such a distinction. When using such signals at sea, care should be taken to see that the vessel has lost all headway (or sternway) before the two prolonged blasts are started.

Sailing vessel The International Rules no longer have unique signals for sailing vessels in restricted visibility, such as are laid down in Article 15 (c), Inland Rules. Under the latter rules a rough estimate of a sailing vessel's course can be obtained by knowing the true direction of the wind and relating it to the one-, two- or three-blast signal heard on a foghorn. However, it is sometimes difficult to distinguish the air whistle of a diesel vessel from the foghorn of a sailing vessel, though normally the unspecified length of the latter's blast is shorter than the prolonged blast of the former.

Vessels at anchor in fog The bell signal for a vessel at anchor on the high seas or in inland waters must be given at least once a minute not only by a single vessel but, when several vessels are anchored together, by every vessel in the nest. This rule is rigidly enforced, however large the number of vessels. The rapid ringing of a ship's bell is a standardized signal, and the substitution of miscellaneous noises such as the beating of a dishpan or the sound of a pneumatic drill is not permitted by the courts, even though such a noise might be heard by the approaching vessel.

Rule 35(f), International Rules, also requires a vessel 100 meters or more in length anchored in fog at sea to sound a gong, the sound of which cannot be confused with the bell. Such vessels must sound the bell in the forepart of the vessel in the manner required and immediately thereafter sound the gong in the after part.

It will be noted that all vessels at anchor in fog on the high seas *may* sound a special sound signal of three blasts (one short, one prolonged, one short) to give an approaching vessel more definite warning of its position and to indicate the possibility of a collision. This signal, which is the letter R in the Morse Code, can be regarded as a special application of Rule 36, and is in addition to the required signals.

Neither the gong signal nor the three-blast warning signal authorized for all vessels anchored in fog on the high seas can be used in the inland waters of the United States.

In inland waters all vessels 65 feet or less in length and nondescript vessels of any size that are anchored in *special anchorage* areas are exempt from sounding the anchor signal. Special anchorage areas are established by the Secretary of Transportation pursuant to Article 11, Inland Rules. They may be found in practically any part of any coast of the United

States. The descriptions are not included in this text due to their bulk and limited relationship to the rules for preventing collisions.

Vessels engaged in special activities in restricted visibility The signal of one prolonged blast followed by two short blasts (letter D in the International Code of Signals) is used in inland waters for a vessel towing in fog. On the high seas this signal, in addition to towing, applies to a vessel fishing, a sailing vessel, a vessel constrained by her draft, a vessel restricted in her ability to maneuver and to a vessel underway which is not under command. It should be noted that the term "vessels restricted in their ability to maneuver" includes vessels engaged in dredging, surveying, underwater operations, minesweeping, underway replenishment, launching or recovery of aircraft and the laying, servicing, or picking up of a navigation mark, submarine cable, or pipeline. In the event of some of these activities being carried out in fog while at anchor, particularly for vessels engaged in underwater operations, it could be assumed that the three-blast signal supersedes the regular anchor signal, though the International Rules do not specifically regulate on this point.

A vessel pushing another ahead that is rigidly connected to it, gives the signal for a power-driven vessel and not that of a vessel towing or pushing.

The signal given by a vessel towing in inland waters in fog may also be used by vessels being towed. Its use by the towed vessel(s) is optional and no other can be used while in inland waters.

A vessel towed at sea, if manned, must sound, in restricted visibility, the signal in Rule 35 (d), International Rules; namely, one prolonged blast followed by three short blasts (letter B of International Code of Signals). If there is more than one vessel towed only the last vessel of the tow should give this signal and, where practicable, it should immediately follow the signal made by the towing vessel.

No special fog signals are prescribed for vessels fishing in inland waters, nor can they use the signals prescribed in the International Rules.

Vessels aground The signal in Rule 35 (g) is peculiar to the International Rules and cannot be used in inland waters. Vessels aground in fog in the inland waters of the United States must sound the prescribed danger signal or distress signals. On the high seas, a vessel aground can, in addition to the required signal, make an appropriate whistle signal which could be a distress signal or a suitable letter from the International Code of Signals.

Pilot vessels in fog Pilot vessels on pilotage duty in inland waters give the same fog signals as other vessels, whether sail or steam driven. The International Rules no longer distinguish between the lighting requirements for sail and power-driven pilot vessels (see Chapter 5), and this intent is apparently carried over to the optional identity signal in Rule

35 (i) where any pilot vessel may now use the four-short-blast signal. However, it is worthy of note that the rule allows it only in addition to the fog signals of Rule 35 (a) (b) or (f), which are for power-driven vessels underway or any vessel at anchor. Perhaps this was an oversight by the rule makers or, more possibly, the sailing pilot vessel is virtually extinct. Be that as it may, the signal is similar to the inland danger signal and might cause confusion at the approaches of busy ports like New York.

Danger signal in fog The courts have decided that the Inland danger signal, Article 18, Rule III, is a fog, as well as a clear weather, signal, and that its use in thick weather is not excluded by Article 18, Rule IX, Inland Rules. In inland waters only, therefore, the four-or-more short blast danger signal should be used whenever the approaching signals of another closing vessel appear to indicate impending collision. The International signal of doubt, Rule 34 (d), can be used by any vessel but is limited to when the vessels are in sight of each other.

8
Conduct of Vessels in Any Condition of Visibility

International Rules

Inland and Pilot Rules

PART B—STEERING AND
SAILING RULES

SECTION I—CONDUCT OF
VESSELS IN ANY CONDITION
OF VISIBILITY

APPLICATION

RULE 4. Rules in this Section apply in any condition of visibility.

LOOKOUT

RULE 5. Every vessel shall at all times maintain a proper lookout by sight and hearing as well as by all available means appropriate in the prevailing circumstances and conditions so as to make a full appraisal of the situation and of the risk of collision.

Art. 29. Nothing in these rules shall exonerate any vessel, or the owner or master or crew thereof, from the consequences of any neglect to carry lights or signals, or of any neglect to keep a proper lookout, or of the neglect of any precaution which may be required by the ordinary practice of seamen, or by the special circumstances of the case.

SAFE SPEED

RULE 6. Every vessel shall at all times proceed at a safe speed so

Art. 16. Every vessel shall, in a fog, mist, falling snow, or heavy

that she can take proper and effective action to avoid collision and be stopped within a distance appropriate to the prevailing circumstances and conditions.

In determining a safe speed the following factors shall be among those taken into account:

(a) By all vessels:

(i) the state of visibility;

(ii) the traffic density including concentrations of fishing vessels or any other vessels;

(iii) the maneuverability of the vessel with special reference to stopping distance and turning ability in the prevailing conditions;

(iv) at night the presence of background light such as from shore lights or from back scatter of her own lights;

(v) the state of wind, sea and current, and the proximity of navigational hazards;

(vi) the draught in relation to the available depth of water.

(b) Additionally, by vessels with operational radar:

(i) the characteristics, efficiency and limitations of the radar equipment;

(ii) any constraints imposed by the radar range scale in use;

(iii) the effect on radar detection of the sea state, weather and other sources of interference:

(iv) the possibility that small vessels, ice and other floating objects may not be detected by radar at an adequate range;

rainstorms, go at a moderate speed, having careful regard to the existing circumstances and conditions.

(v) the number, location and movement of vessels detected by radar;

(vi) the more exact assessment of the visibility that may be possible when radar is used to determine the range of vessels or other objects in the vicinity.

RISK OF COLLISION

RULE 7. (a) Every vessel shall use all available means appropriate to the prevailing circumstances and conditions to determine if risk of collision exists. If there is any doubt such risk shall be deemed to exist.

(b) Proper use shall be made of radar equipment if fitted and operational, including long-range scanning to obtain early warning of risk of collision and radar plotting or equivalent systematic observation of detected objects.

(c) Assumptions shall not be made on the basis of scanty information, especially scanty radar information.

(d) In determining if risk of collision exists the following considerations shall be among those taken into account:

(i) such risk shall be deemed to exist if the compass bearing on an approaching vessel does not appreciably change;

(ii) such risk may sometimes exist even when an appreciable bearing change is evident, particularly when approaching a very large vessel or a tow or when approaching a vessel at close range.

STEERING AND SAILING RULES

PRELIMINARY

Risk of collision can, when circumstances permit, be ascertained by carefully watching the compass bearing of an approaching vessel. If the bearing does not appreciably change, such risk should be deemed to exist.

ACTION TO AVOID COLLISION

RULE 8. (a) Any action taken to avoid collision shall, if the circumstances of the case admit, be positive, made in ample time and with due regard to the observance of good seamanship.

(b) Any alteration of course and/or speed to avoid collision shall, if the circumstances of the case admit, be large enough to be readily apparent to another vessel observing visually or by radar; a succession of small alterations of course and/or speed should be avoided.

(c) If there is sufficient sea room, alteration of course alone may be the most effective action to avoid a close-quarters situation provided that it is made in good time, is substantial and does not result in another close-quarters situation.

(d) Action taken to avoid collision with another vessel shall be such as to result in passing at a safe distance. The effectiveness of the action shall be carefully checked until the other vessel is finally past and clear.

(e) If necessary to avoid collision or allow more time to assess the situation, a vessel shall slacken her speed or take all way off by stopping or reversing her means of propulsion.

NARROW CHANNELS

RULE 9. (a) A vessel proceeding along the course of a narrow chan-

Art. 23. Every steam vessel which is directed by these rules to keep out of the way of another vessel shall, on approaching her, if necessary, slacken her speed or stop or reverse.

NARROW CHANNELS

Art. 25. In narrow channels every steam vessel shall, when it is safe

nel or fairway shall keep as near to the outer limit of the channel or fairway which lies on her starboard side as is safe and practicable.

(b) A vessel of less than 20 metres in length or a sailing vessel shall not impede the passage of a vessel which can safely navigate only within a narrow channel or fairway.

(c) A vessel engaged in fishing shall not impede the passage of any other vessel navigating within a narrow channel or fairway.

(d) A vessel shall not cross a narrow channel or fairway if such crossing impedes the passage of a vessel which can safely navigate only within such channel or fairway. The latter vessel may use the sound signal prescribed in Rule 34(d) if in doubt as to the intention of the crossing vessel.

(e)(i) In a narrow channel or fairway when overtaking can take place only if the vessel to be overtaken has to take action to permit safe passing, the vessel intending to overtake shall indicate her intention by sounding the appropriate signal prescribed in Rule 34(c)(i). The vessel to be overtaken shall, if in agreement, sound the appropriate signal prescribed in Rule 34(c)(ii) and take steps to permit safe passing. If in doubt she may sound the signals prescribed in Rule 34(d).

(ii) This Rule does not relieve the overtaking vessel of her obligation under Rule 13.

(f) A vessel nearing a bend or an

and practicable, keep to that side of the fairway or mid-channel which lies on the starboard side of such vessel. In a narrow channel a power-driven vessel of less than 65 feet in length shall not hamper the safe passage of a vessel which can navigate only inside such channel.

Art. 20. When a steam vessel and a sailing vessel are proceeding in such directions as to involve risk of collision, the steam vessel shall keep out of the way of the sailing vessel. This rule shall not give to a sailing vessel the right to hamper, in a narrow channel, the safe passage of a steam vessel which can navigate only inside that channel.

Art. 26. Sailing vessels underway shall keep out of the way of sailing vessels or boats fishing with nets, lines, or trawls. This rule shall not give to any vessel or boat engaged in fishing the right of obstructing a fairway used by vessels other than fishing vessels or boats.

Rules VIII. When steam vessels are running in the same direction, and the vessel which is astern shall desire to pass on the right or starboard hand of the vessel ahead, she shall give one short blast of the steam whistle, as a signal of such desire, and if the vessel ahead answers with one blast, she shall direct her course to starboard; or if she shall desire to pass on the left or port side of the vessel ahead, she shall give two short blasts of the steam whistle as a signal of such

area of a narrow channel or fairway where other vessels may be obscured by an intervening obstruction shall navigate with particular alertness and caution and shall sound the appropriate signal prescribed in Rule 34(c).

(g) Any vessel shall, if the circumstances of the case admit, avoid anchoring in a narrow channel.

TRAFFIC SEPARATION SCHEMES

RULE 10. (a) This rules applies to traffic separation schemes adopted by the organization.

(b) A vessel using a traffic separation scheme shall:

(i) proceed in the appropriate traffic lane in the general direction of traffic flow for that lane;

(ii) so far as practicable keep clear of a traffic separation line or separation zone;

(iii) normally join or leave a traffic lane at the termination of the lane, but when joining or leaving from the side shall do so at as small an angle to the general direction of traffic flow as practicable.

(c) A vessel shall so far as practicable avoid crossing traffic lanes, but if obliged to do so shall cross as nearly as practicable at right angles to the general direction of traffic flow.

(d) Inshore traffic zones shall not normally be used by through traffic which can safely use the appropriate

desire, and if the vessel ahead answers with two blasts, shall direct her course to port; or if the vessel ahead does not think it safe for the vessel astern to attempt to pass at that point, she shall immediately signify the same by giving several short and rapid blasts of the steam whistle, not less than four, and under no circumstances shall the vessel astern attempt to pass the vessel ahead until such time as they have reached a point where it can be safely done, when said vessel ahead shall signify her willingness by blowing the proper signals. The vessel ahead shall in no case attempt to cross the bow or crowd upon the course of the passing vessel.

traffic lane within the adjacent traffic separation scheme.

(e) A vessel, other than a crossing vessel, shall not normally enter a separation zone or cross a separation line except:

(i) in cases of emergency to avoid immediate danger;

(ii) to engage in fishing within a separation zone.

(f) A vessel navigating in areas near the terminations of traffic separation schemes shall do so with particular caution.

(g) A vessel shall so far as practicable avoid anchoring in a traffic separation scheme or in areas near its terminations.

(h) A vessel not using a traffic separation scheme shall avoid it by as wide a margin as is practicable.

(i) A vessel engaged in fishing shall not impede the passage of any vessel following a traffic lane.

(j) A vessel of less than 20 metres in length or a sailing vessel shall not impede the safe passage of a power-driven vessel following a traffic lane.

NOTES

Application   Rule 4, International Rules, specifies the applicability of the Rules contained in Part B, Section I, and recognizes the fact that vessels do navigate in both clear and restricted visibility.

Lookout   In Rule 5, International Rules, the important subject of a proper lookout is discussed. This new rules goes much further than the old 1960 Rule 29 and present Inland Article 29 that admonishes the mariner for *any neglect to keep a proper lookout.* International Rule 5 specifies that a proper lookout by sight and hearing shall be maintained by all vessels and at all times. In addition, a lookout shall be kept *by all available means appropriate to the prevailing circumstances.* The term *all available means* would certainly include, but not be limited to, intelligent and systematic use of operational radar to detect the location and movement of vessels in the vicinity. The U. S. federal courts have defined the person who is a *proper lookout* to be an experienced seaman, alert and vigilant, without other duties, and properly stationed in the vessel for the prevailing circumstances. In many cases the latter may mean as low down and as far forward on the vessel as circumstances permit.

Safe speed Rule 6, International Rules, is a new rule but is based upon the concept of *moderate speed* found in 1960 Rule 16 and the Radar Annex and Inland Article 16. Rule 6 requires all vessels to proceed at a safe speed in all conditions of visibility in order to allow the maximum possible time for effective action to be taken to avoid a collision. It further specifies factors to be taken into account in determining a safe speed by all vessels and also by those vessels with operational radar. Moderate speed for a vessel under Inland Article 16 has been defined by the Supreme Court as any speed which will enable the vessel to lose all way within half the distance of visibility. This, of course, is so that a vessel on opposite course will have an equal distance in which to stop after the vessels sight each other. When there is little or no visibility, moderate speed becomes bare steerageway, usually not over 3 or 4 knots. In very thick weather, in crowded harbors or other regions of dense traffic, vessels should, if practicable, find an anchorage. Vessels have been held at fault in collision cases for getting underway, or for failing to come to anchor, under conditions of poor visibility. A safe or moderate speed is a matter for individual judgment, but it can only be a speed slow enough to allow time to prevent a collision.

Risk of collision Rule 7, International Rules, is a new rule which combines provisions of the preliminary to the 1960 Steering and Sailing Rules and the Radar Annex. In general, this rule requires the use of all available means to determine if risk of collision exists, and specifically includes the use of radar. The basic method of determining whether risk of collision exists is still by means of compass bearings. The bearings of approaching vessels should be frequently observed and the bearing drift, if any, ascertained as a means for determining risk of collision. If the compass bearing of the other vessel is steady or nearly steady and the range is decreasing, there is risk of collision. Such risk may sometimes exist even when a large bearing change is evident, in the case of a large vessel or a tow at close range.

Action to avoid collision Rule 8, International Rules, contains sound advice for the mariner. It presents specific advice regarding actions to avoid collision. Any action to avoid collision *shall* be positive and made in ample time. Any change of course or speed *must* be large enough to be detected by another vessel either visually or by radar. A new provision is found in 8(d) which requires the mariner to check carefully the effectiveness of any action taken to ensure that safe passage results from that action. Note that International Rule 8 applies to all vessels, rather than just burdened steam vessels as expressed in Inland Article 23.

Narrow channels The 1972 International Rule on narrow channels applies to all vessels, not just power-driven vessels, and requires them to keep as near to the starboard limit of the channel as is safe and practicable. It further admonishes small vessels, sailing vessels, and fishing vessels not to interfere with the safe passage of a vessel restricted to following a narrow channel. Rule 9 also recognizes the problems experienced by large ships in narrow channels when confronted by small vessels crossing the channel. It prescribes the International signal of doubt to be sounded by the restricted vessel in such a situation. The 1972 International Rule 9(e) adopts signals of *proposal and agreement* similar to those currently used under U. S. Inland Rules for steam vessels overtaking in narrow channels. However, such signals are only applicable when the lead vessel must move over to permit safe passing and furthermore are not limited to power-driven vessels. The signals prescribed for this maneuver are laid down in Rule 34 which only applies to vessels in sight of each other. This rule does not change the basic precept of the overtaking vessel being burdened, no matter what the agreement between the two. Rule 9 also extends the bend signal of one prolonged blast to apply to all vessels.

Traffic Separation Schemes Higher concentrations of traffic in various bodies of water have led to the development of traffic separation schemes to keep vessel traffic in lanes flowing in the same general direction. International Rule 10 provides requirements for vessels using those traffic separation schemes adopted by IMCO. Provisions are made in the rule for local traffic, as well as for emergencies and fishing vessels. Other measures affecting the workability and safety of traffic separation schemes are included. The Inland Rules are silent on traffic separation schemes, but the Ports and Waterways Safety Act of 1972 has provided the means to establish similar vessel traffic services for inland waters. (See appendix U.)

Vessel Bridge-to-Bridge Radiotelephone Act This important act went into effect on 1 January 1973 and has the force of law upon inland waters, including the Great Lakes and Western Rivers. (See Appendix S.) It applies to the following categories of vessels in any condition of visibility.

(1) Power-driven vessels of 300 gross tons and upward.

(2) Vessels of 100 gross tons and upward carrying one or more passengers for hire.

(3) Commercial towing vessels of 26 feet or over in length.

(4) Manned dredges and floating plants working in or near a channel or fairway.

All the preceding vessels must guard frequency 156.65 MHZ (Channel 13) for bridge-to-bridge communications. The frequency is for the exclusive use of the person in charge of the vessel for the purpose of transmitting and confirming the intentions of his vessel and any other information necessary for the safe navigation of vessels. However, the use of the radiotelephone in no way relieves any person from the obligation of complying with the Rules of the Road and applicable Pilot Rules.

An extension of similar procedures to the International arena could well be beneficial, especially if the IMCO-recommended trial of a standard marine navigation vocabulary should prove successful and overcome any language barrier.

9
Conduct of Vessels in Sight of One Another

International Rules

Inland and Pilot Rules

SECTION II—CONDUCT OF
VESSELS IN SIGHT OF
ONE ANOTHER

APPLICATION

RULE 11. Rules in this section apply to vessels in sight of one another.

SAILING VESSELS

RULE 12. (a) When two sailing vessels are approaching one another, so as to involve risk of collision, one of them shall keep out of the way of the other as follows:

(i) when each has the wind on a different side, the vessel which has the wind on the port side shall

Rule IX. The whistle signals provided in the rules under this article, for steam vessels meeting, passing, or overtaking, are never to be used except when steamers are in sight of each other, and the course and position of each can be determined in the day time by a sight of the vessel itself, or by night by seeing its signal lights. In fog, mist, falling snow or heavy rain storms, when vessels can not see each other, fog signals only must be given.

Art. 17. When two sailing vessels are approaching one another, so as to involve risk of collision, one of them shall keep out of the way of the other as follows, namely:

(a) A vessel which is running free shall keep out of the way of a vessel which is close-hauled.

(b) A vessel which is close-hauled

keep out of the way of the other;

(ii) when both have the wind on the same side, the vessel which is to windward shall keep out of the way of the vessel which is to leeward;

(iii) if a vessel with the wind on the port side sees a vessel to windward and cannot determine with certainty whether the other vessel has the wind on the port or on the starboard side, she shall keep out of the way of the other.

(b) For the purposes of this rule the windward side shall be deemed to be the side opposite to that on which the mainsail is carried or, in the case of a square-rigged vessel, the side opposite to that on which the largest fore-and-aft sail is carried.

on the port tack shall keep out of the way of a vessel which is close-hauled on the starboard tack.

(c) When both are running free, with the wind on different sides, the vessel which has the wind on the port side shall keep out of the way of the other.

(d) When both are running free, with the wind on the same side, the vessel which is to the windward shall keep out of the way of the vessel which is to the leeward.

(e) A vessel which has the wind aft shall keep out of the way of the other vessel.

OVERTAKING

RULE 13. (a) Notwithstanding anything contained in the rules of this Section any vessel overtaking any other shall keep out of the way of the vessel being overtaken.

(b) A vessel shall be deemed to be overtaking when coming up with another vessel from a direction more than 22.5 degrees abaft her beam, that is, in such a position with reference to the vessel she is overtaking, that at night she would be able to see only the sternlight of that vessel but neither of her sidelights.

(c) When a vessel is in any doubt as to whether she is overtaking an-

Art. 24. Notwithstanding anything contained in these rules every vessel, overtaking any other, shall keep out of the way of the overtaking vessel.

Every vessel coming up with another vessel from any direction more than two points abaft her beam, that is, in such a position, with reference to the vessel which she is overtaking that at night she would be unable to see either of that vessel's side lights, shall be deemed to be an overtaking vessel; and no subsequent alteration of the bearing between the two vessels shall make the overtaking vessel a

other, she shall assume that this is the case and act accordingly.

(d) Any subsequent alteration of the bearing between the two vessels shall not make the overtaking vessel a crossing vessel within the meaning of these rules or relieve her of the duty of keeping clear of the overtaken vessel until she is finally past and clear.

crossing vessel within the meaning of these rules, or relieve her of the duty of keeping clear of the overtaken vessel until she is finally past and clear.

As by day the overtaking vessel can not always know with certainty whether she is forward of or abaft this direction from the other vessels she should, if in doubt, assume that she is an overtaking vessel and keep out of the way.

(See also Sec. 80.6, Pilot Rules— Appendix E.)

HEAD-ON SITUATION

RULE 14. (a) When two power-driven vessels are meeting on reciprocal or nearly reciprocal courses so as to involve risk of collision each shall alter her course to starboard so that each shall pass on the port side of the other.

(b) Such a situation shall be deemed to exist when a vessel sees the other ahead or nearly ahead and by night she could see the masthead lights of the other in a line or nearly in a line and/or both sidelights and by day she observes the corresponding aspect of the other vessel.

(c) When a vessel is in any doubt as to whether such a situation exists she shall assume that it does exist and act accordingly.

Art. 18. Rule I. When steam vessels are approaching each other head and head, that is, end on, or nearly so, it shall be the duty of each to pass on the port side of the other; and either vessel shall give, as a signal of her intention, one short and distinct blast of her whistle which the other vessel shall answer promptly by a similar blast of her whistle, and thereupon such vessels shall pass on the port side of each other. But if the courses of such vessels are so far on the starboard of each other as not to be considered as meeting head and head, either vessel shall immediately give two short and distinct blasts of her whistle, which the other vessel shall answer promptly by two similar blasts of her whistle, and they shall pass on the starboard side of each other.

The foregoing only applies to cases where vessels are meeting

International Rules

CROSSING SITUATION

RULE 15. When two power-driven vessels are crossing so as to involve risk of collision, the vessel which has the other on her own starboard side shall keep out of the way and shall, if the circumstances of the case admit, avoid crossing ahead of the other vessel.

Inland and Pilot Rules

end on, or nearly end on, in such a manner as to involve risk of collision; in other words, to cases in which, by day, each vessel sees the masts of the other in a line, or nearly in a line, with her own, and by night to cases in which each vessel is in such a position as to see both the side lights of the other.

It does not apply by day to cases in which a vessel sees another ahead crossing her own course, or by night to cases where the red light of one vessel is opposed to the red light of the other, or where the green light of one vessel is opposed to the green light of the other, or where a red light without a green light or a green light without a red light, is seen ahead, or where both green and red lights are seen anywhere but ahead.

Art. 19. When two steam vessels are crossing, so as to involve risk of collision, the vessel which has the other on her own starboard side shall keep out of the way of the other.

Sec. 80.7 Vessels approaching each other at right angles or obliquely. (a) When two steam vessels are approaching each other at right angles or obliquely so as to involve risk of collision, other than when one steam vessel is overtaking another, the steam vessel which has the other on her own port side shall hold her course and speed; and the steam vessel which has the other on her own starboard side shall keep out of the way of the other by directing her course to starboard so as to cross the stern of the other steam vessel, or, if necessary to do so, slacken her speed or stop or reverse.

(b) If from any cause the conditions covered by this situation are such as to prevent immediate compliance with each other's signals, the misunderstanding or objection shall be at once made apparent by blowing the danger signal, and both steam vessels shall be stopped and backed if necessary, until signals for passing with safety are made and understood. (Former Pilot Rule VII.)

ACTION BY GIVE-WAY VESSEL

RULE 16. Every vessel which is directed to keep out of the way of another vessel shall, so far as possible, take early and substantial action to keep well clear.

Art. 22. Every vessel which is directed by these rules to keep out of the way of another vessel shall, if the circumstances of the case admit, avoid crossing ahead of the other.

Art. 23. Every steam vessel which is directed by these rules to keep out of the way of another vessel shall, on approaching her, if necessary, slacken her speed, or stop, or reverse.

ACTION BY STAND-ON VESSEL

RULE 17. (a)(i) Where one of two vessels is to keep out of the way, the other shall keep her course and speed.

(ii) The latter vessel may however take action to avoid collision by her manoeuvre alone, as soon as it be-

Art. 21. Where, by any of these rules, one of the two vessels is to keep out of the way, the other shall keep her course and speed.

comes apparent to her that the vessel required to keep out of the way is not taking appropriate action in compliance with these rules.

(b) When, from any cause, the vessel required to keep her course and speed finds herself so close that collision cannot be avoided by the action of the give-way vessel alone, she shall take such action as will best aid to avoid collision.

(c) A power-driven vessel which takes action in a crossing situation in accordance with sub-paragraph (a)(ii) of this rule to avoid collision with another power-driven vessel shall, if the circumstances of the case admit, not alter course to port for a vessel on her own port side.

(d) This rule does not relieve the give-way vessel of her obligation to keep out of the way.

RESPONSIBILITIES BETWEEN
VESSELS

RULE 18. Except where Rules 9, 10 and 13 otherwise require:

(a) A power-driven vessel underway shall keep out of the way of:

(i) a vessel not under command;

(ii) a vessel restricted in her ability to manoeuvre;

(iii) a vessel engaged in fishing;

(iv) a sailing vessel.

(b) A sailing vessel underway shall keep out of the way of:

(i) a vessel not under command;

(ii) a vessel restricted in her ability to manoeuvre;

(iii) a vessel engaged in fishing.

(c) A vessel engaged in fishing

Art. 20. When a steam vessel and a sailing vessel are proceeding in such directions as to involve risk of collision, the steam vessel shall keep out of the way of the sailing vessel.

Art. 26. Sailing vessels underway shall keep out of the way of sailing vessels or boats fishing with nets, lines, or trawls. This rule shall not give to any vessel or boat engaged in fishing the right of obstructing a fairway used by vessels other than fishing vessels or boats.

when underway shall, so far as possible, keep out of the way of:

(i) a vessel not under command;

(ii) a vessel restricted in her ability to manoeuvre.

(d)(i) Any vessel other than a
vessel not under command or a
vessel restricted in her ability to
manoeuvre shall, if the circumstances of the case admit, avoid impeding the safe passage of a vessel
constrained by her draught, exhibiting the signals in Rule 28.

(ii) A vessel constrained by her
draught shall navigate with particular caution having full regard to
her special condition.

(c) A seaplane on the water shall,
in general, keep well clear of all
vessels and avoid impeding their
navigation. In circumstances, however, where risk of collision exists,
she shall comply with the Rules of
this Part.

NOTES

Application   Rule 11, International Rules, specifies the applicability of
Rules 12 through 18.

Sailing vessels   Both Rule 12, International Rules, and Article 17, Inland
Rules, describe the actions required of each of two sailing vessels when
approaching one another and there is risk of collision. Both specify which
vessel is to keep out of the way of the other. Under International Rule 12,
the right-of-way is determined first by point of sail and then, if two
vessels have the wind on the same side, by which vessel is to windward
of the other. International Rule 12, in addition, covers the situation where
a sailing vessel with the wind on the port side cannot determine which
side another sailing vessel has the wind. Article 17, Inland Rules, differs
in that it mentions a sailing vessel "running free" which must keep clear
of a sailing vessel "close-hauled." This old Rule was tailored for square-
rigged vessels which are not often seen today.

Overtaking   Rule 13, International Rules, and Article 24, Inland Rules, are virtually similar in content. An overtaking vessel is defined as one coming up from more than two points abaft the beam of another. The overtaking vessel must keep out of the way of the vessel overtaken and has the option of passing on either side, provided it is safe. Both Rule 13 and Article 24 mention the case where a vessel is in doubt whether she is overtaking or crossing, a common dilemma at sea. The obligation of the overtaking vessel to keep clear lasts not only until she has passed, but until she is "finally past and clear." Note that the two vessels must be in sight for the overtaking situation to exist, as stated in the International Rules and implied in the Inland.

Head-on situation   Both Rule 14, International Rules, and Article 18, Inland Rules, describe a "head-on" or meeting situation in essentially the same terms and require that vessels pass port to port when they are in sight and there is risk of collision. This holds true whether the vessels are already port to port, or are exactly head on, or are a little starboard to starboard but not far enough to pass well clear on that side. In the head-on situation, it is clear that a course change to port is contrary to the intent of both sets of rules although it is not mentioned in either. International Rule 14(c) requires a vessel, when in doubt, to consider a situation a head-on one and alter course to starboard to avoid collision. This should eliminate the possibility of conflicting maneuvers when two vessels are meeting almost end on.

Crossing situation   Rule 15, International Rules, and Articles 19 and 22, Inland Rules, both require the power-driven vessel to port of another crossing power-driven vessel to keep out of the way and avoid, where possible, passing ahead of the other. A crossing situation has usually been defined as what it is not; i.e., neither overtaking nor meeting, but it can generally be considered two power-driven (or steam) vessels in visual sight of one another approaching at right angles or obliquely so as to involve risk of collision.

Action by the give-way vessel   Rule 16, International Rules, and Articles 19, 22, and 23, Inland Rules, apply to the give-way vessel in a crossing situation. Under Rule 16, the give-way vessel is directed to take early and substantial action to keep well clear. By inference, then, the vessel to port in a crossing situation on the high seas is allowed the following actions: turning to starboard, turning to port, or reducing speed by stopping or backing engines. Section 80.7 of the Pilot Rules only allows reduction of speed or turning to starboard, thus eliminating on inland waters the International alternative of turning to port.

Action by the stand-on vessel   Under Rule 17, International Rules, a stand-on (privileged) vessel, i.e., in overtaking and crossing situations, is directed to hold course and speed. If and when she finds herself *in extremis,* that is, so close that collision would be inevitable if she took no action, she is required to take "such action as will best aid to avoid collision." However, a major new provision in the 1972 Rules allows the stand-on vessel the freedom to take action prior to extremis as soon as it becomes apparent to her that the give-way vessel is not taking appropriate action. If the situation is a crossing one, the stand-on vessel is warned against a turn to port for a vessel on her own port side. Rule 17(c) does not specify that this vessel is the give-way one, though presumably this was the intention. The International signal of doubt (five or more short blasts) may always be used by the stand-on vessel to call the other vessel's attention to her duties.

In inland waters, the obligation of the privileged vessel to maintain course and speed is found in Article 21. The term *in extremis* is not mentioned in the Inland Rules but has been defined by the courts as the moment when "it becomes evident that the other vessel will not or cannot keep out of the way." In addition, the requirement of Pilot Rule Section 80.3 for an exchange of whistle signals between passing vessels provides a means by which the privileged vessel may gain advance indications of a burdened vessel that may be failing in her duty to give way.

Responsibilities between vessels Rule 18, International Rules, governs all vessels which are not under command or restricted in their ability to maneuver and admonishes other vessels to keep well clear of them. It also clearly defines a hierarchy among vessels with their mutual responsibilities. Included in the 1972 Rules is the term *vessel constrained by her draught,* which takes into account deep-draft vessels plying shallow seas and straits and their consequent lack of maneuverability.

10
Conduct of Vessels in Restricted Visibility

International Rules   *Inland and Pilot Rules*

SECTION III—CONDUCT OF
VESSELS IN RESTRICTED
VISIBILITY

CONDUCT OF VESSELS IN
RESTRICTED VISIBILITY

RULE 19. (a) This rule applies to vessels not in sight of one another when navigating in or near an area of restricted visibility.

(b) Every vessel shall proceed at a safe speed adapted to the prevailing circumstances and conditions of restricted visibility. A power-driven vessel shall have her engines ready for immediate manoeuvre.

(c) Every vessel shall have due regard to the prevailing circumstances and conditions of restricted visibility when complying with the rules of Section I of this part.

(d) A vessel which detects by radar alone the presence of another vessel shall determine if a close-

Art. 16. Every vessel shall, in a fog, mist, falling snow, or heavy rainstorms, go at a moderate speed, having careful regard to the existing circumstances and conditions.

A steam vessel hearing, apparently forward of her beam, the fog signal of a vessel the position of which is not ascertained shall, so far as the circumstances of the case admit, stop her engines, and then navigate with caution until danger of collision is over.

222

quarters situation is developing and/or risk of collision exists. If so, she shall take avoiding action in ample time, provided that when such action consists of an alteration of course, so far as possible the following shall be avoided:

(i) an alteration of course to port for a vessel forward of the beam, other than for a vessel being overtaken;

(ii) an alteration of course towards a vessel abeam or abaft the beam.

(e) Except where it has been determined that a risk of collision does not exist, every vessel which hears apparently forward of her beam the fog signal of another vessel, or which cannot avoid a close-quarters situation with another vessel forward of her beam, shall reduce her speed to the minimum at which she can be kept on her course. She shall if necessary take all her way off and in any event navigate with extreme caution until danger of collision is over.

NOTES

Conduct of vessels in restricted visibility International Rule 19 and Inland Article 16 apply to vessels not in sight of one another due to some degree of restricted visibility. These rules also apply to vessels navigating near an area of restricted visibility as expressed in Rule 19 and implied in Article 16. Both Rule 19 and Article 16 remind the mariner to proceed at a "safe" or "moderate" speed in restricted visibility with careful regard to the circumstances involved. The term "safe speed" in Rule 19 has been defined more exactly in Rule 6, and the mariner should refer back to it for specific requirements. Also refer to the discussion of safe speed in the notes of chapter 8. In addition to proceeding at a safe speed, the engines of a vessel should be ready for immediate maneuver. The Inland Rules are silent with respect to the action to be taken by a vessel in restricted visibility, on detecting by radar alone another vessel with whom risk of collision exists. International Rule 19, however, requires vessels to take avoiding action when a close-quarters situation is seen to be developing with a vessel detected by radar alone. This action must be taken in ample time, once the situation is so assessed. In taking avoiding action that involves a change of course, specific guidance is given in the rule. The guidelines are such that if two vessels detect each other by radar, their avoiding action will be complementary. To be able to act under this rule it is axiomatic that systematic radar observation or plotting, either manual or automated, is required.

The action required of a vessel upon hearing a fog signal apparently forward of the beam differs between international and inland waters. More flexibility is given the vessel on the high seas which has made efficient use of her radar. She need not stop her engines if her radar plot shows no risk of collision. If the close-quarters situation cannot be avoided, she must reduce her speed to the minimum at which she can hold steerageway, 3–4 knots for most vessels. If this action is not effective she must then take all way off, implicitly by backing her engines and not just letting the ship glide to a halt. Inland Rule, Article 16, remains firm on the requirement to stop engines as soon as another vessel's fog signal is heard ahead. It should be obeyed the instant such a signal is heard, however faintly. Only in the rare case where such action would result in immediate danger is a vessel excused from stopping her engines.

The use of radar may tend to encourage a liberal interpretation of Rule 19 and Article 16. It should be borne in mind, however, that the courts may not agree with such an interpretation. In the cases settled to date, the courts have not been sympathetic to arguments that radar justifies omission of any precaution either stated or implied in the Rules.

The sound signals to be used under conditions of restricted visibility are to be found in Chapter 7.

Examples of action taken under International Rule 19(d)(i) and (ii) Some simple examples of action, involving change of course only, that could be taken in restricted visibility follow. Vessels are considered to be effectively using their radar. All PPI scopes are compass stabilized, with own ship at the center (i.e., a relative picture) and showing a heading marker. No attempt has been made to show more complicated situations, or the effect of speed changes, which more properly belong in radar and collision-avoidance manuals.

(1) Both vessels determine from systematic observation that a close-quarters situation is developing, and that neither is overtaking the other.

Example #1

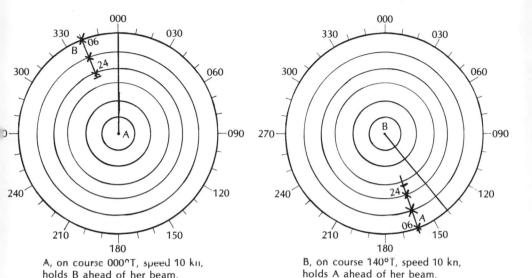

A, on course 000°T, speed 10 kn, holds B ahead of her beam.

B, on course 140°T, speed 10 kn, holds A ahead of her beam.

(2) Both vessels elect to maneuver by making a course change.

(3) The circumstances in this case allow them to comply with Rule 19(d)(i). Therefore they both turn boldly to starboard, though not necessarily at the same moment.

(4) Both continue with systematic observation to ensure their action is effective.

A true motion plot would indicate the situation and the avoiding action taken as shown below:

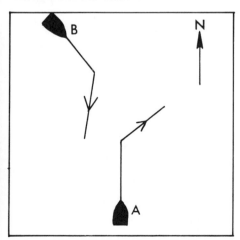

Example #2

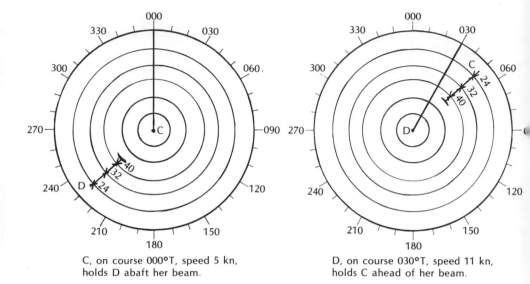

C, on course 000°T, speed 5 kn,
holds D abaft her beam.

D, on course 030°T, speed 11 kn,
holds C ahead of her beam.

(1) Both vessels determine from systematic observation that a close-quarters situation is developing.

(2) C, operating under Rule 19(d)(ii) elects to alter course boldly away from D, i.e., to starboard.

(3) D determines that she is overtaking C. To avoid C she may alter to port or to starboard, there being no preferred direction of alteration specified in Rule 19 (d)(i) in this case.

A true motion plot would indicate the situation and the avoiding action taken as shown below.

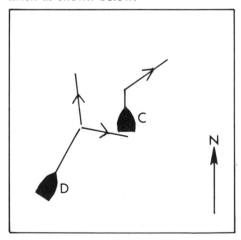

In example #2 it was stated that D was overtaking C. The term *over-taking*, although used, is not defined in the restricted visibility portion of the International Rules.

From Rules 19(d)(i) and (ii), taken together, it *might* be inferred that the term means when coming up generally from abaft the beam of another vessel. The precise meaning laid down in Rule 13(b), of more than 22.5 degrees abaft the beam, is strictly applicable only when vessels are in sight of each other, though it might be considered a reasonable extension to assume it also applies in restricted visibility.

Part II
The Law of the Nautical Road

11
Principles of Marine Collision Law*

Jurisdiction in Collision Cases

Jurisdiction over cases of collision between vessels on public navigable waters is placed by the Constitution of the United States in the hands of federal courts, sitting as courts of admiralty. Public navigable waters may be defined as waters used, or capable of being used, in interstate commerce. This definition excludes from federal jurisdiction collisions occurring on a lake wholly within a state, but includes cases on a navigable river which flows in or between two states or empties into the sea or an inlet of the sea. A collision case ordinarily begins in the federal district court, from whence it may be appealed to the Circuit Court of Appeals and on proper grounds to the United States Supreme Court.

State courts have exclusive jurisdiction over a collision on a lake completely surrounded by territory of the state and concurrent jurisdiction over one occurring on any portion of public navigable waters within the state. Thus, a collision which takes place on Puget Sound may by mutual consent of the parties be adjudicated in a damage suit between the vessels' owners in the Superior Court of the State of Washington. However, such cases are actually tried, in an overwhelming majority, in the federal courts because usually at least one of the litigants regards certain admiralty principles peculiar to these courts as favorable to his side of the case.

* Note.—*Prior to January 1, 1954, both the International and the Inland Rules dealt in terms of "steam vessels." It consequently became the practice on board ship, in textbooks on the subject, and in case work to refer to vessels within the meaning of the term as "steamers." It should be borne in mind in the reading of this text that what is said regarding steamers in cases cited pertains to steam or other power-driven vessels, and that for the purposes of the Steering and Sailing Rules, the International Rules construe a seaplane on the water as being within the meaning of the term "power-driven vessels."*

Cases of collision on public navigable waters, unless action has already been started in a state court, may always be taken to a federal court by either party.

After a collision has occurred on the high seas, an action may be brought in the country of either of the plaintiffs or the defendants, or in any other country where the law permits such action to be brought. Generally speaking, most courts will allow an action to be brought if the defendant vessel is in a port of their country at the time, in which case the proceedings and findings are in accordance with the law of that land.

A valid judgment by a foreign court, delivered abroad before action is brought in another country and given in the presence of both parties, is final and conclusive and a bar to further proceedings between the two same parties in the other country, except possibly for the enforcement, extension, or registration of that judgment.

Legal Personality of a Vessel

In American admiralty cases an important principle applied by the federal courts is the legal personality of the vessel, which is assumed to make the vessel herself the wrongdoer when collision follows a violation of the rules of the road. The action may be, and commonly is, between John Doe and the steamer So-and-So, or it may be between the two vessels. The vessel sued or "libeled" is held until the claims against her are satisfied, unless the owners obtain her release by paying into the court an amount equal to her appraised valuation, or post a bond double the amount of existing liens. If a judgment is obtained against her, the vessel may be sold at public auction by the marshal in order that the proceeds of the sale may place funds in the registry of the court for satisfaction of the judgment. A final recognition of the vessel's personality is seen in the fact that a marshal's sale, properly conducted, divests her of all maritime liens against her, and starts her out with her new owners free of any old claims against her. She thus literally receives a new lease on life.

Division of Damages

Until recently a principle peculiar to American admiralty courts was the doctrine of equal responsibility for unequal fault. When two vessels were in collision and both of them had violated a rule, the liability of each vessel was 50 percent of the total loss, regardless of her degree of guilt. One vessel may have been guilty of what seemed to be only a minor infraction and the other may have violated several rules and been flagrantly and deliberately negligent. The courts were concerned with the *fact* of fault but not, in most cases, with its amount:

Damages from collisions between vessels both at fault must be equally divided, irrespective of degree of fault.[1]

In 1975, the Supreme Court abandoned the equal division of damages and substituted a rule of comparative negligence:

> We hold that when two or more parties have contributed by their fault to cause property damage in a maritime collision or stranding, liability for such damage is to be allocated among the parties proportionately to the comparative degree of their fault, and that liability for such damages is to be allocated equally only when the parties are equally at fault or when it is not possible fairly to measure the comparative degree of their fault.[2]

If one vessel is solely at fault, she is liable for the total damage to the other, subject only to the provisions of the Limited Liability Acts which limit the liability of a vessel to her value after the collision, plus earnings for the voyage, collected or collectible. If neither vessel is at fault, we then have that extremely rare species of collision characterized by the courts as inevitable accident, and each vessel, of course, bears her own loss, be it great or small. It is significant that only about 1 percent of all the cases in the books come under this category. It is evident, therefore, that in a collision between vessel A and vessel B, we have four possibilities as to liability as determined by our admiralty courts: A solely liable; B solely liable; A and B both liable, in which case the damages are proportional to degree of fault; and neither liable, in practice a very rare occurrence.

Limited Liability of a Vessel

The principle of limited liability is a very old one, and was originally based on the high degree of risk that was inherent in any maritime venture. The theory was, and to some extent still is, that capital would be discouraged from investing in a business where an absentee agent, the master, might by his negligence involve his owners in enormous losses through disaster to a ship and her cargo, unless the amount of that loss could be limited somewhat in accordance with the old common-law principle. As described by Justice Holmes in the Supreme Court in a case just after the First World War:

> The notion, as applicable to a collision case, seems to us to be that if you surrender the offending vessel you are free, just as it was said by a judge in the time of Edward III: "If my dog kills your sheep and I, freshly after the fact, tender you the dog, you are without recourse against me."[3]

[1] *The Marian (1933) 66 F(2d) 354.*

[2] *U.S. Reliable Transfer Co., Inc., 1975, 44 L. Ed. 251.*

[3] *Liverpool, Brazil, and River Plate Steam Navigation Co. vs. Brooklyn Eastern District Terminal (1919) 64 L. Ed. 130.*

Under the original statute of 1851 and its later amendments, the law in the United States now provides that where a vessel is at fault without the privity or knowledge of her owners, the limit of her liability is the value of the vessel at the expiration of the voyage, plus any earnings that have accrued or are collectible for the transportation of passengers or cargo. Under a usual form of contract providing that, once the voyage has begun, freight is payable, ship lost or not lost, it frequently happens in the case of a commercial vessel that although the vessel herself is a total loss, these earnings, technically known as "pending freight," may amount to a considerable item. Pending freight is added to the value of the vessel at the end or breaking-up of a voyage, and therefore her value after the accident causing the liability, and not her value before the accident as in English law. This value, including pending freight, may be levied upon for faulty damage to the other vessel or her cargo or for injury to personnel on either vessel. The Harter Act and the later Carriage of Goods by Sea Act, however, excuse the vessel from liability in a faulty collision for damage to her own cargo. It will be seen that where a vessel which is solely at fault in a collision is totally lost and there is no pending freight, the injured vessel can recover nothing for damage either to herself or to her cargo.

An amendment to the Limited Liability Acts, patterned after the English law and passed August 29, 1935, changes the liability for death or personal injury to a maximum of $60 per gross register ton where the remaining value of the ship is less than that amount. The liability for damage to vessels or cargoes was not affected by this amendment.

The term "privity or knowledge of the owners" refers to cases in which damage and consequent liability are incurred through circumstances not beyond the control of the owners or managers. If such guilty knowledge can be implied to the owners or managers, limited liability cannot be invoked, and the injured vessel or cargo owners may bring all the offending owners' resources into that suit. One excellent illustration is the case of the USS *Chicago* and the British freighter, *Silver Palm*, which were in a collision in a fog off the California coast in October 1933. The vessels sighted each other a minute before the collision and both commanding officers ordered their engines full speed astern. The *Chicago* was practically brought to a standstill; but the *Silver Palm*, unknown to her master, had an early type of diesel engine without brakes which could not be reversed at speeds higher than 6 knots until the fuel was shut off and the vessel had lost a substantial part of the headway, the result being that she struck the *Chicago* while still making excessive speed. On the showing of the government that this defect was known to her owners, but they had not warned the master, who was making his first voyage on the vessel, of the conditions, both the District Court and the Circuit Court of Appeals denied the *Silver Palm's* petition for limitation of liability, thus opening the way for the United States to levy on the entire fleet of her owners, if necessary, to make up the difference between the value of the damaged *Silver Palm* and the amount of the judgment.[4]

Naval Vessel Not Subject to Lien

The doctrine of personality of the vessel is modified with respect to navy and other publicly owned vessels, in that it is contrary to public policy to permit such vessels to be libeled and taken into custody of the marshal and thus held out of service. However, the old theory that "The King can do no wrong" is never used as a defense in cases of collision between a ship of the United States Navy and a merchant vessel, even in time of war. Instead, the government permits itself, under a special statutory provision, to be sued as an owner *in personam*, and the damage sustained by both vessels is adjudicated exactly as it would be done were the action *in rem* between the vessels themselves. Indeed, so scrupulously has the United States accepted its responsibility in these cases that it has paid losses in full when the collision occurred because the naval vessel was patrolling without light and fog signals, due to actual war conditions.[5]

Rules of the Road Are Mandatory

At the beginning, it will be well to have in mind certain general principles which govern the action of the courts in determining collision liability. The first of these is that the rules of the road applicable to a particular case are in no sense optional, but are for the most part absolutely mandatory. To avoid liability for a collision the requirements *must* be obeyed. The courts will excuse a departure from the rules on two grounds only, and one of these, to avoid immediate danger, is provided for by the rules themselves.[6] Departure from the rules for any other reason, or for no reason at all, must be justified on the ground that while there was a technical violation, the circumstances were such that it could not possibly have contributed to the collision. As said by the Supreme Court, not only once but in substance many times:

> But when a ship at the time of collision is in actual violation of a statutory rule intended to prevent collision, it is no more than a reasonable presumption that the fault, if not the sole cause, was at least a contributory cause of the disaster.

[4] *Decided October 28, 1937. The Circuit Court found both vessels at fault, thus halving the damage which could be collected under the District Court decision. Certiorari denied (1938) 82 L. Ed. 1539.*

[5] *Watts vs. U.S. (1903) 123 F 105.*

[6] *Special Circumstances, Rule 2 and Arts. 27 and 29, International and Inland Rules, respectively.*

In such a case the burden rests upon the ship of showing, not merely that her fault might not have been one of the causes, or that it probably was not, but that it could not have been.[7]

It will be recognized that a disregard of any rule on the basis of convenience, courtesy, good nature, or disbelief in its efficacy places the navigator under a burden of proof that it is almost impossible for him to carry.

Obedience Must Be Timely

In the second place, not only must the rules be obeyed, but the action prescribed by them must be taken in ample time to carry out their purpose. It must be remembered that the rules are intended not only to prevent collision but to prevent serious and imminent risk of collision. This precept applies with particular force to the use of sound signals, which should always be given in time to be corrected if misunderstood, or as one judge expressed it "in time to maneuver out of a misunderstanding." Obedience to the letter of the rule is not obedience to the spirit of the rule unless it is rendered *before* the vessels are in dangerous proximity, in a sufficiently timely manner so that each vessel is aware of the other's intentions in time to conduct herself in accordance with them and aid in carrying them out.

Rules Apply Alike to All Vessels

A third principle which it is essential to remember is that the rules apply with equal force to all vessels on public navigable waters without regard to flag, ownership, service, size, or speed. A so-called "privileged" vessel is as much under the obligation to hold course and speed as is the "burdened" vessel to keep out of her way. No rights or exemptions, except those conferred by the rule, or amendments thereto, apply under American law to naval vessels, passenger liners, ferries, or towboats with tows, and the same steering and sailing rules govern the USS *America* and a 30-foot trawler. To give the rules their maximum effectiveness this is, of course, precisely as it should be.

Rules Modified by Court Interpretation

A fourth principle of the rules too often overlooked by the mariner in his seagoing practice of collision law is that to avoid liability he must know not only what the rules applicable to a given situation provide but what the federal courts have interpreted them to mean. Judicial interpretation has, in the history of the rules, performed three important functions. First, it has determined the legal meaning of certain phrases not defined

[7] *The* Pennsylvania *(1875) 19 Wall 125.*

in the rules themselves, such as moderate speed, efficient whistle or siren, flare-up light, proper lookout, special circumstances, immediate danger, ordinary practice of seamen, and risk of collision; it is in accordance with the meanings thus established that these terms are construed in collision cases. Second, it has filled certain gaps in the rules sometimes modifying the statute to do this. For example, Article 28, Inland Rules, provides that three short blasts when vessels are in sight of each other shall mean, "My engines are going at full speed astern," while the courts have required the same signal to be given when the engines are going at less than full speed astern or when one engine is going ahead and the other astern, with the vessel actually making sternboard.[8] Again, the courts have determined the proper signals where vessels approach each other in a collision situation stern first, a point on which the rules are silent. Third, judicial interpretation has been used not only to eliminate Pilot Rules found contradictory to the Inland Rules, but to reconcile occasional inconsistencies or conflicts in the latter. This is illustrated in the treatment by the courts of the apparently inconsistent sections of Article 18, Inland Rules, in which Rule III requires the danger signal by an approaching vessel when she fails to understand the course or intention of the other *from any cause*, and Rule IX of the same article provides that in fog, when vessels cannot see each other, *fog signals only must be given*. The courts have decided, in effect, that the danger signal in inland waters must be included as a fog, as well as a clear weather, signal.[9]

Whatever the mariner thinks of the legal setup which has the effect of giving the courts more authority over the rules of the road than the Commandant, U. S. Coast Guard, who enforces them through the local inspectors and supplements them with the Pilot Rules, the mariner must obey the law as he finds it, and that means in practice, as the admiralty judges interpret it. Notwithstanding the fact that in this country we do not have special admiralty courts, but any federal judge may be required to hear a collision case, it will be found that the decisions have been, as a whole, sound in seamanship as well as in law. Of course, the most experienced judges are not infallible, and not infrequently Circuit Courts of Appeal, co-ordinate in rank, will differ on some disputed point of collision law until the issue is settled by the Supreme Court. The basic rules have existed in substantially their present form for so many years that most doubtful questions have long since been decided by that august tribunal and the law for the most part may be regarded as pretty well settled. It remains only for the mariner to familiarize himself with the gist of the important

[8] The Sicilian Prince (CCA NY 1903) 144 F 951; the Deutschland (CCA NY 1904) 137 F 1018; the San Juan (Calif. 1927) A.M.C. 384.
[9] The Celtic Monarch (Wash. 1910) 17 F. 1006.

ruling decisions, many of which are set forth in textbooks dealing with the subject.

The international character of the Collision Regulations require that they should be understood by the seamen of different nations in the same sense. It is therefore of importance that the construction placed on them by courts of different countries should be uniform. This has been distinctly recognized in the United States:

> The paramount importance of having international rules, which are intended to become part of the law of nations, understood alike by all maritime powers, is manifest; and the adoption of any reasonable construction of them by the maritime powers . . . affords sufficient ground for the adoption of a similar construction . . . by the courts of this country.[10]

Rules Apply According to Location of Vessel

A fifth principle to be borne in mind by the mariner is that he must always be careful to observe the particular rules which apply in the locality of his vessel during the approaching situation. There are important differences in the rules to be followed on the high seas and in the inland waters of the United States, these differences extending to sound signals as well as to running and anchor lights. A further complication lies in the fact that different statutes subdivide our inland waters into three sections, with a distinct set of rules for each, and the statutory rules are supplemented in each case by a corresponding body of Pilot Rules, so-called, formulated and issued by the Commandant, U. S. Coast Guard. The three sections of inland waters referred to are (1) the Great Lakes and connecting and tributary waters as far east as Montreal; (2) the Red River of the North and certain other rivers whose waters flow into the Gulf of Mexico and their tributaries; (3) all other inland waters of the United States. In each of these sections, the Pilot Rules, except when they are in conflict with the statutory rules, have coextensive jurisdiction with them, and the mariner must therefore be equally familiar with both. To add to the complexity, Corps of Engineers, Department of the Army, Rules and Regulations supplement the Pilot Rules for the "Great Lakes." They, too, when not in conflict with the statutory rules, have coextensive jurisdiction with them, in the same manner as do the Pilot Rules. Still another special set of inland rules governs the navigation of all vessels in the Panama Canal Zone. The significant point to which attention is drawn here is that obedience to the wrong set of rules, where they are in conflict, constitutes just as serious a breach as does the deliberate disregard of the law altogether. To illustrate, the use of a single short blast of the whistle by a privileged vessel holding her course and speed in a crossing situation is proper in certain

---

[10] *The Sylvester Hale, 6 Bened. 523.*

inland waters, as provided in the Pilot Rules, but might make the vessel solely liable for a collision which followed the use of the same signal on the high seas, where one short blast generally indicates a change of course to the right.

History of the Rules of the Road

The International Rules date back to rules introduced in 1863 by England and France, and similar rules adopted by the United States in 1864, which in turn were adopted, with amendments, before 1886 by the United States, England, France, Germany, Belgium, Norway, and Denmark. These early rules were modified at a conference of representatives of the maritime nations of the world at Washington, D.C., in 1889, and subsequently adopted by the respective nations concerned. In the United States they became effective in 1897. Amended slightly in 1910, unsuccessful attempts were made to amend them further in 1913-1914 and 1929.

In 1948 the International Conference on Safety of Life at Sea at London proposed a revision of the 1889 International Rules as Annex B to its Final Act. The 82nd Congress, by Public Law 172, approved 11 October 1951, adopted this revision and authorized the President to fix its effective date by Presidential Proclamation. Similar legislative steps were taken by the other governments participating in the 1948 Safety Conference. By 19 December 1952, thirty-seven maritime nations had agreed to this revision, at which time the United Kingdom, in accordance with the provisions of the Final Act of the 1948 Conference, fixed 1 January 1954 as the date when the revised International Rules would be in force and effect, making it possible for the individual nations concerned to proclaim that date as the effective date of the 1948 revision of the international rules.

The 1948 Rules, unlike the 1889 Rules, were of short duration. The 1948 Rules were reconsidered and revised again at a similar conference of the same name and scope held in London in 1960. By similar national and international process, the 1960 Rules were made effective 1 September 1965.

In the United States, the 1960 Rules were enacted into law by the 88th Congress as Public Law 131 on 24 September 1963 and proclaimed effective pursuant that law on 1 September 1965 by Presidential Proclamation 3632 of 29 December 1964.

In 1961 a joint working group from the British, French, and German Institutes of Navigation devised Separation Schemes for the Dover Straits. A further working group, with additional representation from other countries, was set up in 1964 to consider similar schemes for other areas of the world. The proposals were accepted by IMCO and recommended for use by mariners in 1967.

The most recent International Conference was held in London during October 1972. As pointed out in Chapter One, the revision was a major one, making the rules more comprehensive, including the provision of mandatory separation schemes, and resulting in a completely new format. The 1972 International Rules are effective July 15, 1977. Executive Order 11964 ratified the rules for the United States, and they are published in Title 33 of the Code of Federal Regulations as Appendix A to Part 87.

The International Rules do not apply to the inland waters of the United States, the authority to make special rules being preserved in Rule 30, and the enacting[11] clause of the Act adopting the 1960 International Rules making them nonapplicable to vessels inshore of the lines of demarcation between the inland waters of the United States and the high seas, nor with respect to aircraft to any territorial waters of the United States.

The rules for the Great Lakes and the St. Lawrence River as far east as Montreal were passed by Congress in 1895, and apply to all vessels in the waters indicated. The rules for the Red River of the North and certain other rivers emptying into the Gulf of Mexico, and their tributaries, known as Western Rivers Rules, were passed by Congress in 1897, as were the so-called Inland Rules which apply to all vessels in such of the inland waters of the United States as are not covered by the two preceding sets of rules. The Pilot Rules applying on the same waters as the Inland Rules were originally promulgated by the Supervising Steamboat Inspectors, but now are and have been promulgated by the Commandant, U. S. Coast Guard, since 1 March 1942 under the authority of Section 157 of Title 33, United States Code, reading as follows:

(a) The Secretary of the Department in which the Coast Guard is operating shall establish such rules to be observed, on the waters described in section 154 of this title, by steam vessels in passing each other and as to the lights and day signals to be carried on such waters by ferryboats, by vessels and craft of all types when in tow of steam vessels or operating by hand power or horsepower or drifting with the current, and by any other vessels not otherwise provided for, not inconsistent with the provisions of this Act, as he from time to time may deem necessary for safety, which rules are hereby declared special rules duly made by local authority. A pamphlet containing such Act and regulations shall be furnished to all vessels and craft subject to this Act. On vessels and craft over sixty-five feet in length the pamphlet shall, where practicable, be kept on board and available for ready reference.

(b) Except in an emergency, before any rules or any alteration, amendment, or repeal thereof are established by the Secretary under the provisions of this section, the said Secretary shall publish the proposed rules, alterations, amend-

---

[11] *Sec. 33 U.S.C. 1051, International Rules, for enacting clause of the 1960 Rules. The enacting clause for the 1972 International Rules can be expected to be of similar intent.*

ments, or repeals, and public hearings shall be held with respect thereto on such notice as the Secretary deems reasonable under the circumstances.

Under this section the Pilot Rules for inland waters, many of which were in use long before the Inland Rules, were given coextensive jurisdiction with those rules, subject only to the legal restriction expressed in the act that they must not conflict with the Inland Rules. Inasmuch as the Inland Rules are statutes passed by Congress, their priority over the rules of the former inspectors, now of the Commandant, U. S. Coast Guard, would probably have been recognized by the courts even without the phrase of 33 U.S.C. 157 specifically limiting their authority to provisions *not inconsistent with the provisions of this act.* Occasionally it has seemed to the courts that a pilot rule has overstepped this authority and conflicted with the meaning or intent of a statutory rule, and they have accordingly invalidated the pilot rule. An example of this was the old Pilot Rule IX, which provided a two-blast signal in inland waters to be exchanged in the crossing situation between the burdened vessel and the privileged vessel when the former could cross the bow of the latter with safety. In 1909, two years after this rule was adopted, it was thrown out by the federal court as inconsistent with Article 19, the statutory crossing rule. As said by the district judge:

> Rule IX of the Board of Inspectors, approved by the Secretary of Commerce and Labor, Feb. 25, 1907, which permits the vessel having the other on her starboard hand to cross the bows of the other if it can be done without risk of collision, is invalid, as repugnant to the starboard hand rule.[12]

In 1972 the Ports and Waterways Safety Act was passed by Congress. The act authorizes the Secretary of the Department in which the Coast Guard is operating, to establish and operate vessel traffic services for navigable waters of the United States, as well as exercising control over environmental quality in the same waters. In some aspects the act is complementary to the traffic separation schemes of the International Rules, and the systems of both dovetail neatly at the boundary of the high seas. (See appendices U, V and W).

Revision and Unification Desirable

The numerous differences between the requirements to be observed by the same vessel when she is in inland waters and when she is outside these waters constitute the chief weakness in our present rules. That many of these differences are far more than mere technicalities is apparent with even a casual reading of the rules. The writer is unable to suggest a single

[12] *The* Pawnee *(NY 1909) 168 F 371. For revised Rule IX, see Sec. 80.9, Pilot Rules for Inland Waters, Appendix E.*

good argument in favor of a system which makes it necessary for a vessel to change the rules governing her conduct in a collision situation whenever she crosses an imaginary line bearing so many degrees from such and such a point. On the other hand there is much to be said in favor of complete uniformity of the rules. The mariner is not legally trained and cannot appreciate fine distinctions of law; in the naval service at least he has so many duties other than those connected with navigation to perform and and so much studying to do to keep up with them that he will do well to keep thoroughly posted on *one* set of rules of the road, and the same argument applies in some degree to the merchant marine officer. At night or in thick weather, the line separating inland waters from the high seas cannot be determined with any degree of accuracy, and an approaching situation is the last place for the mariner to turn his attention from the other vessel to cut in his position in order to be sure which rules apply; numerous border-line situations occur where in the approach one vessel is on one side of the line, under International Rules, and the other on the opposite side, under Inland and Pilot Rules; and finally, there is the ever-present likelihood of a mistake, through the personal equation, in choosing the right rules at the right time. The use of the International Rules in Canadian inland waters, including the tortuous inside passage to Alaska, where they have been applied for many years with a surprisingly low collision rate, should be an effective answer to the argument that those rules are inadequate except on the high seas. While there are certain intrinsic advantages in the Inland Rules, it is the writer's opinion that they may be most safely enjoyed by having them incorporated in the International Rules, not by restricting their application to inland waters and needlessly confusing the mariner who thus has to obey different rules inside and outside an invisible dividing line.

However, changes in law come slowly, particularly in the field of admiralty, which has only in recent years showed a noticeable tendency to undergo change in the face of established tradition. It is conceivable that Congress might be persuaded to abolish the Inland and Pilot Rules altogether, putting in their stead the International Rules and a limited number of supplementary rules required by strictly local conditions. But, we move very slowly in these matters, as illustrated by the fact that the rules adopted by the International Convention of 1889 did not become effective in the United States until 1897, and it was not until 1948 that a successful revision was proposed. Even then, conservative as it was, that revision was held in abeyance for nearly six years, until 1 January 1954 before being put into effect. When the rules were further revised in 1960, it was again nearly six years, 1 September 1965 before the changes were made effective. This dilatoriness is evident again with the 1972 Rules, which came into force internationally on 15 July 1977. Unless and until unification of the rules is an accomplished fact, the professional mariner can protect himself only by making and keeping himself absolutely familiar with the essential details of the International, Inland, and Pilot Rules, with particular emphasis on their points of difference and on interpretive court decisions, and for good measure he must undergo additional study if his vessel goes into the Great Lakes, or up the Mississippi River, or through the Panama Canal.

Two attempts in recent years have been made to unify the Inland and International Rules. The latest, in 1974, was spurred on by the injunction in Rule 1(b) of the 1972 International Rules, requiring special rules to conform as closely as possible to the 1972 Convention. A working paper of proposed U.S. Waters Rules was drawn up by the Coast Guard in recognition of the need for reasonably consistent rules on inland waters and the high seas. Considerable public discussion by interested parties has taken place in Washington, D.C., with some measure of agreement to adopt many of the International Rules while retaining rules unique to local waters. However, the proposed U.S. Waters Rules remain in limbo. Hopefully, either the International Rules or a compromise, such as the proposed U.S. Water Rules, will replace existing statutes after the 1972 International Rules have been in effect for a short period. Ideally, the International Rules should be adopted and the Coast Guard given the authority to supplement the rules with local regulations.

SUMMARY

Federal courts, sitting in Admiralty, have jurisdiction over collisions occurring on public navigable waters, which have been held to be waters navigable, though not necessarily navigated, in interstate commerce. State courts may have concurrent jurisdiction, when provided by local statute, over certain cases on public navigable waters within a state. Admiralty law permits action to be brought against a vessel *in rem* or against her owners *in personam*. Whenever both vessels in a collision are at fault, under United States law the liability must be divided between them. A vessel may be sold at auction to satisfy a judgment against her, but the right to collect for damage may be modified by the provisions of the Limited Liability, Harter, and Carriage of Goods by Sea acts. As a matter of public policy naval and other publicly owned vessels cannot be libeled, but the government permits itself to be sued *in personam* for faulty collision damage by a public vessel.

Vessels on the high seas are subject to the International Rules; and when in specified inland waters various Inland and Pilot Rules, which differ in important respects, govern their action in collision situations. The rules are mandatory, must be obeyed in a timely manner, apply alike to all vessels, must be understood in the light of court interpretation, and have application within fixed geographical limits. While uniformity of the rules is desirable, it does not exist, and the mariner under present law must observe the differences in requirements according to the immediate location of his vessel.

12
Lawful Lights

The Function of Running and Riding Lights

The importance of proper running and riding lights on vessels using public navigable waters can scarcely be over-emphasized. During the hours of darkness it is the function of these lights in clear weather to give such timely and effective notice to one vessel of the proximity of another that all doubt as to her character and intentions will be satisfactorily settled before there is any serious risk of collision. Even in thick fog, with the mariner's safety in an approaching close-quarters situation dependent upon radar and sound rather than upon sight, it is often the welcome glimmer of these same lights through the haze that finally enables each fog-enshrouded vessel safely to feel her way past the other. To the student of collision law it is significant that twelve of the thirty-eight International Rules and sixteen of the thirty-two Inland Rules relate wholly or in part to lights, while the Pilot Rules substitute for the missing Article 4, Inland Rules, a very considerable volume of material regarding special lights in the inland waters of the United States. In cases of collision the courts are as certain to hold a vessel at fault for improper lights as for a violation of signal requirements or for failure to maintain a proper lookout.

Lights at Anchor Must Conform

It is evident from the cases that mere volume of light, even for a vessel at anchor on a clear night, does not constitute the due notice to which approaching vessels are entitled or satisfy the requirement for regulation lights. In an interesting decision affirmed by the Circuit Court of Appeals, the large seagoing tanker *Chester O. Swain* collided with the government cotton carrier *Scantic* on the Mississippi River 600 feet off the docks at New Orleans, and the latter vessel was found equally at fault with the *Swain* because of the irregularity of her anchor lights. It appeared that on the day preceding, fire had spread from a cotton warehouse to the *Scantic* and her cargo, damaging the vessel's running lights before it could be extinguished. The *Scantic* was shifted from her pier to a temporary anchorage across the river from the regular anchorage, so that if the fire in her cargo again broke out, as sometimes happens with cotton, it would not result in damage to other vessels at anchor. The lights were not repaired during the day, as they might have been, but according to the testimony the following lights were shown by the *Scantic* as soon as darkness fell: an oil lantern lashed to the jack staff; an oil lantern on an awning spreader aft; four sets of cargo cluster lights (each containing four large bulbs), one at the center of the bridge, one on the forward part of the boat deck to light No. 3 hatch, one at the after end of the boat deck to light No. 4 and No. 5 hatches, and one on the starboard side near No. 4 hatch to light the pilot ladder which led down to a motorboat tender standing by to render aid in case of the fire's recurring. The *Swain* proceeding down the river from Baton Rouge with a load of oil rounded Algiers Point in charge of a pilot and crossed over to within 600 feet of the left bank, when the lights of the anchored vessel were first sighted against the background of city lights about 1,500 yards ahead. Instead of maneuvering promptly to avoid collision, the *Swain* first continued ahead, then stopped, then backed, then stopped and drifted helplessly into the mass of lights that marked the *Scantic*. The tanker was held at fault for her vacillating conduct and for the lack of vigilance of her lookout; but in also inculpating the *Scantic* the Circuit Court held that:

> while the lights she installed ought to have been discovered by the *Swain* in time to prevent the collision, it cannot be said that better and more conventional lights would not have got the attention of the *Swain* sooner than those which the *Scantic* rigged and would not have averted the trouble.[1]

The importance of having anchor lights conform to the specific requirements was brought out in a number of early cases in which incorrect lights, though visible, proved misleading to approaching vessels. In one such case, a dredge 75 feet in length in New York Harbor exhibited two white lights at anchor instead of the stationary single light and was mistaken by an approaching tug with tow for a tug underway and being overtaken. The tug did not discover her error until within 300 feet of the dredge, when she avoided collision herself by a hard-over helm but was unable to pull her tow clear. Although the tug was held at fault for failure to discover sooner that the dredge was stationary, nevertheless the dredge shared the damages because of technically improper lights.[2]

Notwithstanding this, it seems that a ship will not necessarily be held

[1] *The* Chester O. Swain *(CCA NY 1935) 76 F (2d) 890.*
[2] *The* Arthur *(NY 1901) 108 F 557.*

at fault for a collision caused by improper lights, if her own regulation lights have recently been destroyed. A steamship at anchor with her masthead light up instead of her proper riding lights, was held free from blame in an English court. Her riding light had been broken shortly before the collision in a previous collision for which she was not at fault.[3]

Lights Underway Must Conform; the "S-51"

The tragic collision of the USS *S-51* and the steamship *City of Rome* off Block Island 23 September 1925 affords a striking example of the importance attached by the courts to proper running lights underway. It also indicates the strictness with which the exemptions authorized for vessels of special construction[4] by Rule 2(e), 1972 International Rules, regarding lights, will be construed. This collision, which attracted unusual public interest because of the protracted but futile efforts that were made in the face of Atlantic storms to rescue possible survivors in the sunken submarine, happened on a clear night, and the masthead light of the *S-51* was under continuous observation from the *City of Rome* after being reported by her lookout twenty-two minutes before the collision. It was first made out as a faint white light broad on the starboard bow, and its bearing did not appreciably change until shortly before the collision, when it was observed to be closing in on the steamship's course and to be growing brighter. According to the testimony brought out at the trial, the captain of the *City of Rome* had been watching the light for some twenty minutes without taking any action, although in some doubt as to its character. He concluded at this point that he was overtaking a small tug or fishing vessel and ordered the course changed to the left to give it a wider berth; but a few seconds later the red side light of the submarine appeared a little to the right of the white light, indicating for the first time that she was not an overtaken vessel but was crossing the course of the *City of Rome* from right to left, as she had a right to do under the rules. Although the liner's rudder was ordered put the other way immediately and a few seconds later the engines reversed, it was then too late to avoid the collision. The submarine sank very quickly, and of the three survivors picked up none had been on deck during the approaching situation or could give evidence as to the navigation of the submarine. However, notwithstanding the *City of Rome* was flagrantly at fault for failure to reduce her speed when in doubt regarding the movements of the other vessel and for failure to signal her change of course to the left by two short blasts as required under the then effective International Rules, both the

[3] *The* Kjobenhavn *(1874) 2 Asp. MC 213.*

[4] *See Appendixes Q and R for exemptions granted to Naval and Coast Guard vessels under 1960 Rules.*

district court and the Circuit Court of Appeals found the *S-51* at fault for improper lights. Referring to Article 2 of the 1889 International Rules, then in force, the court said:

> The *S-51* was 240 feet 6 inches long; her beam 25 feet; her surface displacement upwards of 1,000 tons; her forward white light was not 20 feet above the hull but was only 11 feet 2 inches above the deck; the side lights were fixed in a recess on the chariot bridge 7½ feet above the hull; they were not fitted with inboard screens projecting at least 3 feet forward from the lights. There is also testimony that the red light was so constructed and in such close proximity with the masthead light, only 3½ feet apart, that the visibility of the relatively dim red light was materially reduced by the greater brilliancy of the white masthead light.

To the student of collision law a very significant feature of this case was the comments of both trial and appellate courts on the government argument that it was not practicable to have *S*-boats comply with the literal provisions in regard to lights, and moreover as a special type of naval vessel such craft were not under compulsion to comply. The district court said:

> I cannot accept the view that submarines running on the surface through traffic lanes are immune from the usual requirements regarding lights. . . . The obvious answer to the contention that the nature of their construction and operation makes it impractical for them to comply with these rules is that if this be so they should confine their operation to waters not being traversed by other ships. The fact that they are more dangerous should not be a reason for their disregarding rules which other ships must observe. . . . The testimony conclusively shows not only that the failure of the *S-51* to show proper side lights might have contributed but that it was a principal cause of the disaster.

In confirming the decision of the lower court to hold the submarine equally at fault with the liner, the Circuit Court of Appeals added:

> There remains only the contention that the submarine was not subject to the ordinary rules of the road. It does not appear that it was impossible for her to comply with these, but it would make no difference if it did. . . . It is apparent that the rules regulating lights were meant to apply to ships of war; Article 13 would be conclusive if the preamble alone were not enough. If unfortunately it is impossible to equip submarines properly, they must take their chances until some provision has been made for them by law. We have no power to dispense with the statute nor indeed has the Navy. As they now sail they are unfortunately a menace to other shipping and to their own crews, as this unhappy collision so tragically illustrates. We cannot say that they are not to be judged by the same standard as private persons. The safety of navigation depends upon uniformity; only so can reliance be placed upon what masters see at night.[5]

To illustrate the international character of court findings, a similar collision occurred between HM Submarine *Truculent* and a merchantship in

[5] *Ocean SS. Co. of Savannah v. U.S. (CCA NY 1930) 38 F (2d) 782.*

the Thames estuary, with equally tragic loss of life in the submarine. The masthead light of the submarine, like that of the *S-51*, was improperly placed according to the existing rules (also the 1899 ones), and was held to have contributed to the collision and damage. Evidence was accepted showing that the difficulties, in the case of submarines, of complying with the requirement for a masthead light were great, if not insuperable, and that the positioning of lights in submarines of all navies was similar but:

> . . . these considerations afford no answer to the charge that the steaming light of HMS *Truculent* constitutes a breach of the regulations.

It was further held that if it was really impossible in the case of a submarine to fit a masthead light that complied with the rules, then there was a duty to issue a warning to mariners of the fact.[6]

Due warning, in the format of Notices to Mariners, was issued in 1953. The next revision of the International Rules, effective 1 January 1954, provided the basis for the legal exemptions referred to in the *S-51* case. Subsequent revisions of the rules have maintained the exemptions for naval or military vessels unable to comply, and Rule 1(e), 1972 Rules, extends them further to any vessel of special construction approved by her government. The Act of December 3, 1945, as amended, provides the legal exemptions for the inland waters of the United States. Section 1052 of Title 33, U.S. Code, is based on the 1960 Rules, and is limited to naval and Coast Guard vessels of special construction. Similar exemptions for foreign warships are to be found in national notices to mariners and in the appropriate sailing directions. All these vessels must be certified as being unable to comply with the requirements regarding lights *and must be in the closest possible compliance* with the literal requirements of the rules. Should a collision such as was cited occur, it undoubtedly would still be indefensible, on the grounds of inadequate compliance. The variation in the number or position or character of the lights required to be shown cannot be misleading. On the contrary, the obvious intention of the authorized exemptions is to recognize the inability of certain vessels to comply with the literal requirements, while requiring that the nature and spirit of the lighting requirements of the rules be maintained. Thus, it may be presumed the courts will be extremely critical of any unnecessary departure from the literal requirements or failure to give proper notice of the character and position of the lights carried by such vessels of special construction.

Improper Lights May Be a Fault in Naval Vessels

In the United States the courts have held all vessels to a strict observance

---

[6] *The* Truculent, *Admiralty v. SS* Devine *(1951), 2 Lloyds Report 308 w.*

of the rules even in time of war. Thus, when the armored cruiser *Columbia* sank the British freighter *Foscolia* off Fire Island during the Spanish-American War, the *Columbia* was held solely liable for the loss, the court finding that even a vessel of the Navy in time of war cannot be excused for masking her lights, orders of the squadron commander notwithstanding, since there is no statutory authority for such an order.[7] While Article 30, Inland Rules, provides statutory exemption for war vessels and Coast Guard cutters in the inland waters of the United States, there is no corresponding exception under the jurisdiction of the International Rules. Similarly, in a collision off the east coast in 1918 between the privately owned cargo steamships *Proteus* and *Cushing*, both vessels, because of danger from hostile submarines, and under authority of the Navy Department, were proceeding without lights, and both were held at fault because they did not turn on their lights in time to avoid collision;[8] and in still another case, less than three weeks later, the U. S. Navy tanker *Hisko*, running without lights, was held solely at fault for sinking the cargo steamship *Almirante*, which was showing proper side lights, though no masthead light.[9]

During the 1939-45 War, allied convoy orders had statutory force, and, for nations affected, overrode all contrary provisions contained in the International Regulations.[10] Vessels remained otherwise bound to comply with the remainder of their obligations, including the duties of good seamanship, that were not affected by the convoy orders.[11]

General Characteristics of Side Lights

The precise nature of the lights required in inland waters has not always been clear from the wording of the rules, as indeed had been the case previously on the high seas. The requirements of the Inland Rules concerning side lights are such that, if taken literally, they are conflicting. The lights are required to be both visible from directly ahead and to be mounted with screens to prevent them from being seen across the bow. These dictates require some compromise since the side lights, mounted at the sides of a ship, would have to shine across the projected fore-and-aft line of the vessel at some point in order to be visible from ahead, or else there would be a theoretical 'dark lane' ahead which could result in vessels meeting exactly end on being unable to see each others side lights. The revised International Rules cover this eventuality, by allowing a practical cut-off between 1 degree and 3 degrees outside the prescribed sector.

[7] *Watts v. U.S. (NY 1903) 123 F 105.*
[8] *The* Cushing *(CCA NY 1923) 292 F 560.*
[9] *Almirante SS. Corp. v. U.S. (CCA NY 1929) 34 F (2d) 123.*
[10] *The* Vernon City *(1942) 70 Ll.L. Rep. 278.*
[11] *The* Scottish Musician *(1942) 72 Ll.L. Rep. 284.*

The full details concerning arcs of visibility, contained in Annex I to the 1972 International Rules, are shown below, and will have to be ultimately met by all vessels that do not sail exclusively in the inland waters of the United States:

9. Horizontal Sectors
   (a) (i) In the forward direction, sidelights as fitted on the vessel must show the minimum required intensities. The intensities must decrease to reach practical cut-off between 1 degree and 3 degrees outside the prescribed sectors.
   (ii) For sternlights and masthead lights and at 22.5 degrees abaft the beam for sidelights, the minimum required intensities shall be maintained over the arc of the horizon up to 5 degrees within the limits of the sectors prescribed in Rule 21. From 5 degrees within the prescribed sectors the intensity may decrease by 50 percent up to the prescribed limits; it shall decrease steadily to reach practical cut-off at not more than 5 degrees outside the prescribed limits.

Vessels that do operate solely on the inland waters of the United States, must be governed to a certain extent by court interpretations. An analysis of early collision cases involving improper side lights, mostly concerning sailing craft and steamships around the turn of the century, shows that out of the confusing phraseology of the rules, the courts have reached the following definite conclusions:

(1) A vessel in collision is liable if any obstruction prevents the side lights from being visible to a vessel closing from ahead.[12]
(2) A vessel in collision is liable if the inboard screens are not of the prescribed length and if the side lights are seen excessively across the bow.[13]
(3) A vessel in collision is liable if both side lights are visible from a point on her own bow, i.e. both can be seen from the stem of the vessel.[14]

In a crossing collision between two steamers off the Jersey coast on a clear night, the privileged vessel had her side lights set in the rigging in such a manner that they crossed at her stem, and her green light could be seen by the burdened vessel 3 points across the bow. In finding her at fault for improper lights, the Supreme Court made the following emphatic comment:

This rule in regard to setting and screening the colored lights cannot be too highly valued, or the importance of its exact observance be overstated. Better far to have no side lights than to have them so set and screened as to be seen across the bow. In that situation they operate as a snare to deceive even the wary into error and danger.[15]

[12] *The* Vesper *(NY 1881) 9 F 569; The* Johanne Auguste *(NY 1884) 21 F 134;* Carleton v. U.S. *(1874) 10 Ct. Cl. 485.*
[13] *The* North Star *(1882) 27 L. Ed. 91.*
[14] *Clendinin v. the* Alhambra *(NY 1880) 4 F 86.*
[15] *The* Santiago de Cuba *10 Blatch. U.S. 444.*

Modern vessels have far less cluttered superstructure than the earlier ships mentioned in the above cases and are, perhaps, less liable to obstruction or poor fittings of side lights. Nevertheless it is as vital as ever to check that side lights do show over the correct arcs.

The positioning and spacing of side lights are also somewhat loosely described in the Inland Rules. They merely state that the lights shall be on the port and starboard side, which is to say, apparently, that moving the side lights inboard will not make a non-seagoing vessel liable for a collision as long as such lights are visible over the prescribed arcs.[16]

Annex I to the 1972 International Rules is more precise:

> 2. Vertical positioning and spacing of lights
> (g) The sidelights of a power-driven vessel shall be placed at a height above the hull not greater than three quarters of that of the forward masthead light. They shall not be so low as to be interfered with by deck lights.
> (h) The sidelights, if in a combined lantern and carried on a power-driven vessel of less than 20 metres in length, shall be placed not less than 1 metre below the masthead light.
> 3. Horizontal positioning and spacing of lights
> (b) On a vessel of 20 metres or more in length the sidelights shall not be placed in front of the forward masthead lights They shall be placed at or near the side of the vessel.

Vessels constructed while the 1960 International Rules were in effect are exempt from repositioning of sidelights resulting from the prescriptions of Section 3(b) above, until nine years after the date of entry into force of the 1972 Rules, i.e., 15 July 1986.

Masthead and Range Lights; Stern Light

In addition to describing the side lights for steam or other power-driven vessels and sailing vessels, the rules also describe in considerable detail the masthead light and the range lights to be carried by an independent steam or other power-driven vessel. Four important differences may be noted in the requirements for *seagoing vessels*, which are specifically excepted from changing their lights in inland waters and for *non-seagoing vessels*, that is, vessels whose services are limited to the inland waters of the United States. (1) The masthead light, which under both sets of rules is a 20-point white light, under Inland Rules is required merely to be on or in front of the foremast, or if a vessel without a foremast, then in the fore part of the vessel; under International Rules this light must be from 6 to 12 meters above the hull (for vessels 20 meters or more in length), depending on the vessel's beam. (2) Under Inland Rules, steam or other

---

[16] *But see* Samuel H. Crawford *(NY 1881) 6 F 906, which although not faulting the vessel in this instance as the port light did show ahead without obstruction, hevertheless intimated that the fitting of side lights on a deckhouse of a sailing schooner rather than on the rigging "is not to be approved."*

power-driven vessels (except seagoing vessels and ferryboats) must carry an after range light; under International Rules, the after (range) light is optional for vessels under 50 meters in length. (3) On non-seagoing vessels the after range light must be visible all around the horizon; on seagoing vessels, if carried, it must be a 20-point light like the masthead light. (4) Non-seagoing vessels must have the after range light at least 15 feet above the forward masthead light; the International Rules require that the after masthead (range) light be 4.5 meters higher than the forward light (vessels are permanently exempted from repositioning of lights as a result of conversion to metric units and rounding off measurement figures). The International Rules also require that:

> 2. Vertical positioning and spacing of lights
>   (b) The vertical separation of masthead lights of power-driven vessels shall be such that in all normal conditions of trim the after light will be seen over and separate from the forward light at a distance of 1000 metres from the stem when viewed from sea level.

Vessels are given a nine-year exemption on repositioning of lights due to Section 2(b) above.

This, of course, leaves unprovided, in the case of a seagoing vessel, the arc of visibility from 2 points abaft the beam on one side to 2 points abaft the beam on the other. Rule 23 (a), International Rules, therefore, requires a fixed 12-point sternlight on vessels underway on the high seas. On the inland waters, in view of the all around after range light and special lights carried by non-seagoing vessels, Article 10, Inland Rules, is limited to vessels without one or more lights visible from aft.

Importance of After Range Lights

While the combined masthead, stern, and side lights are generally adequate to convey a satisfactory indication of one of the above vessels' movements to another, there is at least one situation peculiarly fraught with the danger of misunderstanding where the arrangement of two white lights in range is invaluable. This is where two steam or other power-driven vessels are crossing at a very fine angle on courses differing by as much as 170°, and the burdened vessel, seeing both side lights of the other a little on the starboard bow, mistakenly assumes that a starboard to starboard meeting is proper. The privileged vessel, seeing only the green light of the other slightly to port and expecting her to give way, maintains course and speed, which may result in a stalemate until the two vessels are in dangerous proximity, particularly if the approaching vessel veers somewhat to port.

The obvious advantage of the after range light here is that, with vessels as nearly end-on as indicated, the slightest change of course by either is instantly revealed to the other. For this reason, notwithstanding its partly optional nature under the International Rules, the after range light should be carried wherever practical.

Visibility of Lights

The 1972 International Rules increased the visibility range requirements of lights, and gave vessels four years from entry of force of the rules to comply.

Rule 22.   Visibility of Lights
The lights prescribed in these rules shall have an intensity as specified in Section 8 of Annex I to these regulations so as to be visible at the following minimum ranges:
(a) In vessels of 50 metres or more in length:
—a masthead light, 6 miles;
—a sidelight, 3 miles;
—a sternlight, 3 miles;
—a towing light, 3 miles;
—a white, red, green or yellow all-round light, 3 miles.
(b) In vessels of 12 metres or more in length but less than 50 metres in length:
—a masthead light, 5 miles; except that where the length of the vessel is less than 20 metres, 3 miles;
—a sidelight, 2 miles;
—a sternlight, 2 miles;
—a towing light, 2 miles;
—a white, red, green or yellow all-round light, 2 miles.
(c) In vessels of less than 12 metres in length:
—a masthead light, 2 miles;
—a sidelight, 1 mile;
—a sternlight, 2 miles;
—a towing light, 2 miles;
—a white, red, green or yellow all-round light, 2 miles.

The Inland Rules require two-mile visibility for side and stern lights and five-mile visibility for masthead and range lights.

Towing Lights

Perhaps next in importance to proper running lights for independent vessels are the lights of vessels towing and being towed. Generally speaking, such vessels move slowly, but tugs are hampered by their tows and relatively unable to maneuver in close situations, while vessels and rafts in tow are, of course, almost completely helpless. The International Rules recognize this when they provide the same fog signal for a tug with a tow as for a vessel not under command.[17] The lights for a vessel towing or pushing as set forth in Rule 24, International Rules, consist of the usual sidelights, a fixed sternlight, and in place of the masthead light a pair of

[17] *Rule 35(c), International Rules, Appendix B.*

similar lights in a vertical line at least 2 meters apart (for a vessel 20 meters or more in length); or if towing *and* the tow extends more than 200 meters astern of the tug, then a third similar white light in line with the others, the three at such a height that the lowest is at least 4 meters above the hull.[18] An after masthead (range) light is mandatory if the towing vessel is 50 meters or more in length; the light is optional in the case of smaller vessels. When towing astern, a yellow towing light is required above the stern light. A vessel towing is not in all respects mistress of her movements and if she is restricted in her ability to deviate from her course she also shows the red-white-red all-round lights in a vertical line.

Referring to Article 3, Inland Rules, we find that five distinct differences apply in the inland waters of the United States: (1) the minimum interval between the towing lights is 3 feet instead of 2 meters, a distinction of questionable practical value; (2) the towing lights may be either 20-point lights carried forward in place of the masthead light, or they may be all around lights carried in the approximate position of the after range light. (3) A tug with one or more vessels alongside or pushed ahead carries two white lights, and with one or more vessels astern, regardless of the length of the tow, three white lights. (4) If the tow is ahead and towing lights are 20-point lights, two 12-point amber lights must be shown aft, in lieu of the stern light, and irrespective of whether the after range light is shown. (5) The after range light is an optional all around light shown only when towing lights are forward.

Lights for Tows

The International Rules make a distinction between vessels towed and vessels being pushed ahead. The latter type vessels are lighted by a single pair of sidelights at the forward end, whether being pushed singly or in a group. However, a modern development is of tugs and barges capable of being mechanically locked so rigidly that they can operate in the pushing mode as one unit even on the high seas. Between them they show only the lights for a single power-driven vessel.

The lights for vessels being towed are the same as for sailing vessels under way, consisting of the usual sidelights and the fixed 12-point stern-light required of all vessels. To distinguish themselves from vessels being towed, sailing vessels may, however, show a special identity signal at the masthead together with these lights. All vessels being towed on the high seas must conform to these requirements, whether sailing vessels, steamers, barges, or even a crib of logs or a dracone of fuel oil. The latter two examples, however, are probably covered by Rule 24(g), which provides:

[18] *See Annex I, International Rules, Appendix B, for definition of "height above the hull."*

Where from any sufficient cause it is impractical for a vessel or object being towed to exhibit the lights prescribed . . . all possible measures shall be taken to light the vessel or object towed or at least indicate the presence of the un-lighted vessel or object.

Article 5, Inland Rules, which formerly applied to sailing vessels only, was amended 1 March 1933 so as to be almost identical with the International Rule in effect at that time, the effect of the amendment being that no longer would a steam or other power-driven vessel being shifted by a tug from one dock to another in a harbor show her range lights.[19] Hence it merely requires side lights to be carried by ordinary vessels being towed. However, the Pilot Rules promulgated by the Commandant, U.S. Coast Guard, under the authority of Section 157 of Title 33, U.S. Code, provide numerous exceptions in inland waters to the standard provisions of Article 5, such as lights for barges, scows, canal boats, and submerged objects in tow of steam or other power-driven vessels. These exceptions, of course, do not apply outside the jurisdiction of the Inland Rules. Any doubt of this fact may be said to have been removed by the Circuit Court of Appeals in the case of the *Helmsman,* a New York tug which towed two loaded dump scows in tandem to sea and had the second scow in the tow in collision with the steamer *Tuscan* outside Scotland Lightship. The night was clear, the steamer identified the tug and barges a long distance away, and the collision was so palpably the result of careless navigation by the *Tuscan* that the courts refused to inculpate the tug and her tow on the technical fault of having the white lights prescribed by the Pilot Rules instead of the colored side lights required by the International Rules. Nevertheless, the district court made it a point to remark that:

If this fact could have contributed to the collision, the *Helmsman* and F.J. 22 are also at fault. . . . No defense of this kind was pleaded, and I find that the failure to comply with the regulation could not have contributed to the collision.[20]

Tug Jointly Responsible for Proper Lights on Tow

The foregoing decision brings out another principle of collision law—that a tug is not only liable for showing improper lights herself which contribute to a collision, but is jointly responsible with the vessel in tow for proper lights on the tow. An interesting case involving in liability both tug

---

[19] *In the* Scandinavia *(NY 1918) 11 F (2d) 542, a steamer and her tug were at fault, under the old rule, for the steamer's being in tow at night in New York Harbor showing side lights only.*

[20] *The Helmsman CCA NY (1925) 11 F (2d) 444. See also the* Cherokee *(NY 1918) 253 F 851, affirmed (CCA 1921) 277 F 1016, a similar case in which the tow was held at fault for navigating outside without side lights, notwithstanding plea of local custom.*

and tow occurred some years ago in Norfolk Harbor when a tug with a covered barge on each side brought one of the barges into collision with a ferry crossing from starboard and therefore having the right of way. On the showing that there were no lights on the barges, which were high enough to blanket the tug's side lights, and that towing lights of the tug, instead of being in a vertical line, were suspended from either end of a horizontal spar across the flagstaff at distances below the spar supposed to differ by three feet, the tug and the tow were found fully liable for the damage to the ferry.[21] Another case confirming the doctrine of the towing vessel's responsibility for the absence of proper lights on her tow was decided in a collision in New York Harbor between a ferryboat which should have kept out of the way and a barge in tow having no light on her bow. In a unique decision, the three vessels involved—ferry, tug, and barge, the last two belonging to the same owner—were found equally liable, with the result that the ferry recovered from the other two an amount equal to two-thirds of her damage.[22]

It should be noted that all of the above cases refer to the towing of barges, presumably with no motive power available, i.e., "dumb" barges. In a situation where the tug is the servant of the tow, i.e., the tug is assisting and responding to the orders from a manned ship, perhaps when maneuvering in confined waters, then it is more probable that it is the tow's responsibility for exhibiting proper lights.[23] In England, the Court of Appeal, in 1953, found the uncompleted aircraft carrier *Albion*, although under tow on the high seas, at fault after a collision in which a merchant vessel was sunk. The carrier, and not the tugs, was held liable for her defective port sidelight, and, also, a failure to show not-under-command lights.[24]

Anchor Lights

Reference has already been made to a case proving that the same strictness in regard to lights is applied to vessels at anchor as when underway.[25] The *Scantic* shared the damages in that case because of her inability to satisfy the court that her irregular lights *could not have contributed to the collision*. It was the same relentless test that is put on every infraction of the rules that precedes a collision.

[21] *Foster v. Merchants and Miners Transportation Co. (Va. 1905) 134 F 964.*
[22] *The* Socony No. 123 *(NY 1935) 10 F Suppl. 341.*
[23] *The* Mary Hounsell *(1879) 4 PD 204.*
[24] *The* Albion; *Thomas Stone (Shipping) Ltd. v. Admiralty (1953) Lloyds Report 239.*
[25] *The* Chester O. Swain *(CCA NY 1935) 76 F(2d) 890.*

The lights for a vessel at anchor are described in Rule 30 and Article 11, International and Inland Rules, respectively, as follows:

Rule 30 Anchored vessels and vessels aground

(a) A vessel at anchor shall exhibit where it can best be seen:

(i) in the fore part, an all-round white light or one ball;

(ii) at or near the stern and at a lower level than the light prescribed in subparagraph (i), an all-round white light.

(b) A vessel of less than 50 metres in length may exhibit an all-round white light where it can best be seen instead of the lights prescribed in paragraph (a) of this rule.

(c) A vessel at anchor may, and a vessel of 100 metres and more in length shall, also use the available working or equivalent lights to illuminate her decks.

(e) A vessel of less than 7 metres in length, when at anchor or aground, not in or near a narrow channel fairway or anchorage, or where other vessels normally navigate, shall not be required to exhibit the lights or shapes prescribed in paragraphs (a), (b) or (d) of this rule.

Art. 11. (a) Except as provided in paragraph (c) of this article, a vessel under one hundred and fifty feet in length when at anchor shall carry forward, where it can best be seen, a white light in a lantern so constructed as to show a clear, uniform, and unbroken light visible all around the horizon at a distance of at least two miles.

(b) Except as provided in paragraph (c) of this article, a vessel of one hundred and fifty feet or upward in length, when at anchor, shall carry in the forward part of the vessel, at a height of not less than twenty feet above the hull, one such light, and at or near the stern of the vessel, and at such a height that it shall be not less than fifteen feet lower than the forward light, another such light.

(c) The Secretary of Transportation may, after investigation, by rule, regulation, or order, designate such areas as he may deem proper as 'special anchorage areas'; such special anchorage areas may from time to time be changed, or abolished, if after investigation the Secretary of Transportation shall deem such change or abolition in the interest of navigation. When anchored within such an area—

(1) a vessel of not more than sixty-five feet in length shall not be required to carry or exhibit the white light required by this article;

(2) a barge, canal boat, scow, or other nondescript craft of one hundred and fifty feet or upward in length may carry and exhibit the single white light prescribed by paragraph (a) of this article in lieu of the two white lights prescribed by paragraph (b) of this article; and

(3) where two or more barges, canal boats, scows, or other nondescript craft are tied together and anchored as a unit, the anchor light prescribed by this article need be displayed only on the vessel having its anchor down.

It will be noted the Inland Rule does not permit a vessel of less than 150 feet to show two anchor lights in the manner of a larger vessel. Nor does the Inland Rule make special provisions for vessels engaged in cable work, servicing navigation marks, or those engaged in surveying or underwater operations. Such craft, as was previously pointed out, conform to the special requirements applicable to them in the Pilot Rules. It is also important to note that there are differences in the prescribed minimum visibilities of the anchor lights and that in inland waters certain vessels at anchor in a special anchorage area may be unlighted.

Especially noteworthy is the fact that anchor lights, like the after range light under Inland Rules, are visible all around the horizon, and that where the length of the vessel requires two lights, or a small vessel under International Rules elects to be lighted as a large vessel, it is the forward light which is the higher, reversing the relative heights of the underway range lights. One practical import of this is that, in maneuvering to avoid a large vessel at anchor forward it should be remembered that any effect of wind or current would be in the direction indicated by a line from the higher (bow) light toward the lower. While the courts failed to find a steamship at fault for having her forward anchor light 10 feet higher than her after light instead of the required 15 feet higher, in a case where the testimony showed the lights were seen by other pilots 5½ miles away and the collision was due to improper lookout on the colliding steamer,[26] nevertheless, the distinction in the requirements due to a vessel's length is likely to be strictly enforced, particularly when the vessel involved is 150 feet in length or longer. Thus, in the case of a 271-foot barge anchored in Chesapeake Bay which was struck by a pilot boat five minutes after her after light had blown out in a puff of wind and while a seaman was overhauling the light, the barge (which was sunk) was held solely at fault for the collision. As said by the court in referring to Article 11:

> The provisions of this article, which requires a vessel of 150 feet or upwards in length when at anchor to carry two lights, one at the forward part and the other at or near the stern at a lower height, to indicate the length of the vessel and the direction in which she is pointing, is of great importance and must be strictly observed, and, if violated, a loss caused by a collision resulting must be borne by the vessel so violating it.[27]

Subject to any local rules, a vessel secured to a buoy may be regarded as a vessel at anchor. She is made fast to moorings which are themselves attached to the ground by an anchor or the equivalent of an anchor.[28]

Vessel Made Fast to Another Must Have Own Lights

Of particular interest to the naval service, with the frequent nesting of vessels at anchor, is the requirement of the courts that a vessel made fast to another at anchor must maintain her own proper anchor lights. It was so held in a collision between one of two barges attached to each other

[26] *The* John G. McCullough *(CCA Va. 1916) 239 F 111.*
[27] *The* Santiago *(Penn. 1908) 160 F 742.*
[28] *The* Dunhelm *(1884) 9 P.D. 164, 171.*

and a car float in Norfolk Harbor.[29] It has long been held by the courts that every vessel in an anchor nest in fog is under the necessity of making proper sound signals for a vessel at anchor whether her own anchor is down or not.[30] On the other hand, in a case with the impressive title Emperor of All the Russias v. the *Heipershausen*, the district court of New York held that a steam launch made fast to a boom projecting sixty feet from the side of a man-of-war at anchor in New York Harbor need not exhibit any light. It seems that the Russian cruiser *Dimitri Donskoi* was visiting the east coast during the Columbian Naval Exposition of 1893, and while she was lying in the North River at anchor with proper lights burning, two tugs with a tow of barges passed between her and the piers, so close that one of the barges struck and sank the steam launch, at the same time knocking the boom around against the captain's gig, which was also damaged. It was argued that the steam launch was not lighted, but the court held that inasmuch as the boom did not project over sixty feet, the minimum passing distance at that time prescribed by statute in New York Harbor, no light was necessary on the launch and the tugs were fully liable for the damage.[31]

Lights for a Vessel Alongside Wharf

Strictly speaking, a vessel moored at a wharf is not at anchor, as implied by the distinction in the rules: "A vessel is 'underway' within the meaning of these rules, when she is not at anchor, or made fast to the shore, or aground." From the standpoint of her ability to maneuver to avoid collision, of course, there is little to distinguish the three not-under-way situations. The practical necessity of lights to give notice to approaching vessels varies according to circumstances. In several cases the courts have decided that a vessel moored in the usual way alongside a wharf and not in the way of other boats need not exhibit lights.[32] But a vessel lying moored at the end of a wharf, on a dark night, in the navigable part of a narrow stream, constantly traversed by different kinds of craft, is required by the special circumstances, in the exercise of common prudence, to carry a light, whether or not it was expressly required by the rules.[33] And, of course, the rule may be further modified by a local harbor regulation, disregard of which is legally as serious as disregard of the Inland or Inter-

---

[29] *The* Prudence *(Va. 1912) 197 F 479.*

[30] *The* Cohocton *(CCA NY 1924) 299 F 319; the* Southway *(NY 1924) 2 F (2d) 1009.*

[31] *The* Dimitri Donskoi *(NY 1894) 60 F 111.*

[32] *Denty v. the* Martin Dallman *(Va. 1895) 70 F 797; City of New York v. the* Express *(NY 1891) 61 F 513.*

[33] *The* Millville *(NJ 1905) 137 F 974.*

national Rules. The following extract from the Seattle Harbor ordinance is typical of the rule which prevails in many organized ports:

> Every vessel or obstruction . . . while lying at any pier or other structure in Seattle Harbor between the hours of sunset and sunrise shall display at least one (1) white light at the outer end of the vessel or obstruction, which white light or lights shall show clearly from seaward and be so constructed and of such character as to be visible at least one (1) mile in clear weather.[34]

Lights for a Vessel Aground

Rule 30(d), International Rules, also contains the following provision not found in the Inland Rules:

> Rule 30. Anchored vessel and vessel aground
> (d) A vessel aground shall exhibit the lights prescribed in paragraph (a) or (b) of this rule and in addition, where they can best be seen:
> (i) two all-round red lights in a vertical line;
> (ii) three balls in a vertical line.

The twofold significance of the rule is, of course, that it provides statutory sanction to the assumption that a vessel aground is in the same category as a vessel at anchor, and that different lights must be carried when aground in waters under the jurisdiction of the International Rules than when under Inland Rules. It is an interesting inconsistency that the courts have decided a steam lighter aground in a narrow channel in inland waters in thick fog is *not*, for the purpose of proper fog signals, a vessel at anchor. The reasoning followed was that an approaching vessel, hearing the signals of a vessel at anchor, would assume that they marked a safe position in the channel, and perhaps hold so close to them as to become stranded herself; consequently, it was held that the proper fog signal for a vessel aground in inland waters is the danger signal.[35] A distress signal is also appropriate *if requiring assistance*. It might be contended with reason that the same argument applies to a vessel aground in a narrow channel in clear weather and that by showing regular anchor lights she invites the near approach of passing vessels. Such, however, was the requirement of the courts, which long ago established the doctrine that for the purpose of proper lights, a vessel aground in inland waters is a vessel at anchor, even if she has a tow.

Red Lights Not Shown by Vessel Aground or Disabled in Inland Waters

In a collision between the *Ant* and the *C. J. Saxe* in New York Harbor in 1881, the tug *Saxe*, which was struck by another vessel while pulling on a tow that had grounded, was held at fault for displaying towing lights

[34] *Seattle Harbor Ordinance (1921).*
[35] *The* Leviathan *(1922) 286 F 745.*

instead of an anchor light which at that time was a globular white light. Referring to the rules then in effect, the court said:

> In navigation, a vessel aground is in circumstances quite similar to a vessel at anchor; and the spirit, if not the letter, of the two rules is best ascertained by holding that a steamer with a tow, whether aground or at anchor, should exhibit the single light required by the tenth rule.[36]

The practical import of this is that only the regular anchor lights and not the two red lights may be shown by a vessel stranded within the jurisdiction of the Inland and Pilot Rules.

As might be inferred, it is also true that the omission of Rule 30(d), International Rules, from the Inland Rules, excludes the use of the two-red-light signals by a disabled vessel in inland waters, and under such circumstances she continues to show the same lights as when normally underway. (A parallel weakness in the Inland Rules requires the same fog signals underway for a vessel broken down as for one not broken down.) This is because neither the Inland Rules nor the Pilot Rules provide specific lights for a vessel not under command.

An interesting attempt was made in a New York Harbor collision case some years ago to hold a disabled vessel liable for failure to show the two international red lights required by the 1889 rules on the basis of the following ingenious argument: (1) Article 4, International Rules, required the two red lights for a vessel not under command; (2) the enacting clause of the International Rules provided that those rules should apply to all public and private vessels of the United States on the high seas and in all waters connected therewith, navigable by seagoing vessels; (3) while Article 30 authorized special rules duly made by local authority relative to the navigation of any harbor, river, or inland waters, and the Inland Rules and the Pilot Rules were such special rules, neither of these sets of rules provided any special signal for a vessel not under command; (4) in the absence of such provision in the Inland or Pilot Rules, the International Rules governed in harbors navigable by seagoing vessels. The case in question was a collision between a barge in tow alongside the motor vessel *Hartford Socony* and a car float in tow alongside the tug *Syossett*. The *Syossett* had been disabled for about forty minutes prior to the collision by fouling her propeller with the chain attached to an unlighted buoy near the entrance to Greenville Channel, and had warned other vessels throughout the period by danger signals repeated at intervals of about one minute. She displayed the regular running lights, for herself and tow, and was libeled for failure to show the two-red-light signal to indicate that she was not under command. Both the district court and the Circuit Court of Appeals dismissed the libel on the grounds that as the Pilot

[36] *The Ant (NJ 1882) 10 F 294.*

Rules already required a signal of two red lights in a vertical line to be shown by a steamer or other vessel moored alongside or over a wreck, a dredge held in position by moorings or spuds, a self-propelling suction dredge under way with the suction on the bottom, and the discharging end of a pipe line attached to a dredge, none of which specific cases fitted the description of the *Syossett*, the *Syossett* could not display such a signal without violating Article 1, Inland Rules, which provided, as it still provides:

> The rule concerning lights shall be complied with in all weathers from sunset to sunrise, and during such time *no other lights which may be mistaken for the prescribed lights shall be exhibited.*[37]

Requirements Regarding Lights Should Be Strictly Observed

In conclusion, it may be said that the courts are strict in enforcing the requirements for proper lights, and rightly; but not unreasonably so. In a case where it was officially after sunset but there was not darkness sufficient to prevent an approaching vessel from seeing a vessel in tow of a tug, it was found that failure of the tug to show towing lights was not a fault.[38] In a collision between two sailing vessels approaching so that one of them had her red light toward the other, it was held to be immaterial that her green light was out, since its presence could not have averted, nor its absence contributed to, the collision.[39] In a very old case the court found that where failure of a vessel to carry a light did not delay the discovery of her presence to the colliding vessel, she was not at fault for the dereliction.[40] On the other hand, in a case almost as old the court announced that a tug with tows carrying but one vertical light would be held in fault without speculating whether absence of the proper light increased the danger of collision.[41] It should be remembered, moreover, that neglect by a vessel to show regulation lights does not relieve another vessel from observing the rules of navigation and using every precaution to avoid collision with her;[42] and that a steamer failing to see lights on a sailing vessel which were clearly visible from the steamer's position was not absolved from responsibility merely because the lights were somewhat faultily placed. This case, like many others, became one of mutual fault.[43]

---

[37] *The* Socony No. 115 *(CCA NY 1933) 63 F (2d) 226.*
[38] *The* City of Troy *(NY 1878) Fed. Cas. No. 2769.*
[39] *The* Robert Graham Dun *(CCA NH 1895) 70 F. 270.*
[40] *Fletcher v. the* Cubana *(NY 1864) Fed. Cas. No. 4863.*
[41] *Elliot v. the Volunteer (CC. Pa. 1870) Fed. Cas. No. 4398.*
[42] *Swift v. Brownell (CC Mass. 1875) Fed. Cas. No. 13,695.*
[43] *The* Samuel H. Crawford *(NY 1881) 6 F 906.*

In any doubtful situation the courts are very likely to have the attitude that:

> The rule requiring lights may as well be disregarded altogether as to be only partially complied with, and in a way which fails to be of any real service in indicating to other vessels the position and course of the one carrying them.[44]

After all, the only safe rule to follow is to be sure that our running or riding lights during the hours from sunset to sunrise conform as closely as possible to the lights specified by the rules *in force where the vessel may happen to be*, remembering that any departure from the rules which is followed by a collision will be subject to the test so often annunciated by the Supreme Court:

> But when a ship at the time of collision is in actual violation of a statutory rule intended to prevent collision, it is no more than a reasonable presumption that the fault, if not the sole cause was at least a contributory cause of the disaster. In such a case the burden rests upon the ship of showing, not merely that her fault might not have been one of the causes, or that it probably was not, but that it could not have been.[45]

If lights are lost or extinguished, then this must be detected by the watch and repair or replacement carried out as soon as possible. Emergency lights, whether oil or battery, should be properly maintained and kept ready for use. If severe weather prevents immediate attention, because of danger to personnel, a delay may be justified, but should be recorded in the official deck log.

SUMMARY

The importance of proper running and riding lights is emphasized by the fact that so many of the International and Inland Rules, and a substantial part of the Pilot Rules, relate to them, and that in collision cases the courts construe strongly against vessels which disregard their requirements.

Side lights are, in practice, a compromise with the literal specifications in the Inland Rules that they be carried on either side of the vessel, visible directly ahead, and not visible across the bow, and are arranged so that their rays cross a short distance ahead of the stem. They may be somewhat inboard of the side, but must be unobstructed from ahead, and must not be visible from the vessel's own bow. The requirements in the International Rules are clearer, avoiding conflicting demands. Five differences are in effect for the running lights of independent steam or other power-

---

[44] *The* Titan *(CC NY 1885) 23 F 413.*
[45] *The* Pennsylvania *(1875) 19 Wall 125.*

driven vessels under International Rules and non-seagoing steam or other power-driven vessels in independent operation under Inland and Pilot Rules, seagoing vessels being specifically exempted from the requirements of inland waters.

(1) the height of the masthead light, for a vessel of 20 meters or more in length, must be 6 to 12 meters under International Rules and is not prescribed under Inland Rules;

(2) the after range light under International Rules is optional for vessels less than 50 meters in length, while under Inland Rules it is required on all non-seagoing vessels, regardless of length;

(3) under International Rules, when carried, it is a 20-point light, while for non-seagoing vessels under Inland Rules it must show all around the horizon; (4) the horizontal separation between the masthead and after range lights must, under International Rules, be at least one-half the length of the vessel but need not be more than 100 meters, while under the Inland Rules the horizontal separation is merely required to be greater than the vertical distance between the lights;

(5) seagoing vessels must carry a fixed 12-point stern light while under way, whereas non-seagoing vessels satisfy the stern light requirements by carrying the all around after range light.

Lights for towboats in inland waters also differ from towing lights under International Rules as follows:

(1) the minimum interval between white lights in a vertical line is 3 feet instead of 2 meters;

(2) the towing lights in inland waters need not be 20-point lights in place of the masthead light, but may be all around lights on the after mast;

(3) two towing lights are used in inland waters to indicate a tow alongside or pushed ahead and three such lights to indicate a tow astern, regardless of length of tow or number of vessels in tow, whereas under International Rules the towing vessel shows three white lights only when towing astern and the length of the tow exceeds 200 meters;

(4) vessels towing on inland waters when showing 20-point lights and pushing ahead show two 12-point amber lights aft and, at other times, a white stern or steering light, while a fixed 12-point sternlight is required of all vessels towing under International Rules, and a yellow towing light is required above the sternlight when towing astern;

(5) in inland waters the all around after range light is optional for all size vessels with 20-point towing lights whereas under International Rules a 20-point after range light is mandatory for towing vessels 50 meters or more in length;

(6) under International Rules only, a vessel engaged in a towing operation such as renders her unable to deviate from her course shows the

red-white-red lights in a vertical line (ball-diamond-ball shapes in day-time) *in addition to* the other lights displayed by a towing vessel.

Vessels towed ordinarily show side lights and the proper stern or steering light with numerous exceptions for special types under Pilot Rules. Proper anchor lights must be shown by all vessels, including individual vessels in a nest. A vessel aground or disabled must show only regular anchor lights in inland waters, the two red lights prescribed under International Rules having been held illegal under Inland Rules and being specifically ex-cluded by the enacting clause to the International Rules.

13
Whistle Signals

Difference in Meaning of Signals

The most important differences to be found in the rules of the road on the high seas and in the inland waters of the United States have to do with the sound signal requirements for vessels approaching one another, both in clear weather and in fog. The purpose of this chapter is to analyze the differences in whistle signals prescribed by the respective rules for vessels meeting, overtaking, or crossing, in good visibility.

As a preliminary consideration, it may be pointed out that there is a fundamental difference in the meaning of the conventional one- and two-short-blast signals in the two jurisdictions, and a consequent difference in the *method* of prescribing each signal in the rules. Under International Rules the signals are purely rudder signals, to be given when, and only when, a change of course is executed. It is therefore unnecessary to specify the use of a signal in a particular situation, a general rule being stated which provides for a signal in every situation when the course is changed. Under the Inland and Pilot Rules, on the other hand, the one- and two-short-blast signals are not for the purpose of announcing a change in course, but to indicate the side on which an approaching vessel will pass. The appropriate signal is not covered by a general rule, but is prescribed in the rule referring to a specific situation.

Signals Compulsory Since 1890

It is interesting to note that it was not until the adoption of the 1889 International Rules in 1890—made effective in the United States by Presidential proclamation 1 July 1897—that the use of sound signals by steam or other power-driven vessels at sea, except in fog, became compulsory. The first international rules, adopted by England and France in 1863, and the revised rules, adopted in 1885 by those countries and the United States, Germany, Belgium, Japan, Norway, and Denmark, authorized certain

266

whistle signals but made their use discretionary with the navigator. At the International Convention of 1889, however, the delegates, after some debate on the subject, decided that they would no longer leave to the discretion of the mariner the question of whether, in a particular case, there was less risk of using the whistle and being misunderstood or in not using it at all. Accordingly, the former Article 28, International Rules, was passed to read:

> Art. 28. The words "short blast" used in this article shall mean a blast of about one second's duration.
> When vessels are in sight of one another, a steam vessel under way, in taking any course authorized or required by these rules, shall indicate that course by the following signals on her whistle or siren, namely:
> One short blast to mean, "I am directing my course to starboard."
> Two short blasts to mean, "I am directing my course to port."
> Three short blasts to mean, "My engines are going at full speed astern."

When the 1889 rules were revised in 1948, the International Conference reiterated the substance of the former Article 28, modifying the three-blast signal's meaning to correspond to the interpretation of the courts, namely, that the backing signal is proper when the engines are going astern at any speed. A limited danger signal was provided and additional special whistle signals were authorized. In 1960 when further revision of the rules occurred at the International Conference on Safety of Life at Sea, 1960, a new optional whistle light was authorized. The International Conference in 1972 added a new set of signals to be given and answered by vessels in an overtaking situation in a narrow channel or fairway, and removed the restriction that the optional danger signal be used only by the privileged vessel, making its use mandatory for all vessels in doubt. The present rule now reads:

> Rule 34. Manoeuvring and warning signals
>   (a) When vessels are in sight of one another, a power-driven vessel under-way, when manoeuvring as authorized or required by these rules, shall indicate that manoeuvre by the following signals on her whistle:
>   —one short blast to mean "I am altering my course to starboard";
>   —two short blasts to mean "I am altering my course to port";
>   —three short blasts to mean "I am operating astern propulsion".
>   (b) Any vessel may supplement the whistle signals prescribed in paragraph (a) of this rule by light signals, repeated as appropriate, whilst the manoeuvre is being carried out.
>   (i) these light signals shall have the following significance:
>   —one flash to mean "I am altering my course to starboard";
>   —two flashes to mean "I am altering my course to port";
>   —three flashes to mean "I am operating astern propulsion";
>   (ii) the duration of each flash shall be about one second, the interval between flashes shall be about one second, and the interval between successive signals shall be not less than ten seconds;
>   (iii) the light used for this signal shall, if fitted, be an all-round white light,

visible at a minimum range of 5 miles, and shall comply with the provisions of Annex I.

(c) When in sight of one another in a narrow channel or fairway:

(i) a vessel intending to overtake another shall in compliance with Rule 9(e)(i) indicate her intention by the following signals on her whistle:

—two prolonged blasts followed by one short blast to mean "I intend to overtake you on your starboard side";

—two prolonged blasts followed by two short blasts to mean "I intend to overtake you on your port side".

(ii) the vessel about to be overtaken when acting in accordance with Rule 9(e)(i) shall indicate her agreement by the following signal on her whistle:

—one prolonged, one short, one prolonged and one short blast, in that order.

(d) When vessels in sight of one another are approaching each other and from any cause either vessel fails to understand the intentions or actions of the other, or is in doubt whether sufficient action is being taken by the other to avoid collision, the vessel in doubt shall immediately indicate such doubt by giving at least five short and rapid blasts on the whistle. Such signal may be supplemented by a light signal of at least five short and rapid flashes.

(e) A vessel nearing a bend or an area of a channel or fairway where other vessels may be obscured by an intervening obstruction shall sound one prolonged blast. Such signal shall be answered with a prolonged blast by any approaching vessel that may be within hearing around the bend or behind the intervening obstruction.

(f) If whistles are fitted on a vessel at a distance apart of more than 100 metres, one whistle only shall be used for giving manoeuvring and warning signals.

If we scrutinize the present rule with a little more than ordinary care, five important provisions will become apparent:

(1) The mandatory use of the signals mentioned in Rule 34(a) is evident in the words "shall indicate." Even if it is thought that the signals may not be heard,[1] or the officer on watch considers they would disturb his own ship, especially the master,[2] does not matter—they still must be given.

(2) The one-blast signal indicates a lawful change of course to the right and the two-blast signal indicates a lawful change of course to the left. That is, both the one- and the two-blast signals are rudder signals and therefore should never be used, either for an original signal or a reply, except when the course is changed. Thus, these signals are not required if the rudder is used to counteract the effect of the wind and tidal current,[3] or if using the rudder to check the swing of the ship when backing,[4] and even, apparently, if a vessel rounds the bend of a river with her rudder amidships.[5]

---

[1] *The* Haugland *(1921) 15 Aspinall MC 318.*
[2] *The* Fremona *(1907) Deane J.*
[3] *The* Gulf of Suez *(1921) 7 Ll.L.Rep. 159.*
[4] *The* Aberdonian *(1910) 11 Aspinall MC 393.*
[5] *The* Heranger *(1937) 58 Ll.L.Rep 377.*

(3) If a change of course is made or the engines are reversed in accordance with the rules, the one-, two-, or three-blast signal must be given by a steam or other power-driven vessel whenever another vessel is in sight. The obligation of signaling is plain, whether the other vessel is ahead, abeam, or astern, and whether she is a steamer with a whistle or a sailing vessel without one.[6] Thus, a tug in collision with a sailing vessel was found at fault for failure to signify by three short blasts the reversal of her engines.[7] And conversely, the use of any of these signals under conditions of visibility so low that neither the other vessel nor her lights can be seen is prohibited.[8] However, a vessel is unlikely to be exonerated for not sounding signals through failure to sight another vessel because of a poor lookout[9] or because the other vessel was momentarily out of sight.[10]

(4) The danger signal of five or more short blasts is required of any vessel in doubt and, like the blind bend and overtaking signals, is not restricted to power-driven vessels. It can, however, be used only by vessels in sight of one another.

(5) The one-, two-, three- and five-blast signals may be supplemented by light signals. The latter need not be synchronized with the sound signals and may be repeated at intervals, without the sound signal, while the immediate maneuver is in progress. If a further alteration is made shortly after the initial maneuver is completed, it is still necessary to make a sound signal for the second maneuver even if it is identical to the first. The light signal alone will not suffice. As the reception of sound signals in other vessels can never be certain, especially in diesel and gas-turbine ships with high noise levels, the visual light signals are an important additional indication of action taken or for the reinforcement of the danger or wake-up signal of five short blasts.

Signals under International Rules

Let us consider the application of the sound signals in Rule 34 when two vessels encounter each other outside the inland waters of the United States.

(1) Vessels meeting under International Rules. Rule 14(a), governing the head-on or meeting situation states: "When two power-driven vessels are meeting on reciprocal or nearly reciprocal courses so as to involve risk of collision each shall alter her course to starboard so that each will pass on the port side of the other." It is clear that when risk of collision exists

---

[6] *The* Comus *(CCA NY 1927) 19 F(2d) 774.*

[7] *The* Triton *(CCA Va 1902) 118 F 329.*

[8] *The* Parthian *(CCA 1893) 55 F 426.*

[9] *The* Lucille Bloomfield *(1966) 2 Ll.L.Rep 245.*

[10] *The* Heire *(1935) 51 Ll.L.Rep 325.*

in this situation, each vessel must turn to the right, at least enough to render safe a port-to-port passing, and when the necessary change in course is made, Rule 34 requires the one-blast signal. It is equally clear, in the language of the rule, that the mandate to change course does not apply if the present course of the two vessels will carry them well clear of each other. If the course is not changed, no whistle signal is authorized or permitted, the one-blast signal being a mandatory rudder signal. Should one vessel be in doubt as to whether holding on will give sufficient clearance and accordingly execute a little right rudder and give the one-blast signal, the other vessel then finding the clearance even more ample without change of course on her part, may lawfully hold her course. But if she does, she cannot use her whistle, since to do so would indicate an action which she is not taking. The practical risk of this apparent ignoring of the other vessel's signal is obvious, and may be avoided by the very simple expedient of keeping within the law by changing course a degree or two to the right and blowing one blast. The point to remember here is that there is legal fault if you use your whistle without at least a slight change in course.

Conversely, you cannot, in the meeting situation under International Rules, lawfully change course at any time without using the one-blast signal. In the collision of the *Anselm* and the *Cyril*, the two vessels met end on in the estuary of the Amazon River, and when they were about two miles apart the *Anselm* changed course slightly to the right. A moment later, seeing that the *Cyril* was apparently changing to port, she again executed right rudder, and this time gave the required one-blast signal. In the collision that followed the *Anselm* was held at fault by the British Court of Appeals for failure to blow one blast the first time she altered her course.[11] Under very similar circumstances the *Malin Head* met the *Corinthian* in the St. Lawrence River. The *Malin Head* changed course to the right and blew one blast, but did not repeat the signal when the failure of the *Corinthian* to go to starboard compelled her again to change course, after steadying for about two minutes, this time with hard-over helm. As in the other case, the Court of Appeals held the offending vessel accountable for the omission, notwithstanding the lower court exonerated her on the grounds that testimony showed the failure did not contribute to the collision.[12] Both these decisions prove that the only safe rule on the high seas is, never change course in sight of another vessel without sounding your whistle.

As indicated in the wording of the rule, vessels meeting end on or nearly end on are bound to pass port to port. It is only when the vessels

[11] *The* Anselm, *10 Aspinall M.C. (N.S.) 438.*
[12] *The* Corinthian, *11 Aspinall M.C. (N.S.) 264 (Admiralty).*

are so far to starboard of each other as not to be considered as meeting head and head, to borrow the language of the Inland Rules, that they escape the requirements to change course to starboard; and in that case no change of course, and therefore no whistle signal, is required. It is difficult to picture a meeting situation at sea where the two-blast signal would be valid, for in any borderline case where there is doubt as to whether the two vessels are meeting end on or are already heading clear for a starboard to starboard passing, then the vessel(s) in doubt must assume it is a head-on situation in accordance with Rule 14(c).

(2) *Overtaking and overtaken vessels under International Rules.* When any vessel is overtaking another vessel at sea her action is governed primarily by Rule 13, International Rules. This rule, which applies not only when the overtaking vessel is coming from well aft but when she is so near the dividing bearing between an overtaking and a crossing vessel as to be in doubt as to her status, provides in part:

Notwithstanding anything contained in the Rules of this Section any vessel overtaking any other shall keep out of the way of the vessel being overtaken.

The overtaken vessel, thus having the right of way, is governed by Rule 17, International Rules, which provides in part:

Where one of two vessels is to keep out of the way the other shall keep her course and speed.

Applying Rule 34 to this situation, it is evident that the overtaking vessel, unless she slows down, must change her course to one side or the other if necessary to clear, announcing any change in course with an appropriate whistle signal. The overtaken vessel, on the other hand, being under compulsion to maintain her course and speed, cannot answer the whistle of the other, though she may, if in doubt as to whether the overtaking vessel is taking sufficient action to avert collision, sound the danger signal of five or more short and rapid blasts to call the attention of the overtaking vessel to its duty to keep clear. Because of the provisions of Rule 34 the use of a rudder or reversing whistle signal here, too, is unlawful where there is no change in course or speed. When the overtaking vessel has passed well clear of the overtaken vessel and changes course a second time in order to return to her original heading, she must again use the proper signal, which will, of course, if the first signal was one blast, be two blasts; and this signal, likewise, must remain unanswered.

In narrow channels or fairways, the overtaken vessel is often required to assist in the maneuver, and the International Rules provide for an *exchange* of whistle signals "when overtaking can take place only if the vessel to be overtaken has to take action to permit safe passing." The vessel intending to overtake shall indicate her intention by sounding one of the following signals on her whistle:

—two prolonged blasts followed by one short blast to mean "I intend to overtake you on your starboard side";

—two prolonged blasts followed by two short blasts to mean "I intend to overtake you on your port side."

The vessel to be overtaken shall, if in agreement, sound the following signal on her whistle: one prolonged, one short, one prolonged, and one short, in that order (International Code group "Charlie" meaning "affirmative"). The overtaken vessel shall then take steps to permit safe passing. If the overtaken vessel is not in agreement, she may sound instead the doubt (danger) signal of five or more short blasts. The overtaken vessel should not attempt passing until an agreement is reached, nor does agreement relieve her of her obligation to keep out of the way until well past and clear.

(3 *Crossing vessels under International Rules.* When two steam or other power-driven vessels are crossing so as to involve risk of collision, Rule 15 requires the vessel which has the other on her own starboard side to keep out of the way of the other. The privileged vessel in the crossing situation, like the overtaken vessel, must hold her course and speed and consequently is forbidden to use the one-, two- or three-blast signals of Rule 34. The burdened vessel, on the other hand, is required to keep out of the way, to take positive early action toward this end, to avoid, if the circumstances admit, crossing ahead of the other, and on approaching her, if necessary, to slacken her speed or stop or reverse. If she turns to starboard to go under the privileged vessel's stern, Rule 34 requires her to sound one blast; if she avoids crossing by sheering to port, a questionable maneuver, two blasts; and if she reverses her engines, three blasts; and all of these signals, so far as the privileged vessel is concerned, must remain unanswered for the reason already given, that the latter can change neither course nor speed.

A vessel doubting the intentions or actions of the other vessel, whether burdened or privileged, is required to give the danger signal prescribed in Rule 34(d). In addition, 1972 Rule 17(a)(ii), subject to the qualification in Rule 17(c), now permits the privileged vessel to "take action to avoid collision by her manoeuvre alone, as soon as it becomes apparent to her that the vessel required to keep out of the way is not taking appropriate action in compliance with these Rules." When taking action under this rule, which applies equally to any stand-on vessel, not just the one in the crossing situation, the appropriate whistle signal in Rule 34 (a) must be given. When, from any cause, the privileged vessel "finds herself so close that collision cannot be avoided by the action of the give-way vessel alone, she *shall* take such action as will best aid to avoid collision." Even in extremis, she may not be excused for failure to indicate such action by the proper whistle if at that point she sheers to starboard or to port, or reverses her engines.[13]

(4) Nearing a bend in a channel under the International Rules. Rule 34(e) prescribes a signal for a vessel approaching a bend or similar obstruction:

> A vessel nearing a bend or an area of a channel or fairway where other vessels may be obscured by an intervening obstruction shall sound one prolonged blast. Such signal shall be answered with a prolonged blast by any approaching vessel that may be within hearing around the bend or behind the intervening obstruction.

A prolonged blast is defined in Rule 32(c) to be a blast of four to six seconds duration. A vessel around the bend hearing the signal must answer with a like signal. Henceforth, no other signals are given by either vessel until and unless one of the vessels changes course or backs down.

Signals under Inland and Pilot Rules

We may next consider the action required of two steam or other power-driven vessels approaching each other so as to involve risk of collision in the inland waters of the United States, with particular reference to sound signals when meeting, overtaking, or crossing. Except that meeting end on is given the additional description of head and head, and that a somewhat larger angle on the bow is included by the courts to take care of vessels proceeding in opposite directions through winding channels, the three situations in Inland Rules are similarly defined. As the rules promulgated by the Commandant, U. S. Coast Guard, commonly called Pilot Rules, have co-extensive jurisdiction with the Inland Rules of 1897, except when they conflict with them, we must be governed here by the requirements of both Inland and Pilot Rules. With the exception noted, the Pilot Rules are valid and binding and have the force of statutory enactment; so far as they may be contrary to the statutory provisions they are null and void.[14]

The first important difference to note in the rules for inland waters is that Article 28, Inland Rules, contains only the three-blast reversing signal, while other whistle signals are provided, each for a specific action, in the subdivisions of Article 18, Inland Rules, designated as Rules, I, III, V, VIII, and IX. In the Pilot Rules, whistle signals are set forth in the so-called signal section (80.03) and in Sections 80.1-80.7. A second important difference is the specific provision for the danger signal found in Article 18 Rule III, Inland Rules, and in Section 80.1, Pilot Rules. The former provides:

> Art. 18, Rule III. If, when steam vessels are approaching each other, either vessel fails to understand the course or intention of the other, from any cause,

[13] *The Comus (CCA NY 1927) 19 F (2d) 774.*

[14] *Belden v. Chase 150 US 674; 37 L. Ed. 1218; the* City of Salem, *2 LRA 380, footnote.*

the vessel so in doubt shall immediately signify the same by giving several short and rapid blasts, not less than four, of the steam whistle.

Section 80.1, Pilot Rules, is identical except for the addition of the words, *the danger signal.* It should be noted that this signal is in no sense optional, but must be used in inland waters whenever either vessel is in doubt as to the course or intention of the other, whether the vessels are meeting, crossing, or one is being overtaken by another. A vessel has been held at fault for failure to use it in clear weather when in doubt as to the course or intention of another vessel whose lights were obscured by a deck load of lumber, but whose whistle was heard somewhere ahead;[15] and despite Article 18, Rule IX, where approaching sound signals in thick fog indicated imminent danger, both vessels were held at fault for failure to sound alarms.[16] The danger signal is thus unlike Article 12, Inland Rules, which *authorizes,* but *does not require,* the use of a flare-up light or detonating signal as a means of attracting the attention of another vessel. The Pilot Rules provide an additional special use for a four-blast signal by a dredge with an outlying pipe line across a navigable channel. The dredge is directed to answer an approaching vessel with four blasts, and when the pipe line is open, to give the approaching vessel the appropriate passing signal (Sec. 80.26).

Another important difference in the rules for inland waters is in the doubly useful bend signal prescribed in Article 18, Rule V, for a steam or other power-driven vessel approaching a sharp bend where the visibility is reduced to less than half a mile, and for a vessel being moved from her dock or berth. This signal is described as a long blast, and is therefore generally interpreted to mean a blast somewhat longer than the four- to six-second "prolonged" blast of the corresponding international rule, Rule 32(c), perhaps eight or ten seconds in length. When used as a bend signal the rule says that if the long blast is answered by a steam or other power-driven vessel on the farther side of such a bend, then the usual signals for meeting and passing shall immediately be given and answered; but in the face of Article 18, Rule IX, prohibiting the use of such signals except when vessels are in sight of each other, this must, of course, be interpreted to mean that they will exchange meeting or passing signals immediately upon sighting each other. This interpretation, in fact, has been published in Section 86.10 of the federal regulations as an interpretive ruling of the Inland Rules. The statement that if the first alarm signal is not answered the vessel blowing it is to consider the channel clear and govern herself accordingly should not be taken seriously, for it is entirely possible that the intervention of a bold headland might prevent the second signal

[15] *The* Virginian *(CCA 1916) 238 F 156.*
[16] *The* Celtic Monarch *(1910) 175 F 1006.*

from being heard, and the rule of good seamanship would certainly not justify any such relaxation of vigilance in rounding a sharp bend in a channel as seems to be implied by the reassuring words. "Govern herself accordingly" should at least be construed to include the admonition to keep a very sharp lookout ahead until the channel is actually seen to be clear.

The use of the bend signal in leaving a berth or dock is required whether the vessel getting under way in inland waters is in view of approaching vessels or not, and whether moving ahead or astern. If she is backing, then the long blast must be followed by the three short blasts of Article 28 as soon as she comes in sight of another vessel. Although the rule says that immediately after clearing her berth so as to be fully in sight she shall be governed by the steering and sailing rules, the courts have held that she is under Article 27, the rule of special circumstances, until she gets upon her settled course.[17]

As a further preliminary to discussing the three situations in inland waters, attention is called to the following Pilot Rules which also have a more or less direct bearing on this problem:

Sec. 80.03, Signals. (a) One short blast of the whistle signifies intention to direct course to own starboard, except when two steam vessels are approaching each other at right angles or obliquely, when it signifies intention of steam vessel which is to starboard of the other to hold course and speed.

(4) Two short blasts of the whistle signify intention to direct course to own port.

(5) Three short blasts of the whistle shall mean, "My engines are going at full speed astern."

Sec. 80.2, Cross Signals. Steam vessels are forbidden to use what has become technically known among pilots as "cross signals," that is, answering one whistle with two, and answering two whistles with one.

Sec. 80.3, Vessels passing each other. (a) The signals for passing, by the blowing of the whistle, shall be given and answered by pilots, in compliance with these rules, not only when meeting "head and head," or nearly so, but at all times, when the steam vessels are in sight of each other, when passing or meeting at a distance within half a mile of each other, and whether passing to starboard or port.

Sec. 80.7, Vessels approaching each other at right angles or obliquely. (a) When two steam vessels are approaching each other at right angles or obliquely so as to involve risk of collision, other than when one steam vessel is overtaking another, the steam vessel which has the other on her own port side shall hold her course and speed; and the steam vessel which has the other on her own starboard side shall keep out of the way of the other by directing her course to starboard so as to cross the stern of the other steam vessel, or, if necessary to do so, slacken her speed or stop or reverse.

(b) If from any cause the conditions covered by this situation are such as to prevent immediate compliance with each other's signals, the misunderstanding or objection shall be at once made apparent by blowing the danger signal, and

[17] The M. Moran (CCA NY 1918) 254 F 766.

both steam vessels shall be stopped and backed if necessary, until signals for passing with safety are made and understood.

Meeting Vessels, Inland Waters

Article 18, Rule I, Inland Rules, and Section 80.4, Pilot Rules, provide:

> When steam vessels are approaching each other head and head, that is, end on, or nearly so, it shall be the duty of each to pass on the port side of the other; and either vessel shall give, as a signal of her intention, one short and distinct blast of her whistle, which the other vessel shall answer promptly by a similar blast of her whistle, and thereupon such vessels shall pass on the port side of each other. But if the courses of such vessels are so far on the starboard side of each other as not to be considered as meeting head and head, either vessel shall immediately give two short and distinct blasts of her whistle, which the other vessel shall answer promptly by two similar blasts of her whistle, and they shall pass on the starboard side of each other.

It is clearly the intent of the above rules to have vessels meeting end on in inland waters pass in the same way as required by the corresponding International Rule. In the case of the *Amolco*, in New York Harbor, the court held that approaching vessels whose courses diverge not more than two points are meeting end on or nearly so within the article and are therefore required to pass port to port.[18] However, a careful comparison with the International Rule discloses two essential points of difference: (1) The one-blast signal must be given in inland waters when meeting head and head, at least if passing within half a mile, whether a change of course is necessary or not, and an answering blast by the other vessel is equally mandatory whether she is changing course or not; (2) The conditions for a starboard to starboard passing, not mentioned in the International Rule, are specifically described as when the vessels are so far to starboard of each other as not to be considered as meeting head and head; yet while such a situation would obviously be very unlikely to result in a change of course by either vessel, a two-blast signal is required to be given and answered.

One- and Two-Blast Signals

It may be argued that the signal section of the Pilot Rules already quoted has done away with this fundamental difference in the meaning of whistle signals in inland and outside waters by stating:

> one short blast of the whistle signifies intention to direct course to own starboard except when two steam vessels are approaching each other at right angles or obliquely . . . two short blasts of the whistle signify intention to direct course to own port.

18 *The* Amolco *(CCA NY 1922) 283 F 890.*

There can be no doubt that this statement seems at first glance to be a very commendable attempt to read into these signals the meaning which they have under International Rules. But when we examine all the evidence that bears on this point, it seems that such a result has not been accomplished. Numerous court decisions have established the doctrine that the Pilot Rules do not repeal or supersede the Inland Rules enacted by Congress. In the *Transfer No. 15* the court, referring to signal requirement in the Pilot Rules, said:

> The power . . . to make rules is restricted to such as are not inconsistent with the provisions of the Act of June 7, 1897.[19]

Now it is certain that there are several situations in inland waters where one short blast under Inland Rules does not mean changing course to the right and two short blasts do not mean changing course to the left. In the meeting situation, as already pointed out, the language of Article 18, Rule I, Inland Rules, makes it plain that the starboard to starboard meeting rule applies only when the vessels are outside the limits of a head and head meeting, that is, when the vessels should pass clear without any change in course; yet two blasts are specified in the rule, and made doubly mandatory by Section 80.3, Pilot Rules, if the vessels pass within one-half mile. In the case of vessel A overtaking vessel B, under Article 18, Rule VIII, Inland Rules (or Section 80.6, Pilot Rules), if she desires to pass on the starboard side of B she blows one blast, and B's signal of assent is also one blast, although her very assent makes it imperative for her not to change course. Similarly, if A desires to pass to port of B the signal is two blasts, and B's answer of two blasts again conveys an implied promise to hold her course, and most certainly cannot be the announcement of a change to port.

However, perhaps the most conclusive evidence that the Pilot Rule definitions of the meaning of one- and two-blast signals are inaccurate is the accompanying diagrams of approaching situations published by the Commandant, U. S. Coast Guard, in Section 80.13 (c), Pilot Rules. It will be noted that three of the diagrams apply to the meeting situation, and that in the second and third situations, requiring a one- and a two-blast signal, respectively, the dotted lines ahead of the vessels indicate that the courses do not change. The obvious conclusion is that, except where vessels are meeting so nearly end on that a change of course is necessary to conform to the rules, any relation in inland waters between the one- or two-blast signal and a change in course is a matter of coincidence and not of cause and effect.

[19] *The* Transfer No. 15 *(CCA NY 1906) 145 F 503.*

FIRST SITUATION

Here the two colored lights visible to each will indicate their direct approach "head and head" toward each other. In this situation it is a standing rule that both shall direct their courses to starboard and pass on the port side of each other, each having previously given one blast of the whistle.

SECOND SITUATION

In this situation the red light only will be visible to each other, the screens preventing the green lights from being seen. Both vessels are evidently passing to port of each other, which is rulable in this situation, each pilot having previously signified his intention by one blast of the whistle.

THIRD SITUATION

In this situation the green light only will be visible to each, the screens preventing the red light from being seen. They are therefore passing to starboard of each other, which is rulable in this situation, each pilot having previously signified his intention by two blasts of the whistle.

FOURTH SITUATION

In this situation one steam vessel is overtaking another steam vessel from some point within the angle of two points abaft the beam of the overtaken steam vessel. The overtaking steam vessel may pass on the starboard or port side of the steam vessel ahead after the necessary signals for passing have been given with assent of the overtaken steam vessel, as prescribed in § 80.6

FIFTH SITUATION

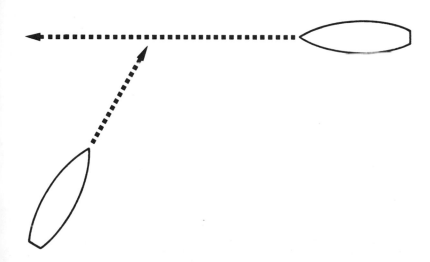

In this situation two steam vessels are approaching each other at right angles or obliquely in such manner as to involve risk of collision, other than where one steam vessel is overtaking another. The steam vessel which has the other on her own port side shall hold course and speed, and the other shall keep clear by crossing astern of the steam vessel that is holding course and speed, or if necessary to do so, shall slacken her speed, stop, or reverse.

"Cross" Signals, Invalid

Section 80.2, Pilot Rules, forbidding the use of cross signals is another regulatory attempt in the promotion of safety which the courts for many years refused to sanction, at least so far as it applied to the use of a valid one-blast signal in reply to an invalid two-blast signal or of a valid two-blast signal in reply to an invalid one-blast signal. Thus, if two vessels met head and head in inland waters, and one of them wrongfully proposed a starboard to starboard meeting by using two whistles, the courts held that the other might reply with one blast;[20] and similarly, if the vessels were so far to starboard of each other as to justify a starboard to starboard passing and one of them sounded the one-blast signal, the other could properly cross it with two blasts.[21] As often stated by the Circuit Court of Appeals, Second Circuit:

> Where a vessel has no right to pursue a particular course without receiving the assent of the vessel she is meeting, the whistles she uses to obtain that assent are merely invitations to an agreement contrary to the usual mode of passing.[22]

This rule was at first worded so as to apply only to vessels meeting head and head, and at that time it was expressly held invalid in a crossing collision where a privileged tug answered the two-blast signal of a burdened vessel with one blast. The Circuit Court made the following general comment on the authority of pilot rules which seemed to exclude the application of Section 80.2, Pilot Rules, to the crossing situation even if the rule had been worded to cover it at the time:

> When under the steering and sailing rules a vessel has the right to make a particular maneuver, she cannot be deprived of that right by any rule . . . forbidding her to sound a signal which would indicate her intention to make that particular maneuver.[23]

When Section 80.2, Pilot Rules, was changed to its present form, apparently making it illegal in *any* situation to answer one blast with two or two blasts with one, the district and circuit courts, through a long line of decisions down to 1939, steadfastly denied its validity in all cases where the "cross" signal was an answer to an improper whistle; of course, if the first whistle is proper, crossing it would be illegal on other grounds and the pilot rule is superfluous. It is true that in all cases of answering one signal with the opposite signal the situation was immediately fraught with doubt as to the course or intention of either vessel with regard to the other, and therefore in inland waters the danger signal was called for; but it seemed to be a matter of indifference to the courts whether the privileged vessel preceded or followed her "cross" signal with the four short blasts.

However, the doctrine that the "cross" signal rule was invalid was for the first time carried up to the United States Supreme Court in January, 1940, and the long-established position of the lower courts was reversed.

[20] *Yamashita Kisen Kabushiki Kaisha (CCA 1927) 20 F (2d) 25.*
[21] *The Terminal (NY 1923) 290 F 533, CCA (1924) 4 F (2d) 1022.*
[22] *The New York (CCA Mich 1898) 86 F 814.*
[23] *The Transfer No. 15 (CCA NY 1906) 145 F 503.*

In a crossing collision between the steamships *Eastern Glade* and the *El Isleo* in a channel approaching Baltimore harbor, in which the privileged *El Isleo* answered a two-blast proposal of the *Eastern Glade* to yield her right of way with the danger signal, followed by one blast, and was exonerated by both the lower courts, the Supreme Court reversed the decree and remanded the case to the Circuit Court of Appeals with the following comment regarding Sections 80.2 and 80.7, Pilot Rules:

> These rules should be construed with Article 27, and are not essentially inconsistent with Articles 19-23 of the Inland Rules and are valid.[24]

Upon a rehearing of this case before the Circuit Court of Appeals, Second Circuit, that court, in obedience to the Supreme Court's opinion, reversed its original decision and held both vessels at fault. It seems highly probable, therefore, that in future cases in inland waters, vessels will be held at fault for using cross signals, at least whenever they are in such proximity to each other that the rule of special circumstances may be construed to apply.

The Half-Mile Rule

Section 80.3, Pilot Rules, often referred to as the half-mile rule, requires that meeting vessels signal if the closest point of approach will be within half a mile. This applies, then, not only to the "head and head" situation, but to all three of the approach situations shown in the Pilot Rule diagrams. In upholding the rule, the District Court said:

> The rule does purport to require signals whenever the projected course of the vessels will bring them within one-half mile of each other, regardless of whether they are end on or nearly so. The rule as construed is not inconsistent with the statutory rule. . . . It does not contradict the statutory rule, but merely supplements it.[25]

The courts have not applied the half-mile rule to the overtaking or crossing situations. Nevertheless, it would be a good practice never to omit signals when the closest point of approach will be within half a mile. However, vessels should not wait until within or reaching half a mile of each other before exchanging signals. It would be prudent for approaching vessels to initiate the proper signals at a reasonable distance in excess of one-half mile once it has been determined that they will pass within half a mile.

[24] *Postal S.S. Corp. v. El Isleo (1940) 308 U.S. 378, 84 L. Ed. 335, reversing (CCA NY 1939) 101 F (2d) 4; rehearing (CCA NY 1940) 112 F (2d) 297.*
[25] *Compania Carreto De Navigation, S.A. v. Tug Sagamore, D.C.N.Y. 1963, 233 F. Supp. 598.*

Overtaking and Overtaken Vessels, Inland Waters

The signal requirements for the overtaking situation in inland waters are similar in principle to the requirements in the International Rules for overtaking in a narrow channel or fairway. The signals themselves, however, are different. If the overtaking vessel desires to overtake on the starboard side of the vessel ahead, she sounds one short blast, sounding two short blasts if she desires to pass on the port side. The overtaken vessel answers with the same signal if in agreement, or she must answer promptly with the danger signal if in disagreement. After a disagreement, signaled by the overtaken vessel with the danger signal, either vessel can initiate a new proposal. The overtaking vessel may not pass, nor is the overtaken vessel required to maintain course and speed, until an agreement is reached.

Crossing Vessels, Inland Waters

The Inland Rules make no mention of one- or two-blast signals in the crossing situation. In Section 80.03 of the Pilot Rules, we find that in the crossing situation one short blast by the privileged vessel indicates her intention to maintain course and speed. The courts have held that this signal is not required but permissive:

> Privileged vessel, which was in plain sight in crossing courses situation, was not under duty to give passing signal and burdened vessel was not entitled to receive any signal.[26]

If the privileged vessel does initiate the signal, she must do it in a timely manner:

> If signals are to be of any value, they must be given with an allowance of a sufficient time to exchange signals and agree on a passing, taking into consideration the speed, power and apparent agility of the vessels.[27]

Sec. 80.7, Pilot Rules, Now Valid

Finally, it should be noted that the Pilot Rules modify the law of crossing in inland waters in two other important respects: (1) Section 80.7 of the Pilot Rules directs the burdened vessel to go to starboard or reduce her speed, thus preventing her taking one other possible action open under International and Inland Rules, namely, sheering to port.

(2) Section 80.7, Pilot Rules, also directs both vessels, whenever there is a "misunderstanding or objection," immediately to stop and back, if necessary, until signals for passing with safety are made and understood.

[26] *Zim Israel Nav. Co. v. S.S. American Press, D.C.N.Y. 1963, 222 F.Supp. 947*
[27] *River Terminals Corp v. U.S., D.C.La. 1954, 121 F.Supp. 98.*

This section has not been applied by the courts to situations where a vessel fails to sound one short blast. The privileged vessel is not relieved of her duty to maintain course and speed, nor is the burdened vessel relieved of her duty to avoid crossing ahead, merely because the other vessel does not sound one short blast. There must be a more positive indication of a misunderstanding or objection. One positive indication is cross signals, and the vessel whose signal is crossed must sound the danger signal and stop. Another situation occurs when a vessel proposes a maneuver which cannot be carried out safely. The vessel receiving the unacceptable proposal is required to sound the danger signal and stop. After a misunderstanding or objection causes the vessels to stop, they must exchange signals, and proceed only after an agreement has been reached.

It was to relieve the vessel having the right of way of the harrowing duty to maintain course and speed until in extremis that the second paragraph of Section 80.7, Pilot Rules, was passed by the former inspectors, in whose seasoned judgment serious danger became apparent in the crossing situation the moment there was a dispute of signals. Their viewpoint was vindicated by the Supreme Court in 1940. The obligation of the privileged, as well as the burdened, vessel to get her way off until the situation is cleared up by a satisfactory exchange of signals, was fully established.[28]

Present System of Signals a Hodge-Podge

Whatever may be said as to the relative merits of the international system of restricting the use of the one- and two-blast signals to indicate changes of course, or the inland system of a specific signal for every maneuver, sufficient discussion has been presented to justify one conclusion—that the present hodge-podge of sound signals, necessitating an accurate knowledge of at least three sets of rules, is a real case for legislative surgery. If there is any valid justification for the present condition of the rules, it certainly is not easily discernible. Cases continue to occur, outside U.S. inland waters, of vessels improperly using whistle signals to express intentions rather than rudder action, in areas where the local rules do not authorize such use.[29] We may hope to find the problem resolved at a future International Conference, but the most practical remedy, as well as the quickest, is to amend the Inland and Pilot Rules into agreement with the International Rules at most important points of difference, particularly in regard to sound signals. This would not only alleviate the situation in a

[28] *Postal SS Corp* v. El Isleo *(1940) 84 L.ED 335 (CCA NY 1940) 112 F(2d) 297.*
[29] *The* Shell Spirit *(1962) 2 L.R. 252; see also The* Friston *(1963) 1 L.R. 74; The* Century *(1963) 1 L.R. 99.*

reasonable period of time, but also decrease by far the difficulty of reconciling differences on an international level. Unless and until some such step is taken, the mariner must continue to use sound signals with the most careful regard to the geographical location of his vessel in any particular situation, and to fall back on good seamanship when he gets into a collision approach where two vessels are on opposite sides of the dividing line and neither set of rules governs both vessels.

SUMMARY

Approaching situations are divided into meeting, overtaking, and crossing. Under International Rules one- and two-blast signals, as provided in Rule 34, are rudder signals which must be given whenever, and only when, a vessel in sight of another changes course, irrespective of the kind of approach. Under Inland and Pilot Rules one- and two-blast signals are prescribed for various particular situations to indicate the manner of passing, and to be given *and answered* regardless of change in course. The inland danger signal, four or more short blasts, must be used in cases of emergency under Inland and Pilot Rules. On the high seas the signal is five or more short blasts. Important differences in the signal requirements of each situation must be observed on the high seas and in inland waters.

In the meeting situation vessels under International Rules sound one blast only when that action is accompanied with a change of course to the right; under Inland and Pilot Rules both vessels sound one blast whether or not either changes course.

In the overtaking situation on the high seas, the overtaking vessel sounds one or two short blasts as she makes course changes to avoid the overtaken vessel. In a narrow channel or fairway subject to the International Rules, or in inland waters, the overtaking vessel must first give a signal indicating the side on which she intends to pass, and receive an answer before carrying out the maneuver. To propose passing on the starboard side, the signal is two prolonged blasts followed by one short blast under the International Rules, or one short blast in inland waters. To propose passing on the port side, the signal is two prolonged blasts followed by two short blasts under the International Rules, or two short blasts in inland waters. In inland waters agreement is signaled by the overtaken vessel by answering with the same signal, while under the International Rules agreement is signaled by one prolonged, one short, one prolonged, one short. Under both sets of rules, disagreement with the proposal is indicated by use of the danger signal.

In the crossing situation under International Rules the privileged vessel may not announce her intention of maintaining course and speed with one blast. She can only question the intentions and actions of the burdened vessel, when in doubt that that vessel will keep clear, by sounding the prescribed danger signal. The one-blast signal is provided in the Pilot Rules for use in inland waters. To be on the safe side the one-blast signal should always be given and answered in the crossing situation in inland waters in a timely manner, and a pilot rule requires that whenever there is a signal dispute in this situation, both vessels shall be stopped and backed, if necessary, until signals for passing with safety are given and understood.

In the Inland Rules the bend signal of one long blast is prescribed for a vessel approaching within half a mile of a bend which it intends to round, or a vessel leaving her mooring. The International bend signal requires a vessel approaching a bend or intervening obstruction to sound a prolonged blast.

The Inland danger signal is a mandatory signal of four or more short blasts required in all cases of doubt or misunderstanding, while the International danger signal can only be used when one vessel is in sight of the other.

14
Head and Head

The Meeting Situation in Inland Waters

Article 18, Inland Rules, and Section 80.4, Pilot Rules, describe with meticulous care an approach situation by two vessels which is to be considered as "head and head" or "meeting end on, or nearly so," the conditions being that: (1) they are approaching in such a manner as to involve risk of collision; (2) by day, each sees the masts of the other in line, or nearly in line, with her own; (3) by night, each sees both side lights of the other.

These rules then proceed to enumerate various tests intended to tell the mariner when a meeting situation is *not* to be considered as meeting head and head. Under these tests, or any one of them, those cases are specifically excluded in which: (1) a vessel sees another ahead crossing her own course; (2) by night: (a) the vessels are red to red or green to green; (b) only one side light is seen ahead; (c) both side lights are seen anywhere but ahead.

The language used in these tests is precise, but it cannot be applied too literally in practice.

Two vessels on exactly opposite courses at night, following tracks which will take them clear of each other, port to port, by 500 yards, will, in the earlier stages of their approach, each see both side lights of the other, almost, though not exactly, ahead; but it is obvious that sooner or later the green light of each vessel will be shut out to the other, leaving the vessels "red to red" yet certainly not removing the application of the head and head rule.

Again, if two vessels are approaching exactly end on, as soon as one of them, in obedience to the rule, makes a marked change of course to starboard, she will at night exhibit one side light ahead as seen by the other vessel, and by day will be seen ahead crossing the course of the other.

Still another discrepancy between the literal phraseology and its practical application may be expected because of the physical imperfections of side lights, which have a certain amount of leakage outside the arc they are supposed to cover and which cannot show from the side of the vessel to points directly ahead without to some extent shining across the bow. This makes it at least questionable if the visibility or invisibility of such lights, in border line cases, can be made an absolute test of whether a situation is head and head within the meaning of the rule.

Under Section 80.3, Pilot Rules, (the "half-mile" rule) passing signals, which do not necessarily mean change of course,

> shall be given and answered by pilots in compliance with these rules, not only when meeting head and head, or nearly so, but at all times, when the steam vessels are in sight of each other, when passing or meeting at a distance within half a mile of each other, and whether passing to the starboard or port.

Section 80.13, Pilot Rules, in turn shows, in the diagram labeled "second situation," two vessels passing port to port *without change of course*, with the explanatory caption:

> In this situation the red light only will be visible to each, the screens preventing the green lights from being seen. Both vessels are evidently passing to port of each other, which is rulable in this situation, each pilot having previously signified his intention by one blast of the whistle.

Thus the requirements which apply only to the "head-and-head" or "meeting end on, or nearly end on" approach situations are that both vessels alter course to starboard and that they pass port to port. In inland waters, the half-mile rule requires that signals be exchanged not only when meeting head and head but when passing or meeting so as *not* to be considered as meeting head and head, if the projected courses bring the vessels within half a mile of each other.

Court decisions have done little to modify the statutory description of vessels meeting end on or nearly end on. In a very old case in the open waters of Lake Erie, when a schooner and a bark collided after approaching each other on within half a point of opposite courses, the Supreme Court held that:

> the variation, in any view of the evidence, did not exceed half a point by the compass, which is clearly insufficient to take the case out of the operation of that (end-on) article.[1]

The writer was unable to find a single case of the type mentioned placing vessels in the head and head category where the courses lacked more than a point of being opposite. On the other hand, the case of a collision in the open sea was found where two vessels approached each

[1] *The* Nichols *(1869) 19 L Ed. 157.*

other so that their courses were within $3/4$ point of opposite, and the court held them to be under the crossing rule. As said by the court:

> These vessels were on crossing courses: as respects the *Knight* because she saw only the other's green light; as respects the *Gulf Stream* because the two colored lights were seen not ahead but from a half a point to a point and a half on her own starboard bow for a considerable time before any risk of collision commenced, so that she showed to the *Knight* only her green light.[2]

The Meeting Situation in International Waters

The International Rules address only the "head-on situation," which is the same as the head-and-head situation in inland waters:

Rule 14 Head-on situation

(a) When two power-driven vessels are meeting on reciprocal or nearly reciprocal courses so as to involve risk of collision each shall alter her course to starboard so that each shall pass on the port side of the other.

(b) Such a situation shall be deemed to exist when a vessel sees the other ahead or nearly ahead and by night she could see the masthead lights of the other in a line or nearly in a line and/or both sidelights and by day she observes the corresponding aspect of the other vessel.

(c) When a vessel is in any doubt as to whether such a situation exists she shall assume that it does exist and act accordingly.

As in inland waters, if the approach situation falls under the definition of a "head-on situation," both vessels are required to alter course to starboard in order to pass port to port. When the course is changed to the right, one short blast is sounded. In other situations, where neither vessel changes course, no signals are sounded.

The specifications in Annex I, 9(a)(i), provide for sidelights to be screened so as to show between one and three degrees across the bow, thus avoiding a theoretical dark lane immediately ahead of the ship. This overlap, plus the effect of any yawing, may make the appreciation of whether a situation is a head-on or a crossing one somewhat uncertain. However, if in doubt a vessel is instructed to assume it is a head-on situation by Rule 14(c). If, in a marginal case, a vessel considers herself to be privileged in a crossing situation, the latitude granted in Rule 17(a)(ii) allows her to take action early rather than having to stand on until in extremis. Such action should be in accordance with Rule 17(c), avoiding an alteration to port. Thus, there is less need to draw a fine distinction between the boundary line between the two situations. In the British Court of Appeals it has been held that, while the rule must always be construed in the strictest accordance with the explanatory words of the rule, construction was a

[2] *The Gulf Stream (NY 1890) 43 F 895.* See also the Comus (2 CCA) 1927 AMC 860, in which two vessels at sea intersecting courses 1° from head and head until within 2 miles of each other were held to be crossing vessels.

matter for the court.[3] In other words, every case should be tested against the explanatory words of the rule itself, rather than solely against previous cases or an arbitrary cut-off point based on differences between the courses of the vessels involved. Nevertheless, the tendency of decisions appears to have been for a difference between courses ($\pm 180°$) of one point or more to be treated as crossing situations, and a difference of half a point or a little more to be treated as head-on situations.[4]

From the wording of Rule 14(b) it is clear that the course referred to in Rule 14(a) is the direction of the ship's head and not the course being made good over the ground. This could be significant where strong cross winds or tidal currents are experienced, transferring what would be, in still waters, a head-on situation into more of a crossing one. The temptation to alter course to port in such circumstances must be resisted, as witnessed by a collision in a swept channel to the approaches of Belfast in 1945. A strong tidal current was sweeping across and two approaching ships were necessarily compensating for it, with the result that their headings were different from their tracks along the channel. The *British Engineer* was found at fault for altering course to port to avoid a green light seen almost dead ahead.[5] *Karanan*, the other ship, altered to starboard as was her duty as give-way vessel.

Crossing Vessels May Be Meeting

A modification in court interpretation of the head-and-head rules relates to the arc of approach included under the rule where vessels meet in a river or winding harbor channel. In a daylight collision between an inbound steamship and an outbound trawler in the New York ship channel it was held that:

> Approaching vessels whose courses diverge not more than one or two points are meeting end on or nearly so within Art. 18 of the Inland Rules and are required to pass port to port.[6]

In a collision on the Delaware River between two ocean steamships, the court similarly ruled that:

> If they are approaching as much as $1\frac{1}{2}$ to 2 points, they are to be considered as head and head and bound to pass port to port.[7]

Remembering that 2 points are equal to $22\frac{1}{2}°$, it will be seen that the head-and-head rule has been made to include, under some circumstances,

[3] *The Kaituna (1933) 46 Ll.L.Rep. 200; also The Gitano (1940) 67 Ll.L.Rep. 339.*
[4] *Marsden, Collisions at Sea, p551.*
[5] *The British Engineer (1945) 78 Ll.L.Rep. 31.*
[6] *The Amolco (CCA Mass. 1922) 283 F 890.*
[7] *The Sabine Sun (Pa 1927) 21 F (2d) 121.*

cases which might have the first appearance of crossing at a considerable angle. Indeed, as pointed out in the case of the *Milwaukee:*

> In determining how vessels are approaching each other, in narrow tortuous channels like the one here in question, their general course in the channel must alone be considered, and not the course they may be on by the compass at any particular time while pursuing the windings and turnings of the channel.[8]

From this it may be seen that vessels' approaching a sharp bend in a river from opposite directions might even be moving at right angles when first mutually sighted, yet still be under the head-and-head rule. One might logically raise the question as to whether vessels are ever crossing in the legal sense, when they approach in the ship channel of a river. The best discussion the writer has found on this point, together with a definite answer to the question in the affirmative, was in a case of collision between two steamships on the Whangpoo River, in which the learned justice of the Supreme (admiralty) Court for China and Japan thus commented on the rules:

> The cases of the *Velocity,* the *Ranger,* and the *Oceano* have explained and illustrated the distinction which exists in the effect of the crossing rule as regards vessels navigating the open sea and those passing along the winding channels of rivers. The crossing referred to is "crossing so as to involve a risk of collision" and it is obvious that while two vessels in certain positions and at certain distances in regard to each other in the open sea may be crossing so as to involve risk of collision it would be completely mistaken to take the same view of two vessels in the same positions and distances in the reaches of a winding river. The reason, of course, is that the vessels must follow, and must be known to intend to follow the curves of the river bank. But vessels may, no doubt, be crossing vessels in a river. It depends on their presumable courses. It at any time, two vessels, not end on, are seen keeping the courses to be expected with regard to them respectively, to be likely to arrive at the same point at or nearly at the same moment, they are vessels crossing so as to involve risk of collision; but they are not so crossing if the course which is reasonably to be attributed to either vessel would keep her clear of the other. The question therefore always turns on the reasonable inference to be drawn as to a vessel's future course from her position at a particular moment, and this greatly depends on the nature of the locality where she is at the moment.[9]

Aside from the doctrine here discussed at some length, it may be pointed out that vessels proceeding up or down a river are usually under Rule 9(a) and Article 25, International and Inland Rules, respectively, and consequently under an additional obligation to keep to the side of the channel which would naturally produce a port-to-port meeting.[10]

[8] *The Milwaukee (1871) Fed. Cas. No. 9,626.*

[9] *The Pekin (1897) AC 532, Supreme Court for China and Japan.*

[10] *See Rule 9(a) International Rules, Art. 25, Inland Rules, and Sec. 80.10, Pilot Rules (Appendixes B, D, and E), requiring that a steam or other power-driven vessel in a narrow channel shall, when it is safe and practicable, keep to that side of the fairway or mid-channel which lies on the starboard side of such vessel.*

Physical Characteristics of Meeting Situation

The head-and-head situation has certain definite characteristics which it would be well to bear in mind before proceeding to a consideration of further illustrative cases. Vessels approach each other in this situation at a rate equal to the sum of their speeds, whereas in the overtaking situation the rate of approach is, of course, the difference of the two speeds, and a varying, but intermediate rate of approach marks the crossing collision. When vessels strike full on, even at slow speed, the result, in accordance with the well-known mathematical rule expressing the respective kinetic energies, is extremely destructive. The rule is $E = W \times V^2 \div {}^2g$; that is, the energy of each vessel (in foot tons) equals the weight (in tons) times the velocity squared (in feet per second) divided by 64.4. There was such a collision on the Columbia River at night between two large, full-powered ocean ships, the steamship *Edward Luckenbach* and the Italian motorship, *Feltre*, in which the latter was said to have been sunk with three distinct gashes in her hull, two of which must have been inflicted after a double recoil by the crumpled bow of the *Edward Luckenbach*. In this situation the least time is allowed for proper action to avoid collision, and hence the primary importance of taking such action in a timely manner. To offset the superior hazard of the most rapid approach it is true that the target is the smallest; that any change of course by one vessel, through changed alignment of masts by day or of range lights by night, should be instantly apparent to the other; and that the smallest change of course will be much more effective than in either the crossing or the overtaking situation, with a strong possibility of a glancing blow if the collision cannot be avoided altogether. However, it is also true that many so-called head-on collisions become physically, though not legally, crossing collisions, as one vessel makes a last desperate attempt to swing clear of the other and succeeds only in attacking or being attacked at a more vulnerable angle.

Legal Characteristics

Legally, the meeting situation resembles the crossing, and differs from the overtaking, situation in that the manner of passing is not optional but prescribed; and it is unlike both of these in that neither vessel has the right of way, and both must therefore take definite and positive action to avoid collision. Under International and Inland Rules alike, vessels meeting head and head *must* pass port to port, and *each must* alter her course to starboard enough to make that maneuver safe, with the concomitant obligation of a proper whistle signal.

Signal Differences

At this point attention is again called to the fundamental difference in the meaning of one- and two-blast whistle signals under International and Inland Rules, discussed in the preceding chapter. Under International Rules, these signals are described in Rule 34(a), and apply alike to all situations in clear weather. Under Inland Rules, Article 28 mentions only the three-blast signal, the one- and two-blast signals being provided in Article 18, Rules I and VIII, and in Section 80.03 of the Pilot Rules, to indicate the manner of passing without reference to changes in course. Section 80.3 of the Pilot Rules has the additional provision that the signals shall be given and answered by pilots in compliance with these rules not only when meeting "head and head" or nearly so, but at all times when the steam vessels are in sight of each other, when passing or meeting at a distance within half a mile of each other, and whether passing to the starboard or port. As explained in Chapter 13, in the meeting situation the practical import of these differences is that:

(1) *Outside the inland waters of the United States*, the one-blast signal is a rudder signal indicating a change of course to the right and two blasts are a similar signal indicating a change of course to the left. Hence, the one-, two-, or three-blast signal *must* be given by a steam or other power-driven vessel in sight of another vessel whenever she changes course, or reverses her engines, the obligation being plain whether the other vessel is ahead, abeam, or astern, and whether she is a power-driven vessel with a whistle or a sailing vessel without one. Additional changes in course require repetition of the signal. Conversely, the one- or two-blast signal can never be used, either for an original signal or a reply, except when the course is changed, nor can either be used under conditions of visibility so low that neither the other vessel nor her lights can be seen.

(2) *In the inland waters of the United States*, the one-blast signal is required of either vessel as an announcement to the other of a port-to-port passing, whether a change in course is made or not. The two-blast signal is required of either vessel as an announcement to the other of a starboard-to-starboard passing, whether a change in course is made or not; this signal is proper only when the courses of the two vessels are so far on the starboard of each other as not to be considered as meeting head and head. It will be noted that the rule requires a prompt reply in each case. Section 80.3, Pilot Rules, already cited, makes an additional obligation to signal and answer if the meeting is within half a mile.

Port-to-Port Passage Required

It will be seen from the rules that when two vessels meet head and head, or nearly so, whether at sea or in inland waters, they are not merely permitted, but are *required*, to pass port to port, and to alter course to starboard *as may be necessary to make such a passage safe*. In this connection it should be noted that the change in course should be both timely and substantial and that *a change of 20° or more is far more effective than one of only 2°*. A sound rule, where circumstances permit, is that the amount of alteration should be more than sufficient to clear the other ship, even if she fails to alter course to starboard. If the vessels are exactly end-on, so that both have to change course to the right, then both the maneuver and the whistle signal of each vessel will be the same under International Rules as under Inland Rules, always bearing in mind that the whistle is blown by each vessel in the first case *because* she is changing course, and in the second case *because* she is proposing or accepting a port-to-port passage. This is the "first situation" in the pilot rule diagrams. In the "second situation," with both vessels so far to port of each other as to pass port to port without a change in course by either, the one-blast signal required in inland waters would be omitted at sea. Similarly, in the third situation in the pilot rule diagrams, with both vessels so far to starboard of each other as to pass starboard to starboard without a change in course by either, the two-blast signal required in inland waters would be omitted at sea.[11]

The first point to be emphasized here is that the obligations to alter course and to signal are mutual in their application, and therefore neither vessel, after a head-on collision, can ever sustain the plea that she was waiting for the other vessel to change course or to signal *first*. The second point is that the injunction to turn to the right or to pass port to port given in all these sets of rules is meant to be obeyed, and should be disregarded for only one purpose—to avoid immediate danger.

It is a common error of experienced mariners to act on the assumption that, since neither vessel in the meeting situation has the right of way or its attendant obligation to hold course and speed, the vessel getting out her signal first properly determines whether the passage shall be port to port or starboard to starboard. In the minds of many, this idea is strengthened by Section 80.2 of the Pilot Rules, which forbids, in inland waters, the use of "cross signals"; i.e., answering one whistle with two or two whistles with one. Certainly the widespread disregard of the port-to-port requirement is not due to any ambiguity in the rules. The International Rules contain no reference whatever to a starboard-to-starboard passage. In the Inland and Pilot Rules, the two-blast signal is especially prescribed for those cases in which the courses of the vessels are so far on the starboard of each other *as not to be considered as meeting head and head*. The rules are therefore unanimous in requiring a port-to-port passage in every genuine head-and-head situation. Moreover, it is interesting to note that numerous court decisions have agreed in upholding this basic provision of the rules. A two-blast signal has been held to be merely a proposal to depart from the rules, not binding upon the other vessel unless and until she assents by a similar signal,[12] and a vessel initiating the two-blast

---

[11] *See pilot rule diagrams, Chapter 13.*
[12] *Southern Pacific Co. v. U.S. (NY 1929) 7 F Supp. 473.*

agreement assumes all risks of the attempt, including a misunderstanding of signals.[13] In the light of these decisions it would seem to be the part of common sense to adhere scrupulously to the rules, and at least never to *propose* a departure unless special circumstance necessitate.

Keynote Is Caution

Referring again to the fact that in the meeting situation neither vessel has the right of way over the other, in the broader sense even a proper port-to-port signal may well be regarded by the vessel giving it as merely a proposal until it is accepted by the whistle of the other. It is true that the other vessel is legally bound to accept it. But the proper keynote of the meeting situation is caution, and the degree of caution required goes much farther than a perfunctory observance of the rule. Indeed it is just about the time of giving the first signal that the real necessity of caution may be said to begin. The other vessel may misunderstand or fail to hear the signal, she may ignore it, she may deliberately disregard it, or she may make a simultaneous counterproposal of two blasts. Unfortunately the first vessel is far from being in a position to say, "We have changed course to starboard and blown one blast. The rest is up to you." The moment the signaling vessel discovers definite evidence of the other's failure to obey the rules, however flagrant the fault, she must take immediate steps to avert collision. The first and most important step, in the eyes of the courts, is to reduce headway to a point where she is under perfect control; if she fails to do this she is practically certain, in the event of collision, to be held guilty of contributory fault. Vessels have been so held for failure to stop or reverse as soon as there was any uncertainty of the other vessel's course,[14] or an apparent misunderstanding of signals,[15] or where the other vessel was seen to be using left rudder in the face of a proper one-blast proposal.[16]

In inland waters it must be remembered that the signal requirements of both Inland and Pilot Rules include the obligation to use the danger signal, four or more short blasts, whenever there is doubt as to the course or intention of another vessel.[17] In a head-and-head approach in inland

---

[13] *The St. Johns (1872) 20 L Ed. 645.*

[14] *The Munaires (CCA NY 1924) 1 F (2d) 13.*

[15] *The Transfer No. 9 (CCA NY 1909) 170 F 944; the Teutonia (La. 1874) 23 L Ed. 44.*

[16] *The Albert Dumois (La. 1900) 44 L Ed. 751.*

[17] *Art. 18, Rule III, Inland Rules: If, when steam vessels are approaching each other, either vessel fails to understand the course or intention of the other from any cause, the vessel so in doubt shall immediately signify the same by giving several short and rapid blasts, not less than four, of the steam whistle. Same as Sec. 80.1, Pilot Rules, except the latter adds the danger signal.*

waters, such doubt should be deemed to exist and the danger signal used whenever a signal is ignored, after one repetition, or disputed; whenever the vessel is slowed or stopped as a precautionary measure; and whenever the other vessel proposes, or is seen attempting to execute, a dangerous maneuver.[18] If the engines are reversed, the three-blast signal in accordance with Article 28 must be sounded whether the danger signal is used or not, and perhaps the addition of the danger signal in that case is unnecessary though its use can do no harm. In a collision below Owl's Head Buoy in New York Harbor between two steamships which sighted each other exactly end on when about a mile apart, it was held that the inbound vessel which blew one whistle, righted her rudder, reversed her engines when the other swung to port, gave a second signal of one whistle, and then blew three whistles, had done all that could be expected of her in efficient endeavor to avoid collision, and the outbound vessel was held solely liable.[19]

If the situation is under International Rules, the one- and two-blast signals denote change in course rather than proposal-agreement on the method of passing. However, if either vessel fails to understand the intentions or actions of the other, she is required to sound the international danger signal of five or more short blasts. In addition she should immediately consider revising her safe speed (Rule 6), which would possibly, in a head-on situation, mean reducing or stopping her way in accordance with Rule 8(e).

The Two-Blast Proposal

Whether to assent when a vessel approaching head and head proposes a two-blast agreement is a question that must be answered very often in practice. The decision of the prudent navigator will be on the basis of what he considers the lesser risk under the circumstances. Many mariners are of the opinion that to dispute a proposal which can safely be accepted is bad practice regardless of the technical invalidity of the proposal. On the other hand, the view is also widely held that the Rules of the Road are so nearly collision-proof that it is always safer to obey them and to refuse to become a part of their nonobservance. When we remember that more than 99 percent of all collisions follow infractions of thse rules by one or both vessels there is some force to this argument. Our first consideration in all cases should be to avoid collision, and our second to avoid liability when the wrongful act of another vessel threatens to force collision upon us. The immediate effect of assenting to a two-blast pro-

[18] *The* Commercial Mariner *(2 CCA) 1933 AMC 489.*
[19] *The* Bilbster *(CCA NY 1925) 6 F (2d) 954.*

posal in the meeting situation is to put both vessels under the rule of special circumstances.[20] As said by the Circuit Court of Appeals:

> A two-whistle agreement varying what would otherwise be the normal method of navigation creates a situation of special circumstances. If the proposal is made when there is reasonable chance of success the other vessel is justified in assenting.[21]

This places an equal burden on both vessels to navigate with caution and to take necessary steps to avoid collision, as agreed, by altering course to port. In effect, the assenting vessel puts the stamp of approval on meeting contrary to law, and thereby assumes an equal responsibility with the proposing vessel to carry out the maneuver in safety. Such assent should therefore never be given when because of current conditions, bends in the channel, speed, proximity of the land, low visibility, or other unfavorable circumstances a starboard-to-starboard passage seems to be hazardous. It will then be much the better procedure, in the writer's opinion, to reply promptly to the two-blast signal with the danger signal, followed by one blast and a substantial change of course to starboard, not forgetting to stop engines until answering signals show that a proper agreement has been reached.

In a head-on, daylight collision in New York Harbor between two ocean steamships, the vessel assenting to a two-blast proposal in a tight situation was found equally at fault with the vessel initiating it. The weather was foggy with a visibility of 500 yards, and the *El Sol*, going up the wrong side of the channel against the tide at 2 knots sighted the *Sac City* almost ahead coming down at 7 knots and immediately blew two blasts. The vessels were then about two minutes and four ship lengths apart. The *Sac City* replied with two blasts, but was unable to swing left fast enough and after one more exchange of two-blast signals, both vessels reversed, but too late to prevent collision. Although the *Sac City* dropped her anchor in a final effort to stop, she struck the *El Sol* in the starboard quarter with sufficient force to penetrate for eighteen feet, sinking her almost at once. The *El Sol* was, of course, primarily at fault for being on the wrong side of the channel in violation of Article 25 and for proposing a starboard-to-starboard passage without justification, but the *Sac City*, which failed to stop her engine when first hearing the *El Sol*'s fog signals and was guilty of excessive speed, was also specifically held at fault:

> for assenting to the two-blast signal of *El Sol* when, having regard to distance between the vessels, she must have known it was risky to try to pass starboard-to-starboard when there was so little time left to swing, and for not stopping,

[20] *The* Newburgh *(CCA NY 1921) 273 F 436.*
[21] *The* Transfer No. 15—Lexington *(2 CCA) 1935 AMC 1163.*

reversing, and blowing alarm signals as soon as she heard *El Sol's* two-blast signal.[22]

When Starboard-to-Starboard Passage Is Proper

The reader should not infer from the foregoing discussion that a starboard-to-starboard passage is never legitimate. If such were the case there would be nothing for meeting vessels to do when approaching each other starboard to starboard within two points but follow the old merchant marine precept (meaning right rudder) of, "port your helm and show your red." Indeed, on the high seas, under International Rules, with the vessels visible to each other through several miles of approach, there is much to justify such a procedure, at least in cases where it is doubtful if the vessels can pass a safe distance off without some change in course. A critical study of the statutory language raises a doubt whether a two-blast signal is ever strictly proper at sea with the vessels on approximately opposite courses. That is to say, if they are so far to starboard of each other as to be able to clear, and actually do clear, without a change of course, no whistle signal is permissible; and if they are somewhat to starboard of each other, but not enough for safe clearance, then they are within the purview of the head-and-head rule and bound to pass port to port. Several collisions have been caused by one vessel altering to port to increase the passing distance and the other vessel turning to starboard. If it is thought necessary to increase the distance of passing starboard to starboard then the implication is that risk of collision exists and the situation should, in a timely manner, be treated as a head-on one. In such a case, the first vessel to alter course to starboard must slightly cross the course of the other, and hence it is increasingly important that both the visible action and the audible notice of it be timely. In the writer's opinion, a sound signal defining any proposed maneuver should be given whenever possible in ample time to be misunderstood once and corrected before the vessels are in *extremis,* or as a federal judge aptly expressed it, in time to maneuver out of a misunderstanding. This is a very practical rule, the observance of which would prevent many collisions. The situation under Inland and Pilot Rules is somewhat different. There we find a specific recognition of a provision for the starboard-to-starboard passage. The two-blast signal is sanctioned both as an original and a reply, regardless of whether there is a change in course. Consequently, when conditions are appropriate, the courts are inclined to enforce this part of the rule almost as strictly as the port-to-port provision.

An examination of the decisions discloses that at least in inland waters a vessel in a proper position for a starboard-to-starboard passage is at

---

[22] *The El Sol (NY 1930) 45 F (2d) 852.*

fault for a collision which occurs because she insists on meeting port to port. The writer is unable to find a corresponding decision under International Rules, and it may be that the courts accept the absence of any reference in the rules to a starboard-to-starboard passage as an indication that it is not an enforceable procedure. In a collision in New York Harbor where two steamers approached each other with ample clearance for meeting starboard to starboard, one of them which proposed a port-to-port passage and then made a wide sheer to starboard was held at fault by the Circuit Court of Appeals.[23] In another case a passenger vessel was held negligent for leaving her course and turning to starboard into the path of an oncoming steam lighter without getting an answer to her one-blast signal.[24] In another case, a steamship and a ferry exchanged two-blast signals and then the steamship, confused by the ferry's whistle to another vessel, suddenly changed course in an attempt to pass port to port, for which she was quite properly held solely liable for the collision.[25]

Similarly, in an old case in Long Island Sound at night between the side-wheeler *Rhode Island* and the steam propeller *Alhambra*, the court found after an analysis of unusually conflicting testimony that the vessels were in a proper position to pass starboard to starboard, and that the *Rhode Island's* red light had already shut in and her green light was widening on the *Alhambra's* bow, when she suddenly blew one blast and swung to starboard. The *Alhambra* reversed, but a collision followed for which the *Rhode Island* was solely liable.[26] When two tugs with tows met in the Delaware River in a starboard-to-starboard approach, one of them made a one-blast proposal when they were only 700 feet apart and the other accepted it. Both were at fault. As said by the court:

> The *Crawford's* fault was in giving the wrong signal, offering to pass on the wrong side, and in attempting to carry out a dangerous maneuver. The *American* was at fault in accepting an obviously improper proposal and in taking part in the effort to carry it out.[27]

In a more recent case, two steamships met above the Delaware River bridge, and the *Manchester Merchant*, bound down the river, had just overtaken a tug and houseboat close aboard to starboard, when in answer to a two-blast signal of the *Margaret*, bound upward, she sounded one blast and went to starboard. Again both were held at fault for the collision, the *Manchester Merchant* for attempting to force a port-to-port

[23] *The North and East River Steamboat Co. v. Jay Street Terminal (CCA NY 1931) 47 F (2d) 474.*

[24] *The Kookaburra (NY 1932) 60 F (2d) 174.*

[25] *The General Putnam (CCA NY 1914) 213 F 613. See also Kiernan v. Stafford (CC NJ 1890) 43 F 542.*

[26] *The Alhambra (CC NY 1887) 33 F 73.*

[27] *The American (Pa. 1912) 194 F 899.*

passing, and the *Margaret* for not sounding the danger signal and for not stopping when the *Manchester Merchant* refused to accept her starboard-to-starboard signals.[28] From these decisions it may be reasonably inferred that the rule is as pointed out many years ago by the Circuit Court of Appeals:

> When two meeting vessels by keeping their courses would pass to the left of each other in safety, one of them, which insists on the naked right of passing to the right, and changes the course when it is attended with danger, is in fault for a collision which results.[29]

The Usual Cause of Head-On Collisions

In conformity with the foregoing discussion it may be said that a striking similarity appears in the causes of most head-and-head collisions. It is preëminently a situation where the surest way to produce a collision is for one vessel to obey, and the other to disobey, the rule. The end-on rule, when obeyed by both, is so nearly collision proof, that it will be no surprise to the reader to be told that the very large majority of collisions of this kind occur simply because *one of the two vessels turns to the left.* While various reasons may be assigned for this disregard of the rule—a misunderstanding of signals, a mistaken notion that the other vessel is intending to turn left, a misapprehension of the requirement to pass port to port, a deliberate usurpation of what is considered the favorable side of a channel—they all point to the same result, and the vessel wrongfully swinging left collides with the vessel properly swinging right. If this obvious cause of disaster could be impressed on the consciousness of every navigator, cases of head-on collision at sea would become extremely rare, being confined largely to those border-line cases at night where there is doubt as to whether the situation is meeting or crossing, and to the even less frequent case where a vessel makes a mistaken attempt to convert a normal starboard-to-starboard passage into one that is port to port.

Illustrative Cases

From a large number of cases bearing out this statement, the following may be selected as typical:

(1) *In re Central Railway of New Jersey* Two side-wheel steamers, the *St. Johns,* and the *Catskill,* met head and head in the North River on a summer evening in 1897, the *Catskill* going up at 10 knots, the *St. Johns* coming down at 13 knots, and both showing regulation lights. Approaching as they were at a combined speed of 23 knots—approximately 2,300 feet per minute—the *Catskill* first signaled with two blasts when the ves-

[28] *The* Margaret *(Pa. 1927) 22 F (2d) 709.*
[29] *The* City of Macon *(CCA Pa. 1899) 92 F 207.*

sels were about 1,800 feet apart, which signal was contradicted almost simultaneously by the *St. Johns* with one blast. Both vessels sheered to the westward, and the *Catskill's* two-blast signal was repeated and again contradicted. Both vessels then reversed and collision followed almost immediately, the *St. Johns* striking the starboard bow of the *Catskill* near her stem at an angle of 30° and cutting into her well across the keel, causing her to sink at once with a large loss of life. Both vessels were quite properly held at fault: the *Catskill* primarily for failure to pass to the right, for failure to signal when half a mile away, for blowing two blasts and for not reducing speed to bare steerageway at once upon the first contradiction of the signal; and the *St. Johns* contributorily for failure to signal as required by the half-mile rule and for failure to reduce headway.[30]

(2) *The Victory* Two British steamships were in a daylight head-and-head collision on the Elizabeth River between Lambert's Point and Craney Island, one of them being so badly damaged that she sank, the total damages to vessels and cargoes amounting to more than $126,000. The steamship *Plymothian* left Lambert's Pier, headed out into the river, rounded a buoy close aboard and headed down the right-hand side of the river on course N¼E for a position off Craney Island Light, a run of 1⅛ miles. Her speed against the tide was about 4 knots over the ground. The *Victory*, coming up past Craney Island with the tide, at 7 or 8 knots, straightened up about mid-river on course S½W. She changed course to the left slightly to avoid two schooners in the river, which would have been unnecessary if she had been near the right bank and then, seeing the *Victory* round the buoy, blew her two blasts for a starboard-to-starboard passage. Her pilot admitted that his object in heading diagonally across the river was to round the black buoy and to save distance. Her signal being unanswered by the *Plymothian*, she repeated it, and the *Plymothian*, hearing it for the first time, promptly replied with the danger signal and reversed her engines so effectively that all her way was off when she was struck by the *Victory*, which reversed too late. The district court found the *Victory* solely liable for her violation of the head and head and narrow channel rules, and the Circuit Court of Appeals found the *Plymothian* jointly liable for holding course without taking positive action until collision was inevitable. But the Supreme Court reversed the appellate court and finally exonerated the *Plymothian*, deciding that she was not bound to change course or reverse earlier than she did, removing all headway before the collision being deemed sufficient.[31]

(3) *The Yoshida Maru–Charles R. McCormack.* This was a collision at night in the lower Columbia River between Astoria and the river

---

[30] In re *Central R.R. of New Jersey* (NY 1899) 92 F 1010.
[31] *The* Victory (Va. 1897) 42 L Ed. 519.

mouth, in which the *Yoshida*, going down the river, attempted to usurp the wrong side of the channel, the excuse of her pilot in court being that he "thought the *McCormack* was going to pass to the left," but the more probable explanation being a preference for the somewhat deeper side of the channel. Each vessel made a turn to her right in entering the straight stretch off Fort Stevens where the collision occurred, and the *Yoshida* sounded two blasts when she first saw the *McCormack's* green light. The latter vessel did not hear the signal—a risk always assumed in this situation by the vessel proposing two blasts—and presently blew one blast when the vessels were still a mile apart, just in time to hear very faintly the *Yoshida's* second two-blast signal. By this time the *Yoshida* was seen to be angling across the river, and as a matter of fact crossed mid-channel when some 2,000 feet from the other vessel; but the *McCormack* continued up her side of the river, without other action, until the vessels were *in extremis*, when both reversed, the *Yoshida* with three blasts, and the *McCormack* with the danger signal. The lower court decided that any faults of the *McCormack* were excusable as *in extremis*, and found the *Yoshida Maru* solely at fault; but the Circuit Court of Appeals, on an interesting and damaging bit of evidence, held the *McCormack* equally liable. It seems that the lookout was on the bridge of the *McCormack* instead of in the bow where he should have been, and the steamer's safety valve, popping off on the smokestack, made it impossible for him to hear the first signal of the *Yoshida*. The signals were distinctly heard and identified, however, by a Coast Guard officer stationed at Hammond, three or four miles away, who had stayed up to take care of a sick member of his family, and who testified that he heard both the two-blast signals, the one-blast signal, the *Yoshida's* three short blasts, and the *McCormack's* danger signal. A proper lookout being a matter of good ears as well as good eyes, this convicted the *McCormack* of negligence before the vessels were *in extremis*, and the Circuit Court also held that she should have sounded the danger signal and taken preventive action as soon as it was apparent that the *Yoshida Maru* was disregarding the rules, when the vessels were at least a mile apart. In this decision, which the Supreme Court declined to review, the Circuit Court of Appeals pointed out that:

(1) A signal for passing starboard-to-starboard, contrary to the rules, given by one of two vessels meeting in a narrow channel gives her no right to attempt such passing unless and until it is assented to.

(2) Initial fault of one vessel does not exempt the other from the duty of complying with the rules of navigation or of using such precautions as good judgment and good seamanship require to meet the emergency.

(3) In the absense of special conditions, the place for the lookout is at the bow.

(4) While the descending vessel was primarily at fault for crossing to the wrong side of the river and attempting to pass starboard to starboard without agreement and in violation of Art. 25, the ascending vessel was guilty of contributory fault in that, on realizing danger of collision when the vessels were a mile apart she did not immediately sound signals required by Art. 18, Rule III, and in failing to hear signals from the other vessel or maintain a proper lookout.[32]

SUMMARY

A head-and-head or head-on approach is the situation where two vessels approach on substantially opposite courses, although in confined waters, because of winding channels, such vessels may first sight each other almost at right angles. The manner of passing is prescribed as port-to-port in both international and inland waters. The International Rules make no mention of a starboard-to-starboard passage; but the Inland Rules prescribe it and provide a two-blast signal when the courses of the vessels are so far on the starboard of each other as not to be considered as meeting head and head. Thus even under Inland Rules the starboard-to-starboard meeting is strictly legal only when the vessels can safely pass without changing course; the Inland Rules require the two-blast signal and the Pilot Rules require the signal any time the projected courses will bring the vessels within a half mile. Rule 9(a) and Article 25, International and Inland Rules respectively, provide an additional reason for vessels meeting port-to-port by requiring vessels to keep to the right in a narrow channel or fairway.

The meeting situation is also characterized by maximum speed of approach, maximum effect of a small change in course by either vessel in avoiding collision, and maximum damage in case of actual collision. Inasmuch as neither vessel has the right of way, neither is under obligation to hold course and speed. On the contrary, both are charged with a positive duty to avoid collision, and hence the keynote of this situation should be extreme caution from the moment the approach becomes evident until collision between the two vessels is no longer possible. By court interpretation each vessel is bound to reduce headway and otherwise bring herself under control whenever it is apparent that the other ignores or disputes her signals or in any other way conducts herself so as to indicate danger of collision. It is important to remember that signals to be effective must be given in plenty of time, and that nearly all head-and-head collisions occur because one vessel holds course or turns to the left in violation of the rule.

[32] *Yamashita Kisen Kabushiki Kaisha (CCA Cal. 1927) 20 F (2d) 25.*

15
The Overtaking Situation

Definition and Characteristics

An overtaking vessel is defined in the rules as a vessel which approaches another from a direction more than two points abaft her beam. Article 24, Inland Rules, describes the overtaking situation in the following clear-cut terms:

> Art. 24. Notwithstanding anything contained in these rules every vessel, overtaking any other, shall keep out of the way of the overtaken vessel.
>
> Every vessel coming up with another vessel from any direction more than two points abaft her beam, that is, in such a position, with reference to the vessel which she is overtaking that at night she would be unable to see either of that vessel's side lights, shall be deemed to be an overtaking vessel; and no subsequent alteration of the bearing between the two vessels shall make the overtaking vessel a crossing vessel within the meaning of these rules, or relieve her of the duty of keeping clear of the overtaken vessel until she is finally past and clear.
>
> As by day the overtaking vessel cannot always know with certainty whether she is forward of or abaft this direction from the other vessel she should, if in doubt, assume that she is an overtaking vessel and keep out of the way.

Rule 13, International Rules, which is practically identical, describes the overtaking situation at sea as follows:

> Rule 13
> (a) Notwithstanding anything contained in the rules of this Section any vessel overtaking any other shall keep out of the way of the vessel being overtaken.
> (b) A vessel shall be deemed to be overtaking when coming up with another

vessel from a direction more than 22.5 degrees abaft her beam, that is, in such a position with reference to the vessel she is overtaking, that at night she would be able to see only the sternlight of that vessel but neither of her sidelights.

(c) When a vessel is in any doubt as to whether she is overtaking another, she shall assume that this is the case and act accordingly.

(d) Any subsequent alteration of the bearing between the two vessels shall not make the overtaking vessel a crossing vessel within the meaning of these rules or relieve her of the duty of keeping clear of the overtaken vessel until she is finally past and clear.

It will be noted both rules attempt to define the overtaking approach at night in terms of the visibility of side lights, and the well known imperfection of these lights will, of course, cause some fluctuation in the actual limits of the overtaking approach in terms of arc of the compass, even if the overtaken vessel is proceeding on a perfectly steady course. However, the exact angle of approach cannot always be determined even in daylight, as frankly conceded by the rules in the admonition to regard all doubtful cases as subject to the overtaking rule.

Providing risk of collision exists and vessels are in sight of each other, there are really two characteristics necessary to any overtaking situation: first, the overtaking vessel must be proceeding in the same general direction as the other, that is within six points of the same course; and second, her speed must be greater. Naval vessels in column are neither overtaking nor overtaken, in the legal sense, as long as their speed remains uniform, though of course a vessel joining such a column is an overtaking vessel until she takes up her position. From the nature of the case, it will be seen that the speed of approach in this situation tends toward the difference in speed of the two vessels, and will be exactly that difference when the vessels approach on identical courses. This fact gives more time for decisive action to avoid collision, and, of course, usually lessens the force of the blow when collision finally occurs. An ocean vessel has, however, been sunk by being overtaken and struck on the quarter by another vessel making only three or four knots more speed.

Where no risk of collision exists, as when a vessel is overhauling another on a parallel course with considerable lateral separation, then clearly overtaking does not exist. If at some subsequent stage either vessel alters course and risk of collision arises, then a crossing situation could exist, and not an overtaking one. For example, if a faster vessel passes a slower vessel on the latter's starboard side and later alters course to port, the slower vessel becomes burdened in a crossing situation. This eventuality was first formulated in the judgment on the collision between the *Baine Hawkins* and the *Moliere*, where, although the latter was found guilty of improperly overtaking, it was said:

. . . It may, on the other hand, be that, when there is no risk of collision at the time (of overhauling)—if, for example the vessel comes within sight of a sidelight at a considerable distance—the crossing rule comes into force; . . .[1]

The actual separation between vessels when such a judgment comes into force probably depends not only on whether risk of collision originally existed, but also on the relative speed of approach once the crossing situation comes into being. For very slow vessels proceeding on similar courses with hardly any difference in their speeds it might be as little as a mile. In one case, two vessels proceeding in approximately the same direction collided after the leading ship, which was two points on the port bow of the second ship, altered course to starboard, flying the correct international flag hoist for adjusting compasses. The ships were between two to three miles apart and it was held that, up to the time of the alteration, the regulations did not apply as there had been no risk of collision and therefore no overtaking situation. After the alteration the vessels were considered to be in a crossing situation before colliding.[2]

It will be seen from the rules that an overtaking vessel has the option of passing on either side of the overtaken vessel, subject only to the modification that in a narrow channel the overtaken vessel should be on the right-hand side of the channel and it would ordinarily be better seamanship in such waters for the overtaking vessel to pass on the left. The overtaking situation thus becomes the only one of the three approaches where any discretion is given as to the lawful manner of passing. Meeting vessels must pass port to port, and in the crossing situation the vessel having the other to starboard must keep out of the way. But while the rule does not prescribe any specific maneuver, this situation is, to a greater degree than any other, one of privilege and burden, and the obligation is put upon the overtaking vessel to keep well clear not only throughout the approach and during the actual passing, but long enough afterward so that she is in the most literal sense "finally past and clear."

It should be noted that International Rule 13, the overtaking rule, takes precedence over all other rules in Part B, Section II, Conduct of Vessels in Sight of One Another. Therefore, sailing vessels and all other vessels given priority in Rule 18, even those hampered in some way by their activity, size, or casualty, must consider themselves bound by Rule 13 and keep out of the way of a vessel they are overtaking. Normally this should be possible by alteration of course or speed; however, some activities do not readily permit an alteration, such as an aircraft carrier recovering aircraft or a minesweeper with gear fully streamed. The special circumstances of the case may then deem it prudent for a vessel being overtaken by the like to get out of the way.

[1] The Molière (1893) 7 Aspinall MC 364.
[2] The Manchester Regiment (1938) 60 L.R. 279.

Although International Rule 13 does override other rules in Part B, Section II, it does not confer on small vessels, sailing vessels, or vessels engaged in fishing, the right to impede the passage of any vessel overtaking them in a narrow channel or following a traffic separation scheme. The rules governing these areas are contained in Part B, Section I, Conduct of Vessels in Any Condition of Visibility, Rules 9 and 10 respectively. Such vessels should conduct themselves so as to keep clear of the deeper part of channels to allow passage for those vessels restricted to the channel. It should be borne in mind by small vessels that many large ships can only transit a channel at certain states of the tide and that they have a limited time to achieve the passage safely. Nevertheless, in the event of coming upon smaller vessels in a channel, the burden of keeping clear still rests with the overtaking vessel, in accordance with Rule 9(e)(ii). If a smaller vessel has not cleared the channel, then it would be necessary for an overtaking vessel to initiate the signals required by International Rule 34(c).

Signals

As pointed out in Chapter 13, one must bear in mind the fundamental difference in the meaning of clear weather sound signals in the overtaking situation as in the meeting and crossing approaches. On the high seas, A overtaking B and desiring to pass her, does not signal unless the approach will be sufficiently close to make advisable a change of course to clear her. Then A blows one blast if changing to the right and two blasts if changing to the left, in accordance with Rule 34 (a). B is required by Rule 17(a)(i) to hold course and speed, and cannot properly give any whistle signal except the danger signal. When A has reached a position well ahead of B, so as to be past and clear within the meaning of the rule, she may return to her course, using the proper signal to indicate the direction she now turns and once again receiving no answering signal from B. Although this last signal of A is nearly always omitted in practice, its use is required by Rule 34(a), International Rules. In a narrow channel or fairway under the jurisdiction of the International Rules, the overtaking vessel sounds a prolonged blast followed by one short blast or two short blasts, indicating a desire to pass on the starboard or port side, respectively. The overtaken vessel signals agreement by sounding a prolonged-short-prolonged-short signal. The overtaken vessel must answer with the danger signal if not in agreement.

In the same situation in inland waters, the overtaking vessel must signal if she will approach the vessel ahead so close that a sudden change of course by the overtaken vessel would bring about a collision. The courts have not applied the half-mile rule to the overtaking situation. Under

Article 18, Rule VIII, Inland Rules,[3] A signifies a desire to pass to starboard with one blast, or to port with two blasts, and B is required to answer promptly, returning A's original signal as assent to the proposed maneuver or blowing the Inland danger signal as dissent to it, and in the latter case A is then expressly forbidden to pass until B's subsequent willingness is made known by a proper signal to indicate on which side she desires to be passed. One short blast by B would mean for A to pass to starboard and two short blasts by B would mean for A to pass to port; and either signal would have to be acknowledged by A by a similar signal. When A is finally past and clear she may come back to her original course, but no whistle signal, such as is required by the International Rules, is provided for announcing the maneuver in inland waters. Perhaps the most important difference to remember in the signal requirements of this situation on the high seas and in inland waters is that under International Rules B cannot properly use her whistle except to warn A of her duty to keep clear, while under Inland and Pilot Rules she must whistle, and has repeatedly been held at fault for failure to answer A's proposal by signal one way or the other.[4]

Rule Applies in All Waters

The overtaking rule has long been recognized by the courts as applying not only in restricted waters but wherever an attempt to pass might mean risk of collision. An early case in point was a collision on a winter night in the wide open waters of Narragansett Bay in which the tug *M. E. Luckenbach* with a tow 2,500 feet long consisting of two coal-laden barges, overtook and passed the tug *Cora L. Staples* with a similar tow of three barges. The *Staples*, with the heavier tow, was making about 4 knots, and the *Luckenbach*, at 6 or 7 knots, overtook and passed the other on the starboard hand without any signal and then crowded to port in

[3] *Art. 18, Rule VIII. When steam vessels are running in the same direction, and the vessel which is astern shall desire to pass on the right or starboard hand of the vessel ahead, she shall give one short blast of the steam whistle, as a signal of such desire, and if the vessel ahead answers with one blast, she shall direct her course to starboard; or if she shall desire to pass on the left or port side of the vessel ahead she shall give two short blasts of the steam whistle as a signal of such desire, and if the vessel ahead answers with two blasts, shall direct her course to port; or if the vessel ahead does not think it safe for the vessel astern to attempt to pass at that point, she shall immediately signify the same by giving several short and rapid blasts of the steam whistle, not less than four, and under no circumstances shall the vessel astern attempt to pass the vessel ahead until such time as they have reached a point where it can be safely done, when said vessel ahead shall signify her willingness by blowing the proper signals. The vessel ahead shall in no case attempt to cross the bow or crowd upon the course of the passing vessel.*

[4] *The* Mesaba *(NY 1901) 111 F 215;* Ocean SS. Co. v. U.S. *(CCA NY 1930) 39 F (2d) 553.*

such a manner that the hawser to her barge fouled the wheelhouse of the *Staples*. Despite frantic danger signals from the latter, the *Luckenbach* held on while her heavy hawser ripped off the wheelhouse roof, smokestack, and mast of the *Staples*, seriously injured the master, and knocked the mate overboard. The mate was picked up by a passing vessel after clinging to the wreckage of the wheelhouse an hour and a half. Both he and the master libeled the *Luckenbach* and the first barge in her tow. The vessels had been on nearly parallel courses, and in holding the *Luckenbach* at fault for close-shaving, for changing course toward the other when passing, for not signaling as required by the Inland Rules, and for attempting to pass without the consent of the *Staples*, and the barge for contributory fault in sheering to port as she was passing and thereby causing the hawser to foul the *Staples*, the court answered the plea of the *Luckenbach* that Article 24 was meant for narrow channels by saying:

> I do not think that the rule was designed for narrow waters only but for any waters where an attempt to pass would involve danger of collision.[5]

Similarly, the overtaking rule was invoked against a steamer which overtook a sailing schooner on the open ocean 60 miles northeast of Cape Hatteras on a dark, overcast night, and collided with her after she failed to show a torch, as at that time was required. While the schooner was unquestionably at fault for this omission, the steamer was held equally at fault when it developed that the mate sighted the schooner less than half a point on the bow, knew from the invisibility of side lights that she was on the port tack, and could easily have cleared her by executing left rudder. The court said:

> Though the overtaken sailing vessel fail to exhibit a torch, as required, the burden is still upon the overtaking vessel to show that she used all reasonable diligence to avoid the other.[6]

Important Significance of Exchanging Signals

There is an important legal significance in this requirement as interpreted by the courts. In one sense it is doubtful whether the prohibition to pass in the face of *B's* dissenting signal really adds anything to the obligation of *A*. It must be remembered that if *B* maintains her course and speed as required under the rule all the burden of avoiding collision by keeping sufficiently clear is put upon *A* whether she has *B's* permission to pass or not, and that in the event of collision under such circumstances *A* would ordinarily be solely liable anyway. To be sure, she would violate one more rule to pass in the face of *B's* danger signal, but if guilty already on the

[5] *The M. E. Luckenbach (NY 1908) 163 F 755.*
[6] *The City of Merida (NY 1885) 24 F 229.*

charge of passing too close, this could not, under American admiralty law, add to *A's* liability. In another sense, however, the requirement in inland waters and in narrow channels and fairways under jurisdiction of the International Rules, that *A* obtain by signal permission to pass the overtaken *B* has a most important bearing on the duty of each vessel to the other. It means that while on the high seas an overtaken vessel incurs the obligation of a privileged vessel to keep her course and speed from the moment the overtaking vessel approaches near enough to involve risk of collision until the latter is finally past and clear, while within the jurisdiction of Inland and Pilot Rules, or International Rules in a narrow channel or fairway, the overtaken vessel is under no obligation unless and until she assents to the overtaking vessel's proposal to pass. If the overtaking vessel neglects her duty to signal, the overtaken vessel is free to reduce speed or alter course, however abruptly, provided, of course, she does not delay such action until the other vessel is so close that it would make collision inevitable, which would violate the rule of good seamanship. But, as held by the Supreme Court in a very early case on the Mississippi above New Orleans, so long as the overtaking vessel can avoid collision by reversing or sheering out, she must pay for her silent approach with full liability for a collision resulting from an unexpected change in course or speed by the vessel ahead.[7]

The best discussion of this point in recent years is by Judge Learned Hand, of the Circuit Court of Appeals in New York in the case between the steam lighter *Industry* and the tug *Viking*, which were in a daylight collision in Kill Van Kull off Myers Wharf at Port Richmond, Staten Island, New York. The *Industry* was overhauling the *Viking* on a parallel course 50 to 60 feet to starboard of her and was about 300 feet astern when the *Viking* swung across her bow to go into her wharf. Although the *Industry* had not signaled, the *Viking* saw her and announced her intention of crossing by a two-blast whistle, a technically improper signal. The *Industry*, instead of stopping, held her speed and likewise executed right rudder, following the *Viking* around until she was boxed in by the wharf alongside which the tug was attempting to land, when she reversed too late to avoid collision and struck the tug on the quarter. There was no question of the fault of the *Industry*, but her owners appealed from the decision of the district court on the grounds that the *Viking* was at fault for her change of course while being overtaken. In denying the appeal and holding the *Industry* solely at fault, despite the improper signal of the *Viking*, which was found not to have contributed to the collision, the court said:

Article 24 puts the burden upon the overtaking vessel to keep out of the way till

[7] *Thompson v. the Great Republic (1874) 23 L Ed. 55.*

she is past and clear and Article 21 in general provides that, whenever one vessel must keep out of the way, the other shall keep her course and speed. Therefore, taken without recourse to the other rules it might be inferred that, whenever one vessel is in fact overtaking another, the vessel ahead must hold her course and speed. However, Article 18, Rule VIII, further modifies the relative duties when each vessel is a steamer. If she would pass, an overtaking steamer must signal, and before passing must get the consent of the steamer ahead. The rule concludes by saying that the steamer ahead shall in no case attempt to cross the bows of the overtaking steamer or to crowd upon her course. It is perhaps possible to read this language as referring to the period before the exchange of signals as well as thereafter, but it seems to us unreasonable to do so. In the first place, so construed, it would add nothing to the general duty prescribed by Article 21. Rather, we think it intended to make clear that it is only after the exchange of signals that the duty of the vessel ahead begins at all.

This is besides the only reasonable construction. The vessel ahead is usually overtaken because she has less speed and cannot avoid it; the overtaking vessel may always slow down and keep astern. The rules provide for no signal by which the overtaken vessel may declare her purpose to change her course and speed, and, if she is bound to keep both, she is, as it were, frozen in her navigation from the moment that risk of collision begins, merely because the overtaking vessel begins to overhaul her, something which it is not always easy to ascertain. Thus, she may be compelled to abandon her intended destination, or to pass her berth, merely because the overtaking vessel insists upon passing. It is therefore fair to suppose that her consent is required, not alone because she may think the passing dangerous in any case, but also because she may need to change her course for her own purposes, to which the interests of the overtaking vessel can hardly be considered equal. The latter should therefore be obliged to hold herself in check against unexpected changes of course, and be prepared to meet them, until by the consent of the vessel ahead, she gets assurance that it is convenient for her to hold on.

And after pointing out that this right of the overtaken vessel to change course or speed in the absence of a signal from the overtaking vessel is questionable only when the latter has crept up so close that any change by the former would instantly create a situation *in extremis*, the court found that:

> while it remains possible for the overtaking vessel by proper navigation to accommodate herself to a change in course or speed of the vessel ahead, that vessel is not held to any duty, but may execute her purpose, regardless of the overtaking vessel and in reliance upon her duty to keep out of her way. That is the situation at bar, for the *Industry*, by starboarding or backing, could, if alert, have avoided collision as soon as the *Viking* began to port.[8]

On the high seas, where no exchange of signals is necessary, similar judgments have been made that the stand-on vessel need not rigidly adhere to its original course and speed. The requirement under International Rules, now Rule 17(a)(i), for the privileged vessel to maintain course

[8] *The* Industry *(CCA NY 1928) 29 F (2d) 29; certiorari denied (1929) 73 L Ed. 985.*

and speed has been interpreted as follows: "Course and speed"—in Rule 17(a)(i)—"mean course and speed in following the nautical manoeuvre in which, to the knowledge of the other vessel, the vessel is at that time engaged."[9] This judgment was given in a case where two steamships were each making to pick up a pilot, and it was held that the burdened vessel was justified in slowing down, as the other vessel should have been aware of her intention to pick up a pilot. This principle has been consistently applied in all situations, whether they be overtaking or crossing.[10]

Equally, in numerous decisions applied to collisions in inland waters, the doctrine outlined in the *Industry-Viking* case, above, has been followed. In several cases where the overtaking vessel was held solely at fault the Circuit Court of Appeals has gone so far as to excuse the overtaken vessel from discovering the presence of the other vessel before the collision. Thus in a case off Pier 4 in New York Harbor, in which a rapidly overhauling steamer which had not announced her approach rammed and sank a small tug which was deflected from her course somewhat by the action of the tide, the appellate court held that:

> An overtaken vessel receiving no signal from an overtaking vessel is not required to look behind before she changes course however abruptly. . . . If the overtaking vessel without signal comes so close to the overtaken vessel that a sudden change of course by the latter may bring about a collision, the fault is that of the overtaking vessel.[11]

However, this approval of what under some circumstances would be an improper lookout aft should not be accepted too literally. It really amounts to little more than a refusal to inculpate a vessel which *is* flagrantly run down by another vessel having no right to overtake her without a signal and still able by smart maneuvering to avoid the collision. It merely says that with respect to a particular offending vessel approaching from more than two points abaft the beam there is no obligation to sight her before hearing her required whistle. It should not be construed as a blanket provision removing the obligation of a proper lookout astern with eyes as well as ears. On the contrary, it is distinctly poor seamanship to change course or reduce speed materially without first checking the situation all around the compass. There may be an overtaking vessel under sail which is not under the signal requirement of Article 18, Rule VIII, and has no means provided of requesting passage. (Similarly the rule does not apply to a steam or other power-driven vessel overtaking a sailing

---

[9] *The* Roanoke *(1908) 11 Aspinall MC 253.*

[10] *The* Echo *(1917) 86 L.J.P. 121; the* Taunton *(1929) 31 Ll.L.Rep 119; the* Manchester Regiment *(1938) 60 L.R. 279; the* Statue of Liberty *(1971) 2 L.R. 277.*

[11] *The* M. J. Rudolph *(CCA NY 1923) 292 F 740; see also the* Holly Park *(CCA NY 1930) 39 F (2d) 572.*

vessel in inland waters because the sailing vessel has no way of assenting or dissenting.) As already pointed out, one steamer overtaking another, whose whistle has not been blown, or whose signal has not been heard, may be so close to the stern of the other that a sudden change in the action of the vessel ahead may make collision inevitable, in which case the latter will be liable for at least part of the damages and may not be able to recover from the other vessel at all.[12] An overtaking vessel following another in a narrow channel and for the time being having no intention to pass is ordinarily under no obligation to signal.[13] The point is that inasmuch as we are bound to observe a vessel astern under some circumstances, the only safe procedure is to look astern under all circumstances where a change in maneuver can be followed by an overtaking collision. As long ago held by the Supreme Court in a case where a steamer was overtaking a schooner in Delaware Bay, and sank her when she tacked unexpectedly across the steamer's bow:

> While a man stationed at the stern as a lookout is not at all times necessary no vessel should change her course materially without having first made such an observation in all directions as will enable her to know how what she is about to do will affect others in her immediate vicinity.[14]

The schooner was solely liable for the collision.

If the overtaking vessel in inland waters signals one or two blasts and the vessel ahead does not answer, it is her duty to repeat the signal. In a very early case it was held that this was necessary, and that even when the signal is repeated and unanswered, the overtaken vessel's silence may not be regarded as acquiescence.[15] If the overtaking vessel persists in passing without receiving the necessary response, both vessels are breaking the rule and will divide the damage.[16] There is thus effective a requirement so rigid with respect to the overtaking vessel in inland waters that unless she signals and receives permission to pass, the only question usually left the courts to decide after a resulting collision is whether she shall pay all the damages or only some proportionate share.

Cases Where Rule Applied

The overtaking rule has been held to apply in a number of cases having

---

[12] *Long Id. R.R. Co. v. Killien (CCA NY 1895) 67 F 365;* the Pleiades *(CCA NY 1926) 9 F (2d) 804.*

[13] *The* Pleiades, *supra.*

[14] *The* Illinois *(1881) 26 L. Ed. 562; see also the* Philadelphian *(CCA NY 1894) 61 F 862.*

[15] *Erwin v. Neversink Steamboat Co. (1882) 88 NY 184.*

[16] *The* Mesaba *(NY 1901) 111 F 215; the M. P. Howlett (CCA Penn. 1932) 58 F (2d) 923.*

certain peculiar points of interest outside the usual run of one vessel trying to pass too close to another on the same course. As early as 1886 a state court in New York brought out the fact that a ship is an overtaking, and not a crossing, vessel within the meaning of the terms used in the navigation rules although there is a difference of three points in the courses of the two vessels.[17] (Of course, under the rule the vessels might differ by any amount less than six points.) In the *George W. Elder*, an ocean steamer, which approached on the quarter of a tug engaged in picking up a tow of barges on the Columbia River at night and sank the tug, was solely at fault for violation of the overtaking rule, although the tug which was properly lighted was stationary at the moment.[18] In an earlier case it was held that a steam vessel coming up with another from a direction more than two points abaft the beam does not cease to be an overtaking vessel merely because during the approach the overtaken vessel takes off all her headway and is at the time of collision actually going astern. The overtaking vessel was liable for not keeping clear.[19]

Similarly, a schooner under sail which ran into the hawser of a barge tow half a mile long in Chesapeake Bay, cutting the hawser in two, was in fault for not keeping clear as an overtaking vessel and liable for the salvage of two of the barges, although during the approach the tow was either motionless, or, because of a 5-knot adverse tide, possibly making sternboard.[20] A steamship which overtook another and attempted to pass her while rounding Corlears Hook, near New York, without obtaining her consent in violation of the overtaking rules and the state law limiting speed at this point, was held liable in part for a collision between the overtaken vessel and a tug caused when the steamship's wrongful acts crowded the overtaken steamer too close to the shore and compelled her to reverse into the following tug; the overtaken steamer was also at fault for failure to recognize the critical situation and take preventive action sooner, as required by the general prudential rule.[21] In a daylight collision on the East River, an overtaking tug with tow which was warned by the exchange of two-blast signals of an overtaken tug with tow and a large steamer they were meeting, was held solely at fault when she failed to conform her movements to the announced change in course by the tug ahead and the two tows were brought into collision.[22] A ferryboat starting out of her slip with her bow pointing astern of a steamer, and then swing-

---

[17] *Aldrich V. Clausen (NY 1886) 42 Hun 473.*
[18] *The George W. Elder (CCA Ore 1918) 249 F 956.*
[19] *The Sicilian Prince (CCA NY 1905) 144 F 951.*
[20] *The Charles C. Lister (CCA NY 1910) 182 F 988.*
[21] *The Plymouth (CCA NY 1921) 271 F 461.*
[22] *O'Brien v. the White Ash and the Winnie (NY 1894) 64 F 893.*

ing across the steamer's bow in a circling course was held to be an overtaking vessel.[23] However, in an old case in the East River, when a steamer had a large steamship to starboard in the act of turning around in such a way as to cross her course, it was held that the larger vessel was entitled to have room to maneuver, and the steamer was in fault when she got across her bows and then claimed to be an overtaken vessel.[24]

Cases Where Rule Did Not Apply

The overtaking rule was held not to apply in a case where it was doubtful whether two tugs were crossing or overtaking, each insisted on the right of way, and both proceeded without regard to the danger of collision. When they collided both vessels were found at fault.[25] In another case, a steamship and a steam pilot boat started almost together, and after first one and then the other had forged ahead, they entered a narrow pass abreast without exchanging signals and were brought into collision when a sudden current sheered the steamship into the pilot boat.[26] Here again the overtaking rule was found not to apply, and both vessels were quite properly held at fault. In a third case, where two steamers were originally on meeting courses but one of them rounded to, to make a landing, and at the time of collision had no definite course, her maneuver did not create an overtaking situation, but rather one of special circumstances and this case, like the two preceding, was really governed by Article 27.[27]

Initial Signal by Overtaken Vessel

An overtaken vessel is ordinarily under no obligation to make an initial signal to a vessel coming up astern if there appears to be ample room for her to pass in safety. It was so held when two tugs with tows in Baltimore Harbor on slightly converging courses, but with one a little in the lead, gradually drew together in broad daylight and finally collided. It developed that the master of the overtaking tug was partially blind in one eye and did not see the other vessel until too late to prevent collision; his tug was, of course, fully liable for the damage.[28] But it is clearly the duty of the overtaken vessel both in inland waters and on the high seas to sound the proper danger signal if she actually sees that collision is imminent. In a somewhat unusual case the steamship *Howard* on her regular run from Baltimore to Providence overtook the seagoing tug

[23] The Venetian *(Mass 1886) 29 F 460.*
[24] The State of Texas *(NY 1884) 20 F 254.*
[25] The Steam Tug No. 15 *(NY 1907) 157 F 142.*
[26] The Joseph Voccaro *(La. 1910) 180 F 272.*
[27] The John Englis *(CCA NY 1910) 176 F 723.*
[28] The Albemarle *(Md. 1927) 22 F (2d) 840.*

Charles F. Mayer with two laden coal barges in a tow on a clear night near Point Judith and sank one of the barges, drowning three of the crew. The watch of the *Howard* had just been changed and the relieving watch officer had his attention suddenly attracted to port by sighting the red light of a steamer, on opposite course altogether too close for comfort. He immediately changed course sharply to the right, which cleared the other steamer, but brought him into dangerous proximity with the barges of the *Mayer*, which he had not noticed. The barges were in tandem on a very long towline, with about a thousand feet between them, and the mate of the *Mayer*, seeing by the *Howard's* lights that she was heading for the barges, called the captain instead of taking preventive action himself. The captain rushed to the bridge and, instead of blowing the danger signal to warn the *Howard*, immediately slowed his engines in the hope that the towline between the barges would sag and that the *Howard* would pass clear above it. Of course, this was a violation of his duty, knowing the other vessel's presence, to keep course and speed; and on the showing that the mate had deferred proper action until the captain had taken charge, this could not be excused as an error *in extremis*. The *Howard's* fault was obvious, but the *Mayer* was also held in fault, not only for her untimely reduction in speed but for her failure to sound the Inland danger signal as soon as the danger became apparent, and for failure to have an officer on watch who was qualified instantly to take the decisive action required.[29]

Legal Effects of Assent to Passing

The International Rule requiring an exchange of signals in a narrow channel or fairway assumes that the overtaken vessel must assist in the maneuver. The legal effect of her assent, therefore, is an agreement to maneuver in such a way as to give the overtaking vessel more room, if necessary. While the overtaken vessel is required to help, the overtaking vessel is still responsible for the safety of the maneuver.

When an overtaken vessel in inland waters assents to the proposal of an overtaking vessel to pass, she neither yields her right of way in the slightest degree nor assumes responsibility for the safety of the maneuver; and the fear that either of these results will follow is not an excuse for failure to answer. As already pointed out, in inland waters she *must* answer, and promptly. She must examine the situation ahead as thoroughly as conditions permit, and immediately express the assent or dissent provided by law. As said by the Circuit Court of Appeals:

The passing signal from an overtaking vessel is not solely a request for permis-

[29] *The* Howard *(CCA Md 1919) 256 F 987.*

sion to pass. It also asks for information which the overtaking vessel is entitled to have. When the overtaken vessel knows of conditions which may make the passing unsafe it has no right to refuse to inform the overtaking vessel of such conditions, and if it does refuse it cannot throw the entire blame for an accident upon the other vessel.[30]

However, this should not be taken to mean that the mere act of assenting to the proposal insures a safe passage, and inculpates the overtaken vessel in an action following collision. The general rule is that it does not inculpate her at all. In narrow channels, where these collisions usually take place, she can be charged with fault for her assent only when it is given in the face of conditions which ought to make it apparent that a safe passage is fraught with serious peril, and is almost certain to cause a collision. In other words, she cannot deliberately lead the following vessel into a trap and escape liability. But if, in her judgment, the overtaking vessel can, with the exercise of a high degree of skill, successfully make her way past, then she is legally justified in giving her signaled consent to the attempt. The burden of clearing her is left almost entirely to the overtaking vessel. As said in a very old case:

> The approaching vessel, when she has command of her movement, takes upon herself the peril of determining whether a safe passage remains for her beside the one preceding her, and must bear the consequences of misjudgment in that respect.[31]

In a typical case illustrating the application of this doctrine by the Supreme Court, the *Gulf Trade*, a single-screw steamship 429 feet long, overtook and attempted to pass on the starboard side of the tug *Taurus*, which was towing in tandem, *i.e.*, in column, four scows, two of them loaded, just as the *Taurus* swung her long tow out of the Delaware River into the quieter waters of the Schuylkill. The *Gulf Trade*, which had previously proposed twice to pass the *Taurus* and had received an assent each time, made the actual attempt, after the third exchange of signals, in time to collide with two of the scows which were swung somewhat in her path by the action of the flood tide as the tug moved out of the Delaware. The district court exonerated the *Taurus* and the Circuit Court of Appeals found both steamers liable, but the Supreme Court held the *Gulf Trade* solely at fault for the collision, reiterating the precedent established by that tribunal many years before. The high court said:

> We cannot conclude that the *Taurus* was in fault. She was prudently navigated in plain view of the *Gulf Trade* who knew the relevant facts; and by assenting that the latter might pass she certainly did not assume responsibility for the maneuver. At most the *Taurus* obligated herself to hold her course and speed so

[30] *The M. P. Howlett (CCA Penn 1932) 58 F (2d) 923.*
[31] *The Rhode Island (NY 1847) Fed. Cas. No. 11,745.*

far as practicable, to do nothing to thwart the overtaking vessel, and that she knew of no circumstances not open to the observation of the *Gulf Trade* which would prevent the latter from going safely by, if prudently navigated. Of course no ship must ever lead another into a trap. There was ample room for the *Gulf Trade* to pass. But if not she should have slowed down and kept at a safe distance. Her fault was the direct and sole cause of the collision. Under these regulations the duty of the *Gulf Trade* was clear. She should have anticipated the effect of the flood tide in the Delaware upon the flotillas as they rounded into the still water of the Schuylkill and kept herself out of the zone of evident danger.[32]

If an overtaking vessel proposes by signal to pass and the overtaken vessel assents under conditions of great and obvious danger, and a collision follows, then both vessels will be at fault. Such a case occurred on the Neches River in Texas, which was governed by Western Rivers Rules and the corresponding Pilot Rules for Western Rivers. The Neches at the time of collision was a narrow and tortuous stream, at the point where the collision occurred about 600 feet in width, reduced for navigation purposes to a dredged channel 30 feet deep, steep-to on one side, and because of a shelving slope on the other side having a bottom width of only 150 feet. In this narrow pass a twin-screw Norwegian steamship, the *Varanger*, assisted by two tugs, one on either side, was overtaken by the *Dora Weems*, a single-screw lake type steamer. The *Varanger* was 489 feet long, 60 feet wide, and at the time drawing nearly 28 feet. The *Dora Weems*, the faster vessel, was 261 feet long, 40 feet wide, and had a maximum draft of nearly 17 feet. She followed the *Varanger* for several miles, and when the channel reached a straight stretch about a mile in length, speeded up and blew two blasts to the larger vessel for a port-side passage. The *Varanger* promptly responded with two blasts, and the *Dora Weems* at full speed attempted the narrow opening between the shelving bank and the *Varanger's* port-side tug. The double suction produced by the bank and the deep-draft *Varanger* caused the *Dora Weems* to sheer to starboard and although her rudder was put hard left and her engines kept at full speed, the break of her forecastle head stuck the port side of the *Varanger* well aft of amidships, and serious damage was done to both vessels. The tug on the collision side of the *Varanger* let go to save herself, the *Varanger* backed her port engine, and by the time the *Dora Weems* scraped clear the *Varanger* had swung into the bank and stranded.

Both vessels in the case were in charge of veteran river pilots, and the district court and the Circuit Court of Appeals agreed in finding them guilty of negligent navigation, the one in proposing what was, in the opinion of various witnesses, a very dangerous maneuver, and the other in

[32] *Charles Warner Co. v. Independent Pier Co. (1928) 73 L Ed. 195.*

sanctioning the proposal. In holding the *Varanger* equally at fault with the *Dora Weems*, the appellate court said:

> Neither a master nor a pilot, whether in charge of a favored or a burdened vessel should acquiesce in a maneuver so inherently dangerous that it cannot likely be accomplished with safety. Both overtaking and overtaken vessels in a river are under duty to avoid collision if possible. The pilot of an overtaken vessel in a narrow channel is charged with knowledge that the force of double suction from a river bank and his vessel will come into play when an overtaking vessel attempts to pass. While the overtaken vessel may acquiesce if the proposed maneuver can, in its judgment, be accomplished with safety, although requiring an unusually high degree of skill, it must not permit the passing if it knows, or has reasonable cause to believe, that passing is fraught with positive danger.[33]

That the overtaken vessel which consents to being passed in a narrow channel is still entitled to use mid channel if necessary was brought out in an early case in Hell Gate, and reiterated in the *Varanger* decision. The overtaken vessel may ease to make more room for the other, without being chargeable with changing her course, but is not obliged to do so if it involved danger for herself. As said in the earlier case referred to, the rule implies:

> that the overtaking vessel will, in passing, fulfill her statutory duty of keeping out of the way of the overtaken vessel, and that the latter will keep her course so far as practicable, consistent with the knowledge that the overtaking vessel is to pass her to port. The overtaken vessel has the right to keep in mid channel so long as there is sufficient room on the port side for the overtaking vessel.[34]

We may sum up the import of these decisions on required signals in the overtaking situation in inland waters by pointing out that while the overtaken vessel will very rarely be held to account for consenting to a proposed passage, she will never be held to account for holding up a following vessel with the prescribed danger signal, and this option should always be used in any situation where a reasonable doubt exists as to the safety of a proposed passage.

Duty of Overtaking Vessel to Keep Clear

The courts have not been more specific than the rule itself in regard to the duration of the overtaking vessel's duty to keep clear. The rule lays that obligation upon her until "she is finally past and clear." Many years ago the point was settled that the rule applies not merely until the overtaken vessel is abeam, but until she has completely passed the other.[35] In a later

[33] *The* Varanger *(CCA Md. 1931) 50 F (2d) 724.*
[34] *The* Dentz *(CC NY 1886) 29 F 525.*
[35] *Kennedy v. American Steamboat Co. (1878) 12 R. I. 23.*

case, when an overtaking steamship, just after passing a tug with barges, lost headway in order to come to anchor, and was struck by one of the barges, the steamship was held not to have fulfilled her duty to keep clear.[36] In a New York Harbor collision between a ferry and a steam lighter, in which the ferry had overtaken and passed the lighter some three-quarters of a mile before the point where they came together, and had been obliged to stop her engines to avoid another vessel cutting across her bow and had herself changed course across the lighter when still from 300 to 500 feet ahead of the lighter, the court held that the ferry was no longer an overtaking vessel, but was, within the meaning of the rule, finally past and clear. The steam lighter, temporarily in charge of a deck hand while the master was at dinner, negligently rammed the ferry, and was held at fault, although what the courts considered an unnecessary change in course by the ferry resulted in her having to pay half the damages.[37] Perhaps the best policy in deciding this point in practice is to fall back on the literal provision of the overtaking rule, and consider that the overtaking vessel must keep clear until far enough ahead so that her maneuver cannot embarrass the vessel she has overtaken, as long as the latter holds course and speed. Of course, if she has to stop in the path of the vessel she has left astern there is an added reason for the prompt use of the danger signal.

Under the International Rules the action by a give-way vessel is covered by Rule 16 and enjoins her to pass "well clear", an injunction that does not prevent her from passing ahead of the stand-on vessel. Thus an overtaking vessel may cross ahead but the stricture of Rule 8(d) makes it imperative that it shall be at a "safe distance," with the maneuver not cut so fine as to result in danger. Where vessels have a large advantage in speed, such as a surface effect ship overtaking a more pedestrian vessel, then such a maneuver is probably safe. However, the constant risk of mechanical breakdown should always be borne in mind in assessing what is a "safe distance" ahead. For more conventional vessels the more prudent action would be to alter course or reduce speed to pass under the stern of the vessel being overtaken. Such action must be taken in good time, for there is a risk that a vessel being overtaken may become sufficiently concerned to take action that might be conflicting under Rule 17(a)(ii). Early action is particularly important in a marginal case, where a vessel to starboard of another may assume herself burdened in an overtaking situation and turn to port to duck under the stern, whereas the vessel to port thinks she is burdened in a crossing case and alters to starboard. Perhaps the best solution is for the vessel to starboard, if she is relatively close to

---

[36] *Brady v. the* Bendo *and the* Sampson *(Va 1890) 44 F 439.*
[37] *The New York Central No. 28 (CCA NY 1919) 258 F 553.*

the other, to turn to a parallel course and pass ahead, or slow and wait for enough room to pass safely under the other vessel's stern, keeping a sharp lookout for any maneuver by the other.

The Usual Cause of Overtaking Collisions

In concluding this discussion, it may be said that the duties of the respective vessels in the overtaking situation are clear and it is only by disregarding them that collision is likely to occur. The burden of keeping a safe distance away is placed on the overtaking vessel. The overtaken vessel has the simple obligation of maintaining course and speed as far as practicable, and in inland waters, or in a narrow channel or fairway under International Rules, the additional duty of answering the other vessel's signals. In an overwhelming majority of overtaking collisions, the cause is the impatience or negligence of the faster vessel, which in an ill-advised effort to save minutes or seconds, crowds the slower vessel too closely, or attempts to pass her when the time and place are not safe. There are numerous cases in the books where vessels have ignored the well-known danger of suction and disaster has resulted. A collision due to suction is nearly always chargeable to the overtaking vessel because it is prima facie evidence that she tried to pass too close. While the effect of suction is undoubtedly strongest, and therefore most properly to be anticipated in shallow channels,[38] it has been alleged to have caused a collision in the deep waters of the Hudson River with vessels more than 200 feet apart.[39]

Suction, or more properly interaction, between two vessels is present whenever they are relatively close aboard each other. When the vessels are moving in the same direction with little difference of speed between them, and especially if they are of dissimilar size, the risk from interaction is greatest. Even in deep water interaction effects may be experienced by fast-moving vessels overtaking at close distances. The collision between the *Queen Mary*, overtaking at 28½ knots, and the cruiser HMS *Curacao*, proceeding at 25 knots, was considered partly due to interaction even though the charted depth was approximately 120 meters. Hence, it is not prudent to attempt to pass close in open waters when there is plenty of sea room available. As was said in the *Queen Mary-Curacao* case:

> . . . the vessels should never have been allowed to approach so closely as to bring the forces of interaction into existence.[40]

In shallow waters, where the flow of water beneath the keel is restricted, the effects of interaction between vessels are enhanced. In addition, with-

---

[38] *The* Sif *(Pa. 1910) 181 F 412; the* Aureole *(CCA Pa. 1902) 113 F 224.*
[39] *The* Cedarhurst *(CCA NY 1930) 42 F (2d) 139; certiorari denied (1930) 75 L Ed. 767.*
[40] *The* Queen Mary *(1949) 82 L.R. 303.*

out another ship being in close proximity, proceeding at a speed too great for the amount of water depth available will cause the rudder to become "sloppy" and, in extreme cases, result in a loss of directional stability; i.e., the ship can take an uncontrollable sheer. When the shallow water is confined to a channel, there is also interaction between a vessel and the channel bank—sometimes called "canal effect"—which can also lead to a sheer to the far bank. For very large vessels with small keel clearances there is also the prospect of "squat" or bodily sinkage that might result in touching the bottom and producing an appreciable trim by the bow, with consequent impairment to shiphandling abilities. The sum effects of all types of interaction are much exaggerated when vessels are overtaking in shallow channels, as the process takes longer than with meeting vessels. Before overtaking another vessel in such waters full consideration should be given to the risk of collision with other marine traffic; to the effects of interaction between vessels; to canal effect causing a possible sheer towards the far bank; to sinkage effect for large vessels and, for all vessels, to the possible loss of control due to proceeding at too high a speed for the water depth available. The first three of these points were specifically mentioned in a recent case dealing with a collision, while overtaking, on the River Schelde, Belgium.[41]

Unlike open waters, where sea room is available, overtaking in shallow channels requires vessels to pass fairly close to each other. The risks involved in overtaking should be carefully weighed against the benefits of getting past the other vessel, especially if she is moving at a high speed, albeit slower than yours, and is of a dissimilar size. Above all, ships should bear in mind that they are less maneuverable in shallow waters, particularly when overtaking or when passing from "deep" to "shallow" water.

In all cases under the rule the keynote is caution, bearing in mind that as the privileged vessel the one ahead has a very strong presumption in her favor. In the eyes of the courts she has an indisputable right to use the public navigable waters in which she is navigating, and so far as that particular stage of the voyage is concerned, she was there first and no one passes but by her leave. Perhaps the whole matter has not been more succinctly stated than by the Supreme Court as to a collision at night more than 100 years ago, when one sailing schooner overtook and sank another in the open waters of Chesapeake Bay:

> The vessel astern, as a general rule, is bound to give way, or to adopt the necessary precautions to avoid a collision. That rule rests upon the principle that the vessel ahead, on that state of facts, has the seaway before her, and is entitled to hold her position; and consequently the vessel coming up must keep out of the way.[42]

41 *The Ore Chief (1974) 2 L.R. 427.*
42 *Whitridge v. Dill (1860) 16 L Ed. 581.*

SUMMARY

An overtaking vessel is one which approaches another from a direction more than two points abaft her beam. The overtaking rule, which requires the overtaking vessel to keep out of the way and thus binds the overtaken vessel to hold course and speed, applies in open waters as well as in narrow channels. In the overtaking situation, the vessels are proceeding in the same general direction and the vessel astern is faster than the vessel ahead. The overtaking vessel may pass on either side, subject to the modification in narrow channels that if the leading vessel is keeping to the right in accordance with Rule 9(a) or Article 25 it may be better seamanship to pass her on her port side.

Under International Rules in open water, the overtaking vessel signals course changes during passing with one or two short blasts. In a narrow channel or fairway under International Rules, a proposal to pass to starboard is signaled by one prolonged and one short blast, and one prolonged and two short blasts for passage to port. The same proposals in inland waters are made without the prolonged blasts, one short to starboard and two short blasts for passage to port. Agreement is signified by answering with the same signal in inland waters, or by a prolonged-short-prolonged-short signal in international waters. Under both sets of rules, disagreement with a proposal must be made known with the appropriate danger signal. In international waters only, agreement signifies that the overtaken vessel will assist in the maneuver.

In inland waters, an overtaken vessel has been found equally at fault with the overtaking vessel when she failed to answer the latter's signal and her silence was mistaken for acquiescence. When the overtaking vessel in inland waters assents, she does not assume responsibility for the safety of the maneuver but merely agrees not to thwart the attempt of the other vessel to pass; however, in the face of apparent danger, it is her duty to prohibit the passage by sounding the prescribed danger signal, and if she assents instead, she will also be held at fault. Even after a proper assent, the overtaking vessel is bound to pass a safe distance off, and will be liable for a collision brought about by passing too close provided the other vessel maintains course and speed. Most overtaking collisions are due to this cause, and particular care must be given to pass far enough off to avoid the effect of suction, especially in shallow water. The obligation of the overtaking vessel to keep clear holds until her maneuvers can no longer embarrass the overtaken vessel, or until she is "finally past and clear."

16
The Crossing Situation

Crossing Situation Most Hazardous

There is no other approach of vessels at sea or in inland waters so trying to the souls of seamen as that of two vessels on a near-collision course in the crossing situation. What navigator of a privileged vessel, about to cross another, has not experienced certain tense moments when it appeared doubtful if the burdened vessel was going to do her duty and give way? Moments when the impulse to reverse or sheer out and yield the right of way was barely balanced by a realization of the risk, legal and physical, of changing course or speed? Or what navigator of a burdened vessel in the same situation has not at some time convinced himself by a pair of bearings that he had plenty of time to cross ahead, and then experienced a harrowing interval wondering whether he was going to make it, conscious that if the race ended in a tie he was hanged higher than a kite? According to the case books, about 40 percent of faulty collisions are crossing cases. When we consider the nervous psychology nearly always present on one or both vessels in these cases, the wonder is that the collision rate is not higher. One is almost inclined to the belief that the crossing situation should have a law against it. It was to reduce, perhaps, this tenseness that the 1972 Conference introduced the most revolutionary change in recent years to the crossing situation; namely, the stand-on vessel may now maneuver before reaching *in extremis*.

Analysis of Differences in Requirements

It is unfortunate that under American law an approach which is naturally fraught with a certain degree of mental hazard should have been made legally so complex that some of its intricacies are puzzling even to admiralty lawyers and are completely baffling to the average mariner,

323

whose duty is not to argue fine distinctions of law but to avoid collision. The writer has attempted to point out in these pages the danger of having differences in the signal requirements of the crossing situation under International Rules and under Inland and Pilot Rules.[1] Briefly summarized, the different requirements are as follows:

(1) Under International Rules, effective in waters outside the prescribed inland waters of the United States,[2] including not only the high seas but the inland waters of countries having no special inland rules, as for example, Canadian waters[3] other than the Great Lakes:

(a) The privileged vessel must hold course and speed, but when she finds herself so close that collision cannot be avoided by the action of the burdened vessel alone, *she is required* to maneuver. As noted above, the privileged vessel *may* take action to avoid collision by her maneuver alone, as soon as it becomes apparent to her that the burdened vessel is not taking appropriate action.[4]

(b) The privileged vessel does not use a one-or two-blast signal until she makes a course change under the conditions in (a) above.

(c) The burdened vessel is required to keep out of the way,[5] to avoid crossing ahead,[6] and if necessary to slacken her speed or stop or reverse.[7]

(d) If the burdened vessel keeps out of the way by turning right, she must sound one blast; if by sheering left, two blasts; if by reversing, three blasts. The privileged vessel does not answer the signals of the burdened vessel.

(e) Either vessel failing to understand the intentions or actions of the other is required to sound the danger signal.

(2) Under Inland and Pilot Rules, effective in prescribed inland waters of the United States and dependencies:

(a) The privileged vessel must hold course and speed until the wrongful action of the burdened vessel forces her into the jaws of a collision or until an improper signal gives positive evidence of a misunderstanding on the part of the burdened vessel.[8]

---

[1] *Chapter 13.*

[2] *For a vessel held at fault for failure to observe the Inland Rules in the waters of Southeastern Alaska see the* Admiral Watson *(Wash 1920) 266 F 122.*

[3] *The International Rules were expressly made to govern in the inland waters of Canada, the Great Lakes excepted, by parliamentary act, Feb. 9, 1897.*

[4] *Rule 17(a)(ii).*

[5] *Rule 16.*

[6] *Rule 15.*

[7] *Rule 8(e).*

[8] *Art. 21, Inland Rules: Where, by any of these rules, one of the two vessels is to keep out of the way, the other shall keep her course and speed.*
Sec. 80.7, Pilot Rules: (a) When two steam vessels are approaching each other

(b) The privileged vessel should announce her intention of holding course and speed by sounding one short blast in a timely manner.[9]

(c) The burdened vessel is required to keep out of the way,[10] to avoid crossing ahead,[11] to cross the stern of the other,[12] or if necessary, to slacken her speed or stop or reverse.[13]

(d) The burdened vessel should answer the privileged vessel's signal of one short blast, or she may initiate the signal.

(e) Either vessel failing to understand the course or intention of the other is required to sound the danger signal.[14] In addition, if the danger signal is sounded in response to an improper or unacceptable signal, such as a cross signal, both vessels must: (1) stop engines, and reverse if necessary;[15] (2) *exchange signals*;[16] and (3) resume speed only after

---

at right angles or obliquely so as to involve risk of collision, other than when one steam vessel is overtaking another, the steam vessel which has the other on her own port side shall hold her course and speed; and the steam vessel which has the other on her own starboard side shall keep out of the way of the other by directing her course to starboard so as to cross the stern of the other steam vessel, or, if necessary to do so, slacken her speed or stop or reverse.

(b) If from any cause the conditions covered by this situation are such as to prevent immediate compliance with each other's signals, the misunderstanding or objection shall be at once made apparent by blowing the danger signal, and both steam vessels shall be stopped and backed if necessary, until signals for passing with safety are made and understood.

[9] Sec. 80.03, Pilot Rules, provides as follows: One short blast of the whistle signifies intention to direct course to own starboard, except when two steam vessels are approaching each other at right angles or obliquely, when it signifies intention of steam vessel which is to starboard of the other to hold course and speed. See the decision of the Circuit Court of Appeals in the Boston Socony (NY 1933) 63 F (2d) 246, in which the signal is held permissive. The navigator in inland waters should act on the theory that he cannot go wrong in using the signal, and may be held at fault if he does not use it.

[10] Art. 19, Inland Rules: When two steam vessels are crossing so as to involve risk of collision, the vessel which has the other on her own starboard side shall keep out of the way of the other. Cf. Sec. 80.7, Pilot Rules.

[11] Art. 22, Inland Rules: Every vessel which is directed by these rules to keep out of the way of another vessel shall, if the circumstances admit, avoid crossing ahead of the other. Same as Sec. 80.9, Pilot Rules, except the latter specifies every steam vessel.

[12] Sec. 80.7, Pilot Rules. See second paragraph, footnote 8.

[13] Art. 23, Inland Rules: Every steam vessel which is directed by these rules to keep out of the way of another vessel shall, on approaching her, if necessary, slacken her speed or stop or reverse.

[14] Art. 18, Rule III: If, when steam vessels are approaching each other, either vessel fails to understand the course or intention of the other, from any cause, the vessel so in doubt shall immediately signify the same by giving several short and rapid blasts, not less than four, of the steam whistle. Same as Sec. 80.1, Pilot Rules, except the latter adds the danger signal.

[15] See second paragraph of Sec. 80.7, Pilot Rules (footnote 8).

[16] Boyers Sons Co. v. U.S. (1912) 15 CCA 400; the Elizabeth (NY 1902) 116 F 225; the Felix Taussig (Ore 1925) 5 F (2d) 612; the Nereus, 23 F 448.

agreement is reached, it being unlawful to continue on while the mis-understanding is unresolved.[17] Either vessel must, of course, accompany any reversal of engines with three blasts.[18]

The privileged vessel may make use of a flare-up light or a detonating signal authorized by Article 12, Inland Rules. However, such a signal is not required, no vessel has ever been held at fault for failure to use it, and its efficiency in arousing the burdened vessel to her duty when the crossing and danger signals are not effective is very questionable. The authority for the privileged vessel to change course when in the jaws of collision comes from Article 27, Inland Rules, and Section 80.7, Pilot Rules.[19]

Both at sea and in the inland waters of the United States, the privileged vessel is expected to cross the burdened vessel's bow and the burdened vessel is to avoid crossing the privileged vessel's bow. However, the proper action of the vessels under International Rules and under Inland and Pilot Rules appears to differ in the following respects:

Under International Rules (1) the privileged vessel maintains whistle silence; (2) the burdened vessel sounds one short blast if turning to starboard, two short blasts if turning to port, and maintains whistle silence unless changing course or reversing engines; (3) the privileged vessel *must* maneuver in extremis or *may* maneuver as soon as it becomes apparent that the burdened vessel is not taking appropriate action; (4) the burdened vessel may clear in any way, avoiding crossing ahead, i.e., by sheering right or left, slowing down, stopping, or reversing.

Under Inland and Pilot Rules (1) the privileged vessel sounds one short blast; (2) the burdened vessel answers one blast with one blast, or she may initiate the one-blast signal; (3) the privileged vessel *must* maneuver in extremis, and both vessels are *required* to sound the danger signal and stop if an improper or unacceptable proposal is heard, or if a signal is crossed; (4) the burdened vessel must clear by altering course

---

[17] *Postal SS. Co. v. El Isleo (1940) 84 L Ed. 335. See same case as re-decided by CCA (1940) 112 F (2d) 297; also see the George S. Schultz (CCA NY 1898) 84 F 508.*

[18] *Art. 28, Inland Rules: When vessels are in sight of one another a steam vessel underway whose engines are going at full speed astern shall indicate that fact by three short blasts on the whistle. (This rule is repeated in the Pilot Rules, Sec. 80.03, last paragraph.*

[19] *Art. 27, Inland Rules (identical with Sec. 80.11, Pilot Rules) provides: In obeying and construing these rules due regard shall be had to all dangers of navigation and collision, and to any special circumstances which may render a departure from the above rules necessary in order to avoid immediate danger. For Sec. 80.7, Pilot Rules, see footnote 8.*

to starboard to go under the stern, or by slowing down, stopping, or reversing.

Special Circumstance Rule Not Substitute at Will for Crossing Rule

An examination of the cases discloses among navigators two common misconceptions of the law in regard to the crossing situation. The first of these is that the application of the crossing rule is modified by the special circumstance rule to such an extent that whenever the privileged vessel recognized any risk of collision whatever, she immediately has complete discretion as to whether or not she will attempt to cross ahead. The second common error, which is confined to inland waters, is the assumption that, by using a two-blast signal *first*, the burdened vessel obtains an enforceable right to cross ahead.

In regard to the first point, there are many navigators who openly express the belief that, even when they have the right of way, in a close situation the safest plan is to yield it at once upon the slightest evidence of dispute. The trouble with this in practice is that oftentimes it may lead us into the very collision we are seeking to avoid, with the stigma of legal liability added to physical injury. The road hog is a notorious bluffer, and there is always the danger that his intention to usurp the right of way may weaken, and he may sheer suddenly to starboard in conformity with the requirement just at the time the privileged vessel slows down or sheers to port to avoid him, with incriminating consequences to the latter if collision ensues. The moral culpability of the privileged vessel in such a case may be slight, but legally she will be held as guilty as the other, and may even be found solely at fault.

With the law on this point as specific as it is the courts could hardly decide otherwise. The crossing rule represents the second of two distinct methods of procedure prescribed in the rules when two vessels approach each other so as to involve risk of collision. The first requires each vessel to take some positive action which has the effect of changing her *status quo*. It is illustrated by the rules that govern when vessels meet head and head. Both must alter course to starboard, both are equally bound to signal, neither can claim, under Inland Rules, that the other should have whistled first. The second method is based on the assumption that one vessel shall maintain her *status quo*, and that any positive action to avoid collision shall be taken by the other. It is illustrated by the rules when one vessel is overtaking another, or a steam or other power-driven vessel meets a sailing vessel, or a sailing vessel running free meets another close-hauled, or two steam or other power-driven vessels meet on crossing courses. The whole theory of such rules is that collision is less likely to occur if one vessel is directed to avoid the other and the other is then required to continue exactly what she is doing. The theory breaks down the moment the burdened vessel cannot rely with certainty on the faithful adherence to course and speed by the privileged vessel. It is for this reason, of course, that the courts invariably excuse an otherwise blameless burdened vessel which can prove it was handicapped in its effort to avoid the other by a change of course or speed on the part of that vessel.[20]

An examination of the decisions on this point should convince the most skeptical as to the validity of the doctrine in the eyes of the courts. As early as 1873, under the 1864 rules, the Federal Court declared:

> Mere apprehension of danger of collision will not justify change of course in a vessel whose duty under the rules is to keep her course. A change should only be made where there is actual danger.[21]

Again, in the case of the *Norfolk*, where a privileged vessel slowed down because of a third vessel with tow, 1,200 feet beyond the intersection point, it was said:

> The duty of the privileged vessel to keep its course and speed is as definite and precise as the duty of the burdened vessel to keep out of the way.[22]

The United States Supreme Court would seem to have decided this question with finality when it declined to review a finding by the New York Circuit Court of Appeals that:

> When two steam vessels are crossing so as to involve risk of collision, it is not only the right, but the duty of the privileged vessel under Pilot Rules, Art. 19, to hold her course and speed until a departure from the rule is necessary to avoid immediate danger, and the fact that subsequent events show that stopping and backing on the part of the privileged vessel would have avoided collision does not prove negligence.[23]

Two cases in the Circuit Court of Appeals, reaffirmed this principle. In the Boston *Socony*, the Circuit Court said:

> The privileged vessel is always in a difficult situation. The rule is that she must keep her course and speed until it becomes apparent that the burdened vessel cannot alone avoid the collision.[24]

and in the *Eastern Glade*, the Circuit Court of Appeals of New York held that:

> Where steamships in inland waters were in the situation of crossing vessels,

---

[20] *The* Morristown *(NY 1922) 278 F 714; the* Elizabeth, *197 F 160; the* Northfield *154 U.S. 629.*

[21] *The* General U.S. Grant *(NY 1873) Fed. Cas. No. 5.320.*

[22] *The* Norfolk *(Md 1924) 297 F 251.*

[23] *The* Boston *(NY 1921) 258 U.S. 622, 66 L Ed. 796.*

[24] *The* Boston Socony *(NY 1933) 63 F (2d) 246.*

privileged steamship was not at fault in holding her course and speed until near the point of collision and then putting rudder hard right instead of reversing engines.[25]

Rule 15, the crossing situation, has consistently been found applicable, not only in the open seas, but in cases in coastal waters where two vessels were approaching some navigational feature, such as a buoy, lightship, headland, or other point, at which each must alter course. However, it has also been held, after a collision in a congested area, where the vessel that would normally be privileged had to constantly change her course, that the crossing rule did not apply. It was only when the give-way vessel was aware, or ought to be aware, of the other's maneuver that the vessels were crossing vessels.

It may be that, in crowded or congested waters, it may not always be possible to ascertain whether the necessary conditions exists. In such cases Articles 19 and 21 cannot apply.[26]

Articles 19 and 21 were, of course, the then extant International Rules on the crossing situation. It was also pointed out that, when maritime traffic was heavy, the rules had always to be considered with the possibility that special circumstances, now International Rule 2(b), might be present— as was the case in this collision. However, a navigational focus by itself, such as an area that is a meeting place of various channels, is not automatically an area of special circumstances. Other factors need to be present to invoke a departure from the rules.[27]

We may sum up the discussion of this point by emphasizing once more that if we find ourselves getting into a crossing situation as a privileged vessel, we cannot safely take the law into our own hands and shirk our duty to hold course and speed unless we stop or haul off so early that a collision cannot possibly ensue, or unless we maneuver under International Rule 17(a)(ii). (See following discussion.)

In inland waters, if we do our duty and collision follows through failure of the burdened vessel to give way, then the all-important testimony for us to be able to give the court after the accident is that we held course and speed unil we reached the point where, according to our well-considered judgment, collision had become inevitable if we continued to do so longer, and that we then took the action which seemed to us most

---

[25] The Eastern Glade (CCA NY 1939) 101 (F 2d) 4. Reversed by Supreme Court on grounds that obligation to hold on does not continue after disputed signals because of former Pilot Rule VII (Sec. 80.7) (1940) 308 U.S. 378, 84 L Ed. 335; (CCA 1940) 112 F (2d) 297.

[26] The Alcoa Rambler (1949) 82 L.R. 359.

[27] The Homer (1972) 1 L.R. 429.

likely to avert collision. That is all the court wants to know, and it will absolve us with nothing less.

Discussion of the Crossing Situation under the 1972 International Rules

The foregoing discussion takes on additional implications with the inclusion of Rule 17(a)(ii) in the 1972 International Rules. By allowing the stand-on vessel to maneuver to avoid collision when it becomes apparent that the burdened vessel is not taking appropriate action, the second method just discussed becomes less distinct. In point of fact, there might be introduced a *third* method whereby in the case of the crossing situation, one vessel is charged with taking positive action to avoid collision while the *status quo* vessel is permitted to take avoiding action in the absence of such action by the first vessel.

The theory just expressed that collision is less likely to occur if one vessel is directed to keep clear of another vessel required to stand-on, is not made invalid in the face of Rule 17(a)(ii). Only when it has become apparent that the burdened vessel has failed to assume her obligation to keep clear is the privileged vessel permitted to deviate from faithful adherence to course and speed. The danger of the theory breaking down lies in the occurrence of delayed compliance of the give-way vessel to maneuver to avoid collision, coincident with the decision of the privileged vessel that the time had come to exercise her prerogative to take avoiding action. Now awakened to a danger, the burdened vessel can no longer rely with certainty that the stand-on vessel is in fact standing-on. In order to avoid this situation, it becomes even more important for the give-way vessel in a crossing situation to adhere strictly to the requirement of Rule 16; that is, to take early action to keep well clear.

And the privileged vessel? When is she advised to proceed under Rule 17(a)(ii)? Certainly not until risk of collision has been established. Probably not until she has sounded the international signal of doubt as a wake-up signal (supplemented by flashes on the signal lamp at night), but definitely prior to *in extremis*. At this writing it is appropriate to leave to the courts to decide at what point the invoking of Rule 17(a)(ii) is deemed prudent. In the meantime, the ordinary practice of good seamanship should serve to guide the mariner.

The important point is to realize that the privileged vessel in a crossing situation has not been granted license to maneuver at will. She is not permitted to alter course or change speed under Rule 17(a)(ii) solely because she thinks it might help the situation or once she observes the other vessel maneuvering to meet her obligations as the burdened vessel.

In considering permissive action, it is well for the privileged vessel to bear in mind that the give-way vessel may belatedly wake up to her responsibilities, probably by altering course to starboard, and to adhere to the provision of Rule 17(c); that is, not alter course to port for a vessel on her own port side. Additionally, a reduction of speed might make it more difficult for the give-way vessel to pass astern. A major alteration to starboard may well be the best course of action, not forgetting to sound the proper sound signal so that the other vessel might speedily understand the intent of the maneuver.

Action to avoid collision becomes compulsory for the privileged vessel when she finds herself so close that collision cannot be avoided by the burdened vessel alone. The distance between the two vessels when this moment arrives will vary with the direction and speed of approach of the other vessel, an estimate of her maneuvering characteristics, and a thorough knowledge of one's own vessel's capabilities and limitations. The precise point of when to cease maintaining course and speed is difficult to determine and some latitude has been allowed in court cases. When it is shown that the other vessel had been carefully watched and that the stand-on vessel had endeavoured to do her best to act at the correct moment, she will not be held to blame, though subsequent analysis shows she waited too long or acted too soon.

> The conduct of a prudent seaman in such circumstances is not to be tried by mathematical calculations subsequently made.[28]

An alteration to starboard to avoid a vessel close on the port bow could be most dangerous, as it will take the stand-on vessel across the other ship's bow. Left too late and she might be struck amidships, the most vulnerable spot. Rule 17(c) therefore does not apply when in extremis is reached, as a vessel is permitted to take any action that might best avert collision. Turning towards the other vessel may well be the best action to take at close quarters, particularly if she is likely to strike abaft the privileged vessel's beam.

When collision, despite all efforts, appears to be inevitable, the aim should be to reduce the effect to a minimum. A glancing blow is normally better than a direct impact, though with tankers and the like it is unlikely to reduce the risk of fire. If a glancing blow is impossible, it is probably best to take the impact on the bow, forward of the collision bulkhead. An alteration away that exposes the vulnerable ship's side might well be the most damaging course of action to take.

Two Blasts by Burdened Vessel Do Not Give Her Right of Way

The belief that an initial two-blast signal by the burdened vessel confers upon her the right of way is a misconception of the rules which seems to

---

[28] *Compagnie des Forges d'Homecourt (1920) S.C. 247; 2 LL.L.Rep 186.*

be common in inland waters, particularly in busy harbors where there is a great deal of cross traffic. Thus, in San Francisco Bay and in New York Harbor this signal is frequently used. Whatever may be a local custom, it is never safe to assume that it can displace a positive statutory provision. As held in a very old case:

> If there is a custom which permits Sound steamers to claim exemption from the operation of this article when approaching the ferries in the East River on the ebb tide, such custom is opposed to law, and cannot prevail.[29]

However, notwithstanding local custom, the practice is at least questionable, and every navigator who makes use of it should fully understand its legal and judicial significance.

In the first place, there is nothing either expressed or implied in the Inland or Pilot Rules to justify a two-blast signal by either vessel in the crossing situation. On the contrary, the privileged vessel is directed to hold her course and speed; the Pilot Rules specifically authorize the one-blast signal as a means of notifying the other vessel that such is her intention. It is true that there was at one time a pilot rule which permitted the vessel having the other on her starboard hand to proceed if it could be done without risk of collision, and provided a two-blast signal therefor; but even this was regarded as contrary to the spirit of the crossing rule, and was repealed after being invalidated by the Federal Court in the following language:

> Rule 9 . . . approved . . . February 25, 1907, which permits the vessel having the other on her starboard hand to cross the bows of the other if it can be done without risk of collision, is invalid, as repugnant to the starboard hand rule.[30]

In the second place, if the burdened vessel, assuming that she has ample time to cross ahead, initiates the two-blast signal which in the absence of any statutory provision can have no sanction but that of local custom, she thereby expresses an admission that risk of collision exists, and lays herself open to the charge of proposing a violation of the law. Recognizing this, the lower courts have repeatedly ruled that such action is at best no more than a proposal which the other vessel is under no obligation to accept; that unless and until the proposal is agreed to by the other, as indicated by a reply of two blasts, the privileged vessel must hold on; and that even after such agreement the burdened vessel assumes any risk of carrying out the maneuver.

The following decisions, some of them antedating the present rules for inland waters, are ample evidence of the attitude of the courts on this question:

[29] The Pequot (1887) 30 F 839; the Mohegan (CCA NY 1900) 105 F 1003.
[30] The Pawnee (NY 1909) 168 F 371.

If a burdened steamer, by her signals, invites a departure from the ordinary rules of navigation she takes the risk both of her own whistles being heard, and, in turn, of hearing the response, if a response is made, and of the success of the maneuver.[31]

Two whistles given in reply to a signal of two whistles from a steamer bound to keep out of the way mean only assent to the latter's course at her own risk, and an agreement to do nothing to thwart her. It does not relieve the latter of her statutory duty to keep out of the way; but when collision becomes imminent, both are bound to do all they can to avoid it whether the previous signals were of two whistles or one. If imminent risk of collision is involved in the maneuver assented to, and the maneuver was unnecessary, both are responsible for agreeing on a hazardous attempt.[32]

When the boat having the right of way fails to respond to the signal of the boat whose duty it is to keep out of the way, the latter has no right to assume, because of such silence, that the former abandons her right of way.[33]

The failure of the privileged vessel to assent to a signal contrary to the rule is equivalent to a dissent which holds the burdened vessel bound to observe the starboard rule.[34]

The privileged vessel is not required . . . to answer the burdened vessel's signals if she does not assent thereto.[35]

The privileged vessel is entitled to assure that, although the burdened vessel may at first propose to exchange rights of way, it will, if such a proposal be rejected, conform to the rules of navigation.[36]

In the light of these decisions the risk in the use of an initial two-blast signal by the burdened vessel is apparent, and should generally be avoided. Certainly it can never be legally justified when the vessels are approaching each other so as to involve risk of collision; and when it is possible for the vessel having the other to starboard to pass so far ahead of the other that risk of collision may be deemed not to exist, whistle signals are not only unnecessary but are better omitted.

Supreme Court Validates Section 80.2 and 80.7, Pilot Rules

It should be pointed out that the foregoing decisions, which were all by district courts or circuit courts of appeal, in effect invalidated former Pilot Rule II (Sec. 80.2) and the second paragraph of former Pilot Rule VII (Sec. 80.7), forbidding the use of "cross" signals, i.e., answering one blast with two or two blasts with one, and directing both vessels in the crossing situation, in case of a misunderstanding of signals, immediately to blow the danger signal and to stop and back, if necessary, until signals for passing with safety are made and understood. For many years these

[31] *Hamilton v. the* John King *(1891) 49 F 469; the* Admiral, *39 F 574.*
[32] *The* Nereus *(NY 1885) 23 F 448.*
[33] *The* Pavonia *(NY 1885) 26 F 106.*
[34] *The* Eldorado *(NY 1896) 32 CCA 464, 89 F 1015.*
[35] *The* Montauk *(NY 1910) 180 F 697.*
[36] *L. Boyers' Sons Co. v. U.S. (NY 1912) 195 F 490.*

courts were agreed that it was always proper to "cross" an improper signal regardless of former Pilot Rule II (Sec. 80.2), and that if a burdened crossing vessel blew two blasts, an improper signal, the privileged vessel, unless she saw fit to assent to the wrongful proposal, could not reverse her engines as directed by the Pilot Rule, but was bound to hold course and speed as required by Article 21 until literally in the jaws of collision. The proper procedure was to respond with the danger signal and the single blast, and then, if the burdened vessel continued to hold on until so close that she could no longer prevent collision unaided, to take such positive action as would best help to avert it.

Such was the decision of both District Court and Circuit Court of Appeals in New York as late as 1939 in the Baltimore harbor collision of the steamships *Eastern Glade* and *El Isleo*. In this case the two vessels sighted each other at night over a mile apart in converging channels, and the *Eastern Glade*, which was the burdened vessel, blew two blasts. The *El Isleo* interpreted this as an announcement of intention to cross her bow and immediately responded with the danger signal, followed by one blast, and continued to hold course and speed until the two vessels were *in extremis*, when she sheered out to starboard in a futile effort to avoid collision, and was rammed nearly amidships at a point about 200 yards outside the buoyed channel. The fault of the *Eastern Glade* was glaring, and in accordance with the long line of its own previous decisions, the Circuit Court of Appeals upheld the District Court in exonerating the *El Isleo* and then finding the *Eastern Glade* solely liable for the collision. The court took the opportunity to express dissatisfaction with the line of reasoning underlying these decisions but felt powerless to change what had become established procedure without an opinion from the Supreme Court. The case was appealed, and the highest tribunal, passing for the first time on the specific question of the validity of former Pilot Rules II and VII (Secs. 80.2 and 80.7), reversed the lower court and held that:

> Under Rules II and VII (Secs. 80.2 and 80.7) . . . when two steamships are on crossing courses, the privileged vessel has no absolute right to keep her course and speed, regardless of danger involved; her right to maintain her privilege ends when there is danger of collision; and in the presence of that danger both vessels must be stopped and backed, if necessary, until signals for passing with safety have been made and understood. . . . These rules should be construed with Art. 27, and are not essentially inconsistent with Arts. 19-23 of the Inland Rules, and are valid.[37]

The case was remanded to the Circuit Court of Appeals, Second Circuit, which reconsidered its former verdict and held both vessels at fault. In its new decision June 3, 1940, the Circuit Court said:

[37] *Postal SS. Corp.* v. *El Isleo (1940) 84 L Ed. 335, reversing (CCA NY 1939) 101 F (2d) 4.*

There can be no doubt that the Supreme Court meant to hold in a crossing case, when the holding-on vessel gets two blasts from the giving way vessel, which are unacceptable to her, she must neither cross the signal, nor keep her speed, but must at least stop her engines, and if necessary back "until signals for passing with safety are made and understood."

This interpretation of the Supreme Court decision evidently indicates a distinctly different course of action in inland waters in future crossing situations. In effect it means that the privileged vessel is deprived of her right and relieved of her duty to hold course and speed the moment there is an unacceptable or disputed signal. But in practice the right referred to has so often proved unenforceable and the duty so difficult that the mariner is, on the whole, much better off under the new requirement. Certainly the former Supervising Inspectors knew what they were about when they formulated the rule. The first paragraph of former Pilot Rule VII (Sec. 80.7) is conclusive evidence that they were not attempting to alter the statutory relation between the vessels of privilege and burden. The duties of both are clearly set forth. The second paragraph, as belatedly interpreted by the Supreme Court, is simply a recognition of what every mariner knows: that when two ships at high speed are on collision courses at their most vulnerable angle of approach, any conflict in the signals provided to ensure a safe passage constitutes ample and positive evidence of immediate danger. With the danger clearly apparent, Section 80.7 of the Pilot Rules offers what is obviously the safest solution of the problem, that is, a prompt and mutual reduction of both vessels to speed zero until an agreement is reached.

Departure from Rules by Agreement

If, as sometimes happens, the privileged vessel offers to yield the right of way by blowing two blasts first, the situation with regard to the burdened vessel is somewhat different. Once the burdened vessel assents to the arrangement by answering with two whistles and the desired agreement is thus established by the interchange of signals, she becomes, in a limited sense, the privileged vessel, though not under the same legal obligation as a privileged vessel to hold her course and speed. In a crossing collision between a tug and a ferryboat in New York Harbor in 1903, where the privileged tug gave two blasts and then failed to go astern of the ferry, the courses being almost at right angles, the Circuit Court of Appeals held that:

An agreement by signal, initiated by the privileged vessel, by which she was to pass under the other's stern, justified the latter in keeping her course and speed.[38]

[38] *The* Edwin J. Berwind *(NY 1906) 144 F 664.*

However, in another crossing collision in the North River, decided fourteen years later, in which the vessels were crossing at a finer angle, the Circuit Court of Appeals held both vessels at fault, involving the burdened vessel for not cooperating with the privileged vessel to avoid collision by also altering course. The court found that:

> When a privileged vessel proposes that the burdened vessel cross her bows and gets an assent to such proposal, she assumes the risk of the proposal . . . the case is one of special circumstances, and the burdened vessel is not rigidly bound to keep her course and speed.[39]

An interesting sidelight on the legal complexities which are introduced when the privileged vessel initiates the two-blast signal, the signal is accepted, and a collision follows, is revealed in the deliberations of the Circuit judges in the case cited:

> It is good law that when the burdened vessel decides to keep out of the way by crossing the bows of the privileged vessel, though she gets an assent to such a proposal, she assumes the risks involved in choosing that method. The duty of the privileged vessel in such cases is to cooperate and she need not keep her course. The situation, at least in this circuit, after the agreement, is one of special circumstances. But such an agreement initiated by the privileged and assented to by the burdened vessel, might be regarded as creating other duties. It could be considered as a proposal that the duties of the vessels should be reversed, and that the burdened (now the privileged) vessel hold her course and speed, so that the privileged (now the burdened) vessel might be able to forecast her positions at future moments precisely as the rule requires when no agreement has been made.
>
> We have been unable to find much in the books that touches on this precise point. In the *Susquehanna*, 35 F 320, the burdened vessel was exonerated because she did not "thwart" the proposal, having apparently kept her course. On the other hand, in the *Columbia*, 29 F 716, Judge Brown thought it a matter of indifference which vessel proposed the change; the burden always remaining upon the vessel originally burdened. In Stetson v. the *Gladiator*, 41 F 927, Judge Nelson said that the exchange justified the burdened vessel in keeping her course.
>
> In none of these cases was the originally burdened vessel held to any duty to keep her course. On the whole we are disposed to think that any agreement to change the usual rules should be treated as creating thereafter a position of special circumstances. If so, we think that, although the proposal emanates from the privileged vessel, and should be taken as meaning that she will undertake actively to keep out of the way, it need not absolve the burdened vessel from her similar and original duty also to keep out of the way, nor will it impose on her a rigid duty to hold her course and speed. It is true that that duty is imposed by the rule generally as a correlative to the duty to keep out of the way, but only in cases where no agreement has been reached. Some convention is essential when neither knows the other's purposes, but where both have agreed upon a maneuver by an exchange of signals their accord should be left for

[39] *The* Newburgh *(NY 1921) 273 F 436.*

execution by movements adapted to the circumstances. For example, if the angle of crossing is wide, it will usually be best for the originally burdened vessel to hold her course and speed; but if it be narrow, it is safest for both to starboard and pass at a greater distance. No doubt the proposal involves the proposer in a duty to give a wide enough margin for safety, even though the assenting vessel does not starboard.

The foregoing discussion shows that even the seasoned admiralty judges of the Circuit Court of Appeals are sometimes compelled to struggle with the intricacies of the law of crossing. If a single useful fact emerges from the involved discussion in this decision, it is that changing the lawful signal by both vessels has the important effect of destroying the right of way of one of them, and making her share with the vessel contemplated by the rules the burden of avoiding collision. This in itself is an excellent argument, in the crossing situation, for sticking to the procedure in practice provided by law.

Two Blasts by Privileged Vessel

From the viewpoint of the privileged vessel, for her to initiate the two-blast signal must appear as a very foolish act. For she is either suggesting that in her opinion the vessel to port already has ample clearance, in which case the signal is superfluous, or else she is giving notice to the burdened vessel that she (the privileged vessel) proposes to waive her privilege and act contrary to the law, in which case, if the other assents by answering with two blasts, she is bound to do her part in carrying out the maneuver. Moreover, she is taking the chance that the burdened vessel may not assent, and until an assent is received she must continue to hold course and speed. As was said in a New York case:

> In order to change a situation of this kind from the situation of a privileged and a burdened vessel to a situation of special circumstances, it is necessary that the burdened vessel should reply with an identical signal and accept the privileged vessel's waiver of the privilege; otherwise the privileged vessel would never know how she should navigate.[40]

In the author's opinion, not only should the privileged vessel scrupulously avoid proposing a two-blast crossing signal but she should be somewhat chary about assenting when it is proposed by the burdened vessel. It would be unwise to lay down an arbitrary rule here, and the individual case must be decided on its merits, remembering that avoidance of collision is always the prime desideratum. The navigator must determine, in the particular instance, which of several actions involves the least risk: (1) agreeing to the proposal with two answering blasts; (2) ignoring the

---

[40] *The Penn. Ry. Co. No. 541 (NY 1934) 7 F Supp 208; also the* Elizabeth, *197 F 160.*

proposal by whistle silence; (3) insisting, by one blast, on obedience to the rules, a procedure formerly upheld by numerous decisions of the circuit courts of appeal but now found by the Supreme Court to be an unlawful violation of Sections 80.2 and 80.7 of the Pilot Rules; (4) promptly reversing, with appropriate danger and three-blast signals, to get the way off, and proceeding only after passing signals are satisfactorily exchanged. This is the procedure approved by the Supreme Court.[41] However, when adopting the first action it should be borne in mind that while a privileged vessel is not in fault, according to the Circuit Court of Appeals, for holding her course even though she fails to receive a response to her first signal of one whistle,[42] if she assents to the crossing of her bows by the other vessel she waives her privilege absolutely.[43] When she assents to this by repeating the two whistles, it is her duty at once to assist the maneuver, a point which the United States Supreme Court, on appeal, declined to review.[44] Finally, a vessel which assents by signal that another shall cross her bows cannot urge the attempted maneuver as a fault, though it results in a collision.[45] These decisions make it evident that even an undisputed acceptance of an irregular proposal carries with it certain risks and that the fourth procedure, compelling both vessels to stop, often has decided merit.

When Crossing Rule Begins to Apply

The navigator is sometimes puzzled to know just how close a vessel approaching from starboard must be to make the law of crossing apply. It will be noted that the same crossing rule[46] is applicable to both inland and outside waters *when vessels are crossing so as to involve risk of collision*. In another part of the rules we are told that risk of collision can, when circumstances permit, be ascertained by carefully watching the compass bearing of an approaching vessel, and that if the bearing does not appreciably change such risk should be deemed to exist. This should not be taken to imply that obtaining a series of bearings of an approaching vessel is an absolute test of risk of collision. It is undoubtedly a valid test to the extent that if the bearings observed are constant, collision will occur if neither vessel changes course or speed, and consequently, vessels

---

[41] *The* Transfer No. 15 *(CCA NY 1906) 145 F 503; Yamashita Kisen Kabushiki (CCA Cal 1927) 20 F (2d) 25; the* Norfolk *(Md 1924) 297 F 251; Postal SS. Corp. v. El* Isleo *(1940) 84 L Ed. 335.*

[42] *The* E. H. Coffin, *Fed. Case No. 4,310.*

[43] *The* Sammie *(NY 1889) 37 F 907; the* Albatross *(1910) 184 F 363.*

[44] *The* Boston *(NY 1922) 258 U.S. 622, 66 L Ed. 796.*

[45] *The* Arthur M. Palmer *(NY 1902) 115 F 417.*

[46] *See footnotes 6 and 10.*

have been held at fault for failure to take such precautionary bearings.[47] But it does not follow that in all cases where the bearing is changing, no risk of collision is involved. As said by the Circuit Court of Appeals:

> This section is not a rule of navigation, but merely a suggestion of one circumstance which denotes that there is danger of collision; and a steamer is not justified in assuming that there is no risk because there is an appreciable change in the compass bearing of the lights of a sailing vessel seen at night, which would manifestly be an unwarranted assumption under some circumstances.[48]

Thus, in the crossing situation, the bearings of a vessel on the starboard bow may be constant, indicating that the two vessels will reach the point of intersection at the same time; they may be drawing ahead, indicating the privileged vessel will reach the point of intersection first; or they may be drawing aft, indicating the burdened vessel will reach that point first. The rapidity of change in bearing depends on the distance apart and the relative speeds of the two vessels. It would be a mistake to assume that only in the first case is there risk of collision. It is true that if the bearings of the privileged vessel draw ahead with a certain degree of rapidity, there is a presumption that she will have clearance across the bow of the burdened vessel; but this does not relieve the latter of her obligation to watch the privileged vessel closely, and to slow down or stop or reverse, if necessary, before coming into dangerous proximity. Conversely, if the bearings of the privileged vessel draw aft with sufficient rapidity, there is a presumption that the burdened vessel might cross with safety; but wide indeed must be the margin in that case before she is legally justified in making the attempt. As a matter of law, it must be wide enough so that no risk of collision is involved; as a matter of practice and of common prudence, it should be wide enough so that no collision can occur no matter what the other vessel does.

This is a sweeping statement, but its validity is established by court decisions in both the United States and in England. As early as 1869 the Supreme Court held:

> Rules of navigation such as have been mentioned (as to the duties of two vessels approaching each other) are obligatory upon such vessels when approaching each other from the time the necessity for precaution begins; and they continue to be applicable as the vessels advance so long as the means and opportunity to avoid the danger remain. They do not apply to a vessel required to keep her course after the approach is so near that collision is inevitable, and are equally inapplicable to vessels of every description while they are yet so distant from each other that measures of precaution have not become necessary to avoid collision.[49]

[47] *The* President Lincoln *(1911) 12 Asp MC 41.*
[48] *Wilders SS. Co. v. Low (Hawaii 1911) 112 F 161.*
[49] *The* Winona *(1873) 19 Wall. 41.*

This decision was referred to by the district court of Michigan in a Great Lakes case a short time later, and amplified in the following unmistakable language:

Risk of collision begins the very moment when the two vessels have approached so near each other and upon such courses that by departure from the rules of navigation, whether from want of good seamanship, accident, mistake, misapprehension of signals, or otherwise, a collision might be brought about. It is true that prima facie each man has a right to assume that the other will obey the law. But this does not justify either in shutting his eyes to what the other may actually do or in omitting to do what he can to avoid an accident made imminent by the acts of the other. I say the right above spoken of is prima facie merely, because it is well known that departure from the law not only may, but does, take place, and often. Risk of collision may be said to begin the moment the two vessels have approached each other so near that a collision might be brought about by any such departure and continues up to the moment when they have so far progressed that no such result can ensue. But independently of this, the idea that there was no risk of collision is fully exploded by the fact that there was a collision.[50]

Similarly, in the case of the *Philadelphia*, the district court said:

The term "risk of collision" has a different meaning from the phrase "immediate danger" and means "chance," "peril," "hazard," or "danger of collision"; and there is risk of collision whenever it is not clearly safe to go on.[51]

Two statements from decisions of Dr. Lushington, famous admiralty jurist of the mid-nineteenth century, will suffice to show the English parallel of this doctrine. In a case of 1851 he said:

This chance of collision is not to be scanned by a point or two. We have held over and over again that if there be a reasonable chance of collision it is quite sufficient.

In another case he said:

The whole evidence shows that it was the duty of the *Colonia*, with the wind free, to have made certain of avoiding the *Susan*. She did not do so, but kept her course till she was at so short a distance of a cable and a half's length (900 feet) in the hope the vessels might pass each other. Now it can never be allowed to a vessel to enter into nice calculations of this kind, which must be attended with some risk, whilst it has the power to adopt, long before the collision, measures which would render it impossible.[52]

It was such an interpretation of the term *risk of collision* which caused the Circuit Court of Appeals to reverse the lower court in a New York Harbor collision between the tug *Ashley* and the tug *Volunteer*. The district court absolved the *Volunteer* on the theory that the starboard hand

[50] *The* Milwaukee *(1871) Fed. Case No. 9,626.*
[51] *The* Philadelphia *(Penn 1912) 199 F 299.*
[52] *Marsden's* Collisions, *11th ed., p. 462.*

rule did not apply to her because it appeared that there was time for her to get across before the courses would intersect; but the Circuit Court of Appeals, in reversing the decision, said:

> The starboard hand rule is intended to avoid just such speculations. When the courses as being steered are crossing courses they involve risk of collision and the burdened vessel is required to keep out of the way and the privileged vessel to hold her course and speed. The account given by the master of the *Volunteer* brings the situation precisely within this article, Arts. 19 and 21.[53]

As clearly pointed out in Chapter 14, *Head to Head*, vessels closing each other in opposite directions in a narrow channel must, local rules apart, keep to the starboard side of the channel, Rule 9(a) and Article 25, even though they might have at first sighting the appearance of a crossing situation. However, in the event of meeting a true crossing vessel, such as a ferry, then in international waters, Rule 15 is effective, though the provisions of Rule 9(d) and any local rules, may confer rights on the vessel following the channel.

No special rights accrue to a vessel lying stopped on the high seas, unless she is in one of the categories of Rule 27. She must keep out of the way of a vessel, with whom risk of collision exists, which approaches from her starboard bow.

Rule 15, the crossing situation on the high seas, is abrogated if one of the two vessels is not under command, restricted in her ability to maneuver, engaged in fishing, or constrained by her draft. Rule 18(a) applies in such circumstances and a vessel that normally would be privileged in a crossing situation is required to keep out of the way. Passing ahead is not ruled out, though an alteration to starboard may prove most prudent. A tow towing is not automatically conferred any rights, unless she shows the shapes or lights authorized by Rule 27(b), but it behooves a privileged vessel to take into account the hampered movements of a tug and tow when contemplating action under Rules 17(a)(ii) or 17(b).

Crossing Rules Equally Binding on Both Vessels

Perhaps in the very nature of the case common sense would permit no other interpretation. For in the final analysis, it is as logical to place an absolute obligation upon one vessel not to cross ahead as upon the other vessel to maintain course and speed. And when a collision occurs because a burdened vessel that thought she had time to get across is hit by a privileged vessel that sheered to the right in an ill-timed attempt to clear her, the courts cannot consistently find that one was under compulsion to hold course and speed if they do not find that the other was equally

---

[53] *The* Ashley *(NY 1915) 221 F 423.*

under compulsion to avoid crossing her bow. In accordance with a very old doctrine when two vessels are at fault, the decision can only be an equal division of damages.

If we exclude all those cases which frequently arise in crowded harbors where the presence of a third, or even other additional vessels, creates special circumstances, modifying the rules, then we may draw a very practical lesson from the foregoing decisions, namely, the manifest danger of crossing a vessel to starboard unless she is so far away that it would be impossible for her to bring about a collision. If she is that far away, the navigator need not worry about proper signals: no crossing signal is either authorized or permitted, for there is no risk of collision.

SUMMARY

In accordance with the theory of privilege and burden the crossing situation requires, both in inland waters and on the high seas, that the vessel having the other to port maintain course and speed, and that the vessel having the other to starboard keep out of the way, avoid crossing ahead, and if necessary slacken speed or stop or reverse. This arrangement creates a serious hazard when, as frequently happens, either vessel fails to do her duty.

On the high seas and in inland waters the privileged vessel is required to maneuver when *in extremis*. Under the International Rules, the privileged vessel *may* maneuver when it becomes apparent to her that the burdened vessel is not taking appropriate action.

In inland waters cross signals or receipt of an unacceptable or improper signal requires both vessels to sound the danger signal and stop. After at least stopping the engines, signals must be exchanged in agreement before proceeding. This action is required under the theory that a dispute of signals in a crossing situation is such positive indication of danger that the injunction of the pilot rule is justified under Article 27, the general prudential rule.

The burdened vessel under International Rules must signal if she alters course or reverses engines, and the same applies (in extremis and in the exercise of Rule 17(a)(ii)) to the privileged vessel. In inland waters, under a Pilot Rule, the privileged vessel should signify her intention to hold course and speed by sounding one short blast in a timely manner, which should be promptly answered by the burdened vessel. Failure of either vessel to sound one short blast does not invoke the requirement to sound the danger signal and stop in inland waters—the more positive indication of a cross signal or improper signal is necessary.

A former Pilot Rule provided a two-blast signal in inland waters by the burdened vessel when she could cross in safety, to be answered, if approved, by the privileged vessel; but this rule was invalidated by the courts as inconsistent with the inland crossing rule. The signal, if used, has only the sanction of custom, therefore, should never be proposed by the privileged vessel, and should be accepted when proposed by the burdened vessel only when the maneuver indicated can be done with a high degree of safety. The effect of such assent is to take the right of way from the privileged vessel without conferring it on the burdened vessel, and thus to put vessels under the rule of special circumstances, with the mutual duty of taking any positive action necessary to avoid collision.

17
The Law in Fog

SUMMARY OF RULES

Despite the concentration of law relating directly to the navigation of vessels in restricted visibility in both the Inland and International Rules and the remarkable advances in recent years in the ability to determine bearings accurately by radar, fog is still a major cause of marine collisions and a prolific source of litigation in admiralty courts arising out of these collisions.

The law in fog deals primarily with three major subjects: sound signals, proper speed, and the approach of other vessels. Rule 35, International Rules, and Article 15, Inland Rules, which prescribe the sound signals to be used, differ in a sufficient number of important details to furnish the usual amount of confusing material to the mariner who is obliged to navigate on both the high seas and inland waters. Similarly, the courts must unscramble the testimony as to what waters the fog-enshrouded vessels were in at the moment of collision, in order to determine which rules to apply.

Rule 6,[1] International Rules, is devoted to giving the mariner factors to

---

[1] *Every vessel shall at all times proceed at a safe speed so that she can take proper and effective action to avoid collision and be stopped within a distance appropriate to the prevailing circumstances and conditions.*

In determining a safe speed the following factors shall be among those taken into account:

    (a) By all vessels:

        (i) the state of visibility;

        (ii) the traffic density including concentrations of fishing vessels or any other vessels;

        (iii) the manoeuvrability of the vessel with special reference to stopping distance and turning ability in the prevailing conditions;

        (iv) at night the presence of background light such as from shore lights or from back scatter of her own lights;

        (v) the state of wind, sea and current, and the proximity of navigational hazards;

take into account in determining a safe speed in any condition of visibility. Article 16, Inland Rules, simply states that for conditions of restricted visibility "every vessel shall . . . go at a moderate speed, having careful regard to the existing circumstances and conditions." A great number of court decisions have defined the term "moderate speed," the major factors taken into account being the distance required to stop and the prevailing visibility.

Rules 5 and 7,[2] International Rules, require a vessel fitted with radar to make proper use of it. While the Inland Rules make no mention of radar, the requirement is as definite in inland waters:

> Dependable radar equipment must be turned on and intelligent and reasonable use made of it.[3]

> Vessel rigging her boom in such a way as to greatly impair effective use of her radar is guilty of gross negligence.[4]

The Inland Rules require a "steam vessel hearing, apparently forward of her beam, the fog signal of a vessel the position of which is not ascer-

---

    (vi) the draught in relation to the available depth of water.
  (b) Additionally, by vessels with operational radar:
    (i) the characteristics, efficiency and limitations of the radar equipment;
    (ii) any constraints imposed by the radar range scale in use;
    (iii) the effect on radar detection of the sea state, weather and other sources of interference;
    (iv) the possibility that small vessels, ice and other floating objects may not be detected by radar at an adequate range;
    (v) the number, location and movement of vessels detected by radar;
    (vi) the more exact assessment of the visibility that may be possible when radar is used to determine the range of vessels or other objects in the vicinity.
  [2]*5. Every vessel shall at all times maintain a proper look-out by sight and hearing as well as by all available means appropriate in the prevailing circumstances and conditions so as to make a full appraisal of the situation and of the risk of collision.*
  7. (a) Every vessel shall use all available means appropriate to the prevailing circumstances and conditions to determine if risk of collision exists. If there is any doubt such risk shall be deemed to exist.
  (b) Proper use shall be made of radar equipment if fitted and operational, including long-range scanning to obtain early warning of risk of collision and radar plotting or equivalent systematic observation of detected objects.
  (c) Assumptions shall not be made on the basis of scanty information, especially scanty radar information.
  (d) In determining if risk of collision exists the following considerations shall be among those taken into account:
    (i) such risk shall be deemed to exist if the compass bearing of an approaching vessel does not appreciably change;
    (ii) such risk may sometimes exist even when an appreciable bearing change is evident, particularly when approaching a very large vessel or a tow or when approaching a vessel at close range.
  [3] *U.S. v. M/V* Wuerttenberg, *(DSC 1963), 219 F Supp 211.*
  [4] *Hess Shipping Corp. v. SS* Charles Lykes, *(DC Ala 1968), 285 F Supp 412.*

tained" to stop her engines. This requirement has been strictly enforced by the courts. Rule 19(e),[5] International Rules, requires the vessel hearing the fog signal to slow to bare steerageway, and relieves her of that requirement where it has been determined (by radar) that a risk of collision does not exist.

The International Rules address the situation where a vessel is detected on radar *before* her fog signal is heard. Rule 19(d)[6] requires the observing vessel to determine if a close-quarters situation is developing and, if so, to take avoiding action in ample time. The courts substitute for the lack of an Inland Rule or Pilot Rule on this point in the following unmistakable language:

> The radar bearing of an approaching vessel which remains fairly constant is indicative of a collision course and requires immediate and radical avoiding action by the observing vessel. . . . When the *Norscot* sighted the *Harrison* on radar, two miles distant, bearing dead ahead, and the *Norscot* was proceeding at a speed of 14 knots, she was already in an emergency situation and her engines should have been backed full, her helm put hard right, and her anchors dropped.[7]

The International Rules apply the requirements to a vessel in fog "navigating in or near an area of restricted visibility." The Inland Rule specifies "fog, mist, falling snow, or heavy rain storms," but the courts will apply the rule to restricted visibility due to any cause, such as smoke.[8] The courts have also required vessels in inland waters to comply with the rules of fog when near a fog bank, even though they are not themselves experiencing the restricted visibility.[9]

When Fog Signals Are Required

When we seek to determine from the cases just when the weather is thick enough to require fog signals to be sounded, we find that a positive defi-

---

[5] *Except where it has been determined that a risk of collision does not exist, every vessel which hears apparently forward of her beam the fog signal of another vessel, or which cannot avoid a close-quarters situation with another vessel forward of her beam, shall reduce her speed to the minimum at which she can be kept on her course. She shall if necessary take all her way off and in any event navigate with extreme caution until danger of collision is over.*

[6] *(d) A vessel which detects by radar alone the presence of another vessel shall determine if a close-quarters situation is developing and/or risk of collision exists. If so, she shall take avoiding action in ample time, provided that when such action consists of an alteration of course, so far as possible the following shall be avoided:*
(i) an alteration of course to port for a vessel forward of the beam, other than for a vessel being overtaken;
(ii) an alteration of course towards a vessel abeam or abaft the beam.

[7] *Norscot Shipping Co. v. SS* President Harrison *(DC Pa 1970), 308 F Supp 1100.*

[8] *The* Gracie, *(DC NY 1900), 106 F 984.*

[9] *The* Papoose, *(CCA NY 1936), 85 F (2d) 54.*

nition is lacking. An early decision ruled that the foghorn must be used by a sailing vessel when there was enough fog to shut out the view of the sails or hull, or at night the lights of a vessel within range of the sound of the horn.[10] Much remains to be defined in this regard, both in inland waters and on the high seas. In the absence of positive court authority, it would be hard to improve upon the very practical suggestion of La Boyteaux that, since the Inland Rules prescribe the minimum visibility of side lights as 2 miles (and these are the only lights shown ahead by a sailing vessel, ordinarily) it is evidently intended that notice of approach shall be given at least at that distance, and that therefore when proper lights cannot be seen by vessels 2 miles apart, fog signals are in order.[11] Such a rule implies the necessity of using the signals not only when actually in a fog, but when steaming toward or near a fog bank which may hide another vessel.

International Rule 35 specifically covers this point by requiring fog signals when navigating near an area of restricted visibility. Again, no definition is given of how poor the visibility should be before signals are sounded. However, the required visibility of sidelights under International Rules (3 miles) and, to a lesser extent, the audibility range of the appliance being used, are useful pointers.

Of particular importance to naval officers is the fact that this rule, like all the other rules, is as binding on ships of the Navy as on commercial vessels. While the old doctrine that the king can do no wrong still applies in many states to damage inflicted on a private vehicle by a speeding fire engine, or police prowl car, the federal government, under special statute, graciously permits itself to be sued in admiralty for damage resulting from the fault of one of its combatant ships. In the eyes of the law, a naval vessel is not excused for damage caused by excessive speed or failure to sound proper signals in fog even in time of war, when the suspected presence of submarines makes both actions imperative. During the Spanish-American War a collision occurred a few miles southeast of Fire Island between the armored cruiser *Columbia*, which was on patrol duty, and a British freight steamer, the latter vessel being sunk. The *Columbia* was making 6 knots in thick fog, and in accordance with the orders of the squadron commander, was running without lights and making no fog signals. The freighter was making 3.5 knots and sounding one blast every minute and a half. In a court action several years later, the cruiser was found solely at fault and liable for the full amount of the loss, one specified point of error being failure to sound the one-blast signal.[12] Again, in a

[10] *Dolner v. the* Monticello *(1870) Fed. Cas. No. 3–971.*
[11] *La Boyteaux, Rules of the Road at Sea, p. 67.*
[12] *Watts v. U.S. (NY 1903) 123 F 105.*

collision in fog in May, 1918, between the Navy collier *Jupiter* and a four-masted schooner at anchor outside Winter Quarter Shoals Lightship, the *Jupiter* was found solely at fault for the same omission, although operating under the following duly authorized naval order:

> During fog, when in areas in which submarines or raiders may be met, vessels when out of the usual track of shipping are not to sound their sirens or whistles unless absolutely necessary.[13]

While these decisions do not mean that it is expected in time of war that our vessels will go about giving due legal notice of their presence to enemy vessels, it does mean that damage to neutral merchantmen which results from any errors of omission or commission must be paid for out of the public treasury. And the decisions certainly add an excellent reason for holding any peace-time maneuvers which may involve temporary nonobservance of the rules with as careful regard to the possible approach of merchant vessels as we now hold target practice, which means a safe distance from any regular commercial track.

Time Intervals Between Signals

The first important difference between the provisions for high seas and for inland waters is in the maximum time interval between signals. Rule 35(a), International Rules, provides:

> A power-driven vessel making way through the water shall sound at intervals of not more than 2 minutes one prolonged blast.

On the other hand, in the Inland Rules and the Pilot Rules the maximum interval is one minute.

When we consider that the purpose of this signal is to give notice to one vessel of the proximity of another, and that such a signal has actual value only when vessels are near each other, the absurdity of changing the requirement as one crosses the line between inland and outside waters is apparent. Presumably, the one-minute interval for steam or other power-driven vessels was established in the Inland Rules on the theory of denser traffic; but from the standpoint of accident prevention, there is, of course, no traffic denser in fog than that which prevails when one vessel approaches another on a collision course. In view of the well-known tendency of shipmasters, however careful they may be in proceeding through inland channels in fog, to speed up as soon as their vessels are clear of the land, it might seem more logical for the shorter interval to apply under International Rules.

However, the 1972 International Conference decided on a standardized

---

[13] *Thurlow v. U.S. (1924) 295 F 905.*

two-minute maximum interval as temporary deafness can be caused by sounding the whistle too frequently. This does not mean signals should not be made at lesser intervals, particularly when other vessels are close, bearing in mind that they might not have operational radar.

The essential objection of the mariner to any such difference in requirement is that it is just one more confusing point to remember. Of course, it should be borne in mind that the foregoing discussion relates only to the maximum interval that may ever lawfully elapse between signals in fog. There are occasions where good seamanship requires signals to be given much oftener. As held in an old case, under an earlier rule requiring a signal every five minutes:

> The requirement of Art. 10 is that the bell shall be sounded at least every five minutes whenever there is a fog. This does not mean that it shall be a sufficient compliance with the law to sound the bell as often as once in five minutes in any fog. It means that it shall not be a sufficient compliance with the law to sound the bell less often than once in five minutes, in any fog.[14]

Similarly, in the case of the schooner *Belle R. Hull*, at anchor in New York in thick fog, that vessel divided damages with the colliding vessel, which was guilty of excessive speed, for not striking her bell oftener than once in two minutes, the maximum interval at that time prescribed in the rules. While the right of vessels to anchor in crowded harbors was upheld, it was said:

> But if they remain there in a dense fog they must exercise the most constant vigilance and activity to make known their position, and if they fail to do this they cannot expect full reparation for damages. Bells must be rung at shorter intervals than two minutes.[15]

In a third case, when a vessel sounding proper fog signals while navigating in Long Island Sound turned into an occupied anchorage, she was found at fault for not increasing the frequency of her whistles to warn vessels already at anchor.[16] And so when vessels are feeling their way past each other in a dense fog, there can be little doubt that legal obligation, as well as good seamanship, may require signals to be given every few seconds until both vessels are past and clear.

Two-blast Signal on High Seas

The second point of difference to remember between Rule 35, International Rules, and Article 15, Inland Rules, is provided in Rule 35(b), International Rules, which reads:

---

[14] *The Chancellor (1870) Fed. Cas. No. 2,589.*
[15] *Brush v. the* Plainfield *(1879) Fed. Cas. No. 2,058.*
[16] *The Quevilly (1918) 253 F 415.*

A power-driven vessel underway, but stopped and making no way through the water, shall sound at intervals of not more than 2 minutes two prolonged blasts in succession with an interval of about 2 seconds between them.

This is omitted in the Inland Rules, there being no distinctive signal in inland waters to indicate that all the way is off a vessel underway. There can be no reasonable doubt that such a signal conveys valuable information to another vessel maneuvering in fog to avoid the steam or other power-driven vessel which is motionless, and this is a strong argument for including it in the Inland Rules. It should be emphasized, however, that the use of the two-prolonged-blast signal in fog is lawful only when all headway has been lost. Great care must be exercised, particularly at night, to ascertain that the vessel is dead in the water before changing from one blast to two; and it is surprising how long some vessels carry way after the engines are stopped. A capital ship making 12 knots has been observed to forge slowly ahead for more than fifteen minutes after ringing a stop bell. The courts are quick to find a vessel guilty when wrongfully using this signal, as evident in the case of the *Ansaldo Savoia*. That vessel, in collision with the American steamer *Ripogenus* in fog at sea off Cape Henry, was found at fault, among other things, for sounding the two-blast signal one minute after stopping her engines, although her original speed was only 4 knots.[17]

Scope of Article 15 (e), Inland Rules

A third point of difference between the rules in force at sea and in inland waters is found in the limited scope of Article 15(e), Inland Rules, which provides:

> A steam vessel when towing, shall, instead of the signals prescribed in subdivision (a) of this article, at intervals of not more than one minute, sound three blasts in succession, namely, one prolonged blast followed by two short blasts. A vessel towed may give this signal and she shall not give any other.

The equivalent subsections of Rule 35, International Rules, provide:

> (c) A vessel not under command, a vessel restricted in her ability to manoeuvre, a vessel constrained by her draught, a sailing vessel, a vessel engaged in fishing and a vessel engaged in towing or pushing another vessel shall, instead of the signals prescribed in paragraphs (a) or (b) of this Rule, sound at intervals of not more than 2 minutes three blasts in succession, namely one prolonged followed by two short blasts.
> (d) A vessel towed or if more than one vessel is towed the last vessel of the tow, if manned, shall at intervals of not more than 2 minutes sound four blasts in succession, namely one prolonged followed by three short blasts. When practicable, this signal shall be made immediately after the signal made by the towing vessel.

[17] *The* Ansaldo Savoia *(1921) 276 F 719.*

(e) When a pushing vessel and a vessel being pushed ahead are rigidly connected in a composite unit they shall be regarded as a power-driven vessel and shall give the signals prescribed in paragraphs (a) or (b) of this Rule.

It will be noted that the Inland Rule, which applies to steam or other power-driven vessels only, is defective in providing no special signal for a vessel not under command—and in a sense, a cable ship at work or a vessel working on a navigation mark or a vessel engaged in fishing is one form of that. The Pilot Rules being equally deficient on this point, such a vessel in inland waters must sound only the one-prolonged-blast signal given in Article 15 (a). Under the International Rule, however, vessels disabled or at work on a telegraph cable or a navigation mark or engaged in fishing, so long as they are wrapped in a veil of fog, are put in the same category as a tug hampered by a tow, with the obvious purpose of causing ordinary vessels to approach them with greater caution and to give them as wide a berth as circumstances permit. A nice question is raised in the case of a vessel at sea which becomes temporarily disabled while making headway in fog as, for example, a destroyer which suddenly loses suction. She becomes for the time being, in as much as circumstances might ensue which would necessitate reversing her engines, a vessel unable to maneuver as required by the Rules, and therefore clearly under the necessity of changing her signal immediately to one prolonged and two short blasts. If she is making 12 knots at the time, she will probably hold some headway for at least ten minutes; when all headway is lost, she does not change her status to a power-driven vessel underway but stopped, with no way upon her, and find herself under the two-prolonged-blast requirement of Rule 35(b). Rule 35(c) is specifically expressed as a substitute for Rule 35(a) and (b). A steam or other power-driven vessel which is both stopped and broken down is recognized as being in a different position from that of one which is merely stopped and able, by a sudden kick ahead or astern, to assist an approaching vessel that looms up in the fog to avoid her.

Understandably, fog signals for vessels being towed are fundamentally optional under both the Inland and International Rules in view of their generally being unmanned. However, it does seem that Article 15 (e) is lacking further in that it does not differentiate between a vessel being towed and one that is towing as does International Rule 35(d), which requires the one-prolonged, three-short signal by the last vessel of a tow, if manned.

Sailing vessels underway on the high seas now give the same signal for hampered vessels found in International Rule 35(c). With the revised requirements for sound signal appliances it was considered that the previous one, two, or three blasts might be confused with maneuvering signals and anyway were of limited value to other vessels. The Inland Rules retain the use of blasts of unspecified length on a foghorn for indicating how a vessel is sailing in relation to the wind.

Danger Signal in Inland Waters

A fourth point of difference peculiar to inland waters is the necessity, under certain conditions, of sounding the Inland danger signal notwithstanding that the fog may be so thick as to prevent either vessel from seeing the other. The average mariner regards the four or more short-blast alarm as a clear weather signal only, and it is surprising that he is misled on this point by Article 18, Rule IX, which provides:

> The whistle signals provided in the rules under this article, for steam vessels meeting, passing, or overtaking, are never to be used except when steamers are in sight of each other, and the course and position of each can be determined in the daytime by a sight of the vessel itself, or by night by seeing its signal lights. In fog, mist, falling snow, or heavy rainstorms, when vessels cannot see each other, fog signals only must be given.

There can be no doubt that this rule excludes the use of one-, two-, and three-short-blast signals as long as the vessels are not in sight of each other. However, as was said in a case of collision at night in Puget Sound, when the lights of one vessel were obscured by a deck load of lumber, and the other vessel argued that, although she heard a whistle somewhere ahead, she could see no lights and was therefore not called upon to give the danger signal:

> Art. 18 Rule IX applies only to the meeting, passing, or overtaking signals specified and does not relieve a vessel of the duty to give alarm signals as required by Rule 3, where from any cause she cannot understand the course or intention of an approaching vessel, although it may be because neither the approaching vessel nor her lights can be seen.[18]

In another Puget Sound case, the *Celtic Monarch*, that vessel was in tow of the tug *Sea Lion*, which collided in thick fog with the passenger steamer *Mainlander* off West Point, sinking the last-named vessel, and both the *Sea Lion* and the *Mainlander* were held at fault for excessive speed and for not sounding the danger signal when fog signals indicated they were rapidly approaching each other but neither could make out the other or her course because of the fog.[19]

At sea, substantially the same signal is an optional identity signal given by pilot vessels on pilotage duty pursuant to Rule 35(i), International Rules, which states:

> A pilot vessel when engaged on pilotage duty may, in addition to the signals

[18] *The* Virginian *(1916) 238 F 156.*
[19] *The* Celtic Monarch *(1910) 175 F 1006.*

prescribed in paragraphs (a), (b) or (f) of this rule, sound an identity signal consisting of four short blasts.

Its main effect, insofar as the United States is concerned, is to create another strong reason for mariners to seek uniformity in the rules of the road.

Alternately, the international danger signal cannot be used where vessels cannot see each other visually.

Anchored Vessels

Another important point of difference between the rules in force at sea and in inland waters is found in Rule 35(f), International Rules, which provides:

> A vessel at anchor shall at intervals of not more than one minute ring the bell rapidly for about 5 seconds. In a vessel of 100 metres or more in length the bell shall be sounded in the forepart of the vessel and immediately after the ringing of the bell the gong shall be sounded rapidly for about 5 seconds in the after part of the vessel.. A vessel at anchor may in addition sound three blasts in succession, namely one short, one prolonged and one short blast, to give warning of her position and of the possibility of collision to an approaching vessel.

The Inland Rule, Article 15 (d) which is partially restated in Section 80.12 of the Pilot Rules for Inland Waters, is a partial application of the first sentence of the International Rule, reading as follows:

> A vessel when at anchor shall, at intervals of not more than one minute, ring the bell rapidly for about five seconds, except that the following vessels shall not be required to sound this signal when anchored in a special anchorage area established pursuant to paragraph (c) of article 11:
> (1) a vessel of not more than sixty-five feet in length; and
> (2) a barge, canal boat, scow, or other nondescript craft.

The difference was brought about by the 1948 revision of the International Rule which introduced the gong and warning signals, and the Act of August 5, 1963, otherwise citable as Public Law 84, 88th Congress, which amended Article 15 (d) to exempt listed vessels. Prior to that time the rules were identical. In the absence of uniformity, the reader can anticipate the strictness with which the courts will hold a vessel to the requirements of the respective rules.

The usual anchorage found in a harbor or designated as such on a chart is rarely a special anchorage area within the meaning of the Inland Rules. To be a *special anchorage area* as meant here the anchorage must be one that is so-designated by the Secretary of the Army, so-described on a chart, and properly published in Title 33, Code of Federal Regulations.

A number of court decisions applicable to vessels at anchor are of particular interest to the naval service. In the first place, the mere assignment of berths to naval ships by local harbor authorities does not excuse the nonobservance of anchor signals unless no other vessels are permitted in the vicinity. As long ago as 1895, it was held that a steam vessel underway in fog must meet whistle requirements in all waters that it does not have the exclusive right to occupy and in which other vessels may be met,[20] and there can be no doubt as to the application of the same interpretation to signals at anchor. Moreover, the law definitely requires the fog signal to be given by every vessel in a flotilla, as in a nest of destroyers or submarines alongside a tender at anchor. So strict is the interpretation of this that in the case of the *Cohocton* the fact that each of three barges anchored in a group in anchorage grounds in New York Harbor sounded its bell in rotation so that there was one bell every minute was held not to be a compliance with the rule.[21] In another New York case, where a steamship collided with one of several barges alongside a properly moored stake boat, it was held that each vessel in a group moored to a stake boat in anchorage grounds in a fog is required to comply with the rules. In denying the claim of the libelants that the stake boat, which was next to the barge that was struck, was sounding proper signals, the court said:

> This claim cannot be sustained because the larger the flotilla the greater the necessity for each boat to give the signal in order to notify any approaching vessel of the number of boats to be avoided, lest by but one boat giving the signal the approaching vessel be misled and in avoiding one come in contact with another.[22]

While one can readily imagine the pandemonium that would result from a strict observance of this requirement on a foggy night in such a harbor as San Diego, it must be recognized that in the event of collision with a merchant vessel the government must pay the usual penalty of any nonobservance, local custom notwithstanding.

Some ambiguities exist in the International Rules for the fog signal of a vessel at anchor that is engaged in fishing, laying or picking up a submarine cable, or engaged in underwater operations. Rule 35(c) is not explicit as to whether such vessels should sound the signals contained therein or the anchor signals in Rule 35(f). It is considered that the vessels engaged in these activities while at anchor would probably be justified in sounding the whistle signals of Rule 35(c) to warn other vessels of her activities and thus to keep well clear.

[20] *The* Princeton *(1895) 67 F 557.*
[21] *The* Cohocton *(1924) 299 F 319.*
[22] *The* Southway *(1924) 2 F (2d) 1009.*

Vessel Aground in Fog

While Rule 35(g), International Rules, requires a vessel aground in fog at sea to give the bell signal and, if required, the gong signal of a vessel at anchor and, in addition, three separate and distinct strokes on the bell immediately before and after such rapid ringing of the bell, the Inland and Pilot Rules are silent in this regard, and we must turn to the courts for guidance. In so doing, we find that although a vessel aground in a fairway has been held, under Inland Rules, to be a vessel at anchor so far as proper lights are concerned, she is apparently *not* a vessel at anchor in regard to fog signals. In the case of the steam lighter *Leviathan*, aground in Cape Cod Canal in thick fog, the court held that while some notice should be given an approaching vessel whose fog signals were heard, the signal of ringing a bell provided in Article 15 (d), Inland Rules, should not be used, as it would tend to confuse the approaching vessel and perhaps cause her to attempt a passage on the shore side of what she would take to be an anchored vessel; and that danger signals were proper.[23] Distress signals are also proper if the vessel actually requires assistance. In numerous cases it has been held that a vessel moored to a pier need not sound fog signals provided she does not project outside her slip, although a tug which made fast to the end of a pier in New York and allowed her tow of eight scows to swing out 200 or 300 feet into the stream without making fog signals was quite properly found at fault when a fire boat answering an alarm collided with one of the scows.[24]

Differences in Fog Unjustifiable

In previous discussions in these pages,[25] emphasis has been given to the needless complexity introduced into the practice of lawful navigation by conflicting sound signals in the different sets of rules. The objections to different requirements in inside and outside waters are especially significant when we consider the manifest difficulty of determining exactly when a vessel passes from the jurisdiction of International Rules to that of Inland and Pilot Rules, or vice versa, under conditions of dense fog. Take, for example, the dividing line in Juan de Fuca Strait, which extends from Angeles Point on the southern shore 23½ miles to Hein Bank Lighted Bell Buoy in the middle of the strait, so far out that it is usually invisible from the regular track of vessels under the finest conditions of visibility. The difficulty of determining the instant of crossing this line is sufficiently great in clear weather; in fog, it is a virtual impossibility. There was recently

[23] *The* Leviathan *(1922) 286 F 745.*
[24] *New York, O., and Western Ry. Co. v. Cornell Steamboat Co. (1911) 193 F 380.*
[25] *Chapter 13.*

a case of minor collision in these waters in which both vessels were inside the dividing line and the liability of one of them was said to have hinged on the fact that, after stopping her engines and losing all way, she sounded the two-pronged-blast signal required under International Rules. Even in narrow entrances, as when rounding Point Loma or the San Pedro breakwater, the line in the latter case being an extension of the breakwater itself, it is not easy, in foggy weather, to establish with certainty the instant of change from one body of rules to the other; and we do not attempt to answer the question of what is proper when one vessel is on one side of the line and the other vessel is on the opposite side. The mariner who thinks that the exact location of his vessel is of minor importance in a collision might read with profit the northwestern case in which, a few miles northward of Hein Bank where the line extends from Kellet Bluff to Turn Point, both navigators acted under the conviction that they were in inland waters, but the court concluded from the evidence and the diagrams constructed therefrom that they were in fact 100 yards west of the line in Canadian waters and subject to International Rules.[26]

Moderate Speed

Rule 19, International Rules, requires vessels in restricted visibility to proceed at a "safe" speed. Article 16, Inland Rules, requires a "moderate" speed.

What constitutes moderate speed, having careful regard to the existing circumstances and conditions, has had a wide variety of construction by the courts, all of which may be characterized as much less liberal than the interpretation put on the term in practice by the most careful naval and commercial navigators. The original reference to existing circumstances and conditions may have intended to leave some discretion on this point to the mariner; but certainly very little discretion has been left by more than seventy years of court decisions.

Two decisions of the United States Supreme Court many years ago established what may perhaps be termed the general rules of moderate speed. In the *Martello*, which vessel was in collision outside New York Harbor while making 6 knots in a fog so dense the visibility was less than half a mile, moderate speed was defined as bare steerageway, which was found in her case to be 3 knots.[27] Three years later, in the *Umbria*, a case in which the fog was intermittent, the Supreme Court said:

The general consensus of opinion in this country is to the effect that a

[26] *Border Line Transportation Co. v. Canadian Pacific Ry. Co. (Wash 1919) 262 F 989.*

[27] *The Martello (1894) 153 U.S. 64.*

steamer is bound to use only such precautions as will enable her to stop in time to avoid a collision, after the approaching vessel comes in sight, provided such approaching vessel is herself going at the moderate speed required by law.[28]

This second definition of moderate speed implies the right to navigate a particular vessel only at such speed as will enable her to stop in half the distance of visibility then existing. The navigator who finds himself in court after a collision must therefore, in order to justify the speed he was making, be able to testify with some accuracy the distance required at that speed to take all the way off his vessel.

It is apparent that the two definitions just quoted must at times approach inconsistency; that is, there are conditions when to maintain even steerageway, a speed is necessary which would make it impossible to stop in time after first sighting an approaching vessel, or even an anchored vessel. In inland waters in such cases, in order to obey the law it is sometimes necessary to come to anchor. In the *Southway*, already cited, the steamship was held at fault for collision in New York Harbor because she did not anchor when the fog became so dense that it was impossible to see ahead any distance. In another case, a vessel attempting to put to sea in thick weather, which was obliged by the density of the fog to anchor in the fairway, was held in fault for a collision with a passing vessel on the grounds that she should not have left her dock under the existing weather conditions.[29] And in a later case a steamship which was caught underway in a thick fog and allowed herself to drift near busy ferry slips for twenty minutes was liable because she did not move to anchorage grounds.[30] In one of the older cases, the Circuit Court of Appeals held that a steamer passing through a narrow, much-used channel in a dense fog must slow down to such a speed as is consistent with the safety of other vessels navigating the channel; and if such speed does not afford sufficient steerageway, it is her duty to come to anchor.[31] More recently, the Circuit Court has ruled that both a fire boat responding to an alarm[32] and a ferryboat may lawfully leave their piers and navigate in fog, although obliged to exercise reasonable care and to have due regard for the rights of other vessels.[33] The consensus seems to be that unless there is an unusual reason for a vessel to start out or continue to navigate in crowded waters in thick fog, she should not thus imperil herself and other vessels.

Moderate speed is a relative term. It cannot be defined so as to apply

---

[28] *The Umbria (1897) 166 U.S. 404.*

[29] *The Georgia (1913) 208 F 635.*

[30] *The Lambs (1926) 17 F (2d) 1010 affirming 14 F (2d) 444.*

[31] *The H. F. Dimock (1896) 77 F 226.*

[32] *New York, O. and W. Ry. Co. v. Cornell Steamboat Co. (1911) 193 F 380.*

[33] *N.Y. Cent. Ry. Co. v. City of New York (1927) 19 F (2d) 294.*

to all cases; it depends on the circumstances of each case. As a general rule speed that is such that another vessel cannot be seen in time to avoid her is unlawful.[34]

Speed that is justifiable in open waters may well be unlawful in restricted waters where more traffic can be expected. What is a moderate or safe speed for one vessel may not be for a different vessel in the same circumstances. The maneuvering characteristics, particularly the rapidity of response from the engines, must be taken into account. A ship's ability to take way off is relevant in considering her speed in fog. "It would be absurd, to take an extreme case, to suggest that a speed of ten knots in a destroyer would be as excessive as ten knots on an old collier."[35] However, not too much weight must be given to this factor, "But . . . it is not enough to say that because a vessel has remarkable pulling-up power she is therefore justified in proceeding at high speed in fog. Regard must be had to the chance other ships have of receiving her fog signals. If two vessels are approaching each other at very high speed, it must be quite obvious that their chances of hearing each other's fog signals are very much reduced."[36]

The object of Inland Rule 16 and International Rule 19(b) and (c) is not merely that ships should proceed at a speed that lessens the likelihood of collision. It is also that they should go at a speed which will give them sufficient time to hear fog signals, indeed at a speed which enables them to listen effectively for signals, as well as a speed that gives as much time as practicable to avoid another vessel that suddenly comes into view at close range.

This speed cannot be stated definitely in terms of knots. As said earlier it depends on the circumstances of each case. The list of considerations in International Rule 6 provides a valuable check-off list of points the courts have considered over the years. To this list might be added that the noise of the engines at different speeds should be taken into account, and the effect of excessive funnel smoke from a ship or her tugs that obscures her lights or the visibility from her deck.[37]

Excessive Speed

Any speed which is not moderate within the judicial construction of the word is excessive; and an examination of the reported cases reveals the interesting fact that vessels colliding in fog have, in an extremely wide range of existing circumstances, been convicted of excessive speed for

[34] *The* City of Brooklyn *(1876) 1 P.O. 276.*
[35] *The Munster (1939) 63 L1. L.Rep. 165.*
[36] *The Arnold Bratt (1955) 1 L.R. 16, 24.*
[37] *The Delius (1954) 1 L.R. 307.*

making every rate of speed from 3 to 18 knots, the first named being a case of striking a vessel at anchor. On the other hand, also in a wide variety of visibility and traffic conditions, speed ranging from 3.5 to a half speed of 7 knots have been specifically approved as moderate, the last named being an instance in a snowstorm at night, with lights visible from a third to a half mile.[38] It is perhaps significant that this is the highest speed ever to receive final court approval in a collision case in thick weather. While it does not follow that all ships of the Navy traveling at higher speeds in fog are *ipso facto* guilty of violating the law, considering the enormous backing power which most of them have in comparison with merchant vessels of like tonnage, yet it might be a common-sense legal precaution for a commanding officer to have on the bridge an approximate deceleration table at various speeds for his vessel, and to set his speed with some reference to the prevailing visibility. An officer who has positive knowledge on this point is in a far better position to defend his vessel on the witness stand than one who can be heckled by the attorney for the other side because he does not know how quickly his ship could be stopped.

With vessels held to the speed requirement described, there is, of course, a double burden of proof put on the luckless ship that collides with a vessel at anchor. Inasmuch as she is supposed to be able to stop in half the visibility, and in the nature of the case has collided after using all of it, she is practically self-convicted of excessive speed. As pointed out in a case where a steamship on known anchorage grounds collided with an anchored schooner on the Delaware:

> The presumption, where a moving vessel comes into collision with one at anchor in a fog, and where there is no evidence of negligence on the part of the anchored vessel, is, by the well-established rule, against the moving vessel.[39]

And so it has repeatedly been held in collisions with one craft at anchor that a vessel navigating in fog must go no faster than will permit her to stop within the distance she can see ahead.[40] In the case of the *Cohocton*, cited previously, the tug *Franks* was found by the Circuit Court of Appeals equally at fault when making 3 knots through anchorage grounds, this speed being proved excessive by the mere fact that she could not stop in time to avoid striking the anchored barge *Cohocton;* moreover, she could not be exonerated on the ground that the *Cohocton* was herself at fault for not ringing the lawful bell.[41] As was the usual custom in cases of mutual fault:

[38] *The* Allianca *(1889) 39 F 476.*
[39] *The* Cananova *(1923) 297 F 658.*
[40] *The* Haven *(1921) 277 F 957.*
[41] *The* Cohocton *(1923) 299 F 319.*

Damages from collision between vessels both at fault must be equally divided, irrespective of degree of fault.[42]

Not only must the precautions as to speed be observed when actually surrounded by fog, but also, like fog-signal requirements, at any time when in dangerous proximity to a fog bank. A steamship was found negligent for failure to discover a fog bank ahead and to moderate her speed before entering it.[43] The Supreme Court held a tug at fault for a collision occurring shortly after she emerged from a bank of thick fog concealing her, because she did not moderate her speed.[44] These decisions are simply the application of the general rule to special circumstances, but they leave no doubt as to the attitude of the courts.

Many have been the excuses offered by mariners for excessive speed in collision cases, and scant indeed has been their judicial consideration. Some of the arguments tried and found wanting were: (1) that full speed was the safest speed, as it enabled the vessel to get through the fog sooner; (2) that the speed was customary for liners; (3) that the vessel was a passenger steamer and obliged to maintain schedule; (4) that the vessel was carrying passengers to whom it was important to get into port; (5) that the vessel was under contract to carry United States mail; (6) that in the opinion of her officers the vessel could not be properly controlled at a lower speed; (7) that the slowest speed of the engines would not drive the vessel at the moderate speed demanded; (8) that the other vessel was more seriously at fault; (9) that the vessel was a ferry; (10) that the regular speed, or at least a speed faster than that allowed, was necessary to keep track of the vessel's position. The judges have listened to these excuses and many more, and have then decided the cases on the coldly practical and unanswerable basis as stated by the Circuit Court of Appeals:

Speed in a fog is always excessive in a vessel that cannot reverse her engines and come to a standstill before she collides with a vessel that she ought to have seen, having regard to fog density.[45]

As a final remark on moderate speed as interpreted by the courts after decisions have been piling up precedent for many years, it will not unduly encourage the mariner who continues to maintain too much speed in fog, perhaps on the hopeful theory that sooner or later public sentiment in favor of more speed will cause the courts somewhat to relax the requirements, to know that the tendency of all the latest decisions is rather towards, than away from, an insistence on speed zero.

[42] The Marian (1933) 66 F (2d) 354.
[43] The Munalbro (1922) 280 F 224.
[44] The William H. Taylor (1922) 258 U.S. 629.
[45] The John F. Bresnahan (1933) 62 F (2d) 1077.

The four decisions which follow show a surprising lack of sympathy for those who navigate at any speed which makes collision possible. A tug was found at fault by the Circuit Court of Appeals for (1) leaving her basin in New York, and (2) navigating at such speed in the harbor as could not be arrested within seeing distance where visibility was fifty feet.[46] The ability to stop within seeing distance as a standard of speed in fog was held to apply to a ferryboat, which was at fault for making 5.5 knots, as well as to other craft.[47] A vessel was held not to be proceeding at moderate speed in fog if she could not be stopped dead in the water in one-half the visibility before her.[48]

Pressure to "catch the tide" or otherwise maintain their schedule sometimes makes masters reluctant to come to a safe moderate speed in poor visibility. The owners and operating authorities have a responsibility in ensuring they exert no such pressure on the master. In a recent case, where a ship underway struck another at anchor and the owners sought to limit their liability, it was held that the owners were guilty of actual fault because their ship had proceeded at excessive speed in fog. It came out in evidence that the master had habitually navigated his vessel in fog at excessive speed over several voyages, and that the marine superintendent, to whom the ship's logs were regularly submitted, failed to check the records, which would have revealed this fact, and thus failed to bring it to the master's attention. Consequently, the owners were unable to limit their liability and the master's certificate was suspended. "Excessive speed in fog is a grave breach of duty, and shipowners should use all their influence to prevent it."[49]

Vessels Must Stop Engines on Hearing Fog Signal Ahead in Inland Waters

While there may still be some iota of discretion left to the seaman on the bridge by the landsman on the bench in regard to moderate speed, at least there is no discretion as to the primary action required in inland waters by the second paragraph of Article 16, either in the law itself or in the decisions enforcing it. That action is for a steam or other power-driven vessel hearing a fog signal ahead to stop her engines, and unless such a proceeding would involve certain and immediate peril, there is no exception to the requirement. As said by the Supreme Court in the case of the *Beaver* and the *Selja*, where the *Selja* slowed to bare steerageway eleven minutes before a collision on the high seas and was held equally

---

[46] *The* John F. Bresnahan *(1933) 62 F (2d) 1077.*
[47] *The* Providence *(1933) 3 F Supp 461.*
[48] *The* Silver Palm *(CCA Calif. 1938) 82 L Ed. 1539.*
[49] *The* Lady Gwendolen *(1965) 1 L.R. 335.*

at fault with the *Beaver* because she did not stop at the first sound of the latter's whistle:

> A steamship which violates this article requiring her to stop her engines on hearing the fog signal of another vessel ahead, can only avoid liability for a following collision by showing that the fault could not have contributed to the collision.[50]

So in a collision on the Atlantic coast between the USS *Conner* and the *Esperanza*, both vessels were held by the Circuit Court of Appeals for failure to stop their engines in accordance with the rule, and the Supreme Court refused to pass further on the matter.[51] The necessity of stopping the engines, though not, ordinarily, the ship, arises not only when there is certainty that the other vessel's signal is forward of the beam, but in all doubtful cases; moreover, except when the apparent imminence of danger makes reversing necessary, the engines should be kept stopped until repeated signals enable the position and course of the other vessel to be known.[52]

Vessel Must Slow to Bare Steerageway under International Rules

The most recent change of the International Rules did away with the requirement to stop engines upon hearing a fog signal. The rules now require that a vessel be slowed to bare steerageway and, if necessary, take all her way off.

A power-driven vessel is required by Rule 19(b) to have her engines ready for immediate maneuver in restricted visibility. This applies in open as well as restricted waters governed by the International Rules. Because it can take some time to round up the necessary personnel and prepare the engines for instant use, forehandedness should be shown in giving the engineers as much warning as possible.

International Rule 19(c) firmly links Section III—conduct of Vessels in Restricted Visibility—with the rules contained in Section I of Part B, namely the conduct of vessels in any condition of visibility. Apart from the safe speed of Rule 6, previously discussed, this injunction particularly applies to Rule 5 (lookout), Rule 7 (risk of collision) and Rule 8 (avoiding action). In addition, the rules for narrow channels and traffic separation schemes apply in all conditions of visibility.

Action to reduce speed to bare steerageway or if necessary to stop the engines, should be initiated, if not already done at longer range, whenever a fog signal is heard apparently forward of the beam. The person in charge

---

[50] *Lie v. San Francisco and Portland SS. Co. (1917) 243 U.S. 291; 61 L Ed. 726.*
[51] *New York and Cuba Mail SS. Co. v. U.S. (CAA NY 1927) 16 F (2d) 945.*
[52] *The* Tillicum *(1916) 230 F 415.*

of a vessel should not delay such action until he himself hears it, but must act on the report of his lookouts.

> I see no excuse for the failure of the master and pilot to act upon the report made to them by the third officer, when he informed them that he had heard the whistle of a vessel ahead. It seems to me that it is no excuse on the part of either pilot or master to say he did not hear it himself. If the officer of the watch, or the lookout, or anybody else, reports the hearing of a whistle from a vessel forward of the beam, it seems to me the imperative duty under Article 16 (1948 Rules) comes into force at once.[53]

International Rule 19(e) requires that "if necessary" a vessel shall take all her way off. The hearing of a fog signal close aboard for the first time, particularly if dead ahead, or the sighting of a vessel of uncertain course looming out of the fog are examples when such action is urgently necessary, particularly if radar is not fitted or operational. The hearing of a higher-frequency whistle fitted to vessels less than 75 meters in length or the alternative efficient sound signal allowed to vessels of less than 12 meters in length, may well be an occasion for immediately backing engines, as such signals have theoretically low audibility ranges.

Also, the detection of the fog signal of an anchored vessel, towards which the tidal current is setting, could well merit reversal of engines.

However, discretion should be used in putting the engines in the astern mode unnecessarily.

> . . . one of the reasons why the Regulations require the stopping of the engines in fog, when a signal is heard from another ship, is so as to enable further signals to be heard the better. It appears . . . that when there is any question of listening for signals one is creating the worst possible conditions for hearing them by working the engines at full speed astern.[54]

In addition, going astern may cause the ship's head to fall off and present her beam to a vessel approaching from ahead. By keeping the bow end-on, or nearly so, to such a vessel a smaller target is presented which may assist avoiding action by the other vessel as well as taking any impact forward of the collision bulkhead.

La Boyteaux's Rules

In La Boyteaux's excellent discussion of the moderate-speed rule, published years ago, the author points out that because the fog signal is faint or may sound a long way off does not excuse failure to stop engines the instant the signal is heard (now applying only to inland waters); that since the rule is meant for vessels presumed to be proceeding at moderate speed, there is probably an additional obligation to check headway by

[53] The Chusan (1955) 2 L.R. 685, 693.
[54] The Monarch (1953) 2 L.R. 151.

reversing if a vessel going at excessive speed hears such a signal; that the position of the vessel ahead is not ascertained to the extent that a stop bell is unnecessary unless its bearing, distance, and course are all known; and that "so far as the circumstances admit" may be invoked as an excuse for not stopping only where some immediate peril other than the approaching vessel actually threatens, such as swirls or swift currents near reefs and rocks.[55] Neither the desire to hasten the voyage nor the fear of losing track of the vessel's position is accepted as the slightest excuse for ignoring the requirement. As said in the *Automatic:*

> A vessel in a fog, hearing a whistle forward of its beam, must stop as soon as it safely can, and ascertain the position of the other vessel.[56]

And in the *Munrio,*

> The duty of a steamer to stop her engines on hearing the fog signal of a vessel ahead is absolute.[57]

Vessels Must Navigate with Caution

"And then navigate with caution," concludes the moderate-speed rule, "until danger of collision is over." There is subtle irony in these closing words to the navigator, already chafing with impatience at his reduced speed and enforced stops, who pushes on too eagerly with his voyage. For the hardest thing to prove to any court after a collision has occurred is that danger of collision was over. It behooves even that exceptional mariner who has conformed to the law up to this point to practice the most scrupulous care in feeling his way past the other vessel. An occasional kick ahead, enough to keep his vessel on her course, with a substantial change in that course only when justified with reasonable certainty by the direction of the other's signals, and with a prompt and vigorous reversal if the latter seem to narrow on the bow, is the action most likely to prevent collision and to win court approval if the inevitable happens.

The courts have held that the obligation to navigate with caution after stopping the engines implies certain very definite additional duties to ensure avoidance of collision. If the speed is immoderate and the other vessel is in apparent proximity, there is an obligation not merely to stop the engines but to reverse full speed until the headway is reduced to a point where the vessel can be stopped dead after sighting the approaching vessel before striking her.[58] While the Supreme Court has said that there is no rigid

---

[55] *La Boyteaux,* Rules of the Road at Sea.

[56] *The* Automatic *(1924) 298 F 607.*

[57] *The* Munrio *(1926) 11 F (2d) 900.*

[58] *The* City of Atlanta *(NY 1886) 26 F 456; the* Wyanoke *(NY 1889) 40 F 702; the* Britannic *(NY 1889) 39 F 395.*

rule requiring a vessel approaching another in fog to hold course until the signals of the other give a clear indication of her direction, and that each case must depend on its own circumstances (which may afford reasonable ground for believing what the direction may be[59]) nevertheless a change in course must not be made blindly and will never be justified when followed by collision unless the vessel making it reversed her engines at the same time to get her way off. In other words we may not speculate on the direction of the other vessel from her signals, alter course in the expectation of dodging her, continue on our way into collision, and then escape liability for the well-intentioned change of course. The vagaries of sound are too uncertain to justify the go-ahead-and-dodge method of avoiding collision in fog. Where a vessel proceeding at moderate speed heard a signal ahead apparently near, steered away from the sound in an effort to escape, but immediately stopped and reversed full speed, she was held to have done everything possible to avoid collision, and was exonerated even though her officers had erred five points in locating the direction of the other vessel's whistle.[60] The conclusion to be drawn from all these decisions is not to make any change in course without an accurate radar plot or before sighting the other vessel or her lights, unless at the same time bringing the headway absolutely under control.

Whether in inland waters or on the high seas, it should be remembered that three short blasts must accompany any reversal of the engines if the other vessel is sighted; otherwise the signal must not be used. In inland waters *only*, navigating with caution includes sounding the danger signal if there seems to be imminent danger of collision, whether the other vessel is sighted or not. And a final rule to remember about navigating with caution is that as long as fog conceals two vessels from each other, neither vessel has the right of way,[61] but after they are clearly in sight the regular rules govern.

Rules in Fog Are for Safety and Should Be Obeyed

The writer is aware that many mariners who read this chapter will render an immediate verdict that with the law in fog as herein described, implicit observance is impossible if voyages are to be carried out as scheduled. Commercial shipmasters will argue that if they stop their engines every time they hear a fog signal ahead all the way from San Francisco to Seattle, for instance, and then proceed each time at bare steerageway until the other vessel is past and clear, they will never reach their destination, even if they "hook her on" between times. It is, of course, self-evident that in

---

[59] *The* Umbria *(NY 1897) 41 L Ed. 1053.*
[60] *The* Lepanto *(NY 1884) 21 F 651.*
[61] *The* D. S. Gregory *(1879) Fed. Cas. No. 4,103.*

foggy weather obedience to the law will occasion some delay, although the amount of that delay is undoubtedly exaggerated in the minds of most navigators. Many have a mistaken form of professional pride in getting their ships in on time regardless of weather conditions, and are influenced also by the fear that their owners will not accept fog as an excuse for any considerable prolongation of the voyage. In some cases this fear is by no means groundless. There is no doubt that the attitude of many passengers, who chafe at any delay and are critical of the company whose ship gets them to their destination late, is another important factor which contributes to excessive speed. In the naval service there is much less incentive to violate the law. The commanding officer of a naval vessel knows that a safe voyage is the prime desideratum, and that delay due to fog is always excused without question by his superior officer.

The law in fog does not merely suggest that voyages must be delayed, it demands it in the interest of the safety of life and property. The navigator who knows the law and deliberately sets himself up as above it is likely sooner or later to come to grief, and to find that his skill in dodging innumerable vessels while he steams at excessive speed does not excuse him for a final collision. It is a well-known fact that many passenger liners have a common practice of making 30 knots or better, sometimes in thick fog. When congratulations on the completion of these fast voyages on schedule in thick weather by passengers and owners are supplemented by suspension of the masters' licenses by the government, the skippers of the ships may be able to exercise a more fitting regard for the safety of other vessels. The law in fog, when obeyed, is practically collision-proof. In time of peace, no naval vessel should be in a collision in fog unless due entirely to the fault of the other vessel. The words of Dr. Lushington, famous Admiralty jurist of England, written over a century ago in the days of sailing ships, are still not only sound legal advice but excellent common sense:

> It is unquestionably the duty of every master of a ship, whether in intense fog or great darkness, to exercise the utmost vigilance, and to put his vessel under command, so as to secure the best chance of avoiding all accidents, even though such precautions may occasion some delay in the prosecution of the voyage.[62]

Radar-equipped Vessels

The first U.S. court case involving a collision of a radar-equipped vessel was the case of *Barry v. Medford* decided in the Eastern District of New York in 1946. In this case the radar-equipped Army transport *Thomas Barry* was running easterly at 18 knots in the North Atlantic near Georges Bank with her radar turned off. She entered a fog bank visible ahead for

[62] *The* Itinerant *(1844) 2 W. Rob Adm. 236.*

twenty-two to twenty-three minutes without turning on the radar or re-ducing speed and on entry commenced sounding fog signals. About two minutes later she struck and sank the fishing trawler *Medford*. Although the *Medford* was sounding the wrong fog signal and did not have a look-out, the court held the *Barry* solely liable and initiated the now-established principle that it is the duty of a radar-equipped vessel with properly functioning radar to make use of it when visibility is restricted:

> The failure of the *Barry* to use her radar is the most serious and sinister aspect of this case. The perfection . . . (of radar) . . . is thought to have invoked a new concept of responsibilities of vessels so equipped . . . in or near a fog area. . . . The offending ship could have informed herself of the presence and track of the *Medford* in abundant time to have avoided by a wide margin any danger of striking her. Under such circumstances, it is impossible to yield to the argument . . . that her conduct is to be condoned to any extent, in view of her failure to employ the very device which was installed to prevent a collision.[63]

Court cases subsequent to the case of *Barry v. Medford* have primarily involved the manner in which radar information has been used. Thus, it is now clearly established that a radar-equipped vessel with her radar in operation must make proper use of radar information that is available, and, if necessary, the vessel must take a succession of ranges and bear-ings to determine the course and speed of any vessel detected by the radar. As the Court said in *The Australia Star*:

> Since the heading of a ship can be plotted from its bearing and distance at two or more points in time, the radar operator can with great accuracy plot the heading of a ship after taking a number of radar readings. . . . The *Australia Star* had ready at hand . . . (radar). . . . By means of her radar *Australia Star* could observe the *Hindoo* and determine her heading and speed. . . . Had the Master made more intelligent use of his radar he would have known . . . that he was almost certainly on a collision course and would have taken precautionary measures. . . . The fault of the *Australia Star* is that she chose to remain blind when she had the means to see. . . . Prudent navigation involves taking advan-tage of all safety devices at hand.[64]

Additionally, the use of radar does not dispense with the necessity of maintaining a visual lookout,[65] and, in the Coast Guard's view, a vessel's position is not ascertained by radar within the meaning of Article 16 nor does a vessel "see" another by radar for purposes of steering and sailing rules.[66]

---

[63] Barry-Medford *(1946)* 65 F Supp 622. See also The Burgan-the Bergechief *(1960)* 274 F 2nd 469.

[64] Australia Star-Hindoo *(1947)* 1947 A.M.C. 1630. See also The Bornholm-the Fort Moultrie *(1960)* 270 F and 419 and the Octo New York-the F. A. Verdon *(1960)* 192 F Supp 295.

[65] The Bucentaur-the Wilson Victory *(1955)* 125 F Supp 42.

[66] Proceedings of the Merchant Marine Council, U.S. Coast Guard, July 1960, Pp. 122.

A radar-equipped vessel is not excused from compliance with any of the rules, and therefore she must: display navigation lights; proceed at a "moderate speed" in inland waters or at a "safe speed" under International Rules; sound fog signals; under Inland Rules, stop the engines when a fog signal is heard; and in all waters, navigate with caution until danger of collision is over.

With the addition of new International Rule 19(d), a vessel which detects by radar alone the presence of another vessel must take action to avoid a close-quarters situation. Such action must be made in ample time and in considering such action many factors must be borne in mind; specifically, the provisions of Rule 8(b), which require any alteration of course and/or speed to be large enough to be readily apparent to the other vessel. In fog, any alterations are likely to be detected only by the other vessel's radar; therefore, larger alterations will be necessary than when vessels are in sight of each other. Additionally, the effectiveness of such alterations must be carefully monitored on one's own radar. Rule 19(d) further stipulates that an alteration to port for a vessel forward of the beam (other than for a vessel being overtaken) and an alteration of course towards a vessel abeam or abaft the beam, should be avoided.

The importance of radar for the avoidance of collisions has been recognized by the specific requirements now included in the 1972 International Rules and by the many court cases over the years for both inland and international waters. There are many types of radar equipment available for use in ships, varying considerably in their cost and complexity. No matter how sophisticated, radar remains an aid, albeit an important one, to collision avoidance. It is not a substitute for the human eye. Its limitations, as well as its advantages, need to be clearly understood. Therefore, those using radar must be knowledgeable in these matters and be competent in using it. Occasional glances will not suffice:

> . . . When reliance is placed on radar, it cannot be too strongly emphasized that a continuous radar watch should be kept by one person experienced in its use.[67]
> . . . if radar is relied upon it must be properly used. If you rely upon the extended and accurate lookout which is provided by radar to justify immoderate speed, you must be careful to see that you use your radar properly and with seamanlike prudence upon the indications and inferences which are given by it, or may be drawn from the data supplied by it.[68]

SUMMARY

The law in fog deals with the three important subjects of sound signals,

[67] Norefoss *(1962) 2 L.R. 113.*
[68] *The* Niceto de Larrinaga *(1960) 1 L.R. 205.*

proper speed, and close-quarters navigation. While the rules do not specify the minimum visibility which makes fog signals unnecessary, they should be used, to be an effective substitute for side lights, whenever the visibilty is less than 2 miles. Naval vessels, even in time of war, are subject to the regulations, and the government accepts liability for infractions resulting in damage to other vessels.

Rule 35, the International fog-signal rule, differs from the corresponding Inland Rule, Article 15, in several important respects. (1) The maximum prescribed interval between sound signals of steam or other power-driven vessels underway on the high seas is two minutes, while in inland waters it is one minute. (2) The signal of two prolonged blasts under the International Rule for a steam or other power-driven vessel underway without way cannot be used in inland waters. (3) Under the International Rule, a signal of one prolonged and two short blasts is sounded by a vessel engaged in fishing, towing or pushing, a vessel restricted in her ability to maneuver or constrained by her draft, a vessel not under command, or a sailing vessel. Under the Inland Rule, this signal is required only of a vessel towing and may be given by a vessel towed. A special signal of one prolonged blast and three short blasts is required of the last vessel being towed at sea, if manned. (4) In inland waters *only*, the danger signal is required whenever imminence of collision is indicated, as when approaching signals from another vessel are narrowing on the bow. At sea, pilot vessels may sound a similar signal as an identity signal, with obvious possible confusion at harbor entrances along the U.S. coasts. (5) Under the International Rule, anchored vessels strike a bell for at least 5 seconds every minute, and if more than 100 meters in length, in addition strike a distinct gong tone for at least 5 seconds immediately after striking the bell; when there is danger of collision with an approaching vessel a special warning of one short, one prolonged, one short blast may be given. The Inland Rule merely requires a vessel at anchor to strike a bell for at least 5 seconds every minute. Some vessels are even exempted from this requirement when at anchor in a *special anchorage area*. (6) A vessel aground at sea gives three separate and distinct strokes of the bell immediately before and after the bell portion of the anchor signal; in inland waters, the Inland Rule being silent regarding a vessel aground in fog, the courts forbid the anchor signal but indicate that the danger signal is proper. If in need of assistance, distress signals are also proper. (7) In inland waters sailing vessels are required to give one-, two-, or three-blast signals on a *foghorn*, while foghorns are not now required under the International Rules, and a sailing vessel gives the signal mentioned in (3) above. A vessel towed also gives her optional signal on a foghorn in inland waters only.

Moderate speed, as prescribed in Article 16, has been defined by the

Supreme Court as bare steerageway or as much speed as will enable a vessel to stop in half the distance of visibility. A moving vessel colliding with a vessel at anchor, is thus self-convicted of excessive speed. The requirement that a vessel hearing such a fog signal apparently forward of the beam stop her engines is strictly enforced by the courts, and departure from this rule is permitted only to avoid immediate danger. Under International Rules, a vessel in inland waters hearing a fog signal is required to slow to bare steerageway rather than stop her engines, and she may be relieved of that responsibility if she can determine by radar that there is no risk of collision.

Radar may tend to encourage a liberal, if not original, interpretation of the rules. It should be borne in mind, however, that the courts may not agree with that interpretation. In the cases settled to date, the courts have not been sympathetic to arguments that radar justifies either omission of a lookout, failure to stop the engines upon hearing a fog signal apparently forward of the beam (inland waters), or speed over that considered moderate for a vessel without radar. As one court said in a case upheld by the Supreme Court, "The notion that a ship, equipped with radar, may . . . plunge through the seas at 15 knots in the hope that all other craft will keep clear of it cannot be accepted as a rule of safe and prudent navigation. . . ."

Under existing decisions a vessel with operable radar on board must (1) turn it on when in or near a restriction of visibility and (2) make proper use of all information available from the radar.

18
Special Circumstances

Two Uses of the Term "Special Circumstances"

The phrase which forms the title of this chapter occurs in Rule 2(b) and Article 27, International and Inland Rules, respectively, known as the general prudential rule; in the corresponding Section 80 11 of the Pilot Rules; and in Rule 2(a) and Article 29, International and Inland Rules, respectively, sometimes called the rule of good seamanship.[1] In Rule 2(b) and Article 27 we are directed to give due regard to any *special circumstances* which may render a departure from the other rules necessary to avoid immediate danger. In Rule 2(a) and Article 29 we are warned against neglecting any precaution required by such *special circumstances*. But none of the statutory provisions gives a real definition of the term. As with several other expressions in the rules, particularly the Inland Rules, such as moderate speed, efficient foghorn, and risk of collision, we must go to the decisions of the admiralty courts to find out just what is meant by special circumstances. In this chapter we consider Rule 2(b) and Article 27.

It will be noted the two rules and articles are basically the same except for the phrase *including the limitations of the vessels involved* found in Rule 2(b). In Rule 2(b) and Article 27 special circumstances are given as a basis for disregarding the other rules, while in Rule 2(a) and Article 29 special circumstances are given as a basis for supplementing the other rules with additional precautions not ordinarily required. On the one hand, to avoid an immediate peril it may be permissible, and even necessary,

---

[1] *Art. 27. In obeying and construing these rules due regard shall be had to all dangers of navigation and collision, and to any special circumstances which may render a departure from the above rules necessary to avoid immediate danger.*

Rule 2(b). In construing and complying with these rules due regard shall be had to all dangers of navigation and collision and to any special circumstances, including the limitations of the vessels involved, which may make a departure from these rules necessary to avoid immediate danger.

to violate a requirement of the other rules and articles; on the other hand, full obedience to these rules or articles may not be enough, and the special circumstances of the case may demand even further action if collision and liability are to be avoided. A single illustration of the latter will suffice. In a very old case the Circuit Court of New York held a steam tug liable for proceeding on a dark and rainy night, with a tow of seven canal boats on a long hawser, through a narrow, crooked channel without signaling her presence to an approaching steamer, although at that time whistle signals, while permitted, were not required. The court said:

> Proof that a vessel has complied with the statute regulations in regard to lights will not necessarily exonerate her from responsibility for a collision. When the special circumstances are such as reasonably to call for extraordinary measures to apprise other vessels of her proximity and character, her omission thereof is culpable negligence.[2]

Rule 2(b) and Article 27 Apply When There Is Immediate Danger

There is a popular fallacy among navigators that whenever a perceptible risk of collision exists the rules, except Rule 2(b) and Article 27, at once cease to apply, and from that moment on it is each man for himself and the devil take the hindmost. A moment's reflection will convince anyone of the folly of having rules which would not hold up in a reasonably close situation. The real key to the matter, as brought out in decision after decision of the courts, is in the words *immediate danger*. As said by the federal court of the Virginia district in an early case under former rules:

> The rules of navigation must be observed, and the courts have no option but to enforce them unless in cases coming clearly under this rule where it is necessary to avoid immediate danger.[3]

As said by the Circuit Court of Appeals of Maryland:

> Where two courses are open to a vessel, one to follow prescribed rules and the other to depart from them, duty is imperative to observe rules and to assume that an approaching vessel will do likewise until after danger has become so manifest as to show there is no proper choice of judgment other than that of departure from the rules. . . . Departure from navigation rules because of special circumstances is only permitted where it is necessary in order to avoid immediate danger, and then only to the extent required to accomplish that object.[4]

And as said by the Supreme Court in still another case:

> Exceptions to the International Rules, provided for by this rule, should be admitted with great caution, and only when imperatively required by the

---

[2] *The* R. W. Burrowes *(NY 1870) Fed. Cas. No. 12,180.*
[3] *The* R. R. Kirkland *(Va 1880) 48 F 760.*
[4] *The* Piankatank *(CCA Md 1937) 87 F (2d) 806.*

particular circumstances. Therefore under all ordinary circumstances, a vessel discharges her full duty and obligations to another by a faithful and literal observance of these rules.[5]

That a danger which justifies a privileged vessel in a collision situation for altering the course and speed which she is required to hold must be very close indeed was brought out in two other decisions, one by the Supreme Court. In the *Illinois*, a steamer collided with a schooner which tacked to avoid floating ice, and on a showing that the schooner could have held on a minute or two longer without striking the ice, and thus allowed the steamer to clear her, she was found solely liable for the collision.[6] In the more recent case of the *Norfolk*, the privileged vessel in a crossing situation slowed down because of a tug with a tow which was seen to be about 1,200 feet beyond the intersection point, and the court, in finding her liable for the collision, remarked that:

> The duty of the privileged vessel to keep its course and speed is as definite and precise as the duty of the burdened vessel to keep out of the way.[7]

These decisions all emphasize the error of considering any situation a special circumstance, within the meaning of the rules, which does not involve a certain and imminent peril.

Cases Held Not to Be Special Circumstances

It may serve to clear up in the reader's mind what the courts recognize as special circumstances if we first consider a number of situations which the courts have held are *not* special circumstances within the meaning of the rule or to a degree entitling a vessel to disregard the ordinary requirements. We have pointed out that there is no such special circumstance if an impending danger is too distant to be considered immediate. In an early New York Harbor collision between the tows of two tugs which met off the Battery in the crossing situation, the burdened vessel was held at fault for failure to comply with the former inspectors' rule requiring her to go under the privileged vessel's stern. The validity of her argument that a special circumstance was created by a strong adverse tide which would have set her far down the river and thus materially delayed her if she had executed right rudder instead of trying to keep out of the way by going left was denied by the Circuit Court of Appeals. In thus deciding, the court, in effect, found that the matter of convenience or inconvenience is not entitled to carry weight in determining special circumstances.[8] Again, in

---

[5] *The* Oregon *(1895) 39 L Ed. 943.*
[6] *Joseph Golding v. the* Illinois *(1881) 26 L Ed. 562.*
[7] *The* Norfolk *(Md 1924) 297 F 251.*
[8] *Scully v. New Jersey Lighterage Co. (CCA NY 1891) 58 F 251.*

another crossing collision in the same harbor between two ferryboats, both were held at fault, and the plea of the burdened ferry that its well-known schedule in connection with railroad trains made a special circumstance entitling it to cross ahead of the privileged vessel was refused.[9]

In a case of head-on collision in 1869, between a brigantine and a schooner in Long Island Sound, conditions of visibility were such that neither lookout, although properly stationed, saw the lights of the other vessel until collision was imminent. The brigantine was running close-hauled on the starboard tack, and the schooner, on the port tack, had the wind a little free, and under the rule effective at that time, each vessel was bound to turn to the right. The brig, however, went to the left, and in the resulting collision sank the schooner; and the Supreme Court denied her plea that the imminence of collision at the moment of discovering the schooner's lights created a special circumstance excusing her violation of the meeting rule.[10]

In a crossing case in 1865, the side-wheeler *America* was in collision off the Battery in New York with the steamship *Corsica*. In this case, the *Corsica*, the privileged vessel, instead of holding her course down the river, swung left under the mistaken assumption that the *America* intended to hold on across her bow; and the *America*, backing down to keep out of the way in conformity with the rule, was actually making sternway when struck. At that time the rule requiring the privileged vessel to hold on contained the stipulation "subject to the next article" which was our present Article 27; and the *Corsica's* counsel contended that special circumstances were created by fear that the *America* would not give way. In denying this plea the Supreme Court thus very early settled the obligation of a privileged vessel to hold course (and under present rules, speed) as long as it is still possible for the burdened vessel to carry out her own obligation and give way.[11]

In another New York Harbor case the *Red Ash*, a burdened tug with a car float on each side, collided with the *Hale*, a privileged tug without tow. The fact that the *Red Ash* was with tow alongside did not excuse her for failure to back down at once when she sighted the *Hale* 500 yards distant on her starboard bow, nor allow her to invoke special circumstances as an excuse for such failure, when as a matter of fact she did back down after an interval, but not soon enough to prevent collision.[12]

[9] *The* Garden City *(NY 1884) 19 F 529.*

[10] *The* Annie Lindsley v. Brown *(1881) 26 L Ed. 716.*

[11] *The* Corsica *(1870) 19 L Ed. 804. See also Postal SS. Co. v. El Isleo (1940) 84 L Ed. 335.*

[12] *Thames Towboat Co. v. Central R. R. of NJ (Conn 1894) 61 F 117.*

The steamer *Dimock* collided with the steam yacht, *Alva*, which was at anchor in the narrow and tortuous channel known as Pollock Rip Slue on Nantucket Shoals, in a dense fog. As she struck an anchored vessel, the *Dimock* was, of course, self-convicted of excessive speed in accordance with the well-known rule of the Supreme Court that if she was going at such a rate as made it dangerous to any craft which she ought to have seen, and might have seen, she had no business to go at that rate.[13] However, she sought to invoke the special circumstance rule on the grounds that running with a swift tide in a crooked channel compelled her to make about 8 knots over the ground in order to have steerageway. While the court admitted that the argument might have had some force had the *Dimock* been compelled to navigate the channel, on a showing that she deliberately entered after the fog set in and kept going instead of anchoring when it failed to abate, it held that special circumstance did not apply.[14]

In still another New York Harbor case, the *Transfer No. 10* was held at fault for a head-on collision with the tug *Mary J.* because she was navigating up the Manhattan side of the East River, in violation of both inland and harbor rules. The court denied that the local custom of keeping on the left-hand side in an ebb tide to make better speed could create a special circumstance as contemplated by the rule.[15]

The tug *Mohawk* collided with the tug *Howard Carroll* in a dense fog while the latter was moored at the end of an East River pier. Her plea was that she had a defective compass and supposed she was navigating in the middle of the river with proper caution, at 3 knots. However, on a showing that the compass was known to be out of order before entering the fog at Brooklyn Bridge, the court declined to find her predicament a special circumstance, and held her solely liable for the collision.[16]

In a Boston Harbor case one passenger vessel collided with another in a thick fog shortly after an earlier collision between one of them and a third vessel. The court failed to accept the confusion that prevailed on board the vessel that had already been through a collision as a special circumstance excusing her for failure to note the other's fog signals, and ruled that she should not have again got under way until everything was shipshape and the officers had regained their composure.[17]

In a collision on the Delaware River at night the sloop yacht *Venture*

---

[13] *The* Nacoochee 137 *U.S. 330 (1890) 34 L Ed. 686.*
[14] *The H. F. Dimock (CCA 1896) 77 F 226.*
[15] *The Transfer No. 10 (NY 1904) 137 F 666.*
[16] *The Mohawk (NY 1890) 42 F 189.*
[17] *The Stamford (Mass 1886) 27 F 227.*

was sunk by a barge in tow of the ocean tug *International*, while drifting in a very light wind of insufficient strength to give her steerageway, and while not keeping a proper lookout. The tug was obviously at fault for failing to keep clear of the sailing vessel; but the court held the yacht also at fault, refusing to excuse her situation on the grounds of special circumstance and holding that she should have anchored near the shore instead of allowing herself to drift into mid-stream and into the regular path of moving vessels.[18]

Rule 2(b) and Article 27 Not Substitute at Will for Other Rules

The foregoing decisions make it very plain to the mariner that Rule 2(b) and Article 27 are far from being a mere substitute at will for the requirements of the other rules. The United States Supreme Court has explicitly limited the application of the special circumstance rule in three well-known decisions:

> It applies only where there is some special cause rendering a departure necessary to avoid immediate danger such as the nearness of shallow water, or a concealed rock, the approach of a third vessel, or something of that kind.[19]

> Nevertheless it is true that there may be extreme cases where departure from their requirements is rendered necessary to avoid impending peril, but only to the extent that such danger demands.[20]

> Exceptions to these rules, though provided for by Rule 24 of the Revised Statutes (now Article 27), should be admitted with great caution, and only when imperatively required by the special circumstances of the case.[21]

Referring to the above opinions of the court of last resort in the *H. F. Dimock*, previously cited, the Circuit Court of Appeals remarks that, taking it altogether, these expressions go little, if any, beyond applying the rule of *in extremis*.[22]

Five Kinds of Cases Where Rule 2(b) and Article 27 Apply

With this discussion as a background, we may now consider a number of decisions where special circumstances have been held to justify a departure from the ordinary rules, and may therefore, under similar conditions, be regarded as a basis of action in a collision situation or of defense after a collision has actually occurred. These may be said to fall into five groups: (1) where the situation is *in extremis*; (2) where other apparent physical conditions make obedience to the ordinary rules impracticable; (3) where

[18] *The* International *(Pa 1906) 143 F 468, 50 L Ed. 1172.*
[19] *The Maggie J. Smith (1887) 123 U.S., 349, 31 L Ed. 175.*
[20] *Belden v. Chase (1893) 150 U.S. 674, 37 L Ed. 1218.*
[21] *The Oregon (1895) 158 U.S. 186, 39 L Ed. 943.*
[22] *The H. F. Dimock (CCA 1896) 77 F 226.*

the ordinary rules must be modified because of the presence of a third, or other additional vessels; (4) where the situation is not specifically covered by the rules; (5) where one of two vessels proposes a departure from the rules and the other assents.

Situations in Extremis

Whenever two moving vessels approach each other so closely that collision is inevitable unless action is taken by both vessels to prevent it, the situation is *in extremis*. Except in thick weather, obedience to the rules will generally prevent vessels from coming into dangerous proximity, it being the intent of the rules to prevent not only collision itself but risk of collision. Hence, it will be found almost invariably that when two vessels reach a situation where collision is imminent, one or both of them has violated the rules. This may be illustrated in the crossing situation. If the burdened vessel fails to give way and both hold on long enough, collision will inevitably occur. It has never been the intent of the rules that the privileged vessel, which is under a specific requirement to maintain course and speed, should hold that course and speed right through the other vessel. On the contrary, as soon as the vessels reach a position where collision is so imminent that it cannot be avoided by the burdened vessel alone, it immediately becomes not only the right but the expressed duty of the privileged vessel to take such action as will, in the judgment of her commanding officer, best aid to avert collision. Rule 17(b), International Rules, is a statutory provision to that effect,[23] applying not only in the crossing situation but in every situation where one vessel is privileged and the other is burdened. While this sentence is not included in Article 21, Inland Rules, nor in the Pilot Rules, it may be regarded as in those rules by construction under Articles 27 and 29, and therefore equally applicable in the inland waters of the United States and dependencies. As stated by the Circuit Court of Appeals in a collision between two tugs at Charleston, South Carolina:

> There is no right of way on which a vessel is entitled to insist when it is obvious that it will result in danger of collision.[24]

And as held by the Circuit Court of Appeals in a collision of two ferryboats in New York Harbor, where the privileged vessel maintained course and speed after it was manifest that departure therefrom could alone prevent collision:

---

[23] *Rule 17(b) When, from any cause, the vessel required to keep her course and speed finds herself so close that collision cannot be avoided by the action of the give-way vessel alone, she shall take such action as will best aid to avoid collision.*
[24] *The* Hercules *(SC 1892) 51 F 452.*

When a collision is imminent, each vessel must do all in her power to avert it, no matter what may have been the previous faults, or which may have the right of way.[25]

A similar opinion was stated by the district court in a more recent case in which a sailing vessel in tow of two tugs collided with an ocean steamship on Puget Sound in foggy weather:

Even improper navigation of another vessel does not excuse adherence to a definite rule, when such adherence plainly invites collision, and stubborn adherence to rule is sometimes culpable fault.[26]

It was probably this line of reasoning which influenced the Supreme Court in its approval of Sections 80.2 and 80.7 of the Pilot Rules in the case of the *Eastern Glade* and *El Isleo* referred to in Chapter 16. In the view of the high court the blowing of a wrongful two-blast signal by the burdened vessel in a crossing situation becomes not merely a proposal, but a positive declaration of intent to depart from the rule and thereby create imminent danger of collision; and the Pilot Rules, considered in conjunction with the general prudential rule, are seen as an effective means of preventing whistle arguments at high speed, and of getting the two endangered vessels under immediate safe control.[26a]

The mariner on a privileged vessel in inland waters is given a nice question to decide whenever he is brought into close proximity with a burdened vessel. For on the one hand, he is required by law to hold course and speed as long as it is possible for the other vessel to conform to the rules in time to escape collision;[27] and on the other hand he is forbidden to hold on the moment the persistence of the other creates an imminence of collision so great as to constitute a special circumstance. There are two things about this situation the seaman will do well to remember. One is that as navigator of a privileged vessel he should make no change in course or speed until he is prepared to testify that in his judgment the burdened vessel had made collision inevitable without such action. The other is that if he does not change before this, then *any action which he takes in good faith to aid in avoiding collision will be upheld by the courts.* Any action except no action; that is, continuing on into a collision without change.

On the high seas, the privileged vessel *may* "take action to avoid collision by her manoeuvre alone, as soon as it becomes apparent to her that the vessel required to keep out of the way is not taking appropriate

---

[25] *The* Mauch Chunk *(NY 1907) 154 F 182.*

[26] *The* Kaga Maru *(Wash 1927) 18 F (2d) 295.*

[26a] *Postal SS. Corp. v. El* Isleo *(1940) 84 L Ed. 335.*

[27] *The* Southern *(Md 1915) 224 F 210.*

action in compliance with these rules." In Rule 17(c) the privileged vessel in a crossing situation is warned not to take advantage of this option by turning left with the burdened vessel on her port hand. Thus on the high seas, where speeds are normally greater, the privileged vessel is not held to such a fine calculation as to when to begin to aid the burdened vessel in avoiding a collision.

Two Kinds of Situations in Extremis

The courts make a distinction here in favor of the vessel which is brought into a situation *in extremis* solely through the fault of another vessel. It is true that she cannot invoke special circumstance to excuse a violation or an improper action unless she comes into court with clean hands. Thus, a merchant vessel may not be excused for an error *in extremis* where at the time she was not under command of a man with a master's license;[28] nor may a vessel navigating without a proper lookout;[29] but almost time without number the courts have accorded with an opinion expressed by the Circuit Court of Appeals more than seventy years ago in a case at sea in which a burdened sailing vessel held on across the bow of a privileged sailing vessel, and the latter, when within a few hundred feet, put her helm up and wore instead of putting it down and coming into the wind, which subsequent events indicated would have been preferable:

> Where the master of a vessel, who is a navigator of experience and good judgment, is confronted with a sudden peril, caused by the action of another vessel, so that he is justified in believing that collision is inevitable, and he exercises his best judgment in the emergency, his action, even though unwise, cannot be imputed to his vessel as a fault.[30]

And so in a long line of decisions, we find a steamer *in extremis* excused for stopping and reversing instead of holding on when the latter course might have avoided collision;[31] a schooner excused for going left when the evidence showed that going right would probably have been more successful;[32] a tug for not stopping her engines and allowing her tow, which was long and cumbersome, to sag and so avoid collision with another tug;[33] a dredge at anchor for a misleading lantern signal to a steamer which was threatening collision;[34] a tug for reversing and immedi-

---

[28] *The* City of Baltimore *(CCA 1922) 282 F 490.*
[29] *The* James A. Lawrence *(NY 1902) 117 F 228.*
[30] *The* Queen Elizabeth *(CCA 1903) 122 F 406.*
[31] *The* Favorita *(1871) Fed. Cas. No. 4,695.*
[32] *Farr v. the* Farnley *(Md 1880) 1 F 631.*
[33] *The* Osceola *(NY 1888) 33 F 719.*
[34] *The* Pacific *(CCA 1907) 154 F 943.*

ately going full ahead, to avoid a schooner making excessive speed in a fog;[35] and a steamship for going full speed ahead in a futile attempt to clear a burdened vessel that failed to give way.[36] As pointed out by both district court and Circuit Court of Appeals in two decisions some fifty years ago:

> If one vessel places another in a position of extreme danger through wrongful navigation, the other is not to be held in fault if she is not navigated with perfect skill and presence of mind.[37]

> The master of a vessel acting *in extremis* is not held to an exercise of that cool and deliberate judgment which facts later developed show would have been a better course.[38]

To conclude this point it may be said that special circumstances exist and vessels are *in extremis* regardless of the cause, whenever the situation becomes one in which, because of the proximity of the vessels, adherence to the ordinary rules is reasonably certain to cause a collision.

When Apparent Physical Conditions Prevent Compliance with Rules

A tug with her engines working full speed astern struck a pier on the East River with such force that the master was knocked unconscious, and then backed out in a semicircle with no one in control, until it struck another tug, with tow, coming up the river. Four minutes elapsed between the collision with the wharf and the collision with the tow; and while the fault of the first tug in miscalculating her speed and striking the pier was not questioned, the Circuit Court of Appeals found the second tug also liable for not sooner recognizing the erratic action of the other, both in her course and in her failure to answer signals, as special circumstances, and for not reversing more promptly to avoid the collision. This is admittedly a border-line case, with only a two to one decision by the Circuit judges, the dissenting opinion agreeing with the lower court that the second tug was not at fault.[39]

A vessel completely disabled is clearly unable to comply with ordinary meeting and passing rules. She is, however, under a corresponding obligation to apprise other vessels that may approach her of her plight. Should she break down outside inland waters her condition should be advertised by the use of the required two black balls or shapes in daytime, the two red lights at night, and the whistle signals of one prolonged and two short

[35] *The* Oceania Vance *(Wash 1914) 217 F 973.*
[36] *The* Munrio *(Calif 1926) 11 F (2d) 900.*
[37] *The* Lafayette *(CCA NY 1920) 269 F 917.*
[38] *Sullivan v. Pittsburgh SS. Co. (1925) 230 Mich 414, 203 NW 126.*
[39] *The* Transfer No. 19 *(CCA NY 1912) 194 F 77.*

blasts when under way in fog.[40] Should the breakdown occur under the exclusive jurisdiction of Inland and Pilot Rules, where none of these signals is authorized, then the vessel's helplessness should be made known to an approaching vessel by a timely use of the Inland danger signal.[41]

A wholly disabled steamer being brought into her slip by two tugs damaged a vessel already moored at a pier. So far as the steamer was concerned, this was a case of special circumstances, and the liability for the damage was attached by the Circuit Court of Appeals to the owner of the tugs.[42]

Presence of More Than Two Vessels

It frequently happens, of course, in crowded harbors that more than two vessels are involved in an approaching situation. The same thing may even happen occasionally at sea. In all such cases, special circumstances may be deemed to exist the moment any of the vessels is prevented from obeying the usual rules. Thus, under the regular rules in inland waters, if vessel A, heading north, is meeting vessel B, heading south while vessel C is approaching from eastward to cross them, a complex situation arises; for A and B with respect to each other should alter course to the right and sound one blast, but with respect to C, B should maintain course and speed. C, on the other hand, is required simultaneously to maintain course and speed with respect to A and to give way with respect to B, and a one-blast signal by her would indicate both maneuvers, a physical impossibility. Similarly, if A is overtaking B and C is crossing from starboard, B would be bound to hold course and speed with respect to A and to yield with respect to C. In such cases, a timely and judicious use of whistle signals will frequently solve the dilemma with a minimum delay to any of the vessels, although great care must be taken to guard against collision resulting from the acceptance by one vessel of a signal intended for another. Thus, in a situation in inland waters where one vessel is heading north to pass between two vessels proceeding south, but far enough apart so that the maneuver is practicable without a change in course by any of them, a signal of one blast will usually be exchanged between the single vessel and the one to be passed to port, and two blasts between the single vessel and the one to be passed to starboard; under International Rules, with the conditions as stated, no signals would be used.

A point to remember is that because special circumstances exist every

---

[40] Rule 27(a) and Rule 35(c), International Rules.
[41] Art. 18, Rule III, Inland Rules, and Sec. 80.1, Pilot Rules.
[42] The Ascutney (CCA NY 1921) 227 F 243.

vessel must, at the first evidence of confusion, be prompt to reduce her headway or to take any other steps necessary to avoid collision. It is a situation where the unpardonable sin is to maintain a dangerous rate of speed on the theory of a preconceived right of way that would apply were there only two vessels involved. As a precaution on the other side, the situation is not one of special circumstances if the relative distances apart and speeds are such that obedience to the ordinary rules will cause the vessels to encounter each other two at a time; in that case these rules must be followed. Thus where there were other vessels in the vicinity which were alleged to have hampered the movement of the privileged vessel, but they were not close enough to prevent her compliance with the steering rules, there was not a case of special circumstances;[43] and in a very early decision it was held that embarrassment by proximity to vessels at anchor was no excuse for the failure of a burdened crossing vessel to keep out of the way of a privileged vessel where there was no justification for her being so close to the anchored vessels.[44]

A number of illustrative decisions will serve to show the treatment by the courts of this type of special circumstance:

The fact that a meeting vessel is in danger from a third which was in full view of the pilot of the other meeting vessel is a "special circumstance," which required the latter to slacken speed or to stop and reverse.[45]

A tug was proceeding up the Delaware River, and a steamer was coming down on an opposite course, so that both were bound to change course to starboard. At this time a schooner was towed out from a pier and ran across the channel. As neither the tug nor the steamer could safely turn across the schooner's bow both turned to cross under her stern as closely as possible and collided. Neither having attempted to stop, both were at fault.[46]

A collision between the tows of two meeting tugs in the East River was held due solely to the fault of the up-bound tug in attempting to pass through the narrow space between two descending tugs instead of passing on the port side of both.[47]

Where a sloop and a lighter were sailing close-hauled on the same tack, on courses varying by only 1½ points, the sloop being the leeward vessel and overtaking the lighter, and a tow lay directly across their course, the lighter was bound to tack in time to keep out of the way of the necessary tack by the leeward vessel regardless of which was privileged.[48]

---

[43] The Morristown (CCA NY 1922) 278 F 714.
[44] The Hansa (CCA NY 1870) Fed. Cas. No. 6,038.
[45] The C. R. Hoyt (NJ 1905) 136 F 671.
[46] The Reading and the David Smith (Pa 1888) 38 F 269.
[47] The Volunteer (CCA NY 1917) 242 F 921.
[48] The Commodore Jones (NY 1885) 25 F 506.

A sheer made suddenly by an overtaking vessel to avoid the one ahead, which caused her to collide with a third vessel coming in the opposite direction before she could recover her course, was a fault.[49]

The situation of three vessels may be further complicated if additional vessels are involved, and of course the greater the number of vessels the greater the necessity of caution by each one. In general the same principle applies: that special circumstances must be deemed to exist until the regular rules can be obeyed with safety. A collision occurred on the East River when the side-wheel passenger steamer *Plymouth*, crowded too close to the shore by the overtaking steamer *Northland* when the latter passed her without an assenting signal, reversed full speed to avoid hitting the Brooklyn ferry slips and was herself hit by a following tug. A half dozen other vessels were in the immediate vicinity, and the Circuit Court of Appeals, while condemning the *Northland*, also found the *Plymouth*, the overtaken vessel, at fault for not reversing sooner when she saw the *Northland* attempting to pass without signal, and knew the traffic ahead made the attempt dangerous.[50]

Situations Not Specifically Covered by the Rules

When any situation arises which is not specifically covered by the steering and sailing rules, the rule of special circumstances governs. For example, there is nothing in the rules about maneuvering around a wharf, except the requirement for the bend signal. A typical decision of the New York Circuit Court of Appeals has held that:

> Where a vessel is entering or leaving a slip and has not yet begun to navigate on a steady course, and a tow is going up or down the river the ordinary steering and sailing rules and signals made for vessels navigating on definite courses do not apply, but each vessel must proceed with due regard to all dangers of navigation and collision.[51]

Where a vessel is coming out of a dock or harbor into the channel she must undock at a proper time, having regard to any vessels navigating outside.

> A ship which is coming out of a dock, or any side channel, into the main stream must, it is clear, do so at the proper time, and in a careful manner, having regard to traffic that may be passing up or down the main channel. The burden is on her not to cause embarrassment to any up-coming ship. That does not, of course, mean that the up-coming ship has anything in the nature of a right of way, because, as has been frequently laid down, there must be some give and take between vessels. What is wrong is for the vessel entering the main

---

[49] *The* Alaska *(NY 1887) 33 F 527.*
[50] *The* Plymouth *(CCA NY 1921) 271 F 461.*
[51] *The* Transfer No. 18 *(CCA NY 1934) 74 F (2d) 256.*

channel from the side to do so at such a time and in such a manner as to require the up-coming ship to take drastic action.[52]

The other vessel should be maneuvered with consideration for the difficulties of the emerging vessel; that is to say, special circumstances apply.

The Circuit Court of Appeals has held in several cases that the starboard-hand rule does not apply to a steamer backing out of a slip before she gets on her definite course; but the special circumstance rule applies to steamers maneuvering to get on their course.[53] Again, where a tug with tow had to pass astern of a steamer backing out from a pier in a narrow channel, the special circumstance rule required the tug, which under the starboard-hand rule would have been privileged, to give the steamer a wider berth, and the court found her at fault for not so doing.[54] In such cases the special circumstance rule applies to both vessels until the maneuvering vessel has proceeded far enough definitely to indicate her course.[55] Similarly, where a vessel is navigating near pier ends while a tug is bringing boats from a near-by slip to make up its tow the case is one of special circumstance,[56] and where a tug is maneuvering with her tow in harbor waters the situation is likewise one of special circumstances, governed by Article 27 of the Inland Rules.[57] In the *Daniel McAllister,* the court held that the *Transfer No. 9,* a tug trying to rescue a drifting barge which had been knocked from her moorings by the *McAllister,* was not chargeable with a collision between the scow and a third vessel, which occurred notwithstanding her efforts. From the standpoint of the *Transfer No. 9* this was a case of special circumstances.[58]

It frequently happens in a harbor that when vessels are maneuvering to change their berths one vessel approaches another while going astern, and occasionally a collision has occurred where both vessels approached each other stern first. The only reference in the rules to signals by a vessel backing is the requirement of Rule 34(a) and Article 28, International and Inland Rules, respectively, that three short blasts be blown if another vessel is in sight, and this signal must, of course, be given before any other maneuvering signal. The rules are silent regarding meeting and passing signals of backing vessels.

While it is the practice of seamen to regard the stern of a vessel as her bow when she is actually proceeding stern first, numerous court decisions

[52] The Adellen *(1954) 1 L.R. 138.*
[53] The M. Moran *(CCA NY 1918) 254 F 766.*
[54] NY Central Tug No. 27 *(NY 1924) 298 F 959.*
[55] The Edouard Alfred *(NY 1919) 261 F 680.*
[56] The William A. Jamison *(CCA NY 1917) 241 F 950.*
[57] The John Rugge *(NY 1916) 234 F 861.*
[58] The Daniel McAllister *(NY 1917) 245 F 183.*

such as those already cited justify the opinion that it is the special circumstance rule which properly governs such a situation. It is true that the stern may be regarded as the bow to the extent that it enables the mariner to determine what passing whistle in inland waters to propose to the other vessel. Thus a steam or other power-driven vessel backing west, desiring to back across a vessel to the southward proceeding north, should sound one blast as a proposal to the other vessel; and the same vessel desiring to back across a vessel to the northward proceeding south should propose a two-blast signal. In the first of these situations there is an important distinction in the meaning of the one-blast signal, depending upon whether the vessel using it is proceeding ahead or astern. If the vessel *heading* west blows one blast it is an announcement of her intention to hold course and speed across the other as required by the rules; while if the vessel *backing* west uses the signal, it is a proposal merely, not enforceable as a matter of right, and the backing vessel must proceed with great caution until her proposal is answered with a whistle of assent by the other.

That the stern of a backing vessel is regarded as the bow only in this limited sense, and that the special circumstance rule replaces the regular meeting and passing rules when one or both vessels approach on a collision course stern first is logical when we remember that vessels maneuver with much less certainty of control when backing and that no mariner can be deceived into mistaking the stern of a vessel for her bow.

From time to time single vessels attempt to pass through, or close ahead, of a squadron of warships or merchant ships in convoy. This can be most dangerous and single vessels are advised to take early measures to keep out of the way. Mariners are expected to take note of the cautions and recommendations given in various national, official publications, details of which can usually be found in Sailing Directions or notices to mariners. Action taken at long range, before risk of collision, to avoid a fleet or convoy on the port bow would not be a departure from the Rules. If, however, a vessel in a formation or convoy is approached close enough for risk of collision to exist, then the Steering and Sailing Rules apply equally to both.

Cautions are usually printed on nautical charts warning mariners of the existence of submarine exercise areas. A vessel should give a wide berth to a warship flying the international code hoist "HP" or "OIY" denoting the presence of submarines submerged in the vicinity, particularly if she is of great draft and in relatively shallow waters

While there is no general rule in the inland statutes limiting the speed of vessels, except in thick weather, every vessel is liable for any damage caused by its swells, either to property along the shore or to passing vessels and their tows. This liability is not excused by the plea that the swells causing the damage were not as large as might have been produced by a high wind, or that the speed was customary for vessels of her class,[59] or that other vessels passed were not injured, or that the vessel injured could have escaped damage by taking unusual precautions. It may be said to apply whenever such speed is used as to cause injury to another vessel of a kind properly in the waters she is navigating in a proper manner.[60] Thus it may become necessary to resort to the special circumstance rule where a privileged cruiser, making 25 knots, is about to cross the bow of a tug with a log raft. To escape liability for breaking up the raft with her swells, the cruiser might be obliged to swing out so as to give the tow a wider berth and to reduce her speed, contrary to the crossing rule.

It has long been a doctrine of the rules that when vessels are approaching so as to involve risk of collision, a subsequent change of course by one of them cannot change a burdened vessel to a privileged vessel. For example, a vessel overtaking another and passing her on her starboard hand cannot then swing across her bow and claim the right of way as a privileged crossing vessel. The situation, which is partially covered by the rules, is one of special circumstances, and the overtaking vessel crosses at her peril.[61]

The rule requiring privileged vessels to hold course and speed is modified whenever required by the approach of the privileged vessel to pier ends, the windings of the channel,[62] or the necessity of stopping at a guard ship or a pilot ship within plain sight of the burdened vessel to report or to pick up a pilot.[63] The action of the privileged vessel in slowing down or stopping is then justified under what is sometimes called the doctrine of presumable course and speed.[64]

Consider this inquiry from the commanding officer of a destroyer: two destroyers moored together and proceeding as one with both using their engines meet a third vessel end on; they alter course to starboard as required by Article 18; should each destroyer sound one blast, or only one of them? This is clearly a case of special circumstances, in which the senior ship which directs the movements of both should alone signal. If both vessels blew, unless the signals were simultaneous, the approaching vessel would erroneously receive a two-blast signal which might easily result in a collision.

[59] *Nelson v. the* Majestic *(NY 1891) 48 F 730.*
[60] *The* Asbury Park *(NY 1905) 144 F 553.*
[61] *The* Horatio Hall *(NY 1904) 127 F 620.*
[62] *The* Interstate *(NY 1922) 280 F 446.*
[63] *The* Roanoke *11 Aspinall M.C. (NS) 253.*
[64] *La Boyteaux.* The Rules of the Road at Sea, *p. 127.*

Departure from Rules by Agreement

In two of the three possible approaching situations between steam or other power-driven vessels, the manner of passing is prescribed by the rules. An overtaking vessel may choose the side on which to pass, but a meeting vessel is required to go to starboard and a crossing vessel must comply with the rules of privilege and burden. The dangers and the occasional advisability of being a party to a departure from the usual procedure in the crossing situation have been discussed in a previous chapter.[65] In a crossing collision in New York Harbor the privileged vessel proposed a two-blast signal, the burdened vessel assented with two blasts, and a collision followed. In finding both vessels at fault the Circuit Court of Appeals pointed out that,

The situation in this circuit, after the agreement, is one of special circumstances.[66]

The same arguments apply when two vessels meet head and head and one of them proposes a starboard-to-starboard passing, contrary to the statute both in inland waters and on the high seas. As a concluding statement these arguments may be summarized as follows:

(a) A proposal to proceed contrary to law is not binding upon the other vessel.

(b) Unless and until such proposal is assented to by the other, both vessels must proceed in accordance with the rules including, in inland waters, the Pilot Rules.

(c) When such proposal is assented to by the other, neither vessel thereafter has the right of way, but both are equally bound to proceed with caution under the rule of special circumstances.

SUMMARY

Rule 2(b) and Article 27, International and Inland Rules, respectively, and the corresponding Section 80.11 of the Pilot Rules, provide for a departure from the ordinary rules when special circumstances make this necessary to avoid immediate danger. Rule 2(a) and Article 29, International and Inland Rules, respectively, suggest that special circumstances may require action in addition to a full observance of the ordinary rules.

That the ordinary rules do not govern close situations is a popular fallacy among mariners. The courts have repeatedly held that these rules do hold and must be obeyed as long as it is reasonably possible for them to prevent collision. They have also held that rules may not be disregarded on the plea of special circumstances if an alleged danger is too distant, or

[65] *The Crossing Situation, Chapter 16.*
[66] *The* Newburgh *(CCA NY 1921) 273 F 436.*

it is suspected that a privileged vessel is not going to perform her duty, or the wrong action is taken because there is not time for protracted deliberation, or the compass is defective, or a vessel unnecessarily enters a narrow channel in foggy weather and is forced by current conditions to proceed at excessive speed.

The Supreme Court has said that the rule of special circumstances "applies only where there is some special cause rendering a departure necessary to avoid immediate danger such as the nearness of shallow water, or a concealed rock, the approach of a third vessel, or something of that kind." It is characteristic of the special circumstance rule that when it is properly invoked, *neither vessel thereafter has the right of way and both are required to navigate with extreme caution.*

The rule of special circumstances applies: (1) Whenever an approaching situation reaches the condition *in extremis*; (2) when physical conditions that should be apparent to both vessels prevent compliance with the ordinary rules; (3) when an approaching situation simultaneously involves more than two vessels; (4) when the situation is not specifically covered by the rules; and (5) when action contrary to the rules is proposed by a signal of one vessel and accepted by a signal of the other. In regard to the last, it should be remembered that such a proposal by one vessel is not binding on the other; that unless and until such proposal is assented to both vessels are bound to proceed in accordance with the rules; and that after such assent both vessels are burdened, under the rule of special circumstances, to the extent that they must then proceed with caution.

19
Good Seamanship

Good Seamanship Defined in Rules

Seamanship, according to the dictionary, is the skill of a good seaman. It is a common experience of mariners to be more or less familiar with the Rules of the Road for many years without discovering that there is a working definition of good seamanship in Rule 2(a) and Article 29, International and Inland Rules, respectively. The definition is simply this: *Any precaution which may be required by the ordinary practice of seamen.* It is one of those things which the mariner may not neglect with impunity, along with the carrying of proper lights and maintaining a sufficient lookout. The rule says in effect that nothing in the rules shall exonerate any vessel or the owner or master or crew thereof from the consequences of any neglect of good seamanship.

To the careful student of the Rules of the Road it is apparent that the lawmakers who formulated the International Rules—and they included the leading professional seamen of their day—were at great pains to make them definite, specific, and comprehensive. Every possible situation was considered, and what was in the opinion of the delegates the most effective course of action to prevent collision in each case was prescribed. Thus certain crossing, overtaken, and other vessels were designated as having the right of way, and vessels encountering them were directed to take all the action necessary to avoid them, with the understanding that such action should be based on the assurance that the privileged vessel would maintain course and speed. Two vessels meeting end on were both specifically directed to avoid collision by turning to the right. Vessels in fog were required to go at moderate speed, to sound fog signals regularly, and to stop their engines on hearing fog signals forward of the beam. It follows that obedience to these rules, which represent the lawmakers' ideas of what is the proper procedure under given circumstances, constitutes the first test of good seamanship; and conversely, disregard of the rules is generally prima-facie evidence of bad seamanship. As pointed out in the preceding chapter, the ordinary rules, including the rule of privilege and burden, might be modified or even temporarily abrogated, when special circumstances made this necessary, as when a situation was *in extremis*, or when physical conditions apparent to both vessels prevented compliance, or when more than two vessels were present, or when a situation arose not specifically covered by the rules, or when action contrary to the rules was proposed by signal by one vessel and accepted by the other. In a sense, the ordinary rules may be said to apply where the lawmakers intended the mariner to have his action laid out for him with little or no discretion in the manner of performance, while the rule of special circumstances represents *par excellence* the bases where, as long as he avoids collision, he is given almost complete discretion in the method used.

If the rule of special circumstances is the first modification of the general rules, the rule of good seamanship is the second. For just as it was recognized in the rules that special circumstances might arise in which a departure would be desirable and necessary to avoid immediate danger, so it was recognized that whether the mariner was operating under a specific rule or under the rule of special circumstances it was proper to put upon him *in all cases* the obligation of good seamanship, *i.e.*, the obligation to act in accordance with the recognized practice of skilled seamen. This obligation might refer to his conduct leading up to, and perhaps even bringing about, the actual collision situation, or to his conduct in avoiding a collision thrust upon him by the fault of the other vessel, or to his conduct in maneuvering to lessen or to aggravate the damage of a collision after it had become inevitable.

Collision Illustrating Good and Bad Seamanship

A collision which occurred between two high-powered ferries in the channel approaching Puget Sound Navy Yard offers a good illustration of both bad and excellent seamanship in the sense contemplated by the rule. The *Chippewa* on a course westward through Rich's Passage was heading to cut inside the turning buoy at Orchard Rocks, while the larger, streamlined ferry *Kalakala*, having rounded Glover Point, was steering an approximate mid-channel course between Orchard Rocks Buoy and Middle Point, with Orchard Point light a little on her starboard bow. The courses of the two vessels were perhaps three points less than opposite, though the fact that they were following the windings of the channel made them technically meeting, rather than crossing, vessels. The *Chippewa*, in charge of her first officer, elected to hold on across the bow of the *Kalakala*, and signified her intention by a two-blast signal. This maneuver was, of course, wrong, whether she regarded herself as a burdened crossing vessel or as a meeting vessel, and was made even less excusable by the fact that she was passing between the buoy and the rocks, and could have started the turn before getting past the buoy into the channel. The justification urged by the officer on watch was that he was afraid to try to veer toward the other vessel because to do so he would be turning against a strong ebb tide. With a handy, full-powered vessel and only a moderate tide, this fear was probably groundless, but even if it were not, putting his vessel in such a situation by cutting inside a buoy would still lay him open to a charge of faulty seamanship. The two-blast signal was misunderstood by the Kalakala, also in charge of her first officer, as a one-blast signal, which she would expect, either as a privileged crossing vessel or as a meeting vessel, to indicate a port to port passing. As the two ferries were approaching each other at a combined speed of more than 30 knots, matters developed very rapidly. As soon as the Chippewa heard the one blast of the Kalakala she blew the danger signal and reversed full speed; the Kalakala followed suit, and a few seconds before the collision, both skippers arrived on their respective bridges.

The steps taken almost instantly by the two seasoned veterans of the ferry line, both arriving on the scene in the jaws of a collision which by that time was inevitable, were impressive. Their testimony agreed on one point: that the two vessels, both backing to port and so preserving the angle of attack, would have struck at an angle of 30 to 40 degrees at a speed of not less than 10 knots, with the result that the Kalakala would have cut the Chippewa in two. However, the skipper of the Chippewa ordered hard right and half speed ahead, and the skipper of the Kalakala hard left and half ahead, with the fortunate result that at the moment of impact, when both engines were again reversed, the vessels were crossing at a finer angle, and the high bow of the Kalakala merely raked the house of the Chippewa for a few feet, with the consequent destruction of three or four automobiles, but no injuries to passengers or hull. This was clearly an instance on the part of both captains of the best practice of seamen under difficult circumstances—a case where seasoned and promptly applied judgment prevented a major casualty.[1]

Proper Lookout Essential

One of the most obvious requirements of good seamanship in a vessel

---

[1] This case was investigated by the local inspectors of the former Bureau of Marine Inspection and Navigation, but as both vessels were owned by the same line, did not reach the courts. Investigations of this type are now conducted by the U. S. Coast Guard.

underway is the maintenance of a proper lookout. In a very early case, which for reasons difficult to determine was carried up to the United States Supreme Court, a schooner was lying at anchor in a proper place one-half mile off the New Jersey shore, on a clear, moonlit night, with an efficient anchor light and the mate on deck as lookout; and another schooner, under full sail, rammed her and cut right through her at the main chains, so that she sank within 15 minutes. The district court, Circuit Court of Appeals, and finally the Supreme Court, were unanimous in finding the colliding vessel at fault for her failure to discover the anchored vessel in time to avoid her.[2] The matter of a proper lookout may perhaps be considered the first rule of good seamanship inasmuch as it is a necessary prerequisite to the observance of all the steering and sailing rules. In fact a proper lookout is so essential that despite the casual reference to it in Article 29, the courts have built up considerable doctrine relating to it, which will be more fully discussed in the following chapter. As said by the Supreme Court:

> The duty of the lookout is of the highest importance. Upon nothing else does the safety of those concerned so much depend. In the performance of this duty the law requires indefatigable care and sleepless vigilance.[3]

Presumption against Moving Vessel

The case of the *Commander-in-Chief* also brings out another rule of good seamanship, often recognized by our courts, which is that there is a definite presumption in favor of a vessel moored or at anchor, as against the vessel which collides with her; and quite properly of course, because of the relative helplessness of the fixed vessel to avoid collision. In foggy weather, as previously pointed out, a vessel striking another at anchor is practically self-convicted of excessive speed, since she has conclusively demonstrated her inability to stop within the distance of visibility.[4] In clear weather, with lights on the anchored vessel at night, the other vessel is equally self-convicted of faulty seamanship, either through improper lookout or bad maneuvering. As frequently held in collision cases:

> A moving vessel is prima facie in fault for a collision with one which is moored.[5]

> Where a collision occurs between a vessel moored to the wharf and another steamer which is under way and susceptible of control and management, the

---

[2] *The* Commander-in-Chief *(NY 1864) 17 L Ed. 609.*
[3] *The Ariadne (1872) 13 Wall. 475.*
[4] *See Chapter 17.*
[5] *The Banner (Ala 1915) 225 F 433.*

presumptions sustained are in favor of the moored vessel, and against the one under way.[6]

So strong is this presumption of fault against the moving vessel that rare indeed is the case where all the liability is put upon the vessel moored or at anchor. Such an exception was the case of the *Jumping Jack* and the *Pinta*, two fishing vessels which collided in the Promised Land Channel near New York, under the following circumstances. The *Jumping Jack*, a sea skiff 32 feet long, with dark-varnished stern, was at anchor in the middle of the channel and her electric riding light had gone out. The moon had set, it was two hours before daylight, and the *Pinta*, a 60-foot oyster schooner, was proceeding down the channel at 6 knots, with her captain at the wheel, a seaman on lookout in the bow, and a second seaman outside the wheelhouse to relay signals from the lookout to the captain because of a noisy Diesel engine, when the *Jumping Jack* was sighted almost under foot. The *Pinta* reversed full speed, and put her rudder hard over, but was unable to avoid sinking the *Jumping Jack*. Flagrant as was the fault of the latter in obstructing a narrow channel without lights, the district court divided the damages, but the Circuit Court, on appeal, exonerated the *Pinta*, finding that she infringed none of the rules and took all reasonable precaution to avoid the collision.[7]

In another case a barge moored to the end of a New York pier was damaged by a Cunard liner attempting to make a landing at an adjacent pier. An hour before the steamship's arrival, the barge was given notice to move out of her dangerous position while the liner landed, and was offered the free services of a tug to aid her in moving out of the way and back again. The court held that she refused to move at her peril and dismissed her libel against the steamship.[8]

These cases are very rare, however, and ordinarily the best that can be hoped for by the vessel unfortunate enough to strike an anchored or moored vessel in clear weather is a division of damages, on one of four grounds: (1) improper position of the anchored vessel; (2) no lights, or improper lights, on the anchored vessel at night; (3) failure of the anchored vessel to maintain anchor watch where circumstances required; (4) failure of the anchored vessel to take proper steps to avoid the collision.

Anchored Vessel Partly Liable for Improper Position

(1) *Improper position of anchored vessel.* In a very early case of some

---

[6] *Wood v. Harbor Towboat Co. (La 1881) 1 McGloin, 121.*

[7] *The* Jumping Jack *(CCA NY 1932) 55 F (2d) 925.*

[8] *The* Etruria *(NY 1898) 88 F 555; see also the* Express *(NY 1892) 49 F 764.*

interest, the Supreme Court emphasized the obligation of a moving vessel to keep clear of an anchored vessel regardless of whether or not the latter lay in a proper anchorage. It seems that on August 1, 1870, the salvage tug *Clara Clarita* saw a fire break out on a ferryboat moored on the Jersey side of New York Harbor and promptly set out to her rescue. After vainly trying to extinguish the flames the tug was engaged by the ferryboat's master to tow the ferry clear of the wharf to prevent the spread of the fire, which she undertook to do with a Manila towline. Shortly after getting under way the flame spread to the towline, the ferry went adrift, and struck the schooner *Clara* which lay at anchor in her path, injuring her by the collision and setting her on fire. The tug extinguished the flames on the schooner and sought to defend the subsequent libel by arguing that the schooner, which had a proper anchor light and a man on deck, was anchored in a wrongful place. While the schooner was able to satisfy the courts that she was not obstructing the channel and was exonerated, the Supreme Court, agreeing with the lower courts, held that:

> Undoubtedly, if a vessel anchors in an improper place, she must take the consequences of her own improper act; but whether she be in an improper place or not, and whether properly or improperly anchored, the other vessel must avoid her if it be reasonably practicable and consistent with her own safety.[9]

In another early case, a 28-ton oyster schooner was improperly anchored in a harbor channel some 500 yards from a wharf and directly in the path of a sidewheel steamer approaching to make her regular landing, anchorage in this locality being forbidden by a law of the state of Maryland. The evidence showed the schooner's anchor light was burning. The steamer was proceeding at about 7 knots, and did not discover the schooner until too late, though she attempted to avoid collision by reversing. The damage was slight, but the court held the side-wheeler at fault for excessive speed in a crowded harbor, declaring that:

> Where a steamer collides with a vessel unlawfully anchored in an improper and dangerous place, while negligently maintaining too high a rate of speed, the damages will be equally divided.[10]

In a later case a launch moored outboard of two other launches was struck by a passenger ship attempting to land at the city dock in the harbor of Juneau, Alaska. It was shown that the launch projected at least half her width outside a line drawn from the corner of the pier to a dolphin against which the stern of incoming steamers was expected to swing, but nevertheless the court found the steamship fully liable for the damage,

[9] *The* Clarita *and the* Clara *(1875) 23 L Ed. 146.*
[10] *Green v. the* Helen *(Md 1880) 1 F 916.*

holding that the launch's position was not legally improper, and that the steamer must be treated as a moving vessel colliding with a vessel at anchor and without fault.[11]

In the case of the *Westernland*, that steamer was in collision with a schooner in New York Harbor which was anchored in an improper place too close to the wharf where the steamer had been lying. The steamer notified the schooner to move, but did not offer to provide a tug or to assist her. The schooner refused, and instead of calling on the harbor master to enforce the regulations and compel the schooner to move, the steamer attempted to back out of her slip in a strong ebb tide, and was carried against the schooner. Both vessels were held at fault, the schooner for being in an improper place and refusing to move, and the steamer for proceeding into obvious danger, a violation of good seamanship.[12]

Anchored Vessel Partly Liable for Improper Lights

(2) *No lights, or improper lights, on an anchored vessel at night.* A vessel at anchor at night without lights is prima facie at fault; nevertheless, there have been numerous decisions inculpating the moving vessel with the anchored vessel, the courts finding that even an unlighted vessel would have been discovered by a vigilant lookout in time to avoid her.[13] If a steam or other power-driven vessel maintaining a proper lookout and otherwise navigating properly reverses as soon as she picks up the un-lighted vessel she would not be at fault, and in most cases the unlighted vessel at anchor has been held solely liable for the collision.[14] Where the anchored vessel has lights, but they do not conform to the specific require-ments for vessels of her class, she will share the liability for a collision unless it can be proved the faulty lights could not have misled the ap-proaching vessel or have been a contributing factor. Reference has already been made to several such cases.[15] In one case, a steamship at anchor at New Orleans, following a fire, with makeshift oil lanterns and electric cargo cluster lights, was struck by an oil tanker coming down the river, and both were at fault;[16] and in another case of mutual liability, a 75-foot dredge wrongfully exhibiting two white lights at anchor was mis-taken by a tug with tow for a tug being overtaken.[17]

[11] Haho v. the Northwestern (1920) 6 Alaska 268.
[12] The Westernland (NY 1885) 24 F 703.
[13] The Cambridge v. the Omega (Md 1866) Fed. Cas. No. 2336; the Premier (Wash 1892) 51 F 766.
[14] The Westfield (NY 1889) 38 F 366.
[15] See Chapter 12.
[16] The Chester O. Swain (CCA NY 1935) 76 F (2d) 890.
[17] The Arthur (NY 1901) 108 F 557.

Failure to Maintain Necessary Anchor Watch

(3) *Failure of anchored vessel to maintain an anchor watch where circumstances required.* As said by the court in a very old case:

A small vessel at anchor in a safe harbor in ordinary weather is not required by any rule or custom of navigation to set an anchor watch.[18]

In the case of the *Clara Clarita*, already cited, the Supreme Court, in absolving the anchored schooner from fault, made the comment that the statute does not require a watch on a vessel at anchor.[19] A vessel in the naval service is required by regulations to have an anchor watch, and in many harbors such a watch is specified for all vessels at anchor by harbor ordinance, which has the full force of law. However, despite the absence of any specific provision in the International, Inland, or Pilot Rules, the courts have found that an anchor watch is sometimes required under the rule of good seamanship. Thus it was held in the Supreme Court that a schooner at anchor inside the Delaware breakwater during a storm, when numerous vessels were seeking shelter, was in fault for not having a watch on deck, and when sunk by another vessel which was properly navigated and on her way to anchor could not recover damages.[20] Again, in a Massachusetts case it was held that when a vessel is at anchor where other vessels are frequently passing, and navigation is difficult and dangerous because of shoals and a channel only 1½ miles wide, special vigilance is required, including not only a watch on deck but someone on lookout to warn off an approaching vessel.[21] In foggy weather, there is, of course, a special reason for requiring an anchor watch on a vessel in a busy harbor;[22] but even in clear weather, if the night is dark and the anchored vessel is in the way of traffic, good seamanship demands it. As said by the court when a schooner barge at anchor in the middle of the Elizabeth River below Norfolk, with an anchor light but no anchor watch, was run down and sunk by a steamship bound down the river:

Anchored where she was on such a night, she was bound to take every precaution to warn approaching vessels of her presence. A vigilant watch on her deck might by shouting and swinging a lantern have attracted the attention of those on the steamboat to her presence in the locality where she lay at anchor in time to have enabled the steamship to have avoided her. . . . Both vessels being found in fault the damages will be apportioned.[23]

---

[18] *The* Fremont *(Cal 1876) Fed. Cas. No. 5,094.*

[19] *The* Clarita *and the* Clara *(1875) 23 L Ed. 146.*

[20] *The* Clara *(NY 1880) 26 L Ed. 145.*

[21] *The* Henry Warner *(Mass 1886) 29 F 601.*

[22] *The* Lydia *(CC NY 1873) Fed. Cas. No. 8,615.*

[23] *The* Guyandotte *(NY 1889) 39 F 575; see also the* Lehigh *(NY 1935) 12 F Supp 75.*

Finally, inasmuch as a vessel is liable for any damage she may do to another vessel by dragging, whenever weather, current conditions, or poor holding ground are such as to indicate that possibility, a competent anchor watch becomes essential to prevent it.[24]

Failure to Veer Chain

(4) *Failure of anchored vessel to take proper steps to avoid the collision.* While a vessel at anchor is relatively unable to maneuver, there are two acts which may be required of her under certain circumstances, and omission of either of them may involve her in fault for a collision under the rule of good seamanship. In the first place she must not anchor too close to another vessel, the legal presumption being that the vessel anchored first has a right to ample swinging room, upon which the later arrival must not infringe. She must anchor securely, that is with sufficient chain out, and if heavy weather or a strong current make it necessary, she must drop a second anchor to prevent dragging into another vessel. Failure to do this has resulted in numerous decisions holding the dragging vessel at fault for collision.[25] In one such case, the steamship *Bragdo*, at anchor off Staten Island in a December gale with 45 fathoms out, dragged across the chain of the steamship *British Isles* and set her adrift. In finding the *Bragdo* at fault, despite the fact that the gale had reached hurricane strength, the Circuit Court of Appeals cited the rule from Knight's *Seamanship,* recommending a length of cable equal to seven times the depth of water for ordinary circumstances with more if weather conditions cause the vessel to put excessive strain on the chain.[26]

Another step sometimes required of an anchored vessel to avoid collision is to move out of the way of the vessel threatening her by paying out her chain. While ordinarily this is a futile maneuver and in most collisions the courts have recognized that the need for veering chain becomes apparent too late for the anchored vessel to avert the collision by doing it,[27] two old cases will serve to illustrate its occasional requirement. In one instance a tug and helper were going up the Hudson River at night in a flood tide, with a tow 1,600 feet in length consisting of nine tiers of canal boats, when a steamship was discovered half a mile ahead and anchored somewhat outside the prescribed anchorage. The tug and her helper went right somewhat, but not promptly enough to avoid collision between the last tier in the tow and the steamship, and one of the

---

[24] *The Forde (CCA NY 1919) 262 F 127.*
[25] *The Bertha (Va 1917) 244 F 319;* the Djerissa *CCA (1920) 267 F 115.*
[26] *The British Isles (CCA 1920) 264 F 318.*
[27] *The Ceylon Maru (Md 1920) 266 F 396;* the Beaverton *(NY 1919) 273 F 539.*

canal boats was sunk. The anchor watch on the steamship saw the flotilla approaching in ample time so that if he had given her chain the tide would have carried his vessel back and out of danger. He failed to do this, and on that point, and not because she was technically in an unlawful anchorage, the Circuit Court of Appeals found the steamship liable for half the damages.[28]

In another somewhat different case of mutual fault, which is of particular interest because of the emphasis laid by the court on good seamanship in its comments to both parties, the three-master steamer *Cochico*, lying at anchor near the outer entrance to Hampton Roads in a strong ebb tide, was in the act of heaving up her anchor, preparatory to getting underway. The day was fair, and a large fleet of perhaps 150 vessels, which had put in for shelter the day before and anchored from one to seven miles above the *Cochico*, was proceeding to sea *en masse*, impelled by a light following breeze and a 1- or 2-knot tide. The *Cochico* was in the middle of a 2-mile channel, and the fleet was so numerous that the colliding vessel, the *Kelsey*, did not see her until within 250 yards, when an intervening vessel hauled out of line. The *Kelsey* changed course about a point, enough barely to clear the *Cochico*, but the latter sheered slightly and the *Kelsey*, striking her at a fine angle, knocked off her bowsprit and did some other damage. Just before the impact, the master of the *Kelsey* hailed the *Cochico* to starboard her helm and pay out chain, but she did neither. In finding both vessels liable, the *Kelsey* for not avoiding the *Cochico* which on evidence she might easily have done by prompt and effective measures, and the *Cochico* for her entire lack of prudence, attention, and assistance in avoiding danger, while voluntarily remaining as an obstruction in the midst of a fleet of moving vessels, Judge Brown made the following significant observations:

> (To the *Kelsey*) Such a sheer should have been expected: hence her master was at fault for not allowing a sufficient margin of safety, amid the contingencies of navigation, and not taking in time the decisive measures at his easy command. As I must find that the master had sufficient time and space to keep out of the way had he acted with the promptness and decision that reasonable prudence demanded, and as there was no other vessel that prevented his doing so, the *Kelsey* must be found in fault.

> (To the *Cochico*) Ordinarily a vessel anchored in a proper place in the daytime and in fair weather, is not expected, or legally required, to be on the watch, and to stand prepared to take measures to avoid vessels under way, and having control of their motions. But under exceptional circumstances, where the vessel under way is subject to special difficulties or embarrassments in her navigation, some care and precautions on the part of the vessel at anchor may become

[28] *Riley v. the* Richmond *and the* E. Heipershausen *(CCA NY 1894) 63 F 1020.*

obviously prudent and necessary that would not otherwise be obligatory. Such I think is plainly this case.[29]

The same line of reasoning which presumes it bad seamanship to hit a vessel that is moored or at anchor applies when a collision occurs between a vessel with way upon her and one which is lying dead in the water. Thus, when a steamship which had stopped off the quarantine station on the Delaware River for examination, but was not at anchor, was approached so closely by a passing tug that the two heavy scows in her tow both struck and injured the steamship, the court held the tug solely liable for the damage.[30] As said in another case:

> The obligation on the part of free vessels to avoid risk of collision with those incumbered, or at rest, is imperative, and one that the admiralty courts must enforce, having regard to the perils of navigation and the importance of the rule of the road in respect thereto.[31]

However, while it may be good seamanship and manners to avoid a vessel stopped in the water, on the high seas, it must be made clear that the latter does not have the privileges of a ship at anchor. She is underway and where risk of collision exists should comply with the regulations as far as she is able.[32]

Restriction of Speed in Good Visibility

The International Rules contain a list of factors which must be taken into consideration in determining a safe speed under *any* condition of visibility:

Rule 6   Safe speed
Every vessel shall at all times proceed at a safe speed so that she can take proper and effective action to avoid collision and be stopped within a distance appropriate to the prevailing circumstances and conditions.
  In determining a safe speed the following factors shall be among those taken into account:
  (a) By all vessels:
  (i) the state of visibility;
  (ii) the traffic density including concentrations of fishing vessels or any other vessels;
  (iii) the manoeuvrability of the vessel with special reference to stopping distance and turning ability in the prevailing conditions;
  (iv) at night the presence of background light such as from shore lights or from back scatter of her own lights;
  (v) the state of wind, sea and current, and the proximity of navigational hazards;

---

[29] *Wells v. Armstrong (NY 1886) 29 F 216;* also the Bacchus *(Va 1920) 267 F 468.*
[30] *The* John F. Gaynor *(Pa 1902) 115 F 382.*
[31] *The* Shinsei Maru *(Va 1920) 266 F 548.*
[32] *Marsden's* Collisions, 11th Ed. p 612.

(vi) the draught in relation to the available depth of water.

(b) Additionally, by vessels with operational radar:

(i) the characteristics, efficiency and limitations of the radar eqluipment;

(ii) any constraints imposed by the radar range scale in use;

(iii) the effect on radar detection of the sea state, weather and other sources of interference;

(iv) the possibility that small vessels, ice and other floating objects may not be detected by radar at an adequate range;

(v) the number, location and movement of vessels detected by radar;

(vi) the more exact assessment of the visibility that may be possible when radar is used to determine the range of vessels or other objects in the vicinity.

While moderate speed in restricted visibility is a very definite requirement of the Inland Rules, they are silent on the subject of speed in clear weather. It is true that in most canals and in many rivers and harbors a specific speed limit is fixed by local statute or ordinance, and such a regulation unquestionably has the force of law. When a speed regulation exists, it invariably means speed over the ground and allowance must therefore be made when the rate is accelerated by a favorable current.[33] One of the important applications of the rule of good seamanship as interpreted by the courts is in the restriction of speed. An examination of the cases shows numerous vessels at fault for excessive speed in inland waters in the absence of any specific speed limit, these speeds ranging all the way from 4 to 17 knots. It may be stated as a general rule that any speed in a harbor or narrow channel is excessive (1) if it causes damage to other property by the vessel's swell, or (2) if it renders the vessel herself unmanageable in maneuvering to avoid collision.

(1) *Damage caused by vessel's swell.* In one of the earliest cases decided on this point, the Circuit Court of New York declined to find a steamer at fault for damage to a number of canal boats in a tow, caused by the steamer's swells when she passed the tow on the Hudson River. The court held that, there being at that time no rule of law prescribing the speed a boat might use or the swell it might make or how near it might pass to another, any reasonable speed was justifiable, and 17 knots, the steamer's regular speed, was proper.[34] But in a case a few years later, court interpretation changed this rule considerably, and for more than eighty years now the opposite view has prevailed, namely, that a large steam or other power-driven vessel which proceeds at such speed as to create a swell causing injury to another vessel of a kind properly in the waters which she is navigating, and which is properly handled, is liable for such injury, even if that speed is only 5 or 6 miles an hour.[35] In the case referred to, the

---

[33] *The Plymouth (CCA NY 1921) 271 F 461.*

[34] *The Daniel Drew (CC NY 1876) Fed. Cas. No. 3565.*

[35] *The New York (NY 1888) 34 F 757.*

offending steamer, which passed within a few feet of a scow loading at an icehouse, with her engines on dead slow ahead, was held for failure to stop her engine entirely. In another case two or three years later an ocean liner passed a river tug with a scow in tow on each side in upper New York Bay, and her swells caused the tug to seriously damage one of the scows. She passed the two within half a mile at a speed of about 11 knots; but notwithstanding the steamship's argument that the tug contributed to the damage by failure to present her stern to the swell of the overtaking vessel the latter was found fully liable.[36] (Incidentally, while a meeting vessel is under obligation to head into a swell with her tow if it will lessen damage, the courts have steadfastly refused to require an overtaken vessel, which is privileged, thus to alter her course.) The opinion of the court included the following excellent statement of the rule, which still holds:

> Such waters are not to be appropriated to the exclusive use of any one class of vessels. We do not mean to hold that ocean steamers are to accommodate their movements to craft unfit to navigate the bay, either from inherent weakness, or overloading, or improper handling, or which are carelessly navigated. But of none of these is there any proof here, and in the absence of such proof we do hold that craft such as the libelant's have the right to navigate there without anticipation of any abnormal dangerous condition, produced solely by the wish of the owners of exceptionally large craft to run them at such a rate of speed as will insure the quickest passage. To hold otherwise would be virtually to exclude smaller vessels, engaged in a legitimate commerce, from navigating the same waters.

Even in lower New York Bay substantially the same rule has been applied. As said by the Circuit Court of Appeals when a Cunard liner, coming in at night, caused a swell which damaged two scows in a tow by making one scow override the other:

> The rule that large vessels navigating New York Bay must so regulate their speed as not to injure by their swells small craft, which are seaworthy and properly loaded and navigated, is also applicable to the lower bay, though not with the same strictness. Owing to its less crowded condition and nearer proximity to the sea, incoming steamers may there proceed at greater speed, provided the channel is free, but not when it is full of boats, at night, or in a fog.[37]

In this case the tug was found contributorily negligent in having towlines only 6 feet in length between the scows, and only half damages were allowed.

In a more recent case a barge loading on the St. Lawrence River just west of Quebec was injured by pounding on the bottom when she was struck by a heavy swell from the Cunard steamer *Andania*, which passed her at a speed over the ground of about 17 knots, though there is a legal

[36] *The Majestic (CCA NY 1891) 48 F 730.*
[37] *The Campania (NY 1913) 203 F 855.*

speed limit in that part of the river of 9 knots. Ascertaining the extent of the damage after the barge had completed a voyage to New York, the owner sued the Cunard Line *in personam*, and was met with the interesting defense that the steamship was in charge of a compulsory pilot, and that the company through its agent, the master, was therefore not liable. However, the court held that the master, who was also on the bridge, was negligent in not exercising his superior authority and ordering the pilot to slow down in conformity with the government speed regulation.[38]

As a matter of practical seamanship it is well to remember that to reduce the swell of a speeding steam or other power-driven vessel, it is necessary to slow down a considerable distance before reaching the vessel it is intended to protect. In a New York case where the passing steamer in a narrow channel did not slow sufficiently or in time, it is reported that the tow was actually broken up by the swell which piled up *ahead* before the steamer had come abeam.[39]

Commanding officers of naval vessels who find themselves under the necessity of making high-speed trial or post-repair runs in more or less confined waters will be interested in cases where the following defenses have *not* been accepted by the courts: (1) that a vessel's waves did not render navigation more perilous than would a high wind;[40] (2) that a vessel was navigating at a speed customary for ships of her class,[40] (3) that other vessels passed on that or other similar occasions were not injured;[41] (4) that the vessel injured did not sound a warning signal to the other vessel to slow down.[42] (5) that the vessel injured might have saved herself by taking unusual precautions.[43]

(2) *Speed excessive under particular conditions.* It has long been held by the Supreme Court that a steam or other power-driven vessel in a crowded harbor or river should not be operated at a higher speed than will keep her under perfect control. This is, of course, merely a rule of common sense. In a collision between two early steamships off the Battery, with numerous other vessels in the immediate vicinity either underway or at anchor, a speed of 6 knots was held excessive;[44] and in another collision the next year between a steamship and a schooner, near the same spot under like conditions, 7 knots was held excessive. In the latter case,

[38] The Emma Grimes *(NY 1933) 2 F Supp 319; see also the* Hendrick Hudson *(NY 1933) 3 F Supp 317.*

[39] The Luke *(CCA NY 1927) 19 F (2d) 925.*

[40] The New York *(NY 1888) 34 F 757.*

[41] The Asbury Park *(NY 1905) 144 F 553; the* Hendrick Hudson *(NY 1908) 159 F 581.*

[42] The Chester W. Chapin *(NY 1907) 155 F 854.*

[43] The Emma Grimes *(NY 1933) 2 F Supp 319.*

[44] The Corsica *(NY 1870) 19 L Ed. 804.*

the schooner was standing over to the Jersey shore to anchor and await a fair tide up the East River; and the old steamship *City of Paris*, bound out at 7 or 8 knots, headed to pass through a 300-foot opening between a brig and a sailing ship, and did not see the schooner until the latter passed at right angles under the stern of the brig. The steamship immediately reversed, but although the schooner luffed slightly in a futile effort to escape, she was almost cut in two by the impact and sank so quickly as to imperil the lives of all her crew. In upholding both lower courts in their condemnation of the steamship, the Supreme Court said:

> She ought not to have entered upon the narrow track between the ship and the brig without being very careful first to see that her passage would involve no danger to any approaching vessel in its transit. The results proved that the speed of the steamer was higher than was consistent with the safety of other vessels in so crowded a thoroughfare and hence higher than she was warranted to assume.[45]

The high court dismissed the argument that the schooner contributed to the disaster by luffing, in the following brief, but pointed, comment:

> The acts complained of were done in the excitement of the moment and *in extremis*. Whether they were wise it is not material to inquire. If unwise they were errors and not faults. In such cases the law in its wisdom gives absolution.

Similarly, in numerous other decisions vessels in collision have been held liable for excessive speed where it was found that they approached other vessels in restricted waters at speeds which the results showed were imprudent. In a collision between two steamships on the Patapsco River, near Baltimore, on a clear day, one of them, the *Acilia*, attempted to blow two blasts for a starboard-to-starboard meeting, and the whistle cord stuck, causing a single whistle of 5 or 6 minutes' duration. The other vessel, the *Crathorne*, which was making about 6 knots, tried to pass port to port; the *Acilia* executed left rudder, both vessels reversed, and they came together with some $50,000 damage to the *Crathorne*. The *Acilia* was found solely liable for the damage for going at her ordinary cruising speed of 10 knots, the Circuit Court of Appeals remarking that:

> Full speed in these dredged channels when about to pass other vessels is undeniably a fault which increases every risk of navigation.[46]

It is a well-known fact that vessels in shallow water have a tendency to sheer and become unmanageable; and that if they attempt to pass too closely they are likely to be brought into collision by suction. Hence,

---

[45] *The Liverpool, New York, and Philadelphia SS. Co. v. Henry P. Simmons (NY 1870) 19 L Ed. 751; see also the* George H. Jones *(CCA NY 1928) 27 F (2d) 665.*
[46] *The* Acilia *(CCA Md 1903) 120 F 455.*

vessels colliding from either of these causes are often convicted of excessive speed. A typical case occurred at Horseshoe Bend on the Delaware River between the steamship *Saratoga*, going down light and the steamship *Taunton* coming up from sea. It was a clear day; the vessels saw each other 2 miles apart, signaled a port-to-port meeting when a mile apart, and were about to clear each other in the usual manner, when the *Saratoga* touched a mud bank at the side of the channel, the existence of which was well known and marked, and sheered into the other vessel before she could be stopped. On a showing that the *Taunton* was properly navigated on her own side of the channel, but that the *Saratoga's* speed of not less than 8 knots caused her to "smell the bottom" as she rounded the buoy, the latter was found solely liable for the collision.[47]

In another case a steamship 314 feet long anchored for the night in Brewerton channel below Baltimore, at a point where the channel is 600 feet wide, so that when she swung around her stern was about 100 feet from one side and her anchor chain extended toward the other. Another steamship, heavily loaded with iron, coming up from sea, attempted to pass under her stern at 8 knots, and as she reached the shallow edge of the channel, took an uncontrollable sheer toward the anchored vessel. While the anchored steamship was held liable for unnecessarily obstructing a navigable channel, in violation of the Act of March 3, 1899, the colliding vessel was held equally at fault for a speed that prevented her overcoming the effects of a sheer which might reasonably have been expected.[48]

The question of good seamanship is also involved when vessels make their way at too great speed along a city waterfront and fail to keep a safe distance off the pierheads. Many harbors have local regulations prohibiting such movements within a specific distance of the piers, and in New York a statute requires vessels navigating the East River to go up and down in mid-channel. But regardless of such local rules, the courts have again and again held vessels at fault which collided with vessels properly emerging from their slips. As already explained, vessels maneuvering around piers are under the rule of special circumstances, and the greatest caution must be observed when there is a possibility of encountering them.[49] This doctrine was enunciated by the United States Supreme Court as long ago as 1873, when a case was carried up involving a collision between a side-wheel excursion steamer hugging the Brooklyn piers to avoid a tug with tow, at a speed of 8 knots, and a ferry which emerged from her slip, saw the steamer bearing down from port, and

[47] The Saratoga *(Pa 1910) 180 F 620; see also Appleby v. the* Kate Irving *(Md 1880) 2 F 919.*

[48] The Caldy *(CCA Md 1907) 153 F 837.*

[49] *See Chapter 20.*

reversed in a frantic, though perhaps mistaken, attempt to escape disaster. The decision of the Supreme Court, condemning the excursion vessel and exonerating the ferry, included much that would apply in greater or lesser degree to any busy harbor:

> In the East River, vessels cannot with safety run across the mouths of ferry slips in going to or from their wharves, but they should occupy as near as possible the middle of the river. . . . If the middle of the river be previously occupied and the ship is obliged to go nearer to shore in order to avoid other vessels pursuing the same track she must run at such a slow rate of speed as to be easily stopped, so as not to endanger boats pursuing their regular and accustomed occupation.[50]

And in clearing the ferry on the charge of failure to hold her course and speed, the court reiterated the opinion expressed three years earlier:[51]

> In a moment of sudden danger, caused by the misconduct of the colliding vessel, the law will not hold the pilot of the injured vessel, acting in good faith, guilty of a fault, if it should turn out after the event that he chose the wrong means to avoid the collision, unless his seamanship was clearly unskillful.[52]

In concluding this point it may perhaps be unnecessary to point out that it is no defense to a collision a few feet off the piers to argue that the speed was less than the statutory limit. As said by the court in finding a side-wheel steamer solely liable for a collision while navigating within a ship length of the piers at 9 knots:

> A statute imposing a penalty for running along the piers of the East River at a speed exceeding 10 knots does not necessarily render a less rate of speed prudent. The speed must be regulated by the dangers attending the navigation under the particular circumstances of the case.[53]

Among other decisions inculpating vessels for excessive speed under the rule of good seamanship may be mentioned the case of a steamer, about to meet a sailing vessel beating through a 300-foot channel in the Penobscot River, which failed to anticipate the sailing vessel's tack and held to a speed of 8 knots;[54] the case of a steam yacht which approached the blind bend at Horn's Hook, near New York, at 15 knots and was in collision with a tow coming down the river;[55] the case of a steamship which approached a confusion of lights, part of them improper, which turned out

---

[50] The Favorita v. Union Ferry Co. (NY 1873) 21 L Ed. 856; see also the Shady Side (NY 1899) 93 F 507.

[51] The Sif (NY 1920) 266 F 166.

[52] The Favorita v. Union Ferry Co. (NY 1873) 21 L Ed. 856; see also the Shady Side (NY 1899) 93 F 507.

[53] Greenman v. Narragansett (NY 1880) 4 F 244.

[54] The Northern Warrior (Me 1870) Fed. Cas. No. 10,325.

[55] The Hoquendaqua (CCA NY 1918) 251 F 562.

to be a single tow of two tugs and seven barges, off Governor's Island, and in trying to go through them at more than 4 knots, sank two of them;[56] the case of a government lighthouse tender coming down the East River at night which approached at 10 knots a group of three vessels crossing the river both ways ahead of her;[57] and the case of a Puget Sound steamer which entered Port Townsend Harbor at full speed, and in approaching her wharf, failed to distinguish the flickering lantern of an anchored bark with its background of bright city lights, until collision was inevitable.[58]

Special Right of Way under Rule of Good Seamanship

In the discussion of special circumstances[59] it was pointed out that it sometimes happens that one of two vessels in an approaching situation, given the right of way by the rules, must surrender this right of way, with its attendant obligation to maintain course and speed, because of adverse physical conditions, as, for example, a steamer otherwise privileged crossing a tug coming down a current with a tow. The rule of good seamanship sometimes goes a step farther, and creates a right of way in one of two vessels where neither would ordinarily be privileged. Thus, in a narrow channel with a swift current in one direction, it has been held in several cases that when vessels meet, the one moving with the current is the favored vessel.[60] This rule was applied in a collision between a tug and tow on a long hawser coming down the Hudson River and rounding the sharp bend at West Point, where the current sweeps rapidly toward the opposite bank, and a similar tug and tow coming up the river, in favor of the former and against the latter.[61] It was applied when two steamships met in the Delaware River, in the narrow channel above Horseshoe Buoy, when one of them, running light and stemming the tide, tried to cross the bow of the other, deeply laden, and coming with the tide. The former was held solely liable.[62] The Supreme Court, applying it to a collision between a steamer and three barges in a tow which the steamer sank in Hell Gate with the tide running 7 knots, thus definitely stated the rule:

Where two steamers about to meet are running one with and the other against

[56] The Corsica (NY 1870) 19 L Ed. 804.

[57] U.S. v. the Mineola (NY 1879) Fed. Cas. No 15,779a.

[58] Fristad v. the Premier (Wash 1892) 51 F 766.

[59] See Chapter 18.

[60] For recognition of this doctrine in the rules for the Great Lakes and for Western Rivers, see Rule 18, Western Rivers Rules, and Sec. 90.5, Pilot Rules for the Great Lakes, in Appendixes N and J.

[61] The Marshall (NY 1882) 12 F 921.

[62] The Scots Greys v. the Santiago de Cuba (CC Pa 1883) 19 F 213.

the tide, if it be necessary that one or the other should stop in order to avoid a collision, the one proceeding against the tide should stop.[63]

Vessel Must Be Properly Manned and Steered

The obligation of good seamanship requires that a vessel should be properly manned and properly steered. When a small schooner moored at New Orleans in a gale sought to change her position in the absence of the captain, with only a man and a boy to handle her, she was held responsible for her own injuries when impaled on the bow of a steamer and sunk.[64] In a collision at sea between a schooner and a steamer, off Sea Girt, New Jersey, at night in clear weather, the erratic actions of the former were adjudged due to the incompetence of her helmsman, who managed to display on the witness stand a profound ignorance of the duties of a seaman, and the schooner was held solely at fault for the collision.[65] And similarly when a vessel in a tow on the Saint Mary's River turned toward an approaching steamer because the helmsman made a mistake in executing the master's orders, putting the wheel hard right instead of hard left, she was found liable for the resulting damage.[66]

It is often necessary to supplement an emergency maneuver with the dropping of one or both anchors. In order to do this, a man must be standing by, as said by a district court:

> In waters well frequented by small tows, a ship must have a competent person standing by in the forecastle ready at a moment's notice to let go the anchors.[67]

Vessel Must Not Navigate with Defective Equipment

Vessels are often found liable for a collision where they have chosen to get underway even though there was a defective compass or lights which were not operating properly. In some cases vessels are convicted because a failure occurred a second time, such as a steering failure, and the cause was not determined and corrected after the first failure. An unexpected failure of equipment which contributes to a collision will not be excused if the equipment had not been submitted to periodic inspection and preventive maintenance.

Navigator Must Know His Vessel and the Conditions to Be Encountered

Particularly in close quarters, a navigator must be familiar with the advance

---

[63] The Galatea (NY 1876) 23 L Ed. 727.
[64] The Sarah v. Bellais (CCA La 1892) 52 F 233.
[65] The Tallahassee (CAA NY 1903) 125 F 1005.
[66] The Sitka (NY 1904) 132 F 861.
[67] River Terminals Corp. v. U.S. (DC La 1954) 121 F Supp 98.

and transfer which is characteristic of his vessel for the speed at which he is traveling. He must also be knowledgeable of the effectiveness of a backing bell depending on the speed. Allowance must be made, in both cases, for the effect of wind and current. As expressed by the court:

> A navigator is chargeable with knowledge of the maneuvering capacity of his vessel. He is bound to know the character of his vessel and how she would turn in ordinary conditions.[68]

A vessel will not be excused for a collision caused by weather conditions if those conditions could have been avoided. As stated by a district court in a recent case:

> Tug's obligation includes responsibility to utilize available weather reports so that it can operate in manner consistent with foreseeable risk and captain of tug is chargeable with knowledge of weather predictions whether he knows them or not.[69]

Similarly, a vessel cannot be excused for striking a navigational hazard if the cause of the navigator's ignorance is failure to carry up-to-date charts.

Rules Modified by Requirements of Good Seamanship

As final evidence of the legal importance of good seamanship, cases may be cited in which this factor has caused a statutory rule to be modified distinctly by court interpretation. The requirement of Article 28, Inland Rules, that when vessels are in sight of one another a "steam vessel" underway whose engines are going at full speed astern shall indicate that fact by three short blasts of the whistle. Because of the value of the information given by this signal in close situations, the courts have extended its use to cases where engines are reversed less than full speed, notwithstanding the wording of the statute. In the case of the *Sicilian Prince*, that vessel was maneuvering to turn around in upper New York Bay, and sighting the steamer *Jefferson* approaching at a distance of a mile or less, blew three blasts to indicate her engines were going full speed astern. Immediately after signaling, the *Sicilian Prince* stopped her engines, but continued to move slowly astern; then, seeing the *Jefferson* approaching rapidly and hearing her blow one blast, she went full ahead, though too late to avoid being struck. The *Jefferson* contended that the *Sicilian Prince's* stern was for the moment her bow and that she was therefore a burdened crossing vessel, but this was denied by the court, which found the *Jefferson* at fault as an overtaking vessel for not keeping clear. The *Sicilian Prince*, however, was also held for failure to repeat the

---

[68] *City of New York v. Morania No. 12 Inc. (1973) 357 F Supp 234.*
[69] *M. P. Howlett Inc. v. Tug* Dalzellido *(DC NY 1971) 324 F Supp 912.*

three-blast signal later when it was evident the *Jefferson* had not heard the first signal, although the engines were no longer reversing.[70] In another New York case an ocean steamship maneuvering to turn around, with one engine full ahead and the other partly astern, but with the ship, because of a strong tide, actually making some sternboard, was in collision with a small sailing vessel; again the steamship was held at fault for failure to use the backing signal, and this decision, like the preceding, was affirmed by the Circuit Court of Appeals.[71] In a third case, the *Harry Luckenbach*, a 14,000-ton freighter, was maneuvering with the aid of two tugs in Los Angeles inner harbor. Backing slowly out of her slip with one prolonged blast, she sighted the steamer *San Juan* in a turning basin three quarters of a mile away, and blew three blasts, although one engine was actually going ahead to check her way astern. The *San Juan*, coming down at full speed, rammed her, and was held solely at fault, the court upholding the three-blast signal of the *Harry Luckenbach* as proper under the circumstances to indicate slow movement astern.[72]

First Rule of Good Seamanship

In the final analysis, good seamanship becomes a factor in collision prevention in so far as it influences the navigator, in observing the Rules of the Road, to conduct his vessel where it is safe, when it is safe, and in the manner of a prudent seaman. Such is the test placed upon him by the courts, as typically expressed by the Circuit Court of Appeals:

> No man is infallible, and there are certain errors for which the law does not hold a navigator liable; but he is liable for an error of judgment *which a careful and prudent navigator would not have made.*[73]

SUMMARY

Good seamanship as defined in the rules of the road means the practice of every precaution which may be required by the ordinary practice of seamen. The first test of good seamanship is obedience to the rules, whether an ordinary rule or the rule of special circumstances. It is under the rule of good seamanship that vessels are required to have a proper lookout, which the courts have held must be stationed as low down and as far forward as circumstances permit. Similarly under the rule of good seamanship there is always a presumption of fault against a vessel anchored

---

[70] *The* Sicilian Prince *(CCA NY 1905) 144 F 951*
[71] *The* Deutschland *(CAA NY 1904) 137 F 1018.*
[72] *The* San Juan *(Cal 1927) A.M.C. 384.*
[73] *The* Old Reliable *(CCA Pa 1921) 269 F 725.*

in an improper place; against a moving vessel which collides with a vessel moored or at anchor; against a vessel going up a swift stream which collides with a vessel going down stream; against a free vessel which collides with a vessel disabled or hampered with a tow.

While there is no Inland Rule limiting speed in clear weather, under the rule of good seamanship a vessel may be held at fault for damage done by her swell, or for maintaining such speed that because of the proximity of piers or of crowded traffic collision results. It is an obligation of good seamanship that a vessel be properly manned and steered, and to have a man standing by to let go the anchors under certain conditions. A vessel must not navigate with defective equipment, and a navigator is charged with knowledge of the maneuvering characteristics of his vessel, weather predictions, and the information on *up-to-date* charts. The courts have applied the principle of good seamanship when they have construed Article 28 to mean the three-short-blast signal is proper when going *less* than full speed astern. Good seamanship is a factor in collision prevention whenever it influences the mariner, in observing the Rules of the Road, to conduct his vessel where it is safe, when it is safe, and in the manner of a prudent seaman.

20
A Proper Lookout

Requirement of Proper Lookout Positive

In the naval service there is probably no rule of the road more con-scientiously observed than the implied admonition of Rule 5 and Article 29, International and Inland Rules, respectively, to keep a proper lookout.[1] In the merchant service, where vessels of corresponding tonnage carry much smaller crews, the relative scarcity of men results in many more cases of collision attributable at least in part, according to the case books, to improper lookout. It is interesting to note that of some 200 such cases in the records very few involved vessels of the Navy. As might be expected, about three times as many cases occur in inland waters as on the high seas, a fact no doubt due to the relative congestion of shipping and not to the maintenance of a less efficient lookout in crowded waters. How-ever, as evidenced by more than fifty specific findings of faulty lookout on the high seas, there is apparently some tendency by navigators to let down on the requirements once a vessel is clear of the land.

But if the provision of Article 29 in regard to keeping a proper lookout is negative in form, nothing could be more positive than the obligation as construed by the civil courts and, it might be added, by naval courts and boards. As early as 1833 an American sailing vessel was held liable for a collision with another sailing vessel having the right of way because

---

[1] *Art. 29, Inland Rules, provides: Nothing in these rules shall exonerate any vessel, or the owner or master or crew thereof, from the consequences of any neglect to carry lights and signals, or of any neglect to keep a proper lookout, or of the neglect of any precaution required by the ordinary practice of seamen, or by the special circumstances of the case. Rule 5, International Rules, provides: Every vessel shall at all times maintain a proper lookout by sight and hearing as well as by all available means appropriate in the prevailing circumstances and conditions so as to make a full appraisal of the situation and of the risk of collision.*

she was navigating at sea, in daylight in clear weather, with no watch on deck but the man at the wheel,[2] and for more than a hundred years our courts have been enforcing careful vigilance by those entrusted with the navigation of vessels as a requisite of common seamanship. It is an obligation that applies to all vessels of a size capable of committing injuries.[3] As held in a collision between two small vessels on a clear night many years ago:

> The failure to keep a lookout is a violation of the general rule to prevent collisions between vessels, and nothing can exonerate a vessel from such failure, unless it should appear that the collision would have occurred notwithstanding such failure. This rule is undoubtedly as applicable to the boats of the motor class as to ocean vessels.[4]

The obligation should be regarded as applying at all times when underway, day or night, and even, under some circumstances, when at anchor. For while the statute does not specify a watch on a vessel at anchor, and a vessel securely anchored in a safe harbor, with proper lights, in ordinary weather need not have one, yet it was held in an old case that a schooner at anchor inside the Delaware breakwater during a storm, when numerous vessels were seeking shelter, was in fault for not having a watch on deck and when sunk by another vessel which was properly navigated was unable to recover damages. The decision was affirmed by the United States Supreme Court.[5] Again, in a Massachusetts case it was held that when a vessel is at anchor in a place where other vessels are frequently passing, and where navigation is difficult and dangerous because of shoals and a channel only a mile and a half wide, special care and vigilance are required, and she must have a good lookout and an anchor light of the regular pattern lighted and burning. To have a watch on deck is not sufficient if there is no one on lookout at the time of the collision to warn off an approaching vessel.[6] And of course the well-known liability of a vessel for any damage which it may do to another through dragging anchor makes a proper lookout imperative whenever conditions create a risk of such an occurrence, as when a vessel was anchored in New York Harbor during a winter gale that reached a velocity of 88 miles an hour.[7]

Lookout Defined

A lookout has been defined by the federal court as a person who is

[2] *The* Rebecca *(NY 1833) Fed. Cas. No. 11,168.*
[3] *The* Harry Lynn *(Wash 1893) 56 F 271.*
[4] *Brindle v. the* Eagle *(Alaska 1922) 6 Alaska 503.*
[5] *The* Clara *(NY 1880) 26 L Ed. 145.*
[6] *The* Henry Warner *(Mass 1886) 29 F 601.*
[7] *The* Forde *(CCA 1919) 262 F 127.*

specially charged with the duty of observing the lights, sounds, echoes, or any obstruction to navigation with that thoroughness which the circumstances permit.[8] The words *specially charged* imply that such person shall have no other duties which detract in any way from the keeping of a proper lookout. Thus it has been held in numerous cases that because the lookout must devote his attention to this duty, the officer of the deck or the helmsman cannot properly serve as lookout.[9] Even on a slow moving tug with a tow, the duty is not legally complied with by the officer in charge of navigation keeping a lookout from the pilot house.[10] Where the captain of a steamer is acting at the same time as pilot and lookout, the vessel has not a proper lookout, and the owners may be liable for the damage caused by such omission.[11] A seaman who had been dividing his attention between looking out and reefing sail was held not to be a vigilant lookout,[12] and where the only two men on the deck of a schooner navigating at night were engaged in taking down sail, it was held that neither one nor both seamen constituted a proper lookout, and accordingly the schooner was at fault for colliding with another schooner having the right of way.[13] A vessel backing out from a pier in a fog was at fault for requiring the lookout in her bow to take in the bow line, since this interfered with the degree of vigilance required under such conditions.[14] In still another case, where the lookout on a car float alongside a tug was directed to concentrate his attention on the East River piers, so that he did not see a large block of floating ice which forced tug and tow to collide with a steamer alongside a pier, it was held that the tug should have detailed an additional man for the general lookout duty.[15] However, in a very early decision the Supreme Court found that the man blowing the foghorn on a sailing vessel was a proper lookout,[16] and in 1911 the Circuit Court of Appeals in New York rendered a similar decision in refusing to hold a schooner guilty of contributory fault for colliding with a steamer when it was shown that the mate, in a dense fog, was acting

[8] *The* Tillicum *(Wash 1914) 217 F 976.*

[9] *The* Kaga Maru *(Wash 1927) 18 F (2d) 295; the* Donau *(Wash 1931) 49 F (2d) 799.*

[10] *The* City of Philadelphia *(Pa. 1894) 62 F 617; the* Sea Breeze *Fed. Cas. No. 12,572a.*

[11] *Bill v. Smith (1872) 39 Conn 206; Dahlmer v. Bay State Dredging & Contracting Co. (CCA Mass 1928) 26 F (2d) 603.*

[12] *The* Twenty-one Friends *(Pa 1887) 33 190.*

[13] *The* Fannie Hayden *(Me 1905) 137 F 280.*

[14] *The* Albatross *(Mass 1921) 273 F 285.*

[15] *New York and Oriental SS. Co. v. N.Y., N.H., and H. Ry. (NY 1906) 143 F 991.*

[16] *The* Nacoochee v. Mosely *(NY 1890) 34 L Ed. 687.*

as lookout and sounding the foghorn at the same time, but that all his duties were properly done.[17]

In addition to maintaining "a proper lookout by sight and hearing," the International Rules also require a proper lookout "by all available means appropriate in the prevailing circumstances and conditions so as to make a full appraisal of the situation and of the risk of collision." Therefore under certain circumstances on the high seas, the use of radar information is required in order to have a proper lookout.

International Rule 5 places greater emphasis than hitherto on the need for a proper lookout; the requirement is positive rather than implied. Guidance on the maintenance of a proper lookout is given in the IMCO Recommendation On Navigational Watchkeeping, Section I, paragraph 11.[18] This guidance distills much of the wisdom the courts have pronounced over the years on this subject.

The expression "all available means appropriate" means that effective use must be made of suitable instruments and equipment, and is not confined to the use of radar only to supplement a visual and aural watch. Binoculars should be used, not only by the lookout, but by the bridge personnel, and if necessary, used on the bridge wing or through an open window.

> It is difficult, in my view, in any event, to understand why he did not use binoculars on seeing the approaching *Gorm*. Apparently he remained behind closed windows in the wheelhouse.[19]

In addition to keeping a radar lookout, vessels should not neglect to listen to the radio:

> I find that the *Antonio Carlos* was at fault for bad look-out in the broadest sense; namely, faulty appreciation of VHF information and total absence of radar look-out.[20]

Where shore-based radar stations are operating, it has been held that use should be made of them:

> . . . these facilities of radar advice are made and supplied and established for the greater safety of shipping in general and for greater accuracy in navigation. . . . A vessel which deliberately disregards such an aid when available is exposing not only herself, but other shipping to undue risks, that is, risks which with seamanlike prudence could, and should, be eliminated. . . . there

---

[17] *The* Pallanza *(NY 1811) 189 F 43.*
[18] *See Appendix X.*
[19] *The* Gorm *(1961) 1 L.R. 196.*
[20] *The* Bovenkerk *(1973) 1 L.R. 70.*

is a duty upon shipping to use such aids when readily available—and if they elect to disregard such aids they do so at their own risk.[21]

Clear visibility does not dispense with the need to keep a radar lookout. In the United States courts, ships have been found at fault for not using radar as a general lookout at night, after colliding with offshore oil-drilling rigs, even though the visibility was clear. However, a vessel is not obliged to use radar, even in restricted visibility, if it is not working properly, though active efforts should be made to have repairs completed as soon as possible.

> There might well be times when the continued use of radar by a navigator who was uncertain of the results he was observing and unwilling to place reliance thereon might well be foolhardy and hazardous.[22]

However, Judge Medina in the U.S. Appeals Court, when reviewing this case in 1959, gave the following caution:

> This does not mean that, in the face of the fact that a properly functioning radar will give useful and necessary information, the master had a discretion to decide that it will not give such information and turn off his radar. A master has no more discretion to disregard this aid to navigation than he has to disregard the use of charts, current tables and soundings where the circumstances require the use thereof.

The use of a radar as a general lookout does not dispense with the need to maintain a visual lookout:

> The question . . . on this occasion was: "Was it seamanlike for the *Arietta* to rely on relative motion radar observation only and to have no visual look-out?" and the answer was: "No."[23]

Lookout comprises not only the proper use of sight and hearing, augmented by equipment such as radar, but also a proper appreciation of a situation by the person in charge of the watch. The officer of the deck must be alert to what is happening in his own vessel, checking the steering, the correct functioning of equipment and, not least, that the correct lights continue to be shown at night. Several collisions in recent years have occurred due to dilatory discovery of equipment defects.

> Where, in my judgement, she was at fault, was in having a very bad look-out, and a bad look-out in every possible sense of the term. It seems to me that it comes within the term "bad look-out" when I say that she was at fault for failing to take proper precautions to meet the situation in the event of the

---

[21] *The* Vechtstroom *(1964) 1 L.R. 118.*
[22] *The Pocahontas Steamship Co. v. Esso Aruba (1950).*
[23] *The* Arietta *(1970) 1 L.R. 70.*

compass breaking down again, as it in fact did. It was, in my judgement, bad look-out on the part of this young third officer in failing to appreciate, long before he did appreciate it, what was happening, namely that his vessel was falling off to starboard, and in failing to appreciate what the probable cause of the falling off was. It was bad look-out on the part of the quartermaster, when he knew perfectly well that the compass had stuck again, not to report the matter at once to the officer in charge. It was bad look-out on the part of the officer to take no steps himself, whether by going to the standard compass or otherwise, to check up on what was happening and what was the course of his vessel.[24]

Many similar judgments have followed in subsequent cases.[25] The advent of modern aids in ships seems sometimes to lead to an unfounded belief in their reliability and a too-casual attitude towards keeping a proper lookout. In the Mediterranean, in 1964, the cargo ship *Trentbank* suffered a failure of her automatic steering as she was overtaking the tanker *Fogo* and swung across the bow of the latter.

> I ought not to leave this part of the case without observing how lamentable was the attitude of the master of the *Trentback* and her chief officer towards the system of automatic steering. The master had given no orders to ensure that somebody was on the look-out all the time. The chief officer, according to his own story, saw nothing wrong in undertaking a clerical task and giving only an occasional glance forward when he knew that there was other shipping about and that he was the only man on board his ship who was keeping any semblance of a look-out at all. Automatic steering is a most valuable invention if properly used. It can lead to disaster when it is left to look after itself while vigilance is relaxed. It is on men that safety at sea depends and they cannot make a greater mistake than to suppose that machines can do all their work for them.[26]

Immaterial Absence of Proper Lookout Not a Fault

It is not meant to imply that whenever two vessels collide, the mere proof of improper lookout on either vessel, in the technical sense, will *ipso facto* condemn that vessel for the collision. On the contrary, it has been held by the Supreme Court that the absence of a lookout is unimportant where the approaching vessel was seen long before the collision occurred;[27] that it is immaterial where it does not appear that the collision could in any way be attributed to his absence;[28] and that the absence of a lookout stationed where he should be will not render a vessel in fault

[24] *The Staffordshire (1948) 81 L.R. 141.*

[25] *The Chusan (1955) 2 L.R. 685; The Esso Plymouth (1955) 1 L.R. 429; The Indus (1957) 1 L.R. 335; The Greathope (1957) 2 L.R. 197; The British Tenacity (1963) 2 L.R. 1; The Salaverry (1968) 1 L.R. 53.*

[26] *The Trentback (1967) 2 L.R. 208.*

[27] *The Dexter (Md 1875) 23 L Ed. 84; the George W. Elder (CCA 1918) 249 F 9656.*

[28] *The Tacoma (Wash 1888) 36 L Ed. 469.*

for a collision where she was navigated exactly as she should have been had there been a lookout reporting the situation.[29] As said by the Circuit Court of Appeals in a later case, where an overtaking vessel rammed the vessel ahead:

> Absence of a lookout is not entitled to weight in cases where the proof is satisfactory that the vessel in fault saw the other in time to have taken every precaution it was its duty to take, and which, if taken, would have avoided the collision.[30]

But the difficulty in practice is, of course, to overcome the presumption of fault which the absence of a proper lookout entails and furnish such saitsfactory proof. It is only when it can be made clear that the lack of a lookout could not have contributed to the collision that it will be excused.[31] Two illustrative cases may be mentioned here. In one of them, a dredge at work in a channel during a dense fog, while sounding a fog bell at intervals of less than a minute which could be heard many times the distance of visibility, was run down by a stern-wheel steamer making 15 knots, and the presence or absence of an efficient lookout on the dredge was held immaterial.[32] In another case, in a crossing situation on the East River, a burdened ferry stopped well off the course of a privileged tug to let her pass, but was rammed when the latter suddenly changed her course; it was held with some degree of reason that the want of a proper lookout on the burdened vessel was not a contributory fault.[33]

Notwithstanding such occasional exceptions, the navigator should always adhere to the general admiralty rule that:

> The strict performance of a vessel's duty to maintain proper lookout is required and failure to do so, especially when other craft are known to be in the vicinity, is culpable negligence.[34]

Many court decisions on the subject indicate that the strict performance referred to means, at least in most circumstances, not only that lookouts shall be free from other duties but that they shall be (1) qualified by a certain amount of experience as seamen, (2) vigilant and alert, (3) properly stationed, and (4) in such numbers as circumstances require in order that the vessel may avoid risk of collision.[35]

[29] *Elcoate v. the* Plymothian *(Va 1897) 42 L Ed. 519.*

[30] *The* M. J. Rudolph *(NY 1923) 292 F 740; the* Lehigh *(NY 1935) 12 F Supp 75.*

[31] *The* Titan *(CC 1885) 23 F 413.*

[32] *The* Bailey Gatzert *(Ore 1910) 179 F 44.*

[33] *The* N and W No. 2 *(NY 1903) 122 F 171.*

[34] *The* Kaga Maru *(Wash 1927) 18 F (2d) 295.*

[35] *For a discussion of court interpretation of "risk of collision," see Chapter 16.*

Lookout Should Be Experienced Seaman

No definite minimum experience requirement has been laid down by the courts as qualifying a man for duty as lookout, but several decisions have shown the necessity of some attention to this point. In an early case the District Court of New York held that the steward, who was standing by the companion way, and was no mariner, and had not been stationed as a lookout, was not a proper lookout;[36] and fourteen years later the district court of Pennsylvania held that it is doubtful whether a steward is a competent lookout, and he certainly is not when his attention is divided between such duty and the duties belonging to his employment as steward, such as serving coffee to the crew.[37] The Circuit Court of Appeals has said that besides watching for lights ahead and on crossing courses a lookout should also be watchful for things adrift, such as a disabled launch, so near as to be likely to drift against his vessel, and a tug with a long tow must extend this watchfulness the full length of the tow;[38] in another decision the Circuit Court found that a steamer should have a "trustworthy" lookout.[39] It was held a fault rendering a steamship liable for a collision with a schooner to have as the only lookout in a dense fog, on a frequented part of the Atlantic coast, a boy of sixteen years who had been on the water but a few weeks.[40] When the lookout on a moving vessel confused the lights of an anchored vessel with others on the shore five miles distant, the vessel was not relieved from liability for collision with the anchored vessel.[41] In two other decisions implying that a lookout must have some knowledge of his responsibilities that comes with experience, the Circuit Court of Appeals in New York held:

> The failure of the lookout of a steamer to report a vessel when discovered is negligence, though the master and pilot were on the bridge.[42]
> A lookout's duty is to report as soon as he sees any vessel with which there is danger of collision or which in any way may affect the navigation of his own; and he cannot speculate on the probabilities of collision, such responsibility being for the master.[43]

This does not suggest that a lookout should report everything he sees; in crowded waters he could not be expected to cope. In such a case

---

[36] The Gratitude (NY 1868) Fed. Cas. No. 5,704.
[37] The Bessie Morris (Pa 1882) 13 F 397.
[38] Cook v. Moran Towing Co. (CCA NY 1911) 193 F 48.
[39] The Pilot Boy (SC 1902) 115 F 873.
[40] The Pottsville (Pa 1882) 12 F 631.
[41] The John G. McCullough (CCA Va 1916) 239 F 111.
[42] The Hansa (CCA NY 1870) Fed. Cas. No. 6,036.
[43] The Madison (CCA NY 1918) 250 F 850.

consideration should be given to placing additional lookouts. Certainly the courts will take into account the number of seamen available on board when considering whether a proper lookout was maintained.[44] Even if this is done, a lookout must use his discretion to some extent in reporting what he sees. As was said in one case:

> You cannot report every light you see in the River Thames. You have to watch until you see a light, which, perhaps, you have seen before, becoming material, because if you are going to report every light in Gravesend Reach when coming up the Thames the confusion would be something appalling to those in charge of the navigation; but you have to have a look-out to report every material light as soon as it becomes material.[45]

This heightens the need for a lookout to be experienced, well trained and thoroughly briefed on every occasion before taking up his duty.

In the naval service it is suggested that except on the smallest vessels the lookout might well be a petty officer. On a capital ship, when we consider the value of the property at risk, the intelligence that should be demanded in reporting various kinds of lights, with correct bearings, and the legal importance attached to a proper performance, the duty should by no means be regarded as beneath the dignity of a chief petty officer. It goes without saying that the choice of a competent lookout is only half the requirement, the other half being an insistence by the officer of the deck that reports to him be made promptly and correctly, at times of good visibility as well as bad, so that in darkness or in thick weather they will be rendered as a matter of habit. Perhaps it is significant that more than 70 percent of the cases cited in this chapter were clear weather collisions.

Lookout Should Be Vigilant

That a high degree of vigilance is constantly required of the lookout is evident from the findings in numerous cases; a high degree, though not an unreasonable degree. Thus, the district court of Maryland declined to condemn a steamer for failure to discover a sailing vessel without lights on a dark night, merely because the sailing vessel might have been discovered in time to avoid collision if an officer had been constantly observing the horizon with a good pair of glasses.[46] But a vessel's failure to see the lights on another vessel, properly set and burning, due to want of

---

[44] The Spirality (1954) 2 L.R. 59; also the Saxon Queen (1954) 2 L.R. 286; the Mode (1954) 2 L.R. 26.

[45] The Shakkeborg (1911) Sh. Gaz. Apr. 11.

[46] The Leversons (Md 1882) 10 F.753.

vigilance, renders it liable for the resulting collision;[47] and a vessel's failure to discover the lights of a passing vessel in time to avoid collision is tantamount to having no lookout.[48] An overtaking vessel without lights in a convoy during the war was liable for a collision with the ship ahead because the lookout failed to keep under close observation the other vessel, and to give warning of the close approach in time to avoid collision.[49]

That it is incumbent on a vessel navigating New York Harbor and vicinity, even in the daytime, to maintain a vigilant lookout, is a requirement which the Supreme Court declined to review.[50] In another New York case, this time in the harbor of Buffalo, it was said by the district court:

It is the imperative duty of a steamship when making a landing at a dock in a river where other vessels are constantly passing, to maintain an efficient lookout, and the absence of such lookout cannot be excused on the ground that all the crew were otherwise engaged.[51]

And in an Alaska case, where a tug negligently allowed a loaded barge to be cast upon the rocks during a snowstorm, the Supreme Court affirmed the decision of the Circuit Court of Appeals awarding a decree to the barge owners which held that:

The strict rules with respect to the necessity of having a lookout properly stationed and devoting his whole attention to the situation ahead is not limited to vessels navigating harbors, but applies as well to a vessel navigating along the coast, where danger from striking the land is as great as the danger of collision in harbor.[52]

In a collision between a steamship and a sailing vessel the Circuit Court of Appeals found that the duty of the steamship to maintain a constant lookout is especially imperative in favor of a vessel which under the rules has the right of way.[53] Other decisions emphasize the fact that the degree of vigilance exercised by the lookout is quite likely to be judged by the single standard of its effectiveness in preventing collision:

The failure of a steamer to see a sailing vessel which she ought to have discovered, in time to give her sufficient room, is a fault rendering the steamer liable if it results from insufficient lookout.[54]

[47] *The* Buenos Aires *(CCA NY 1924) 5 F (2d) 425.*
[48] *Pendleton Bros. v. Morgan (Md 1926) 11 F (2d) 67.*
[49] *The* War Pointer *(CCA Va 1921) 277 F 718.*
[50] *The* Transfer No. 15 *(CCA NY 1917) 243 F 174.*
[51] *The* Northland *(NY 1903) 125 F 58.*
[52] *The British Columbia Mills Tug and Barge Co. v. Mylroie 66 L Ed. 807.*
[53] *The* Dorchester *(1908) 167 F 124.*
[54] *The* Belgenland *(1885) 29 L Ed. 152.*

The excuse that a vessel is unable to determine (by reason of the darkness and the direction of the wind) from the lights of the other vessel, on what course she is sailing, and which is the privileged vessel, cannot be invoked where, by reason of the inefficiency of her lookout, she failed to discover the approaching vessel until the two were in close proximity, and she had no time to study the situation.[55]

A burdened vessel which fails, through the inexcusable absence of her lookout, to maintain it steadily, and thus causes a collision, is liable.[56]

Where the evidence leaves no doubt that two blasts of a whistle were given by one steamer, which were heard on the other as only a single blast, the distance being such that both ought to have been heard, the court must conclude, in the absence of other explanation, that the officers and lookout were inattentive.[57]

It is a fault for the lookout of a vessel to leave his post after reporting the light of another vessel.[58]

Lookout Specially Necessary in Fog

The degree of vigilance required is, of course, greatly increased underway in foggy weather, and absence or insufficency of lookout under such conditions underway can never be justified by the plea that visibility was so low as to render a lookout useless. If he cannot see, at least he can hear. Under the general admiralty rules it is the duty of every vessel, when navigating in a fog, to maintain a lookout in a proper position, who shall be charged with no other duty.[59] A local custom cannot excuse a vessel from observing this rule.[60] As said by the Circuit Court of Appeals:

The denser the fog and the worse the weather are greater cause for vigilance, and a vessel cannot excuse failure to maintain lookout on the ground that the weather was so thick that another vessel could not be seen until actually in collision.[61]

However, as brought out by the Circuit Court in the collision of the *Bailey Gatzert* with a Columbia River dredge, already cited, this injunction apparently does not apply with the same force to a vessel at anchor in fog, provided she is making proper fog signals.[62]

---

[55] The Queen Elizabeth *100 F 874 (reversed on other grounds), 122 F 406.*
[56] The Robert Graham Dun *(CCA 1895) 70 F 270.*
[57] The Ottoman *(CCA Mass 1896) 74 F 316.*
[58] *Wilders SS. Co. v. Low (Hawaii 1901) 112 F 161;* the Havre *(NY 1868) Fed. Cas. 6,232.*
[59] The Wilbert L. Smith *(Wash 1914) 217 F 981.*
[60] The Tillicum *(Wash 1914) 217 F 976.*
[61] The Sagamore *(Mass 1917) 247 F 743.*
[62] The Bailey Gatzert *(CCA Ore 1910) 179 F 44.*

The degree of vigilance required is in no way lessened because a vessel in a collision situation may happen to have the right of way. In a number of very early decisions it was held that if a vessel having the right of way held her course, it was all an approaching vessel had a right to require, and in the case of a small sailing schooner run down by a large steamship in Chesapeake Bay the Supreme Court held that whether she had a proper lookout or not was immaterial.[63] But as early as 1874 the district court of Maine established the rule that:

> A vessel having the right of way must keep a proper lookout and use proper seamanship to avoid collision.[64]

Accordingly, as said by the federal court in the *Kaga Maru*, a vessel is not relieved of her obligation to maintain a proper lookout because she is the preferred vessel, if prudent navigation with the aid of a good lookout would have avoided the collision,[65] and in a New York Harbor collision decided in 1928, a steamer without a lookout was held equally at fault with an army dredge on the wrong side of the channel with which it collided.[66] Similarly, the failure of a tug to keep a lookout rendered it liable for the death of a man in a rowboat on the Delaware River, on the showing that notwithstanding the latter's contributory negligence in attempting to cross the tug's course, a vigilant lookout would have discovered his peril in time for the tug to avoid him. In this case the tug was flanked on either side by a loaded car float, neither float having a lookout.[67]

The old idea that to be efficient a seaman must be uncomfortable is happily disappearing in the naval service. In this connection it might be well to remember that a lookout who is freezing from exposure in a cold wind can scarcely be expected to be vigilant. The author remembers with some feeling his early service as a merchant seaman, with winter night watches in northern waters, out on the unprotected bow of a fast passenger steamer. After a few moments of this, there would be little thought given to approaching lights, or of anything else except getting in out of the weather. A canvas dodger would have worked wonders, as indeed it will with the lookout on the nose of a present-day cruiser, heading into a breeze at 20 knots. The officer of the deck who expects his lookouts to be alert will do well to assure himself that the men performing this duty are

---

[63] *The* Fannie *(Md 1871) 20 L Ed. 114.*
[64] *The* Mary C *(Me 1874) Fed. Cas. No. 9,201.*
[65] *The* Kaga Maru *(Wash 1927) 18 F (2d) 295.*
[66] *A. H. Bull SS. Co. v. U.S. (NY 1928) 29 F (2d) 765.*
[67] *Klutt v. Philadelphia and Reading Ry. Co. (CCA Penn 1906) 142 F 394.*

adequately clothed and as well protected from the weather as conditions will permit.

Lookout Should Be Properly Stationed

Although the statute is silent as to the specific location of the lookout, a long line of court decisions has well established his proper position to be as low down and as far forward in the ship as conditions allow. As said by the Circuit Court of Appeals:

> He is required by good navigation to be placed at the point best suited for the purpose alike of hearing and observing the approach of objects likely to be brought into collision with the vessel, having regard to the circumstances of the case and the conditions of the weather.[68]

Accordingly, the *Vedamore*, a large ocean steamship navigating Chesapeake Bay at night in fog, was at fault because her only lookout was in the crow's nest 60 feet above the deck and 100 feet from the stem. It was held to be the duty of another ocean steamer passing out of the Delaware at night to maintain her lookout as far forward and as near the water as possible.[69] In a collision in Boston Harbor in which a ferryboat was sunk by a mud scow the pilot house was declared not a proper place for the former's lookout;[70] and in another case, stationing the lookout on top of the pilot house 140 feet from the bow of a steamship navigating in a dense fog, with visibility of 100 feet, was a gross fault.[71] A lookout on the bridge without any in the bow is insufficient;[72] and in another collision in fog previously cited the steamship *Sagamore* was held at fault for not maintaining a lookout from the forecastle head despite lookouts both in the crow's nest and on the bridge.[73] In a collision on a clear night at sea, when the usual order was reversed by having a sailing vessel sink a steamship, the Circuit Court of Appeals held that every steamer must have at least one lookout in the eyes of the ship.[74] In a collision in a dense fog on Puget Sound the court found a tug at fault for having the lookout by the pilot house, but only 12 feet from the stem.[75] In the *Winnisimmet*, mentioned above, the judicial attitude was thus summarized:

The courts have been rigid in holding vessels to maintaining lookout as far

---

[68] *The* Vedamore *(1905) 137 F 844.*
[69] *The* Prinz Oskar *(1915) 219 F 483.*
[70] *Eastern Dredging Co. v.* Winnisimmet *162 F 860.*
[71] *The* Campania *(La 1927) 21 F (2d) 233.*
[72] *Neally v. the* Michigan *63 F 280.*
[73] *The* Sagamore *(CCA Mass 1917) 247 F 743.*
[74] *The* Stifinder *(CAA NY 1921) 275 F 271.*
[75] *The* Kaga Maru *(Wash 1927) 18 F (2d) 295.*

forward and as near the water as possible. Especially where the water is dark, with otherwise a fairly clear night, it is important that the lookout should be as near it as possible, in order that his eye may follow the surface, and thus be in position to detect anything low down which may be approaching.[70]

A United States submarine was held solely at fault for sinking a small schooner near the western end of the Cape Cod Canal shortly after World War I, on a clear night with smooth sea and all lights burning brightly, a charge of improper lookout being sustained. In its decision, the court recognized the extremely limited space available for a lookout on the bow of an R-boat, but declared that every moving vessel must maintain a competent, careful, and efficient lookout stationed on the forward part of the vessel, and that the rule applies with equal force to submarines or other naval vessels, in the absence of statutory exception.[76]

When physical conditions prevent, of course, a lookout need not be kept forward of the bridge. An ocean tug whose lookout was in the pilot house because green seas were sweeping over the bow,[77] and a steamship navigating the Atlantic on a clear night with her lookout on the bridge because of the coldness of the weather and the freezing spray forward[76] were both absolved from blame. If the weather is clear and the lookout is sufficiently vigilant it really matters little where he is stationed; but the practical catch that goes with failure to place him away forward is, the burden of proof devolves upon the offender to show that the lookout functioned as well as he would have done if properly placed. As an example in point, the fact that the lookout on a steamer at sea on a clear night was stationed on the bridge instead of forward was held not to be at fault in a collision with a fishing vessel where the evidence showed that each vessel reasonably discovered the other and kept her under continuous observation.[78] But in another case, involving a tug and a sailing vessel on the Hudson River, it was held that:

> The position of the captain of a schooner abaft the wheel is not a proper position for a lookout, when sailing full and free with a strong wind; and in case of a conflict of testimony, observation reported from such a position must be deemed partial, interrupted, and incomplete, and entitled to far less weight than that of a lookout properly stationed.[79]

The decisions are clear in requiring that the lookout have unobstructed visibilty ahead and on both bows. Hence it has been held that an old rule of the former Board of Supervising Inspectors, requiring passenger steamers

---

[76] U.S. v. Black (CCA 1936) 82 F (2d) 394.

[77] The Caro (NY 1884) 23 F 734; the Kaiserin Marie Theresa (CCA NY 1906) 147 F 97.

[78] The Lake Monroe (CCA 1921) 271 F 474.

[79] The Excelsior (NY 1882) 12 F 195.

and ferryboats to keep one of the crew on watch in or near the pilot house could not supersede the general rule requiring a lookout forward.[80] In the case of the *Scandinavia* it was pointed out that the duty to maintain a lookout on the lower deck of a ferryboat is not statutory but is imposed by the general maritime law.[81] The same principle was established in several decisions requiring that a tug must keep a lookout at the bow of a tow alongside where it projects beyond the tug;[82] and where other traffic may be expected, a vessel towing astern of a tug should maintain as careful a lookout as the tug herself, and be prepared, if necessary to avoid collision, to sheer out or cut her hawser.[83] Because the tow cannot always see ahead, the vessel towing should keep a specially vigilant lookout. In addition to having an unobstructed view, a further reason for placing the lookout forward is to keep his hearing as unimpaired as much as is possible by the noise from the engines,[84] especially in diesel and gas turbine-powered ships.

However, should a collision occur, it is well to bear in mind that clear visibility, rather than technical location, is the essential thing, and that after all, as expressed by the district court of Virginia in a collision between a government steam launch and a fishing steamer near Norfolk:

> All that the law requires with respect to a lookout is that there shall be someone properly stationed to best observe, see, and hear the approach of other vessels; and a small launch, only 61 feet long, having her pilot house, in which her navigator stood, well forward, with open windows all around, and other members of the crew on the deck, cannot be held in fault for a collision in the daytime, in fair weather, because she did not have a lookout specially stationed where she was the privileged vessel, entitled to keep her course and speed, and the absence of such lookout did not contribute to the collision.[85]

While in the absence of special conditions the place for the lookout is at the bow,[86] there are circumstances which require a lookout also at the stern. Thus it has been held that an ocean steamer starting her propeller in order to leave her slip, in which there are other vessels, should have a lookout at the stern to give warning of danger to such vessels from the

---

[80] *The* Tillicum *(Wash 1914) 217 F 976.*

[81] *The* Scandinavia *(NY 1918) 11 F (2d) 542.*

[82] *The* Pennsylvania *(NY 1878) Fed. Cas. No. 10,949; the* A. P. Skidmore *(NY 1901) 108 F 972.*

[83] *The* Virginia Ehrman *and the* Agnese *24 L Ed. 890; the* American *102 F 767.*

[84] Cabo Santo Tome *(1933) 46 L.R. 165.*

[85] *The* Pocomoke *(Va 1906) 150 F 193.*

[86] *Yamashita Kisen Kabushiki Kaisha v. McCormick Intercoastal SS. Co. (CCA Cal 1927) 20 F (2d) 25.*

motion of the propeller;[87] that a vessel backing out of her slip must keep a lookout astern;[88] as must a tug floating downstream bow towards the shore,[89] a vessel drifting backwards with the tide,[90] or in fact a vessel making sternway for any purpose, as when backing and filling to turn around,[91] or when backing into her slip.[92] And a steam tug which towed a barge past a vessel at anchor so close as to cause a collision between her tow and the vessel without keeping a proper lookout at the stern, was solely liable.[93]

In general, an overtaken vessel is under no duty to keep a lookout aft to prevent being run down by the overtaking vessel, but has a right to act on the presumption that the latter will keep clear.[94] The Circuit Court of Appeals in New York has gone so far as to rule that in inland waters, where the overtaking vessel has no right to pass without a signal being given and answered, the overtaken vessel is not required to discover her before she changes course, however abruptly; if the overtaking vessel comes so close without signaling that a sudden change of course by the vessel ahead brings about a collision, the fault is that of the overtaking vessel.[95] However, good seamanship would seem to go a step further here, and require the precaution of always at least looking aft before changing course or reducing speed, because of the possibility of embarrassing an overtaking vessel. As said by the Supreme Court in the case of the *Illinois*, when a sailing vessel, failing to notice a following steamship, tacked to avoid floating ice in Delaware Bay and was sunk by the steamship:

> While a man stationed at the stern as a lookout is not at all times necessary, no vessel should change her course materially without having first made such an observation in all directions as will enable her to know how what she is about to do will affect others in her immediate vicinity.[96]

In a collision between the USS *Bell* and a steam lighter, both vessels were leaving Boston Harbor in a thick fog, with the destroyer leading. The *Bell* stopped without warning when it appeared that the gate in a steel

---

[87] *The* Nevada v. Quick *(NY 1882) 27 L Ed. 149.*

[88] *The* Luzerne *(CCA NY 1912) 197 F 162; the* Herbert L. Pontin *(CCA NY 1931) 50 F (2d) 177.*

[89] *The* Mary J. Kennedy *(CCA 1924) 11 F (2d) 169.*

[90] *The* Senator D. C. Chase *(CCA NY 1901) 108 F 110.*

[91] *The* Deutschland *(CCA NY 1905) 137 F 1018.*

[92] *Greenwood v. the* William Fletcher *and the* Grapeshot *(NY 1889) 38 F 156.*

[93] *The* Cement Rock *and the* Venture *(NY 1876) Fed. Cas. No. 2,544.*

[94] *The* Greystoke Castle *(Cal 1912) 199 F 521.*

[95] *The* Merrill C. Hart *(CCA 1911) 188 F 49; the* M. J. Rudolph *292 F 740.*

[96] *The* Illinois *(1881) 26 L Ed. 563.*

submarine net stretched across the north channel during the war was closed; and the lighter, attempting to sheer out, collided with the depth charge sponson, injuring both vessels. The Circuit Court of Appeals found both at fault: the lighter for excessive speed in striking a vessel which was dead in the water, and the destroyer for not keeping a proper lookout astern when she knew another vessel was following, although she had two depth-charge men aft who had not been instructed to report approaching vessels.[97]

Lookouts Must Be Adequate for Circumstances

There can be no doubt from the decisions that under some circumstances more than one lookout is required, although ordinarily one with that exclusive duty will be sufficient. In a collision at sea in a dense fog at night where, besides a man forward, stationed as a lookout, there were two persons on watch in the pilot house of a large ocean steamer, the lookout was held sufficient.[98] On the other hand, in a decision of the Supreme Court relating to a collision on the Columbia River between a passenger steamship and a dredge at anchor, it was held that:

> Where the circumstances require more than ordinary care, as in the case of a steamer running at a speed of 15 miles an hour, on a dark night, in a narrow channel, where there is a great probability of meeting other vessels, a deck watch composed of the river pilot in command, stationed upon the bridge just above the pilot house, a man at the wheel, and a lookout upon the forecastle head, is insufficient, and prudent navigation requires a lookout to be stationed on either bow.[99]

In a collision during the Spanish-American War a few miles off Fire Island at night in a thick fog, the armored cruiser *Columbia* sank a British freighter. The *Columbia* was making 6 knots, and in accordance with the orders of the squadron commander showing no lights and making no fog signals. The freighter was making 3½ knots and sounding regular fog signals. In an action several years later the cruiser was found solely at fault, the court commenting on the fact that under such circumstances unusual vigilance was required, and that her lookouts were quite insufficient, being only those usually maintained in clear weather—one at each end of the bridge, 94 feet from the stem and 38 feet above the water, and two farther aft.[100] While it is true that in this case the real fault lay in not

---

[97] *Boston Sand and Gravel Co. v. U.S. (CCA 1925) 7 F (2d) 278.*
[98] *Watts v. U.S. (1903) 123 F 105.*
[99] *The Oregon (Ore 1895) 39 L Ed. 943.*
[100] *Watts v. U.S. (1903) 123 F 105.*

having the forward lookouts out on the bow, yet it is significant that here was an instance of improper lookout with four men detailed to exclusive lookout duty. On a large vessel in thick weather there is a positive obligation to have lookouts stationed so as to give the earliest warning of approaching vessels from whatever direction they may come.

It may seem to the reader that the courts have given undue emphasis to the necessity of lookouts when their function is a duty already laid on the officer of the deck. It may be argued that an officer of the deck who is worth his salt will be the first to discover the approach of anything which might endanger his vessel. The explanation can only be the obvious one that the commissioned or licensed watch stander has other concurrent duties which he cannot neglect, and the law contemplates that every vessel underway shall exercise vigilance *which is continuous and unbroken,* both for her own protection and that of other vessels. However, it is doubtful if the civil courts are more exacting in this regard than are the naval courts and boards which must be encountered by an officer in the service whenever a naval vessel is involved in collision. With them the question of proper lookout in collision cases is inevitable. In a recent hearing that followed a collision between a naval vessel and a merchant ship, the board of investigation found the commanding officer at fault for improper lookout on the technical point that the quartermaster of the watch was serving as lookout while the vessel was leaving port, although the collision occurred in broad daylight with excellent visibility, and the testimony showed that the approaching vessel, as she emerged from a channel entrance, was sighted by the commanding officer, the officer of the deck, the man at the wheel, and the lookout himself. This illustrates the importance that may be attached by one's brother-officers to maintaining a technically proper lookout even when visibility is unquestionably good.

Importance of Lookouts

From the standpoint of the navigator who is interested in avoiding liability for collision, which usually means avoiding the collision itself, perhaps there could be no more appropriate conclusion to these remarks on a proper lookout than the following words of the United States Supreme Court, delivered in a case that arose out of a collision between a steamship and a brig outside New York Harbor on a foggy night in 1865:

> The duty of the lookout is of the highest importance. Upon nothing else does the safety of those concerned so much depend. A moment's negligence on his part may involve the loss of his vessel with all the property and the lives of all on board. The same consequence may ensue to the vessel with which his shall collide. In the performance of this duty the law requires indefatigable care and sleepless vigilance. . . . It is the duty of all courts charged with the administration

of this branch of our jurisprudence to give it the fullest effect whenever the circumstances are such as to call for its application. Every doubt as to the performance of the duty and the effect of nonperformance, should be resolved against the vessel sought to be inculpated until she vindicates herself by testimony to the contrary.[101]

SUMMARY

A lookout has been defined by the federal court as a person who is specially charged with the duty of observing the lights, sounds, echoes, or any obstruction to navigation with that thoroughness which the circumstances permit. The statement in Article 29 that nothing in the rules shall exonerate any vessel from the consequence of any neglect to keep a proper lookout has caused the courts to hold a vessel in collision without a proper lookout at fault unless it can be proved that the other vessel was discovered as soon as a proper lookout would have discovered her.

Numerous court decisions have built up a considerable doctrine with reference to what constitutes a proper lookout. Such a lookout must have no other duties, such as conning or steering the vessel; he must be constantly alert and vigilant, he must have had a reasonable amount of experience as a seaman; he must report what he sees or hears to the officer of the watch; and he must ordinarily be stationed as low down and as far forward on the vessel as circumstances permit. In conditions of crowded traffic and in thick weather enough lookouts must be posted to detect the approach of another vessel from any direction.

[101] *The Ariadne (1872) 13 Wall 475.*

21
Inevitable Accident

Collision Liability under American Admiralty Law

In a previous chapter it was pointed out that whenever two vessels are in a collision which results in litigation there are precisely four possibilities, under American maritime law, as to the judicial determination of liability: (1) vessel *A* may be held solely at fault and liable for all the damage to both vessels; (2) the same may be true of vessel *B*; (3) both may be at fault, with the invariable result of a division of damages; (4) or neither may be at fault, in which case each must bear her own damage, be it great or small.[1] While the question of legal liability does not ordinarily arise in a collision between two naval vessels which have a common owner, it does arise, and is settled in the same manner, when a naval vessel collides with a merchant vessel; and even in a collision between two vessels of the Navy, the rules of the road and governing court decisions which apply in a civil action are to a large extent followed by naval courts and boards in fixing the culpability of officers involved in the collision. A proper understanding of collision law as administered by the courts therefore becomes of as much importance to officers in the naval service as it is to ship operators and to officers of the Merchant Marine.

A casual examination of the case books will show that of the over 8,000 cases that have come before our courts only about 70 have fallen in the fourth-mentioned category, or less than 1 percent of the total. There are

---

[1] *The ability of the wronged vessel to collect may, of course, be modified by the Limited Liability Acts, which limit the liability of a vessel to her value after the collision plus pending freight; i.e., earnings collected or collectible for the voyage on which the collision occurs; and which limit aggregate recovery for personal injury or loss of life to $15 per gross ton where value of the vessel plus pending freight is not more.*

numerous collisions in which only one vessel is at fault, but the surprising fact to the uninitiated is that in the majority of cases *both* vessels are at fault.

Cases of Inevitable Accident Are Rare

It is well known that collisions are not brought about intentionally, and that comparatively few of them, moreover, occur because of thick fog. Despite the wide-spread practice of maintaining excessive speed with low visibility, vessels navigating in fog successfully dodge each other most of the time. Probably at least three-fourths of the collisions take place in clear weather, with each vessel or her lights plainly visible to the other for a considerable time before the casualty, and are the result of some misunderstanding. When we consider that the rules of the road were carefully drawn up for the express purpose of preventing not only actual collision but even serious risk of collision, perhaps the prevalence of double culpability is not surprising. It would seem to indicate that the rules as interpreted are almost air-tight; that if they do not always prevent collision, at least they make it impossible in most cases for a collision to occur unless both vessels fail to obey them. This is, indeed, the opinion of the admiralty courts, which rightly or wrongly, are the final arbiters of collision liability. As pointed out by the Circuit Court of Appeals in the well-known case of the *West Hartland*, when a privileged ocean freighter making not over 6 knots sank a 15-knot passenger liner which attempted to cross her bow on a clear night in Puget Sound, with the loss of several lives, largely because the liner's pilot mistook the freighter's port light for a more distant pier light and the master of the freighter overestimated his distance from the liner:

> There can seldom be a collision in the open sea in clear weather, where there is no obstruction and the vessels are plainly visible to each other for a long distance, without fault on the part of both vessels.[2]

From this introduction the reader will realize that the present chapter considers an extremely rare type of marine collision. Nevertheless, it is well for the professional mariner to know the characteristics of what the courts call inevitable, or unavoidable, accident for two reasons: (1) an appreciation of its rarity should incline him to a stricter observance of the rules; and (2) if he is ever involved in such a case he can take what comfort there may be in the judicial assurance that:

> The civil law, the common law, the maritime law, and the law of Great Britain and the United States agree that where a collision takes place by unavoidable

---

[2] *The* West Hartland *(CCA 1924) 2 F (2d) 834.*

accident, without blame being imputable to either party, the consequences of the misfortune must be borne by the party upon whom it happens to fall.[3]

Under the common law an accident was said to be inevitable when it was not occasioned in any degree, either remotely or directly, by the want of such care and skill as the law holds every man bound to exercise. Similarly, under the maritime law:

> An inevitable accident is something that human skill and foresight could not, in the exercise of ordinary prudence, have provided against.[4]

> The term "inevitable accident" as applied to a collision means a collision which occurs when both parties have endeavored by every means in their power, with due care and caution and a proper display of nautical skill, to prevent the occurrence of the accident, and where the proofs show that it occurred in spite of everything that nautical skill, care, and precaution could do to keep the vessels from coming together.[5]

The matter of establishing the vessel's innocence by satisfactory proofs is even more emphatically stated in a later decision holding that:

> To sustain the defense of inevitable accident in a suit for collision, the defendant has the burden of proof and must show either what was the cause of the accident, and that cause was inevitable, or he must show all the possible causes and in regard to every one of such possible causes that the result could not have been avoided.[6]

It is not enough for a vessel to show that all that could be done was done as soon as the need to take action to avoid collision was determined. The point is whether actions should not have been taken earlier. When two ships are shown to have been in a position in which collision became inevitable, the question is, by whose fault, if there was fault, did the vessels get into such a position?[7]

In the light of these interpretations of inevitable accident, it will readily be understood that most of the cases determined by the courts have been due either to (1) *vis major*, or superior force of the elements, or (2) to a mechanical failure, in a collision situation, of steering gear or other machinery which due diligence could not prevent. The few cases that remain may for want of a better term be classed as miscellaneous, due either to a

---

[3] *The* Olympia *(CCA 1894) 61 F 120, aff. 52 F 985.*

[4] *The* Drum Craig *(1904) 133 F 804;* the Pennsylvania *(1861) 16 L Ed. 699.*

[5] *New York and Oriental SS. Co. v. N. Y., N.H., and H. Ry. Co. (NY 1906) 143 F 991;* the Mabey and Cooper *(1872) 20 L Ed. 881.*

[6] *The* Edmund Moran *(CCA NY 1910) 180 F 700, adopted from* The Merchant Prince *(1892) P 179, 189; see also* Southport Corporation v. Esso Petroleum Company Ltd. *(1955) 2 L.R. 655.*

[7] *Marsdens: Collisions, 11th Ed. p. 8, p. 9*

special combination of circumstances, or to causes which could not be ascertained from the evidence and were therefore not chargeable to either vessel.

Vis Major—Inevitable Accident Due to "Vis Major"

Vis major has been defined as an irresistible, natural cause which cannot be guarded against by the ordinary exertions of human skill and prudence.[8] An injury caused by a *vis major* is equivalent to an act of God.[9] It has been held that as respects the liability of carriers for loss or damage of goods the term *vis major* is used in the civil law in the same way that the words "act of God" are used in the common law, meaning inevitable accident or casualty.[10] Thus, storms of great and unexpected violence, unusual tidal currents, abnormal river floods, unpredictable ice conditions, or very dense fog may bring about marine collisions classed as inevitable. In this connection, it is fortunate that the word inevitable is considered as a relative term and construed not absolutely, but reasonably, with regard to the circumstances of the particular case.[11] In the case just cited, the steamer *Anna C. Minch* was broken from her moorings in the Buffalo River by a spring freshet, during which a huge mass of ice subjected her to such pressure that all her lines were parted at once, and she was carried down stream at 8 to 10 knots against other moored vessels. It being shown that her lines were sufficient under any conditions ordinarily to be anticipated, the accident was held inevitable.

Similarly, in a New York case, a tier of six canal boats was knocked from its moorings by another group of boats which had gone adrift as a combined result of a fresh wind and a strong tide, and one of the boats, the *Nora Costello*, struck and damaged a vessel at another pier, and was libeled. In dismissing the libel, the court held that:

> Vessels in making fast to piers are bound to provide only against ordinary contingencies such as they can anticipate; that they are not bound to make fast by lines so strong or numerous as to resist the impact of such a fleet of vessels as got adrift in this case; and that as there was no negligence in the *Costello* as to her mode of fastening, the libel against her should be dismissed.[12]

Again, when a sudden and extraordinary flood in the Monongahela River tore a fleet of water craft from its mooring at night, and crashed it at 10 knots or more into a fleet of coal boats, the courts dismissed a libel

[8] *Evans v. Wabash Ry. Co. 12 SW (2d) 767.*
[9] *Southern Pacific v. Schuyler 135 F 1015.*
[10] *Lehman, Stern, and Co. v. Morgan's La. and Tex. R.R. and SS. Co. 38 South 873.*
[11] *The* Anna C. Minch *(CCA 1921) 271 F 192.*
[12] *The* Nora Costello *(1890) 46 F 869.*

charging negligent moorings, and cited the following opinion of the Supreme Court:

> Inevitable accident is where a vessel is pursuing a lawful avocation in a lawful manner using the proper precautions against danger, and an accident occurs. The highest degree of caution that can be used is not required. It is enough that it is reasonable under the circumstances, such as is usual in similar cases, and has been found by long experience to be sufficient to answer the end in view —the safety of life and property. Neel v. Blythe (1890) 42 F 457, citing the *Grace Girdler* (1869) 19 L Ed. 113.

Other Cases of Vis Major at Anchor

In still another case, when a car float moored in a slip in the East River at the beginning of an extraordinary blizzard demonstrated the security of her mooring by remaining through two full tides, but was finally wrenched free by a floe of ice of a size not reasonably to be anticipated coming up the river, the court held that damage done by the car float to another vessel was due to inevitable accident;[13] and as a final illustration, when the bow lines of a steamship were carried away by a storm in New York Harbor which gave no more warning than the usual thunderstorm, but the wind actually reached a velocity for half a minute of 125 miles an hour, and a canal boat was damaged by the steamship, the latter was held free from fault.[14]

But an early case in Galveston was decided quite differently. It seems that three vessels, a brig, a schooner, and a bark, lay moored at a wharf when a heavy storm arose, breaking the brig adrift from the wharf. By quick work she was brought up by her anchors 100 yards or less from the schooner. Not long afterward, the bark was driven against the schooner, crushing in her stern and putting her in a sinking condition. The master of the schooner, to save her from sinking with her cargo in the deep water at the wharf, cut her adrift; whereupon, despite all efforts to the contrary, she struck and injured the brig. In the action brought against her by the brig the court denied the schooner's plea of inevitable accident inasmuch as the act of her master in cutting her adrift had been a voluntary one.[15]

When vessels at anchor fail to hold their position and are brought into collision with other vessels through dragging, it is very unusual for the courts to excuse them on the plea of inevitable accident. It is apparent from the decisions that in such cases a heavy burden is put upon the offending vessel to show that she was properly anchored. In a December

---

[13] *The* Transfer No. 2 and Car Float No. 12 *(1893) 56 F 313.*

[14] *The* Campanello *(NY 1917) 244 F 312.*

[15] *Sherman v. Mott (1871) Fed. Cas. No. 12,767 (affirmed by CCA, 1873).*

gale in New York the steamship *Bragdo*, at anchor off Staten Island with 45 fathoms out, dragged across the chain of the steamship *British Isles* and set her adrift. The plea of the *Bragdo* when libeled for the damage, was that she did not come to anchor with more chain out for fear of hitting piers half a length astern. The gale reached hurricane strength and in finding her liable for the collision the Circuit Court of Appeals cited the following passage from Knight's *Seamanship:*

> It is a common rule to give, under ordinary circumstances, a length of cable equal to seven times the depth of water. This is perhaps enough for a ship riding steadily and without any great tension of her cable, but it should be promptly increased if, for any reason, she begins to sheer about or jump, for it is always easier to prevent an anchor from dragging than to make it hold after it has once begun to drag.[16]

In the *Djerissa*, an ocean steamship of that name was at anchor in the James River when she was damaged by the *Neva*, a second steamship, which anchored subsequently and dragged into her. The storm which caused the mishap was evidently approaching for several hours, and aside from the fact that the first of two vessels to anchor is naturally the favored vessel, the courts found the *Neva* at fault for not dropping a second anchor.[17] An ocean tug left two seagoing barges at anchor in a storm off the Rhode Island coast for thirty-six hours while she took shelter in Newport Harbor. One barge dragged into the other, and was held at fault when the evidence showed that although she was forewarned as to the storm, she had only one anchor out until after she began to drag. Incidentally, on a showing that the tug could have stood by without danger to herself, the tug was held to share the liability because of contributory negligence.[18]

An excellent case to illustrate the distinction between negligence and necessary prudence in a similar situation was the *Herm*, decided by the Circuit Court of Appeals after being carried up from the district court of Virginia. Three barges anchored off the Newport News coal piers, after dragging for more than an hour under the pressure of drifting ice, struck and damaged a vessel moored at one of the piers, with her stern projecting 40 feet into the fairway. Two of the barges were held at fault for failure to drop a second anchor, while the third barge, which had lost her second anchor the night before and had been unable to replace it, was exonerated. The moored vessel recovered only half damages, however, for although it is not ordinarily a fault for a vessel's stern to project into the fairway beyond a pier end unless she obstructs navigation, it was con-

---

[16] *The* British Isles *(CCA 1920) 264 F 318.*
[17] *The* Djerissa *(CCA 1920) 267 F 115.*
[18] *The* Sea King *(NY 1926) 14 F (2d) 684.*

tributory negligence in this case where anchored barges subject to the action of drifting ice were in plain sight.[19]

However, in a unique collision between two anchored steamships in New York Harbor in a thick fog no fault was found with either vessel. The White Star liner *Adriatic* left her pier on the East River late on a November afternoon intending to proceed to sea, there being at the time sufficient visibility to see across the river. Near the Statue of Liberty the liner encountered fog of unprecedented density and was compelled to come to anchor. She proceeded very cautiously to a position off the Battery, dropped her hook, and swung around on it so as to contact the stem of the *Saint Michael*, an anchored vessel, about 125 feet forward of her own stern, with damage to both vessels. Each vessel libeled the other, the *Adriatic* being charged with negligence for leaving her pier in fog and for failing to try to return to it; and the *Saint Michael* being charged for lack of promptness in paying out her chain when the *Adriatic* appeared; but both the district and the appellate courts ruled that under all the attendant circumstances the accident was inevitable.[20]

Cases of Vis Major Underway

Not all cases of *vis major*, of course, occur while vessels are moored or at anchor, though they are less likely to happen to vessels with way on and fully capable of maneuvering. For the same reason not a few of these cases are responsible for collisions of tugs and of tows with which they are encumbered. Thus, two long tows of vessels with a combined length of 3,200 feet were in the act of passing starboard to starboard, as customary, about 200 feet apart below the Poughkeepsie Bridge on the Hudson River, when a terrific windstorm came up and drove some of the boats in the tows together.[21] A similar case of inevitable accident under the *vis major* rule occurred when a flotilla of vessels crossing Newark Bay in charge of two capable tugs was set down on two steamers lying at the National Drydock pier by the combined action of wind and tide of unpredictable violence.[22] A tug, maneuvering a barge in the ice off Delaware Breakwater, was carried by tide and ice into an anchored schooner, and having convinced the court that she was managed with ordinary care and skill under the circumstances was exonerated on the same grounds,[23] as was a tug that was libeled by a vessel in her tow which was forced ashore

[19] *The Herm (CCA 1920) 267 F 373.*
[20] *The Adriatic (CCA 1922) 287 F 259.*
[21] *The Cornell (1905) 134 F 694.*
[22] *The Mary Tracy (CCA 1925) 8 F (2d) 591.*
[23] *The Harold (NY 1922) 287 F 757.*

in the Hudson when a large mass of ice caught on a point near Piermont was turned by the tide and pocketed the slow-moving tug before it could escape.[24]

A steamer overtook and passed another in a river clogged with ice. She then maintained her lead for some time until the amount of ice increased so as to impede her progress; it finally forced her to stop and she immediately sounded the danger signal. The other steamer, although she was keeping a sharp lookout and although she reversed full speed and executed left full rudder, was unable because of the ice to get out of the way. The damage, which was slight, was held due to inevitable accident.[25]

When vessels navigating with due caution and without fault in thick fog collide, the accident may be said to result from a form of *vis major*. A ferryboat is a class of vessel which because of the nature of her service is permitted to leave her wharf in the thickest weather. A New York ferry, while feeling her way into her slip, with a lookout properly stationed, drifted into a car float which had been moored outside her tug at the face of a pier, with several other tugs and tows, all of which had been forced to take refuge there because of an unusually heavy fog. In the collision the car float was knocked from her moorings, whence she drifted down the river and collided with several barges moored ten piers below. Both collisions under the circumstances were held inevitable.[26]

In another New York Harbor case, the tug *Edwin Hawley*, learning that a ferry was disabled out in the river, put out in the fog to rescue her. Finding that the ferry had lost her rudder, the tug took her in tow on a bridle secured to the port and starboard bitts, respectively. In a collision a few days before a steamship had been sunk in the harbor, and her steel masts formed an obstruction in the channel. The tug laid a course which would have cleared these masts, but when almost up with them the ferry took a sheer in the strong tide and knocked off one of the masts. The owners of the steamship libeled the tug. In finding the accident inevitable the court held that:

> There was no negligence on the part of the tug in going to the aid of the disabled vessel, notwithstanding the fog; there was no negligence in her method of towing, which was the only method possible; and as the sheer of the tug which was the immediate and sole cause of the accident was occasioned by the disabled vessel and the latter was unable to prevent it, or the tug to anticipate or withstand it, the tug was not liable for the damage.[27]

---

[24] *The* General William McCandless *(NY 1879) Fed. Cas. No. 5,322.*

[25] *The* Erandio *(1908) 163 F 435.*

[26] *Wright and Cobb Lighterage Co. v. New England Nav. Co. (CCA 1913) 204 F 762.*

[27] *The* Edwin Hawley *(NY 1890) 41 F 606.*

Vis Major Not Excuse if Incurred Through Negligence

However, the mere presence of *vis major* does not excuse a vessel if she has been negligent in bringing herself into a critical situation. A number of very old decisions shows that such has long been the policy of the federal courts. As long ago as 1868, a tug tied up at the pier in New York with her stern projecting several feet into a ferry slip was struck by a ferry trying to get into her slip, due to a strong tide. Both vessels were held at fault, the tug for obstructing the slip, and the ferry for attempting a landing under the circumstances.[28] About a year later the British steamship *Russia*, passing through the heavy tide rips which occur because the ebb begins to run out of the North River an hour and a half before it runs out of the East River, took a sheer and rammed and sank an Austrian ship at anchor off the battery. As a pilot is presumed to know the action of the tides, this collision was held solely the fault of the *Russia*.[29] A schooner was aground and partially athwart a 150-foot channel in Hatteras Inlet and a steamer, whose pilot had taken soundings the day before and thought he could get around her, scraped bottom and sheered into the schooner. Notwithstanding that she reversed immediately she began to sheer, the steamer was found at fault for going at such speed as to put a hole in the schooner.[30] An ice boat owned by the city of Baltimore, in coming along-side with a vessel's engineer and stores which she had taken off a disabled tug, miscalculated the strength of the ice and the effect of backing her starboard screw, and struck the steamship just forward of the poop. Although the ice boat was performing a purely gratuitous service, the court held the city of Baltimore liable for the damage.[31] In the case of the *Columbia*, a large steam elevator having a high tower which presented a large surface to the wind, attempted to get alongside some barges on the exposed side of the river and sank one of them. The court held that while inevitable accident may arise from sudden gusts of wind, the evidence in this case showed lack of sufficient caution by the pilot, when the wind was rising and a 10-knot wind was known to make handling this elevator dangerous.[32]

Numerous attempts have been made to invoke inevitable accident under the *vis major* rule as an excuse for collision when the courts have found one or both vessels guilty of contributory fault. An Army transport proceeding down the Elizabeth River from Norfolk Navy Yard at 8 knots,

---

[28] *The* Baltic *(NY 1868) Fed. Cas. No. 823.*
[29] *The* Russia *(NY 1869) Fed. Cas. No. 12,168.*
[30] *The* Ellen S. Terry *(NY 1874) Fed. Cas. No. 4,378.*
[31] *The* F. C. Latrobe *(Md 1886) 28 F 377.*
[32] *The* Columbia *(NY 1891) 48 F 325.*

after dodging a tug with barges in tow, sagged into the Southern Railway docks at Town Point and sank a lighter loaded with valuable cargo. The immediate cause of the accident was failure of the steamship to answer her rudder promptly because of the combined effect of a wind on her port bow and an ebb tide on her starboard quarter; but the Court of Claims called attention to local regulations limiting speed to 4 knots and pointed out that:

> Inevitable accident cannot be maintained as a defense unless it be shown that the master acted reasonably, that he did everything which an experienced mariner could do, and that the collision ensued in spite of ordinary caution and his exertions.[33]

A tug with a car float was proceeding through San Francisco Bay in a dense fog at night, with lookout properly stationed and alert, at a speed of about 7 knots, when she collided with a properly anchored barkentine whose fog bell she mistook for the bell on the mole. The district court accepted the tug's plea of inevitable accident or inscrutable fault but was reversed by the Circuit Court of Appeals which found contributory fault because of excessive speed.[34] A steamship which was very light was being docked in Mobile Harbor by two tugs whose movements were directed from her bridge; she struck and damaged another vessel moored at a pier; and the court found that while a wind squall was undoubtedly the proximate cause of the collision, the weather conditions were well known, storm warnings had been hoisted, and the landing should not have been attempted.[35] As was said in a similar case in New Orleans where the damage, however, was done by a steamer attempting a landing under her own power:

> In a collision case defense of inevitable accident will not avail unless the vessel was free from fault, and such defense cannot be maintained if a vessel voluntarily put herself in a situation where she received the effect of natural forces, the result of which should have been foreseen and might reasonably have been anticipated.[36]

The same attitude was shown in a case in New York, where failure of a tug to make preparations for an impending storm, or even to observe the approach of the storm, precluded a plea of inevitable accident, when, after the storm broke, her tow was swept into collision with another tow.[37]

---

[33] *Southern Ry. Co. v. U.S. (1910) 45 Ct. Cl. 322.*
[34] *The* Fullerton *(Cal 1914) 211 F 833.*
[35] *Coello v. U.S. (La 1925) 9 F (2d) 931.*
[36] *The* Mendocino *(La 1929) 34 F (2d) 783.*
[37] *The* Patrick A. Dee *(CCA 1931) 50 F (2d) 393.*

Court Treatment of Mechanical Failure

Inevitable accident due to mechanical failure Inevitable accident may result at a critical moment from unforeseen casualty to main engines or steering gear, the latter being more likely, of course, to cause collision with another vessel. One case of inevitable accident occurred in Craighill Channel, Baltimore Harbor, between the passenger steamer *City of Baltimore* and the tanker *Beacon*. The *City of Baltimore* outbound and the *Beacon* inbound approached each other near Buoy 9 at a combined speed of 23 knots, each on the proper side of the 600-foot channel, and exchanged one-blast signals for the usual port-to-port passing. When the vessels were not more than four or five lengths apart the *City of Baltimore*, from a cause later discovered to be the slipping of the yoke on a steering engine valve stem, suddenly began sheering to port. She immediately reversed full speed and sounded the danger signal; the *Beacon* did not reply to her signals or alter her course but promptly reversed her own engines; and approximately a minute and a half after her first sheer began the *City of Baltimore*, almost dead in the water, was struck by the *Beacon* at about 6 knots just abaft her chain locker, and both vessels were damaged. Although both omitted the three-blast reversing signals, it was established to the satisfaction of the court that the omission did not affect the action of either vessel and that the mechanical failure, which had never occurred before, was of a nature so unpredictable as to free the vessel from fault.[38]

But in a similar collision some years earlier on the St. Clair River, not only did the sheering vessel fail to justify her involuntary change of course but the steamer and towed barge with which she collided were held for contributory fault for not taking steps to avoid the disaster when after exchanging meeting signals the disabled vessel, then nearly half a mile distant, began to sheer and twice sounded the danger signal. While the court accepted testimony that failure of her steering gear was due either to fouling of steering cables by cargo in the hold or because some foreign substance had been carried into a steam valve, preventing it from closing, it held that this could not be classed as inevitable accident where the steering gear had stuck within half an hour of the collision and the vessel had proceeded without any attempt to ascertain the cause.[39]

Somewhat similar was the line of reasoning followed in the case of a collision between the USS *O-7* and the passenger vessel *Lexington* which was en route from New York to Providence one evening shortly after World War I. The submarine was rounding Hallet's Point, when the

[38] *The Beacon (Md 1934) 6 F Supp 779.*
[39] *Australia Transit Co. v. Lehigh Valley Transp. Co. (1916) 235 F 53.*

Lexington, after sounding the bend signal of one long blast, appeared well clear on the port hand. The *O-7's* electric steering gear jammed, causing her to sheer sharply to port; and though she blew the danger signal, stopped both engines, threw in the hand gear, and backed on her motors and although the *Lexington*, which had stopped her engines before sighting the submarine when she heard the bend signal, also backed full speed, the submarine struck her near the stern, doing considerable damage. The government contended the trouble was caused by the dynamic contact breaker in the panel, fusing and sticking; but on the admission of the commanding officer that similar trouble had been experienced before (though not since the contactor panel had recently been overhauled) and the nature of the trouble had been reported to the Bureau of Construction and Repair for the preceding two quarters, it was held that it was a fault to attempt the crowded and turbulent waters of Hell Gate without shifting to hand gear, and the accident was not therefore inevitable.[40]

In a second collision near the end of the first World War involving a submarine, this time the *R-19*, and a barge anchored in San Francisco Bay, the plea of the submarine that she was rendered helpless by the blowing out of a fuse, which made her electric steering gear inoperable and enabled the tide to throw her against the barge, was held not to establish the defense of the inevitable accident. The night was clear, and the court declared that the vessel need not have been maneuvered in such a manner as to be suddenly put up against a strong running flood tide, throwing on the steering apparatus a load too great for the fuse to carry. She was accordingly found solely liable for the collision.[41]

In the famous English case of the *Merchant Prince*, that vessel came down the River Mersey in a gale of wind and approached the ship *Catalonia* which was at anchor and because of the direction of the wind lying somewhat athwart the channel. Due to a kink in some new chain in her tiller lines the rudder of the *Merchant Prince* jammed so as to make her sheer into the *Catalonia*. She pleaded inevitable accident, but on appeal Lord Esher, speaking for the higher court, called attention to the fact that the tendency of new chain to stretch with use is well known and to be guarded against by taking in the slack so frequently that kinking will not occur. To quote the decision:

> If that is so, is not that stretching of the chain a thing which they could have foreseen, which they ought to have foreseen, and which if they had foreseen— not that it would do it but that it might do it—ought not they to have taken means on that morning to have had the other steerages ready to act in a

---

[40] *Colonial Nav. Co. v. U.S. (NY 1926) 14 F (2d) 480.*
[41] *U.S. v. King Coal Co. (CCA 1925) 5 F (2d) 780.*

moment, even if they ought not to have used those other steerages, and those other steerages alone? It seems to me in this case, from what one can see of the facts proved of the conduct of the ships here, to show a probable cause, and if that was the cause it could have been avoided.[42]

Even if the cause of mechanical breakdown is found to have not been caused by negligence, a plea of inevitable accident does not necessarily follow. In the *Norwalk Victory* the steering gear of the vessel failed without any negligence on her part and she came into collision with another vessel she met on the bend of the River Scheldt. She was, nevertheless, held at fault for failure to monitor her helm indicator and for not detecting earlier the fact she had a breakdown, and for not letting go an anchor. It was held that the collision itself was not inevitable.[43] Similarly, a vessel that was disabled by the failure of her steering gear, was held at fault for not giving warning of the fact in due time, and the other vessel was blamed for bad lookout, which resulted in her failing to take action to avoid the disabled vessel.[44]

When Breaking of Tiller Rope Is Inevitable Accident

A number of collisions have been caused by the sudden breaking of a vessel's tiller ropes, and in these cases, too, the question is not merely one of proving the fact but of showing that the breaking was unavoidable. The usual attitude of the courts in such circumstances was well expressed by the Circuit Court in the old case of the schooner *John Sherman* and the steamer *Olympia*, which collided on the Detroit River in 1891:

> When a collision results from the breaking of a steamer's tiller rope, the burden is upon her to rebut the presumption of negligence, either by showing the cause which broke the rope, and that the result of that cause was inevitable, or by showing all the possible causes which might have produced the break and then showing that the result of each one of them could not have been avoided.[45]

The court enumerated four possible causes of the breaking of a tiller rope as follows: (1) patent defects, due either to original unfitness or to use; (2) mismanagement of steering engine, too sudden spinning of the wheel, etc.; (3) extraordinary strain, as unexplained caprice of steam, or obstruction encountered by rudder; (4) latent defects due to negligence of manufacturer or to use, not discoverable by such examination as can ordinarily be made. On the showing that in this case the tiller rope was of charcoal iron wire of suitable size, of the usual kind, and externally sound; that it had been bought from a reputable outfitter and used less

---

[42] *The* Merchant Prince *(1892) Eng. Law Rep. (PD) 179.*
[43] *The* Norwalk Victory *(1949) 82 Ll.L.Rep 539.*
[44] *The* Nevitina *(1946) 79 Ll.L.Rep 531.*
[45] *The* Olympia *(1894) 61 F 120.*

than two seasons, while the usual life of such a wire was three years; that it had been inspected a few hours before the accident, and that when the broken ends were seen afterwards by witnesses there were no indications of defects; and finally, that although the steering engines were capable of putting a severe strain on the tiller ropes, in this instance the wheel was not suddenly handled, it was held that the collision was due to inevitable accident and not to the steamer's fault.

In the case of the *Jumna*, three tugs were engaged in turning a steamship in the East River a short distance above Brooklyn Bridge. Signals had been exchanged with an up-bound tow to pass starboard to starboard, when without warning the hawser with which one of the tugs was pulling on the stem of the steamship parted, allowing the tug to crash into the tows, which in turn struck and injured the piers on the Manhattan side. The court held that the collisions resulted solely from the breaking of the hawser, which was attributable in a legal sense to inevitable accident.[46]

Mechanical Failure Not Excuse if Due to Negligence

However, the breaking of a hawser by a tug was not inevitable accident when it was due to unskillfulness on the part of the tug in getting her tow into strong tide rips, knowing they were present, so that it would sheer violently, and the tug was liable for damage done immediately afterward by her tow to an anchored dredge which it failed to clear. This decision the Supreme Court, on appeal, declined to review.[47] In another case a tug with a tow of twenty-seven boats suddenly rounded to, putting such a heavy strain on the steel wire towing bridle that the port hawser broke. The tug was held liable for collision damage to vessels in her tow. As held by the Circuit Court of Appeals:

> To sustain defense of inevitable accident, defendant must prove, if the cause of the accident is shown, that he did not, by want of care and skill, contribute to it, or that he could not have prevented it by the exercise of such care and skill; and if the cause is not shown, he must show all possible causes, and that he was not responsible for any of them.[48]

Hence the courts have declined to attribute collision to inevitable accident where a tug's wheel jammed as the result of spinning it too suddenly to avoid a schooner which a proper lookout would have discovered in time to make such action unnecessary;[49] where a steering cable parted when a burdened vessel went hard right within 60 or 70 feet of a privi-

---

[46] *The* Jumna *(NY 1906) 149 F 171.*
[47] *Petition of Red Star Towing and Transp. Co. (CCA 1929) 30 F (2d) 454.*
[48] *The* Osceola *(CCA 1927) 18 F (2d) 418.*
[49] *Brigham v. Luckenbach (Me 1905) 140 F 322.*

leged canal boat,[50] where a steering gear shaft broke under similar circumstances;[51] where a steering gear failed because of a set screw coming loose, when it had not been inspected for more than two years.[52]

A similar treatment occurs in cases where a collision follows failure of the main engines. A steamboat with a side-wheel engine was approaching her wharf at a speed of about 2 knots, and when the signal to reverse was given the exhaust valve failed to operate and the steamer struck a ferry which was just leaving her slip. No trouble with the engine was experienced either before or after the accident and it was thought probable that it was caused by sediment in the steam. Recognizing that while failure of an exhaust valve in that type of engine may happen, it cannot be foreseen or prevented, the court exonerated the steamer.[53] But where a tug was maneuvering to turn around in Port Arthur, Texas, and struck a steamer moored at a wharf when a bolt broke in the reversing machinery, on a showing that the bolt had not been inspected for six years, the Circuit Court of Appeals held the tug liable.[54]

Miscellaneous Cases of Inevitable Accident

Inevitable accident due to combination of circumstances A considerable variety of cases occurs under this category, of which a few will be given by way of illustration. Perhaps they may be appropriately characterized by those stirring words in the old melodramas, "It was the hand of Fate!" It was doubtless on this theory that in a very early case a tug was exonerated from liability for the destruction of her tow when the latter was brought into contact with an uncharted rock while navigating a regularly used river channel.[55] In another case a tug was coming through Hell Gate on a fair tide with a tow of five boats and a length of 800 feet when she suddenly came upon a stranded steamer with a derrick alongside lightering cargo. She was prevented from swinging into Harlem River by an approaching schooner, and was forced to try to go between the stern of the wrecked vessel and Hallet's Point, a passage perhaps 500 feet in width. Despite all her efforts to avoid disaster, the tug was unable to prevent the tide from carrying her tow into the derrick,

[50] *The* Edmund Moran *(CCA 1910) 180 F 700.*

[51] *The* Stimson *(Va 1919) 257 F 762.*

[52] *Van Eyken v. Erie R.R. Co. (NY 1902) 117 F 712.*

[53] *The* Rose Standish *(Mass 1928) 26 F (2d) 480.*

[54] *The* J. N. Gilbert *(CCA 1915) 222 F 37.*

[55] *The* Angelina Corning *(NY 1867) Fed. Cas. No. 384; also the* America *(NY 1872).*

which was sunk with the lightered cargo. This was quite properly held to be inevitable accident.[56] In an old case occurring in Boston Harbor in fair weather and in broad daylight, the Cunard steamship *Java* was approaching her wharf and was about to pass a large school ship which was at anchor, when a small schooner that had been dropped by her tug and was completely concealed from the liner by the school ship while she hoisted her sails, suddenly drifted into the path of the Cunarder. The latter had lookouts properly posted, was making only 2 knots, and was immediately reversed, but nevertheless she struck and seriously damaged the schooner. The Supreme Court upheld the district court and reversed the Circuit Court of Appeals, holding that the circumstances justified the contention of inevitable accident.[57] As a final illustration, consider the unusual case of the schooner *Southern Home*, en route from Santo Domingo to New York with most of her crew stricken with yellow fever. The captain and the mate were confined to their bunks, the steward had died, and the second mate had turned in exhausted after standing a continuous watch for thirty hours, leaving only a convalescent seaman at the wheel and in charge of the deck. There was no one left to stand lookout, and when the man at the wheel sighted the lights of a privileged sailing vessel close aboard he was too weak to put over the wheel, though his shouts of alarm were successful in arousing the second mate. The ensuing collision was, of course, proximately due to failure of the burdened schooner to keep out of the way, and it was argued by the libelants that the stricken schooner should have come to anchor off the Jersey coast instead of attempting to proceed. However, it was shown that the weakened crew, while it could have dropped anchor, would have been unable afterward to heave it up, and the court, considering all the circumstances, held that reasonable precautions had been taken and the accident was inevitable.[58]

Collision can be inevitable as far as a ship sued is concerned, where the fault lies elsewhere, such as in a case where a ship is thrust or rolled against another by the swell of a passing vessel or by a third vessel fouling her[59] or causing her suddenly to alter courses.[60]

---

[56] *Merritt and Chapman Derrick and Wrecking Co. v. Cornell Steamboat Co.* (CCA 1911) 185 F 261.

[57] *The Java (1872) 20 L Ed. 834.*

[58] *The Southern Home (CC NY 1879) Fed. Cas. No. 13,187.*

[59] *The Sisters (1876) 1 P.D. 117; the* Hibernia *(1858) 4 Jur. (NS) 1244.*

[60] *The Schwan and the* Albano *(1892) p. 419; The* Thames *(1874) 2 Asp. MC 512.*

SUMMARY

Inevitable accident has been defined as something that human skill and foresight could not, in the exercise of ordinary prudence, have provided against. The term as applied to a marine collision means one which occurs when both parties have tried by every means in their power, with due care and caution and a proper display of nautical skill, to prevent the occurrence of the accident and it occurred in spite of everything that nautical skill, care, and precaution could do to keep the vessels from coming together. Thus a collision between vessels falls in this category only when neither vessel has violated a rule and both vessels are free from fault. Such collisions are rare, numbering fewer than 1 percent of the cases coming into court; when they occur, each vessel bears her own damage and has no recourse against the other.

Most collisions of this kind are due to *vis major*, i.e., superior force of the elements, or to mechanical failure of engines or steering gear which due diligence could not anticipate or prevent. *Vis major* is illustrated when a storm of great violence, a spring freshet, an extraordinary fog, or an unexpected heavy movement of ice brings one vessel into collision with another. Mechanical failure as a cause of inevitable accident is illustrated where a steering gear, despite originally proper construction and frequent periodical inspection, carries away in the crucial moment of an approaching situation and precipitates a collision. In none of these cases can the doctrine of inevitable accident be invoked where legal fault, which could have contributed to the collision, can be imputed to either vessel.

It is significant that many of the cases of inevitable accident shown in this chapter were decided over fifty years ago, and that there are very few recent cases where the plea of inevitable accident has been successful.

Appendices

APPENDIX A
Lines of Demarcation of Inland Waters[1]

PART 82—Colregs Demarcation Lines

General

[1] *Authority: (Rule 1, International Regulations for Preventing Collisions at Sea, 1972 (as rectified); E.O. 11964, 14 U.S.C. 2; 49 CFR 1.46 (b)).*

General

82.710 Charleston Harbor, SC.
82.712 Morris Island, SC to Hilton Head Island, SC.
82.715 Savannah River.
82.717 Tybee Island, GA to St. Simons Island, GA.
82.720 St. Simons Island, GA to Amelia Island, FL.
82.723 Amelia Island, FL to Cape Canaveral, FL.
82.727 Cape Canaveral, FL to Miami Beach, FL.
82.730 Miami Harbor, FL.
82.735 Miami, FL to Long Key, FL.

Puerto Rico and Virgin Islands

82.738 Puerto Rico and Virgin Islands.

Gulf Coast

82.740 Long Key, FL to Cape Sable, FL.
82.745 Cape Sable, FL to Cape Romano, FL.
82.748 Cape Romano, FL to Sanibel Island, FL.
82.750 Sanibel Island, FL to St. Petersburg, FL.
82.753 St. Petersburg, FL to the Anclote, FL.
82.755 Anclote, FL to the Suncoast Keys, FL.
82.757 Suncoast Keys, FL to Horseshoe Point, FL.
82.760 Horseshoe Point, FL to Rock Island, FL.
82.805 Rock Island, FL to Cape San Blas, FL.
82.810 Cape San Blas, FL to Perdido Bay, FL.

Gulf Coast (cont.)

82.815 Mobile Bay, AL to the Chandeleur Islands, LA.
82.820 Mississippi River.
82.825 Mississippi Passes, LA.
82.830 Mississippi Passes, LA to Point Au Fer, LA.
82.835 Point Au Fer, LA to Calcasieu Pass, LA.
82.840 Sabine Pass, TX to Galveston, TX.
82.845 Galveston, TX to Freeport, TX.
82.850 Brazos River, TX to the Rio Grande, TX.

Pacific Coast

82.1105 Santa Catalina Island, CA.
82.1110 San Diego Harbor, CA.
82.1115 Mission Bay, CA.
82.1120 Oceanside Harbor, CA.
82.1125 Dana Point Harbor, CA.
82.1130 Newport Bay, CA.
82.1135 San Pedro Bay–Anaheim Bay, CA.
82.1140 Redondo Harbor, CA.
82.1145 Marina Del Rey, CA.
82.1150 Port Hueneme, CA.
82.1155 Channel Islands Harbor, CA.
82.1160 Ventura Marina, CA.
82.1165 Santa Barbara Harbor, CA.

82.1205 San Luis Obispo Bay, CA.
82.1210 Estero–Morro Bay, CA.
82.1215 Monterey Harbor, CA.
82.1220 Moss Landing Harbor, CA.
82.1225 Santa Cruz Harbor, CA.
82.1230 Pillar Point Harbor, CA.
82.1250 San Francisco Harbor, CA.
82.1255 Bodega and Tomales Bay, CA.

Pacific Coast (cont.)

82.1260 Albion River, CA.
82.1265 Noyo River, CA.
82.1270 Arcato–Humboldt Bay, CA.
82.1275 Crescent City Harbor, CA.

82.1305 Chetco River, OR.
82.1310 Rogue River, OR.
82.1315 Coquille River, OR.
82.1320 Coos Bay, OR.
82.1325 Umpqua River, OR.
82.1330 Sinslaw River, OR.
82.1335 Alsea Bay, OR.
82.1340 Yaquina Bay, OR.
82.1345 Depoe Bay, OR.
82.1350 Netarts Bay, OR.
82.1360 Nehalem River, OR.
82.1365 Columbia River Entrance, OR/WA.
82.1370 Willapa Bay, WA.
82.1375 Grays Harbor, WA.
82.1380 Quillayute River, WA.
82.1385 Strait of Juan de Fuca.
82.1390 Haro Strait and Strait of Georgia.

Pacific Islands

82.1410 Hawaiian Island Exemption from General Rule.
82.1420 Mamala Bay, Oahu, HI.
82.1430 Kaneohe Bay, Oahu, HI.
82.1440 Port Allen, Kauai, HI.

Pacific Islands (cont.)

82.1450 Nawiliwili Harbor, Kauai, HI.
82.1460 Kahului Harbor, Maui, HI.
82.1470 Kawaihae Harbor, Hawaii, HI.
82.1480 Hilo Harbor, Hawaii, HI.
82.1490 Apra Harbor, U.S. Territory of Guam.
82.1495 U.S. Pacific Island Possessions.

Alaska

82.1705 Canadian (BC) and United States (AK) borders to Cape Muzon, AK.
82.1710 Cape Muzon, AK to Cape Bartolome, AK.
82.1715 Cape Bartolome, AK to Cape Ulitka, AK.
82.1720 Cae Ulitka, AK to Cape Ommaney, AK.
82.1725 Cape Ommaney, AK to Cape Edgecumbe, AK.
82.1730 Cape Edgecumbe, AK to Cape Spencer, AK.
82.1735 Cape Spencer, AK to Point Whitshed, AK.
82.1740 Prince William Sound, AK.
82.1750 Alaska West and North of Prince William Sound.

General

General Basis and Purpose of Demarcation Lines

SEC. 82.01 (a) The regulations in this part establish the lines of demarcation delineating those waters upon which mariners must comply with the International Regulations for Preventing Collisions at Sea, 1972 (72 COLREGS) and those waters upon which mariners must comply with the Navigation Rules for Harbors, Rivers, and Inland Waters (Inland Rules).

(b) The waters inside of the lines are INLAND RULES WATERS. The waters outside the lines are COLREGS WATERS.

(c) The regulations in this part do not apply to the Great Lakes or their connecting and tributary waters as described in Part 90 of this Chapter, or the Western Rivers as described in Part 95 of this Chapter.

Atlantic Coast

Calais, ME to Cape Small, ME

SEC. 82.105 The 72 COLREGS shall apply on the harbors, bays, and inlets on the east coast of Maine from International Bridge at Calais, ME to the southwesternmost extremity of Bald Head at Cape Small.

Casco Bay, ME

SEC. 82.110 (a) A line drawn from the southwesternmost extremity of Bald Head at Cape Small to the southernmost extremity of Ragged Island; thence to the southern tangent of Jaquish Island thence to Little Mark Island Monument Light; thence to the northernmost extremity of Jewell Island.

(b) A line drawn from the tower on Jewell Island charted in approximate position latitude 43°40.6′ N. longitude 70°05.9′ W. to the northeasternmost extremity of Outer Green Island.

(c) A line drawn from the southwesternmost extremity of Outer Green Island to Ram Island Ledge Light to Portland Head Light.

Portland Head, ME to Cape Ann, MA

SEC. 82.115 (a) Except inside lines specifically described in this section, the 72 COLREGS shall apply on the harbors, bays, and inlets on the east coast of Maine, New Hampshire, and Massachusetts from Portland Head to Halibut Point at Cape Ann.

(b) A line drawn from the southernmost tower on Gerrich Island charted in approximate position latitude 43°04.0′ N. longitude 70°41.2′ W. to Whaleback Light; thence to the northeasternmost extremity of Frost Point.

(c) A line drawn from the northernmost extremity of Farm Point to Annisquam Harbor Light.

Cape Ann, MA to Marblehead Neck, MA

SEC. 82.120 (a) Except inside lines specifically described in this section, the 72 COLREGS shall apply on the harbors, bays and inlets on the east coast of Massachusetts from Halibut Point at Cape Ann to Marblehead Neck.

(b) A line drawn from Gloucester Harbor Breakwater Light to the twin towers charted in approximate position latitude 42°35.1' N. longitude 70°41.6' W.

(c) A line drawn from the westernmost extremity of Gales Point to the easternmost extremity of House Island; thence to Bakers Island Light; thence to Marblehead Light.

Marblehead Neck, MA to Winthrop Head, MA

SEC. 82.125 The 72 COLREGS shall apply on the bays, harbors and inlets on the east coast of Massachusetts from Marblehead Neck to Winthrop Head.

Boston Harbor Entrance

SEC. 82.130 A line drawn from the standpipe on Winthrop Head charted in approximate position latitude 42°22.1' N. longitude 70°58.1' W. to Great Faun Bar Daybeacon; thence to Boston Light; thence to the tower on Point Allerton charted in approximate position latitude 42°18.4' N. Longitude 70°53.1' W.

Point Allerton, MA to Race Point, MA

SEC. 82.135 (a) Except inside lines specifically described in this section, the 72 COLREGS shall apply on the harbors, bays and inlets on the east coast of Massachusetts from Point Allerton to Race Point on Cape Cod.

(b) A line drawn from Cape Cod Canal Breakwater Light south to the shoreline.

Race Point, MA to Marthas Vineyard, MA

SEC. 82.140 (a) The 72 COLREGS apply to the harbors, bays and inlets along the coast of Cape Cod from Race Point to the southernmost extremity of Nauset Beach.

(b) A line drawn from the southernmost extremity of Nauset Beach to the northernmost extremity of Monomoy Island.

(c) A line drawn from the abandoned lighthouse tower on the southern end of Monomoy Island to Nantucket (Great Point Light).

(d) A line drawn from the westernmost extremity of Nantucket Island to the southernmost tangent of Wasque Point on Marthas Vineyard.

Marthas Vineyard, MA to Watch Hill, RI

SEC. 82.145 (a) Except lines specifically described in this section, the 72 COLREGS shall apply on the harbors, bays and inlets on the south coast of Massachusetts and Rhode Island from Marthas Vineyard to Watch Hill.

Watch Hill, RI to Montauk Point, NY

SEC. 82.305 (a) A line drawn from Watch Hill Light to East Point on Fishers Island.

(b) A line drawn from Race Point to Race Rock Light; thence to Little Gull Island Light thence to East Point on Plum Island.

(c) A line drawn from Plum Island Harbor East Dolphin Light and Plum Island Harbor West Dolphin Light.

(d) A line drawn from Plum Island Light to Orient Point Light; thence to Orient Point.

(e) A line drawn from the lighthouse ruins at the southwestern end of Long Beach Point to Cornelius Point.

(f) A line drawn from Coecles Harbor Entrance Light to Sungie Point.

(g) A line drawn from Nichols Point to Cedar Island Light.

(h) A line drawn from Three Mile Harbor West Breakwater Light to Three Mile Harbor East Breakwater Light.

(i) A line drawn from Montauk West Jetty Light to Montauk East Jetty Light.

Montauk Point, NY to Atlantic Beach, NY

SEC. 82.310 (a) A line drawn from Shinnecock Inlet East Breakwater Light to Shinnecock West Breakwater Light.

(b) A line drawn from Moriches Inlet East Breakwater Light to Moriches Inlet West Breakwater Light.

(c) A line drawn from Fire Island Inlet Breakwater Light 348° true to the southernmost extremity of the spit of land at the western end of Oak Beach.

(d) A line drawn from Jones Inlet Light 142° true across the southwest tangent of the island on the north side of Jones Inlet to the shoreline.

New York Harbor

SEC. 82.315 A line drawn from East Rockaway Inlet Breakwater Light to Sandy Hook Light.

Sandy Hook, NJ to Cape May, NJ

SEC. 82.320 (a) A line drawn from Shark River Inlet North Breakwater Light to Shark River Inlet South Breakwater Light.

(b) A line drawn from Manasquan Inlet North Breakwater Light to Manasquan Inlet South Breakwater Light.

(c) A line drawn from Barnegat Inlet North Breakwater Light to Barnegat Inlet South Breakwater Light. Lines formed by the submerged Barnegat Breakwaters.

(d) A line drawn from the seaward tangent on Long Beach Island to the seaward tangent to Pullen Island across Beach Haven and Little Egg Inlets.

(e) A line drawn from the seaward tangent of Pullen Island and Brigantine Island across Brigantine Inlet.

(f) A line drawn from the seaward extremity of Absecon Inlet North Jetty and Atlantic City Light.

(g) A line drawn from the southernmost point of Longport at latitude 39°18.2′ N. longitude 74°32.2′ W. to the northeasternmost point of Ocean City at latitude 39°17.6′ N. longitude 74°33.1′ W. across Great Egg Harbor Inlet.

(h) A line formed by the centerline of the Townsend Inlet Highway Bridge.

(i) A line formed by the shoreline of Seven Mile Beach and Hereford Inlet Light.

(j) A line drawn from Cape May Inlet East Jetty Light to Cape May Inlet West Jetty Light.

Delaware Bay

SEC. 82.325 A line drawn from Cape May Light to Harbor of Refuge Light; thence to the northernmost extremity of Cape Henlopen.

Cape Henlopen, DL to Cape Charles, VA

SEC. 82.505 (a) A line drawn from Indian River Inlet North Jetty Light to Indian River Inlet South Jetty Light.

(b) A line drawn from Ocean City Inlet Light 6 234° true across Ocean City Inlet to the submerged south breakwater.

(c) A line drawn from Assateague Beach Tower Light to the tower charted at latitude 37°52.6′ N. longitude 75°26.7′ W.

(d) A line formed by the range of Wachapreague Inlet Light 3 and Parramore Beach Lookout Tower drawn across Wachapreague Inlet.

(e) A line drawn from the lookout tower charted on the northern end of Hog Island to the seaward tangent of Parramore Beach.

(f) A line drawn 207° true from the lookout tower charted on the southern end of Hog Island across Great Machipongo Inlet.

(g) A line formed by the range of the two cupolas charted on the southern end of Cobb Island drawn across Sand Shoal Inlet.

(h) Except as provided elsewhere in this section from Cape Henlopen to Cape Charles, lines drawn parallel with the general trend of the highwater shoreline across the entrances to small bays and inlets.

Chesapeake Bay Entrance, VA

SEC. 82.510 A line drawn from Cape Charles Light to Cape Henry Light.

Cape Henry, VA to Cape Hatteras, NC

SEC. 82.515 (a) A line drawn from Rudee Inlet Jetty Light 2 to Rudee Inlet Jetty Light 1.

(b) A line formed by the centerline of the highway bridge across Oregon Inlet.

Cape Hatteras, NC to Cape Lookout, NC

SEC. 82.520 (a) A line drawn from Hatteras Inlet Light 255° to the eastern end of Ocracoke Island.

(b) A line drawn from the westernmost extremity of Ocracoke Island at latitude 35°04.0′ N. longitude 76°00.8′ W. to the northeastern extremity of Portsmouth Island at latitude 35°03.7′N. longitude 76°02.3′ W.

(c) A line drawn across Drum Inlet parallel with the general trend of the highwater shoreline.

Cape Lookout, NC to Cape Fear, NC

SEC. 82.525 (a) A line drawn from Cape Lookout Light to the seaward tangent of the southeastern end of Shackleford Banks.

(b) A line drawn from Morehead City Channel Range Front Light to the seaward extremity of the Beaufort Inlet west jetty.

(c) A line drawn from the southernmost extremity of Bogue Banks at latitude 34°38.7′ N. longitude 77°06.0′ W. across Bogue Inlet to the northernmost extremity of Bear Beach at latitude 34°38.5′ N. longitude 77′07.1° W.

(d) A line drawn from the tower charted in approximate position latitude 34°31.5′ N. longitude 77°20.8′ W. to the seaward tangent of the shoreline on the northeast side of New River Inlet.

(e) A line drawn across New Topsail Inlet between the closest extremities of the shore on either side of the inlet from latitude 34°20.8′ N. longitude 77°39.2′ W. to latitude 34°20.6′ N. longitude 77°39.6′ W.

(f) A line drawn from the seaward extremity of the jetty on the northeast side of Masonboro Inlet west to the shoreline approximately 0.6 mile southwest of the inlet.

(g) Except as provided elsewhere in this section from Cape Lookout to Cape Fear, lines drawn parallel with the general trend of the highwater shoreline across the entrance of small bays and inlets.

Cape Fear, NC to New River Inlet, NC

SEC. 82.530 (a) A line drawn from the abandoned lighthouse charted in approximate position latitude 33°52.4′ N. longitude 78°00.1′ W. across the Cape Fear River Entrance to Oak Island Light.

(b) Except as provided elsewhere in this section from Cape Fear to New River Inlet, lines drawn parallel with the general trend of the highwater shoreline across the entrance to small inlets.

Little River Inlet, SC to Cape Romain, SC

SEC. 82.703 (a) A line drawn from the westernmost extremity of the sand spit on Bird Island to the easternmost extremity of Waties Island across Little River Inlet.

(b) Lines drawn parallel with the general trend of the highwater shoreline across Hog Inlet, Muriels Inlet, Midway Inlet, Pawleys Inlet, and North Inlet.

(c) A line drawn from the charted position of Winyah Bay North Jetty End Buoy 2N south to the Winyah Bay South Jetty.

(d) A line drawn from Santee Point to the seaward tangent of Cedar Island.

(e) A line drawn from Cedar Island Point west to Murphy Island.

(f) A north-south line (longitude 79°20.3' W.) line drawn from the southern extremity of Murphy Island to the northernmost extremity of Cape Island Point.

Cape Romain, SC to Sullivans Island, SC

SEC. 82.707 (a) A line drawn from the western extremity of Cape Romain 292° true to Racoon Key on the west side of Racoon Creek.

(b) A line drawn from the northwesternmost extremity of Sandy Point across Bull Bay to the northernmost extremity of Northeast Point.

(c) A line drawn from the southernmost extremity of Bull Island to the easternmost extremity of Capers Island.

(d) A line formed by the overhead power cable from Capers Island to Dewees Island.

(e) A line formed by the overhead power cable from Dewees Island to Isle of Palms.

(f) A line formed by the centerline of the highway bridge between Isle of Palms and Sullivans Island over Beach Inlet.

Charleston Harbor, SC

SEC. 82.710 (a) A line drawn from across the seaward extremity of the Charleston Harbor Jetties.

(b) A line drawn from the west end of the South Jetty across the South Entrance to Charleston Harbor to shore on a line formed by the submerged south jetty.

Morris Island, SC to Hilton Head Island, SC

SEC. 82.712 (a) A line drawn from the Folly Island Loran Tower charted in approximate position latitude 32°41.0' N. longitude 79°53.2' W. to the abandoned lighthouse tower on the northside of Lighthouse Inlet; thence west to the shoreline of Morris Island.

(b) A straight line drawn from the seaward tangent of Folly Island through Folly River Daybeacon 10 across Stono River to the shoreline of Sandy Point.

(c) A line drawn from the southernmost extremity of Seabrook Island 257° true across the North Edisto River Entrance to the shore of Botany Bay Island.

(d) A line drawn from the microwave antenna tower on Edisto Beach charted in approximate position latitude 32°29.3' N. longitude 80°19.2' W. across St. Helena Sound to the abandoned lighthouse tower on Hunting Island.

(e) A line formed by the centerline of the highway bridge between Hunting Island and Fripp Island.

(f) A line drawn from the westernmost extremity of Bull Point on Capers Island to Port Royal Sound Channel Rear Range Light; thence 245° true to the easternmost extremity of Hilton Head at latitude 32°13.2' N. longitude 80°40.1' W.

Savannah River

SEC. 82.715 A line drawn from the southernmost tank on Hilton Head Island charted in approximate position latitude 32°06.7' N. longitude 80°49.3' W. to Bloody Point Range Rear Light; thence to Tybee (Range Rear) Light.

Tybee Island, GA to St. Simons Island, GA

SEC. 82.717 (a) A line drawn from the southernmost extremity of Savannah Beach on Tybee Island 255° true across Tybee Inlet to the shore of Little Tybee Island south of the entrance to Buck Hammock Creek.

(b) A straight line drawn from the northeasternmost extremity of Wassaw Island 031° true through Tybee River Daybeacon 1 to the shore of Little Tybee Island.

(c) A line drawn approximately parallel with the general trend of the highwater shorelines from the seaward tangent of Wassaw Island to the seaward tangent of Bradley Point on Ossabaw Island.

(d) A north-south line (longitude 81°8.4' W.) drawn from the southernmost extremity of Ossabaw Island to St. Catherines Island.

(e) A north-south line (longitude 81°10.6′ W.) drawn from the southern-most extremity of St. Catherines Island to Northeast Point on Blackbeard Island.

(f) A north-south line (longitude 81°16.9′ W.) drawn from the southwest-ernmost point on Sapelo Island to Wolf Island.

(g) A north-south line (longitude 81°17.1′ W.) drawn from the southeast-ernmost point of Wolf Island to the northeasternmost point on Little St. Simons Island.

(h) A line drawn from the northeastern extremity of Sea Island 045° true to Little St. Simons Island.

St. Simons Island, GA to Amelia Island, FL

SEC. 82.720 (a) A line drawn from St. Simons Light to the northernmost tank on Jekyll Island charted in approximate position latitude 31°05.9′ N. longitude 81°24.5′ W.

(b) A line drawn from the southernmost tank on Jekyll Island charted in approximate position latitude 31°01.6′ N. longitude 81°25.2′ W. to coordi-nate latitude 30°59.4′ N. longitude 81°23.7′ W. (0.5 nautical mile east of the charted position of St. Andrew Sound Lighted Buoy 32); thence to the abandoned lighthouse tower on the north end of Little Cumberland Island charted in approximate position latitude 30°58.5′ N. longitude 81°24.8′ W.

(c) A line drawn across the seaward extremity of the St. Marys River Entrance Jetties.

Amelia Island, FL to Cape Canaveral, FL

SEC. 82.723 (a) A line drawn from the southernmost extremity of Amelia Island to the northeasternmost extremity of Little Talbot Island.

(b) A line drawn across the seaward extremity of the St. Johns River En-trance Jetties.

(c) A line drawn across the seaward extremity of the St. Augustine Inlet Jetties.

(d) A line formed by the centerline of the highway bridge over Matanzas Inlet.

(e) A line drawn across the seaward extremity of the Ponce de Leon Inlet Jetties.

Cape Canaveral, FL to Miami Beach, FL

SEC. 82.727 (a) A line drawn across the seaward extremity of the Port Canaveral Entrance Channel Jetties.

(b) A line drawn across the seaward extremity of the Sebastian Inlet Jetties.

(c) A line drawn across the seaward extremity of the Fort Pierce Inlet Jetties.

(d) A north-south line (longitude 80°09.8' W.) drawn across St. Lucie Inlet through St. Lucie Inlet Entrance Range Front Daybeacon.

(e) A line drawn from the seaward extremity of Jupiter Inlet North Jetty to the northeast extremity of the concrete apron on the south side of Jupiter Inlet.

(f) A line drawn across the seaward extremity of the Lake Worth Inlet Jetties.

(g) A line drawn across the seaward extremity of the South Lake Worth Inlet Jetties.

(h) A line drawn from Boca Raton Inlet North Jetty Light 2 to Boca Raton Inlet South Jetty Light 1.

(i) A line drawn from Hillsboro Inlet Entrance Light 2 to Hillsboro Inlet Entrance Light 1; thence west to the shoreline.

(j) A line drawn across the seaward extremity of the Port Everglades Entrance Jetties.

(k) A line formed by the centerline of the highway bridge over Bakers Haulover Inlet.

Miami Harbor, FL

SEC. 82.730 A line drawn across the seaward extremity of the Miami Harbor Government Cut Jetties.

Miami, FL to Long Key, FL

SEC. 82.735 (a) A line drawn from the southernmost extremity of Fisher Island 211° true to the point latitude 25°45.1' N. longitude 80°08.6' W. on Virginia Key.

(b) A line formed by the centerline of the highway bridge between Virginia Key and Key Biscayne.

(c) A line drawn from the abandoned lighthouse tower on Cape Florida to Biscayne Channel Light 8; thence to the northernmost extremity on Soldier Key.

(d) A line drawn from the southernmost extremity on Soldier Key to the northernmost extremity of the Ragged Keys.

(e) A line drawn from the Ragged Keys to the southernmost extremity of Angelfish Key following the general trend of the seaward shoreline.

(f) A line drawn on the centerline of the Overseas Highway (U.S. 1) and bridges from latitude 25°19.3' N. longitude 80°16.0' W. at Little Angelfish Creek to the radar dome charted on Long Key at approximate position latitude 24°49.3' N. longitude 80°49.2' W.

Puerto Rico and Virgin Islands

SEC. 82.738 (a) Except inside lines specifically described in this section, the 72 COLREGS shall apply on all other bays, harbors, and lagoons of Puerto Rico and the U.S. Virgin Islands.

(b) A line drawn from Puerto San Juan Light to Cabras Light across the entrance of San Juan Harbor.

Gulf Coast

Long Key, FL to Cape Sable, FL

SEC. 82.740 A line drawn from the radar dome charted on Long Key at approximate position latitude 24°49.3′ N. longitude 80°49.2′ W. to Long Key Light 2; thence to Arsenic Bank Light 1; thence to Arsenic Bank Light 2; thence to Sprigger Bank Light 5; thence to Schooner Bank Light 6; thence to Oxfoot Bank Light 10; thence to East Cape Light 2; thence through East Cape Daybeacon 1A to the shoreline at East Cape.

Cape Sable, FL to Cape Romano, FL

SEC. 82.745 (a) A line drawn following the general trend of the mainland, highwater shoreline from Cape Sable at East Cape to Little Shark River Light 1; thence to westernmost extremity of Shark Point; thence following the general trend of the mainland, highwater shoreline crossing the entrances of Harney River, Broad Creek, Broad River, Rodgers River First Bay, Chatham River, Huston River, to the shoreline at coordinate latitude 25°41.8′ N. longitude 81°17.9′ W.

(b) The 72 COLREGS shall apply to the waters surrounding the Ten Thousand Islands and the bays, creeks, inlets, and rivers between Chatham Bend and Marco Island except inside lines specifically described in this part.

(c) A north-south line drawn at longitude 81°20.2′ W. across the entrance to Lopez River.

(d) A line drawn across the entrance to Turner River parallel to the general trend of the shoreline.

(e) A line formed by the centerline of Highway 92 Bridge at Goodland.

Cape Romano, FL to Sanibel Island, FL

SEC. 82.748 (a) Lines drawn across Big Marco Pass parallel to the general trend of the seaward, highwater shoreline.

(b) A line drawn through Capri Pass Daybeacons 2A and 3 across Capri Pass.

(c) Lines drawn across Hurricane and Little Marco Passes parallel to the general trend of the seaward, highwater shoreline.

(d) A straight line drawn from Gordon Pass Light 4 through Daybeacon 5 to the shore.

(e) A line drawn across the seaward extremity of Doctors Pass Jetties.

(f) Lines drawn across Wiggins, Big Hickory, New, and Big Carlos Passes parallel to the general trend of the seaward, highwater shoreline.

(g) A straight line drawn from Sanibel Island Light through Matanzas Pass Channel Light 2 to the shore of Estero Island.

Sanibel Island, FL to St. Petersburg, FL

SEC. 82.750 (a) Lines drawn across Redfish and Captiva Passes parallel to the general trend of the seaward, highwater shorelines.

(b) A line drawn from La Costa Test Pile North Light to Port Boca Grande Light.

(c) Lines drawn across Gasparilla and Stump Passes parallel to the general trend of the seaward, highwater shorelines.

(d) A line across the seaward extremity of Venice Inlet Jetties.

(e) A line drawn across Midnight Pass parallel to the general trend of the seaward, highwater shoreline.

(f) A line drawn from Big Sarasota Pass Light 14 to the southernmost extremity of Lido Key.

(g) A line drawn through Sarasota Bay Channel Light 7A across New Pass parallel to the seaward, highwater shoreline of Longboat Key.

(h) A line drawn across Longboat Pass parallel to the seaward, highwater shoreline.

(i) A line drawn from the northwesternmost extremity of Bean Point to the southeasternmost extremity of Egmont Key.

(j) A straight line drawn from Egmont Key Light through Egmont Channel Range Rear Light to the shoreline on Mullet Key.

(k) A line drawn from the northernmost extremity of Mullet Key across Bunces Pass and South Channel to Pass-a-Grille Daybeacon 9; thence to the southwesternmost extremity of Long Key.

St. Petersburg, FL to the Anclote, FL

SEC. 82.753 (a) A line drawn across Blind Pass parallel with the general trend of the seaward, highwater shoreline.

(b) Lines formed by the centerline of the highway bridges over Johns and Clearwater Passes.

(c) A line drawn across Dunedin and Hurricane Passes parallel with the general trend of the seaward, highwater shoreline.

(d) A line drawn from the northernmost extremity of Honeymoon Island to Anclote Anchorage South Entrance Light 7; thence to Anclote Keys Light; thence a straight line through Anclote River Cut B Range Rear Light to the shoreline.

Anclote, FL to the Suncoast Keys, FL

SEC. *82.755* (a) Except inside lines specifically described in this section, the 72 COLREGS shall apply on the bays, bayous, creeks, marinas, and rivers from Anclote to the Suncoast Keys.

(b) A north-south line drawn at longitude 82°38.3' W. across the Chassahowitgka River Entrance.

Suncoast Keys, FL to Horsehoe Point, FL

SEC. *82.757* (a) Except inside lines specifically described in this section, the 72 COLREGS shall apply on the bays, bayous, creeks, and marinas from the Suncoast to Horseshoe Point.

(b) A line formed by the centerline of Highway 44 Bridge over the Salt River.

(c) A north-south line drawn through Crystal River Entrance Daybeacon 25 across the river entrance.

(d) A north-south line drawn through the Cross Florida Barge Canal Daybeacon 38 across the canal.

(e) A north-south line drawn through Withlacoochee River Daybeacon 40 across the river.

(f) A line drawn from the westernmost extremity of South Point north to the shoreline across the Waccasassa River Entrance.

(g) A line drawn from position latitude 29°16.6' N. longitude 83°06.7' W. 300° true to the shoreline of Hog Island.

(h) A north-south line drawn through Suwanee River West Pass Daybeacons 27 and 28 across the Suwannee River.

Horseshoe Point, FL to Rock Islands, FL

SEC. *82.760* (a) Except inside lines specifically described provided in this section, the 72 COLREGS shall apply on the bays, bayous, creeks, marinas, and rivers from Horseshoe Point to the Rock Islands.

(b) A north-south line drawn through Steinhatchee River Light 21.

(c) A line drawn from Fenholloway River Approach Light FR east across the entrance to Fenholloway River.

Rock Island, FL to Cape San Blas, FL

SEC. *82.805* (a) A south-north line drawn from the Econfina River Light to the opposite shore.

(b) A line drawn from Gamble Point Light to the southernmost extremity of Cabell Point.

(c) A line drawn from St. Marks (Range Rear) Light to St. Marks Channel Light 11; thence to Live Oak Point; thence to Ochlockonee Point; thence to Bald Point.

(d) A line drawn from the south shore of Southwest Cape at longitude 84°22.7′ W. to Dog Island Reef East Light 1; thence to Turkey Point Light 2; thence to the easternmost extremity of Dog Island.

(e) A line drawn from the westernmost extremity of Dog Island to the easternmost extremity of St. George Island.

(f) A line drawn across the seaward extremity of the St. George Island Channel Jetties.

(g) A line drawn from the northwesternmost extremity of Sand Island to West Pass Light 7.

(h) A line drawn from the westernmost extremity of St. Vincent Island to the southeast, highwater shoreline of Indian Peninsula at longitude 85°13.5′ W.

Cape San Blas, FL to Perdido Bay, FL

SEC. 82.810 (a) A line drawn from St. Joseph Range A Rear Light through St. Joseph Range B Front Light to St. Joseph Point.

(b) A line drawn across the mouth of Salt Creek as an extension of the general trend of the shoreline.

(c) A line drawn from the northernmost extremity of Crooked Island 000° T. to the mainland.

(d) A line drawn from the easternmost extremity of Shell Island 120° true to the shoreline across the east entrance to St. Andrews Bay.

(e) A line drawn between the seaward end of the St. Andrews Bay Entrance Jetties.

(f) A line drawn between the seaward end of the Choctawhatchee Bay Entrance Jetties.

(g) A west-east line drawn from Fort McGee Leading Light across the Pensacola Bay Entrance.

(h) A line drawn between the seaward end of the Perdido Pass Jetties.

Mobile Bay, AL to the Chandeleur Islands, LA

SEC. 82.815 (a) A line drawn across the inlets to Little Lagoon as an extension of the general trend of the shoreline.

(b) A line drawn from Mobile Point Light to Dauphin Island Spit Light to the eastern corner of Fort Gaines at Pelican Point.

(c) A line drawn from the westernmost extremity of Dauphin Island to the easternmost extremity of Petit Bois Island.

(d) A line drawn from Horn Island Pass Entrance Range Front Light on Petit Bois Island to the easternmost extremity of Horn Island.

(e) An east-west line (latitude 30°14.7' N.) drawn between the westernmost extremity of Horn Island to the easternmost extremity of Ship Island.

(f) A curved line drawn following the general trend of the seaward, highwater shoreline of Ship Island.

(g) A line drawn from Ship Island Light; thence to Chandeleur Light; thence in a curved line following the general trend of the seaward, highwater shorelines of the Chandeleur Islands to the island at coordinate latitude 29°31.1' N. longitude 89°05.7' W.; thence to Breton Island Light located at latitude 29°29.1' N. longitude 89°09.7' W.

Mississippi River

SEC. 82.820 The Pilot Rules for Western Rivers are to be followed in the Mississippi River and its tributaries above the Huey P. Long Bridge.

Mississippi Passes, LA

SEC. 82.825 (a) A line drawn from Breton Island Light to coordinate latitude 29°21.5' N. thence to coordinate latitude 29°21.5' N. longitude 89°11.7' W.

(b) A line drawn from coordinate latitude 29°21.5' N. longitude 89°11.7' W. following the general trend of the seaward, highwater shoreline in a southeasterly direction to coordinate latitude 29°12.4' N. longitude 89°06.0' W.; thence following the general trend of the seaward, highwater shoreline in a northeasterly direction to coordinate latitude 29°13.0' N. longitude 89°01.3' W. located on the northwest bank of North Pass.

(c) A line drawn from coordinate latitude 29°13.0' N. longitude 89°01.3' W.; thence coordinate latitude 29°12.7' N. longitude 89°0.9' W.; thence coordinate latitude 29°10.6' N. longitude 88°59.8' W.; thence coordinate latitude 29°03.5' N. longitude 89°59.8' W.; thence coordinate latitude 29°03.5' N. longitude 89°03.7' W., thence Mississippi River South Pass East Jetty Light 4.

(d) A line drawn from Mississippi River South Pass East Jetty Light 4; thence following the general trend of the seaward, highwater shoreline in a northwesterly direction to coordinate latitude 29°03.4' N. longitude 89°13.0' W.; thence following the general trend of the seaward, highwater shoreline in a southwesterly direction to Mississippi River Southwest Pass Entrance Light.

(e) A line drawn from Mississippi River Southwest Pass Entrance Light; thence to the seaward extremity of the Southwest Pass West Jetty located at coordinate latitude 28°54.5' N. longitude 89°26.1' W.

Mississippi Passes, LA to Point Au Fer, LA

SEC. 82.830 (a) A line drawn from the seaward extremity of the Southwest Pass West Jetty located at coordinate latitude 28°54.5′ N. longitude 89°26.1′ W.; thence following the general trend of the seaward, highwater jetty and shoreline in a north-northeasterly direction to Old Tower latitude 28°58.8′ N. longitude 89°23.3′ W.; thence to West Bay Light; thence to coordinate latitude 29°05.2′ N. longitude 89°24.3′ W.; thence a curved line following the general trend of the highwater shoreline to Point Au Fer Island except as otherwise described in this section.

(b) A line drawn across the seaward extremity of the Empire Waterway (Bayou Fontanelle) entrance jetties.

(c) A line drawn from Barataria Bay Light to the Grand Isle Fishing Jetty Light.

(d) A line drawn between the seaward extremity of the Belle Pass Jetties.

(e) A line drawn from the westernmost extremity of the Timbolier Island to the easternmost extremity of Isles Dernieres.

(f) A south-north line drawn from Caillou Bay Light 13 across Caillou Boca.

(g) A line drawn 107° true from Caillou Bay Boat Landing Light across the entrances to Grand Bayou du Large and Bayou Grand Caillou.

(h) A line drawn on an axis of 103° true through Taylors Bayou Light across the entrances to Jack Stout Bayou, Taylors Bayou, Pelican Pass, and Bayou de West.

Point Au Fer, LA to Calcasieu Pass, LA

SEC. 82.835 (a) A line drawn from Point Au Fer to Atchafalaya Channel Light 32; thence Point Au Fer Reef Light; Atchafalaya Bay Pipeline Light D latitude 29°25.0′ N. longitude 91°31.7′ W.; thence Atchafalaya Bay Light 1 latitude 29°25.3′ N. longitude 91°35.8′ W.; thence South Point.

(b) Lines following the general trend of the highwater shoreline drawn across the bayou canal inlet from the Gulf of Mexico between South Point and Calcasieu Pass except as otherwise described in this section.

(c) A line drawn on a axis of 130° T. through Vermillion Bay Light 2 across Southwest Pass.

(d) A line drawn across the seaward extremity of the Freshwater Bayou Canal Entrance Jetties.

(e) A line drawn from Mermentau River Channel Light 4 to Mermentau River Channel Light 5.

(f) A line drawn from the radio tower in approximate position latitude 29°45.7′ N. longitude 93°06.3′ W. 160° true across Mermentau

(g) A line drawn across the seaward extremity of the Calcasieu Pass Jetties.

Sabine Pass, TX to Galveston, TX

SEC. 82.840 (a) A line drawn from the Sabine Pass East Jetty Light to the seaward end of the Sabine Pass West Jetty.

(b) Lines drawn across the small boat passes through the Sabine Pass East and West Jetties.

(c) A line formed by the centerline of the highway bridge over Rollover Pass at Gilchrist.

Galveston, TX to Freeport, TX

SEC. 82.845 (a) A line drawn from Galveston North Jetty Light to Galveston South Jetty Light.

(b) A line formed by the centerline of the highway bridge over San Luis Pass.

(c) Lines formed by the centerlines of the highway bridges over the inlets to Christmas Bay (Cedar Cut) and Drum Bay.

(d) A line drawn from the seaward extremity of the Freeport North Jetty to Freeport Entrance Light 6; thence Freeport Entrance Light 7; thence the seaward extremity of Freeport South Jetty.

Brazos River, TX to the Rio Grande, TX

SEC. 82.850 (a) Except as otherwise described in this section lines drawn continuing the general trend of the seaward, highwater shorelines across the inlets to Brazos River Diversion Channel, San Bernard River, Cedar Lakes, Brown Cedar Cut, Colorado River, Matagorda Bay Cedar Bayou, Corpus Christi Bay, and Laguna Madre.

(b) A line drawn across the seaward extremity of Matagorda Ship Channel North Jetties.

(c) A line drawn from the seaward tangent of Matagorda Peninsula at Decros Point to Matagorda Daybeacon 2; thence to Matagorda Light.

(d) A line drawn across the seaward extremity of the Aransas Pass Jetties.

(e) A line drawn across the seaward extremity of the Port Mansfield Entrance Jetties.

(f) A line drawn across the seaward extremity of the Brazos Santiago Pass Jetties.

Pacific Coast

Santa Catalina Island, CA

SEC. 82.1105 The 72 COLREGS shall apply to the harbors on Santa Catalina Island.

San Diego Harbor, CA

SEC. 82.1110   A line drawn from Zunica Jetty Light "V" to Zunica Jetty Light "Z"; thence to Point Loma Light.

Mission Bay, CA

SEC. 82.1115 A line drawn from Mission Bay South Jetty Light 2 to Mission Bay North Jetty Light 1.

Oceanside Harbor, CA

SEC. 82.1120 A line drawn from Oceanside South Jetty Light 4 to Oceanside Breakwater Light 3.

Dana Point Harbor, CA

SEC. 82.1125 A line drawn from Dana Point Jetty Light 6 to Dana Point Breakwater Light 5.

Newport Bay, CA

SEC. 82.1130 A line drawn from Newport Bay East Jetty Light 4 to Newport Bay West Jetty Light 3.

San Pedro Bay–Anaheim Bay, CA

SEC. 82.1135 (a) A line drawn from Anaheim Bay East Jetty Light 6 to Anaheim Bay West Jetty Light 5; thence to Long Beach Breakwater East End Light.

(b) A line drawn from Long Beach Channel Entrance Light 2 to Long Beach Light.

(c) A line drawn from Los Angeles Main Entrance Channel Light 2 to Los Angeles Light.

Redondo Harbor, CA

SEC. 82.1140 A line drawn from Redondo Beach East Jetty Light 2 to Redondo Beach West Jetty Light 3.

Marina Del Rey, CA

SEC. 82.1145 (a) A line drawn from Marina Del Rey Breakwater South Light 1 to Marina Del Rey Light 4.

(b) A line drawn from Marina Del Rey Breakwater North Light 2 to Marina Del Rey Light 3.

(c) A line drawn from Marina Del Rey Light 4 to the seaward extremity of the Ballona Creek South Jetty.

Port Hueneme, CA

SEC. 82.1150 A line drawn from Port Hueneme East Jetty Light 4 to Port Hueneme West Jetty Light 3.

Channel Islands Harbor, CA

SEC. 82.1155 (a) A line drawn from Channel Islands Harbor South Jetty Light 2 to Channel Islands Harbor Breakwater South Light 1.

(b) A line drawn from Channel Islands Harbor Breakwater North Light to Channel Islands Harbor North Jetty Light 5.

Ventura Marina, CA

SEC. 82.1160. A line drawn from Ventura Marina South Jetty Light 2 to Ventura Marina Breakwater South Light 1; thence to Ventura Marina North Jetty Light 3.

Santa Barbara Harbor, CA

SEC. 82.1165 A line drawn from Santa Barbara Harbor Light 4 to Santa Barbara Harbor Breakwater Light.

San Luis Obispo Bay, CA

SEC. 82.1205 A line drawn from the southernmost extremity of Fossil Point to the seaward extremity of Whaler Island Breakwater.

Estero–Morro Bay, CA

SEC. 82.1210 A line drawn from the seaward extremity of the Morro Bay East Breakwater to the Morro Bay West Breakwater Light.

Monterey Harbor, CA

SEC. 82.1215 A line drawn from Monterey Harbor Breakwater Light to the northern extremity of Monterey Municipal Wharf 2.

Moss Landing Harbor, CA

SEC. 82.1220 A line drawn from the seaward extremity of the pier located 0.3 mile south of Moss Landing Harbor Entrance to the seaward extremity of the Moss Landing Harbor North Breakwater.

Santa Cruz Harbor, CA

SEC. 82.1225 A line drawn from the seaward extremity of the Santa Cruz Harbor East Jetty to the seaward extremity of the Santa Cruz Harbor West Jetty; thence to Santa Cruz Light.

Pillar Point Harbor, CA

SEC. 82.1230 A line drawn from Pillar Point Harbor Light 6 to Pillar Point Harbor Light 5.

San Francisco Harbor, CA

SEC. 82.1250 A straight line drawn from Point Bonita Light through Mile Rocks Light to the shore.

Bodega and Tomales Bay, CA

SEC. 82.1255 (a) An east-west line drawn through Tomales Bay Daybeacon 3 from Sand Point to Avalis Beach.
(b) A line drawn from the seaward extremity of Bodega Harbor North Breakwater to Bodega Harbor Entrance Light 1.

Albion River, CA

SEC. 82.1260 A line drawn on an axis of 030° true through Albion River Light 1 across Albion Cove.

Noyo River, CA

SEC. 82.1265 A line drawn from Noyo River Entrance Daybeacon 4 to Noyo River Entrance Light 5.

Arcata–Humboldt Bay, CA

SEC. 82.1720 A line drawn from Humboldt Bay Entrance Light 4 to Humboldt Bay Entrance Light 3.

Crescent City Harbor, CA

SEC. 82.1275 A line drawn from Crescent City Outer Breakwater Light to the southeasternmost extremity of Whaler Island.

Chetco River, OR

SEC. 82.1305 A line drawn from the seaward extremity of the Chetco River South Jetty to Chetco River Entrance Light 5.

Rogue River, OR

SEC. 82.1310 A line drawn from the seaward extremity of the Rogue River Entrance South Jetty to Rogue River North Jetty Light 3.

Coquille River, OR

SEC. 82.1315 A line drawn across the seaward extremity of the Coquille River Entrance Jetties.

Coos Bay, OR

SEC. 82.1320 A line drawn across the seaward extremity of the Coos Bay Entrance Jetties.

Umpqua River, OR

SEC. 82.1325 A line drawn across the seaward extremity of the Umpqua River Entrance Jetties.

Siuslaw River, OR

SEC. 82.1330 A line drawn from the seaward extremity of the Siuslaw River Entrance South Jetty to Siuslaw River Light 9.

Alsea Bay, OR

SEC. 82.1335 A line drawn from the seaward shoreline on the north of the Alsea Bay Entrance 165° true across the channel entrance.

Yaquina Bay, OR

SEC. 82.1340 A line drawn from the seaward extremity of Yaquina Bay Entrance South Jetty to Yaquina Bay North Jetty Light 5.

Depoe Bay, OR

SEC. 82.1345 A line drawn across the Depoe Bay Channel entrance parallel with the general trend of the highwater shoreline.

Netarts Bay, OR

SEC. 82.1350 A line drawn from the northernmost extremity of the shore on the south side of Netarts Bay north to the opposite shoreline.

Tillamook Bay, OR

SEC. 82.1355 A north-south line drawn from the lookout tower charted on the north side of the entrance to Tillamook Bay south to the Tillamook Bay South Jetty.

Nehalem River, OR

SEC. 82.1360 A line drawn approximately parallel with the general trend of the highwater shoreline across the Nehalem River Entrance.

Columbia River Entrance, OR/WA

SEC. 82.1365 A line drawn from the seaward extremity of the Columbia

River North Jetty (above water) 155°true to the seaward extremity of the Columbia River South Jetty (above water).

Willapa Bay, WA

SEC. 82.1370 A line drawn from Willapa Bay Light 171° true to the westernmost tripod charted 1.6 miles south of Leadbetter Point.

Grays Harbor, WA

SEC. 82.1375 A line drawn from across the seaward extremity, (above water) of the Grays Harbor Entrance Jetties.

Quillayute River, WA

SEC. 82.1380 A line drawn from the seaward extremity of the Quillayute River Entrance East Jetty to the overhead power cable tower charted on James Island; thence a straight line through Quillayute River Entrance Light 3 to the shoreline.

Strait of Juan de Fuca

SEC. 82.1385 (a) The 72 COLREGS shall apply on Neah Bay and the waters inside Ediz Hook (Port Angeles Harbor).

(b) A line drawn from New Dungeness Light through Puget Sound Traffic Lane Entrance Lighted Buoy S to Rosario Strait Traffic Lane Entrance Lighted Horn Buoy R; through Hein Bank Lighted Bell Buoy to Cattle Point Light.

Haro Strait and Strait of Georgia

SEC. 82.1390 (a) The 72 COLREGS shall apply on the bays of the southwest coast of San Juan Island from Cattle Point Light to Lime Kiln Light.

(b) A line drawn from Lime Kiln Light to Kellett Bluff Light; thence to Turn Point Light; thence to Skipjack Island Light; thence to Sucia Island Daybeacon 1.

(c) A line drawn from the shoreline of Sucia Island at latitude 48°46.1' N. longitude 122°53.5' W. through Clements Reef Buoy 2 to Alden Bank Lighted Gong Buoy A; thence to the westernmost tip of Birch Point at latitude 48°56.6' N. longitude 122°49.2' W.

(d) The 72 COLREGS shall apply in Semiamoo Bay and Drayton Harbor.

Pacific Islands

Hawaiian Island Exemption from General Rule

SEC. 82.1410 Except as provided elsewhere in this part for Mamala Bay and Kaneohe Bay on Oahu; Port Allen and Nawiliwili Bay on Kauai; Kahului Harbor on Maui; and Kawailae and Hilo Harbors on Hawaii, the 72 COLREGS shall apply on all other bays, harbors, and lagoons of the Hawaiian Islands (including Midway).

Mamala Bay, Oahu, HI

SEC. 82.1420 A line drawn from Barbers Point Light to Diamond Head Light.

Kaneohe Bay, Oahu, HI

SEC. 82.1430 A straight line drawn from Pyramid Rock Light across Kaneohe Bay through the center of Mokolii Island to the shoreline.

Port Allen, Kauai, HI

SEC. 82.1440 A line drawn from Hanapepe Light to Hanapepe Bay Breakwater Light.

Nawiliwili Harbor, Kauai, HI

SEC. 82.1450 A line drawn from Nawiliwili Harbor Breakwater Light to Kukii Point Light.

Kahului Harbor, Maui, HI

SEC. 82.1460 A line drawn from Kahului Harbor Entrance East Breakwater Light to Kahului Harbor Entrance West Breakwater Light.

Kawaihae Harbor, Hawaii, HI

SEC. 82.1470 A line drawn from Kawaihae Light to the seaward extremity of the Kawaihae South Breakwater.

Hilo Harbor, Hawaii, HI

SEC. 82.1480 A line drawn from the seaward extremity of the Hilo Breakwater 265° true (as an extension of the seaward side of the breakwater) to the shoreline 0.2 nautical mile north of Alealea Point.

Apra Harbor, U.S. Territory of Guam

SEC. 82.1490 A line drawn from the westernmost extremity of Orote Island to the westernmost extremity of Glass Breakwater.

U.S. Pacific Island Possessions

SEC. 82.1495 The 72 COLREGS shall apply on the bays, harbors, lagoons, and waters surrounding the U.S. Pacific Island Possessions of American Soma, Baker, Canton, Howland, Jarvis, Johnson, Palmyra, Swains and Wake Island. (The Trust Territory of the Pacific Islands it not a U.S. possession, and therefore PART 82 does not apply thereto.)

Alaska

Canadian (BC) and United States (AK) borders to Cape Muzon, AK

SEC. 82.1705 (a) A line drawn from the northeasternmost extremity of Point Mansfield, Sitklan Island 040° true to the mainland.

(b) A line drawn from the southernmost extremity of Sitklan Island to the southernmost extremity of Garnet Point, Kanagunut Island.

(c) A line drawn from the westernmost extremity of Tingbeg Island to the southwesternmost extremity of Tongass Island.

(d) A line drawn from the northern shoreline of Tongass Island at longitude 130°44.6′ W. to Tongass Reef Daybeacon; thence to Boat Rock Light; thence to the shoreline.

(e) A line drawn from Tree Point Light to Barren Island Light; thence to Cape Chacon Light; thence to Cape Muzon Light.

Cape Muzon, AK to Cape Bartolome, AK

SEC. 82.1710 (a) The 72 COLREGS shall apply on the harbors and bays of the west coast of Doll Island from Cape Muzon to Cape Lookout.

(b) A line drawn from the westernmost extremity of Cape Lookout to Diver Islands Light; thence to the southernmost extremity of Cape Felix; thence to Cape Bartolome Light.

Cape Bartolome, AK to Cape Ulitka, AK

SEC. 82.1715 A line drawn from the westernmost extremity of Outer Point on Baker Island to the southernmost extremity of St. Nicholas Point on Noyes Island.

Cape Ulitka, AK to Cape Ommaney, AK

SEC. 82.1720 (a) A line drawn from Cape Ulitka Light to the southwesternmost extremity of St. Joseph Island.

(b) A line drawn from south-north line (longitude 133°42.8′ W.) from the northernmost extremity of St. Joseph Island to the southernmost extremity of the Wood Islands.

(c) A line drawn from the northwesternmost extremity of Wood Island to Cape Lynch Light; thence to the southwesternmost extremity of Boot Point on Warren Island.

(d) A line drawn from the northwesternmost extremity of Point Borlase on Warren Island to the northeastern extremity of the Spanish Islands.

(e) A line drawn from Spanish Islands Light to Cape Decision Light; thence through Cape Ommaney Light to the shoreline.

(f) The 72 COLREGS shall apply on the bays and harbors of Coronation Island.

Cape Ommaney, AK to Cape Edgecumbe, AK

SEC. 82.1725 (a) The 72 COLREGS shall apply on the bays, inlets, and harbors of the west coast of Baranof Island from Cape Ommaney to Cape Burunof.

(b) A line drawn from the westernmost extremity of Cape Burunof to Kulichkof Rock; thence to Vitskari Island Light; thence to the southeasternmost extremity of Shoals Point on Kruzof Island.

Cape Edgecumbe, AK, to Cape Spencer, AK

SEC. 82.1730 (a) The 72 COLREGS shall apply on the bays and harbors of the south and west coasts of Kruzof Island from Shoals Point to Cape Georgiana.

(b) A line drawn from the northwesternmost extremity of Cape Georgiana on Kruzof Island to Klokachef Island Light.

(c) A line drawn from the northernmost extremity of Fortuna Point on Klokachef Island 055° true to the shoreline of Khaz Peninsula.

(d) The 72 COLREGS shall apply on the bays, inlets and harbors of the west coast of Chichogof Island from Fortuna Strait to Easter Island.

(e) A line drawn from Lisianski Strait Entrance Light to the southernmost extremity of Point Theodore on Yakobi Island.

(f) The 72 COLREGS shall apply on the bays and harbors of the west coast of Yakobi Island from Point Theodore to Soapstone Point.

(g) A line drawn from Lisianski Inlet Light to Cape Spencer Light; thence to the southernmost extremity of Cape Spencer.

Cape Spencer, AK to Point Whitshed, AK

SEC. 82.1735 The 72 COLREGS shall apply on the bays and harbors from Cape Spencer to Point Whitshed on the coast of Alaska Mainland.

Prince William Sound, AK

SEC. 82.1740 (a) Hawkins Island Cutoff: A line drawn from Point Whitshed on the Alaska Mainland at position 60°26.7′ N. 145°52.7′ W. west-southwesterly to Point Bentinck aerobeacon on Hinchinbrook Island.

(b) Hinchinbrook Entrance: A line drawn from Cape Hinchinbrook Light northerly to Schooner Rock Light.

(c) Montague Strait: A line drawn from a point on the western end of Montague Island at position 59°50.2′ N. 147°54.4′ W. northwesterly to Point Elrington Light on Elrington Island thence due west to the Alaska Mainland at Cape Puget.

Alaska west and north of Prince William Sound

SEC. 82.1750 The 72 COLREGS shall apply on the sounds, bays, inlets, and harbors of Alaska west of Cape Puget, Kodiak Island, Aleutian Islands, and the west and north coasts of Alaska.

APPENDIX B

Convention on the International Regulations for Preventing Collisions at Sea, 1972[1]

The Convention, as signed on October 20, 1972, and as rectified on December 1, 1973, together with the International Regulations attached thereto are as follows:

CONVENTION ON THE INTERNATIONAL REGULATIONS FOR PREVENTING COLLISIONS AT SEA, 1972

The Parties to the present Convention,

Desiring to maintain a high level of safety at sea,

Mindful of the need to revise and bring up to date the International Regulations for Preventing Collisions at Sea annexed to the Final Act of the International Conference on Safety of Life at Sea, 1960,

Having considered those Regulations in the light of developments since they were approved,

Have agreed as follows:

Article I

General Obligations

The Parties to the present Convention undertake to give effect to the

[1] *The United States' domestic enabling legislation for the 1972 Rules has been omitted. An enrolled bill, HR No. 94-973, was passed by both houses and transmitted to the President. On 10 October 1976, the President vetoed the bill on constitutional grounds. There was no objection to the collision regulations themselves, but to the powers that Congress proposed using over amendment procedures. Meanwhile, the President has deposited U.S. ratification. Thus the convention will apply to U.S. mariners when it becomes effective on 15 July 1977, leaving enabling legislation to follow and tie up details.*

Rules and other Annexes constituting the International Regulations for Preventing Collisions at Sea, 1972, (hereinafter referred to as "the Regulations") attached hereto.

Article II

Signature, Ratification, Acceptance, Approval and Accession

1. The present Convention shall remain open for signature until 1 June 1973 and shall thereafter remain open for accession.

2. States Members of the United Nations, or of any of the Specialized Agencies, or the International Atomic Energy Agency, or Parties to the Statute of the International Court of Justice may become Parties to this Convention by:

(a) signature without reservation as to ratification, acceptance or approval;

(b) signature subject to ratification, acceptance or approval followed by ratification, acceptance or approval; or

(c) accession.

3. Ratification, acceptance, approval or accession shall be effected by the deposit of an instrument to that effect with the Inter-Governmental Maritime Consultative Organization (hereinafter referred to as "the Organization") which shall inform the Governments of States that have signed or acceded to the present Convention of the deposit of each instrument and of the date of its deposit.

Article III

Territorial Application

1. The United Nations in cases where they are the administering authority for a territory or any Contracting Party responsible for the international relations of a territory may at any time by notification in writing to the Secretary-General of the Organization (hereinafter referred to as "the Secretary-General"), extend the application of this Convention to such a territory.

2. The present Convention shall, upon the date of receipt of the notification or from such other date as may be specified in the notification, extend to the territory named therein.

3. Any notification made in accordance with paragraph 1 of this Article may be withdrawn in respect of any territory mentioned in that notification and the extension of this Convention to that territory shall cease to apply after one year or such longer period as may be specified at the time of the withdrawal.

4. The Secretary-General shall inform all Contracting Parties of the notification of any extension or withdrawal of any extension communicated under this Article.

Article IV

Entry into Force

1. (a) The present Convention shall enter into force twelve months after the date on which at least 15 States, the aggregate of whose merchant fleets constitutes not less than 65 percent by number or by tonnage of the world fleet of vessels of 100 gross tons and over have become Parties to it, whichever is achieved first.

(b) Notwithstanding the provisions in subparagraph (a) of this paragraph, the present Convention shall not enter into force before 1 January 1976.

2. Entry into force for States which ratify, accept, approve or accede to this Convention in accordance with Article II after the conditions prescribed in subparagraph 1 (a) have been met and before the Convention enters into force, shall be on the date of entry into force of the Convention.

3. Entry into force for States which ratify, accept, approve or accede after the date on which this Convention enters into force, shall be on the date of deposit of an instrument in accordance with Article II.

4. After the date of entry into force of an amendment to this Convention in accordance with paragraph 4 of Article VI, any ratification, acceptance, approval or accession shall apply to the Convention as amended.

5. On the date of entry into force of this Convention, the Regulations replace and abrogate the International Regulations for Preventing Collisions at Sea, 1960.

6. The Secretary-General shall inform the Governments of States that have signed or acceded to this Convention of the date of its entry into force.

Article V

Revision Conference

1. A Conference for the purpose of revising this Convention or the Regulations or both may be convened by the Organization.

2. The Organization shall convene a Conference of Contracting Parties for the purpose of revising this Convention or the Regulations or both at the request of not less than one-third of the Contracting Parties.

Article VI

Amendments to the Regulations

1. Any amendment to the Regulations proposed by a Contracting Party shall be considered in the Organization at the request of that Party.

2. If adopted by a two-thirds majority of those present and voting in the Maritime Safety Committee of the Organization, such amendment shall be communicated to all Contracting Parties and Members of the Organization at least six months prior to its consideration by the Assembly of the Organization. Any Contracting Party which is not a Member of the Organization shall be entitled to participate when the amendment is considered by the Assembly.

3. If adopted by a two-thirds majority of those present and voting in the Assembly, the amendment shall be communicated by the Secretary-General to all Contracting Parties for their acceptance.

4. Such an amendment shall enter into force on a date to be determined by the Assembly at the time of its adoption unless, by a prior date determined by the Assembly at the same time, more than one-third of the Contracting Parties notify the Organization of their objection to the amendment. Determination by the Assembly of the dates referred to in this paragraph shall be by a two-thirds majority of those present and voting.

5. On entry into force any amendment shall, for all Contracting Parties which have not objected to the amendment, replace and supersede any previous provision to which the amendment refers.

6. The Secretary-General shall inform all Contracting Parties and Members of the Organization of any request and communication under this Article and the date on which any amendment enters into force.

Article VII

Denunciation

1. The present Convention may be denounced by a Contracting Party at any time after the expiry of five years from the date on which the Convention entered into force for that Party.

2. Denunciation shall be effected by the deposit of an instrument with the Organization. The Secretary-General shall inform all other Contracting Parties of the receipt of the instrument of denunciation and of the date of its deposit.

3. A denunciation shall take effect one year, or such longer period as may be specified in the instrument, after its deposit.

Article VIII

Deposit and Registration

1. The present Convention and the Regulations shall be deposited with the Organization, and the Secretary-General shall transmit certified true copies thereof to all Governments of States that have signed this Convention or acceded to it.

2. When the present Convention enters into force, the text shall be transmitted by the Secretary-General to the Secretariat of the United Nations for registration and publication in accordance with Article 102 of the Charter of the United Nations.

Article IX

Languages

The present Convention is established, together with the Regulations, in a single copy in the English and French languages, both texts being equally authentic. Official translations in the Russian and Spanish languages shall be prepared and deposited with the signed original.

IN WITNESS WHEREOF the undersigned being duly authorized by their respective Governments for that purpose have signed the present Convention.

DONE AT LONDON this twentieth day of October one thousand nine hundred and seventy-two.

Procès-Verbal of Rectification

Whereas a Convention on the International Relations for Presenting Collisions at Sea was done at London on 20 October 1972 and is deposited with the Inter-Governmental Maritime Consultative Organization; and

Whereas certain errors in English and in French have been discovered in the original signed copy of the said Convention and brought to the notice of the interested Governments; and

Whereas no objection to the correction of these errors having been raised by any of the Governments which were represented at the International conference on Revision of the International Regulations for Preventing Collisions at Sea, 1972, which adopted the Convention, the said errors should be corrected as indicated. . . . :

Now, therefore, I the undersigned, Colin Goad, Secretary-General of the Inter-Governmental Maritime Consultative Organization, acting for the depositary of the Convention on the International Regulations for Preventing Collisions at Sea, 1972, have caused the original text of the Convention to be modified by the corrections indicated above, and initialled in the margin thereof.

In witness whereof, I have signed the present Procès-Verbal at the Headquarters of the Organization this first day of December 1973, in the English and French languages, in a single copy which shall be kept in the archives of the Organization with the original signed copy of the Convention on the International Regulations for Preventing Collisions at Sea, 1972.

A certified copy of this Procès-Verbal shall be communicated to each Government which has signed or acceded to the aforementioned Convention.

Colin Goad.

INTERNATIONAL REGULATIONS FOR PREVENTING COLLISIONS AT SEA, 1972

(As rectified by Procès-Verbal of December 1, 1973)

PART A—GENERAL

Application

RULE 1 (a) These Rules shall apply to all vessels upon the high seas and in all waters connected therewith navigable by seagoing vessels.

(b) Nothing in these Rules shall interfere with the operation of special rules made by an appropriate authority for roadsteads, harbours, rivers, lakes or inland waterways connected with the high seas and navigable by seagoing vessels. Such special rules shall conform as closely as possible to these Rules.

(c) Nothing in these Rules shall interfere with the operation of any special rules made by the Government of any State with respect to additional station or signal lights or whistle signals for ships of war and vessels proceeding under convoy, or with respect to additional station or signal lights for fishing vessels engaged in fishing as fleet. These additional station or signal lights or whistle signals shall, so far as possible, be such that they cannot be mistaken for any light or signal authorized elsewhere under these Rules.

(d) Traffic separation schemes may be adopted by the Organization for the purpose of these Rules.

(e) Whenever the Government concerned shall have determined that a vessel of special construction or purpose cannot comply fully with the provisions of any of these Rules with respect to the number, position, range or arc of visibility of lights or shapes, as well as to the disposition and characteristics of sound-signalling appliances, without interfering with the special function òf the vessel, such vessel shall comply with such other provisions in regard to the number, position, range or arc of visibility of lights or shapes, as well as to the disposition and characteristics of sound-signalling appliances, as her Government shall have determined to be the closest possible compliance with these Rules in respect to that vessel.

Responsibility

RULE 2 (a) Nothing in these Rules shall exonerate any vessel, or the owner, master or crew thereof, from the consequences of any neglect to comply with these Rules or of the neglect of any precaution which may be required by the ordinary practice of seamen, or by the special circumstances of the case.

(b) In construing and complying with these Rules due regard shall be had to all dangers of navigation and collision and to any special circumstances, including the limitations of the vessels involved which may make a departure from these Rules necessary to avoid immediate danger.

General Definitions

RULE 3 For the purpose of these Rules, except where the context otherwise requires:

(a) The word "vessel" includes every description of water craft, including non-displacement craft and seaplanes, used or capable of being used as a means of transportation on water.

(b) The term "power-driven vessel" means any vessel propelled by machinery.

(c) The term "sailing vessel" means any vessel under sail provided that propelling machinery, if fitted, is not being used.

(d) The term "vessel engaged in fishing" means any vessel fishing with nets, lines, trawls or other fishing apparatus which restrict manoeuvrability, but does not include a vessel fishing with trolling lines or other fishing apparatus which do not restrict manoeuvrability.

(e) The word "seaplane" includes any aircraft designed to manoeuvre on the water.

(f) The term "vessel not under command" means a vessel which through some exceptional circumstance is unable to manoeuvre as required by these Rules and is therefore unable to keep out of the way of another vessel.

(g) The term "vessel restricted in her ability to manoeuvre" means a vessel which from the nature of her work is restricted in her ability to manoeuvre as required by these Rules and is therefore unable to keep out of the way of another vessel.

The following vessels shall be regarded as vessels restricted in their ability to manoeuvre:

(i) a vessel engaged in laying, servicing or picking up a navigation mark, submarine cable or pipeline;

(ii) a vessel engaged in dredging, surveying or underwater operations;

(iii) a vessel engaged in replenishment or transferring persons, provisions or cargo while underway;

(iv) a vessel engaged in the launching or recovery of aircraft;

(v) a vessel engaged in minesweeping operations;

(vi) a vessel engaged in a towing operation such as severely restricts the towing vessel and her tow in their ability to deviate from their course.

(h) The term "vessel constrained by her draught" means a power-driven vessel which because of her draught in relation to the available depth of water is severely restricted in her ability to deviate from the course she is following.

(i) The word "underway" means that a vessel is not at anchor, or made fast to the shore, or aground.

(j) The words "length" and "breadth" of a vessel mean her length overall and greatest breadth.

(k) Vessels shall be deemed to be in sight of one another only when one can be observed visually from the other.

(l) The term "restricted visibility" means any condition in which visibility is restricted by fog, mist, falling snow, heavy rainstorms, sandstorms or any other similar causes.

PART B—STEERING AND SAILING RULES

Section I—Conduct of Vessels in Any Condition of Visibility

Application

RULE 4 Rules in this Section apply in any condition of visibility.

Look-out

RULE 5 Every vessel shall at all times maintain a proper look-out by sight and hearing as well as by all available means appropriate in the prevailing circumstances and conditions so as to make a full appraisal of the situation and of the risk of collision.

Safe Speed

RULE 6 Every vessel shall at all times proceed at a safe speed so that she can take proper and effective action to avoid collision and be stopped within a distance appropriate to the prevailing circumstances and conditions.

In determining a safe speed the following factors shall be among those taken into account:

(a) By all vessels:

(i) the state of visibility;

(ii) the traffic density including concentrations of fishing vessels or any other vessels;

(iii) the manoeuvrability of the vessel with special reference to stopping distance and turning ability in the prevailing conditions;

(iv) at night the presence of background light such as from shore lights or from back scatter of her own lights;

(v) the state of wind, sea and current, and the proximity of navigational hazards;

(vi) the draught in relation to the available depth of water.

(b) Additionally, by vessels with operational radar:

(i) the characteristics, efficiency and limitations of the radar equipment;

(ii) any constraints imposed by the radar range scale in use;

(iii) the effect on radar detection of the sea state, weather and other sources of interference;

(iv) the possibility that small vessels, ice and other floating objects may not be detected by radar at an adequate range;

(v) the number, location and movement of vessels detected by radar;

(vi) the more exact assessment of the visibility that may be possible when radar is used to determine the range of vessels or other objects in the vicinity.

Risk of Collision

RULE 7 (a) Every vessel shall use all available means appropriate to the prevailing circumstances and conditions to determine if risk of collision exists. If there is any doubt such risk shall be deemed to exist.

(b) Proper use shall be made of radar equipment if fitted and operational, including long-range scanning to obtain early warning of risk of collision and radar plotting or equivalent systematic observation of detected objects.

(c) Assumptions shall not be made on the basis of scanty information, especially scanty radar information.

(d) In determining if risk of collision exists the following considerations shall be among those taken into account:

(i) such risk shall be deemed to exist if the compass bearing of an approaching vessel does not appreciably change;

(ii) such risk may sometimes exist even when an appreciable bearing change is evident, particularly when approaching a very large vessel or a tow or when approaching a vessel at close range.

Action to Avoid Collision

RULE 8 (a) Any action taken to avoid collision shall, if the circumstances of the case admit, be positive, made in ample time and with due regard to the observance of good seamanship.

(b) Any alteration of course and/or speed to avoid collision shall, if the circumstances of the case admit, be large enough to be readily apparent to another vessel observing visually or by radar; a succession of small alterations of course and/or speed should be avoided.

(c) If there is sufficient sea room, alteration of course alone may be the most effective action to avoid a close-quarters situation provided that it is made in good time, is substantial and does not result in another close-quarters situation.

(d) Action taken to avoid collision with another vessel shall be such as to result in passing at a safe distance. The effectiveness of the action shall be carefully checked until the other vessel is finally past and clear.

(e) If necessary to avoid collision or allow more time to assess the situation, a vessel shall slacken her speed or take all way off by stopping or reversing her means of propulsion.

Narrow Channels

RULE 9 (a) A vessel proceeding along the course of a narrow channel or fairway shall keep as near to the outer limit of the channel or fairway which lies on her starboard side as is safe and practicable.

(b) A vessel of less than 20 metres in length or a sailing vessel shall not impede the passage of a vessel which can safely navigate only within a narrow channel or fairway.

(c) A vessel engaged in fishing shall not impede the passage of any other vessel navigating within a narrow channel or fairway.

(d) A vessel shall not cross a narrow channel or fairway if such crossing impedes the passage of a vessel which can safely navigate only within such channel or fairway. The latter vessel may use the sound signal prescribed in Rule 34(d) if in doubt as to the intention of the crossing vessel.

(e)(i) In a narrow channel or fairway when overtaking can take place only if the vessel to be overtaken has to take action to permit safe passing, the vessel intending to overtake shall indicate her intention by sounding the appropriate signal prescribed in Rule 34(c)(i). The vessel to be overtaken shall, if in agreement, sound the appropriate signal prescribed in Rule 34(c) (ii) and take steps to permit safe passing. If in doubt she may sound the signals prescribed in Rule 34(d).

(ii) This Rule does not relieve the overtaking vessel of her obligation under Rule 13.

(f) A vessel nearing a bend or an area of narrow channel or fairway where other vessels may be obscured by an intervening obstruction shall navigate with particular alertness and caution and shall sound the appropriate signal prescribed in Rule 34(e).

(g) Any vessel shall, if the circumstances of the case admit, avoid anchoring in a narrow channel.

Traffic Separation Schemes

RULE 10 (a) This Rule applies to traffic separation schemes adopted by the Organization.

(b) A vessel using a traffic separation scheme shall:

(i) proceed in the appropriate traffic lane in the general direction of traffic flow for that lane;

(ii) so far as practicable keep clear of a traffic separation line or separation zone;

(iii) normally join or leave a traffic lane at the termination of the lane, but when joining or leaving from the side shall do so at as small an angle to the general direction of traffic flow as practicable.

(c) A vessel shall so far as practicable avoid crossing traffic lanes, but if obliged to do so shall cross as nearly as practicable at right angles to the general direction of traffic flow.

(d) Inshore traffic zones shall not normally be used by through traffic which can safely use the appropriate traffic lane within the adjacent traffic separation scheme.

(e) A vessel, other than a crossing vessel, shall not normally enter a separation zone or cross a separation line except:

(i) in cases of emergency to avoid immediate danger;

(ii) to engage in fishing within a separation zone.

(f) A vessel navigating in areas near the terminations of traffic separation schemes shall do so with particular caution.

(g) A vessel shall so far as practicable avoid anchoring in a traffic separation scheme or in areas near its terminations.

(h) A vessel not using a traffic separation scheme shall avoid it by as wide a margin as is practicable.

(i) A vessel engaged in fishing shall not impede the passage of any vessel following a traffic lane.

(j) A vessel of less than 20 metres in length or a sailing vessel shall not impede the safe passage of a power-driven vessel following a traffic lane.

Section II—Conduct of Vessels in Sight of One Another

Application

RULE 11 Rules in this Section apply to vessels in sight of one another.

Sailing Vessels

RULE 12 (a) When two sailing vessels are approaching one another, so as to involve risk of collision, one of them shall keep out of the way of the other as follows:

(i) when each has the wind on a different side, the vessel which has the wind on the port side shall keep out of the way of the other;

(ii) when both have the wind on the same side, the vessel which is to windward shall keep out of the way of the vessel which is to leeward;

(iii) if a vessel with the wind on the port side sees a vessel to windward and cannot determine with certainty whether the other vessel has the wind on the port or on the starboard side, she shall keep out of the way of the other.

(b) For the purposes of this Rule the windward side shall be deemed to be the side opposite to that on which the mainsail is carried or, in the case of a square-rigged vessel, the side opposite to that on which the largest fore-and-aft sail is carried.

Overtaking

RULE 13 (a) Notwithstanding anything contained in the Rules of this Section any vessel overtaking any other shall keep out of the way of the vessel being overtaken.

(b) A vessel shall be deemed to be overtaking when coming up with another vessel from a direction more than 22.5 degrees abaft her beam, that is, in such a position with reference to the vessel she is overtaking, that at night she would be able to see only the sternlight of that vessel but neither of her sidelights.

(c) When a vessel is in any doubt as to whether she is overtaking another, she shall assume that this is the case and act accordingly.

(d) Any subsequent alteration of the bearing between the two vessels shall not make the overtaking vessel a crossing vessel within the meaning of these Rules or relieve her of the duty of keeping clear of the overtaken vessel until she is finally past and clear.

Head-on Situation

RULE 14 (a) When two power-driven vessels are meeting on reciprocal or nearly reciprocal courses so as to involve risk of collision each shall alter her course to starboard so that each shall pass on the port side of the other.

(b) Such a situation shall be deemed to exist when a vessel sees the other ahead or nearly ahead and by night she could see the masthead lights of the other in a line or nearly in a line and/or both sidelights and by day she observes the corresponding aspect of the other vessel.

(c) When a vessel is in any doubt as to whether such a situation exists she shall assume that it does exist and act accordingly.

Crossing Situation

RULE 15 When two power-driven vessels are crossing so as to involve risk of collision, the vessel which has the other on her own starboard side shall keep out of the way and shall, if the circumstances of the case admit, avoid crossing ahead of the other vessel.

Action by Give-Way Vessel

RULE 16 Every vessel which is directed to keep out of the way of another vessel shall, so far as possible, take early and substantial action to keep well clear.

Action by Stand-On Vessel

RULE 17 (a)(i) Where one of two vessels is to keep out of the way the other shall keep her course and speed.

(ii) The latter vessel may however take action to avoid collision by her manoeuvre alone, as soon as it becomes apparent to her that the vessel required to keep out of the way is not taking appropriate action in compliance with these Rules.

(b) When, from any cause, the vessel required to keep her course and speed finds herself so close that collision cannot be avoided by the action of the give-way vessel alone, she shall take such action as will best aid to avoid collision.

(c) A power-driven vessel which takes action in a crossing situation in accordance with sub-paragraph (a)(ii) of this Rule to avoid collision with another power-driven vessel shall, if the circumstances of the case admit, not alter course to port for a vessel on her own port side.

(d) This Rule does not relieve the give-way vessel of her obligation to keep out of the way.

Responsibilities Between Vessels

RULE 18 Except where Rules 9, 10 and 13 otherwise require:
(a) A power-driven vessel underway shall keep out of the way of:
(i) a vessel not under command;
(ii) a vessel restricted in her ability to manoeuvre;
(iii) a vessel engaged in fishing;
(iv) a sailing vessel.
(b) A sailing vessel underway shall keep out of the way of:
(i) a vessel not under command;
(ii) a vessel restricted in her ability to manoeuvre;
(iii) a vessel engaged in fishing.
(c) A vessel engaged in fishing when underway shall, so far as possible, keep out of the way of:
(i) a vessel not under command;
(ii) a vessel restricted in her ability to manoeuvre.
(d)(i) Any vessel other than a vessel not under command or a vessel restricted in her ability to manoeuvre shall, if the circumstances of the case admit, avoid impeding the safe passage of a vessel constrained by her draught, exhibiting the signals in Rule 28.
(ii) A vessel constrained by her draught shall navigate with particular caution having full regard to her special condition.
(e) A seaplane on the water shall, in general, keep well clear of all vessels and avoid impeding their navigation. In circumstances, however, where risk of collision exists, she shall comply with the Rules of this Part.

Section III—Conduct of Vessels in Restricted Visibility

Conduct of Vessels in Restricted Visibility

RULE 19 (a) This Rule applies to vessels not in sight of one another when navigating in or near an area of restricted visibility.
(b) Every vessel shall proceed at a safe speed adapted to the prevailing circumstances and conditions of restricted visibility. A power-driven vessel shall have her engines ready for immediate manoeuvre.
(c) Every vessel shall have due regard to the prevailing circumstances and conditions of restricted visibility when complying with the Rules of Section I of this Part.
(d) A vessel which detects by radar alone the presence of another vessel shall determine if a close-quarters situation is developing and/or risk of collision exists. If so, she shall take avoiding action in ample time, provided that when such action consists of an alteration of course, so far as possible the following shall be avoided:

(i) an alteration of course to port for a vessel forward of the beam, other than for a vessel being overtaken;

(ii) an alteration of course towards a vessel abeam or abaft the beam.

(e) Except where it has been determined that a risk of collision does not exist, every vessel which hears apparently forward of her beam the fog signal of another vessel, or which cannot avoid a close-quarters situation with another vessel forward of her beam, shall reduce her speed to the minimum at which she can be kept on her course. She shall if necessary take all her way off and in any event navigate with extreme caution until danger of collision is over.

PART C—LIGHTS AND SHAPES

Application

RULE 20 (a) Rules in this Part shall be complied with in all weathers.

(b) The Rules concerning lights shall be complied with from sunset to sunrise, and during such times no other lights shall be exhibited, except such lights as cannot be mistaken for the lights specified in these Rules or do not impair their visibility or distinctive character, or interfere with the keeping of a proper look-out.

(c) The lights prescribed by these Rules shall, if carried, also be exhibited from sunrise to sunset in restricted visibility and may be exhibited in all other circumstances when it is deemed necessary.

(d) The Rules concerning shapes shall be complied with by day.

(e) The lights and shapes specified in these Rules shall comply with the provisions of Annex I to these Regulations.

Definitions

RULE 21 (a) "Masthead light" means a white light placed over the fore and aft centreline of the vessel showing an unbroken light over an arc of the horizon of 225 degrees and so fixed as to show the light from right ahead to 22.5 degrees abaft the beam on either side of the vessel.

(b) "Sidelights" means a green light on the starboard side and a red light on the port side each showing an unbroken light over an arc of the horizon of 112.5 degrees and so fixed as to show the light from right ahead to 22.5 degrees abaft the beam on its respective side. In a vessel of less than 20 metres in length the sidelights may be combined in one lantern carried on the fore and aft centreline of the vessel.

(c) "Sternlight" means a white light placed as nearly as practicable at the stern showing an unbroken light over an arc of the horizon 135 degrees and so fixed as to show the light 67.5 degrees from right aft on each side of the vessel.

(d) "Towing light" means a yellow light having the same characteristics as the "sternlight" defined in paragraph (c) of this Rule.

(e) "All-round light" means a light showing an unbroken light over an arc of the horizon of 360 degrees.

(f) "Flashing light" means a light flashing at regular intervals at a frequency of 120 flashes or more per minute.

Visibility of Lights

RULE 22 The lights prescribed in these Rules shall have an intensity as specified in Section 8 of Annex I to these Regulations so as to be visible at the following minimum ranges:

(a) In vessels of 50 metres or more in length:

a masthead light, 6 miles;

a sidelight, 3 miles;

a sternlight, 3 miles;

a towing light, 3 miles;

a white, red, green or yellow all-round light, 3 miles.

(b) In vessels of 12 metres or more in length but less than 50 metres in length:

a masthead light, 5 miles; except that where the length of the vessel is less than 20 metres, 3 miles;

a sidelight, 2 miles;

a sternlight, 2 miles;

a towing light, 2 miles;

a white, red, green or yellow all-round light, 2 miles.

(c) In vessels of less than 12 metres in length:

a masthead light, 2 miles;

a sidelight, 1 mile;

a sternlight, 2 miles;

a towing light, 2 miles;

a white, red, green or yellow all-round light, 2 miles.

Power-Driven Vessels Underway

RULE 23 (a) A power-driven vessel underway shall exhibit:

(i) a masthead light forward;

(ii) a second masthead light abaft of and higher than the forward one; except that a vessel of less than 50 metres in length shall not be obliged to exhibit such light but may do so;

(iii) sidelights;

(iv) a sternlight.

(b) An air-cushion vessel when operating in the nondisplacement mode shall, in addition to the lights prescribed in paragraph (a) of this Rule, exhibit an all-round flashing yellow light.

(c) A power-driven vessel of less than 7 metres in length and whose maximum speed does not exceed 7 knots may, in lieu of the lights prescribed in paragraph (a) of this Rule, exhibit an all-round white light. Such vessel shall, if practicable, also exhibit sidelights.

Towing and Pushing

RULE 24 (a) A power-driven vessel when towing shall exhibit:

(i) instead of the light prescribed in Rule 23(a)(i), two masthead lights forward in a vertical line. When the length of the tow, measuring from the stern of the towing vessel to the after end of the tow exceeds 200 metres, three such lights in a vertical line;

(ii) sidelights;

(iii) a sternlight;

(iv) a towing light in a vertical line above the sternlight;

(v) when the length of the tow exceeds 200 metres, a diamond shape where it can best be seen.

(b) When a pushing vessel and a vessel being pushed ahead are rigidly connected in a composite unit they shall be regarded as a power-driven vessel and exhibit the lights prescribed in Rule 23.

(c) A power-driven vessel when pushing ahead or towing alongside, except in the case of a composite unit, shall exhibit:

(i) instead of the light prescribed in Rule 23(a)(i), two masthead lights forward in a vertical line;

(ii) sidelights;

(iii) a sternlight.

(d) A power-driven vessel to which paragraphs (a) and (c) of this Rule apply shall also comply with Rule 23(a)(ii).

(e) A vessel or object being towed shall exhibit:

(i) sidelights;

(ii) a sternlight;

(iii) when the length of the tow exceeds 200 meters, a diamond shape where it can best be seen.

(f) Provided that any number of vessels being towed alongside or pushed in a group shall be lighted as one vessel,

(i) a vessel being pushed ahead, not being part of a composite unit, shall exhibit at the forward end, sidelights;

(ii) a vessel being towed alongside shall exhibit a sternlight and at the forward end, sidelights.

(g) Where from any sufficient cause it is impracticable for a vessel or object being towed to exhibit the lights prescribed in paragraph (e) of this Rule, all possible measures shall be taken to light the vessel or object towed or at least to indicate the presence of the unlighted vessel or object.

Sailing Vessels Underway and Vessels Under Oars

RULE 25 (a) A sailing vessel underway shall exhibit:
  (i) sidelights;
  (ii) a sternlight.

(b) In a sailing vessel of less than 12 metres in length the lights prescribed in paragraph (a) of this Rule may be combined in one lantern carried at or near the top of the mast where it can best be seen.

(c) A sailing vessel underway may, in addition to the lights prescribed in paragraph (a) of this Rule, exhibit at or near the top of the mast, where they can best be seen, two all-round lights in a vertical line, the upper being red and the lower green, but these lights shall not be exhibited in conjunction with the combined lantern permitted by paragraph (b) of this Rule.

(d)(i) A sailing vessel of less than 77 metres in length shall, if practicable, exhibit the lights prescribed in paragraph (a) or (b) of this Rule, but if she does not, she shall have ready at hand an electric torch or lighted lantern showing a white light which shall be exhibited in sufficient time to prevent collision.

(ii) A vessel under oars may exhibit the lights prescribed in this Rule for sailing vessels, but if she does not, she shall have ready at hand an electric torch or lighted lantern showing a white light which shall be exhibited in sufficient time to prevent collision.

(e) A vessel proceeding under sail when also being propelled by machinery shall exhibit forward where it can best be seen a conical shape, apex downwards.

Fishing Vessels

RULE 26 (a) A vessel engaged in fishing, whether underway or at anchor, shall exhibit only the lights and shapes prescribed in this Rule.

(b) A vessel when engaged in trawling, by which is meant the dragging through the water of a dredge net or other apparatus used as a fishing appliance, shall exhibit:
  (i) two all-round lights in a vertical line, the upper being green and the lower white, or a shape consisting of two cones with their apexes together in a vertical line one above the other; a vessel of less than 20 metres in length may instead of this shape exhibit a basket;
  (ii) a masthead light abaft of and higher than the all-round green

light; a vessel of less than 50 metres in length shall not be obliged to exhibit such a light but may do so;

(iii) when making way through the water, in addition to the lights prescribed in this paragraph, sidelights and a sternlight.

(c) A vessel engaged in fishing, other than trawling, shall exhibit:

(i) two all-round lights in a vertical line, the upper being red and the lower white, or a shape consisting of two cones with apexes together in a vertical line one above the other; a vessel of less than 20 metres in length may instead of this shape exhibit a basket;

(ii) when there is outlying gear extending more than 150 metres horizontally from the vessel, an all-round white light or a cone apex upwards in the direction of the gear;

(iii) when making way through the water, in addition to the lights prescribed in this paragraph, sidelights and a sternlight.

(d) A vessel engaged in fishing in close proximity to other vessels engaged in fishing may exhibit the additional signals described in Annex II to these Regulations.

(e) A vessel when not engaged in fishing shall not exhibit the lights or shapes prescribed in this Rule, but only those prescribed for a vessel of her length.

Vessels Not Under Command or Restricted in
Their Ability to Manoeuvre

RULE 27 (a) A vessel not under command shall exhibit:

(i) two all-round red lights in a vertical line where they can best be seen;

(ii) two balls or similar shapes in a vertical line where they can best be seen;

(iii) when making way through the water, in addition to the lights prescribed in this paragraph, sidelights and a sternlight.

(b) A vessel restricted in her ability to manoeuvre, except a vessel engaged in minesweeping operations, shall exhibit:

(i) three all-round lights in a vertical line where they can best be seen. The highest and lowest of these lights shall be red and the middle light shall be white;

(ii) three shapes in a vertical line where they can best be seen. The highest and lowest of these shapes shall be balls and the middle one a diamond;

(iii) when making way through the water, masthead lights, sidelights and a sternlight, in addition to the lights prescribed in subparagraph (i);

(iv) when at anchor, in addition to the lights or shapes prescribed in sub-paragraphs (i) and (ii), the light, lights or shape prescribed in Rule 30.

(c) A vessel engaged in a towing operation such as renders her unable to deviate from her course shall, in addition to the lights or shapes prescribed in subparagraph (b)(i) and (ii) of this Rule, exhibit the lights or shape prescribed in Rule 24(a).

(d) A vessel engaged in dredging or underwater operations, when restricted in her ability to manoeuvre, shall exhibit the lights and shapes prescribed in paragraph (b) of this Rule and shall in addition, when an obstruction exists, exhibit:

(i) two all-round red lights or two balls in a vertical line to indicate the side on which the obstruction exists;

(ii) two all-round green lights or two diamonds in a vertical line to indicate the side on which another vessel may pass;

(iii) when making way through the water, in addition to the lights prescribed in this paragraph, masthead lights, sidelights and a sternlight; light;

(iv) a vessel to which this paragraph applies when at anchor shall exhibit the lights or shapes prescribed in subparagraphs (i) and (ii) instead of the lights or shape prescribed in Rule 30.

(e) Whenever the size of a vessel engaged in diving operations makes it impracticable to exhibit the shapes prescribed in paragraph (d) of this Rule, a rigid replica of the International Code flag "A" not less than 1 metre in height shall be exhibited. Measures shall be taken to ensure all-round visibility.

(f) A vessel engaged in minesweeping operations shall, in addition to the lights prescribed for a power-driven vessel in Rule 23, exhibit three all-round green lights or three balls. One of these lights or shapes shall be exhibited at or near the foremast head and one at each end of the fore yard. These lights or shapes indicate that it is dangerous for another vessel to approach closer than 1,000 metres astern or 500 metres on either side of the minesweeper.

(g) Vessels of less than 7 metres in length shall not be required to exhibit the lights prescribed in this Rule.

(h) The signals prescribed in this Rule are not signals of vessels in distress and requiring assistance. Such signals are contained in Annex IV to these Regulations.

Vessels Constrained by Their Draught

RULE 28 A vessel constrained by her draught may, in addition to the lights prescribed for power-driven vessels in Rule 23, exhibit where they can best be seen three all-round red lights in a vertical line, or a cylinder.

Pilot Vessels

RULE 29 (a) A vessel engaged on pilotage duty shall exhibit:

(i) at or near the masthead, two all-round lights in a vertical line, the upper being white and the lower red;

(ii) when underway, in addition, sidelights and a sternlight;

(iii) when at anchor, in addition to the lights prescribed in sub-paragraph (i), the anchor light, lights or shape.

(b) A pilot vessel when not engaged on pilotage duty shall exhibit the lights or shapes prescribed for a similar vessel of her length.

Anchored Vessels and Vessels Aground

RULE 30 (a) A vessel at anchor shall exhibit where it can best be seen:

(i) in the fore part, an all-round white light or one ball;

(ii) at or near the stern and at a lower level than the light prescribed in sub-paragraph (i), an all-round white light.

(b) A vessel of less than 50 metres in length may exhibit an all-round white light where it can best be seen instead of the lights prescribed in paragraph (a) of this Rule.

(c) A vessel at anchor may, and a vessel of 100 metres and more in length shall, also use the available working or equivalent lights to illuminate her decks.

(d) A vessel aground shall exhibit the lights prescribed in paragraph (a) or (b) of this Rule and in addition, where they can best be seen:

(i) two all-round red lights in a vertical line;

(ii) three balls in a vertical line.

(e) A vessel of less than 7 metres in length, when at anchor or aground, not in or near a narrow channel, fairway or anchorage, or where other vessels normally navigate, shall not be required to exhibit the lights or shapes prescribed in paragraphs (a), (b) or (d) of this Rule.

Seaplanes

RULE 31 Where it is impracticable for a seaplane to exhibit lights and shapes of the characteristics or in the positions prescribed in the Rules of this Part she shall exhibit lights and shapes as closely similar in characteristics and position as is possible.

PART D—SOUND AND LIGHT SIGNALS

Definitions

RULE 32 (a) The word "whistle" means any sound signalling appliance capable of producing the prescribed blasts and which complies with the specifications in Annex III to these Regulations.

(b) The term "short blast" means a blast of about one second's duration.

(c) The term "prolonged blast" means a blast of from four to six seconds' duration.

Equipment for Sound Signals

RULE 33 (a) A vessel of 12 metres or more in length shall be provided with a whistle and a bell and a vessel of 100 metres or more in length shall, in addition, be provided with a gong, the tone and sound of which cannot be confused with that of the bell. The whistle, bell and gong shall comply with the specifications in Annex III to these Regulations. The bell or gong or both may be replaced by other equipment having the same respective sound characteristics, provided that manual sounding of the required signals shall always be possible.

(b) A vessel of less than 12 metres in length shall not be obliged to carry the sound signalling appliances prescribed in paragraph (a) of this Rule but if she does not, she shall be provided with some other means of making an efficient sound signal.

Manoeuvring and Warning Signals

RULE 34 (a) When vessels are in sight of one another, a power-driven vessel underway, when manoeuvring as authorized or required by these Rules, shall indicate that manoeuvre by the following signals on her whistle:

One short blast to mean "I am altering my course to starboard";

—two short blasts to mean "I am altering my course to port";

—three short blasts to mean "I am operating astern propulsion."

(b) Any vessel may supplement the whistle signals prescribed in paragraph (a) of this Rule by light signals, repeated as appropriate, whilst the manoeuvre is being carried out:

(i) these light signals shall have the following significance:

—one flash to mean "I am altering my course to starboard";

—two flashes to mean "I am altering my course to port";

—three flashes to mean "I am operating astern propulsion";

(ii) the duration of each flash shall be about one second, the interval between flashes shall be about one second, and the interval between successive signals shall be not less than ten seconds;

(iii) the light used for this signal shall, if fitted, be an all-round white light, visible at a minimum range of 5 miles, and shall comply with the provisions of Annex I.

(c) When in sight of one another in a narrow channel or fairway:

(i) a vessel intending to overtake another shall in compliance with Rule 9(e)(i) indicate her intention by the following signals on her whistle:

—two prolonged blasts followed by one short blast to mean "I intend to overtake you on your starboard side";

—two prolonged blasts followed by two short blasts to mean "I intend to overtake you on your port side".

(ii) the vessel about to be overtaken when acting in accordance with Rule 9(e)(i) shall indicate her agreement by the following signal on her whistle:

—one prolonged, one short, one prolonged and one short blast, in that order.

(d) When vessels in sight of one another are approaching each other and from any cause either vessel fails to understand the intentions or actions of the other, or is in doubt whether sufficient action is being taken by the other to avoid collision, the vessel in doubt shall immediately indicate such doubt by giving at least five short and rapid blasts on the whistle. Such signal may be supplemented by a light signal of at least five short and rapid flashes.

(e) A vessel nearing a bend or an area of a channel or fairway where other vessels may be obscured by an intervening obstruction shall sound one prolonged blast. Such signal shall be answered with a prolonged blast by any approaching vessel that may be within hearing around the bend or behind the intervening obstruction.

(f) If whistles are fitted on a vessel at a distance apart of more than 100 metres, one whistle only shall be used for giving manoeuvring and warning signals.

Sound Signals in Restricted Visibility

RULE 35 In or near an area of restricted visibility, whether by day or night, the signals prescribed in this Rule shall be used as follows:

(a) A power-driven vessel making way through the water shall sound at intervals of not more than 2 minutes one prolonged blast.

(b) A power-driven vessel underway but stopped and making no way through the water shall sound at intervals of not more than 2 minutes two prolonged blasts in succession with an interval of about 2 seconds between them.

(c) A vessel not under command, a vessel restricted in her ability to manoeuvre, a vessel constrained by her draught, a sailing vessel, a vessel engaged in fishing and a vessel engaged in towing or pushing another vessel shall, instead of the signals prescribed in paragraphs (a) or (b) of this

Rule, sound at intervals of not more than 2 minutes three blasts in succession, namely one prolonged followed by two short blasts.

(d) A vessel towed or if more than one vessel is towed the last vessel of the tow, if manned, shall at intervals of not more than 2 minutes sound four blasts in succession, namely one prolonged followed by three short blasts. When practicable, this signal shall be made immediately after the signal made by the towing vessel.

(e) When a pushing vessel and a vessel being pushed ahead are rigidly connected in a composite unit they shall be regarded as a power-driven vessel and shall give the signals prescribed in paragraphs (a) or (b) of this Rule.

(f) A vessel at anchor shall at intervals of not more than one minute ring the bell rapidly for about 5 seconds. In a vessel of 100 metres or more in length the bell shall be sounded in the forepart of the vessel and immediately after the ringing of the bell the gong shall be sounded rapidly for about 5 seconds in the after part of the vessel. A vessel at anchor may in addition sound three blasts in succession, namely, one short, one prolonged and one short blast, to give warning of her position and of the possibility of collision to an approaching vessel.

(g) A vessel aground shall give the bell signal and if required the gong signal prescribed in paragraph (f) of this Rule and shall, in addition, give three separate and distinct strokes on the bell immediately before and after the rapid ringing of the bell. A vessel aground may in addition sound an appropriate whistle signal.

(h) A vessel of less than 12 metres in length shall not be obliged to give the above-mentioned signals but, if she does not, shall make some other efficient sound signal at intervals of not more than 2 minutes.

(i) A pilot vessel when engaged on pilotage duty may in addition to the signals prescribed in paragraphs (a), (b) or (f) of this Rule sound an identity signal consisting of four short blasts.

Signals to Attract Attention

RULE 36 If necessary to attract the attention of another vessel any vessel may make light or sound signals that cannot be mistaken for any signal authorized elsewhere in these Rules, or may direct the beam of her searchlight in the direction of the danger, in such a way as not to embarrass any vessel.

Distress Signals

RULE 37 When a vessel is in distress and requires assistance she shall use or exhibit the signals prescribed in Annex IV to these Regulations.

PART E—EXEMPTIONS

Exemptions

RULE 38 Any vessel (or class of vessels) provided that she complies with the requirements of the International Regulations for Preventing Collisions at Sea, 1960, the keel of which is laid or which is at a corresponding stage of construction before the entry into force of these Regulations may be exempted from compliance therewith as follows:

(a) The installation of lights with ranges prescribed in Rule 22, until four years after the date of entry into force of these Regulations.

(b) The installation of lights with colour specifications as prescribed in Section 7 of Annex I to these Regulations, until four years after the date of entry into force of these Regulations.

(c) The repositioning of lights as a result of conversion from Imperial to metric units and rounding off measurement figures, permanent exemption.

(d)(i) The repositioning of masthead lights on vessels of less than 150 metres in length, resulting from the prescriptions of Section 3(a) of Annex I, permanent exemption.

(ii) The repositioning of masthead lights on vessels of 150 metres or more in length, resulting from the prescriptions of Section 3(a) of Annex I to these Regulations, until nine years after the date of entry into force of these Regulations.

(e) The repositioning of masthead lights resulting from the prescriptions of Section 2(b) of Annex I, until nine years after the date of entry into force of these Regulations.

(f) The repositioning of sidelights resulting from the prescriptions of Sections 2(g) and 3(b) of Annex I, until nine years after the date of entry into force of these Regulations.

(g) The requirements for sound signal appliances prescribed in Annex III, until nine years after the date of entry into force of these Regulations.

ANNEX I

Positioning and Technical Details of Lights and Shapes

1. Definition

The term "height above the hull" means height above the uppermost continuous deck.

2. Vertical Positioning and Spacing of Lights

(a) On a power-driven vessel of 20 metres or more in length the mast-head lights shall be placed as follows:

(i) the forward masthead light, or if only one masthead light is car-ried, then that light, at a height above the hull of not less than 6 metres, and, if the breadth of the vessel exceeds 6 metres, then at a height above the hull not less than such breadth, so however that the light need not be placed at a greater height above the hull than 12 metres;

(ii) when two masthead lights are carried the after one shall be at least 4.5 metres vertically higher than the forward one.

(b) The vertical separation of masthead lights of power-driven vessels shall be such that in all normal conditions of trim the after light will be seen over and separate from the forward light at a distance of 1000 metres from the stem when viewed from sea level.

(c) The masthead light of a power-driven vessel of 12 metres but less than 20 metres in length shall be placed at a height above the gunwale of not less than 2.5 metres.

(d) A power-driven vessel of less than 12 metres in length may carry the uppermost light at a height of less than 2.5 metres above the gunwale. When however a masthead light is carried in addition to sidelights and a sternlight, then such masthead light shall be carried at least 1 metre higher than the sidelights.

(e) One of the two or three masthead lights prescribed for a power-driven vessel when engaged in towing or pushing another vessel shall be placed in the same position as the forward masthead light of a power-driven vessel.

(f) In all circumstances the masthead light or lights shall be so placed as to be above and clear of all other lights and obstructions.

(g) The sidelights of a power-driven vessel shall be placed at a height above the hull not greater than three quarters of that of the forward masthead light. They shall not be so low as to be interfered with by deck lights.

(h) The sidelights, if in a combined lantern and carried on a power-driven vessel of less than 20 metres in length, shall be placed not less than 1 metre below the masthead light.

(i) When the Rules prescribe two or three lights to be carried in a vertical line, they shall be spaced as follows:

(i) on a vessel of 20 metres in length or more such lights shall be spaced not less than 2 metres apart, and the lowest of these lights shall, except where a towing light is required, not be less than 4 metres above the hull;

(ii) on a vessel of less than 20 metres in length such lights shall be spaced not less than 1 metre apart and the lowest of these lights shall, except where a towing light is required, not be less than 2 metres above the gunwale;

(iii) when three lights are carried they shall be equally spaced.

(j) The lower of the two all-round lights prescribed for a fishing vessel when engaged in fishing shall be at a height above the sidelights not less than twice the distance between the two vertical lights.

(k) The forward anchor light, when two are carried, shall not be less than 4.5 metres above the after one. On a vessel of 50 metres or more in length this forward anchor light shall not be less than 6 metres above the hull.

3. Horizontal Positioning and Spacing of Lights

(a) When two masthead lights are prescribed for a power-driven vessel, the horizontal distance between them shall not be less than one half of the length of the vessel but need not be more than 100 metres. The forward light shall be placed not more than one quarter of the length of the vessel from the stem.

(b) On a vessel of 20 metres or more in length the sidelights shall not be placed in front of the forward masthead lights. They shall be placed at or near the side of the vessel.

4. Details of Location of Direction-Indicating Lights for Fishing Vessels, Dredgers and Vessels Engaged in Underwater Operations

(a) The light indicating the direction of the outlying gear from a vessel engaged in fishing as prescribed in Rule 26(c)(ii) shall be placed at a horizontal distance of not less than 2 metres and not more than 6 metres away from the two all-round red and white lights. This light shall be placed not higher than the all-round white light prescribed in Rule 26(c)(i) and not lower than the sidelights.

(b) The lights and shapes on a vessel engaged in dredging or underwater operations to indicate the obstructed side and/or the side on which it is safe to pass, as prescribed in Rule 27(d)(i) and (ii), shall be placed at the maximum practical horizontal distance, but in no case less than 2 metres, from the lights or shapes prescribed in Rule 27(b)(i) and (ii). In no case shall the upper of these lights or shapes be at a greater height than the lower of the three lights or shapes prescribed in Rule 27(b)(i) and (ii).

5. Screens for Sidelights

The sidelights shall be fitted with inboard screens painted matt black, and meeting the requirements of Section 9 of this Annex. With a combined lantern, using a single vertical filament and a very narrow division between the green and red sections, external screens need not be fitted.

6. *Shapes*

(a) Shapes shall be black and of the following sizes:
(i) a ball shall have a diameter of not less than 0.6 metre;
(ii) a cone shall have a base diameter of not less than 0.6 metre and a height equal to its diameter;
(iii) a cylinder shall have a diameter of at least 0.6 metre and a height of twice its diameter;
(iv) a diamond shape shall consist of two cones as defined in (ii) above having a common base.
(b) The vertical distance between shapes shall be at least 1.5 metre.
(c) In a vessel of less than 20 metres in length shapes of lesser dimensions but commensurate with the size of the vessel may be used and the distance apart may be correspondingly reduced.

7. *Colour Specification of Lights*

The chromaticity of all navigation lights shall conform to the following standards, which lie within the boundaries of the area of the diagram specified for each colour by the International Commission on Illumination (CIE).

The boundaries of the area for each colour are given by indicating the corner co-ordinates, which are as follows:

(i) *White*

x	0.525	0.525	0.452	0.310	0.310	0.443
y	0.382	0.440	0.440	0.348	0.283	0.382

(ii) *Green*

x	0.028	0.009	0.300	0.203
y	0.385	0.723	0.511	0.356

(iii) *Red*

x	0.680	0.660	0.735	0.721
y	0.320	0.320	0.264	0.259

(iv) *Yellow*

x	0.612	0.618	0.575	0.575
y	0.382	0.382	0.425	0.406

8. *Intensity of Lights*

(a) the minimum luminous intensity of lights shall be calculated by using the formula:
$$I = 3.43 \times 10^6 \times T \times D^2 \times K^{-D}$$

where I is luminous intensity in candelas under service conditions.

T   is threshold factor 2×10^{-7} lux,

D   is range of visibility (luminous range)
of light in nautical miles,

K   is atmospheric transmissivity.
For prescribed lights the value of
K shall be 0.8, corresponding to a
meteorological visibility of
approximately 13 nautical miles.

(b) A selection of figures derived from the formula is given in the following table:[1]

Range of visibility (luminous range) of light in nautical miles D	Luminous intensity of light in candelas for K=0.8 I
1	0.9
2	4.3
3	12.0
4	27.0
5	52.0
6	94.0

9. Horizontal Sectors

(a)(i) In the forward direction, sidelights as fitted on the vessel must show the minimum required intensities. The intensities must decrease to reach practical cut-off between 1 degree and 3 degrees outside the prescribed sectors.

(ii) For sternlights and masthead lights and at 22.5 degrees abaft the beam for sidelights, the minimum required intensities shall be maintained over the arc of the horizon up to 5 degrees within the limits of the sectors prescribed in Rule 21. From 5 degrees within the prescribed sectors the intensity may decrease by 50 per cent up to the prescribed limits; it shall decrease steadily to reach practical cut-off at not more than 5 degrees outside the prescribed limits.

(b) All-round lights shall be so located as not to be obscured by masts, topmasts or structures within angular sectors of more than 6 degrees, except anchor lights, which need not be placed at an impracticable height above the hull.

10. Vertical Sectors

(a) The vertical sectors of electric lights, with the exception of lights on sailing vessels shall ensure that:

[1] *The maximum luminous intensity of navigation lights should be limited to avoid undue glare.*

(i) at least the required minimum intensity is maintained at all angles from 5 degrees above to 5 degrees below the horizontal;

(ii) at least 60 per cent of the required minimum intensity is maintained from 7.5 degrees above to 7.5 degrees below the horizontal.

(b) In the case of sailing vessels the vertical sectors of electric lights shall ensure that:

(i) at least the required minimum intensity is maintained at all angles from 5 degrees above to 5 degrees below the horizontal;

(ii) at least 50 per cent of the required minimum intensity is maintained from 25 degrees above to 25 degrees below the horizontal.

(c) In the case of lights other than electric these specifications shall be met as closely as possible.

11. Intensity of Non-Electric Lights

Non-electric lights shall so far as practicable comply with the minimum intensities, as specified in the Table given in Section 8 of this Annex.

12. Manoeuvring Light

Notwithstanding the provisions of paragraph 2(f) of this Annex the manoeuvring light described in Rule 34(b) shall be placed in the same fore and aft vertical plane as the masthead light or lights and, where practicable, at a minimum height of 2 metres vertically above the forward masthead light, provided that it shall be carried not less than 2 metres vertically above or below the after masthead light. On a vessel where only one masthead light is carried the manoeuvring light, if fitted, shall be carried where it can best be seen, not less than 2 metres vertically apart from the masthead light.

13. Approval

The construction of lanterns and shapes and the installation of lanterns on board the vessel shall be to the satisfaction of the appropriate authority of the State where the vessel is registered.

ANNEX II

Additional Signals for Fishing Vessels Fishing in Close Proximity

1. General

The lights mentioned herein shall, if exhibited in pursuance of Rule 26(d), be placed where they can best be seen. They shall be at least 0.9 metre apart but at a lower level than lights prescribed in Rule 26(b)(i) and (c)(i). The lights shall be visible all round the horizon at a distance of at least 1 mile but at a lesser distance than the lights prescribed by these Rules for fishing vessels.

2. Signals for Trawlers

(a) Vessels when engaged in trawling, whether using demersal or pelagic gear, may exhibit:

(i) when shooting their nets: two white lights in a vertical line;

(ii) when hauling their nets: one white light over one red light in a vertical line;

(iii) when the net has come fast upon an obstruction: two red lights in a vertical line.

(b) Each vessel engaged in pair trawling may exhibit:

(i) by night, a searchlight directed forward and in the direction of the other vessel of the pair;

(ii) when shooting or hauling their nets or when their nets have come fast upon an obstruction, the lights prescribed in 2(a) above.

3. Signals for Purse Seiners

Vessels engaged in fishing with purse seine gear may exhibit two yellow lights in a vertical line. These lights shall flash alternately every second and with equal light and occultation duration. These lights may be exhibited only when the vessel is hampered by its fishing gear.

ANNEX III

Technical Details of Sound Signal Appliances

1. Whistles

(a) *Frequencies and range of audibility*—The fundamental frequency of the signal shall lie within the range 70–700 Hz.

The range of audibility of the signal from a whistle shall be determined by those frequencies, which may include the fundamental and/or one or more higher frequencies, which lie within the range 180–700 Hz ($\pm$1 percent) and which provide the sound pressure levels specified in paragraph 1(c) below.

(b) *Limits of fundamental frequencies*—To ensure a wide variety of whistle characteristics, the fundamental frequency of a whistle shall be between the following limits:

(i) 70–200 Hz, for a vessel 200 metres or more in length;

130–350 Hz, for a vessel 75 metres but less than 200 metres in length;

(iii) 250–700 Hz, for a vessel less than 75 metres in length.

(c) *Sound signal intensity and range of audibility*—A whistle fitted in a vessel shall provide, in the direction of maximum intensity of the whistle and at a distance of 1 metre from it, a sound pressure level in at least $1/3$-octave band within the range of frequencies 180–700 Hz ($\pm$ 1 percent) of not less than the appropriate figure given in the table below.

Length of vessel in meters	$1/3$d-octave band level at 1 meter in dB referred to 2×10^{-5} N/m²	Audibility range in nautical miles
200 or more	153	2.0
75 but less than 200	138	1.5
20 but less than 75	130	1.0
Less than 20	120	.5

The range of audibility in the table above is for information and is approximately the range at which a whistle may be heard on its forward axis with 90 percent probability in conditions of still air on board a vessel having average background noise level at the listening posts (taken to be 68 dB in the octave band centred on 250 Hz and 63 dB in the octave band centred on 500 Hz).

In practice the range at which a whistle may be heard is extremely variable and depends critically on weather conditions; the values given can be regarded as typical but under conditions of strong wind or high ambient noise level at the listening post the range may be much reduced.

(d) *Directional properties*—The sound pressure level of a directional whistle shall not be more than 4 dB below the sound pressure level on the axis at any direction in the horizontal plane within $\pm$45 degrees of the axis. The sound pressure level at any other direction in the horizontal plane shall be not more than 10 dB below the ground pressure level on the axis, so that the range in any direction will be at least half the range on the forward axis. The sound pressure level shall be measured in that $1/3$rd-octave band which determines the audibility range.

(e) *Positioning of whistles*—When a directional whistle is to be used as the only whistle on a vessel, it shall be installed with its maximum intensity directed straight ahead.

A whistle shall be placed as high as practicable on a vessel, in order to reduce interception of the emitted sound by obstructions and also to minimize hearing damage risk to personnel. The sound pressure level of the vessel's own signal at listening posts shall not exceed 110 dB (A) and so far as practicable should not exceed 100 dB (A).

(f) *Fitting of more than one whistle*—If whistles are fitted at a distance apart of more than 100 metres, it shall be so arranged that they are not sounded simultaneously.

(g) *Combined whistle systems*—If due to the presence of obstructions the sound field of a single whistle or of one of the whistles referred to in paragraph 1(f) above is likely to have a zone of greatly reduced signal level, it is recommended that a combined whistle system be fitted so as to overcome this reduction. For the purposes of the Rules a combined whistle system is to be regarded as a single whistle. The whistles of a combined system shall be located at a distance apart of not more than 100 metres and arranged to be sounded simultaneously. The frequency of any one whistle shall differ from those of the others by at least 10 Hz.

2. Bell or Gong

(a) *Intensity of signal*—A bell or gong, or other device having similar sound characteristics shall produce a sound pressure level of not less than 110 dB at 1 metre.

(b) *Construction*—Bells and gongs shall be made of corrosion-resistant material and designed to give a clear tone. The diameter of the mouth of the bell shall be not less than 300 mm for vessels of more than 20 metres in length, and shall be not less than 200 mm for vessels of 12 to 20 metres in length. Where practicable, a power-driven bell striker is recommended to ensure constant force but manual operation shall be possible. The mass of the striker shall be not less than 3 percent of the mass of the bell.

3. Approval

The construction of sound signal appliances, their performance and their installation on board the vessel shall be to the satisfaction of the appropriate authority of the State where the vessel is registered.

ANNEX IV

Distress Signals

1. The following signals, used or exhibited either together or separately, indicate distress and need of assistance:

(a) a gun or other explosive signal fired at intervals of about a minute;

(b) a continuous sounding with any fog-signalling apparatus;

(c) rockets or shells, throwing red stars fired one at a time at short intervals;

(d) a signal made by radiotelegraphy or by any other signalling method consisting of the group ... - - - ... (SOS) in the Morse Code;

(e) a signal sent by radiotelephony consisting of the spoken word "Mayday";

(f) the International Code Signal of distress indicated by N.C.;

(g) a signal consisting of a square flag having above or below it a ball or anything resembling a ball;

(h) flames on the vessel (as from a burning tar barrel, oil barrel, etc.)

(i) a rocket parachute flare or a hand flare showing a red light;

(j) a smoke signal giving off orange-coloured smoke;

(k) slowly and repeatedly raising and lowering arms outstretched to each side;

(l) the radiotelegraph alarm signal;

(m) the radiotelephone alarm signal;

(n) signals transmitted by emergency position—indicating radio beacons.

2. The use or exhibition of any of the foregoing signals except for the purpose of indicating distress and need of assistance and the use of other signals which may be confused with any of the above signals is prohibited.

3. Attention is drawn to the relevant sections of the International Code of Signals, the Merchant Ship Search and Rescue Manual and the following signals:

(a) a piece of orange-coloured canvas with either a black square and circle or other appropriate symbol (for identification from the air);

(b) a dye marker.

APPENDIX C
Interpretive Rulings, International Rules[1]

PART 85[2]

Scope

SEC. 85.01–1 The regulations in this part are interpretive rulings with respect to the "Rules of the Road" requirements applicable to all public and private vessels of the United States while upon the high seas and in waters connected therewith when subject to the "International Rules" as set forth in the Act of September 24, 1963 (77 Stat. 195–210; 33 U.S.C. 1061–1094).

Sternlight for Motorboats Operating on the High Seas Carried on Centerline

SEC. 85.05–1 Rule 10[3] of the "International Rules" (33 U.S.C. 1070) states, "A vessel when underway shall carry at her stern a white light, . . ." This 12-point white stern light shall be carried on the centerline of every motorboat of Class A, 1, 2, or 3, except that on a motorboat of Class A or 1 this light may be carried off the centerline.

---

[1] *Code of Federal Regulations: Title 33—Navigation and Navigable Waters; Part 85—Interpretive Rulings—International Rules.*

[2] *Authority: The provisions of this Part 85, issued under sec. 1, 80 Stat. 383, as amended, sec. 1, 63 Stat. 545, sec. 6(b)(1), 80 Stat. 937; 5 U.S.C. 552, 14 U.S.C. 633, 49 U.S.C. 1655 (b)(1); 49 CFR 1.46(b).*

[3] *Rule 10, 1960 International Rules, has been replaced by Rule 21(c), 1972 International Rules, which requires the sternlight to be "placed as nearly as practicable at the stern."*

APPENDIX D
Inland Rules[1]

APPLICATION OF INLAND RULES OF THE ROAD
(33 U.S.C. 154)

The following regulations for preventing collisions shall be followed by all vessels upon the harbors, rivers, and other inland waters of the United States, except the Great Lakes and their connecting and tributary waters as far east as Montreal, and the waters of the Mississippi River between its source and the Huey P. Long Bridge and all of its tributaries emptying thereinto and their tributaries and that part of the Atchafalaya River above its junction with the Plaquemine-Morgan City alternate waterway, and the Red River of the North; and are hereby declared special rules duly made by local authority.

NAVY AND COAST GUARD VESSEL EXCEPTIONS
(33 U.S.C. 360)

Any requirement as to the number, position, range of visibility, or arc of visibility of lights required to be displayed by vessels under . . . sections 154-231 of this title . . . and all laws amendatory thereto, shall not apply to any vessel of the Navy or of the Coast Guard, where the Secretary of the Navy, or the Secretary of Transportation in the case of Coast Guard vessels operating under the Department of Transportation, or such official or officials as either may designate, shall find or certify that, by reason of special construction, it is not possible with respect to such vessel or class of vessels to comply with the statutory provisions as to the number, position, range of visibility, or arc of visibility of lights. The lights of any such exempted vessel or class of vessels shall, however, comply as closely to the requirements of the applicable sections as the Secretary shall find to be feasible.

[1] *Title 33, U.S. Code, Section 154-159, 171-183, 191-192, 201-213, 222, 231, 232.*

PUBLICATION OF NAVY AND COAST GUARD VESSEL EXCEPTIONS (33 U.S.C. 360a)

When the Secretary of the Navy or the Secretary of Transportation, or such official or officals as either may designate, shall make any finding or certification as prescribed in section 360 of this title, notice of such finding or certification and the character and position of the lights to be displayed on such vessel shall be published in "Notice to Mariners."

AUTHORITY FOR PILOT RULES (33 U.S.C. 157)

(a) The Secretary of the Department in which the Coast Guard is operating shall establish such rules to be observed, on the waters described in section 154 of this title, by steam vessels in passing each other and as to the lights and day signals to be carried on such waters by ferryboats, by vessels and craft of all types when in tow of steam vessels or operating by handpower or horsepower or drifting with the current, and by any other vessels not otherwise provided for, not inconsistent with the provisions of this Act, as he from time to time may deem necessary for safety, which rules are declared special rules duly made by local authority. A pamphlet containing such Act and regulations shall be furnished to all vessels and craft subject to this Act. On vessels and craft over sixty-five feet in length the pamphlet shall, where practicable, be kept on board and available for ready reference.

(b) Except in an emergency, before any rules or any alteration, amendment, or repeal thereof are established by the Secretary under the provisions of this section, the said Secretary shall publish the proposed rules, alterations, amendments, or repeals, and public hearings shall be held with respect thereto on such notice as the Secretary deems reasonable under the circumstances.

AUTHORITY FOR SPECIAL REGULATIONS NEAR LOW BRIDGES (33 U.S.C. 157a)

(a) The Secretary of the Department in which the Coast Guard is operating may permit vessels desiring to navigate or operate under bridges constructed over navigable waters of the United States to temporarily lower any lights, day signals, or other navigational means and appliances prescribed or required pursuant to law, rule, or regulation, and, if necessary, may authorize vessels so navigating or operating to depart from the rules to prevent collisions as prescribed by law, rule, or regulation. The Secretary of the Department in which the Coast Guard is operating may also prescribe such special regulations to be observed by vessels so navigating or operating as in his judgment the public safety may require for the prevention of collisions.

(b) Notice of the regulations to accomplish the purposes of this section shall be published in the Federal Register and in the Notice to Mariners, and after the effective date specified in such notices, such regulations shall have the force of law.

(c) Any person who navigates or operates a vessel in violation of the regulations established pursuant to this section shall be liable to a penalty not exceeding $500. In addition, any vessel navigated or operated in violation of the regulations established pursuant to this section shall be liable to a penalty of $500, for which sum such vessel may be seized and proceeded against, by way of libel, in the district court of the United States for any district within which such vessel may be found.

AUTHORITY FOR INLAND/INTERNATIONAL LINE OF DEMARCATION (33 U.S.C. 151)

The Commandant of the Coast Guard is authorized, empowered, and directed from time to time to designate and define by suitable bearings or ranges with lighthouses, light vessels, buoys, or coast objects, the lines dividing the high seas from rivers, harbors, and inland waters.

PENALTY FOR VIOLATIONS BY PILOT, ENGINEER, MATE OR MASTER (33 U.S.C. 158)

Every licensed and unlicensed pilot, engineer, mate, or master of any vessel[2] who violates the provisions of this Act or the regulations established pursuant hereto shall be liable to a penalty of not exceeding $500, and for all damages sustained by any passenger, in his person or baggage, as a result of such violation: Provided, That nothing herein shall relieve any vessel, owner, or corporation from any liability incurred by reason of such violation.

PENALTY FOR VIOLATIONS BY VESSEL (33 U.S.C. 159)

Every vessel which is navigated in violation of any of the provisions of this Act or the regulations established pursuant hereto shall be liable to a penalty of $500, one-half to go to the informer, for which sum such vessel may be seized and proceeded against by action in any district court of the United States having jurisdiction of the offense.

[2] For a definition of the word "vessel," see Rule 3(a), International Rules.

PRELIMINARY AND DEFINITIONS

In the following rules every steam vessel which is under sail and not under steam is to be considered a sailing vessel, and every vessel under steam, whether under sail or not, is to be considered a steam vessel.

The words "steam vessel" shall include any vessel propelled by machinery.

A vessel is "underway," within the meaning of these rules, when she is not at anchor, or made fast to the shore, or aground.

The word "visible" in these rules, when applied to lights, shall mean visible on a dark night with a clear atmosphere.

Art. 1. The rules concerning lights shall be complied with in all weathers from sunset to sunrise, and during such time no other lights which may be mistaken for the prescribed lights shall be exhibited.

LIGHTS AND SHAPES

Art. 2.[3] A steam vessel when underway shall carry (a) On or in the front of the foremast, or if a vessel without a foremast then in the fore part of the vessel, a bright white light so constructed as to show an unbroken light over an arc of the horizon of twenty points of the compass, so fixed as to throw the light ten points on each side of the vessel, namely, from right ahead to two points abaft the beam on either side, and of such a character as to be visible at a distance of at least five miles.

Steam Vessels—Side Lights

(b) On the starboard side a green light so constructed as to show an unbroken light over an arc of the horizon of ten points of the compass, so fixed as to throw the light from right ahead to two points abaft the beam on the starboard side, and of such a character as to be visible at a distance of at least two miles.

(c) On the port side a red light so constructed as to show an unbroken light over an arc of the horizon of ten points of the compass, so fixed as to throw the light from right ahead to two points abaft the beam on the port side, and of such a character as to be visible at a distance of at least two miles.

(d) The said green and red side lights shall be fitted with inboard screens projecting at least three feet forward from the light, so as to prevent these lights from being seen across the bow.

---

[3] *Article 2 is amended by an act of Congress approved April 25, 1940, describing lights required to be carried by every vessel propelled by machinery and not more than 65 feet in length except tugboats and towboats propelled by steam.*

Steam Vessels—Range Lights

(e) A seagoing steam vessel under way may carry an additional white light similar in construction to the light mentioned in subdivision (a). These two lights shall be so placed in line with the keel that one shall be at least fifteen feet higher than the other, and in such a position with reference to each other that the lower light shall be forward of the upper one. The vertical distance between these lights shall be less than the horizontal distance.

(f) All steam vessels (except seagoing vessels and ferryboats), shall carry in addition to green and red lights required by article two (b) and (c), and screens as required by article two (d), a central range of two white lights; the after light being carried at an elevation at least fifteen feet above the light at the head of the vessel. The headlight shall be so constructed as to show an unbroken light through twenty points of the compass, namely, from right ahead to two points abaft the beam on either side of the vessel, and the after light so as to show all around the horizon.

Steam Vessels—When Towing or Pushing

Art. 3. (a) A steam vessel when towing another vessel or vessels alongside or by pushing ahead shall, in addition to her side lights, carry two bright white lights in a vertical line, one over the other, not less than three feet apart, and when towing one or more vessels astern, regardless of the length of the tow, shall carry an additional bright white light three feet above or below such lights. Each of these lights shall be of the same construction and character, and shall be carried in the same position as the white light mentioned in article 2 (a) or the after range light mentioned in article 2 (f).

(b) A steam vessel carrying towing lights the same as the white light mentioned in article 2(a), when pushing another vessel or vessels ahead, shall also carry at or near the stern two bright amber lights in a vertical line, one over the other, not less than three feet apart; each of these lights shall be so constructed as to show an unbroken light over an arc of the horizon of twelve points of the compass, so fixed as to show the light six points from right aft on each side of the vessel, and of such a character as to be visible at a distance of at least two miles. A steam vessel carrying towing lights the same as the white light mentioned in article 2 (a) may also carry, irrespective of the position of the tow, the after range light mentioned in article 2 (f); however, if the after range light is carried by such a vessel when pushing another vessel or vessels ahead, the amber lights shall be carried in a vertical line with and at least three feet lower than the after range light. A steam vessel carrying towing lights the same as the white light mentioned in article 2 (a), when towing one or more vessels astern, may also carry, in lieu of the stern light specified in article 10, a small white light abaft the funnel or aftermast for the tow to steer by, but such light shall not be visible forward of the beam.

Lights for Sailing Vessels and Vessels in Tow

Art. 5. A sailing vessel underway and any vessel being towed, except barges, canal boats, scows, and other vessels of nondescript type, when in tow of steam vessels, shall carry the same lights as are prescribed by article 2 for a steam vessel underway, with the exception of the white lights mentioned therein, which they shall never carry.

Lights for Small Vessels in Bad Weather

Art. 6. Whenever, as in the case of vessels of less than ten gross tons underway during bad weather, the green and red side lights cannot be fixed, these lights shall be kept at hand, lighted and ready for use; and shall, on the approach of or to other vessels, be exhibited on their respective sides in sufficient time to prevent collision, in such manner as to make them most visible, and so that the green light shall not be seen on the port side nor the red light on the starboard side, nor, if practicable, more than two points abaft the beam on their respective sides. To make the use of these portable lights more certain and easy lanterns containing them shall each be painted outside with the color of the light they respectively contain, and shall be provided with proper screens.

Lights for Rowing Boats

Art. 7. Rowing boats, whether under oars or sail, shall have ready at hand a lantern showing a white light which shall be temporarily exhibited in sufficient time to prevent collision.

Lights for Pilot Vessels

Art. 8. Pilot vessels when engaged on their stations on pilotage duty shall not show the lights required for other vessels, but shall carry a white light at the masthead, visible all round the horizon, and shall also exhibit a flare-up light or flare-up lights at short intervals, which shall never exceed fifteen minutes.

On the near approach of or to other vessels they shall have their side lights lighted, ready for use, and shall flash or show them at short intervals, to indicate the direction in which they are heading, but the green light shall not be shown on the port side or the red light on the starboard side.

A pilot vessel of such a class as to be obliged to go alongside of a vessel to put a pilot on board may show the white light instead of carrying it at the masthead, and may, instead of the colored lights above mentioned, have at hand ready for use, a lantern with a green glass on the one side and a red glass on the other, to be used as prescribed above.

Pilot vessels, when not engaged on their station on pilotage duty, shall carry lights similar to those of other vessels of their tonnage.

A steam pilot vessel, when engaged on her station on pilotage duty and in waters of the United States, and not at anchor, shall in addition to the lights required for all pilot boats, carry at a distance of eight feet below her white masthead light a red light, visible all around the horizon and of such a character as to be visible on a dark night with a clear atmosphere at a distance of at least two miles, and also the colored side lights required to be carried by vessels when underway.

When engaged on her station on pilotage duty and in waters of the United States, and at anchor, she shall carry in addition to the lights required for all pilot boats the red light above mentioned, but not the colored side lights. When not engaged on her station on pilotage duty, she shall carry the same lights as other steam vessels.

Lights for Fishing Vessels

Art. 9 (a) Fishing vessels of less than ten gross tons, when underway and when not having their nets, trawls, dredges, or lines in the water, shall not be obliged to carry the colored side lights; but every such vessel shall, in lieu thereof, have ready at hand a lantern with a green glass on one side and a red glass on the other side, and on approaching to or being approached by another vessel such lantern shall be exhibited in sufficient time to prevent collision, so that the green light shall not be seen on the port side nor the red light on the starboard side.

(b) All fishing vessels and fishing boats of ten gross tons or upward, when underway and when not having their nets, trawls, dredges, or lines in the water, shall carry and show the same lights as other vessels underway.

(c) All vessels, when trawling, dredging, or fishing with any kind of drag nets or lines, shall exhibit, from some part of the vessel where they can be best seen, two lights. One of these lights shall be red and the other shall be white. The red light shall be above the white light, and shall be at a vertical distance from it of not less than six feet and not more than twelve feet; and the horizontal distance between them, if any, shall not be more than ten feet. These two lights shall be of such a character and contained in lanterns of such construction as to be visible all around the horizon, the white light a distance of not less than three miles and the red light of not less than two miles.

Lights For Rafts or Other Craft Not Provided For

(d) Rafts, or other water craft nor herein provided for, navigating by hand power, horse power, or by the current of the river, shall carry one or more good white lights, which shall be placed in such manner as shall be prescribed by the Commandant of the Coast Guard.

Stern Lights for Vessels

Art. 10. (a) A vessel when underway, if not otherwise required by these rules to carry one or more lights visible from aft, shall carry at her stern a white light, so constructed that it shall show an unbroken light over an arc of the horizon of twelve points of the compass, so fixed as to show the light six points from right aft on each side of the vessel, and of such a character as to be visible at a distance of at least two miles. Such light shall be carried as nearly as practicable on the same level as the side lights.

(b) In a small vessel, if it is not possible on account of bad weather or other sufficient cause for this light to be fixed, an electric torch or a lighted lantern shall be kept at hand ready for use and shall, on the approach of an overtaking vessel, be shown in sufficient time to prevent collision.

Anchor Lights

Art. 11.[4] (a) Except as provided in paragraph (c) of this article, a vessel under one hundred and fifty feet in length when at anchor shall carry forward, where it can best be seen, a white light in a lantern so constructed as to show a clear, uniform, and unbroken light visible all around the horizon at a distance of at least two miles.

(b) Except as provided in paragraph (c) of this article, a vessel of one hundred and fifty feet or upward in length, when at anchor, shall carry in the forward part of the vessel, at a height of not less than twenty feet above the hull, one such light, and at or near the stern of the vessel, and at such a height that it shall be not less than fifteen feet lower than the forward light, another such light.

(c) The Secretary of the Army may, after investigation, by rule, regulation, or order, designate such areas as he may deem proper as "special anchorage areas"; such special anchorage areas may from time to time be changed, or abolished, if after investigation the Secretary of the Army shall deem such change or abolition in the interest of navigation. When anchored within such an area—

---

[4] *Functions, powers, and duties of the Secretary of the Army re water vessel anchorage under Art. 11 were transferred to the Secretary of Transportation on October 15, 1966 by Public Law 89-670, 49 U.S.C. 1655 (g) (1) (B), (C) and (D).*

(1) a vessel of not more than sixty-five feet in length shall not be required to carry or exhibit the white light required by this article;

(2) a barge, canal boat, scow, or other nondescript craft of one hundred and fifty feet or upward in length may carry and exhibit the single white light prescribed by paragraph (a) of this article in lieu of the two white lights prescribed by paragraph (b) of this article; and

(3) where two or more barges, canal boats, scows, or other nondescript craft are tied together and anchored as a unit, the anchor light prescribed by this article need be displayed only on the vessel having its anchor down.

Signals to Attract Attention

Art. 12. Every vessel may, if necessary, in order to attract attention, in addition to the lights which she is by these rules required to carry, show a flare-up light or use any detonating signal that cannot be mistaken for a distress signal.

Naval Lights and Recognition Signals

Art. 13. Nothing in these rules shall interfere with the operation of any special rules made by the Government of any nation with respect to additional station and signal lights for two or more ships of war or for vessels sailing under convoy, or with the exhibition of recognition signals adopted by shipowners, which have been authorized by their respective Governments, and duly registered and published.

Steam Vessel under Sail by Day

Art. 14. A steam vessel proceeding under sail only, but having her funnel up, may carry in daytime, forward, where it can best be seen, one black ball or shape two feet in diameter.

SOUND SIGNALS AND CONDUCT IN RESTRICTED VISIBILITY

Preliminary

Art. 15. All signals prescribed by this article for vessels underway shall be given:

1. By "steam vessels" on the whistle or siren.

2. By "sailing vessels" and "vessels towed" on the foghorn.

The words "prolonged blast" used in this article shall mean a blast of from four to six seconds' duration.

A steam vessel shall be provided with an efficient whistle or siren, sounded by steam or by some substitute for steam, so placed that the sound may not be intercepted by any obstruction, and with an efficient fog horn; also with an efficient bell. A sailing vessel of twenty tons gross tonnage or upward shall be provided with a similar foghorn and bell.

In fog, mist, falling snow, or heavy rain storms, whether by day or night, the signals described in this article shall be used as follows, namely:

Steam Vessel Underway

(a) A steam vessel underway shall sound, at intervals of not more than one minute, a prolonged blast.

Sailing Vessel Underway

(c) A sailing vessel underway shall sound, at intervals of not more than one minute, when on the starboard tack, one blast; when on the port tack, two blasts in succession, and when with the wind abaft the beam, three blasts in succession.

Vessel at Anchor

(d) A vessel when at anchor shall, at intervals of not more than one minute, ring the bell rapidly for about five seconds, except that the following vessels shall not be required to sound this signal when anchored in a special anchorage area established pursuant to paragraph (c) of article 11:

(1) a vessel of not more than sixty-five feet in length; and

(2) a barge, canal boat, scow, or other nondescript craft.

Vessels Towing or Towed

(e) A steam vessel when towing, shall, instead of the signals prescribed in subdivision (a) of this article, at intervals of not more than one minute, sound three blasts in succession, namely, one prolonged blast followed by two short blasts. A vessel towed may give this signal and she shall not give any other.

Rafts, or Other Craft Not Provided For

(f) All rafts or other water craft, not herein provided for, navigating by hand power, horse power, or by the current of the river, shall sound a blast of the foghorn, or equivalent signal, at intervals of not more than one minute.

Speed in Fog

Art. 16. Every vessel shall, in a fog, mist, falling snow, or heavy rain-storms, go at a moderate speed, having careful regard to the existing circumstances and conditions.

A steam vessel hearing, apparently forward of her beam, the fog signal of a vessel the position of which is not ascertained shall, so far as the circumstances of the case admit, stop her engines, and then navigate with caution until danger of collision is over.

STEERING AND SAILING RULES

Preliminary

Risk of collision can, when circumstances permit, be ascertained by carefully watching the compass bearing of an approaching vessel. If the bearing does not appreciably change, such risk should be deemed to exist.

Sailing Vessels

Art. 17. When two sailing vessels are approaching one another, so as to involve risk of collision, one of them shall keep out of the way of the other as follows, namely:

(a) A vessel which is running free shall keep out of the way of a vessel which is closehauled.

(b) A vessel which is closehauled on the port tack shall keep out of the way of a vessel which is closehauled on the starboard tack.

(c) When both are running free, with the wind on different sides, the vessel which has the wind on the port side shall keep out of the way of the other.

(d) When both are running free, with the wind on the same side, the vessel which is to the windward shall keep out of the way of the vessel which is to the leeward.

(e) A vessel which has the wind aft shall keep out of the way of the other vessel.

Rules and Whistle Signals for Vessels Meeting, Nearing Bends, Leaving Berths and Overtaking

Art. 18. Rule 1. When steam vessels are approaching each other head and head, that is, end on, or nearly so, it shall be the duty of each to pass on the port side of the other; and either vessel shall give, as a signal of her intention, one short and distinct blast of her whistle which the other vessel shall answer promptly by a similar blast of her whistle, and thereupon such vessels shall pass on the port side of each other. But if the courses of such vessels are so far on the starboard of each other as not to be considered as meeting head and head, either vessel shall immediately give two short and distinct blasts of her whistle, which the other vessel shall answer promptly by two similar blasts of her whistle, and they shall pass on the starboard side of each other.

The foregoing only applies to cases where vessels are meeting end on, or nearly end on, in such a manner as to involve risk of collision; in other words, to cases in which, by day, each vessel sees the masts of the other in a line, or nearly in a line, with her own, and by night to cases in which each vessel is in such a position as to see both the side lights of the other.

It does not apply by day to cases in which a vessel sees another ahead crossing her own course, or by night to cases where the red light of one vessel is opposed to the red light of the other, or where the green light of one vessel is opposed to the green light of the other, or where a red light without a green light or a green light without a red light, is seen ahead, or where both green and red lights are seen anywhere but ahead.

Rule III. If, when steam vessels are approaching each other, either vessel fails to understand the course or intention of the other, from any cause, the vessel so in doubt shall immediately signify the same by giving several short and rapid blasts, not less than four, of the steam whistle.

Rule V. When a steam vessel is nearing a short bend or curve in the channel, where, from the height of the banks or other cause, a steam vessel approaching from the opposite direction can not be seen for a distance of half a mile, such steam vessel, when she shall have arrived within half a mile of such curve or bend, shall give a signal by one long blast of the steam whistle, which signal shall be answered by a similar blast given by any approaching steam vessel that may be within hearing. Should such signal be so answered by a steam vessel upon the farther side of such bend, then the usual signals for meeting and passing shall immediately be given and answered; but, if the first alarm signal of such vessel be not answered, she is to consider the channel clear and govern herself accordingly.

When steam vessels are moved from their docks or berths, and other boats are liable to pass from any direction toward them, they shall give the same signal as in the case of vessels meeting at a bend, but immediately after clearing the berths so as to be fully in sight they shall be governed by the steering and sailing rules.

Rule VIII. When steam vessels are running in the same direction, and the vessel which is astern shall desire to pass on the right or starboard hand of the vessel ahead, she shall give one short blast of the steam whistle, as a signal of such desire, and if the vessel ahead answers with one blast, she shall direct her course to starboard; or if she shall desire to pass on the left or port side of the vessel ahead, she shall give two short blasts of the steam whistle as a signal of such desire, and if the vessel ahead answers with two blasts, shall direct her course to port; or if the vessel ahead does not think it safe for the vessel astern to attempt to pass at that point, she shall immediately signify the same by giving several short and rapid blasts of the steam whistle, not less than four, and under no circumstances shall the vessel astern attempt to pass the vessel ahead until such time as they have reached a point where it can be safely done, when said vessel ahead shall signify her willingness by blowing the proper signals. The vessel ahead shall in no case attempt to cross the bow or crowd upon the course of the passing vessel.

Rule IX. The whistle signals provided in the rules under this article, for steam vessels meeting, passing, or overtaking, are never to be used except when steamers are in sight of each other, and the course and position of each can be determined in the day time by a sight of the vessel itself, or by night by seeing its signal lights. In fog, mist, falling snow or heavy rain storms, when vessels can not see each other, fog signals only must be given.

Two Steam Vessels Crossing

Art. 19. When two steam vessels are crossing, so as to involve risk of collision, the vessel which has the other on her own starboard side shall keep out of the way of the other.

Sailing Vessel Right-of-Way

Art. 20. When a steam vessel and a sailing vessel are proceeding in such directions as to involve risk of collision, the steam vessel shall keep out of the way of the sailing vessel. This rule shall not give to a sailing vessel the right to hamper, in a narrow channel, the safe passage of a steam vessel which can navigate only inside that channel.

Privileged Vessel Duty

Art. 21. Where, by any of these rules, one of the two vessels is to keep out of the way, the other shall keep her course and speed.

[See articles 27 and 29.]

Burdened Vessel Duty

Art. 22. Every vessel which is directed by these rules to keep out of the way of another vessel shall, if the circumstances of the case admit, avoid crossing ahead of the other.

Art. 23. Every steam vessel which is directed by these rules to keep out of the way of another vessel shall, on approaching her, if necessary, slacken her speed or stop or reverse.

Overtaking Vessels

Art. 24. Notwithstanding anything contained in these rules every vessel, overtaking any other, shall keep out of the way of the overtaken vessel.

Every vessel coming up with another vessel from any direction more than two points abaft her beam, that is, in such a position, with reference to the vessel which she is overtaking that at night she would be unable to see either of that vessel's sidelights, shall be deemed to be an overtaking vessel; and no subsequent alteration of the bearing between the two vessels shall make the overtaking vessel a crossing vessel within the meaning of these rules, or relieve her of the duty of keeping clear of the overtaken vessel until she is finally past and clear.

As by day the overtaking vessel can not always know with certainty whether she is forward of or abaft this direction from the other vessels she should, if in doubt, assume that she is an overtaking vessel and keep out of the way.

Narrow Channels

Art. 25. In narrow channels every steam vessel shall, when it is safe and practicable, keep to that side of the fairway or midchannel which lies on the starboard side of such vessel. In narrow channels a steam vessel of less than sixty-five feet in length shall not hamper the safe passage of a vessel which can navigate only inside that channel.

Right of Way of Fishing Vessels

Art. 26. Sailing vessels underway shall keep out of the way of sailing vessels or boats fishing with nets, lines, or trawls. This rule shall not give to any vessel or boat engaged in fishing the right of obstructing a fairway used by vessels other than fishing vessels or boats.

General Prudential Rule

Art. 27. In obeying and construing these rules due regard shall be had to all dangers of navigation and collision, and to any special circumstances which may render a departure from the above rules necessary in order to avoid immediate danger.

SOUND SIGNALS FOR VESSELS IN SIGHT OF ONE ANOTHER

Backing Signal

[See article 18.]

Art. 28. When vessels are in sight of one another a steam vessel underway whose engines are going at full speed astern shall indicate that fact by three short blasts on the whistle.

MISCELLANEOUS

Rule of Good Seamanship

Art. 29. Nothing in these rules shall exonerate any vessel, or the owner or master or crew thereof, from the consequences of any neglect to carry lights or signals, or of any neglect to keep a proper lookout, or of the neglect of any precaution which may be required by the ordinary practice of seamen, or by the special circumstances of the case.

Lights on United States Naval Vessels and Coast Guard Cutters

Art. 30. The exhibition of any light on board of a vessel of war of the United States or a Coast Guard cutter may be suspended whenever, in the opinion of the Secretary of the Navy, the commander in chief of a squadron, or the commander of a vessel acting singly, the special character of the service may require it.

Distress Signals

Art. 31. When a vessel is in distress and requires assistance from other vessels or from the shore the following shall be the signal to be used or displayed by her, either together or separately, namely:

In the daytime—

A continuous sounding with any fog-signal apparatus, or firing a gun.

At night—

First. Flames on the vessel as from a burning tar barrel, oil barrel, and so forth.

Second. A continuous sounding with any fog-signal apparatus, or firing a gun.

Orders to Helmsmen

Art. 32. All orders to helmsmen shall be given as follows:

"Right Rudder" to mean "Direct the vessel's head to starboard."

"Left Rudder" to mean "Direct the vessel's head to port."

APPENDIX E
Pilot Rules for Inland Waters[1]

PART 80

[1] *Code of Federal Regulations:—Title 33—Navigation and Navigable Waters; Part 80—Pilot Rules for Inland Waters.*

80.16b Lights for barges, canal boats, scows, and other nondescript vessels temporarily operating on waters requiring different lights.

80.17 Lights for barges and canal boats in tow of steam vessels on the Hudson River and adjacent waters and Lake Champlain.

Lights and Day Signals for Vessels, Dredges of all Types, and Vessels Working on Wrecks and Obstructions, Etc.

80.18 Signals to be displayed by a towing vessel when towing a submerged or partly submerged object upon a hawser when no signals can be displayed upon the object which is towed.

80.19 Steam vessels, derrick boats, lighters, or other types of vessels made fast alongside a wreck, or moored over a wreck which is on the bottom or partly submerged, or which may be drifting.

80.20 Dredges held in stationary position by moorings or spuds.

80.21 Dredges underway and engaged in dredging operations.

80.22 Vessels moored or anchored and engaged in laying cables or pipe, submarine construction, excavation, mat sinking, bank grading, dike construction, revetment, or other bank protection operations.

80.23 Lights to be displayed on pipe lines.

80.24 Lights generally.

80.25 Vessels moored or at anchor.

Passing Floating Plant Working in Navigable Channels

80.26 Passing signals.

80.27 Speed of vessels passing floating plant working in channels.

80.28 Light-draft vessels passing floating plant.

80.29 Aids to navigation marking floating-plant moorings.

80.30 Obstruction of channel by floating plant.

80.31 Clearing of channels.

80.31a Protection of marks placed for the guidance of floating plant.

Lights For Rafts and Other Craft Not Provided For

80.32 Lights for rafts and other craft.

Special Day or Night Signals

80.32a Day marks for fishing vessels with gear out.

80.33 Special signals for vessels employed in hydrographic surveying.

80.33a Warning signals for Coast Guard vessels while handling or servicing aids to navigation.

General[2]

General Instructions

SEC. 80.01 The regulations in this part apply to vessels navigating the harbors, rivers, and inland waters of the United States, except the Great Lakes and their connecting and tributary waters as far east as Montreal, the Red River of the North, the Mississippi River and its tributaries above Huey P. Long Bridge, and that part of the Atchafalaya River above its junction with the Plaquemine-Morgan City alternate waterway.

Definition of Steam Vessel and Vessel Underway; Risk of Collision

SEC. 80.02 In the rules in this part the words "steam vessel" shall include any vessel propelled by machinery. A vessel is underway, within the meaning of the rules in this part, when she is not at anchor, or made fast to the shore, or aground. Risk of collision can, when circumstances permit, be ascertained by carefully watching the compass bearing of an approaching vessel. If the bearing does not appreciably change, such risk should be deemed to exist.

Signals

SEC. 80.03 (a) The whistle signals provided in the rules in this part shall

[2] *The provisions of this Part 80 issued under sec. 2, 30 Stat. 102, as amended, sec. 6(b)(1), 80 Stat. 937; 33 U.S.C. 157, 49 U.S.C. 1655(b)(1); 49 CFR 1.46(b), unless otherwise noted.*

be sounded on an efficient whistle or siren sounded by steam of by some substitute for steam.

(1) A short blast of the whistle shall mean a blast of about one second's duration.

(2) A prolonged blast of the whistle shall mean a blast of from 4 to 6 seconds' duration.

(3) One short blast of the whistle signifies intention to direct course to own starboard, except when two steam vessels are approaching each other at right angles or obliquely, when it signifies intention of steam vessel which is to starboard of the other to hold course and speed.

(4) Two short blasts of the whistle signify intention to direct course to own port.

(5) Three short blasts of the whistle shall mean, "My engines are going at full speed astern."

(b) When vessels are in sight of one another a steam vessel underway whose engines are going at full speed astern shall indicate that fact by three short blasts on the whistle.

Danger Signal

SEC. 80.1 If, when steam vessels are approaching each other, either vessel fails to understand the course or intention of the other, from any cause, the vessel so in doubt shall immediately signify the same by giving several short and rapid blasts, not less than four, of the steam whistle, the danger signal.

Cross Signals

SEC. 80.2 Steam vessels are forbidden to use what has become technically known among pilots as "cross signals," that is, answering one whistle with two, and answering two whistles with one.

Vessels Passing Each Other

SEC. 80.3 (a) The signals for passing, by the blowing of the whistle, shall be given and answered by pilots, in compliance with the rules in this part, not only when meeting "head and head," or nearly so, but at all times when the steam vessels are in sight of each other, when passing or meeting at a distance within half a mile of each other, and whether passing to the starboard or port.

(b) The whistle signals provided in the rules in this part for steam vessels meeting, passing, or overtaking are never to be used except when steam vessels are in sight of each other, and the course and position of each can be determined in the daytime by a sight of the vessel itself, or by night by seeing its signal lights. In fog, mist, falling snow, or heavy rainstorms, when vessels cannot so see each other, fog signals only must be given.

Situations

Vessels Approaching Each Other Head and Head, End On

SEC. 80.4 (a) When steam vessels are approaching each other head and head, that is, end on, or nearly so, it shall be the duty of each to pass on the port side of the other, and either vessel shall give, as a signal of her intention one short and distinct blast of her whistle, which the other vessel shall answer promptly by a similar blast of her whistle, and thereupon such vessels shall pass on the port side of each other. But if the courses of such vessels are so far on the starboard of each other as not to be considered as meeting head and head, either vessel shall immediately give two short and distinct blasts of her whistle, which the other vessel shall answer promptly by two similar blasts of her whistle, and they shall pass on the starboard side of each other.

(b) The foregoing only applies to cases where vessels are meeting end on or nearly end on, in such a manner as to involve risk of collision; in other words, to cases in which, by day, each vessel sees the masts of the other in a line, or nearly in a line, with her own, and by night to cases in which each vessel is in such a position as to see both the side lights of the other.

(c) It does not apply by day to cases in which a vessel sees another ahead crossing her own course, or by night to cases where the red light of one vessel is opposed to the red light of the other, or where the green light of one vessel is opposed to the green light of the other, or where a red light without a green light or a green light without a red light is seen ahead, or where both green and red lights are seen anywhere but ahead.

Vessels Nearing Bend or Curve in Channel; Moving From Docks

SEC. 80.5 (a) Whenever a steam vessel is nearing a short bend or curve in the channel, where, from the height of the banks or other cause, a steam vessel approaching from the opposite direction cannot be seen for a distance of half a mile, such steam vessel, when she shall have arrived within half a mile of such curve or bend, shall give a signal by one long blast of the steam whistle, which signal shall be answered by a similar blast, given by any approaching steam vessel that may be within hearing. Should such signal be so answered by a steam vessel upon the farther side of such bend, then the usual signals for meeting and passing shall immediately be given and answered; but, if the first alarm signal of such vessel be not answered, she is to consider the channel clear and govern herself accordingly.

(b) When steam vessels are moved from their docks or berths, and other boats are liable to pass from any direction toward them, they shall give the same signal as in the case of vessels meeting at a bend, but immediately after clearing the berths so as to be fully in sight they shall be governed by the steering and sailing rules.

Vessels Running in Same Direction; Overtaking Vessel

SEC. 80.6 (a) When steam vessels are running in the same direction, and the vessel which is astern shall desire to pass on the right or starboard hand of the vessel ahead, she shall give one short blast of the steam whistle, as a signal of such desire, and if the vessel ahead answers with one blast, she shall direct her course to starboard; or if she shall desire to pass on the left or port side of the vessel ahead, she shall give two short blasts of the steam whistle as a signal of such desire, and if the vessel ahead answers with two blasts, shall direct her course to port; or if the vessel ahead does not think it safe for the vessel astern to attempt to pass at that point, she shall immediately signify the same by giving several short and rapid blasts of the steam whistle, not less than four, and under no circumstances shall the vessel astern attempt to pass the vessel ahead until such time as they have reached a point where it can be safely done, when said vessel ahead shall signify her willingness by blowing the proper signals. The vessel ahead shall in no case attempt to cross the bow or crowd upon the course of the passing vessel.

(b) Every vessel coming up with another vessel from any direction more than two points abaft her beam, that is, in such a position with reference to the vessel which she is overtaking that at night she would be unable to see either of that vessel's side lights, shall be deemed to be an overtaking vessel; and no subsequent alteration of the bearing between the two vessels shall make the overtaking vessel a crossing vessel within the meaning of the rules in this part, or relieve her of the duty of keeping clear of the overtaken vessel until she is finally past and clear.

(c) As by day the overtaking vessel cannot always know with certainty whether she is forward of or abaft this direction from the other vessel she should, if in doubt, assume that she is an overtaking vessel and keep out of the way.

Vessels Approaching Each Other at Right Angles or Obliquely

SEC. 80.7 (a) When two steam vessels are approaching each other at right angles or obliquely so as to involve risk of collision, other than when one steam vessel is overtaking another, the steam vessel which has the other on her own port side shall hold her course and speed; and the steam vessel which has the other on her own starboard side shall keep out of the way of the other by directing her course to starboard so as to cross the stern of the other steam vessel, or, if necessary to do so, slacken her speed or stop or reverse.

(b) If from any cause the conditions covered by this situation are such as to prevent immediate compliance with each other's signals, the misunderstanding or objection shall be at once made apparent by blowing the danger signal, and both steam vessels shall be stopped and backed if necessary, until signals for passing with safety are made and understood.

Meeting of Steam and Sailing Vessels; Right-Of-Way

SEC. 80.8 When a steam vessel and a sailing vessel are proceeding in such directions as to invoke risk of collision, the steam vessel shall keep out of the way of the sailing vessel.

Avoidance of Crossing Ahead

SEC. 80.9 Every steam vessel which is directed by the rules of this part to keep out of the way of another vessel shall, if the circumstances of the case admit, avoid crossing ahead of the other.

Keeping to Right in Narrow Channels

SEC. 80.10 In narrow channels every steam vessel shall, when it is safe and practicable, keep to that side of the fairway or mid-channel which lies on the starboard side of such vessel.

Departure From Rules

SEC. 80.11 In obeying and construing the rules in this part due regard shall be had to all dangers of navigation and collision, and to any special circumstances which may render a departure from said rules necessary in order to avoid immediate danger.

Fog Signals

SEC. 80.12 In fog, mist, falling snow, or heavy rainstorms, whether by day or night, signals shall be given as follows:

(a) A steam vessel underway, except when towing other vessels or being towed, shall sound, at intervals of not more than 1 minute, on the whistle or siren, a prolonged blast.

(b) A steam vessel when towing other vessels shall sound, at intervals of not more than 1 minute, on the whistle or siren, three blasts in succession, namely, one prolonged blast followed by two short blasts.

(c) A vessel towed may give, at intervals of not more than 1 minute, on the foghorn, a signal of three blasts in succession, namely, one prolonged blast followed by two short blasts, and she shall not give any other.

(d) A vessel when at anchor shall, at intervals of not more than 1 minute, ring the bell rapidly for about 5 seconds.

Speed in Fog; Pamphlet Containing Pilot Rules; Diagrams

SEC. 80.13 **(a) Moderate speed in fog.** (1) Every steam vessel shall, in a fog, mist, falling snow, or heavy rainstorms, go at a moderate speed, having careful regard to the existing circumstances and conditions.

(2) A steam vessel hearing, apparently forward of her beam, the fog signal of a vessel the position of which is not ascertained shall, so far as the circumtsances of the case admit, stop her engines and then navigate with caution until danger of collision is over.

(b) Pamphlet containing Pilot Rules. All vessels and craft over 65 feet in length upon the waters described in Section 80.01 shall, where practicable, carry on board and maintain for ready reference copies of the current edition of Coast Guard pamphlet CG-169. Nothing in this section shall require copies of this pamphlet to be carried on board any motorboat as defined by section 1 of the Act of April 25, 1940, as amended (54 Stat. 163; 46 U.S.C. 526).

(c) Diagrams. The following diagrams are intended to illustrate the working of the system of colored lights and pilot rules: (Former Pilot Rule XIII).

FIRST SITUATION

Here the two colored lights visible to each will indicate their direct approach "head and head" toward each other. In this situation it is a standing rule that both shall direct their courses to starboard and pass on the port side of each other, each having previously given one blast of the whistle.

SECOND SITUATION

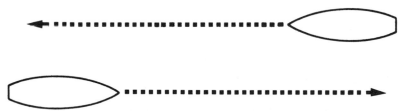

In this situation the red light only will be visible to each, the screens preventing the green light being seen. Both vessels are evidently passing to port of each other, which is rulable in this situation, each pilot having previously signified his intention by one blast of the whistle.

THIRD SITUATION

In this situation the green light only will be visible to each, the screens preventing the red light from being seen. They are therefore passing to starboard of each other, which is rulable in this situation, each pilot having previously signified his intention by two blasts of the whistle.

FOURTH SITUATION

In this situation one steam vessel is overtaking another steam vessel from some point within the angle of two points abaft the beam of the overtaken steam-vessel. The overtaking steam vessel may pass on the starboard or port side of the steam vessel ahead after the necessary signals for passing have been given with assent of the overtaken steam vessel, as prescribed in § 80.6.

FIFTH SITUATION

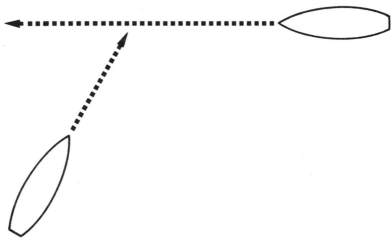

In this situation two steam vessels are approaching each other at right angles or obliquely in such a manner as to involve risk of collision, other than where one steam vessel is overtaking another. The steam vessel which has the other on her own port side shall hold course and speed, and the other shall keep clear by crossing astern of the steam vessel that is holding course and speed, or, if necessary to do so, shall slacken her speed, stop, or reverse.

Lights for Certain Classes of Vessels

Lights; Time for

SEC. 80.14 The following rules in this part concerning lights shall be complied with in all weathers from sunset to sunrise.

Ferryboats

SEC. 80.15 (a) Ferryboats propelled by machinery and navigating the harbors, rivers, and other inland waters of the United States, except the Great Lakes and their connecting and tributary waters as far east as Montreal, the Red River of the North, the Mississippi River and its tributaries above Huey P. Long Bridge, and that part of the Atchafalaya River above its junction with the Plaquemine-Morgan City alternate waterway, shall carry the range lights and the colored sidelights required by law to be carried on steam vessels navigating those waters, except that double-end ferryboats shall carry a central range of clear, bright, white lights, showing all around the horizon, placed at equal altitudes forward and aft, also on the starboard side a green light, and on the port side a red light of such a character as to be visible on a dark night with a clear atmosphere at a distance of at least 2 miles, and so constructed as to show a uniform and unbroken light over an arc of the horizon of 10 points of the compass, and so fixed as to throw the light from right ahead to 2 points abaft the beam on their respective sides.

(b) The green and red lights shall be fitted with inboard screens projecting at least 3 feet forward from the lights, so as to prevent them from being seen across the bow.

(c) Officers in Charge, Marine Inspection,[3] in districts having ferryboats shall, whenever the safety of navigation may require, designate for each line of such boats a certain light, white or colored, which will show all around the horizon, to designate and distinguish such lines from each other, which light shall be carried on a flagstaff amidships, 15 feet above the white range lights.

Lights for Barges, Canal Boats, Scows, and Other Nondescript Vessels on Certain Inland Waters on the Atlantic and Pacific Coasts

SEC. 80.16 (a) On the harbors, rivers, and other inland waters of the United States except the Great Lakes and their connecting and tributary waters as far east as Montreal, the Red River of the North, the Mississippi River and its tributaries above the Huey P. Long Bridge, and that part of the Atchafalaya River above its junction with the Plaquemine-Morgan City

---

[3] *For definition of an Officer in Charge, Marine Inspection, see Title 46, Code of Federal Regulations, Section 70.10-33.*

alternate waterway, and the waters described in §§ 80.16a and 80.17, barges, canal boats, scows, and other vessels of nondescript type not otherwise provided for, when being towed by steam vessels, shall carry lights as set forth in this section.

(b) Barges and canal boats towing astern of steam vessels, when towing singly, or what is known as tandem towing, shall each carry a green light on the starboard side and a red light on the port side, and a white light on the stern, except that the last vessel of such tow shall carry two lights on her stern, athwartship, horizontal to each other, not less than 5 feet apart, and not less than 4 feet above the deck house, and so placed as to show all around the horizon. A tow of one such vessel shall be lighted as the last vessel of a tow.

(c) When two or more boats are abreast, the colored lights shall be carried at the outer sides of the bows of the outside boats. Each of the outside boats in last tier of a hawser tow shall carry a white light on her stern.

(d) The white light required to be carried on stern of a barge or canal boat carrying red and green sidelights except the last vessel in a tow shall be carried in a lantern so constructed that it shall show an unbroken light over an arc of the horizon of 12 points of the compass, namely, for 6 points from right aft on each side of the vessel, and shall be of such a character as to be visible on a dark night with a clear atmosphere at a distance of at least 2 miles.

(e) Barges, canal boats, or scows towing alongside a steam vessel shall, if the deck, deck houses, or cargo of the barge, canal boat or scow be so high above water as to obscure the sidelights of the towing steamer when being towed on the starboard side of the steamer, carry a green light upon the starboard side; and when towed on the port side of the steamer, a red light on the port side of the barge, canal boat, or scow; and if there is more than one barge, canal boat or scow abreast, the colored lights shall be displayed from the outer barges, canal boats, or scows.

(f) Barges, canal boats, or scows shall, when being propelled by pushing ahead of a steam vessel, display a red light on the port bow and a green light on the starboard bow of the head barge, canalboat or scow, carried at a height sufficiently above the superstructure of the barge, canalboat or scow as to permit said sidelights to be visible; and if there is more than one barge, canal boat or scow abreast, the colored lights shall be displayed from the outer side of the outside barges, canal boats or scows.

(g) The colored sidelights referred to in this section shall be fitted with inboard screens so as to prevent them from being seen across the bow, and of such a character as to be visible on a dark night, with a clear atmosphere, at a distance of at least 2 miles, and so constructed as to show a uniform and unbroken light over an arc of the horizon of 10 points of the compass, and so fixed as to throw the light from right ahead to 2 points abaft the beam on either side. The minimum size of glass globes shall not be less than 6 inches in diameter and 5 inches high in the clear.

(h) Scows not otherwise provided for in this section on waters described in paragraph (a) of this section shall carry a white light at each end of each scow, except that when such scows are massed in tiers, two or more abreast, each of the outside scows shall carry a white light on its outer bow, and the outside scows in the last tier shall each carry, in addition, a white light on the outer part of the stern. The white light shall be carried not less than 8 feet above the surface of the water, and shall be so placed as to show an unbroken light all around the horizon, and shall be of such a character as to be visible on a dark night with a clear atmosphere at a distance of at least 5 miles.

(i) Other vessels of nondescript type not otherwise provided for in this section shall exhibit the same lights that are required to be exhibited by scows by this section.[4]

Light for Barges, Canal Boats, Scows, and Other Nondescript Vessels on Certain Inland Waters on the Gulf Coast and the Gulf Intracoastal Waterway

SEC. 80.16a (a) On the Gulf Intracoastal Waterway and on other inland waters connected therewith or with the Gulf of Mexico from the Rio Grande, Texas, to Cape Sable (East Cape), Florida, barges, canal boats, scows, and other vessels of nondescript type not otherwise provided for, when being towed by steam vessels shall carry lights as set forth in this section.

(b) When one or more barges, canal boats, scows, or other vessels of nondescript type not otherwise provided for, are being towed by pushing ahead of a steam vessel, or by a combination of pushing ahead and towing alongside of a steam vessel, such tow shall be lighted by a flashing amber light at the extreme forward end of the tow, so placed as to be as nearly as practicable on the centerline of the tow, a green light on the starboard side of the tow, so placed as to mark the maximum projection of the tow to starboard, and a red light on the port side of the tow, so placed as to mark the maximum projection of the tow to port.

(c) When one or more barges, canal boats, scows, or other vessels of nondescript type not otherwise provided for, are being towed alongside a steam vessel, there shall be displayed a white light at each outboard corner of the tow. If the deck, deck house, or cargo of such barge, etc., obscures

---

[4] The regulations in §§ 80.16 to 80.17, inclusive, are not applicable to rafts. The requirements regarding lights for rafts are in § 80.32.

the sidelight of the towing vessel, such barge, etc., shall also carry a green light upon the starboard side when being towed on the starboard side of a steam vessel or shall carry a red light on the port side of the barge, etc., when being towed on the port side of the steam vessel. If there is more than one such barge, etc., being towed abreast, the appropriate colored sidelight shall be displayed from the outer side of the outside barge.

(d) When one barge, canal boat, scow, or other vessel of nondescript type not otherwise provided for, is being towed singly behind a steam vessel, such vessel shall carry four white lights, one on each corner or outermost projection of the bow and one on each corner or outermost projection of the stern.

(e) When two or more barges, canal boats, scows, or other vessels of nondescript type not otherwise provided for, are being towed behind a steam vessel in tandem, with a hawser length, between vessels, of 75 feet or more, such vessels shall carry white lights as follows:

(1) The first vessel in the tow shall carry three white lights, one on each corner or outermost projection of the bow and a white light at the stern amidships.

(2) Each intermediate vessel shall carry two white lights, one at each end amidships.

(3) The last vessel in the tow shall carry three white lights, one on each corner or outermost projection of the stern and a white light at the bow amidships.

(f) When two or more barges, canal boats, scows, or other vessels of nondescript type not otherwise provided for, are being towed behind a steam vessel in tandem, with a hawser length between vessels of less than 75 feet, such vessels shall carry white lights as follows:

(1) The first vessel in the tow shall carry three white lights, one on each corner or outermost projection of the bow and a white light at the stern amidships.

(2) Each intermediate vessel shall carry a white light at the stern amidships.

(3) The last vessel in the tow shall carry two white lights, one on each corner or outermost projection of the stern.

(g) When two or more barges, canal boats, scows, or other vessels of nondescript type not otherwise provided for, are being towed behind a steam vessel in tandem, with a hawser length between vessels of less than vessels in each tier shall carry a white light on the outboard corner of the bow, and each of the outside vessels in the last tier shall carry, in addition, a white light on the outboard corner of the stern.

(h) Lights for moored barges shall be as described in this paragraph.

(1) The following barges, when moored in or near a fairway, shall dis-

play between the hours of sunset and sunrise the barge lights described in subparagraph (2) of this paragraph:

(i) Every barge projecting into a buoyed or restricted channel.

(ii) Every barge so moored that it reduces the available navigable width of any channel to less that 250 feet.

(iii) Barges moored in fleets more than two barges wide or to a maximum width of over 80 feet, parallel to the bank.

(iv) Every barge moored to the bank in any manner other than parallel thereto.

(2) Barges required to be lighted under subparagraph (1) of this paragraph shall carry two white lights of such character as to be visible on a dark night with a clear atmosphere at a distance of at least 1 mile, so located as to give unobstructed view and arranged as follows:

(i) On a single moored barge, a light on each outboard or channelward corner.

(ii) On barges moored in group formation, a light on the upstream outboard or channelward corner of the outer upstream barge and a light on the downstream outboard or channelward corner of the outer downsteam barge. In addition, any barge projecting toward or into the channel in such a group formation shall have two white lights similarly placed on the outboard or channelward corners of the barge.

(3) Barges moored in any slip or slough which is used primarily for mooring purposes are exempt from the lighting requirements of this paragraph.

(i) The colored sidelights shall be so constructed as to show a uniform and unbroken light over an arc of the horizon of 10 points of the compass, so fixed as to show the light from right ahead to 2 points abaft the beam on their respective sides, and of such a character as to be visible at a distance of at least 2 miles, and shall be fitted with inboard screens so as to prevent either lights from being seen more than a half a point across the centerline of the tow.

(j) The amber light shall flash 50 to 70 times per minute and be so constructed as to show a uniform light over an arc of the horizon of 20 points of the compass, so fixed as to show the light 10 points on each side of the tow, namely, from right ahead to 2 points abaft the beam on either side, and of such a character as to be visible at a distance of at least 2 miles.

(k) The white lights shall be so constructed and so fixed as to show a clear, uniform, and unbroken light all around the horizon, and of such a character as to be visible at a distance of at least 2 miles.

(l) All the lights shall be carried at approximately the same height above the surface of the water and, except as provided in paragraph (h) of this section, shall be so placed with respect thereto as to be clear of and above all obstructions which might tend to interfere with the prescribed arc or distance of visibility.

Lights for Barges, Canal Boats, Scows, and Other Nondescript Vessels Temporarily Operating on Waters Requiring Different Lights

SEC 80.16b Nothing in §§ 80.16, 80.16a, or 80.17 shall be construed as compelling barges, canal boats, scows, or other vessels of nondescript type not otherwise provided for, being towed by steam vessels, when passing through any waters coming within the scope of any regulations where lights for such boats are different from those of the waters whereon such boats are usually employed, to change their lights from those required on the waters on which their trip begins or terminates; but should such boats engage in local employment on waters requiring different lights from those where they are customarily employed, they shall comply with the local rules where employed.

Lights for Barges and Canal Boats in Tow of Steam Vessels on the Hudson River and Adjacent Waters and Lake Champlain

SEC. 80.17 (a) All nondescript vessels known as scows, car floats, lighters, and vessels of similar type, navigating the waters referred to in this section, shall carry the lights required to be carried by barges and canal boats in tow of steam vessels, as prescribed in this section.

(b) Barges and canal boats, when being towed by steam vessels on the waters of the Hudson River and its tributaries from Troy to the boundary lines of New York Harbor off Sandy Hook, as defined pursuant to section 2 of the act of Congress of February 19, 1895 (28 Stat. 672; 33 U.S.C. 151), the East River and Long Island Sound (and the waters entering thereon, and to the Atlantic Ocean), to and including Narragansett Bay, R.I., and tributaries, and Lake Champlain, shall carry lights as follows:

(1) Barges and canal boats being towed astern of steam vessels when towing singly shall carry a white light on the bow and a white light on the stern.

SINGLY

(2) When towing in tandem, with a hawser length, between vessels, of less than 75 feet, each boat shall carry a white light on its stern and the first or hawser boat shall, in addition, carry a white light on its bow.

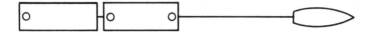

(3) When towing in tandem with a hawser length of 75 feet or more, between the various boats in the tow, each boat shall carry a white light on the bow and a white light on the stern, except that the last vessel in the tow shall carry two white lights on her stern, athwartship, horizontal to each other, not less than 5 feet apart and not less than 4 feet above the deck house, and so placed as to show all around the horizon: Provided, That seagoing barges shall not be required to make any change in their seagoing lights (red and green) on waters coming within the scope of this section, except that the last vessel of the tow shall carry two white lights on her stern, athwartship, horizontal to each other, not less than 5 feet apart, and not less than 4 feet above the deck house, and so placed as to show all around the horizon.

TANDEM (WITH A HAWSER LENGTH, BETWEEN VESSELS,
OF 75 FEET OR MORE)

(4) Barges and canal boats when towed at a hawser, two or more abreast, when in one tier, shall each carry a white light on the stern and a white light on the bow of each of the outside boats.

TWO OR MORE ABREAST IN ONE TIER

(5) When in more than one tier, each boat shall carry a white light on its stern and the outside boats in the hawser or head tier shall each carry, in addition, a white light on the bow.

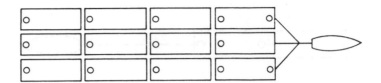

(6) The white bow lights for barges and canal boats referred to in this section shall be carried at least 10 feet and not more than 30 feet abaft the stem or extreme forward end of the vessel. On barges and canal boats required to carry a white bow light, the white light on bow and the white light on stern shall each be so placed above the hull or deck house as to show an unbroken light all around the horizon, and of such a character as to be visible on a dark night with a clear atmosphere at a distance of at least 2 miles.

(7) When nondescript vessels known as scows, car floats, lighters, barges, or canal boats, and vessels of similar type, are towed alongside a steam vessel, there shall be displayed a white light at the outboard corners of the tow.

TOWED ALONGSIDE—VARIOUS POSITIONS

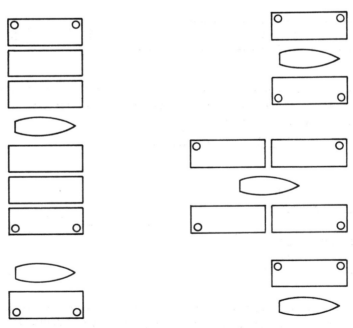

(8) When underway between the hours of sunset and sunrise there shall

be displayed a red light on the port bow and a green light on the starboard bow of the head barge or barges, properly screened and so arranged that they may be visible through an arc of the horizon of 10 points of the compass; that is, from right ahead to 2 points abaft the beam on either side and visible on a dark night with a clear atmosphere at a distance of at least 2 miles, and be carried at a height sufficiently above the superstructure of the barge or barges pushed ahead as to permit said sidelights to be visible.

PROPULSION OF BARGE OR BARGES BY PUSHING

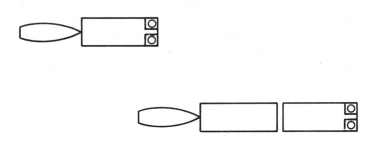

(9) Dump scows utilized for transportation and disposal of garbage, street sweepings, ashes, excavated material, dredging, etc. when navigating on the Hudson River or East River or the Waters tributary thereto between loading points on these waters and the dumping grounds established by competent authority outside the line dividing the high seas from the inland waters of New York Harbor, shall, when towing in tandem, carry, instead of the white lights previously required, red and green side lights on the respective and appropriate sides of the scow in addition to the white light required to be shown by an overtaken vessel.

(10) The red and green lights prescribed in this section shall be carried at a height at which they can readily be seen, the lights properly screened and so arranged as to show through an arc of the horizon of 10 points of the compass, that is, from right ahead to 2 points abaft the beam on either side and visible on a dark night with a clear atmosphere a distance of at least 2 miles.

Provided, That nothing in this section shall be construed as compelling barges or canal boats in tow of steam vessels, passing through any waters coming within the scope of this section where lights for barges or canal boats are different from those of the waters whereon such vessels are usually employed, to change their lights from those required on the waters from which their trip begins or terminates; but should such vessels engage in local employment on waters requiring different lights from those where they are customarily employed, they shall comply with the local rules where employed.

Lights and Day Signals for Vessels, Dredges of all Types, and Vessels Working on Wrecks and Obstructions, etc.[5]

Signals To Be Displayed by a Towing Vessel When Towing a Submerged or Partly Submerged Object upon a Hawser When No Signals Can Be Displayed upon the Object Which Is Towed

SEC. 80.18 (a) The vessel having the submerged object in tow shall display by day, where they can best be seen, two shapes, one above the other, not less than six feet apart, the lower shape to be carried not less than 10 feet above the deck house. The shapes shall be in the form of a double frustum of a cone, base to base, not less than two feet in diameter at the center nor less than eight inches at the ends of the cones, and to be not less than four feet lengthwise from end to end, the upper shape to be painted in alternate horizontal stripes of black and white, eight inches in width, and the lower shape to be painted a solid bright red.

(b) By night the towing vessel shall display the regular sidelights but in lieu of the regular white towing lights shall display four lights in a vertical position no less than 3 feet nor more than 6 feet apart, the upper and lower of such lights to be white and of the same character as the regular towing lights and the middle of such lights to be red and of such a character as to be visible on a dark night with a clear atmosphere for a distance of at least 2 miles.

Steam Vessels, Derrick Boats, Lighters, or Other Types of Vessels Made Fast Alongside a Wreck, or Moored over a Wreck Which Is on the Bottom or Partly Submerged, or Which May Be Drifting

SEC. 80.19 (a) Steam vessels, derrick boats, lighters or other types of vessels made fast alongside a wreck, or moored over a wreck which is on the bottom or partly submerged, or which may be drifting, shall display by day two shapes of the same character and dimensions and displayed in the same manner as required by §80.18 (a), except that both shapes shall be painted a solid bright red, but where more than one vessel is working

---

[5] *The regulations in Sections 80.18 to 80.31a are applicable on the harbors, rivers, and inland waters along the Atlantic and Pactific Coasts and the Coast of the Gulf of Mexico as described in Section 80.01. Similar regulations in Sections 95.51 to 95.66 are applicable on the "western rivers" as described in Section 95.01. Similar Department of the Army (Corps of Engineers) regulations in Sections 201.1 to 201.16 of this title are applicable on the Great Lakes and their connecting and tributary waters as far east as Montreal. The provisions of Section 80.21 now apply to all dredges underway and engaged in dredging operations while the similar provisions in Sections 95.55 and 201.5 apply to self-propelled suction dredges underway and engaged in dredging operations.*

under the above conditions, the shapes need be displayed only from one vessel on each side of the wreck from which they can best be seen from all directions.

(b) By night this situation shall be indicated by the display of a white light from the bow and stern of each outside vessel or lighter not less than six feet above the deck, and in addition thereto there shall be displayed in a position where they can best be seen from all directions two red lights carried in a vertical line not less than three feet nor more than six feet apart, and not less than 15 feet above the deck.

Dredges Held in Stationary Position by Moorings or Spuds

SEC. 80.20 (a) Dredges which are held in stationary position by moorings or spuds shall display by day two red balls not less that two feet in diameter and carried in a vertical line not less than three feet nor more than six feet apart, and at least 15 feet above the deck house and in such a position where they can best be seen from all directions.

(b) By night they shall display a white light at each corner, not less than six feet above the deck, and in addition thereto there shall be displayed in a position where they can best be seen from all directions two red lights carried in a vertical line not less than three feet nor more than six feet apart, and not less than 15 feet above the deck. When scows are moored alongside a dredge in the foregoing situation they shall display a white light on each outboard corner, not less than six feet above the deck.

Dredges Underway and Engaged in Dredging Operations

SEC. 80.21 (a) Dredges underway and engaged in dredging operations shall display by day two black balls not less than two feet in diameter and carried in a vertical line not less than three feet nor more than six feet apart, where they can best be seen from all directions. The term "dredging operations" shall include maneuvering into or out of position at the dredging site but shall not include proceeding to or from the site.

(b) By night self-propelled dredges underway and engaged in dredging operations shall carry, in addition to the regular running lights, two red lights in a vertical line beneath the white masthead light. These red lights shall be not less than three feet nor more than six feet apart and the upper red light shall be not less than three feet nor more than six feet below the masthead light. They shall also carry on or near the stern two red lights in a vertical line not less than three feet nor more than six feet apart, to show through twelve points of the compass; that is, from right astern to six points on each quarter. The forward red lights and after red lights shall be of such character as to be visible on a dark night with a clear atmosphere for a distance of at least 2 miles.

(c) By night, a non-self-propelled dredge which is underway and engaged in dredging operations while being pushed ahead by a towboat shall be considered, with such towboat, for the purpose of compliance with Rules of the Road requirements for lights and shapes, as a single vessel. This vessel shall carry the lights described in paragraph (b) of this section, except that both the dredge and towboat shall carry the sidelights normally required for a barge towed by being pushed ahead and a vessel towing, respectively. When not engaged in dredging operations, this unit shall carry the regular lights for vessels towing and being towed.

Vessels Moored or Anchored and Engaged in Laying Cables or Pipe, Submarine Construction, Excavation, Mat Sinking, Bank Grading, Dike Construction, Revetment, or Other Bank Protection Operations

SEC. 80.22 (a) Vessels which are moored or anchored and engaged in laying cables or pipe, submarine construction, excavation, mat sinking, bank grading, dike construction, revetment, or other bank protection operations, shall display by day, not less than 15 feet above the deck, where they can best be seen from all directions, two balls not less than two feet in diameter, in a vertical line not less than three feet nor more than six feet apart, the upper ball to be painted in alternate black and white vertical stripes six inches wide, and the lower ball to be painted a solid bright red.

(b) By night they shall display three red lights, carried in a vertical line not less than three feet nor more than six feet apart, in a position where they can best be seen from all directions, with the lowermost light not less than 15 feet above the deck.

(c) Where a stringout of moored vessels or barges is engaged in the operations, three red lights carried as prescribed in paragraph (b) of this section shall be displayed at the channelward end of the stringout. Where the stringout crosses the navigable channel and is to be opened for the passage of vessels, the three red lights shall be displayed at each side of the opening instead of at the outer end of the stringout. There shall also be displayed upon such stringout one horizontal row of amber lights not less than six feet above the deck, or above the deck house where the craft carries a deck house, in a position where they can best be seen from all directions, spaced not more than 50 feet apart so as to mark distinctly the entire length and course of the stringout.

Lights to Be Displayed on Pipe Lines

SEC. 80.23 Pipe lines attached to dredges, and either floating or supported on trestles, shall display by night one row of amber lights not less than eight feet nor more than 12 feet above the water, about equally spaced and in such number as to mark distinctly the entire length and course of the line, the intervals between lights where the line crosses navigable channels to be not more than 30 feet. There shall also be displayed on the shore or discharge end of the line two red lights, three feet apart, in a vertical line with the lower light at least eight feet above the water, and if the line is to be opened at night for the passage of vessels, a similar arrangement of lights shall be displayed on each side of the opening.

Lights Generally

SEC. 80.24 (a) All the lights required by §§ 80.18 to 80.23, inclusive, except as provided in §§ 80.18 (b) shall be of such character as to be visible on a dark night with a clear atmosphere for a distance of at least two miles. The white lights provided for in § 80.18 (b) shall be visible for at least 5 miles.

(b) The lights required by § 80.18 (b) shall be of the same construction as the regular towing lights. The lights required by § 80.21 (b) shall be of the same construction as the masthead light.

(c) All floodlights or headlights which may interfere with the proper navigation of an approaching vessel shall be so shielded that the lights will not blind the pilot of such vessel.

Vessels Moored or at Anchor

SEC. 80.25 Vessels of more than 65 feet in length when moored or anchored in a fairway or channel shall display between sunrise and sunset on the forward part of the vessel where it can best be seen from other vessels one black ball not less than two feet in diameter.

Passing Floating Plant Working in Navigable Channels[6]

Passing Signals

SEC. 80.26 (a) Vessels intending to pass dredges or other types of floating plant working in navigable channels, when within a reasonable distance therefrom and not in any case over a mile, shall indicate such intention by one long blast of the whistle, and shall be directed to the proper side for passage by the sounding, by the dredge or other floating plant, of the signal prescribed in the local pilot rules for vessels underway and approaching each other from opposite directions, which shall be answered in the usual manner by the approaching vessel. If the channel is not clear, the floating plant shall sound the alarm or danger signal and the approaching vessel shall slow down or stop and await further signal from the plant.

[6] The term "floating plant" as used in Sections 80.26 to 80.31a, includes dredges, derrick boats, snag boats, drill boats, pile drivers, maneuver boats, hydraulic graders, survey boats, working barges, and mat sinking plant.

(b) When the pipe line from a dredge crosses the channel in such a way that an approaching vessel cannot pass safely around the pipe line or dredge, there shall be sounded immediately from the dredge the alarm or danger signal and the approaching vessel shall slow down or stop and await further signal from the dredge. The pipe line shall then be opened and the channel cleared as soon as practicable; when the channel is clear for passage the dredge shall so indicate by sounding the usual passing signal as prescribed in paragraph (a) of this section. The approaching vessel shall answer with a corresponding signal and pass promptly.

(c) When any pipe line or swinging dredge shall have given an approaching vessel or tow the signal that the channel is clear, the dredge shall straighten out within the cut for the passage of the vessel or tow.

Speed of Vessels Passing Floating Plant Working in Channels

SEC. 80.27 Vessels, with or without tows, passing floating plant working in channels, shall reduce their speed sufficiently to ensure the safety of both the plant and themselves, and when passing within 200 feet of the plant their speed shall not exceed five miles per hour. While passing over lines of the plant, propelling machinery shall be stopped.

Light-Draft Vessels Passing Floating Plant

SEC. 80.28 Vessels whose draft permits shall keep outside of the buoys marking the end of mooring lines of floating plant working in channels.

Aids to Navigation Marking Floating Plant Moorings

SEC. 80.29 Breast, stern, and bow anchors of floating plant working in navigable channels shall be marked by barrel or other suitable buoys. By night approaching vessels shall be shown the location of adjacent buoys by throwing a suitable beam of light from the plant on the buoys until the approaching vessel has passed, or the buoys may be lighted by red lights, visible in all directions, of the same character as specified in § 80.24 (a): *Provided,* That the foregoing provisions of this section shall not apply to the following waters of New York Harbor and adjacent waters: the East River, the North River (Battery to Spuyten Duyvil), the Harlem River and the New York and New Jersey Channels (from the Upper Bay through Kill Van Kull, Newark Bay, Arthur Kill, and Raritan Bay to the Lower Bay).

Obstruction of Channel by Floating Plant

SEC. 80.30 Channels shall not be obstructed unnecessarily by any dredge or other floating plant. While vessels are passing such plant, all lines running therefrom across the channel on the passing side, which may interfere with or obstruct navigation, shall be slacked to the bottom of the channel.

Clearing of Channels

SEC. 80.31 When special or temporary regulations have not been pre-scribed and action under the regulations contained in §§ 20.26 to 80.30, inclusive, will not afford clear passage, a floating plant in narrow channels shall, upon notice, move out of the way of vessels a sufficient distance to allow them a clear passage. Vessels desiring passage shall, however, give the master of the floating plant ample notice in advance of the time they expect to pass.[7]

Protection of Marks Placed for the Guidance of Floating Plant

SEC. 80.31a Vessels shall no run over anchor buoys, or buoys, stakes, or other marks placed for the guidance of floating plant working in channels; and shall not anchor on the ranges of buoys, stakes, or other marks placed for the guidance of such plant.

Lights For Rafts and Other Craft Not Provided For

Lights for Rafts and Other Craft

SEC. 80.32 (a) Any vessel propelled by hand power, horsepower, or by the current of the river, except rafts and rowboats, shall carry one white light forward not less than 8 feet above the surface of the water.

(b) Any raft while being propelled by hand power, by horsepower, or by the current of the river, while being towed, or while anchored or moored in or near a channel or fairway, shall carry white lights as follows:

(1) A raft of one crib in width shall carry one white light at each end of the raft.

(2) A raft of more than one crib in width shall carry 4 white lights, one on each outside corner.

(3) An unstable log raft of one bag or boom in width shall carry at least 2 but not more than 4 white lights in a fore and aft line, one of which shall be at each end. The lights may be closely grouped clusters of not more than 3 white lights rather than single lights.

(4) An unstable log raft of more than one bag or boom in width shall

---

[7] If it is necessary to prohibit or limit the anchorage or movement of vessels within certain areas in order to facilitate the. work of improvement, application should be made through official channels for establishment by the Secretary of the Army of special or temporary regulations for this purpose.

carry 4 white lights, one on each outside corner. The lights may be closely grouped clusters of not more than 3 white lights rather than single lights.

(c) The white lights required by this section shall be carried from sunset to sunrise, in a lantern so fixed and constructed as to show a clear, uniform, and unbroken light, visible all around the horizon, and of such intensity as to be visible on a dark night with a clear atmosphere at a distance of at least one mile. The lights for rafts shall be suspended from poles of such height that the lights shall not be less than 8 feet above the surface of the water, except that the lights prescribed for unstable log rafts shall not be less than 4 feet above the water.

Special Day or Night Signals

Day Marks for Fishing Vessels with Gear Out

SEC. 80.32a All vessels or boats fishing with nets or lines or trawls, when underway, shall in daytime indicate their occupation to an approaching vessel by displaying a basket where it can best be seen. If the vessels or boats at anchor have their gear out, they shall, on the approach of other vessels, show the same signal in the direction from the anchor back towards the nets or gear.

Special Signals for Vessels Employed in Hydrographic Surveying

SEC. 80.33 By day a surveying vessel of the Coast and Geodetic Survey, underway and employed in hydrographic surveying, may carry in a vertical line, one over the other not less than 6 feet apart where they can best be seen, three shapes not less than 2 feet in diameter of which the highest and lowest shall be globular in shape and green in color and the middle one diamond in shape and white.

(a) Vessels of the Coast and Geodetic Survey shall carry the above-prescribed marks while actually engaged in hydrographic surveying and underway, including drag work. Launches and other boats shall carry the prescribed marks when necessary.

(b) It must be distinctly understood that these special signals serve only to indicate the nature of the work upon which the vessel is engaged and in no way give the surveying vessel the right-of-way over other vessels or obviate the necessity for a strict observance of the rules for preventing collisions of vessels.

(c) By night a surveying vessel of the Coast and Geodetic Survey, underway and employed in hydrographic surveying, shall carry the regular lights prescribed by the rules of the road.

(d) A vessel of the Coast and Geodetic Survey, when at anchor in a fairway on surveying operations, shall display from the mast during the daytime two black balls in a vertical line not less than 6 feet apart. At night two red lights shall be displayed in the same manner. In the case of a small vessel the distance between the balls and between the lights may be reduced to not less than 3 feet if necessary.

(e) Such vessels, when at anchor in a fairway on surveying operations, shall have at hand and show, if necessary, in order to attract attention, a flareup light in addition to the lights which are, by this section, required to be carried.

*Warning Signals for Coast Guard Vessels While Handling
or Servicing Aids to Navigation*

SEC. 80.33a (a) Coast Guard vessels while engaged in handling or servicing an aid to navigation during the daytime may display from the yard two orange and white vertically striped balls in a vertical line not less than 3 feet nor more than 6 feet apart, and during the nighttime may display, in a position where they may best be seen, two red lights in a vertical line not less than 3 feet nor more than 6 feet apart.

(b) Vessels, with or without tows, passing Coast Guard vessels displaying this signal, shall reduce their speed sufficiently to insure the safety of both vessels, and when passing within 200 feet of the Coast Guard vessel displaying this signal, their speed shall not exceed 5 miles per hour.

Miscellaneous

Rule Relating to the Use of Searchlights or Other Blinding Lights

SEC. 80.34 Flashing the rays of a searchlight or other blinding light onto the bridge or into the pilothouse of any vessel underway is prohibited. Any person who shall flash or cause to be flashed the rays of a blinding light in violation of the above may be proceeded against in accordance with the provisions of R.S. 4450, as amended, looking to the revocation or suspension of his license or certificate.

Rule Prohibiting Unnecessary Sounding of the Whistle

SEC. 80.35 Unnecessary sounding of the whistle is prohibited within any harbor limits of the United States. Whenever any licensed officer in charge of any vessel shall authorize or permit such unnecessary whistling, such officer may be proceeded against in accordance with the provisions of R.S. 4450, as amended, looking to a revocation or suspension of his license.

Rule Prohibiting the Carrying of Unauthorized Lights on Vessels

SEC. 80.36 Any master or pilot of any vessel who shall authorize or permit the carrying of any light, electric or otherwise, not required by law, that in any way will interfere with distinguishing the signal lights, may be proceeded against in accordance with the provisions of R.S. 4450, as amended, looking to a suspension or revocation of his license.

Distress Signals

SEC. 80.37 (a) Daytime (1) Slowly and repeatedly raising and lowering arms outstretched to each side.

Warning Signals

Warning Signal Displayed While Transferring Dangerous Cargoes

SEC. 80.38 (a) *At a dock.* While fast to a dock, a vessel during the loading or unloading of hazardous or dangerous cargoes, such as explosives, combustible or inflammable liquids or gases, or certain chemicals in bulk, is required to display a red flag by day or a red light by night.

(b) *At anchor.* When at anchor, a vessel during the loading or unloading of such hazardous or dangerous cargoes is required to display a red flag by day. (No special warning signal is displayed at night.)[8]

Exceptions to the Statutory and Regulatory Requirements for Lights, Day Signals, or Other Navigational Means and Appliances When Operating under Bridges

SEC. 80.40 (a) Any vessel while passing under a bridge may temporarily lower any lights, day signals, or other navigational means and appliances when required to do so because of the restricted vertical clearance under the bridge. Immediately when clear of the bridge, all lights, days signals, or other navigational means and appliances shall be exhibited as required by law or regulation.

Distinctive Blue Lights Authorized for Use by Law Enforcement Vessels

SEC. 80.45 (Identical to Sec. 90.30 paragraphs a, b, and c, Pilot Rules for the Great Lakes, p. 576.)

---

[8] *The regulations in 46 CFR 35.30—1(a), 98.05—50(h), 98.10—45(g), 98.15—45(h), 98.25—90(f), and 146.29—25(o) require vessels to display warning signals when loading or unloading bulk cargoes of inflammable or combustible liquids or gases, elemental phosphorus in water, sulfuric acid, hydrochloric acid, liquid chlorine, or anhydrous ammonia, or military explosives.*

APPENDIX F
Interpretive Rulings, Inland Rules[1]

PART 86[2]

Scope

SEC. 86.01–1 The regulations in this part are interpretive rulings with respect to "Rules of the Road" requirements applicable to all vessels while in the harbors, rivers, and other inland waters of the United States except the Great Lakes and their connecting and tributary waters as far east as Montreal and the waters of the Mississippi River between its source and the Huey P. Long Bridge and all of the tributaries emptying thereinto and their tributaries, and that part of the Atchafalaya River above its junction with the Plaquemine-Morgan City alternate waterway, and the Red River of the North.

[1] Code of Federal Regulations: Title 33—Navigation and Navigable Waters; Part 86—Interpretive Rulings—Inland Waters.

[2] Authority: The provisions of this Part 86 issued under Sec. 1, 80 Stat. 383, as amended, sec. 1, 63 Stat. 545, sec. 6(b)(1), 80 Stat. 937; 5 U.S.C. 552, 14 U.S.C. 633, 49 U.S.C. 1655 (b)(1); 49 CFR 1.46(b), unless otherwise noted.

Penalties and Violations

SEC. 86.01–10 (a) Failure to comply with any law as interpreted will be considered as a violation of such law and the penalty may be assessed as provided by law.

(b) The reports of violations of the "Rules of the Road," as well as the assessment, collection, mitigation or remission of civil penalties authorized by law, shall be in accordance with 46 CFR 2.50–20 to 2.50–30, inclusive (Subchapter A—Procedures Applicable to the Public).

White Lights for Motorboats Carried on Centerline

SEC. 86.05–1 Every white light required by section 3 of the Act of April 25, 1940, as amended (46 U.S.C. 526b), shall be carried on the centerline of the motorboat, except that the all-around white light aft on a motorboat of Class A or 1 may be carried off the centerline.

Stern Lights for All Vessels

SEC. 86.05–5 Article 10 of section 1 of the Act of June 7, 1897, as amended by the Act of August 14, 1958 (33 U.S.C. 179), requires "A vessel when underway, if not otherwise required by these rules to carry one or more lights visible from aft, shall carry at her stern a while light, . . ." and this requirement shall be applied to all vessels, including but not limited to, tugs, barges, sail vessels, motorboats when propelled by sail alone, etc.

*Navigational Lights for Barges Traversing Both International
and Inland Waters*

SEC. 86.05–10 Notwithstanding the provisions of Section 80.16b of this chapter, every barge which shall have occasion during its voyage to operate upon waters to which the International Regulations for Prevention of Collisions at Sea pertain, may, for the duration of said voyage, display the navigational lights and shapes required by International Rule 5 (33 U.S.C. 1065).[3]

Bend Signal and Subsequent Meeting Situation

SEC. 86.10–1 Article 18, Rule V, and Article 18, Rule IX, of section 1, of the Act of June 7, 1897, as amended (33 U.S.C. 203), must be read together and followed after a bend signal is answered and the word "immediately" as used in Rule V shall be construed to require the exchange of sound signals for passing immediately upon sighting the other vessel.

---

[3] *Rule 5, 1960 International Rules, has been replaced by Rule 24(e)(f) and (g),
1972 International Rules.*

APPENDIX G
Towing of Barges, Inland Waters[1]

PART 84[2]

Application

SEC. 84.01 (a) The regulations in this part apply to vessels navigating the harbors, rivers, and inland waters of the United States, except the Great Lakes and their connecting and tributary waters as far east as Montreal, the Red River of the North, the Mississippi River and its tributaries above Huey P. Long Bridge, and that part of the Atchafalaya River above its junction with the Plaquemine-Morgan City alternate waterway.

(b) Seagoing barges and their towing vessels shall be subject to the requirements in this part under the provisions of section 14 of the Act of May 28, 1908, as amended (sec. 14, 35 Stat. 428, as amended; 33 U.S.C. 152). Under the provisions of section 15 of the Act of May 28, 1908, as amended (sec. 15, 35 Stat. 429; 33 U.S.C. 153), the penalty for use of an unlawful towline shall be an action against the master of the towing vessel seeking the suspension or revocation of his license.

---

[1] *Code of Federal Regulations: Title 33—Navigation and Navigable Waters; Part 84—Towing of Barges—Inland Waters.*

[2] *Authority: The provisions of this Part 84 issued under sec. 14, 35 Stat. 428, as amended, sec. 6(b)(1), 80 Stat. 937; 33 U.S.C. 152, 49 U.S.C. 1655(b)(1); 49 CFR 1.46(b).*

Tows of Seagoing Barges Within Inland Waters

SEC. 84.05 (a) The tows of seagoing barges when navigating the inland waters of the United States shall be limited in length to five vessels, including the towing vessel or vessels.

Hawser Lengths for All Tows on Inland Waters

SEC. 84.10 (a) The length of hawsers between vessels shall be limited to no more than 450 feet (75 fathoms).This length shall be the distance measured from the stern of one vessel to the bow of the following vessel. The distance between two vessels should in all cases be as much shorter as the weather or sea will permit: *Provided,* That where, in the opinion of the master of the towing vessel, it is dangerous or inadvisable, whether on account of the state of weather or sea or otherwise, to limit hawser lengths, the 450-foot limitation need not apply.

(b) In any event the hawsers between vessels must be shortened to the prescribed length of not more than 450 feet (75 fathoms) when the tows with inland or seagoing barges are operating in the following named localities:

(1) The James River and Hampton Roads westward of Thimble Shoal Light.

(2) The Chesapeake Bay north of the Chesapeake Bay Bridge.

(3) New York Harbor north of West Bank Light and west of Fort Schuyler.

(4) Delaware Bay north of Elbow of Cross Ledge Light.

(5) Narragansett Bay north of Brenton Reef Light.

(6) Puget Sound south of West Point.

Bunching of Tows

SEC. 84.20 (a) In all cases where tows can be bunched, it should be done.

(b) Tows navigating in the North and East Rivers of New York must be bunched above a line drawn between Robbins Reef Light and Owls Head, Brooklyn, but the quarantine anchorage and the north entrance to Ambrose Channel shall be avoided in the process of bunching tows.

(c) Tows must be bunched above the mouth of the Schuylkill River, Pa.

Excerpts from Motorboat Act of April 25, 1940;[1]

AN ACT TO AMEND LAWS FOR PREVENTING COLLISIONS OF VESSELS, TO REGULATE THE EQUIPMENT OF CERTAIN MOTORBOATS ON THE NAVIGABLE WATERS OF THE UNITED STATES, AND FOR OTHER PURPOSES

Motorboat Defined; Inspection

Be it enacted by the Senate and House of Representatives of the United States of America in Congress assembled, That the word "motorboat" where used in this Act shall include every vessel propelled by machinery and not more than sixty-five feet in length except tugboats and towboats propelled by steam. The length shall be measured from end to end over the deck, excluding sheer: Provided, That the engine, boiler or other operating machinery shall be subject to inspection by the Coast Guard, and to their approval of the design thereof, on all said motorboats, which are more than forty feet in length, and which are propelled by machinery driven by steam.

Classes of Motorboats

SEC. 2 Motorboats subject to the provisions of this Act shall be divided into four classes as follows:

Class A. Less than sixteen feet in length.

Class 1. Sixteen feet or over and less than twenty-six feet in length.

---

[1] Title 46 U.S. Code. Section 526—526u.

Class 2. Twenty-six feet or over and less than forty feet in length.

Class 3. Forty feet or over and not more than sixty-five feet in length.

Lights[2]

SEC. 3 Every motorboat in all weathers from sunset to sunrise shall carry and exhibit the following lights when under way, and during such time no other lights which may be mistaken for those prescribed shall be exhibited:

(a) Every motorboat of Classes A and 1 shall carry the following lights:

First. A bright white light aft to show all around the horizon.

Second. A combined lantern in the fore part of the vessel and lower than the white aft, showing green to starboard and red to port, so fixed as to throw the light from right ahead to two points abaft the beam on their respective sides.

(b) Every motorboat of classes 2 and 3 shall carry the following lights:

First. A bright white light in the fore part of the vessel as near the stem as practicable, so constructed as to show an unbroken light over an arc of the horizon of twenty points of the compass, so fixed as to throw the light ten points on each side of the vessel; namely, from right ahead to two points abaft the beam on either side.

Second. A bright white light aft to show all around the horizon and higher than the white light forward.

Third. On the starboard side a green light so constructed as to show an unbroken light over an arc of the horizon of ten points of the compass, so fixed as to throw the light from right ahead to two points abaft the beam on the starboard side. On the port side a red light so constructed as to show an unbroken light over an arc of the horizon of ten points of the compass, so fixed as to throw the light from right ahead to two points abaft the beam on the port side. The said side lights shall be fitted with inboard screens of sufficient height so set as to prevent these lights from being seen across the bow.

(c) Motorboats of Classes A and 1 when propelled by sail alone shall carry the combined lantern, but not the white light aft, prescribed by this section. Motorboats of Classes 2 and 3, when so propelled, shall carry the colored side lights, suitably screened, but not the white lights, prescribed

---

[2] *Administrative interpretations of November 22, 1940:*

Running Lights. *These lights are running lights for motorboats in inland waters, the western rivers, and the Great Lakes and are to be carried in lieu of the running lights prescribed by the Inland, Western Rivers, and Great Lakes Rules. Motorboats when on the high seas must exhibit the lights prescribed by the International Rules.*

Running lights not in conflict with other lights. *These lights are not in conflict with lights, other than running lights, prescribed by Inland, Western Rivers, or Great Lakes Rules. Motorboats must carry such other lights as may be prescribed by applicable Inland, Western Rivers, or Great Lakes Rules.*

by this section. Motorboats of all classes, when so propelled, shall carry, ready at hand, a lantern or flashlight showing a white light which shall be exhibited in sufficient time to avert collision.[3]

(d) Every white light prescribed by this section shall be of such character as to be visible at a distance of at least two miles. Every colored light prescribed by this section shall be of such character as to be visible at a distance of at least one mile. The word "visible" in this Act, when applied to lights, shall mean visible on a dark night with clear atmosphere.

(e) When propelled by sail and machinery any motorboat shall carry the lights required by this section for a motorboat propelled by machinery only.

(f) Any motorboat may carry and exhibit the lights. . . . [This paragraph will be modified to conform with the Regulations for Preventing Collisions at Sea, 1972, as amended, in lieu of the lights required by this section when enabling legislation is effected.][4]

Whistles

SEC. 4 Every motorboat of class 1, 2, or 3 shall be provided with an efficient whistle or other sound-producing mechanical appliance.

Bells

SEC. 5 Every motorboat of class 2 or 3 shall be provided with an efficient bell.

Exemptions for Outboard Racing Motorboats

SEC. 9 The provisions of sections 4, 5, and 8 of this Act shall not apply to motorboats propelled by outboard motors while competing in any race previously arranged and announced or, if such boats be designed and intended solely for racing, while engaged in such navigation as is incidental to the tuning up of the boats and engines for the race.

Pilot Rules Not Required

SEC. 12 Motorboats shall not be required to carry on board copies of the pilot rules.

Authority to Arrest for Negligent Operation

SEC. 15 Any officer of the United States authorized to enforce the navi-

---

[3] *On motorboats of classes A and 1 the aft white all around light or the 12-point white stern light may be located off the centerline.*

[4] *Refer to Rule 22(b)(c) in the 1972 International Rules.*

gation laws of the United States shall have power and authority to swear out process and to arrest and take into custody, with or without process, any person who may commit any act or offense prohibited by section 13, or who may violate any provision of said section: Provided, That no person shall be arrested without process for any offense not committed in the presence of some one of the aforesaid officials: Provided, further, That whenever an arrest is made under the provisions of this act, the person so arrested shall be brought forthwith before a commissioner, judge, or court of the United States for examination of the offense alleged against him, and such commissioner, judge, or court shall proceed in respect thereto as authorized by law in cases of crimes against the United States.

Penalty for Other Violations of Act

SEC. 16 If any motorboat or vessel subject to any of the provisions of this Act is operated or navigated in violation of this Act or any regulation issued thereunder, the owner or operator, either one or both of them, shall, in addition to any other penalty prescribed by law, be liable to a penalty of $100: Provided, That in the case of motorboats or vessels subject to the provisions of this Act carrying passengers for hire, a penalty of $200 shall be imposed on the owner or operator, either one or both of them, thereof for any violation of section 6, 7, or 8 of this Act or of any regulations pertaining thereto. For any penalty incurred under this section the motorboat or vessel shall be held liable and may be proceeded against by way of libel in the district court of any district in which said motorboat or vessel may be found.

Regulations; Enforcement

SEC. 17 The Commandant of the Coast Guard shall establish all necessary regulations required to carry out in the most effective manner all of the provisions of this Act, and such regulations shall have the force of law. The Commandant of the Coast Guard or any officer of the Coast Guard authorized by the Commandant may, upon application therefore, remit or mitigate any fine, penalty, or forfeiture incurred under this Act or any regulation thereunder relating to motorboats or vessels, except the penalties provided for in section 14 hereunder. The Commandant of the Coast Guard shall establish such regulations as may be necessary to secure the enforcement of the provisions of this Act by any officer of the United States authorized to enforce the navigation laws of the United States.

Exemptions

SEC. 18 The proviso contained in the last paragraph of section 2 of the

Act of May 11, 1918 (40 Stat. 549), shall apply also with like force and effect to motorboats as defined in this Act.

Motorboats as defined in this Act are hereby exempted from the provisions of Revised Statutes 4399, as amended (48 Stat. 125; 46 U.S.C. 361).

Application of Act; "State" Defined

SEC. 22 (a) This Act applies to every motorboat or vessel on the navigable waters of the United States, Guam, the Virgin Islands, the Commonwealth of Puerto Rico, and the District of Columbia, and every motorboat or vessel owned in a State and using the high seas except that the provisions of this Act other than sections 12, 18, and 19 do not apply to boats as defined in and subject to the Federal Boat Safety Act of 1971.

(b) As used in this Act—

The term "State" means a State of the United States, Guam, the Virgin Islands, the Commonwealth of Puerto Rico, and the District of Columbia.

APPENDIX I
Great Lakes Rules[1]

AN ACT TO REGULATE NAVIGATION ON THE GREAT LAKES AND THEIR CONNECTING AND TRIBUTARY WATERS, AS AMENDED

Be it enacted by the Senate and House of Representatives of the United States of America in Congress assembled, That the following rules for preventing collisions shall be followed in the navigation of all public and private vessels of the United States upon the Great Lakes and their connecting and tributary waters as far east as Montreal and in the navigation of all other vessels upon such lakes and waters while within the territorial waters of the United States.

Steam and Sail Vessels

RULE 1 Every steam vessel which is under sail and not under steam shall be considered a sail vessel; and every steam vessel which is under steam, whether under sail or not, shall be considered a steam vessel. The words "steam vessel" shall include any vessel propelled by machinery. A vessel is under way within the meaning of these rules when she is not at anchor or made fast to the shore or aground.

LIGHTS

When Exhibited

RULE 2 The lights mentioned in the following rules, and no others which may be mistaken for the prescribed lights, shall be exhibited in all weathers from sunset to sunrise. The word "visible" in these rules, when applied to lights, shall mean visible on a dark night with a clear atmosphere.

[1] *Act of February 8, 1895, as amended, 33 U.S.C. 241-294.*

Steam Vessels

RULE 3 Except in the cases hereinafter expressly provided for, a steam vessel when under way shall carry:

Masthead Lights

(a) On or in front of the foremast, or if a vessel without a foremast, then in the fore part of the vessel, a bright white light so constructed as to show an unbroken light over an arc of the horizon of twenty points of the compass, so fixed as to throw the light ten points on each side of the vessel, namely, from right ahead to two points abaft the beam on either side, and of such a character as to be visible at a distance of at least five miles. Such light shall be at a greater height above the water than the side lights required by subdivisions (b) and (c).

Starboard Side Light

(b) On the starboard side, a green light, so constructed as to throw an unbroken light over an arc of the horizon of ten points of the compass, so fixed as to throw the light from right ahead to two points abaft the beam on the starboard side, and of such a character as to be visible at a distance of at least two miles.

Port Side Light

(c) On the port side, a red light, so constructed as to show an unbroken light over an arc of the horizon of ten points of the compass, so fixed as to throw the light from right ahead to two points abaft the beam on the port side, and of such a character as to be visible at a distance of at least two miles.

Side Light Screens

(d) The said green and red lights shall be fitted with inboard screens projecting at least three feet forward from the light, so as to prevent these lights from being seen across the bow.

Range Lights: Vessels Over 100 Feet in Length

(e) A steamer of over 100 feet register length shall carry also, when under way, a bright white light so fixed as to throw the light all around the horizon, and of such a character as to be visible at a distance of at least three miles. Such light shall be placed in line with the keel at least 15 feet higher than, and more than 50 feet abaft, the light mentioned in subdivision (a) of this rule; or in lieu thereof two such lights of the same character and height as herein described placed not over 30 inches apart horizontally, one on either side of the keel, and so arranged that one or the other or both shall be visible from any angle of approach.

Range Lights: Vessels 100 Feet or Less in Length

(f) A steam vessel not more than 100 feet in length shall carry also a bright white light aft to show all around the horizon. Such light shall be placed in line with the keel higher than the light required by subdivision (a) of this rule.

Vessels Having a Tow, Other Than Rafts

RULE 4 A steam vessel having a tow other than a raft shall in addition to the forward bright light mentioned in subdivision (a) of rule three carry in a vertical line not less than six feet above or below that light a second bright light of the same construction and character and fixed and carried in the same manner as the forward bright light mentioned in said subdivsion (a) of rule three. Such steamer shall also carry a small bright light abaft the funnel or aftermast for the tow to steer by, but such light shall not be visible forward of the beam.

Vessels Towing Rafts

RULE 5 A steam vessel having a raft in tow shall, instead of the forward lights mentioned in rule four, carry on or in front of the foremast, or if a vessel without a foremast then in the fore part of the vessel, at a height above the hull of not less than twenty feet, and if the beam of the vessel exceeds twenty feet, then at a height above the hull not less than such beam, so however that such height need not exceed forty feet, two bright lights in a horizontal line athwartships and not less than eight feet apart, each so fixed as to throw the light all around the horizon and of such character as to be visible at a distance of at least five miles. Such steamer shall also carry the small bright steering light aft, of the character and fixed as required in rule four.

Sail Vessels

RULE 6 A sailing vessel under way and any vessel being towed shall carry the side lights mentioned in rule three.

A vessel in tow shall also carry a small bright light aft, but such light shall not be visible forward of the beam.

Tugs, etc.

RULE 7 The lights for tugs under 100 tons register (net), whose principal business is harbor towing, and for boats navigating only on the River Saint

Lawrence, also ferryboats, rafts, and canal boats, shall be regulated by rules which have been or may hereafter be prescribed by the Commandant of the Coast Guard.

Small Vessels

RULE 8 Whenever, as in the case of small vessels under way during bad weather, the green and red side lights cannot be fixed, these lights shall be kept at hand lighted and ready for use, and shall, on the approach of or to other vessels, be exhibited on their respective sides in sufficient time to prevent collision, in such manner as to make them most visible, and so that the green light shall not be seen on the port side, nor the red light on the starboard side, nor, if practicable, more than two points abaft the beam on their respective sides. To make the use of these portable lights more certain and easy, they shall each be painted outside with the color of the light they respectively contain, and shall be provided with suitable screens.

Anchor Lights

RULE 9[2] A vessel under 150 feet register length, when at anchor, shall carry forward, where it can best be seen, but at a height not exceeding 20 feet above the hull, a white light constructed so as to show a clear, uniform, and unbroken light visible all around the horizon at a distance of at least 1 mile: Provided, That the Secretary of the Army may, after investigation, by rule, regulation, or order designate such areas as he may deem proper as "special anchorage areas"; such special anchorage areas may from time to time be changed, or abolished, if after investigation the Secretary of the Army shall deem such change or abolition in the interest of navigation: Provided further, That vessels not more than 65 feet in length, when at anchor, in any such special anchorage area shall not be required to carry or exhibit the white light required by this article.

A vessel of 150 feet or upward in register length, when at anchor, shall carry in the forward part of the vessel, two white lights at the same height of not less than 20 and not exceeding 40 feet above the hull and not less than 10 feet apart horizontally and athwartships, except that each need not be visible all around the horizon but so arranged that one or the other, or both, shall show a clear, uniform, and unbroken light and be visible from any angle of approach at a distance of at least 1 mile; and at or near the stern of the vessel two similar lights, similarly arranged and at such a height that they shall not be less than 15 feet lower than the forward lights. In addition, the four anchor lights above specified, at least one white deck

---

[2] *Functions, powers, and duties of Secretary of the Army re water vessel anchorage under Rule 9 were transferred to the Secretary of Transportation on October 15, 1966, by Public Law 89-670, 49 U.S.C. 1655 (g) (1) (B), (C), and (D).*

light shall be displayed in every interval of 100 feet along the deck measuring from the forward lights, said deck lights to be not less than 2 feet above the deck and arranged, so far as intervening structures will permit, so as to be visible from any angle of approach.

Miscellaneous Craft

RULE 10 Produce boats, canal boats, fishing boats, rafts, or other water craft navigating any bay, harbor, or river by hand power, horsepower, sail or by the current of the river, or which shall be anchored or moored in or near the channel or fairway of any bay, harbor, or river, and not otherwise provided for in these rules, shall carry one or more good white lights, which shall be placed in such manner as shall be prescribed by the Commandant of the Coast Guard.

Open Boats

RULE 11 Open boats shall not be obliged to carry the side lights required for other vessels, but shall, if they do not carry such lights, carry a lantern having a green slide on one side and a red slide on the other side; and on the approach of or to other vessels, such lantern shall be exhibited in suffcient time to prevent collision, and in such a manner that the green light shall not be seen on the port side, nor the red light on the starboard side. Open boats, when at anchor or stationary, shall exhibit a bright white light. They shall not, however, be prevented from using a flare-up in addition if considered expedient.

Sail Vessels

RULE 12 Sailing vessels shall at all times, on the approach of any steamer during the nighttime, show a lighted torch upon that point or quarter to which such steamer shall be approached.

Public Vessels: Exemptions

RULE 13 The exhibition of any light on board of a vessel of war or Coast Guard vessel of the United States may be suspended, whenever, in the opinion of the Secretary of the Navy, the commander in chief of a squadron, or the commander of a vessel acting singly, the special character of the service may require it.

Fog Signals

RULE 14 A steam vessel shall be provided with an efficient whistle, sounded by steam or by some substitute for steam, placed before the funnel not less than 8 feet from the deck, or in such other place as the

Coast Guard shall determine, and of such character as to be heard in ordinary weather at a distance of at least two miles, and with an efficient bell, and it is made the duty of the United States Coast Guard when inspecting the same to require each steamer to be furnished with such whistle and bell. A sailing vessel shall be provided with an efficient fog horn and with an efficient bell.

Whenever there is thick weather by reason of fog, mist, falling snow, heavy rainstorms, or other causes, whether by day or by night, fog signals shall be used as follows:

(a) A steam vessel under way, excepting ony a steam vessel with raft in tow, shall sound at intervals of not more than 1 minute three distinct blasts of her whistle.

(b) Every vessel in tow of another vessel shall, at intervals of 1 minute, sound four bells on a good and efficient and properly placed bell as follows: By striking the bell twice in quick succession, followed by a little longer interval, and then again striking twice in quick succession (in the manner in which four bells is struck in indicating time).

(c) A steamer with a raft in tow shall sound at intervals of not more than 1 minute a screeching or Modoc whistle for from 3 to 5 seconds.

(d) A sailing vessel under way and not in tow shall sound at intervals of not more than 1 minute—

If on the starboard tack with wind forward of abeam, one blast of her fog horn;

If on the port tack with wind forward of the beam, two blasts of her fog horn;

If she has the wind abaft the beam on either side, three blasts of her fog horn.

(e) A vessel at anchor and a vessel aground in or near a channel or fairway shall at intervals of not more than 2 minutes ring the bell rapidly for from 3 to 5 seconds and, in addition, at intervals of not more than 3 minutes shall sound on the whistle or horn a signal of one short blast, two long blasts, and one short blast in quick succession.

(f) Vessels of less than 10 tons registered tonnage, not being steam vessels, shall not be obliged to give the above-mentioned signals, but if they do not they shall make some other efficient sound signal at intervals of not more than 1 minute.

(g) Produce boats, fishing boats, rafts, or other water craft navigating by hand power or by the current of the river, or anchored or moored in or near the channel or fairway and not in any port, and not otherwise provided for in these rules, shall sound a fog horn, or equivalent signal, at intervals of not more than 1 minute.

RULE 15 Every vessel shall, in thick weather, by reason of fog, mist, falling snow, heavy rainstorms, or other causes, go at moderate speed. A steam vessel hearing, apparently not more than four points from right ahead, the fog signal of another vessel shall at once reduce her speed to bare steerageway, and navigate with caution until the vessels shall have passed each other.

Steering and Sailing Rules
Sailing Vessels

RULE 16 When two sailing vessels are approaching one another so as to involve risk of collision, one of them shall keep out of the way of the other, as follows, namely:

(a) A vessel which is running free shall keep out of the way of a vessel which is close-hauled.

(b) A vessel which is close-hauled on the port tack shall keep out of the way of a vessel is close-hauled on the starboard tack.

(c) When both are running free, with the wind on different sides, the vessel which has the wind on the port side shall keep out of the way of the other.

(d) When they are running free, with the wind on the same side, the vessel which is to windward shall keep out of the way of the vessel which is to leeward.

Steam Vessels

Meeting End On

RULE 17 When two steam vessels are meeting end on, or nearly end on, so as to involve risk of collision each shall alter her course to starboard, so that each shall pass on the port side of the other.

Crossing

RULE 18 When two steam vessels are crossing so as to involve risk of collision the vessel which has the other on her own starboard side shall keep out of the way of the other.

Steam and Sail Vessels Meeting

RULE 19 When a steam vessel and a sailing vessel are proceeding in such directions as to involve risk of collision the steam vessel shall keep out of the way of the sailing vessel. This rule shall not give to a sailing vessel the right to hamper, in a narrow channel, the safe passage of a steam vessel which can navigate only inside that channel.

Right of Way

RULE 20 Where, by any of the rules herein prescribed, one of two vessels shall keep out of the way, the other shall keep her course and speed.

Duty to Slacken Speed or Stop

RULE 21 Every steam vessel which is directed by these rules to keep out of the way of another vessel shall, on approaching her, if necessary, slacken her speed or stop or reverse.

Overtaking Vessel

RULE 22 Notwithstanding anything contained in these rules every vessel overtaking any other shall keep out of the way of the overtaken vessel.

Signals Indicating Course

RULE 23 In all weathers every steam vessel under way in taking any course authorized or required by these rules shall indicate that course by the following signals on her whistle, to be accompanied whenever required by corresponding alteration of her helm; and every steam vessel receiving a signal from another shall promptly respond with the same signal or, as provided in rule twenty-six:

One blast to mean, "I am directing my course to starboard."

Two blasts to mean, "I am directing my course to port." But the giving or answering signals by a vessel required to keep her course shall not vary the duties and obligations of the respective vessels.

[See Rule 29 for orders to helmsmen.]

Rivers and Channels

RULE 24 That in all narrow channels where there is a current, and in the rivers Saint Marys, Saint Clair, Detroit, Niagara, and Saint Lawrence, when two steamers are meeting, the descending steamer shall have the right-of-way, and shall, before the vessels shall have arrived within the distance of one-half mile of each other, give the signal necessary to indicate which side she elects to take. In all narrow channels a steam vessel of less than sixty-five feet in length shall not hamper the safe passage of a vessel which can navigate only inside that channel.

Narrow Channels

RULE 25 In all channels less than five hundred feet in width, no steam vessel shall pass another going in the same direction unless the steam vessel ahead be disabled or signify her willingness that the steam vessel astern shall pass, when the steam vessel astern may pass, subject, however, to the other rules applicable to such a situation. And when steam vessels proceeding in opposite directions are about to meet in such channels, both such vessels shall be slowed down to a moderate speed, according to the circumstances.

Dissent to Signal Given

RULE 26 If the pilot of a steam vessel to which a passing signal is sounded deems it unsafe to accept and assent to said signal, he shall not sound a cross signal; but in that case, and in every case where the pilot of one steamer fails to understand the course or intention of an approaching steamer, whether from signals being given or answered erroneously, or from other causes, the pilot of such steamer so receiving the first passing signal, or the pilot so in doubt, shall sound several short and rapid blasts of the whistle; and if the vessels shall have approached within half a mile of each other both shall reduce their speed to bare steerageway, and, if necessary, stop and reverse.

Departure from Rules

RULE 27 In obeying and construing these rules due regard shall be had to all dangers of navigation and collision and to any special circumstances which may render a departure from the above rules necessary in order to avoid immediate danger.

Precautions

RULE 28 Nothing in these rules shall exonerate any vessel, or the owner or master or crew thereof, from the consequences of any neglect to carry lights or signals, or of any neglect to keep a proper lookout, or of a neglect of any precaution which may be required by the ordinary practice of seamen, or by the special circumstances of the case.

Orders to Helmsmen

RULE 29 All orders to helmsmen shall be given as follows:
"Right Rudder" to mean "Direct the vessel's head to starboard."
"Left Rudder" to mean "Direct the vessel's head to port."

Anchor Lights, Shapes, etc.

RULE 30 (a) Between sunrise and sunset every vessel over 65 feet in length when at anchor shall carry forward, where it can best be seen, one black ball not less than two feet in diameter.

(b) A vessel over 65 feet in length which is not under command shall carry where they can best be seen and, if a steam vessel, in lieu of the white light required by rule 3 (a), two red lights in a vertical line one over the other not less than three feet apart, and of such a character as to be visible all around the horizon at a distance of at least two miles. By day such vessel shall carry in a vertical line one over the other not less than three feet apart, where they can best be seen, two black balls, each two feet in diameter. Such vessel, when not making way through the water, shall not carry the side lights required by rule 3 (b) and (c), but when making way shall carry them.

(c) A vessel aground over 65 feet in length shall carry by night the white light or lights prescribed for a vessel at anchor and in addition shall carry, where they can best be seen by approaching vessels, two red lights in a vertical line one over the other, not less than three feet apart, visible all around the horizon at a distance of at least two miles. By day such vessel shall carry in a vertical line one over the other not less than three feet apart, where they can best be seen, three black balls, each two feet in diameter.

Penalty

SEC. 2 (a) Every licensed or unlicensed pilot, engineer, mate, or master of any vessel subject to section 1 of this Act who neglects or refuses to observe the provisions of this Act or the regulations established pursuant hereto shall be liable to a penalty not exceeding $500.

(b) Every private vessel subject to section 1 of this Act that shall be navigated without complying with the provisions of this Act or the regulations established pursuant hereto shall be liable to a penalty of $500, for which sum such vessel may be seized and proceeded against by way of libel in any district court of the United States of any district within which such vessel may be found.

Regulations

That the Commandant of the Coast Guard shall have authority to establish all necessary regulations, not inconsistent with the provisions of this Act, required to carry the same into effect.

The Commandant of the Coast Guard of the United States shall have authority to establish such regulations to be observed by all steam vessels in passing each other, not inconsistent with the provisions of his Act, as he shall from time to time deem necessary; and all regulations adopted by the said Commandant of the Coast Guard under the authority of this Act shall have the force of law. Two printed copies of any such regulations for passing, signed by him, shall be furnished to each steam vessel, and shall at all times be kept posted up in conspicuous places on board.

Anchorage and General Regulations for St. Marys River

The Commandant of the Coast Guard is authorized and directed to adopt and prescribe suitable rules and regulations governing the movements and anchorage of vessels and rafts in Saint Marys River from Point Iroquois, on Lake Superior, to Point Detour, on Lake Huron, and for the purpose of enforcing the observance of such regulations the Secretary of

Transportation is authorized to detail one or more Coast Guard cutters for duty upon the request of the Commandant of the Coast Guard on said river.

All officers of the Coast Guard who are directed to enforce the regulations prescribed by the above rules are hereby empowered and directed, in case of necessity, or when a proper notice has been disregarded, to use the force at their command to remove from channels or stop any vessel found violating the prescribed rules.

In the event of the violation of any such regulations or rules of the Commandant of the Coast Guard by the owners, master, or person in charge of such vessel, such owners, master, or person in charge shall be liable to a penalty not exceeding two hundred dollars: *Provided*, That the Commandant of the Coast Guard may remit said fine on such terms as he may prescribe: *Provided also*, That nothing in this section shall be construed to amend or repeal chapter 4 of this title regulating navigation on the Great Lakes and their connecting and tributary waters as far east as Montreal.

(Sec 1–3, 29 Stat. 54–55, as amended; 33 U.S.C. 474.)

APPENDIX J
Pilot Rules for the Great Lakes[1]

PART 90[2]

---

[1] *Code of Federal Regulations: Title 33—Navigation and Navigable Waters; Part 90—Pilot Rules for the Great Lakes.*

[2] *Authority: §§ 90.01 to 90.21, 90.25, and 90.30 issued under 33 U.S.C. 243, 256, and 259. §§ 90.22 to 90.24 issued under 46 U.S.C. 375.*

General Instructions

SEC. 90.01 The regulations in this part govern pilots of vessels propelled by steam, gas, fluid, naphtha, or electric motors, and of other vessels propelled by machinery, navigating the Great Lakes and their connecting and tributary waters as far east as Montreal.

Definitions and Risk of Collision

SEC. 90.02 (a) In this part the words "steam vessel" and "steamer" shall include any vessel propelled by machinery.

(b) A vessel is under way within the meaning of the rules in this part when she is not at anchor or made fast to the shore or aground.

(c) Risk of collision can, when circumstances permit, be ascertained by carefully watching the bearing of an approaching vessel. If the bearing does not appreciably change, such risk should be deemed to exist.

Demarcation Lines between "Rules of the Road—Great Lakes"
and "Rules of the Road—Western Rivers"

SEC. 90.03 (a) The demarcation lines between the "Rules of the Road—Great Lakes" and "Rules of the Road—Western Rivers" are as follows:

(1) On the Calumet River at the Thomas J. O'Brien Lock and Controlling Works (between mile 326 and 327).

(2) On the Chicago River at the east side of the Ashland Avenue Bridge (between mile 321 and 322).

Signals and Rules of the Road

Signals

SEC. 90.1 (a) In all weathers every steam vessel under way, in taking any course authorized or required by the rules in this part, shall indicate that course by the following signals on her whistle, to be accompanied, whenever required, by corresponding alteration of her course; and every steam vessel receiving a signal from another shall promptly respond with the same signal or sound the danger signal as provided in § 90.2.

(b) Except as otherwise provided in the rules in this part, one blast shall mean, "I am directing my course to starboard"; two blasts shall mean, "I am directing my course to port."

Danger Signal

SEC. 90.2 If, when steamers are approaching each other, the pilot of either vessel fails to understand the course or intention of the other, whether from signals being given or answered erroneously or from other causes, the pilot so in doubt shall immediately signify the same by giving the danger signal of several short and rapid blasts of the whistle not less than five; and if both vessels shall have approached within half a mile of each other, both shall be immediately slowed to a speed barely sufficient for steerageway, and, if necessary, stopped and reversed, until the proper signals are given, answered, and understood, or until the vessels shall have passed each other.

Cross Signals

SEC. 90.3 Steam vessels are forbidden to use what has become technically known among pilots as "cross signals"—that is, answering one whistle with two, and answering two whistles with one. In all cases, and under all circumstances, a pilot receiving either of the whistle signals provided in the rules in this part, which for any reason he deems injudicious to comply with, instead of answering it with a cross signal, shall at once sound the danger signal and observe the rule applying thereto (§ 90.2).

Vessels Passing Each Other

SEC. 90.4 The whistle signals indicating course shall be given and answered in accordance with the rules, not only when an alteration of course is required, but at all times before vessels approach within half a mile of each other, from whatever direction, if their courses will bring them within that distance from each other.

Vessels Approaching Each Other "Head and Head"

SEC. 90.5 When steam vessels are meeting end on, or nearly end on, it shall be the duty of each steam vessel to pass on the port side of the other; and the pilot of either steam vessel may be first in determining to pursue this course, and thereupon shall give, as a signal of this intention, one distinct blast of his whistle, which the pilot of the other steam vessel shall answer promptly by a similar blast of his whistle, and thereupon such steam vessels shall pass on the port side of each other. But if the courses of such steam vessels are so far on the starboard of each other as not to be considered by pilots as meeting end on, or nearly end on, the pilot so first deciding shall immediately give two distinct blasts of his whistle, which the pilot of the other steam vessel shall answer promptly by two similar blasts of his whistle, and they shall pass on the starboard side of each other: Provided, however, That in all narrow channels where there is a current, and in the rivers St. Marys, St. Clair, Detroit, Niagara, and St. Lawrence, when two steam vessels are meeting, the descending steam vessel shall have the right of way and shall, before the vessels shall have arrived within the distance of half a mile of each other, give the signal necessary to indicate which side she elects to take.

Vessels Nearing Short Bend or Curve in Channel

SEC. 90.6 Whenever a steam vessel is nearing a short bend or curve in the channel, where, from the height of the banks or other cause, a steam vessel approaching from the opposite direction cannot be seen for a distance of half a mile, the pilot of such steam vessel, when he shall have arrived within half a mile of such curve or bend, shall give a signal by one blast of the whistle, of at least 8 seconds' duration, which signal shall be answered by a similar blast, given by the pilot of any steam vessel within hearing that may be approaching on the other side, and within half a mile, of such bend or curve. Should such signal be so answered by a steam vessel upon the farther side of such bend, then the usual signals for meeting and passing shall immediately be given and answered.

Vessel Leaving a Dock

SEC. 90.7 When a steam vessel is leaving her dock or berth, she shall give a signal of one blast of the whistle, of at least 8 seconds' duration, which signal shall be answered by a similar blast given by any approaching steam vessel, but she and any approaching vessel shall be governed by Rule 27, the general prudential rule, until her course is apparent, and then both vessels shall be governed by the applicable steering and sailing rules.

Vessels Running in Same Direction; Signals for Overtaking

SEC. 90.8 (a) When one steam vessel is overtaking another and the steam vessel astern shall desire to pass on the right or starboard side of the steam vessel ahead, she shall give one distinct blast of the whistle as a signal of such desire and, if the vessel ahead answers with one blast, she shall direct her course to starboard; or if she shall desire to pass on the left or port side of the vessel ahead, she shall give two distinct blasts of the whistle as a signal of such desire and, if the vessel ahead answers with two blasts, she shall direct her course to port; or if the vessel ahead does not think it safe for the vessel astern to pass at that time, she shall immediately signify the same by giving the danger signal of several short and rapid blasts of the whistle, not less than five. It shall then be the duty of the steam vessel astern to hold back and, after an appropriate interval, if she still desires to pass, to make the proper signal so indicating; but under no circumstances shall the steam vessel attempt to pass the steam vessed ahead until such time as they have reached a point where it can be safely done, and the steam vessel ahead shall signify her willingness by blowing the proper answering signal. The steam vessel ahead shall in no case attempt to cross the bow or crowd upon the course of the other steam vessel.

(b) Every vessel coming up with another vessel from any direction more than two points abaft her beam; that is, in such a position, with reference to the vessel which she is overtaking, that at night she would be unable to see either of that vessel's side lights, shall be deemed to be an overtaking vessel, and no subsequent alteration of the bearing between the two vessels shall make the overtaking vessel a crossing vessel within the meaning of the rules in this part, or relieve her of the duty of keeping clear of the overtaken vessel until the overtaken vessel is finally passed and cleared.

(c) As the overtaking vessel cannot always know with certainty whether she is forward or abaft this direction from the other vessel, she should, if in doubt, assume that she is an overtaking vessel and keep out of the way.

Vessels Approaching Each Other at Right Angles or Obliquely

SEC. 90.10 (a) When two steam vessels are approaching each other at right angles or obliquely so as to involve risk of collision, other than when one steam vessel is overtaking another, the steam vessel which has the other on her own port side shall hold her course and speed; and the steam vessel which has the other on her own starboard side shall keep out of the way of the other by directing her course to starboard so as to cross the stern of the other steam vessel; or, if necessary to do so, slacken her speed or stop or reverse. The steam vessel having the other on her own port side shall blow one distinct blast of her whistle as a signal of her intention to cross the bow of the other, holding her course and speed, which signal shall be promptly answered by the other steam vessel by one distinct blast of her whistle as a signal of her intention to direct her course to starboard so as to cross the stern of the other steam vessel or otherwise keep clear.

(b) If from any cause whatever the conditions covered by this situation are such as to prevent immediate compliance with each other's signals, the misunderstanding or objection shall be at once made apparent by blowing the danger signal, and both steam vessels shall be stopped, and backed if necessary, until signals for passing with safety are made and understood.

Departure from the Rules

SEC. 90.12 In obeying and construing the rules in this part due regard shall be had to all dangers of navigation and collision and to any special circumstances which may render a departure from the above rules necessary in order to avoid immediate danger.

Distress Signals; Posting of Rules; Diagrams; Starting, Stopping, and Backing Signals—(a) Distress Signals

SEC. 90.15 When a vessel is in distress and requires assistance from other vessels or from the shore, the following shall be the signals to be used or displayed by her, either together or separately, namely:

(1) In the daytime:

(i) A gun or other explosive signal fired at intervals of about a minute.

(ii) The distant signal consisting of a square flag having either above or below it a ball or some object resembling a ball.

(iii) A continuous sounding with any fog-signal apparatus.

(iv) Slowly and repeatedly raising and lowering arms outstretched to each side.

(2) At night:

(i) A gun or other explosive signal fired at intervals of about a minute.

(ii) Flames from the vessel (as from burning a tar barrel, oil barrel, etc.).

(iii) Rockets or shells, throwing stars of any color or description fired one at a time at short intervals.

(iv) A continuous sounding with any fog-signal apparatus.

Posting of Pilot Rules

(b)(1) On every vessel, two copies of the pamphlet containing the Pilot Rules for the Great Lakes (CG-172) or two copies of a placard containing these rules shall be kept posted, wherever practicable, in conspicuous places, one copy of which shall be in the pilothouse. When the pamphlet is secured in plain sight in such a manner that it can be used as a reference, it is considered to be posted.

(2) Nothing in this section shall require copies of the pilot rules to be carried on board any motorboat as defined by section 1 of the Act of April 25, 1940 (54 Stat. 163; 46 U.S.C. 526-526t).

Diagrams

(c) The following diagrams are intended to illustrate the working of the system of colored lights and pilot rules:

Here the two colored lights visible to each will indicate their direct approach "head and head" toward each other. In this situation it is a standing rule that both shall direct their courses to starboard and pass on the port side of each other, each having previously given one distinct blast of the whistle.

SECOND SITUATION

In this situation the red light only will be visible to each, the screens preventing the green light being seen. Both vessels are evidently passing to port of each other, which is rulable in this situation, each pilot having previously signified his intention by one distinct blast of the whistle.

THIRD SITUATION

In this situation the green light only will be visible to each, the screens preventing the red light from being seen. They are therefore passing to starboard of each other, which is rulable in this situation, each pilot having previously signified his intention by two distinct blasts of the whistle.

FOURTH SITUATION

In this situation one steamer is overtaking another steamer from some point within the angle of two points abaft the beams of the overtaken steamer. The overtaking steamer may pass on the starboard or port side of the steamer ahead after the necessary signals for passing have been given, with assent of the overtaken steamer, as prescribed in § 90.8.

FIFTH SITUATION

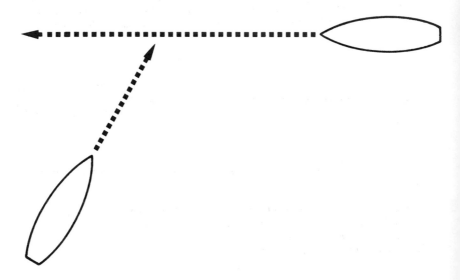

In this situation two steamers are approaching each other at right angles or obliquely in such a manner as to involve risk of collision, other than where one steamer is overtaking another.

The steamer which has the other on her own port side shall hold course and speed, and the other shall keep clear by crossing astern of the steamer that is holding course and speed, or, if necessary to do so, shall slacken her speed or stop or reverse.

Both steamers shall otherwise observe the provisions of §§ 90.10 and 90.2 with respect to the signals for passing and the danger signal.

Starting, Stopping, and Backing Signals

(d)(1) The signals between the master or pilot and the engineer, when made by a bell, gong or whistle, shall be as follows:

1 whistle, bell or gong	Go ahead.
1 whistle, bell or gong	Stop.
2 whistles, bells or gongs	Back.
3 whistles, bells or gongs	Check.
4 whistles, bells or gongs	Strong.
4 whistles, bells or gongs	All right.

(2) Two whistles, two bells or two gongs shall always mean back, irrespective of other signals previously given.

Warning Signals for Coast Guard Vessels While Handling or Servicing Aids to Navigation

SEC. 90.15a. (a) Coast Guard vessels while engaged in handling or servicing an aid to navigation during the daytime may display from the yard two orange and white vertically striped balls in a vertical line not less than three feet nor more than six feet apart, and during the nighttime may display, in a position where they may best be seen, two red lights in a vertical line not less than three feet nor more than six feet apart.

(b) Vessels, with or without tows, passing Coast Guard vessels displaying this signal, shall reduce their speed sufficiently to insure the safety of both vessels, and when passing within 200 feet of the Coast Guard vessel displaying this signal, their speed shall not exceed 5 miles per hour.

Rules for Lights for Certain Classes of Vessels

Lights for Tugs under 100 Tons Register (Net) Whose Principal Business Is Harbor Towing

SEC. 90.16 (a) Tugs under 100 tons register (net) whose principal business is harbor towing, navigating the Great Lakes and their connecting and tributary waters as far east as Montreal, shall carry the red and green side lights carried by other steamers; and, at the foremast head, or, if the steamers have no foremast, then on top of the pilothouse, a white light so constructed as to show a uniform and unbroken light over an arc of the horizon of 20 points of the compass, and so fixed as to throw the light 10 points on each side of the vessel, namely, from right ahead to 2 points abaft the beam on either side, and of such a character as to be visible at a distance of at least 3 miles; and when towing, except when towing a raft, shall carry an additional white light of same character and construction as the headlight, and hung not less than 3 feet vertically above or below the headlight.

(b) When towing a raft, the two headlights shall be carried in a horizontal line athwartships not less than 4 feet apart, each so fixed as to throw the light all around the horizon, and of such character as to be visible at a distance of at least 3 miles.

Lights for Boats Navigating Only on the River St. Lawrence

SEC. 90.17 The lights for boats of all kinds navigating only on the River St. Lawrence as far east as Montreal shall be the same as required by law for vessels navigating the Great Lakes, and as required by the rules of the Commandant, for ferryboats, rafts, canal boats, and watercraft propelled by hand power, horsepower, or by the current of the river.

Lights for Ferryboats

SEC. 90.18 (a) Ferryboats propelled by steam or machinery and navigating the waters of the Great Lakes and their connecting and tributary waters as far east as Montreal shall carry the white light or lights and the colored side lights required by law to be carried on steam vessels navigating those waters, except that double-end ferryboats shall carry a central range of clear, bright, white lights, showing all around the horizon, placed at equal altitudes forward and aft, also on the starboard side a green light, and on the port side a red light, of such character as to be visible on a dark night with a clear atmosphere at a distance of at least 2 miles, and so constructed as to show a uniform and unbroken light over an arc of the horizon of ten points of the compass, and so fixed as to throw the light from right ahead to 2 points abaft the beam on their respective sides.

(b) The green and red lights shall be fitted with inboard screens projecting at least 3 feet forward from the lights, so as to prevent them from being seen across the bow.

(c) Officers in Charge, Marine Inspection,[3] in districts having ferryboats shall, whenever the safety of navigation may require, designate for each line of such boats a certain light, white or colored, which shall show all around the horizon, to designate and distinguish such lines from each other, which light shall be carried on a flagstaff amidships, 15 feet above the white range lights.

Lights for Canal Boats in Tow of Steam Vessels

SEC. 90.19 (a) Canal boats when in tow of steam vessels on the Great Lakes and their connecting and tributary waters as far east as Montreal shall carry lights as follows:

(1) Canal boats when towed astern of steam vessels and towed singly

---

[3] *For definition of an Officer in Charge, Marine Inspection, see Title 46, Code of Federal Regulations, Section 70.10-33.*

or tandem shall each carry a green light on the starboard side, a red light on the port side, and a small bright white light aft.

(2) When canal boats are towed at a hawser in one or more tiers, two or more abreast, the boat on the starboard side of each tier shall carry a green light on her starboard side, and the boat on the port side of each tier shall carry a red light on her port side, and each of the outside boats in the last tier shall also carry a small bright white light aft.

(3) When a canal boat is towed alongside and on the starboard side of a steamer, the boat towed shall carry a green light on the starboard side; and when towed on the port side of a steamer, the boat towed shall carry a red light on the port side.

(4) When two canal boats are towed alongside of a steamer, one on the starboard and one on the port side, the starboard boat shall carry a green light on the starboard side and the port boat shall carry a red light on the port side.

(b) The colored side lights referred to in this section for canal boats in tow of steam vessels shall be fitted with inboard screens, so as to prevent them from being seen across the bow, and of such a character as to be visible on a dark night, with a clear atmosphere, at a distance of at least 2 miles, and so constructed as to show a uniform and unbroken light over an arc of the horizon of 10 points of the compass, and so fixed as to throw the light from right ahead to 2 points abaft the beam on either side. The minimum size of glass globe shall not be less than 6 inches in diameter and 5 inches high in the clear.

(c) The small bright white light aft required to be carried on canal boats in tow shall not be visible forward of the beam.

Lights for Canal Boats Towed by Being Pushed Ahead

SEC. 90.19a When a tow of one or more canal boats is towed by being pushed ahead of a steam vessel such tow shall carry a green light on the starboard side and a red light on the port side so placed that they mark the tow at its maximum projection to starboard and port, respectively, and may carry an amber light at the extreme forward end of the tow as near the centerline as it is practicable to carry such light. The term "canal boats" as used in this section shall be construed to include barges, scows, and other craft of nondescript type not otherwise provided for by statute or regulations in this part. The amber light described shall show an unbroken light over an arc of the horizon of 20 points of the compass, so fixed as to throw the light ten points on each side, namely, from right ahead to 2 points abaft the beam on either side, and be of such a character as to be visible at a distance of at least three miles. The colored side lights shall be fitted with inboard screens, so as to prevent them from being seen across the bow, and of such a character as to be visible on a dark night, with a clear atmosphere, at a distance of at least 2 miles, and so constructed as to show a uniform and unbroken light over an arc of the horizon of 10 points of the compass, and so fixed as to throw the light from right ahead to 2 points abaft the beam on either side.

Lights for Watercraft Propelled by Hand Power, Horsepower, or by Current

SEC. 90.20 (a) Any vessel propelled by hand power, horsepower, or by the current of the river, navigating any bay, harbor, or river, of the Great Lakes, or which shall be anchored or moored in or near the channel or fairway of any bay, harbor, or river, of the Great Lakes, except rafts and rowing boats under oars, shall carry one white light forward not less than 8 feet above the surface of the water, which light shall be carried, from sunset to sunrise, in a lantern so fixed and constructed as to show a clear, uniform, and unbroken light, visible all around the horizon, and of such intensity as to be visible on a dark night with a clear atmosphere at a distance of at least 1 mile.

(b) Rowing boats under oars shall have ready at hand a lantern showing a white light which shall be temporarily exhibited in sufficient time to prevent collision.

Lights for Rafts

SEC. 90.21 (a) Rafts on the Great Lakes and their connecting and tributary waters as far east as Montreal, propelled by hand power, horsepower, or by the current of the river, or in tow, or which shall be anchored or moored in or near a channel or fairway of other vessels, shall carry lights as follows:

(1) Rafts of one crib and not more than two in length shall carry one white light. Rafts of three or more cribs in length and one crib in width shall carry one white light at each end of the raft. Rafts of more than one crib abreast shall carry one white light on each outside corner of the raft, making four lights in all.

(2) Bag or boom rafts navigating or anchored in the fairway of any bay, harbor, or river shall carry a bright white light at each end of the raft, and one of such lights on each side midway between the forward and after ends.

(b) The white lights required by this section for rafts shall be carried, from sunset to sunrise, in a lantern so fixed and constructed as to show a clear, uniform, and unbroken light, visible all around the horizon, and of such intensity as to be visible on a dark night with a clear atmosphere at a distance of at least 1 mile; which lights shall be suspended from poles of such height that the light shall not be less than 8 feet above the surface of the water.

Unauthorized Use of Lights; Unnecessary Whistling

Rule Relating to the Use of Searchlights or Other Blinding Lights

SEC. 90.22 Flashing the rays of a searchlight or other blinding light onto the bridge or into the pilothouse of any vessel under way is prohibited. Any person who shall flash or cause to be flashed the rays of a blinding light in violation of the above may be proceeded against in accordance with the provisions of R.S. 4450, as amended (46 U.S.C. 315), looking to the revocation or suspension of his license or certificate.

Rule Prohibiting Unnecessary Sounding of the Whistle

SEC. 90.23 Unnecessary sounding of the whistle is prohibited within any harbor limits of the United States. Whenever any licensed officer in charge of any vessel shall authorize or permit such unnecessary whistling, such officer may be proceeded against in accordance with the provisions of R.S. 4450, as amended (46 U.S.C. 375), looking to a revocation or suspension of his license.

Rule Prohibiting the Carrying of Unauthorized Lights on Vessels

SEC. 90.24 Any master or pilot of any vessel who shall authorize or permit the carrying of any light, electric or otherwise, not required by law, that in any way will interfere with distinguishing the signal lights, may be proceeded against in accordance with the provisions of R.S. 4450, as amended (46 U.S.C. 375), looking to a suspension or revocation of his license.

Warning Signals

Warning Signal Displayed While Transferring Dangerous Cargoes

SEC. 90.25 (a) *At a dock.* While fast to a dock, a vessel during the loading or unloading of hazardous or dangerous cargoes, such as explosives, combustible or inflammable liquids or gases, or certain chemicals in bulk, is required to display a red flag by day or a red light by night.

(b) *At anchor.* When at anchor, a vessel during the loading or unloading of such hazardous or dangerous cargoes is required to display a red flag by day. (No special warning signal is displayed at night.)[4]

---

[4] *The regulations in 46 CFR 35.30—1(a), 98.05—50(h), 98.10—45(g), 98.15—45(h), 98.25—90(f), and 146.29—25(o) require vessels to display warning signals when loading or unloading bulk cargoes of inflammable or combustible liquids or gases, elemental phosphorus in water, sulfuric acid, hydrochloric acid, liquid chlorine, or anhydrous ammonia, or military explosives.*

Distinctive Blue Light Authorized for Use by Law Enforcement Vessels

SEC. 90.30 (a) The use of a distinctive light described in paragraph (b) of this section is authorized for law enforcement vessels, and may be displayed during the day or night, whenever the vessel may be engaged in direct law enforcement activities where identification of the law enforcement vessel is desirable or where necessary for safety reasons. This light when used would be in addition to prescribed lights and day signals required by law or regulations in this part.

(b) The distinctive light prescribed is a blue colored, revolving horizontal beam, low intensity light, rotating or appearing to rotate because of a pulsating effect gained by means of a rotating reflector which causes a flashing or periodic peak intensity effect. The light shall be located at any effective point on the forward exterior of the vessel. A shield or other device, fixed or movable, to restrict the arc of visibility may be used if desired.

(c) The distinctive blue light described in this section may be displayed by law enforcement vessels of the United States, a State, or its political subdivisions, including municipalities, having administrative control over use of navigable waters, duly authorized by a controlling Federal or State governmental agency.

Interpretive Rulings, Great Lakes Rules[1]

PART 91[2]

Scope

SEC. 91.01–1 The regulations in this part are interpretive rulings with respect to "Rules of the Road" requirements applicable to all vessels of the United States while in the Great Lakes and their connecting and tributary waters as far east as Montreal and in the navigation of all other vessels upon such lakes and waters while within the territorial waters of the United States.

Penalties and Violations

SEC. 91.01–10 (a) Failure to comply with any law as interpreted will be considered as a violation of such law and the penalty may be assessed as provided by law.

(b) The reports of violations of the "Rules of the Road," as well as the

---

[1] *Code of Federal Regulations: Title 33—Navigation and Navigable Waters; Part 91—Interpretive Rulings—Great Lakes Rules.*

[2] *Authority: The provisions of this Part 91 issued under 80 Stat. 383, as amended, sec. 1, 63 Stat. 545 sec. 6(b)(1); 80 Stat. 937; 5 U.S.C. 552, 14 U.S.C. 633, 49 U.S.C. 1655(b)(1); 49 CFR 1.46(b).*

assessment, collection, mitigation or remission of civil penalties authorized by law, shall be in accordance with 33 CFR, Subpart 1.07.

White Lights for Motorboats Carried on Centerline

SEC. 91.05–1 Every white light required by section 3 of the Act of April 25, 1940, as amended (46 U.S.C. 526b), shall be carried on the centerline of the motorboat, except that the all-around white light aft on a motorboat of Class A or 1 may be carried off the centerline.

Anchorage and Navigation Regulations, St. Marys River, Michigan[1]

PART 92[2]

[1] Code of Federal Regulations: Title 33—Navigation and Navigable Waters; Part 92—Anchorage and Navigation Regulations, St. Marys River, Michigan.

[2] Authority: The provisions of this Part 92 issued under secs. 1–3, 29 Stat. 54–55, as amended sec. 6(b)(1), 80 Stat. 937; 33 U.S.C. 474, 49 U.S.C. 1655(b)(1); 49 CFR 1.46(b).

General Instructions

SEC. 92.01 The regulations in this part control vessel traffic in the United States waters of the St. Marys River between Point Iroquois and Point Detour, except the waters of the St. Marys Falls Canal. These regulations in this part shall not be considered to cover all of the obligations imposed by the law upon vessels and their operators, and shall not be construed as relieving the owners or persons operating vessels from any penalties which might be incurred in the violation of any of the general laws relating to shipping on the Great Lakes and tributary waters, or a violation of regulations issued pursuant to such laws.

Captain of the Port

SEC. 92.03 The Coast Guard officer to whom is assigned the duty of enforcing the rules and regulations in this part is designated "Captain of the Port." His office is at Sault Ste. Marie, Mich.

St. Marys River Patrol

SEC. 92.05 The St. Marys River patrol comprises all of the personnel and equipment of the Coast Guard employed by the captain of the port in the enforcement of the rules and regulations in this part.

District Engineer

SEC. 92.07 The officer of the United States Army Engineers in charge of the district is authorized to declare any channel closed when by reason of low water, obstruction, or obscurity in the channel or other cause, he deems such action necessary for the safety of shipping; and under contrary circumstances, or for the expediting of vessel passage, to declare any channel open. He or his local representative decides the proper disposition of dredging and wrecking outfits legally engaged in improving or clearing a channel, and the allowable maximum speed and draft of vessels in channels which are impaired temporarily. His decisions with respect to the foregoing are duly communicated to the Captain of the Port. The movements of vessels in the St. Marys Falls Canal are under the direction of the district engineer or his local representative.

Lookout Stations

SEC. 92.09 Lookout stations of the St. Marys River patrol are numbered and located as follows:
No. 3 off Mission Point, Little Rapids Cut.
No. 4 at upper end of Rock Cut, West Neebish Channel.

Routing of Traffic in Channels

SEC. 92.13 The routing of traffic through the several dredged channels is contingent upon the physical conditions in them; and the vessel masters should be prepared upon notice from the patrol, or through published notification, to follow such alternate route as may be prescribed, or to proceed with caution. Under normal conditions traffic passes up the Middle Neebish Channel, and down the West Neebish Channel; but it may be necessary in emergency to pass two-way traffic in either of those channels. It may also become necessary to close either or both channels for a short time owing to obscurity of navigation marks, in which case vessels should be prepared to anchor and wait a clearing away of obscurity.

Visual Signals at Lookout Stations

SEC. 92.15 (a) The following signals are hoisted at Lookout Station No. 4 to indicate changes in the conditions of channel passage, and masters of vessels approaching the entrances to the several channels should be on the alert for such signals:
(1) Closure of channel. Indicated by two red balls by day, two red lights by night, hoisted vertically about 6 feet apart.
(2) Channel partially obstructed. Indicated by a red ball over a white ball by day, a red light over a white light by night, hoisted vertically about 6 feet apart.
(b) Boats of the patrol may carry the signal described in paragraph (a) (1) of this section, as required.

Temporary Closure of West Neebish Channel

SEC. 92.19 (a) In the event the West Neebish Channel is temporarily closed to navigation (due to dredging, grounding of vessels, or other reasons), the resulting two-way navigation will pass through the Middle Neebish, Munuscong, and Sailors Encampment Channels. The closure and obstruction signals shall be shown from Lookout Station No. 4.

(b) In these channels between Lake Munuscong and Lake Nicolet, the westerly 300-foot portion of these channels provides a 27-foot depth and the easterly 200-foot portion provides a 21-foot depth. When vessel drafts permit upbound vessels shall use the easterly (21-foot depth) portion of these channels. All downbound vessels shall use the westerly (27-foot depth) portion of these channels.

(c) All the range lights marking the downbound or westerly (27-foot depth) portion of these channels will be white lights on red structures. All the range lights marking the upbound or easterly (21-foot depth) portion of these channels will be red lights on white structures.

(d) A downbound vessel when abeam of Nine-Mile Point may make a "Securité Call" to inform all traffic that she is now entering the two-way traffic channels.

Sound Signals Used by Patrol

SEC. 92.21 (a) Two short blasts and one long blast of whistle or horn indicate that the signalling unit desires to speak a passing vessel, and the signaled vessel will check speed and await orders. Vessels should use this signal to speak a lookout station or passing patrol boat.

(b) Three long blasts of whistle or horn indicate that the vessel signaled is moving at too high a rate of speed. This signal may be used by dredging and wrecking plants working in channels.

Definitions

SEC. 92.23 (a) The word "vessel," as used in this part, shall be held to include all types of floating craft and equipment. Where special provisions apply only to rafts, dredges, etc., the type will be specified by its class designation.

(b) Speed limits established in this part are expressed in terms of statute miles per hour over the ground.

Obedience to Instructions

SEC. 92.25 All persons in charge of or operating vessels in the St. Marys River are required to yield prompt and implicit obedience to the directions of the captain of the port and the officers and men of the St.

Marys River patrol, acting under his instructions, in connection with the enforcement of the rules and regulations in this part.

Reporting Procedures for Vessels Transiting the St. Marys River

SEC. *92.26* (a) Every upbound vessel, when abeam of Detour Reef Light shall notify the Coast Guard Control Office, St. Marys River Patrol (Radiotelephone call: "Soo Control"), of her time of passage at Detour Reef Light and her draft.

(b) Similarly, every downbound vessel, when abeam of Parisienne Island (Ile Parisienne), shall notify the Coast Guard Control Office, St. Marys River Patrol (Radiotelephone call: "Soo Control"), of her time of passage at Parisienne Island and her draft. Such vessel when making the turn from the Birch Point Range on to the Brush Point Range shall make a second call to "Soo Control" reporting her position. Such vessel when turning on to the Point aux Pins Channel Range at Brush Point (old Coast Guard Lookout Station No. 6) shall make a third call to "Soo Control" reporting her position.

Anchorage Grounds

SEC. *92.27* The authorized anchorage grounds are those areas outside of the dredged channels, and clear of the steering courses in other portions of the St. Marys River, between Point Iroquois and Point Detour. Vessels shall be anchored so as not to swing into channel limits or across steering courses.

Emergency Anchoring

SEC. *92.29* A vessel may be permitted in an emergency, due to breakdown of machinery or other accident or obscurity of navigation marks, to anchor in a dredged channel; but the vessel shall be anchored as near the edge of the channel as possible, and shall get under way and proceed as soon as the emergency ceases, unless otherwise directed.

Forbidden Anchorage

SEC. *92.31* It is forbidden to anchor a vessel at any time in the area to the southward of the Point aux Pins Range, lying between Brush Point and the waterworks intake crib off Big Point; also within a quarter mile of the said intake crib in any direction.

Dredging and Wrecking Plants in Channel

SEC. *92.33* Duly authorized dredging and wrecking plants, when engaged in improving or clearing a channel, will be permitted to anchor or moor in the channel under such conditions as may be prescribed by the district engineer or his local representative.

Shifting Anchorage When Directed

SEC. 92.35 The captain of the port, or the St. Marys River Patrol acting under his instructions, is empowered to cause any anchored vessel to shift anchorage when and as directed, whenever in the judgment of the enforcing officer such action is deemed necessary for the safety of vessels, the safe or expeditious passage of shipping, or the preservation or effective operation of Government installations. In enforcing this section the officer will have due regard for the hazards of navigation and vessel handling which may exist at the time, and under such circumstances will permit a reasonable delay in compliance by the vessel directed to move.

Order of Departure From Anchorage

SEC. 92.37 (a) Whenever vessels collect in any part of the river or on anchorage grounds, by reason of temporary closure of channel or impediment to navigation, the order of getting under way and proceeding by the vessels so collected shall be the order in which they arrived at the place of assembly, unless otherwise directed by a unit of the patrol. The patrol is authorized to advance any vessel in the order of procedure to expedite the movement of mails, passengers, or cargo of a perishable nature, or to facilitate passage of vessels through any channel when partially obstructed by ice or by other causes, or to facilitate passage through the locks as indicated to the patrol by the officer in charge of the St. Marys River Canal.

(b) When by reason of ice or other special conditions, it is obvious that low-power vessels, vessels of particular construction, tows or rafts cannot maintain their order of proceeding and constitute a hazard to other vessels capable of proceeding, the Captain of the Port may declare emergency conditions existing and temporarily refuse such vessel permission to enter or proceed in the river.

Visual Signals for Dredges and Wrecking Plants

SEC. 92.39 Dredges and wrecking plants while engaged in working on the St. Marys River shall display the visual signals prescribed for them by the Department of the Army.

Visual Signals on Vessel Aground in Channel

SEC. 92.41 A vessel aground in a dredged channel shall carry from sunset to sunrise in addition to the white light or lights prescribed for a vessel at anchor, two red lights hoisted vertically not less than 3 feet apart, in such position and height as to be readily visible to vessels bound up and down the channel.

Sound Signals for Vessel Aground in the Channel

SEC. 92.43 A vessel aground in a channel shall sound several short and rapid blasts of her whistle, not less than five, upon the approach of another vessel bound up or down the channel. If the approaching vessel cannot pass with safety, she shall stop and make proper dispositions to avoid fouling the grounded vessel, and shall upon the approach of another vessel coming up astern sound the same signal. Should additional vessels approach from that same direction, it shall be the duty of the last vessel in line to sound this signal. In times of low visibility, the signal described herein shall be in addition to the prescribed fog signal.

Special Sound Signal for Middle Neebish Channel

SEC. 92.45 When two-way traffic is prescribed for Middle Neebish Channel, a downbound vessel when abreast of Coyle Point shall sound a blast of her whistle of at least 8 seconds' duration, and an upbound vessel when abreast of Everens Point shall sound the same signal.

Temporary Closure of Channel

SEC. 92.47 When any channel is closed or under limited traffic conditions, no vessel shall proceed in accordance with the provisions of § 92.37, without specific orders from the patrol.

Speed Limit for Vessels of 50 Gross Tons or Over

SEC. 92.49 This section applies to any vessel of 50 gross tons or over navigating the stated reaches of the St. Marys River. (a) Except as modified by paragraphs (c) and (d) of this section and §§ 92.53 and 92.55, a vessel shall not exceed a speed of 12 statute miles per hour over the ground between the following points:
(1) Upbound:
(i) Everens Point and Nine Mile Point.
(ii) Six Mile Point Range Rear Light and Big Point.
(2) Downbound:
(i) Big Point and Six Mile Point Range Rear Light.
(ii) Nine Mile Point and lower end of West Neebish Channel.
(b) Except as modified by paragraph (d) of this section a vessel shall not exceed a speed of 10 statute miles per hour over the ground in the Sailors Encampment Channel between Everens Point and Johnson Point, the Middle Neebish Dike Cut (Middle Neebish Channel Light 50 to Lake

Nicolet Lighted Buoy 62), or the West Neebish Rock Cut (West Neebish Channel Light 33 to West Neebish Channel Light 25).

(c) Except as modified by paragraph (d) of this section, a vessel shall not exceed a speed of 15 statute miles per hour over the ground between the following points:

(1) Upbound between Nine Mile Point and Six Mile Point Range Rear Light.

(2) Downbound between Six Mile Point Range Rear Light and Nine Mile Point.

(d) The Commander, Ninth Coast Guard District is delegated authority to reduce any or all speed limits specified in paragraphs (a), (b), or (c) of this section. In exercising this authority the District Commander shall consider all interests affected by the speed of vessels in the river, including the protection of the property of riparian owners. The regulations issued by the District Commander shall be published in the *Federal Register* and in the *Notice to Mariners.*

Speed Limits; Two-Way Traffic

SEC. 92.53 When one of the lower channels is closed, making it necessary to accommodate two-way traffic in the Middle Neebish or the West Neebish Channel, vessels of 500 gross tons or over shall not exceed a speed of 10 statute miles per hour in the following named reaches:

(a) Between Everens Point, Lake Munuscong, and Nine-Mile Point, Lake Nicolet.

(b) Between Nine-Mile Point, Lake Nicolet, and the lower end of West Neebish Channel in Lake Munuscong.

Speed Limit Approaching St. Marys Falls Canal

SEC. 92.55 Vesels approaching the St. Marys Falls Canal shall at all times reduce speed to the extent of being under full control with ability to maneuver in accordance with the instructions of the officers in charge of the St. Marys Falls Canal before entering the canal.

Pipe Island Passages

SEC. 92.57 Vessels of 500 gross tons or over shall leave Pipe Island Shoal and Pipe Island on the port hand in passing them, except that an upbound vessel which will stop at one of the Detour Coal Wharves above Watson Reefs may pass to the westward of the shoal and island.

Directional Neebish Channels

SEC. 92.59 When both the Middle Neebish Channel and the West

Neebish Channel are available to traffic, vessels of 100 gross tons or over shall pass upbound through Middle Neebish Channel and downbound through West Neebish Channel. Vessels over the prescribed tonnage making regular local stops in either of those channels may run counter to the general traffic direction only on written permit issued by the captain of the port, for such term and under such conditions of renewal or revocation as he may prescribe. A vessel thus running counter to the general traffic shall keep off the channel range when an approaching vessel is on or entering that range.

Passing and Approach in Channels

SEC. 92.61 (a) In a channel where the speed is restricted to 12 miles an hour or less, no vessel of 500 gross tons or over shall approach nearer than one-quarter of a mile to a vessel bound in the same direction, nor pass such a vessel except between Little Rapids Cut Lighted Buoy No. 105 and the St. Marys Falls Canal, and for upbound vessels, only between Vidal Shoal and Big Point or except as provided in paragraph (b) of this section and § 92.63.

(b) In order to facilitate passing in Lake Nicolet, upbound vessels may, after passing Lake Nicolet Lighted Buoy No. 68 off Shingle Bay, approach not nearer than 500 feet to a vessel bound in the same direction.

Vessel Passing Towing Tug Going in Same Direction

SEC. 92.63 A vessel at normal speed coming up on a tug towing a dredge or scow bound in the same direction as the overtaking vessel in a restricted channel may pass such tow, after the prescribed exchange of signals. Under such circumstances the tug shall not increase speed during the passing, and shall haul with its tow to the proper side of the channel to allow passing room.

Vessels Going in Same Direction; When Passing Prohibited

SEC. 92.65 No vessels shall pass or attempt to pass another vessel bound in the same direction, when such passing would bring more than two vessels abreast, in any of the passages between Lake Munuscong Junction Lighted Bell Buoy in Upper Lake Munuscong and Big Point in upper St. Marys River, except that such passing is permitted between Little Rapids Cut Lighted Buoy No. 105 and the St. Marys Falls Canal.

Towing Vessels; Hauling Clear of Ranges; Tow Lines

SEC. 92.67 (a) Towing vessels engaged in shortening or lengthening tows or dropping or making up tows, mooring or unmooring or anchoring or hoisting anchor, loading or discharging stores or cargo from boats alongside, or awaiting supply boats, shall haul clear of the ranges and permit unobstructed passage to other vessels.

(b) On the connecting waters of the Great Lakes between Point Iroquois, upper St. Marys River and Frying Pan Island, lower St. Marys River, the length of tow lines shall not exceed by more than 50 feet the length of the scow, barge, vessel, or other craft being towed: Provided, That no scow, barge, vessel, or other craft shall be required to have a tow line less than 250 feet. The length of the tow line shall be measured from the stern of one vessel to the bow of the following vessel.

Dropping of Towed Vessels

SEC. 92.69 Towed vessels shall not be dropped in any of the usual steering courses, but shall be hauled clear of the course before being left by the towing vessel.

Speed Through Dredged Channels

SEC. 92.71 The minimum speed at which any vessel or tow will be permitted to make regular passage through any dredged channel shall be 5 miles an hour over the ground; and any craft which cannot make this speed shall not enter any of the channels until the patrol has been communicated with, and directions received as to further procedure.

Navigation of Dredged Channels by Sail

SEC. 92.73 Vessels of 10 gross tons or over shall not navigate any dredged channel under sail power; and such vessel capable of propulsion by both machinery and sail shall not carry sail in any of the dredged channels.

Obstruction of Traffic; Retarding Other Vessels

SEC. 92.75 No vessel shall maneuver so as to affect adversely the relative position of another vessel when entering any of the cuts, nor attempt to obstruct traffic, nor unnecessarily retard a following vessel, nor increase speed after having signaled permission to an overtaking vessel to pass.

Rafts in Channels

SEC. 92.77 No raft shall enter any of the dredged channels between Everens Point and the improved channel above Round Island without first having communicated with the patrol and obtained permission and directions as to route and procedure. So long as rafts are in any portion of the passages between the points named they shall be under the control of the patrol, and shall obey all instructions as to time and manner of movement or stoppage. They shall use the Lake George Channel when it will serve their passage toward destination.

Reporting Obstruction of Channel

SEC. 92.79 Any person having knowledge of an obstruction in the channel, or the loss of an anchor, or the grounding of a vessel in or out of the channel, or the striking of any obstruction, or any other hazard or danger to navigation, at any point in the St. Marys River between Point Detour and Point Iroquois, shall report the same without delay to the Captain of the Port and also to the Corps of Engineers' Control Tower, St. Marys Falls Canal.

Government Vessels

SEC. 92.81 Vessels when signaled to do so shall give way to boats of the St. Marys River patrol, and to United States vessels on duty in connection with the maintenance of channels, and accord the right of way to such boats and vessels.

Small Craft

SEC. 92.83 (a) Motorboats as defined by section 1 of an act of Congress approved April 25, 1940 (54 Stat. 163; 46 U.S.C. 526), shall be considered amenable to the provisions of §§ 92.25 to 92.31, inclusive, 92.35, 92.79, and 92.81.

(b) Sail vessels under 10 gross tons shall be considered amenable to the provisions of §§ 92.25 to 92.31, inclusive, and 92.35.

APPENDIX M

Corps of Engineers, Regulations for the Great Lakes[1]

PART 201[2]

Sec.

201.1 Scope and applicability of regulations.

Lights and Day Signals

201.2 Signals to be displayed by a towing vessel when towing a submerged or partly submerged object upon a hawser when no signals can be displayed upon the object which is towed.

201.3 Steam vessels, derrick boats, lighters, or other types of vessels made fast alongside a wreck, or moored over a wreck which is on the bottom or partly submerged, or which may be drifting.

201.4 Dredges held in stationary position by moorings or spuds.

201.5 Self-propelling suction dredges underway and engaged in dredging operations.

201.6 Vessels moored or anchored and engaged in laying cables or pipe, submarine construction, excavation, mat sinking, bank grading, dike construction, revetment, or other bank protection operations.

[1] *Code of Federal Regulations: Title 33—Navigation and Navigable waters; Part 201—General Regulations.*

[2] *Authority: The provisions of this Part 201, issued under sec. 4, 28 Stat. 362 as amended; 33 U.S.C. 1.*

Section 7 of the River and Harbor Act of August 8, 1917, as amended (33 U.S.C. 1), provides as follows:

It shall be the duty of the Secretary of the Army to prescribe such regulations for the use, administration, and navigation of the navigable waters of the United States as in his judgment the public necessity may require for the protection of life and property, or of operations of the United States in channel improvement, covering all matters not specifically delegated by law to some other executive department. Such regulations shall be posted, in conspicuous and appropriate places, for the information of the public; and every person and every corporation which shall violate such regulations shall be deemed guilty of a misdemeanor and, on conviction thereof in any district court of the United States within whose territorial jurisdiction such offense may have been committed, shall be punished by a fine not exceeding $500, or by improvement (in the case of a natural person) not exceeding six months, in the discretion of the court.

In pursuance of the above-quoted law, the following regulations have been prescribed.

Scope and Applicability of Regulations[3]

SEC. 201.1 (a) The regulations contained in this part govern night and day signals to be displayed by towing vessels with tows on which no signals can be displayed, vessels working on wrecks, dredges, and vessels engaged in laying cables or pipe or in submarine or bank protection operations, lights to be displayed on dredge pipe lines, and day signals to be displayed by vessels of more than 65 feet in length moored or

---

[3] *These regulations, despite omitted language to the contrary in Sec. 201.1 (b), are now applicable only to the Great Lakes and their connecting and tributary waters. Their application has been limited by Coast Guard Pilot Rules for other waters. For Inland Waters, see Sections 80.18 to 80.31a. For Western Rivers, see Sections 95.51 to 95.66.*

anchored in a fairway or channel (§§ 201.2 to 201.9, inclusive), and the passing by other vessels of floating plant working in navigable channels (§§ 201.10 to 201.16, inclusive).

(b) The regulations contained in this part are applicable on the Great Lakes and their connecting and tributary waters as far east as Montreal.

Lights and Day Signals

Signals to Be Displayed by a Towing Vessel When Towing a Submerged or Partly Submerged Object Upon a Hawser When No Signals Can Be Displayed Upon the Object Which is Towed

SEC. 201.2 (a) The vessel having the submerged object in tow shall display by day, where they can best be seen, two shapes, one above the other, not less than six feet apart, the lower shape to be carried not less than 10 feet above the deck house. The shapes shall be in the form of a double frustum of a cone, base to base, not less than two feet in diameter at the center nor less than eight inches at the ends of the cones, and to be not less than four feet lengthwise from end to end, the upper shape to be painted in alternate horizontal stripes of black and white, eight inches in width, and the lower shape to be painted a solid bright red.

(b) By night the towing vessel shall display the regular side lights, but in lieu of the regular white towing lights shall display four lights in a vertical position not less than three feet nor more than six feet apart, the upper and lower of such lights to be white, and the two middle lights to be red, all of such lights to be the same character as the regular towing lights.

Steam Vessels, Derrick Boats, Lighters, or Other Types of Vessels Made Fast Alongside a Wreck, or Moored Over a Wreck Which Is on the Bottom or Partly Submerged, or Which May Be Drifting

SEC. 201.3 (a) Steam vessels, derrick boats, lighters, or other types of vessels made fast alongside a wreck, or moored over a wreck which is on the bottom or partly submerged, or which may be drifting, shall display by day two shapes of the same character and dimensions and displayed in the same manner as required by § 201.2 (a), except that both shapes shall be painted a solid bright red, but where more than one vessel is working under the above conditions, the shapes need be displayed only from one vessel on each side of the wreck from which they can best be seen from all directions.

(b) By night this situation shall be indicated by the display of a white light from the bow and stern of each outside vessel or lighter not less than six feet above the deck, and in addition thereto there shall be displayed in a position where they can best be seen from all directions two red lights carried in a vertical line not less than three feet nor more than six feet apart, and not less than 15 feet above the deck.

Dredges Held in Stationary Position by Moorings or Spuds

SEC. 201.4 (a) Dredges which are held in stationary position by moorings or spuds shall display by day two red balls not less than two feet in diameter and carried in a vertical line not less than three feet nor more than six feet apart, and at least 15 feet above the deck house and in a position where they can best be seen from all directions.

(b) By night they shall display a white light at each corner, not less than six feet above the deck, and in addition thereto there shall be displayed in a position where they can best be seen from all directions two red lights carried in a vertical line not less than three feet nor more than six feet apart, and not less than 15 feet above the deck. When scows are moored alongside a dredge in the foregoing situation they shall display a white light on each outboard corner, not less than six feet above the deck.

Self-propelling Suction Dredges Under Way and Engaged in Dredging Operations

SEC. 201.5 (a) Self-propelling suction dredges under way and engaged in dredging operations shall display by day two black balls not less than two feet in diameter and carried in a vertical line not less than 15 feet above the deck house, and where they can best be seen from all directions. The term "dredging operations" shall include maneuvering into or out of position at the dredging site, but shall not include proceeding to and from the site.

(b) By night they shall carry, in addition to the regular running lights, two red lights of the same character as the white masthead lights and in a vertical line beneath that light, the red lights to be not less than three feet nor more than six feet apart and the upper red light to be not less than four feet nor more than six feet below the masthead light, and on or near the stern two red lights in a vertical line not less than four feet nor more than six feet apart, to show through four points of the compass; that is, from right astern to two points on each quarter.

Vessels Moored or Anchored and Engaged in Laying Cables or Pipe, Submarine Construction, Excavation, Mat Sinking, Bank Grading, Dike Construction, Revetment, or Other Bank Protection Operations

SEC. 201.6 (a) Vessels which are moored or anchored and engaged in laying cables or pipe, submarine construction, excavation, mat sinking, bank grading, dike construction, revetment, or other bank protection operations, shall display by day, not less than 15 feet above the deck, where they can best be seen from all directions, two balls not less than two feet in diameter, in a vertical line not less than three feet nor more than six feet apart, the upper ball to be painted in alternate black and white vertical stripes six inches wide, and the lower ball to be painted a solid bright red,

(b) By night they shall display three red lights, carried in a vertical line not less than three feet nor more than six feet apart, in a position where they can best be seen from all directions, with the lowermost light not less than 15 feet above the deck.

(c) Where a stringout of moored vessels or barges is engaged in the operations, three red lights carried as prescribed in paragraph (b) of this section shall be displayed at the channelward end of the stringout. Where the stringout crosses the navigable channel and is to be opened for the passage of vessels, the three red lights shall be displayed at each side of the opening instead of at the outer end of the stringout. There shall also be displayed upon such stringout one horizontal row of amber lights not less than six feet above the deck, or above the deck house where the craft carries a deck house, in a position where they can best be seen from all directions, spaced not more than 50 feet apart so as to mark distinctly the entire length and course of the stringout.

Lights to Be Displayed on Pipe Lines

SEC. 201.7 Pipe lines attached to dredges, and either floating or supported on trestles, shall display by night one row of amber lights not less than eight feet nor more than 12 feet above the water, about equally spaced and in such number as to mark distinctly the entire length and course of the line, the intervals between lights where the line crosses navigable channels to be not more than 30 feet. There shall also be displayed on the shore or discharge end of the line two red lights, three feet apart, in a vertical line with the lower light at least eight feet above the water, and if the line is to be opened at night for the passage of vessels, a similar arrangement of lights shall be displayed on each side of the opening.

Lights Generally

SEC. 201.8 (a) All the lights required by §§ 201.2 to 201.7, inclusive, except as provided in §§ 201.2 (b) and 201.5 (b), shall be of such character as to be visible on a dark night with a clear atmosphere for a distance of at least two miles.

(b) The lights required by § 201.2 (b) to be of the same character as the regular towing lights, and the lights required by § 201.5 (b) to be of the same character as the masthead light, shall be of such character as to be visible on a dark night with a clear atmosphere for a distance of at least five miles.

(c) All floodlights or headlights which may interfere with the proper navigation of an approaching vessel shall be so shielded that the lights will not blind the pilot of such vessel.

Vessels Moored or at Anchor

SEC. 201.9 Vessels of more than 65 feet in length when moored or anchored in a fairway or channel shall display between sunrise and sunset on the forward part of the vessel where it can best be seen from other vessels one black ball not less than two feet in diameter.

Passing Floating Plant Working in Navigable Channels[4]

Passing Signals

SEC. 201.10 (a) Vessels intending to pass dredges or other types of floating plant working in navigable channels, when within a reasonable distance therefrom and not in any case over a mile, shall indicate such intention by one long blast of the whistle, and shall be directed to the proper side for passsage by the sounding, by the dredge or other floating plant, of the signal prescribed in the local pilot rules for vessels under way and approaching each other from opposite directions, which shall be answered in the usual manner by the approaching vessel. If the channel is not clear, the floating plant shall sound the alarm or danger signal and the approaching vessel shall slow down or stop and await further signal from the plant.

(b) When the pipe line from a dredge crosses the channel in such a way that an approaching vessel cannot pass safely around the pipe line or dredge, there shall be sounded immediately from the dredge the alarm or danger signal and the approaching vessel shall slow down or stop and await further signal from the dredge. The pipe line shall then be opened and the channel cleared as soon as practicable; when the channel is clear for passage the dredge shall so indicate by sounding the usual passing signal as prescribed in paragraph (a) of this section. The approaching vessel shall answer with a corresponding signal and pass promptly.

(c) When any pipe line or swinging dredge shall have given an approaching vessel or tow the signal that the channel is clear, the dredge shall straighten out within the cut for the passage of the vessel or tow.

[4] *The term "floating plant" as used in §§ 201.10 to 201.16 inclusive, includes dredges, derrick boats, snag boats, drill boats, pile drivers, maneuver boats, hydraulic graders, survey boats, working barges, and mat sinking plant.*

Speed of Vessels Passing Floating Plant Working in Channels

SEC. 201.11 Vessels, with or without tows, passing floating plant working in channels, shall reduce their speed sufficiently to insure the safety of both the plant and themselves, and when passing within 200 feet of the plant their speed shall not exceed five miles per hour. While passing over lines of the plant, propelling machinery shall be stopped.

Lightdraft Vessels Passing Floating Plant

SEC. 201.12 Vessels whose draft permits shall keep outside the buoys marking the ends of mooring lines of floating plant working in channels.

Aids to Navigation, Marking Floating Plant Moorings

SEC. 201.13 Breast, stern, and bow anchors of floating plant working in navigable channels shall be marked by barrel or other suitable buoys. By night approaching vessels shall be shown the location of adjacent buoys by throwing a suitable beam of light from the plant on the buoys until the approaching vessel has passed, or the buoys may be lighted by red lights, visible in all directions, of the same character as specified in § 201.8 (a).

Obstruction of Channel by Floating Plant

SEC. 201.14 Channels shall not be obstructed unnecessarily by any dredge or other floating plant. While vessels are passing such plant all lines running therefrom across the channel on the passing side which may interfere with or obstruct navigation shall be slacked to the bottom of the channel.

Clearing of Channels

SEC. 201.15 When special or temporary regulations have not been prescribed and action under the regulations contained in sections 201.10 to 201.14, will not afford clear passage, floating plant in narrow channels shall, upon notice, move out of the way of vessels a sufficient distance to allow them a clear passage. Vessels desiring passage shall, however, give the master of the floating plant ample notice in advance of the time they expect to pass.[5]

Protection of Marks Placed for the Guidance of Floating Plant

SEC. 201.16 Vessels shall not run over anchor buoys, or buoys, stakes,

[5] *If it is necessary to prohibit or limit the anchorage or movement of vessels within certain areas in order to facilitate the work of improvement, application should be made through official channels for establishment by the Secretary of the Army of special or temporary regulations for this purpose.*

or other marks placed for the guidance of floating plant working in channels; and shall not anchor on the ranges of buoys, stakes, or other marks placed for the guidance of such plant.

Lights for Great Lakes Pilot Vessels

SEC. 201.20 (a) A power-driven pilot vessel engaged in pilotage duty and under way:

(1) Shall carry a white light at the masthead at a height of not less than 20 feet above the hull visible all round the horizon at a distance of at least 3 miles and at a distance of 8 feet below it a red light similar in construction and character. If such a vessel is of less than 65 feet in length the vessel may carry the white light at a height of not less than 9 feet above the gunwale and the red light at a distance of 4 feet below the white light.

(2) Shall carry the sidelights prescribed by Great Lakes Rule 3 (33 U.S.C. 252) or by the Act of April 25, 1940 (46 U.S.C. 526b), as appropriate, and a white light at the stem showing an unbroken light over an arc of the horizon of 135°, so fixed as to show the light 6/1/2° from right aft on each side of the vessel, and of such character as to be visible at a distance of at least 2 miles.

(3) Shall show one or more flareup lights at intervals not exceeding 10 minutes. An intermittant white light visible all round the horizon may be used in lieu of flareup lights.

(b) A sailing pilot vessel when engaged on pilotage duty and under way:

(1) Shall carry a white light at the masthead visible all round the horizon at a distance of at least 3 miles.

(2) Shall be provided with the sidelights prescribed in paragraph (a)(2) of this section or the portable lanterns prescribed by Great Lakes Rule 8 (33 U.S.C. 257), as appropriate, and shall, on the near approach of or to other vessels, have such lights ready for use, and shall show them at short intervals to indicate the direction in which the pilot vessel is heading, but the green light shall not be shown on the port side nor the red light on the starboard side. The vessel shall also carry the stern light prescribed in paragraph (a)(2) of this section.

(3) Shall show one or more flareup lights at intervals not exceeding 10 minutes.

(c) A pilot vessel when engaged on pilotage duty and not under way shall carry the lights and show the flares prescribed in paragraphs (a)(1) and (3) or (b)(1) and (3) of this section, as appropriate, and if at anchor shall also carry the anchor lights prescribed in Great Lakes Rule 9 (33 U.S.C. 258).

(d) A pilot vessel when not engaged on pilotage duty shall show the lights or shapes for a similar vessel of the same length.

APPENDIX N
Western Rivers Rules[1]

SECTIONS OF THE REVISED STATUTES OF THE UNITED STATES TO THE NAVIGATION OF VESSELS ON THE MISSISSIPPI, ATCHAFALAYA, AND THE RED RIVER OF THE NORTH

All Vessels

SEC. 4233 The following regulations for preventing collisions shall be followed by all vessels upon the waters of the Mississippi River between its source and the Huey P. Long Bridge and all of the tributaries emptying thereinto and their tributaries, and that part of the Atchafalaya River above its junction with the Plaquemine-Morgan City alternate waterway, and the Red River of the North; and are hereby declared special rules duly made by local authority.

I—Preliminary Definitions

RULE NUMBERED 1 In the following rules every steam vessel which is under sail and not under power is to be considered a sailing vessel, and every vessel under power, whether under sail or not, is to be considered a steam vessel.

The words "steam vessel" shall include any vessel propelled by machinery.

A vessel is "under way" within the meaning of these rules when she is not at anchor, or made fast to the shore, or aground.

The word "visible" in these rules, when applied to lights, shall mean visible on a dark night with a clear atmosphere.

The words "distinct blast" in these rules, when applied to whistle signals shall mean a clearly audible blast of any length.

[1] R. S. 4233, 4233A, 4233B, 4233C, and 4487, as amended; 33 U.S.C. 301-356, 46 U.S.C. 480.

II—Lights, and So Forth

RULE NUMBERED 2 The rules concerning lights shall be complied with in all weathers from sunset to sunrise, and during such time no other lights which may be mistaken for the prescribed lights, or impair their visibility, shall be exhibited.

RULE NUMBERED 3 A steam vessel when towing another vessel or vessels alongside or by pushing ahead shall carry—

(a) On the starboard side a green light so constructed and fixed as to show the light from ahead and not more than half a point on the port bow to two points abaft the beam on the starboard side, and of such a character as to be visible at a distance of at least three miles.

(b) On the port side a red light so constructed and fixed as to show the light from ahead and not more than half a point on the starboard bow, to two points abaft the beam on the port side, and of such a character as to be visible at a distance of at least three miles.

(c) The said green and red side lights shall be fitted with inboard screens painted black and projecting at least three feet forward from the light, so as to prevent these lights from being seen more than half a point across the bow.

(d) At or near the stern, where they can best be seen, two amber lights in a vertical line, one over the other, not less than three feet apart, of such a character as to be visible from aft for a distance of at least two miles, and so screened as not to be visible forward of the beam.

RULE NUMBERED 4 A steam vessel when towing another vessel or vessels on a hawser astern shall carry, in addition to the side lights described in rule 3 (a), (b), and (c) and at a greater height than those lights, in the forward half of the vessel, two bright white lights in a vertical line, one over the other, at least three feet apart. Each of these lights shall be so constructed as to show an unbroken light over an arc of twenty points of the compass, so fixed as to throw the light ten points on each side of the vessel, namely, from right ahead to two points abaft the beam on either side and of such a character as to be visible at a distance of at least three miles.

RULE NUMBERED 5 A seagoing steam vessel under way shall carry lights as required by article 2, International Rules, as amended.[2]

RULE NUMBERED 6 A river steamer, by which is meant a river-type steam vessel with two smokestacks in an athwartship line, may carry, in lieu of the lights prescribed by rule 7 (a), the following lights, namely: One red light on the outboard side of the port smokestack and one green light

---

[2] *Now Rule 23, 1972 International Rules.*

on the outboard side of the starboard smokestack. Such lights shall show forward, aft, and abeam on their respective sides.

RULE NUMBERED 7 (a) A steam vessel under way, except as otherwise provided in these rules, shall carry, in addition to side lights as described in rule 3 (a), (b), and (c), a central range of two white lights, the after light being carried at an elevation higher than the light at the head of the vessel. The headlight shall be so constructed as to show an unbroken light through twenty points of the compass, namely, from right ahead to two points abaft the beam on either side of the vessel, and the after light so as to show all around the horizon.

(b) The lights for barges, canal boats, scows, and other vessels of non-descript type, when in tow of steam vessels, and for ferryboats, shall be as prescribed by the Commandant, United States Coast Guard.

RULE NUMBERED 8 A sailing vessel under way, and any vessel being towed except barges, canal boats, scows, and other vessels of nondescript type when in tow of steam vessels, shall carry screened side lights as prescribed by rule 3, sections (a), (b), and (c), for a steam vessel, and a stern light as prescribed by rule 10.

RULE NUMBERED 9 Whenever, as in the case of small vessels during bad weather, the green and red lights cannot be fixed, these lights shall be kept on deck, on their respective sides of the vessel, ready for instant exhibition, and shall, on the approach of or to other vessels, be exhibited on their respective sides in sufficient time to prevent collision, in such manner as to make them most visible, and so that the green light shall not be seen on the port side, nor the red light on the starboard side. To make the use of these portable lights more certain and easy, they shall each be painted outside with the color of the light they respectively contain, and shall be provided with suitable screens.

RULE NUMBERED 10 (a) A vessel when under way, if not otherwise required by these rules to carry one or more lights visible from aft, shall carry at her stern a white light, so constructed that it shall show an unbroken light over an arc of the horizon of twelve points of the compass, so fixed as to show the light six points from right aft on each side of the vessel, and of such a character as to be visible at a distance of at least two miles. Such light shall be carried as nearly as practicable on the same level as the side lights.

(b) In a small vessel, if it is not possible on account of bad weather or other sufficient cause for this light to be fixed, an electric torch or a lighted lantern shall be kept at hand ready for use and shall, on the approach of an overtaking vessel, be shown in sufficient time to prevent collision.

RULE NUMBERED 11 (a) Sailing pilot vessels, when engaged on their station on pilotage duty, and not at anchor, shall not show the lights required for other vessels, but shall carry a white light at the masthead, visible all around the horizon, at a distance of at least three miles, and shall also exhibit a flare-up light or flare-up lights at short intervals, which shall never exceed ten minutes.

On the near approach of or to other vessels, they shall have their side lights lighted, ready for use, and shall flash or show them at short intervals to indicate the direction in which they are heading, but the green light shall not be shown on the port side, nor the red light on the starboard side.

A sailing pilot vessel of such a class as to be obliged to go alongside of a vessel to put a pilot on board may show the white light instead of carrying it at the masthead, and may, instead of the side lights above mentioned, have at hand, ready for use, a lantern with a green glass on the one side and a red glass on the other, to be used as prescribed above.

(b) A steam pilot vessel when engaged on her station on pilotage duty and not at anchor shall, in addition to the lights and flares required for sailing pilot vessels, carry, at a distance of eight feet below her white masthead lights, a red light, visible all around the horizon at a distance of at least three miles, and also the side lights required to be carried by vessels when under way.

(c) All pilot vessels, when engaged on their stations on pilotage duty and at anchor, shall carry the lights and show the flares prescribed above, except that the side lights shall not be shown.

When not engaged on their stations on pilotage duty they shall carry the same lights as other vessels of their class and tonnage.

RULE NUMBERED 12 Motorboats, when not engaged in towing, shall be lighted as provided by the Motorboat Act of April 25, 1940, as amended. When towing, they shall be subject to the same provisions for lighting as other steam vessels towing.

RULE NUMBERED 13[3] (a) Except as provided in paragraph (c) of this rule, a vessel under one hundred and fifty feet in length, when at anchor, shall carry forward, where it can best be seen, a white light in a lantern so constructed as to show a clear, uniform, and unbroken light visible all around the horizon at a distance of at least two miles.

(b) Except as provided in paragraph (c) of this rule, a vessel of one hundred and fifty feet or upward in length, when at anchor, shall carry in the forward part of the vessel, at a height of not less than twenty feet above the hull, one such light, and at or near the stern of the vessel, at such a height that it shall not be less than fifeen feet lower than the forward light, another such light.

---

[3] *Functions, powers, and duties of Secretary of the Army re water vessel anchorage under Rule Number 13 were transferred to Secretary of Transportation on October 15, 1966, by Public Law 89-670, 49 U.S.C. 1655 (g) (1) (B), (C), and (D).*

(c) The Secretary of the Army may, after investigation, by rule, regulation, or order, designate such areas as he may deem proper as "special anchorage areas"; such special anchorage areas may from time to time be changed, or abolished, if after investigation the Secretary of the Army shall deem such change or abolition in the interests of navigation. When anchored within such an area—

(1) a vessel of not more than sixty-five feet in length shall not be required to carry or exhibit the white light required by this rule;

(2) a barge, canal boat, scow, or other nondescript craft of one hundred and fifty feet or upward in length may carry and exhibit the single white light prescribed by paragraph (a) of this rule in lieu of the two white lights prescribed by paragraph (b) of this rule; and

(3) where two or more barges, canal boats, scows, or other nondescript craft are tied together and anchored as a unit, the anchor light prescribed by this rule need be displayed only on the vessel having its anchor down.

RULE NUMBERED 14 The exhibition of any light on board of a vessel of war of the United States or a Coast Guard cutter may be suspended whenever, in the opinion of the Secretary of the Navy, the commander in chief of a squadron, or the commander of a vessel acting singly, the special character of the service may require it.

RULE NUMBERED 15 All signals prescribed by this article for vessels under way shall be given —

By "steam vessels" on the whistle or siren.

By sailing vessels and "vessels towed" on the foghorn.

A steam vessel shall be provided with an efficient whistle or siren, sounded by steam or by some substitute for steam, so placed that the sound may not be intercepted by any obstruction; also with an efficient bell. A sailing vessel of twenty gross tons or upward shall be provided with a similar bell.

In fog, mist, falling snow, heavy rainstorms, or any other condition similarly restricting visibility, whether by day or night, the signals described by this article shall be used as follows, namely:

(a) A steam vessel under way and towing another vessel or vessels shall sound, at intervals of not more than one minute, three distinct blasts of the whistle, of approximately equal length.

(b) A steam vessel under way without a tow shall sound, at intervals of not more than one minute, three blasts of the whistle, the first two blasts to be approximately of equal length, the last blast to be longer.

(c) A steam vessel, with or without a tow, lying to, by which is meant holding her position near or against the bank, by using her engines, or temporarily moored to the bank, when a fog signal or other sound is heard indicating the approach of another vessel, shall, if lying to on the right bank, give one tap of the bell to indicate her presence, and if lying to on the left bank, two taps of the bell, at intervals of not more than one minute, such signals to continue until the approaching steam vessel has passed. Right and left bank is understood as facing downstream or with the flow of the current.

(d) A vessel when at anchor shall, at intervals of not more than one minute, ring the bell rapidly for about five seconds, except that the following vessels shall not be required to sound this signal when anchored in a special anchorage area established pursuant to paragraph (c) of rule 13:

(1) a vessel of not more than sixty-five feet in length; and

(2) a barge, canal boat, scow or other nondescript craft.

RULE NUMBERED 16 Every steam vessel shall, in fog, mist, falling snow, heavy rainstorms, or any other condition similarly restricting visibility, whether by day or night, go at a moderate speed. A steam vessel hearing, apparently forward of her beam, the fog signal of another vessel shall at once reduce her speed to bare steerageway, and navigate with caution until the vessels shall have passed each other.

RULE NUMBERED 17 When two sailing vessels are approaching one another, so as to involve risk of collision, one of them shall keep out of the way of the other, as follows, namely:

(a) A vessel which is running free shall keep out of the way of a vessel which is close-hauled.

(b) A vessel which is close-hauled on the port tack shall keep out of the way of a vessel which is close-hauled on the starboard tack.

(c) When both are running free, with the wind on different sides, the vessel which has the wind on the port side shall keep out of the way of the other.

(d) When both are running free, with the wind on the same side, the vessel which is to the windward shall keep out of the way of the vessel which is to the leeward.

(e) A vessel which has the wind aft shall keep out of the way of the other vessel.

III—Steering and Sailing Rules

Preliminary—Risk of Collision

Risk of collision can, when circumstances permit, be ascertained by carefully watching the bearing of an approaching vessel. If the bearing does not appreciably change such risk should be deemed to exist.

RULE NUMBERED 18 (a) When two steam vessels are meeting end on, or nearly end on, so as to involve risk of collision, except when one steam vessel is ascending and the other descending a river, it shall be the duty of each to pass on the port side of the other, and to alter course to starboard sufficiently so that this can be done in safety. This maneuver shall require an exchange of one-blast signals when the vessels are not less than one-half mile apart, and either vessel shall blow the first signal which the other shall promptly answer.

(b) When an ascending steam vessel is approaching a descending steam vessel on a river, the signals for passing shall be one distinct blast of the whistle by each vessel if passing port to port, and two distinct blasts of the whistle if passing starboard to starboard.

The pilot of the ascending steam vessel shall give the first signal for passing, which shall promptly be answered by the same signal by the pilot of the descending steam vessel, if safe to do so, and both shall be governed accordingly; but if the pilot of the descending steam vessel deems it dangerous to take the side indicated by the ascending steam vessel, he shall immediately signify that fact by sounding four or more short and rapid blasts, the danger signal, and it shall be the duty of the pilot of the ascending steam vessel to answer by a similar danger signal and the engines of both shall immediately be stopped and backed, if necessary, until signals for passing are given, answered, and understood. After sounding the danger signal by both vessels, the pilot of the descending steam vessel shall indicate by his whistle the side on which he desires to pass, and the pilot of the ascending steam vessel shall govern himself accordingly, the descending steam vessel being entitled to the right-of-way.

The pilot of the descending steam vessel shall not blow the first signal, except that if the other vessel has not whistled when the steam vessels, or the forward end of their tows, if being pushed ahead, are within one-half mile of each other, he shall blow the first danger signal, which shall be promptly answered by a danger signal by the ascending vessel; but whether answered or not, the pilot of the descending vessel shall indicate the side on which he desires to pass, and both vessels shall be governed accordingly.

RULE NUMBERED 19 (a) When two steam vessels are crossing so as to involve risk of collision, other than when one vessel is overtaking another, the vessel which has the other to starboard shall keep out of the way of the other. Either vessel shall give, as a signal of intention to comply with this rule, one distinct blast of her whistle, which the other vessel shall answer with a similar blast: Provided, however, That a steam vessel descending a river and towing another vessel or vessels shall be deemed to have the right-of-way over any steam vessel crossing the river, and shall give as a signal of her intention to hold on across the bow of the other vessel, three distinct blasts of the whistle. The crossing vessel shall immediately reply with a similar signal, and shall keep clear by stopping or going under the stern of the descending vessel.

(b) If from any cause the conditions covered by these situations are such as to prevent immediate compliance with each other's signals, the misunderstanding or objection shall be at once made apparent by blowing four or more short and rapid blasts, the danger signal, and both steam vessels shall be stopped and backed if necessary until signals for passing with safety in accordance with these rules are given, answered, and understood.

RULE NUMBERED 20 When a steam vessel and a sailing vessel are proceeding in such directions as to involve risk of collision, except when the sailing vessel is overtaking the steam vessel, the steam vessel shall keep out of the way of the sailing vessel. This rule shall not give to a sailing vessel the right to hamper the safe passage of a large steam vessel or vessel with tow that is ascending or descending a river.

RULE NUMBERED 21 Every steam vessel, when approaching another vessel so as to involve risk of collision, shall slacken her speed, or, if necessary, stop and reverse.

RULE NUMBERED 22 (a) Nothwithstanding anything contained in these rules, every vessel, overtaking any other, shall keep out of the way of the overtaken vessel.

Every vessel coming up with another vessel from any direction more than two points abaft her beam shall be deemed to be an overtaking vessel; and no subsequent alteration of the bearing between the two vessels shall make the overtaking vessel a crossing vessel within the meaning of these rules, or relieve her of the duty of keeping clear of the overtaken vessel until she is finally past and clear.

As the overtaking vessel cannot always know with certainty whether she is forward of or abaft this direction from the other vessel, she should, if in doubt, assume that she is an overtaking vessel and keep out of the way.

(b) When one steam vessel is overtaking another steam vessel, so as to involve risk of collision, and the overtaking vessel shall desire to pass on the right or starboard side of the other vessel, she shall give, as a signal of such desire, one distinct blast of her whistle, and if the overtaken vessel answers with one blast, shall direct her course to starboard; or if the overtaking vessel shall desire to pass on the left or port side of the other vessel, she shall give, as a signal of such desire, two distinct blasts of her whistle and if the overtaken vessel answers with two blasts, shall direct her course to port. However, if the overtaken vessel does not think it is safe for the overtaking vessel to attempt to pass at that time, she shall immediately so signify by giving several short and rapid blasts of her whistle, not less than four, and under no circumstances shall the overtaking vessel attempt to pass until such time as they have reached a point where it can be safely done, and the overtaken vessel shall have signified her willingness by blowing the proper signal, two blasts for the overtaking vessel to pass on the port side, one blast to pass on the starboard side, which signal shall be answered with a similar signal by the overtaking vessel before passing. After an agreement has been reached the overtaken vessel shall in no case attempt to cross the bow or crowd upon the course of the overtaking vessel.

RULE NUMBERED 23 Where by rules 17, 19, 20, and 22 one of two vessels shall keep out of the way, the other shall keep her course, subject to the qualifications of rule 25.

RULE NUMBERED 23A A steam vessel of less than sixty-five feet in length which can maneuver easily shall not hamper the safe passage of a large vessel or vessel with tow that is ascending or descending a river.

RULE NUMBERED 24 (a) If, when steam vessels are approaching each other either vessel for any reason fails to understand, or regards as unsafe, the course or intention of the other, the vessel in doubt shall immediately so signify by giving several short and rapid blasts of her whistle, at least four, the danger signal.

(b) Whenever a steam vessel, whether ascending or descending, is nearing a bend in a channel where, from the height of the banks or other cause, a steam vessel approaching from the other direction cannot be seen for a distance of six hundred yards such steam vessel, when within six hundred yards of such bend—or if she have a tow projecting ahead, then when the head of such tow is within six hundred yards of the bend—shall give a signal by three distinct blasts of her whistle, which signal shall be answered by a similar signal given by any approaching steam vessel that may be within hearing around the bend. Should such signal be so answered by a steam vessel upon the farther side of such bend, then, immediately upon sighting each other, the usual signals for meeting and passing shall be given and answered. Regardless of whether an approaching vessel on the farther side of the bend is heard, such bend shall be rounded with alertness and caution.

(c) When a steam vessel is moved from her dock, or anchorage, she shall give the same signal as in the case of a steam vessel nearing a bend, but she and any approaching vessel shall be governed by rules 25 and 26 until her course is apparent, and then both vessels shall be governed by the other steering and sailing rules.

(For additional whistle signals and other regulations established by the Commandant, United States Coast Guard, see Pilot Rules for Western Rivers as prescribed under section 4233A.)

RULE NUMBERED 25 In obeying and construing these rules due regard shall be had to all dangers of navigation and collision and to any special circumstances which may render a departure from the above rules necessary in order to avoid immediate danger. When such departure becomes necessary neither vessel shall have the right-of-way and both shall navigate with caution until danger of collision is over.

RULE NUMBERED 26 Nothing in these rules shall exonerate any vessel, or the owner or master or crew thereof, from the consequences of any neglect to carry lights or signals, or of any neglect to keep a proper lookout, or of the neglect of any precaution which may be required by the ordinary practice of seamen, or by the special circumstances of the case.

RULE NUMBERED 27 All orders to helmsmen shall be given as follows:

"Right rudder" to mean "Direct the vessel's head to starboard."

"Left rudder" to mean "Direct the vessel's head to port."

Regulations

SEC. 4322A (a) The Secretary of the Department in which the Coast Guard is operating shall establish such rules to be observed, on the waters described in section 4233, by steam vessels in passing each other and as to the lights and day signals to be carried on such waters by ferryboats, by vessels and craft of all types when in tow of steam vessels or operating by hand power or horsepower or drifting with the current, and by any other vessels not otherwise provided for, not inconsistent with the provisions of this Act, as he from time to time may deem necessary for safety, which rules are hereby declared special rules duly made by local authority. A pamphlet containing such Act and regulations shall be furnished to all vessels and craft subject to this Act. On vessels and craft over sixty-five feet in length the pamphlet shall, where practicable, be kept on board and available for ready reference.

(b) Except in an emergency, before any rules or any alteration, amendment, or repeal thereof, are established by the Secretary under the provisions of this section, the said Secretary shall publish the proposed rules, alterations, amendments, or repeals, and public hearings shall be held with respect thereto on such notice as the Secretary deems reasonable under the circumstances.

Penalties

SEC. 4233B Every licensed or unlicensed pilot, engineer, mate, or master of any steam vessel, and every master or mate of any barge, canal boat, scow, or other nondescript craft, who neglects or refuses to observe the provisions of section 4233, or the regulations established in pursuance of section 4233A, shall be liable to a penalty not exceeding $500, and for all damages sustained by any passenger in his person or baggage by such neglect or refusal: Provided, That nothing herein shall relieve any vessel, owner, or corporation from any liability incurred by reason of such neglect or refusal.

SEC. 4233C Every vessel that shall be navigated without complying with the provisions of section 4233, or the regulations established in pursuance of section 4233A, shall be liable to a penalty of $500, one-half to go to the informer, for which sum the vessel so navigated shall be liable and may be seized and proceeded against by action in any district court of the United States having jurisdiction of the offense.

Safe Navigation

SEC. 4487 On any steamers navigating rivers only, when from darkness, fog, or other cause the pilot or [on] watch shall be of opinion that the navigation is unsafe, or from accident to or derangement of the machinery of the boat the chief engineer shall be of the opinion that the further navigation of the vessel is unsafe, the vessel shall be brought to anchor or moored as soon as it can prudently be done: Provided, That if the person in command shall, after being so admonished by either of such officers, elect to pursue such voyage, he may do the same; but in such case both he and the owners of such steamer shall be answerable for all damages which shall arise to the person of any passenger or his baggage from such causes in so pursuing the voyage, and no degree of care or diligence shall in such case be held to justify or excuse the person in command or the owners. (46 U.S.C. 480)

Navy or Coast Guard Vessels

SEC. 5 Where any Navy or Coast Guard vessel of special construction, as certified to by the Secretary of the Navy, or the Secretary of Transportation in the case of Coast Guard vessels operating under the Transportation Department, or such official or officials as either may designate, is now or may hereafter by virtue of statute, convention, or treaty, be exempt from compliance with any requirements of the International Rules of the Road, such type of vessel shall similarly be exempt from compliance with any corresponding requirements under the rules specified in this Act. (Sec. 5, 62 Stat. 257; 33 U.S.C. 356.)

Pilot Rules for Western Rivers[1]

PART 95[2]

Sec.

General

[1] Code of Federal Regulations: Title 33—Navigation and Navigable Waters; Part 95—Pilot Rules for Western Rivers.

[2] Authority: The provisions of this Part 95 issued under R.S. 4233 A, as amended, Sec. 46(b)(i), 80 Stat. 937 33 U.S.C. 353, 49 U.S.C. 1655(b)(l); 49 C.F.R. 146(b), unless otherwise noted.

while transferring dangerous cargoes.

nals, or other navigational
means and appliances
when operating under
bridges.

General

General Instructions

SEC. 95.01 The regulations in this part apply to vessels navigating the
Red River of the North, the Mississippi River and its tributaries above Huey
P. Long Bridge, and that part of the Atchafalaya River above its junction
with the Plaquemine-Morgan City alternate waterway.

*Demarcation Lines between "Rules of the Road—Western Rivers"
and "Rules of the Road—Great Lakes"*

SEC. 95.02 (a) The demarcation lines between the "Rules of the Road—
Western Rivers" and the "Rules of the Road—Great Lakes" are as follows:

(1) On the Calumet River at the Thomas J. O'Brien Lock and Controlling
Works (between mile 326 and 327).

(2) On the Chicago River at the east side of the Ashland Avenue Bridge
(between mile 321 and 322).

Definitions

SEC. 95.03 (a) In this part the words "steam vessel" or "steamer" shall
include any vessel propelled by machinery; and the word "barge" shall include barge, canal boat, scow, and any other vessel of nondescript type not
otherwise provided for herein.

(b) The phrase "Western Rivers" shall include only the Red River of the
North, the Mississippi River and its tributaries above Huey P. Long Bridge,
and that part of the Atchafalaya River above its junction with the Plaquemine-Morgan City alternate waterway.

Risk of Collision

SEC. 95.05 Risk of collision can, when circumstances permit, be ascertained by carefully watching the bearing of an approaching vessel. If the
bearing does not appreciably change, such risk should be deemed to exist.

Vessels Passing Each Other

Vessels Meeting at Confluence of Two Rivers

SEC. 95.07 When two steam vessels meet at the confluence of two rivers, the steam vessel which has the other to port shall give the first signal; but in no case shall pilots on steam vessels attempt to pass each other until there has been a thorough understanding as to the side each steam vessel shall take.

Danger and Cross Signals

SEC. 95.09 (a) The alarm or danger signal shall consist of four or more short and rapid blasts. Steam vessels are forbidden to use what has become technically known among pilots as "cross signals," that is, answering one whistle with two, and answering two whistles with one. In all cases and under all circumstances, a pilot receiving either of the whistle signals provided in the rules in this part with which for any reason, he deems it injudicious to comply, instead of answering it with a cross signal, shall at once observe the provisions of this section.

(b) The pilot of any steam vessel shall sound the alarm or danger signal whenever required by the law, or any of the regulations hereinafter contained; that is to say, as follows:

(1) Whenever it is dangerous to take the side indicated by the passing signal of another vessel; or,

(2) Whenever any steam vessel does not understand or is in doubt regarding the signal of another steam vessel; or,

(3) Whenever, from any cause, one steam vessel is imperiled by another.

Narrow Channels

SEC. 95.11 When two steam vessels are about to enter a narrow channel at the same time, the ascending steam vessel shall be stopped below such channel until the descending steam vessel shall have passed through it; but should two steam vessels unavoidably meet in such narrow channel, then it shall be the duty of the pilot of the ascending steam vessel to make the proper signals, and when answered, the ascending steam vessel shall lie as close as possible to the side of the channel and either stop the engines or move them so as to give the boat only steerageway; and the pilot of the descending steam vessel shall cause his steam vessel to be worked slowly until he has passed the ascending steam vessel.

Approaching Bridge Span or Draw

SEC. 95.13 (a) When two steam vessels are approaching a bridge span or draw from opposite directions and the passing signals have been given and understood, should the pilot of the descending steam vessel deem it dangerous for the steam vessels to pass each other between the piers of such span or draw, he shall sound the alarm or danger signal and it shall then be the duty of the pilot of the ascending steam vessel to answer with a similar alarm signal, and to slow or stop his engines below such span or draw until the descending steam vessel shall have passed.

(b) If the ascending steam vessel is already in the bridge span or draw, and the descending steam vessel sounds the danger or alarm signal, it shall be the duty of the ascending steam vessel, if practicable, to drop below the bridge span or draw, and wait until the other steam vessel shall have passed.

Ascending, Descending Steam Vessels Crossing River

SEC. 95.15 The pilot of an ascending steam vessel shall in no case attempt to cross the river when an ascending or descending steam vessel shall be so near that it would be possible for a collision to ensue therefrom; and conversely, the pilot of a descending steam vessel shall in no case attempt to cross the river when an ascending or descending steam vessel shall be so near that it would be possible for a collision to ensue therefrom.

Overtaking Situation

SEC. 95.17 When two steam vessels are in the overtaking situation, it is the duty of the steam vessel being overtaken to answer immediately a passing signal of the overtaking steam vessel, either by assenting with the same number of blasts or by dissenting with the danger signal.

Passing Signals

SEC. 95.19 The passing signals, by the blowing of the whistle, shall be given and answered by pilots, in all weathers, when approaching each other; and, wherever possible, the signals shall be given and answered before the steam vessels, or if towboats pushing tows, the heads of such tows, have arrived at a distance of half a mile of each other.

Visual Signal

SEC. 95.21 All whistle signals shall be further indicated by a visual signal consisting of an amber colored light so located as to be visible all around the horizon for a distance of not less than one mile. This light shall be so devised that it will operate simultaneously and in conjunction with the whistle sounding mechanism, and remain ignited or visible during the same period as the sound signal: Provided, That the installation, use, or employment of the amber visual signal required by this section shall be optional in the case of (a) vessels operating upon the Gulf Intracoastal Waterway; (b) vessels operating on the Mississippi River below mile 237 AHP (Belmont Landing) as set forth in map No. 40, "Maps of the Mississippi River, Cairo, Illinois, to the Gulf of Mexico, Louisiana (1944 ed.)," published by the Mississippi River Commission; (c) newly constructed vessels while en route from point of construction to a point in waters where the aforementioned amber visual signal is not required; (d) motorboats of class A and class 1; and (e) motorboats of class 2 and class 3 not engaged in trade or commerce.

Pamphlet Containing Pilot Rules

SEC. 95.23 All vessels and craft over 65 feet in length upon the waters described in Section 95.01 shall, where practicable, carry on board and maintain for ready reference copies of the current edition of Coast Guard pamphlet CG-184. Nothing in this section shall require copies of this pamphlet to be carried on board any motorboat as defined by section 1 of the Act of April 25, 1940, as amended (*54 Stat. 163; 46 U.S.C. 526*).

Diagrams

SEC. 95.25 The following diagrams are intended to illustrate the working of the system of colored lights and the pilot rules:

FIRST SITUATION

Here the two colored lights visible to each will indicate their meeting end on, or nearly end on, so as to involve risk of collision. In this situation it is a standing rule that both shall direct their courses to starboard and pass on the port of each other, each having previously given one blast of the whistle, except that, when an ascending steam vessel is approaching a descending steam vessel, the descending steam vessel has the right-of-way and the vessels shall pass each other on the side determined by the descending steam vessel. The necessary signals for passing shall be given as provided in Rule 18.

SECOND SITUATION

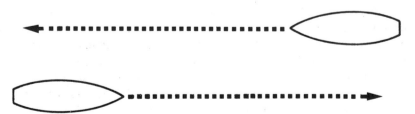

In this situation the red light only will be visible to each. Both vessels are evidently passing to port of each other; however, the vessels shall pass each other on the side determined by the descending steam vessel.

THIRD SITUATION

In this situation the green light only will be visible to each. They are there-fore passing to starboard of each other; however, the vessels shall pass each other on the side determined by the descending vessel.

FOURTH SITUATION

In this situation one steam vessel is overtaking another steam vessel from some point within the angle of two points abaft the beam of the overtaken steam vessel. The overtaking steam vessel may pass on the starboard or port side of the steam vessel ahead after the necessary signals for passing have been given, with assent of the overtaken steam vessel as prescribed in Rule 22.

FIFTH SITUATION

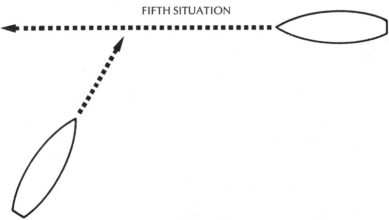

In this situation two steam vessels are crossing so as to involve risk of colli-sion, other than where one steam vessel is overtaking another. The steam vessel which has the other to starboard shall keep out of the way of the other. Either vessel shall give one distinct blast of her whistle, as a signal of her intention, which the other vessel shall answer with a similar blast. However, a steam vessel with tow descending a river shall be deemed to have the right-of-way over any steam vessel crossing the river.

SEC. 95.26 (a) Coast Guard vessels while engaged in handling or servicing an aid to navigation during the daytime may display from the yard two orange and white vertically striped balls in a vertical line not less than three feet nor more than six feet apart, and during the nighttime may display, in a position where they may best be seen, two red lights in a vertical line not less than three feet nor more than six feet apart.

(b) Vessels, with or without tows, passing Coast Guard vessels displaying this signal, shall reduce their speed sufficiently to insure the safety of both vessels, and when passing within 200 feet of the Coast Guard vessel displaying the signal, their speed shall not exceed 5 miles per hour.

Lights for Ferryboats and Barges

Lights for Ferryboats

SEC. 95.27 (a) The signal lights on ferryboats shall be the same as those of similar steamboats, except that double-end ferryboats shall carry a central range of clear, bright, white lights, showing all around the horizon, placed at equal altitudes forward and aft, also on the starboard side a green light, and on the port side a red light, of such character as to be visible on a dark night with a clear atmosphere at a distance of at least 3 miles, and so constructed as to show a uniform and unbroken light over an arc of the horizon of 10 points of the compass, and so fixed as to throw the light from right ahead to 2 points abaft the beam on their respective sides.

(b) The green and red lights shall be fitted with inboard screens projecting at least 3 feet forward from the lights, so as to prevent them from being seen more than half a point across the bow.

(c) Officers in Charge, Marine Inspection,[3] in districts having ferryboats shall, whenever the safety of navigation may require, designate for each line of such boats a certain light, white or colored, which shall show all around the horizon, to designate and distinguish such lines from each other, which light shall be carried on a flagstaff amidships 15 feet above the white range lights.

Lights for Barges Towed Ahead or Alongside

SEC. 95.29 (a) When one or more barges are being towed by pushing ahead of a steam vessel, or by a combination of pushing ahead and towing

---

[3] *For definition of an Officer in Charge, Marine Inspection, see Title 46, Code of Federal Regulations, Section 70.10-33.*

alongside of a steam vessel, such tow shall be lighted by a flashing amber light at the extreme forward end of the tow, so placed as to be as nearly as practicable on the centerline of the tow, a green light on the starboard side of the tow, so placed as to mark the maximum projection of the tow to starboard, and a red light on the port side of the tow, so placed as to mark the maximum projection of the tow to port.

(b) When one or more barges are being towed alongside a steam vessel, there shall be displayed a white light at each outboard corner of the tow. If the deck, deck house, or cargo of such barge obscures the sidelight of the towing steam vessel, such barge shall also carry a green light upon the starboard side when being towed on the starboard side of a steam vessel; or shall carry a red light on the port side of the barge when being towed on the port side of the steam vessel. If there is more than one such barge being towed abreast, the appropriate colored sidelight shall be displayed from the outer side of the outside barge.

(c) The colored side lights shall be so constructed as to show a uniform and unbroken light over an arc of the horizon of 10 points of the compass, so fixed as to show the light from right ahead to 2 points abaft the beam on their respective sides and of such a character as to be visible at a distance of at least 2 miles, and shall be fitted with inboard screens so as to prevent either light from being seen more than half a point across the centerline of the tow.

(d) The amber light shall flash 50 to 70 times per minute and be so constructed as to show a uniform and unbroken light over an arc of the horizon of 20 points of the compass, so fixed as to show the light 10 points on each side of the tow, namely, from right ahead to 2 points abaft the beam on either side, and of such a character as to be visible at a distance of at least 2 miles.

(e) The white lights shall be so constructed and so fixed as to show a clear, uniform, and unbroken light all around the horizon, and of such a character as to be visible at a distance of at least 2 miles.

(f) All the lights shall be carried at approximately the same height above the surface of the water and shall be so placed with respect thereto as to be clear of and above all obstructions which might tend to interfere with the prescribed arc or distance of visibility.

Lights for Barges Towed Astern

SEC. 95.31 (a) When one barge is being towed singly behind a steam vessel, such vessel shall carry four white lights, one on each corner or outermost projection of the bow and one on each corner or outermost projection of the stern.

(b) When two or more barges are being towed behind a steam vessel in tandem, with a hawser length, between vessels, of 75 feet or more, such vessels shall carry white lights as follows:

(1) The first vessel in the tow shall carry three white lights, one on each corner or outermost projection of the bow and a white light at the stern amidships.

(2) Each intermediate vessel shall carry two white lights, one at each end amidships.

(3) The last vessel in the tow shall carry three white lights, one on each corner or outermost projection of the stern and a white light at the bow amidships.

(c) When two or more barges are being towed behind a steam vessel in tandem, with a hawser length, between vessels, of less than 75 feet, such vessels shall carry white lights as follows:

(1) The first vessel in the tow shall carry three white lights, one on each corner or outermost projection of the bow and a white light at the stern amidships.

(2) Each intermediate vessel shall carry a white light at the stern amidships.

(3) The last vessel in the tow shall carry two white lights, one on each corner or outermost projection of the stern.

(d) When two or more barges are being towed behind a steam vessel two or more abreast, in one or more tiers, each of the outside barges in each tier shall carry a white light on the outboard corner of the bow and each of the outside barges in the last tier shall carry, in addition, a white light on the outboard corner of the stern.

(e) The white lights shall be so constructed and so fixed as to show a clear, uniform, and unbroken light all around the horizon and of such a character as to be visible at a distance of at least 2 miles. The lights shall be carried at approximately the same height above the surface of the water and shall be so placed with respect thereto as to be clear of and above all obstructions which might tend to interfere with the prescribed arc or distance of visibility.

Lights for Barges Temporarily Operating within or without Western Rivers

SEC. 95.33 Nothing in §§ 95.29 and 95.31 shall be construed as compelling barges being towed, when passing through any waters coming within the scope of any regulation where lights for barges are different from those of the waters whereon such barges are usually employed, to change their lights from those required on the waters from which their trip begins or terminates; but should such barges engage in local employment on waters requiring different lights from those where they are customarily employed, they shall comply with the local rules where employed: Provided, That such barges (including canal boats) being towed on the Great Lakes and their connecting waters and the St. Marys River shall comply with the rules prescribing lights for craft being towed on such waters.

Lights for Barges at Bank or Dock

SEC. 95.36 (a) Lights for barges at bank or dock in the Mississippi River and its tributaries and in the Atchafalaya River above its junction with the Plaquemine-Morgan City Alternate Waterway shall be as required by this section.

(b) The following barges, when moored in or near a fairway, except those barges exempted under the provisions of paragraph (e) of this section, shall display between the hours of sunset and sunrise the barge lights described in paragraph (c) of this section:

(1) Every barge projecting into a buoyed or restricted channel.

(2) Every barge so moored that it reduces the available navigable width of any channel to less than 250 feet.

(3) Barges moored in fleets more than two barges wide or to a maximum width of over 80 feet, parallel to the bank.

(4) Every barge moored to the bank in any manner other than parallel thereto.

(c) Barges required to be lighted under paragraph (b) of this section shall carry two white lights of such character as to be visible on a dark night with a clear atmosphere at a distance of at least 1 mile, so located as to give unobstructed view and arranged as follows:

(1) On a single moored barge, a light on each outboard or channelward corner.

(2) On barges moored in group formation, a light on the upstream outboard or channelward corner of the outer upstream barge and a light on the downstream outboard or channelward corner of the outer downstream barge. In addition, any barge projecting toward or into the channel in such a group formation shall have two white lights similarly placed on the outboard or channelward corners of the barge.

(d) Barges moored in any ship or slough which is used primarily for mooring purposes are exempt from the lighting requirements of this section.

(e) Barges moored in well-illuminated areas of the Illinois River north of Brandon Lock and Dam at Joliet, Ill., shall not be required to display the lights prescribed in paragraph (c) of this section. These areas are as follows:

Chicago Sanitary Ship Canal

(1) Mile 293.2 to 293.9—Material Service Corp.

(3) Mile 295.2 to 296.1—Material Service Corp. and Commonwealth Edison Co.

(5) Mile 297.5 to 297.8—Pure Oil Docks.

(7) Mile 298 to 298.2—Ceco Steel Docks.

(9) Mile 298.6 to 298.8—Lemont Manufacturing Co.

(11) Mile 299.3 to 299.4—Mechmar Development Co.

(13) Mile 299.8 to 300.5 (Stephen St. Bridge)—Tri-Central Oil Co.

(15) Mile 303 to 303.2—North American Car Corp.

(17) Mile 303.7 to 303.9—Hannah Inland Waterways Transportation Co.

(19) Mile 305.7 to 305.8—Publicker Chemical Co.

(21) Mile 310.7 to 310.9—Shell Oil Co.

(23) Mile 311 to 311.2—General American Tank Storage Terminal.

(25) Mile 312.5 to 312.6—Trumbull Asphalt Co.

(27) Mile 313.8 to 314.2—Lake River Oil Terminal.

(29) Mile 314.6—Waterways Terminals, Inc.

(31) Mile 314.8 to 315.3—Commonwealth Edison Co. and Material Service Corp.

(33) Mile 315.7 to 316—Sanitary District Dock.

(35) Mile 316.8—Whitewater Petroleum Terminal Co.

(37) Mile 316.85 to 317.05—Hughes Oil Co.

(39) Mile 317.5—Socony Vacuum Oil Co.

(41) Mile 318.4 to 318.9—Commonwealth Edison Co.

(43) Mile 318.7 to 318.8—Bell Oil Co.

(45) Mile 320 to 320.3—Globe Fuel & Humble Oil.

(47) Mile 320.6—American Sugar Refining Co., South Branch of Chicago River and Chicago River.

(49) Mile 322.3 to 322.4—Commonwealth Edison Co.

(51) Mile 322.8—Time, Inc.

(53) Mile 322.9 to 327.2.

Calumet Sag Channel

(61) Mile 316.5—Marine Oil Co. unloading piers.

Little Calumet River

(71) Mile 321.2—Pump house outfall.

(73) Mile 322.3—South bank.

Calumet River

(81) Mile 328.5 to 328.7—Cargill Grain Elevator.

(83) Mile 329.2 to 329.4—Continental Grain Elevator.

(85) Mile 330, west bank to 330.2.

(87) Mile 331.4 to 331.6—Rail to Water Transfer Corp.

(89) Mile 332.2 to 332.4—Dundee Cement Co.

(91) Mile 332.6 to 332.8—Material Service Corp.

Lights For Rafts and Other Craft Not Provided For

Lights For Rafts and Other Craft

SEC. 95.37 (a) All watercraft, except as herein otherwise provided, navigating any bay, harbor, or river, propelled by hand power, horsepower, or by the current of the river, or which shall be anchored or moored in or near the channel or fairway of any bay, harbor, or river, shall carry one white light forward, not less than 8 feet above the surface of the water.

(b) Rafts propelled by hand power or by the current of the river, or when being towed, or which shall be anchored or moored in or near a channel or fairway, shall carry white lights, as follows:

(1) Rafts of one crib and not more than two in length shall carry one white light.

(2) Rafts of three or more cribs in length and one crib in width shall carry one white light at each end of the raft.

(3) Rafts of more than one crib abreast shall carry one white light on each outside corner of the raft, making four lights in all.

(c) The white light required by this section for rafts and other watercraft shall be carried from sunset to sunrise, in a lantern so fixed and constructed as to show a clear, uniform, and unbroken light, visible all around the horizon, and of such intensity as to be visible on a dark night with a clear atmosphere at a distance of at least 1 mile. The lights for rafts shall be suspended from poles of such height that the light shall not be less than 8 feet above the surface of the water.

(d) Rowing boats under oars shall have ready at hand a lantern showing a white light which shall be temporarily exhibited in sufficient time to prevent collision.

Towing of Barges

Hawser Lengths for All Tows

SEC. 95.38 The length of hawsers, between vessels, shall be limited to no more than 450 feet (75 fathoms). This length shall be the distance measured from the stern of one vessel to the bow of the following vessel. The distance between two vessels should in all cases be as much shorter as the weather or sea will permit.

Distress Signals

Distress Signals—(a) In the Daytime

SEC. 95.39

(1) A gun fired at intervals of about a minute.

(2) The International Code signal of distress indicated by N.C.

(3) The distant signal, consisting of a square flag, having either above or below it a ball or anything resembling a ball.

(4) Rockets or shells as prescribed below for use at night.

(5) A continuous sounding with a steam whistle or any fog-signal apparatus.

(6) Slowly and repeatedly raising and lowering arms outstretched to each side.

(b) At night. (1) A gun fired at intervals of about a minute.

(2) Flames on the vessel (as from a burning tar barrel, oil barrel, etc.).

(3) Rockets or shells, bursting in the air with a loud report and throwing stars of any color or description, fired one at a time at short intervals.

(4) A continuous sounding with a steam whistle or any fog-signal apparatus.

Unauthorized Use of Lights; Unnecessary Whistling

Rule Relating to the Use of Searchlights or Other Blinding Lights

SEC. 95.41 Flashing the rays of a searchlight or other blinding light onto the bridge or into the pilothouse of any vessel under way is prohibited. Any person who shall flash or cause to be flashed the rays of a blinding light in violation of the above may be proceeded against in accordance with the provisions of section 4450 R. S., as amended, looking to the revocation or suspension of his license or certificate.

Rule Prohibiting Unnecessary Sounding of the Whistle

SEC. 95.43. Unnecessary sounding of the whistle is prohibited within any harbor limits of the United States. Whenever any licensed officer in charge of any vessel shall authorize or permit such unnecessary whistling, such officer may be proceeded against in accordance with the provisions of section 4450 R. S., as amended, looking to a revocation or suspension of his license.

Rule Prohibiting the Carrying of Unauthorized Lights on Vessels

SEC. 95.45 Any master or pilot of any vessel who shall authorize or permit the carrying of any light, electric or otherwise, not required by law, that in any way will interfere with distinguishing the signal lights, may be proceeded against in accordance with the provisions of section 4450, R. S., as amended, looking to a suspension or revocation of his license.

Lights and Day Signals for Vessels, Dredges of All Types, and Vessels Working on Wrecks and Obstructions, etc.

Scope and Applicability

SEC. 95.51 (a) The regulations contained in Sections 95.51 to 95.66, inclusive, govern lights and day signals to be displayed by towing vessels with tows on which no signals can be displayed, vessels working on wrecks, dredges, and vessels engaged in laying cables or pipe or in submarine or bank protection operations, lights to be displayed on dredge pipeline, and day signals to be displayed by vessels of more than 65 feet in length moored or anchored in a fairway or channel (Sections 95.52 to 95.59, inclusive), and the passing by other vessels of floating plant working in navigable channels (Sections 95.60 to 95.66, inclusive).[4]

(b) The regulations contained in Sections 95.51 to 95.66, inclusive, are applicable on the western rivers.

Lights and Day Signals

Signals to Be Displayed by a Towing Vessel When Towing a Submerged or Partly Submerged Object upon a Hawser When No Signals Can Be Displayed upon the Object Which Is Towed

SEC. 95.52 (a) The vessel having the submerged object in tow shall display by day, where they can best be seen, two shapes, one above the other, not less than six feet apart, the lower shape to be carried not less than 10 feet above the deckhouse. The shapes shall be in the form of a double frustum of a cone, base to base, not less than two feet in diameter at the center nor less than eight inches at the ends of the cones, and to be not less than four feet lengthwise from end to end, the upper shape to be painted in alternate horizontal stripes of black and white, eight inches in width, and the lower shape to be painted a solid bright red.

(b) By night the towing vessel shall display the regular side lights, but in lieu of the regular white towing lights shall display four lights in a vertical position not less than three feet, nor more than six feet apart, the upper

---

[4] *The regulations in Sections 95.51 to 95.66, inclusive, are applicable on the western rivers as described in Section 95.01. The same regulations in Sections 80.18 to 80.31a of this chapter are applicable on the harbors, rivers, and inland waters along the Atlantic and Pacific Coasts and the Coast of the Gulf of Mexico. Similar Department of the Army regulations are applicable on the Great Lakes and their connecting and tributary waters as far east as Montreal and are contained in Sections 201.1 to 201.16 of this title.*

and lower of such lights to be white and of the same character as the regular towing lights and the middle of such lights to be red and of such a character as to be visible on a dark night with a clear atmosphere for a distance of at least 2 miles.

Steam Vessels, Derrick Boats, Lighters, or Other Types of Vessels Made Fast Alongside a Wreck, or Moored over a Wreck Which Is on the Bottom or Partly Submerged, or Which May Be Drifting

SEC. 95.53 (a) Steam vessels, derrick boats, lighters, or other types of vessels made fast alongside a wreck, or moored over a wreck which is on the bottom or partly submerged, or which may be drifting, shall display by day two shapes of the same character and dimensions and displayed in the same manner as required by Paragraph 95.52 (a), except that both shapes shall be painted a solid bright red, but where more than one vessel is working under the above conditions, the shapes need be displayed only from one vessel on each side of the wreck from which they can best be seen from all directions.

(b) By night this situation shall be indicated by the display of a white light from the bow and stern of each outside vessel or lighter not less than six feet above the deck, and in addition thereto there shall be displayed in a position where they can best be seen from all directions two red lights carried in a vertical line not less than three feet nor more than six feet apart, and not less than 15 feet above the deck.

Dredges Held in Stationary Position by Moorings or Spuds

SEC. 95.54 (a) Dredges which are held in stationary positions by moorings or spuds shall display by day two red balls not less than two feet in diameter and carried in a vertical line not less than three feet nor more than six feet apart, and at least 15 feet above the deckhouse and in a position where they can best be seen from all directions.

(b) By night they shall display a white light at each corner, not less than six feet above the deck, and in addition thereto there shall be displayed in a position where they can best be seen from all directions two red lights carried in a vertical line not less than three feet nor more than six feet apart, and not less than 15 feet above the deck. When scows are moored alongside a dredge in the foregoing situation they shall display a white light on each outboard corner, not less than six feet above the deck.

Self-propelling Suction Dredges Under Way and Engaged in Dredging Operations

SEC. 95.55 (a) Self-propelling suction dredges under way and engaged in dredging operations shall display by day two black balls not less than two feet in diameter and carried in a vertical line not less than 15 feet above the deckhouse, and where they can best be seen from all directions. The term "dredging operations" shall include maneuvering into or out of position at the dredging site, but shall not include proceeding to and from the site.

(b) By night self-propelling dredges underway and engaged in dredging operations shall carry, in addition to the regular running lights, two red lights in a vertical line beneath the white masthead light. These red lights shall be not less than three feet apart and the upper red light to be not less than three feet nor more than six feet below the masthead light. They shall also carry on or near the stern two red lights in a vertical line not less than three feet nor more than six feet apart, to show through twelve points of the compass; that is, from right astern to six points on each quarter. The forward red lights and after red lights shall be of such character as to be visible on a dark night with a clear atmosphere for a distance of at least two miles.

Vessels Moored or Anchored and Engaged in Laying Cables or Pipe,
Submarine Construction, Excavation, Mat Sinking,
Bank Grading, Dike Construction, Revetment,
or Other Bank Protection Operations

SEC. 95.56 (a) Vessels which are moored or anchored and engaged in laying cables or pipe, submarine construction, excavation, mat sinking, bank grading, dike construction, revetment, or other bank protection operations, shall display by day, no less than 15 feet above the deck, where they can best be seen from all directions, two balls not less than two feet in diameter, in a vertical line not less than three feet nor more than six feet apart, the upper ball to be painted in alternate black and white vertical stripes six inches wide, and the lower ball to be painted a solid bright red.

(b) By night they shall display three red lights, carried in a vertical line not less than three feet nor more than six feet apart, in a position where they can best be seen from all directions, with the lowermost light not less than 15 feet above the deck.

(c) Where a stringout of moored vessels or barges is engaged in the operations, three red lights carried as prescribed in paragraph (b) of this section shall be displayed at the channelward end of the stringout. Where the stringout crosses the navigable channel and is to be opened for the passage of vessels, the three red lights shall be displayed at each side of the opening instead of at the outer end of the stringout. There shall also be displayed upon such stringout one horizontal row of amber lights not less than six feet above the deck, or above the deckhouse where the craft carries a deckhouse, in a position where they can best be seen from all directions, spaced not more than 50 feet apart so as to mark distinctly the entire length and course of the stringout.

Lights to Be Displayed on Pipelines

SEC. 95.57 Pipelines attached to dredges, and either floating or supported on trestles, shall display by night one row of amber lights not less than eight feet nor more than 12 feet above the water, about equally spaced and in such number as to mark distinctly the entire length and course of the line, the intervals between lights where the line crosses navigable channels to be not more than 30 feet. There shall also be displayed on the shore or discharge end of the line two red lights, three feet apart, in a vertical line with the lower light at least eight feet above the water, and if the line is to be opened at night for the passage of vessels, a similar arrangement of lights shall be displayed on each side of the opening.

Lights Generally

SEC. 95.58 (a) All the lights required by Sections 95.52 to 95.57, except as provided in Paragraph 95.52(b), shall be of such character, as to be visible on a dark night with a clear atmosphere for a distance of at least two miles. The white lights provided for in § 95.52(b), shall be visible for at least 3 miles.

(b) The lights required by Paragraph 95.52(b) shall be of the same construction as the regular towing lights. The lights required by Paragraph 95.55(b) shall be of the same construction as the masthead light.

(c) All floodlights or headlights which may interfere with the proper navigation of an approaching vessel shall be so shielded that the lights will not blind the pilot of such vessel.

Vessels Moored or at Anchor

SEC. 95.59 Vessels of more than 65 feet in length when moored or anchored in a fairway or channel shall display between sunrise and sunset on the forward part of the vessel where is can best be seen from other vessels one black ball not less than two feet in diameter.

Passing Floating Plant Working in Navigable Channels[5]

Passing Signals

SEC. 95.60 (a) Vessels intending to pass dredges or other types of float-

---

[5] The term "floating plant," as used in Sections 95.60 to 95.66, includes dredges, derrick boats, snag boats, drill boats, pile drivers, maneuver boats, hydraulic graders, survey boats, working barges, and mat sinking plant.

ing plant working in navigable channels, when within a reasonable distance therefrom and not in any case over a mile, shall indicate such intention by one long blast of the whistle, and shall be directed to the proper side for passage by the sounding, by the dredge or other floating plant, of the signal prescribed in the local pilot rules for vessels under way and approaching each other from opposite directions, which shall be answered in the usual manner by the approaching vessel. If the channel is not clear, the floating plant shall sound the alarm or danger signal and the approaching vessel shall slow down or stop and await further signal from the plant.

(b) When the pipeline from a dredge crosses the channel in such a way that an approaching vessel cannot pass safely around the pipeline or dredge, there shall be sounded immediately from the dredge the alarm or danger signal and the approaching vessel shall slow down or stop and await further signal from the dredge. The pipeline shall then be opened and the channel cleared as soon as practicable; when the channel is clear for passage the dredge shall so indicate by sounding the usual passing signal as prescribed in paragraph (a) of this section. The approaching vessel shall answer with a corresponding signal and pass promptly.

(c) When any pipeline or swinging dredge shall have given an approaching vessel or tow the signal that the channel is clear, the dredge shall straighten out within the cut for the passage of the vessel or tow.

Speed of Vessels Passing Floating Plant Working in Channels

SEC. 95.61 Vessels, with or without tows, passing floating plant working in channels, shall reduce their speed sufficiently to insure the safety of both the plant and themselves, and when passing within 200 feet of the plant their speed shall not exceed five miles per hour. While passing over lines of the plant, propelling machinery shall be stopped.

Light-draft Vessels Passing Floating Plant

SEC. 95.62 Vessels whose draft permits shall keep outside the buoys marking the ends of mooring lines of floating plant working in channels.

Aids to Navigation Marking Floating-plant Moorings

SEC. 95.63 Breast, stern, and bow anchors of floating plant working in navigable channels shall be marked by barrel or other suitable buoys. By night approaching vessels shall be shown the location of adjacent buoys by throwing a suitable beam of light from the plant on the buoys until the approaching vessel has passed, or the buoys may be lighted by red lights, visible in all directions, of the same character as specified in Paragraph 95.58(a).

Obstruction of Channel by Floating Plant

SEC. 95.64 Channels shall not be obstructed unnecessarily by any dredging or other floating plant. While vessels are passing such plant all lines running therefrom across the channel on the passing side which may interfere with or obstruct navigation shall be slacked to the bottom of the channel.

Clearing of Channels

SEC. 95.65. When special or temporary regulations have not been prescribed and action under the regulations contained in Sections 95.60 to 95.64, will not afford clear passage, floating plant in narrow channels shall, upon notice, move out of the way of vessels a sufficient distance to allow them a clear passage. Vessels desiring passage shall, however, give the master of the floating plant ample notice in advance of the time they expect to pass.[6]

Protection of Marks Placed for the Guidance of Floating Plant

SEC. 95.66 Vessels shall not run over anchor buoys, or buoys, stakes, or other marks placed for the guidance of floating plant working in channels; and shall not anchor on the ranges of buoys, stakes, or other marks placed for the guidance of such plant.

Warning Signals

Warning Signal Displayed While Transferring Dangerous Cargoes

SEC. 95.70 (a) *At a dock.* While fast to a dock, a vessel during the loading or unloading of hazardous or dangerous cargoes, such as explosives, combustible or inflammable liquids or gases, or certain chemicals in bulk, is required to display a red flag by day or a red light by night.

(b) *At anchor.* When at anchor, a vessel during the loading or unloading of such hazardous or dangerous cargoes is required to display a red flag by day. (No special warning signal is displayed at night.)[7]

---

[6] *If it is necessary to prohibit or limit the anchorage or movement of vessels within certain areas in order to facilitate the work of improvement, application should be made through official channels for establishment by the Secretary of the Army of special or temporary regulations for this purpose.*

[7] *The regulations in 46 CFR 3530—1 (a), 98.05—50(h), 98.10—45(g), 98.15—45(h), 98.25—90(f), and 146.29—25(o) require vessels to display warning signals when loading or unloading bulk cargoes of inflammable or combustible liquids or gases, elemental phosphorus in water, sulfuric acid, hydrochloric acid, liquid chlorine, or anhydrous ammonia, or military explosives.*

Miscellaneous

*Exceptions to the Statutory and Regulatory Requirements for Lights,
Day Signals, or Other Navigational Means and Appliances
When Operating under Bridges*

SEC. 95.75 (a) Any vessel while passing under a bridge may temporarily lower any lights, day signals, or other navigational means and appliances when required to do so because of the restricted vertical clearance under the bridge. Immediately when clear of the bridge, all lights, day signals, or other navigational means and appliances shall be exhibited as required by law or regulation.

Distinctive Blue Light Authorized for Use by Law Enforcement Vessels

SEC. 95.80 (a) The use of a distinctive light described in paragraph (b) of this section is authorized for law enforcement vessels, and may be displayed during the day or night, whenever the vessel may be engaged in direct law enforcement activities where identification of the law enforcement vessel is desirable or where necessary for safety reasons. This light when used would be in addition to prescribed lights and day signals required by law or regulation in this part.

(b) The distinctive light prescribed is a blue colored, revolving horizontal beam, low intensity light, rotating or appearing to rotate because of a pulsating effect gained by means of a rotating reflector which causes a flashing or periodic peak intensity effect. The light shall be located at any effective point on the forward exterior of the vessel. A shield or other device, fixed or movable, to restrict the arc of visibility may be used if desired.

(c) The distinctive blue light described in this section may be displayed by law enforcement vessels of the United States, a State, or its political subdivisions, including municipalities, having administrative control over use of navigable waters, duly authorized by a controlling Federal or State governmental agency.

APPENDIX P
Interpretive Rulings, Western Rivers Rules[1]

PART 96[2]

Scope

SEC. 96.01–1 The regulations in this part are interpretive rules with respect to "Rules of the Road" requirements applicable to all vessels while in the waters of the Mississippi River between its source and the Huey P. Long Bridge and all of the tributaries emptying thereinto and their tributaries and that part of the Atchafalaya River above its junction with the Plaquemine-Morgan City alternate waterway, and the Red River of the North.

[1] Code of Federal Regulations: Title 33—Navigation and Navigable Waters; Part 96—Interpretive Rulings—Western Rivers Rules.

[2] Authority: Provisions for this Part 96 issued under 80 Stat. 383, as amended, sec. 1, 63 Stat. 545, sec. 6(b)(1), 80 Stat. 937; 5 U.S.C. 552, 14 U.S.C. 633, 49 U.S.C. 1655(b)(1); 49 CFR 1.46(b).

Penalties and Violations

SEC. 96.01–10 (a) Failure to comply with any law as interpreted will be considered as a violation of such law and the penalty may be assessed as provided by law.

(b) The reports of violations of the "Rules of the Road," as well as the assessment, collection, mitigation or remission of civil penalties authorized by law, shall be in accordance with 33 CFR Subpart 1.07.

White Lights for Motorboats Carried on Centerline

SEC. 96.05–1 Every white light required by section 3 of the Act of April 25, 1940, as amended (46 U.S.C. 526b), shall be carried on the centerline of the motorboat, except that the all-around white light aft on a motorboat of Class A or 1 may be carried off the centerline.

Stern Lights for All Vessels

SEC. 96.05–5 Rule Numbered 10 of section 4233 of the Revised Statutes of the United States, as amended by the Act of August 14, 1958 (33 U.S.C. 319), requires "a vessel when underway, if not otherwise required by these rules to carry one or more lights visible from aft, shall carry at her stern a white light, . . . and this requirement shall be applied to all vessels, including but not limited to, tugs, barges, sail vessels, motorboats when propelled by sail alone, etc.

Vessel Moved From Dock or Anchorage

SEC. 96.10–1 (a) Rule Numbered 24(c) of section 4233 of the Revised Statutes as amended (33 U.S.C. 349), requires "when a vessel is moved from her dock, or anchorage," to give a prescribed signal of three distinct blasts on her whistle. The phrase "moved from her dock, or anchorage," includes moving from a riverbank mooring or from a mooring of any type.

APPENDIX Q
Exemptions for Naval Vessels[1]

PART 706

Sec.

706.1 Purpose of regulations.

706.2 Certifications of the Secre-

tary of the Navy under 33 U.S.C. 360 and 1052.

Navigational Light Waivers[2]

Purpose of Regulations

SEC. 706.1 (a) All ships are warned that, when U.S. naval vessels are met on the high seas or on navigable waters of the United States during periods when navigational lights may be displayed, certain navigational lights of some naval vessels may vary from the requirements of the Regulations for Preventing Collisions at Sea, 1960, 33 U.S. Code sections 1061-1094, and rules applicable to the navigable waters of the United States, as to number, position, range of visibility or arc of visibility. These differences are necessitated by reasons of military function or special construction of the naval ships. An example is the aircraft carrier where the two white lights are in most instances on the island superstructure considerably displaced from the center or keel line of the vessel when viewed from ahead. Certain other naval vessels cannot comply with the horizontal separation requirements of the white lights, and the two white lights on even large naval vessels, such as some cruisers, will thus appear to be crowded together when viewed from a distance. Other naval vessels may

---

[1] *Code of Federal Regulations: Title 32—National Defense; Part 706—Navigational Light Waivers; Part 707—Distinctive Lights Authorized for Submarines.*

[2] *At the time of writing, no updating of these regulations to correspond with the 1972 International Rules has been issued. It is expected that the present exemptions in CG-169 will be replaced in time.*

also have unorthodox navigational light arrangements or characteristics when seen either underway or at anchor.

(b) Naval vessels may also be expected to display certain other lights. These lights include, but are not limited to, different colored recognition light signals, landing lights on carriers, and pulsating red lights to indicate speed to other naval ships. These lights may sometimes be shown in combination with navigational lights.

(c) During peacetime naval maneuvers, naval ships, alone or in company, may also dispense with showing any lights, though efforts will be made to display lights on the approach of shipping.

(d) 33 U.S. Code, sections 360 and 1052 provide that the requirements of the Regulations for Preventing Collisions at Sea, 1960, the Inland Rules, the Great Lakes Rules, and Western River Rules, as to the number, position, range of visibility, or arc of visibility of lights required to be displayed by vessels, shall not apply to any vessel or class of vessels of the Navy where the Secretary of the Navy shall find or certify that, by reason of special construction or purpose, it is not possible for such vessel or class of vessels to comply with the statutory provisions as to lights.

(e) This part consolidates and codifies certificates of the Secretary of the Navy under 33 U.S.C. 360 and 1052. It has been determined that, because of their construction, it is not possible for the classes or types of naval vessels listed in this part to comply with all of the requirements of the statutes enumerated in sections 360 and 1052, Title 33, United States Code.

Certifications of the Secretary of the Navy under 33 U.S.C. 360 and 1052

SEC. 706.2 The Secretary of the Navy hereby finds and certifies that the classes or types of vessels listed in this section are naval vessels of special construction and that, with respect to the position of the navigation lights listed in this section, it is not possible to comply with the requirements of the statutes enumerated in sections 360 and 1052 of Title 33, United States Code. The Secretary of the Navy further finds and certifies that the navigation lights listed in this section conform as closely as feasible to the applicable statutory requirements.

Submarines

SEC. 706.2 (a) One, 20-point white light is generally carried in the forward part of the vessel and will not be less than 15 feet above the hull. This light is visible over a maximum arc of 27 points, that is from right ahead to 5½ points (62 degrees) abaft the beam on either side.

(b) A second, 20-point or other white light is not installed.

(c) Side lights may be visible simultaneously across the bow. The side lights may also be visible 30 degress abaft the beam.

TABLE ONE

Vessel class or type	Distance in feet of the forward 20-point white light below minimum required height (based on requirements of International Rule 2(a)(iii))	Distance in feet below minimum required vertical separation between forward and after 20-point white lights (based on requirements of International Rule 2(a)(iii))	Ratio of horizontal to vertical separation of the two 20-point white lights (based on International Rule 2(a)(iii) which requires ratio of 3.0 to 1))	Minimum distance horizontally in feet between forward and after 20-point white lights
Cruisers: CA (Heavy Cruiser) CAG (Guided Missile Heavy Cruiser) CG(N) (Guided Missile Cruiser) CL (Light Cruiser) CLG (Guided Missile Light Cruiser)	None	None	0.9 or greater to 1	29 or greater.
AIRCRAFT CARRIERS: T-AKV (MSTS Auxiliary Cargo Ship) LPH (Amphibious Assault Ship) CVA (Attack Aircraft Carrier) CVS (ASW Support Aircraft Carrier)	11 or less	2 or less	0.7 or greater to 1	20 or greater.
CC2 (Command Ship converted from aircraft carrier).	25	None	2.0 or greater to 1	30 or greater.
AGMR-2 (Major Communications Relay Ship converted from aircraft carrier)	25 or less	None	3.0 or greater to 1	30 or greater.
AVT (Auxiliary Aircraft Transport)	14 or less		3.0 or greater to 1	45 or greater.
AUXILIARIES: ADG (Degaussing Vessel) AG (Miscellaneous) AGB (Icebreaker) AGS (Surveying Ship) AKS (General Stores Issue Ship) AN (Net Laying Ship) APB (Self-Propelled Barracks Ship)	40 or less	3 or less	0.9 or greater to 1	19 or greater.

Vessel				
ARSD (Salvage Lifting Vessel)				
AVB (Advanced Aviation Base Ship)	40 or less	3 or less	0.9 or greater to 1	19 or greater.
AVM (Guided Missile Ship)				
AVP (Small Seaplane Tender)				
DESTROYERS:				
DD (Destroyer)				
DDE (Escort Destroyer)				
DDG (Guided Missile Destroyer)	18 or less	3 or less	0.9 or greater to 1	17 or greater.
DDR (Radar Picker Destroyer)				
DL (Frigate)				
DLG (Guided Missile Frigate)				
AMPHIBIOUS WARFARE VESSELS:				
APD (High Speed Transport)				
IFS (Inshore Fire Support Ship)				
LSD (Dock Landing Ship)	40 or less	5 or less	1.0 or greater to 1	21 or greater.
LST (Tank Landing Ship)				
LSM (Medium Landing Ship)				
LSMR (Landing Ship Medium Rocket)	19 or less	None	3.0 or greater to 1	158 or greater.
PATROL VESSELS:				
DE (Escort Vessel)				
DER (Radar Picket Escort Vessel)	17 or less	5 or less	1.0 or greater to 1	19 or greater.
PC (Submarine Chaser)				
PCE (Escort)				
PCER (Rescue Escort)	After white light not carried.			
PC(H) (Hydrofoil Patrol Craft)	None	None	1.0 or greater to 1	19 or greater.
PGM (Motor Gunboat)	7 or less	None	1.3 or greater to 1	19 or greater.
MINE VESSELS:				
MHC (Minehunter Coastal)				
MSF (Minesweeper Fleet)	16 or less	3 or less	0.6 or greater to 1	8 or greater.
MSO (Minesweeper Ocean)				
MSS (Minesweeper Special)				
SERVICE VESSELS:				
YG (Garbage Lighter Self-Propelled)				
YV (Drone Aircraft Catapult) (Control Craft)	16 or less	5 or less	0.6 or greater to 1	12 or greater.
Self-Propelled Crane (No hull classification)				
SUBMERSIBLES:				
NR-1 (Nuclear Powered Research Vehicle)	10	After white light neither required nor carried.		

(d) Lights required by International Rule 4 are not installed.

(e) The white light showing to the stern will be visible over a maximum arc of 23 points of the compass, that is from right astern 11½ points (approximately 126 degrees) to either side. This light is not installed at the stern but may be located from 20 to 190 feet forward of the stern.

(f) The forward anchor light may be carried up to a maximum of 60 feet aft of the stem and is carried at a height not less than 6 feet above the hull. The after anchor light may be carried at a greater height.

NOTES

1. The after range light when carried by naval vessels is a 20-point white light as required by International Rule 2(a) (ii).

2. The arc of visibility of the after 20-point white light on certain heavy cruisers (CA) may be obstructed by as much as one point when viewed from ahead.

3. On aircraft carriers (CVA and CVS) and aircraft carrier types (LPH, T-AKV and AVT), the following additional variations exist:

a. The two 20-point white lights (masthead light and range light) are located at a maximum distance of 94 feet to the left of the keel line when viewed from ahead. (This distance is measured perpendicularly from the keel line to the two white lights.)

b. The forward anchor lights are located a maximum of 8 feet vertically below the uppermost continuous deck (two lights at the same level). These lights are located forward and on either side of the vessel.

c. The after anchor lights are located a maximum of 31 feet vertically below the uppermost continuous deck (two lights at the same level). These lights are located aft and on either side of the vessel.

4. On certain Command Ships and major Communications Relay Ships (CC-2 and AGMR-2 types) converted from aircraft carrier hull, the following additional variations exist:

a. Towing lights, when displayed, will meet the requirements for vertical separation; however, the lower light will be located 3-9 feet above the hull.

b. Five degrees of the arc of visibility of the range light on CC-2 type ships is obstructed at a point commencing approximately 2½ points forward of the port beam.

c. The number and position of the forward and after anchor lights for CC-2 type ships are the same as those of other classes of aircraft carriers described in Notes 3b and 3c of this section.

d. The lights mentioned in Table One with respect to CC-2 and AGMR-2 type ships are located on the center or keel line.

e. The masthead light shall be carried at a height of 15 feet or more above the hull.

5. On mechanized landing craft (LCM) and certain utility landing craft (LCU) only one 20-point white light is installed and is located in the after part of the ship. Also in certain utility landing craft, the 20-point white light is located 11 feet or less to the left of the keel line when viewed from ahead.

6. On 94-feet aircraft rescue boats (no hull classification) and motor-torpedo boats (PT), the 20-point white light is located at a maximum of 14 feet below the required height (based on International Rule 2 (a) (iii)).

7. On motor-torpedo boats (PT) the lower towing light is located at a maximum of 4 feet below the required height (based on International Rule 3(a)).

8. On hydrofoil patrol craft (PC(H) class):

a. The masthead and anchor lights shall be located on the centerline and two feet aft of the amidship point instead of in the forepart of such vessels.

b. The anchor light shall be carried at a height above the hull of more than 20 feet.

9. On self-propelled crane (no hull classification) considerable reduction in the all around visibility of anchor lights exists. Two sets of "not under command" lights are installed, one set on either side of the super-structure (based on International Rule 4(a)).

10. Great Lakes—Naval vessels operating on the Great Lakes shall carry their navigational lights and shapes at the positions complying with the Regulations for Preventing Collisions at Sea, 1960, except as follows: For naval vessels under 150 feet in length requiring only one white light under the Regulations for Preventing Collisions at Sea, 1960, an additional all around white light will be carried which in some cases may be carried less than 50 feet abaft the forward light. In addition, the after white range light required by Rule 3(c), Great Lakes Rules, is a 20-point white light, so fixed as to show the light 10 points on each side of the vessel, that is, from right ahead to two points abaft the beam on either side. These vessels will, however, carry the white stern light required by Rule 10, Regulations for Preventing Collisions at Sea, 1960, to light the vessel aft. At anchor these vessels will display in lieu of the two lights forward and two lights aft, Rule 9, Great Lakes Rules, a single all around white anchor light forward and a single all around white anchor light aft located in accordance with Rule 11 (a) and (b), Regulations for Preventing Collisions at Sea, 1960, as modified for aircraft carriers and aircraft carrier types by Note 3 of this section. Submarines will be lighted as provided by Table Two.

11. On guided missile destroyers known as the DDG–2 Class, and on destroyer-type vessels when engaged in towing vessels or objects exceeding 600 feet in length, the two lower of the three towing 20-point white

lights will be separated from 3 feet to 15 feet vertically in lieu of the prescribed 6-foot separation. On motor gunboats (PGM) the three towing lights shall be carried in a vertical line, equally spaced and not less than 3 feet apart in lieu of the prescribed 6-foot separation (based on International Rule 3(a)).

12. On Mine Countermeasures Support Ships (MCS 1 Class), the after anchor light will be carried at a height not less than 4 feet lower than the forward anchor light in lieu of the required 15 feet (based on International Rule 11(b)). The after 20-point white light will be obstructed, in arc of visibility, for approximately 1° when viewed from dead ahead.

13. On motor gunboats (PGM), the three task lights shall be carried in a vertical line, equally spaced and not less than 3 feet apart in lieu of the prescribed 6-foot separation (based on International Rule 4(c)).

14. On Side Loaded Warping Tugs, the 20-point white light (masthead light) will be located 55½ feet, or approximately two-thirds of the vessel's length, aft on the bow, rather than in the forepart of the vessel (based on International Rule 2(a)(i) and Inland Article 2(a)). Also, this light will be located 5 feet to starboard of the vessel's centerline.

15. On Landing Craft Repair Ships (ARL) the lower two towing lights in the three-light presentation (based on International Rule 3(a) and Inland Article 3(a)) will be obstructed when viewed from off the vessel's port and starboard bow. There will be a 1.5° arc of obstruction, from 10° through 11.5°, relative to vessel's head; and a 2.5° arc of obstruction, from 346° through 348.5°, relative to the vessel's head.

DISTINCTIVE LIGHTS AUTHORIZED FOR SUBMARINES

PART 707

Display of Distinctive Lights by Submarines

SEC. 707.1 (a) In accordance with Rule 13(a), International Rules, and Article 13, Inland Rules, the Secretary of the Navy has authorized the display of a distinctive light by U.S. Naval submarines in international waters and in the inland waters of the United States. The light will be exhibited in addition to the presently prescribed navigational lights for submarines.

(b) The normal navigational lights of submarines have been found to be easily mistaken for those of small vessels when in fact submarines are large deep draft vessels with limited maneuvering characteristics while they are on the surface. The newly authorized light is expected to promote safety at sea by assisting in the identification of submarines.

(c) U.S. submarines may therefore display an amber rotating light producing 90 flashes per minute visible all around the horizon at a distance of at least 3 miles, the light to be located not less than 2 feet, and not more than 6 feet above the masthead light.

APPENDIX R
Exemptions for Coast Guard Vessels[1]

PART 135

Purpose of Regulations[2]

SEC. 135.01 The regulations in this part set forth findings, certificates, exemptions from certain statutory requirements, and those requirements found or certified to be feasible for Coast Guard vessels, by reason of

[1] *Code of Federal Regulations: Title 33—Navigation and Navigable Waters; Part 135—Lights for Coast Guard Vessels of Special Construction; Part 136—Shapes (Day Signals) for Coast Guard Vessels of Special Construction.*

[2] *At the time of writing, no updating of these regulations to correspond with the 1972 International Rules has been issued. It is expected that the present exemptions in CG-169 for Coast Guard vessels will be replaced in time. New exemptions for nonpublic vessels of special construction that qualify under Rule 1(e), 1972 International Rules, can also be expected to be made public record in some form.*

special construction, with respect to the number, position, range of visibility, or arc of visibility of the lights required to be displayed by vessels when navigating on the high seas or navigable waters of the United States, its territories or possessions.

Definition of Terms Used in This Part—(a) International Rules

The term "International Rules" means the "Regulations for Preventing Collisions at Sea, 1960," as set forth in Section 4 of the act of September 24, 1963 (77 Stat. 195–210; 33 U.S.C. 1061–1094).

(b) Inland Rules

The term "Inland Rules" means the rules for the navigation of rivers, harbors, and inland waters of the United States, except (1) the Great Lakes and their connecting and tributary waters as far east as Montreal, (2) the waters of the Mississippi River between its source and the Huey P. Long Bridge and all of its tributaries emptying thereinto and their tributaries, (3) that part of the Atchafalaya River above its junction with the Plaquemine-Morgan City alternate waterway and (4) the Red River of the North, as set forth in the act of June 7, 1897, as amended (30 Stat. 96–103, as amended; 33 U.S.C. 154–232).

(c) Great Lakes Rules

The term "Great Lakes Rules" means the act to regulate navigation on the Great Lakes and their connecting and tributary waters of February 8, 1895, as amended (28 Stat. 645–650, as amended; 33 U.S.C. 241–294).

General Findings and Certifications

SEC. 135.15 (a) It is hereby found that the Coast Guard vessels of special construction described in this part cannot comply with certain applicable statutory requirements, enumerated in various sections of this part, relating to the lights required to be displayed by vessels when navigating on the high seas or navigable waters of the United States, its territories or possessions, without seriously affecting the military characteristics and functions of the vessels concerned.

(b) It is hereby found and certified that the requirements regarding lights, as stated in the various sections of this part, which will be carried by the Coast Guard vessels described, conform as closely as feasible to the applicable statutory requirements.

Extent of Compliance

SEC. 135.20 Except as provided otherwise in this part, the Coast Guard vessels described in this part are in full compliance with the other provisions of the applicable International Rules, Inland Rules, or Great Lakes Rules governing the areas where the vessels are being operated.

Horizontal Separation of Range Lights

SEC. 135.25 (a) Rule 2(a)(iii), International Rules, requires in part that the minimum horizontal separation between the forward masthead light and the after range light shall be at least 45 feet (33 U.S.C. 1062(a) (iii)). Because of special construction, the Coast Guard vessels named in this section cannot comply with this requirement and are therefore exempted.

(b) The following Auxiliary vessel shall carry the forward masthead light and the after range light with a horizontal separation of 34 feet:

USCGC *Storis* (WAGB–38).

(c) The following Icebreakers carry the forward masthead light and after range light with a horizontal separation of 23 feet or more:

USCGC *Burton Island* (WAGB–283).

USCGC *Edisto* (WAGB–284).

USCGC *Glacier* (WAGB–4).

USCGC *Northwind* (WAGB–282).

USCGC *Southwind* (WAGB–280).

USCGC *Staten Island* (WAGB–278).

USCGC *Westwind* (WAGB–281).

(d) [Reserved.]

(e) The following Buoy Tenders, Class 180–A, shall carry the forward masthead light and after range light with a horizontal separation of 24 feet:

USCGC *Balsam* (WLB–62).

USCGC *Cactus* (WLB–270).

USCGC *Citrus* (WLB–300).

USCGC *Clover* (WLB–292).

USCGC *Conifer* (WLB–301).

USCGC *Cowslip* (WLB–277).

USCGC *Evergreen* (WAGO–295).

USCGC *Gentian* (WLB–290).

USCGC *Laurel* (WLB–291).

USCGC *Madrona* (WLB–302).

USCGC *Sorrel* (WLB–296).

(f) The following Buoy Tenders, Class 180–B, shall carry the forward masthead light and after range light with a horizontal separation of 16 feet:

USCGC *Buttonwood* (WLB–306).

USCGC *Ironwood* (WLB–297).

USCGC *Papaw* (WLB–308).

USCGC *Planetree* (WLB–307).

USCGC *Sweetgum* (WLB–309).

(g) The following Buoy Tenders, Class 180–C, shall carry the forward masthead light and after range light with a horizontal separation of 16 feet:

USCGC *Basswood* (WLB–388).
USCGC *Bittersweet* (WLB–389).
USCGC *Blackhaw* (WLB–390).
USCGC *Blackthorn* (WLB–391).
USCGC *Firebush* (WLB–393).
USCGC *Hornbeam* (WLB–394).
USCGC *Iris* (WLB–395).
USCGC *Mallow* (WLB–396).
USCGC *Mariposa* (WLB–397).
USCGC *Sagebrush* (WLB–399).
USCGC *Salvia* (WLB–400).
USCGC *Sassafras* (WLB–401).
USCGC *Sedge* (WLB–402).
USCGC *Spar* (WLB–403).
USCGC *Sweetbriar* (WLB–405).

(h) All patrol cutters, medium endurance, 210-foot class, shall carry the forward masthead light and the after range light with a horizontal separation of not less than 18 feet.

(i) The following patrol cutters, medium endurance, 143' class, carry the forward masthead light and the after range light with a horizontal separation of 40 feet or more:

USCGC *Modoc* (WMEC–194).
USCGC *Comanche* (WMEC–202).

International Rules and Inland Rules; Height and Arc of Visibility of After Anchor Light

SEC. 135.35 (a) Rule 11(b), International Rules, and Article 11, Inland Rules, require that the anchor light at the stern shall be not less than 15 feet lower than the forward anchor light, and also require that this light shall be visible all around the horizon (33 U.S.C. 1071(b), 180). Because of special construction the Coast Guard vessel named in this section cannot comply with these requirements and is therefore exempted.

(b) The following Auxiliary vessel shall carry the after anchor light at a height of 10 feet below the forward anchor light and the arc of visibility of the after anchor light shall be an arc of approximately 240 degrees, that is, from right aft to 120 degrees to port and 120 degrees to starboard:

USCGC *Courier* (WTR–410).

Vertical Separation of Range Lights

SEC. 135.40 (a) Rule 2(a)(iii), International Rules, and Article 2 (a), (e), Inland Rules, require that the vertical separation between the forward masthead light and the after range light shall be at least 15 feet (33 U.S.C. 1062(a)(iii), 172 (a) (e)). Because of special construction the Coast Guard vessels named in this section cannot comply with this requirement and are therefore exempted.

(b) The vertical separation between the forward masthead light and the after range light for the following Coast Guard Cutters is:

USCGC *Modoc* (WMEC–194) .... 10'7¹/₂"
USCGC *Comanche* (WMEC–202) .... 10'7¹/₂"

Height of Forward Masthead Light

SEC. 135.45 (a) Because of special construction, the Coast Guard Cutters named in paragraph (b) of this section cannot comply with the requirements of Rule 2(a)(iii) of the International Regulations (33 U.S.C. 1062(a)(iii)) and are exempted as allowed by 33 U.S.C. 1052.

(b) The height of the forward masthead light for the Coast Guard Cutter in the following class is:

143' WMEC CLASS................................. at least 28'0"

Vertical Separation of Towing Lights

SEC. 135.47 (a) Rule 3(a), International Rules, requires in part that "A power-driven vessel . . . when towing and the length of the tow, measuring from the stern of the towing vessel to the stern of the last vessel towed, exceeds 600 feet, shall carry three white lights in a vertical line one over the other, so that the upper and lower lights shall be the same distance from, and not less than 6 feet above or below the middle light. . . ." (33 U.S.C. 1063.) Because of special construction, the Coast Guard vessels described in this section cannot comply with this requirement and are therefore exempted.

(b) All Coast Guard cutters of the 82-foot and 95-foot WPB Classes, and of the 65-foot WYTL Class, when required to display towing lights consisting of three white lights in a vertical line one over the other, display such lights in a vertical line so that the upper and lower lights are the same distance from, and not less than 3 feet above or below the middle light.

Great Lakes Rules; Horizontal Separation of Range Lights

SEC. 135.50 (a) Rule 3(e), Great Lakes Rules, requires in part that the minimum horizontal separation between the forward masthead light and the after range light shall be more than 50 feet (33 U.S.C. 252 (e)). Because of special construction, the Coast Guard vessels named in this section cannot comply with this requirement and are therefore exempted.

(b) The following Buoy Tenders, Class 180–A, shall carry the forward masthead light and after range light with a horizontal separation of 24 feet:

USCGC *Tupelo* (WLB–303).

USCGC *Woodbine* (WLB–289).

(c) The following Buoy Tender, Class 180–B, shall carry the forward masthead light and after range light with a horizontal separation of 16 feet:

USCGC *Mesquite* (WLB–305).

(d) The following Buoy Tenders, Class 180–C, shall carry the forward masthead light and after range light with a horizontal separation of 16 feet:

USCGC *Acacia* (WLB–406).

USCGC *Bramble* (WLB–392).

USCGC *Sundew* (WLB–404).

USCGC *Woodrush* (WLB–407).

(e) The following Icebreaker shall carry the forward masthead light and after range light with a horizontal separation of 36 feet:

USCGC *Mackinaw* (WAGB–83).

(f) The following Icebreakers carry the forward masthead light and after range light with a horizontal separation of 23 feet:

USCGC *Burton Island* (WAGB–283).

USCGC *Edisto* (WAGB–284).

USCGC *Glacier* (WAGB–4).

USCGC *Northwind* (WAGB–282).

USCGC *Southwind* (WAGB–280).

USCGC *Staten Island* (WAGB–278).

USCGC *Westwind* (WAGB–281).

PART 136

Purpose of Regulations

SEC. *136.01* (a) The regulations in this part set forth findings, certifications, and exemptions from certain statutory requirements, and those requirements found or certified to be feasible for Coast Guard vessels, by reason of special construction, with respect to the number, position, range of visibility or arc of visibility of shapes (day signals) required to be displayed during the daytime by vessels when navigating on the high seas or navigable waters of the United States, its territories or its possessions.

Definition of Terms Used in This Part

SEC. 136.10 (a) *International Rules.* The term "International Rules" means the "Regulations for Preventing Collisions at Sea, 1960," as set forth in section 4 of the Act of September 24, 1963 (77 Stat. 195–210; 33 U.S.C. 1061–1094).

(b) *Inland Rules.* The term "Inland Rules" meaning the rules for the navigation of rivers, harbors, and other inland waters of the United States, except (1) the Great Lakes and their connecting and tributary waters as far east as Montreal, (2) the waters of the Mississippi River between its source and the Huey P. Long Bridge and all of its tributaries emptying thereinto and their tributaries, (3) that part of the Atchafalaya River above its junction with the Plaquemine-Morgan City alternate waterway, and (4) the Red River of the North; as set forth in the act of June 7, 1897, as amended (30 Stat. 96–103, as amended, 33 U.S.C. 154–232).

General Findings and Certification

SEC. 136.15 (a) It is hereby found that the Coast Guard vessels of special construction described in this part cannot comply with certain applicable statutory requirements, enumerated in various sections of this part, relating to the shapes (day signals) required to be displayed by vessels when navigating on the high seas or navigable waters of the United States, its territories or possessions, without seriously affecting the military characteristics and functions of the vessels concerned.

(b) It is hereby found and certified that the requirements regarding shapes (day signals), as stated in the various sections of this part, which will be carried by the Coast Guard vessels described, conform as closely as feasible to the applicable statutory requirements.

Extent of Compliance

SEC. 136.20 (a) Except as provided otherwise in this subchapter, the Coast Guard vessels described in this part are in full compliance with the other provisions regarding shapes (day signals) of the applicable International Rules or Inland Rules governing the areas where the vessels are being operated.

*International Rules; Vessels Not under Command or Engaged in
Certain Operations and Displaying Two Black Balls*

SEC. 136.25 (a) Rule 4(a), International Rules, requires in part that a
vessel which is not under command shall by day carry "in a vertical line
one over the other not less than 6 feet apart, where they can best be seen,
two black balls or shapes each not less than 2 feet in diameter" (33 U.S.C.
1064). Because of special construction, the Coast Guard vessels of the
82-foot and 95-foot WPB classes cannot comply with such requirements
and are therefore exempt.

(b) All Coast Guard vessels of the 82-foot and 95-foot WPB classes
shall carry and when necessary display the required two black balls or
shapes with a vertical separation of not less than 4 feet between them.

*International Rules; Vessels Engaged in Certain Occupations
and Displaying Three Shapes*

SEC. 136.30 (a) Rule 4(c) and Rule 11(d), International Rules, require
in part that a vessel "engaged in laying or picking up a submarine cable
or navigation mark, or a vessel engaged in surveying or underwater operations," including "when at anchor," shall carry and display 3 shapes, each
2 feet in diameter, in a vertical line one over the other so the upper and
lower shapes shall be the same distance from, and not less than 6 feet
above or below, the middle shape (33 U.S.C. 1064(c), 1071(d)). Because
of special construction, the Coast Guard vessels of the 82-foot and 95-foot
WPB classes cannot comply with these requirements and are therefore
exempt.

(b) Rule 11(e), International Rules, requires in part that a vessel aground
by day "shall carry, where they can best be seen, 3 black balls, each not
less than 2 feet in diameter, placed in a vertical line one over the other,
not less than 6 feet apart" (33 U.S.C. 1071(e)). Because of special construction, the Coast Guard vessels of the 82-foot and 95-foot WPB classes
cannot comply with this requirement and are therefore exempt.

(c) All Coast Guard vessels of the 82-foot and 95-foot WPB classes shall
carry and when necessary shall display where they can best be seen, three
black balls or shapes required by Rule 4(c) and Rule 11 (d) or (e), International Rules, in a vertical line with a vertical separation of not less than
1 foot between them.

APPENDIX S

Vessel Bridge-to-Bridge Radiotelephone Act[1]

TO REQUIRE A RADIOTELEPHONE ON CERTAIN VESSELS WHILE NAVIGATING UPON SPECIFIED WATERS OF THE UNITED STATES

Be it enacted by the Senate and House of Representatives of the United States of America in Congress assembled, That this Act may be cited as the "Vessel Bridge-to-Bridge Radiotelephone Act".

SEC. 2 It is the purpose of this Act to provide a positive means whereby the operators of approaching vessels can communicate their intentions to one another through voice radio, located convenient to the operator's navigation station. To effectively accomplish this, there is need for a specific frequency or frequencies dedicated to the exchange of navigational information, on navigable waters of the United States.

SEC. 3. (1) "Secretary" means the Secretary of the Department in which the Coast Guard is operating;

(2) "power-driven vessel" means any vessel propelled by machinery; and

(3) "towing vessel" means any commercial vessel engaged in towing another vessel astern, alongside, or by pushing ahead.

SEC. 4. (a) Except as provided in section 7 of this Act—

(1) every power-driven vessel of three hundred gross tons and upward while navigating;

(2) every vessel of one hundred gross tons and upward carrying one or more passengers for hire while navigating;

(3) every towing vessel of twenty-six feet or over in length while navigating; and

(4) every dredge and floating plant engaged in or near a channel or fairway in operations likely to restrict or affect navigation of other vessels— shall have a radiotelephone capable of operation from its navigational bridge or, in the case of a dredge, from its main control station and capable

[1] *85 Stat. 164; 33 U.S.C. Sec. 1201-1208.*

of transmitting and receiving on the frequency or frequencies within the 156–162 Mega-Hertz band using the classes of emissions designated by the Federal Communications Commission, after consultation with other cognizant agencies, for the exchange of navigational information.

(b) The radiotelephone required by subsection (a) shall be carried on board the described vessels, dredges, and floating plants upon the navigable waters of the United States inside the lines established pursuant to section 2 of the Act of February 19, 1895 (28 Stat. 672), as amended.

SEC. 5. The radiotelephone required by this Act is for the exclusive use of the master or person in charge of the vessel, or the person designated by the master or person in charge to pilot or direct the movement of the vessel, who shall maintain a listening watch on the designated frequency. Nothing contained herein shall be interpreted as precluding the use of portable radiotelephone equipment to satisfy the requirements of this Act.

SEC. 6. Whenever radiotelephone capability is required by this Act, a vessel's radiotelephone equipment shall be maintained in effective operating condition. If the radiotelephone equipment carried aboard a vessel ceases to operate, the master shall exercise due diligence to restore it or cause it to be restored to effective operating condition at the earliest practicable time. The failure of a vessel's radiotelephone equipment shall not, in itself, constitute a violation of this Act, nor shall it obligate the master of any vessel to moor or anchor his vessel; however, the loss of radiotelephone capability shall be given consideration in the navigation of the vessel.

SEC. 7. The Secretary may, if he considers that marine navigational safety will not be adversely affected or where a local communication system fully complies with the intent of this concept but does not conform in detail, issue exemptions from any provisions of this Act, on such terms and conditions as he considers appropriate.

SEC. 8. (a) The Federal Communications Commission shall, after consultation with other cognizant agencies, prescribe regulations necessary to specify operating and technical conditions and characteristics including frequencies, emission, and power of radiotelephone equipment required under this Act.

(b) The Secretary shall, subject to the concurrence of the Federal Communications Commission, prescribe regulations for the enforcement of this Act.

SEC. 9. (a) Whoever, being the master or person in charge of a vessel subject to this Act, fails to enforce or comply with this Act or the regulations hereunder; or

Whoever, being designated by the master or person in charge of a vessel subject to this Act to pilot or direct the movement of the vessel, fails to enforce or comply with this Act or the regulations hereunder—

Is liable to a civil penalty of not more than $500 to be assessed by the Secretary.

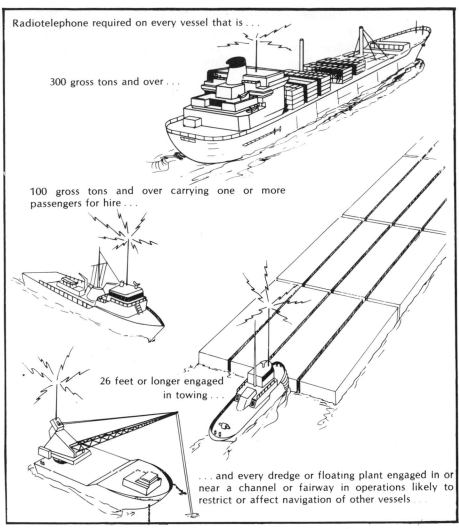

Radiotelephone required on every vessel that is . . .

300 gross tons and over . . .

100 gross tons and over carrying one or more passengers for hire . . .

26 feet or longer engaged in towing . . .

. . . and every dredge or floating plant engaged in or near a channel or fairway in operations likely to restrict or affect navigation of other vessels . . .

FIG. S1. Some examples of vessels required to have radiotelephones.

(b) Every vessel navigating in violation of this Act or the regulations hereunder is liable to a civil penalty of not more than $500 to be assessed by the Secretary for which the vessel may be proceeded against in any district court of the United States having jurisdiction.

(c) Any penalty assessed under this section may be remitted or mitigated by the Secretary upon such terms as he may deem proper.

SEC. 10. This Act shall become effective May 1, 1971, or six months after the promulgation of regulations which implement its provisions, whichever is later.

Vessel Bridge-to-Bridge Radiotelephone Regulations[1]

PART 26[2]

Purpose

SEC. 26.01 (a) The purpose of this part is to implement the provisions of the Vessel Bridge-to-Bridge Radiotelephone Act. This part—

(1) Requires the use of the vessel bridge-to-bridge radiotelephone;

(2) Provides the Coast Guard's interpretation of the meaning of important terms in the Act;

(3) Prescribes the procedures for applying for an exemption from the Act and the regulations issued under the Act and a listing of exemptions.

(b) Nothing in this part relieves any person from the obligation of complying with the rules of the road and the applicable pilot rules.

---

[1] *Code of Federal Regulations: Title 33—Navigation and Navigable Waters; Part 26—Vessel bridge-to-bridge radiotelephone Regulations.*

[2] *Authority: The provisions of this Part 26 issued under 85 stat. 164: 33 U.S.C.A. secs. 1201-1208, 49 CFR 1.46(o)(2).*

Definitions

SEC 26.02 For the purpose of this part and interpreting the Act—

"Secretary" means the Secretary of the Department in which the Coast Guard is operating;

"Act" means the "Vessel Bridge-to-Bridge Radiotelephone Act", 33 U.S.C.A. sections 1201–1208;

"Length" is measured from end to end over the deck excluding sheer;

"Navigable waters of the United States inside the lines established pursuant to section 2 of the Act of February 19, 1895 (28 Stat. 672), as amended," means those waters governed by the Navigation Rules for Harbors, Rivers, and Inland Waters (33 U.S.C. sec. 151 et seq.), the Navigation Rules for Great Lakes and their Connecting and Tributary Waters (33 U.S.C. sec. 241 et seq.), and the Navigation Rules for Red River of the North and Rivers emptying into Gulf of Mexico and Tributaries (33 U.S.C. sec. 301 et seq.);

"Power-driven vessel" means any vessel propelled by machinery; and

"Towing vessel" means any commercial vessel engaged in towing another vessel astern, alongside, or by pushing ahead.

Radiotelephone Required

SEC. 26.03 (a) Unless an exemption is granted under Section 26.09 and except as provided in subparagraph (4) of this paragraph, section 4 of the Act provides that:

(1) Every power-driven vessel of 300 gross tons and upward while navigating:

(2) Every vessel of 100 gross tons and upward carrying one or more passengers for hire while navigating:

(3) Every towing vessel of 26 feet or over in length while navigating: and

(4) Every dredge and floating plant engaged in or near a channel or fairway in operations likely to restrict or affect navigation of other vessels: *Provided,* That an unmanned or intermittently manned floating plant under the control of a dredge need not be required to have separate radiotelephone capability:

Shall have a radiotelephone capable of operation from its navigational bridge, or in the case of a dredge, from its main control station, and capable of transmitting and receiving on the frequency or frequencies within the 156–162 Mega-Hertz band using the classes of emissions designated by the Federal Communications Commission, after consultation with other cognizant agencies, for the exchange of navigational information.

(b) The radiotelephone required by paragraph (a) of this section shall be carried on board the described vessels, dredges, and floating plants upon the navigable waters of the United States inside the lines established pursuant to section 2 of the Act of February 19, 1895 (28 Stat. 672), as amended.

Use of the Designated Frequency

SEC. 26.04 (a) No person may use the frequency designated by the Federal Communications Commission under section 8 of the Act, 33 U.S.C.A. section 1207(a), to transmit any information other than information necessary for the safe navigation of vessels or necessary tests.

(b) Each person who is required to maintain a listening watch under section 5 of the Act shall, when necessary, transmit and confirm, on the designated frequency, the intentions of his vessel and any other information necessary for the safe navigation of vessels.

(c) Nothing in these regulations may be construed as prohibiting the use of the designated frequency to communicate with shore stations to obtain or furnish information necessary for the safe navigation of vessels.[3]

Use of Radiotelephone

SEC. 26.05 Section 5 of the Act states:

(a) The radiotelephone required by this Act is for the exclusive use of the master or person in charge of the vessel, or the person designated by the master or person in charge of the vessel, or the person designated by the master or person in charge to pilot or direct the movement of the vessel, who shall maintain a listening watch on the designated frequency. Nothing contained herein shall be interpreted as precluding the use of portable radiotelephone equipment to satisfy the requirements of this Act.

Maintenance of Radiotelephone; Failure of Radiotelephone

SEC. 26.06 Section 6 of the Act states:

(a) Whenever radiotelephone capability is required by this Act, a vessel's radiotelephone equipment shall be maintained in effective operating condition. If the radiotelephone equipment carried aboard a vessel ceases to operate, the master shall exercise due diligence to restore it or cause it to be restored to effective operating condition at the earliest practicable time. The failure of a vessel's radiotelephone equipment shall not, in itself, constitute a violation of this Act, nor shall it obligate the master of any vessel to moor or anchor his vessel; however, the loss of radiotelephone capability shall be given consideration in the navigation of the vessel.

---

[3] The Federal Communications Commission has designated the frequency 156.65 MHz for the use of bridge-to-bridge radiotelephone stations.

English Language

SEC. 26.07 No person may use the services of, and no person may serve as a person required to maintain a listening watch under section 5 of the Act, 33 U.S.C.A. section 1204 unless he can speak the English language.

Exemption Procedures

SEC. 26.08 (a) Any person may petition for an exemption from any provision of the Act or this part;

(b) Each petition must be submitted in writing to U. S. Coast Guard (M), 400 Seventh Street SW., Washington, DC 20590, and must state:

(1) The provisions of the Act or this part from which an exemption is requested; and

(2) The reasons why marine navigation will not be adversely affected if the exemption is granted and if the exemption relates to a local communication system how that system would fully comply with the intent of the concept of the Act but would not conform in detail if the exemption is granted.

List of Exemptions

SEC. 26.09 (Reserved)

Penalties

SEC. 26.10 Section 9 of this Act states:

(a) Whoever, being the master or person in charge of a vessel subject to the Act, fails to enforce or comply with the Act or the regulations hereunder; or whoever, being designated by the master or person in charge of a vessel subject to the Act to pilot or direct the movement of a vessel fails to enforce or comply with the Act or the regulations hereunder—is liable to a civil penalty of not more than $500 to be assessed by the Secretary.

(b) Every vessel navigated in violation of the Act or the regulations hereunder is liable to a civil penalty of not more than $500 to be assessed by the Secretary, for which the vessel may be proceeded against in any District Court of the United States having jurisdiction.

(c) Any penalty assessed under this section may be remitted or mitigated by the Secretary, upon such terms as he may deem proper.

This amendment shall become effective January 1, 1973.

Ports and Waterways Safety Act of 1972[1]

Be it enacted by the Senate and House of Representatives of the United States of America in Congress assembled, That:
This Act may be cited as the "Ports and Waterways Safety Act of 1972."

TITLE I—PORTS AND WATERWAYS SAFETY AND ENVIRONMENTAL QUALITY

SEC. 101 In order to prevent damage to, or the destruction or loss of any vessel, bridge, or other structure on or in the navigable waters of the United States, or any land structure or shore area immediately adjacent to those waters; and to protect the navigable waters and the resources therein from environmental harm resulting from vessel or structure damage, destruction, or loss, the Secretary of the department in which the Coast Guard is operating may—

(1) establish, operate, and maintain vessel traffic services and systems for ports, harbors, and other waters subject to congested vessel traffic;

(2) require vessels which operate in an area of a vessel traffic service or system to utilize or comply with that service or system, including the carrying or installation of electronic or other devices necessary for the use of the service or system;

(3) control vessel traffic in areas which he determines to be especially hazardous, or under conditions of reduced visibility, adverse weather, vessel congestion, or other hazardous circumstances by—

(i) specifying times of entry, movement, or departure to, from, within, or through ports, harbors, or other waters;

[1] *Public Law 92-340, July 10, 1972 (Title 33 U.S. Code).*

(ii) establishing vessel traffic routing schemes;

(iii) establishing vessel size and speed limitations and vessel operating conditions; and

(iv) restricting vessel operation, in a hazardous area or under hazardous conditions, to vessels which have particular operating characteristics and capabilities which he considers necessary for safe operation under the circumstances;

(4) direct the anchoring, mooring, or movement of a vessel when necessary to prevent damage to or by that vessel or her cargo, stores, supplies, or fuel;

(5) require pilots on self-propelled vessels engaged in the foreign trades in areas and under circumstances where a pilot is not otherwise required by State law to be on board until the State having jurisdiction of an area involved establishes a requirement for a pilot in that area or under the circumstances involved;

(6) establish procedures, measures, and standards for the handling, loading, discharge, storage, stowage, and movement, including the emergency removal, control and disposition, of explosives or other dangerous articles or substances (including the substances described in section 4417a(2) (A), (B), and (C) of the Revised Statutes of the United States (46 U.S.C. 391a(2) (A), (B), and (C) on structures subject to this title;

(7) prescribe minimum safety equipment requirements for structures subject to this title to assure adequate protection from fire, explosion, natural disasters, and other serious accidents or casualties;

8) establish water or waterfront safety zones or other measures for limited, controlled, or conditional access and activity when necessary for the protection of any vessel, structure, waters, or shore area; and

(9) establish procedures for examination to assure compliance with the minimum safety equipment requirements for structures.

SEC. 102 (a) For the purpose of this Act, the term "United States" includes the fifty States, the District of Columbia, Puerto Rico, the territories and possessions of the United States, and the Trust Territory of the Pacific Islands.

(b) Nothing contained in this title supplants or modifies any treaty or Federal statute or authority granted thereunder, nor does it prevent a State or political subdivision thereof from prescribing for structures only higher safety equipment requirements or safety standards than those which may be prescribed pursuant to this title.

(c) In the exercise of his authority under this title, the Secretary shall consult with other Federal agencies, as appropriate, in order to give due consideration to their statutory and other responsibilities, and to assure consistency of regulations applicable to vessels, structures, and areas covered by this title. The Secretary may also consider, utilize, and incorporate regulations or similar directory materials issued by port or other State and local authorities.

(d) This title shall not be applicable to the Panama Canal. The authority granted to the Secretary under section 101 of this title shall not be delegated with respect to the Saint Lawrence Seaway to any agency other than the Saint Lawrence Seaway Development Corporation. Any other authority granted the Secretary under this title shall be delegated to the Saint Lawrence Seaway Development Corporation to the extent that the Secretary determines such delegation is necessary for the proper operation of the Seaway.

(e) In carrying out his duties and responsibilities under this title to promote the safe and efficient conduct of maritime commerce the Secretary shall consider fully the wide variety of interests which may be affected by the exercise of his authority hereunder. In determining the need for, and the substance of, any rule or regulation or the exercise of other authority hereunder the Secretary shall, among other things, consider—

(1) the scope and degree of the hazards;

(2) vessel traffic characteristics including minimum interference with the flow of commercial traffic, traffic volume, the sizes and types of vessels, the usual nature of local cargoes, and similar factors;

(3) port and waterway configurations and the differences in geographic, climatic, and other conditions and circumstances;

(4) environmental factors;

(5) economic impact and effects;

(6) existing vessel traffic control systems, services, and schemes; and

(7) local practices and customs, including voluntary arrangements and agreements within the maritime community.

SEC. 103 The Secretary may investigate any incident, accident, or act involving the loss or destruction of, or damage to, any structure subject to this title, or which affects or may affect the safety or environmental quality of the ports, harbors, or navigable waters of the United States. In any investigation under this title, the Secretary may issue a subpoena to require the attendance of any witness and the production of documents and other evidence. In case of refusal to obey a subpoena issued to any person, the Secretary may request the Attorney General to invoke the aid of the appropriate district court of the United States to compel compliance. Witnesses may be paid fees for travel and attendance at rates not exceeding those allowed in a district court of the United States.

SEC. 104 The Secretary may issue reasonable rules, regulations, and standards necessary to implement this title. In the exercise of his rulemaking authority the Secretary is subject to the provisions of chapters 5 and 7 of title 5, United States Code. In preparing proposed rules, regulations, and standards, the Secretary shall provide an adequate opportunity for consultation and comment to State and local governments, representatives of the marine industry, port and harbor authorities, environmental groups, and other interested parties.

SEC. 105 The Secretary shall, within one year after the effective date of this Act, report to the Congress his recommendations for legislation which may be necessary to achieve coordination and/or eliminate duplication between the functions authorized by this Act and the functions of any other agencies.[2]

SEC. 106 Whoever violates a regulation issued under this title shall be liable to a civil penalty of not more than $10,000. The Secretary may assess and collect any civil penalty incurred under this title and, in his discretion, remit, mitigate, or compromise any penalty. Upon failure to collect or compromise a penalty, the Secretary may request the Attorney General to commence an action for collection in any district court of the United States. A vessel used or employed in a violation of a regulation under this title shall be liable in rem and may be proceeded against in any district court of the United States having jurisdiction.

SEC. 107 Whoever willfully violates a regulation issued under this title shall be fined not less than $5,000 or more than $50,000 or imprisoned for not more than five years, or both.

Title II, dealing with vessels carrying certain cargoes in bulk and pollution prevention, is not included herein.

[2] *No report has been made, as the Coast Guard had no recommendations for legislative corrections or additions.*

Vessel Traffic Services[1]

PART 161[2]

Puget Sound Vessel Traffic Service[3]

Sec.

[1] *Code of Federal Regulations: Title 33—Navigation and Navigable Waters; Part 161—Vessel Traffic Services.*
[2] *Authority: Sec. 104, Pub. L. 92-340, 86 Stat. 424 (33 U.S.C. 1224); 37 FR 21943, 49 CFR 1.46(o)(4).*
[3] *Regulations have been published as of this writing only for the Puget Sound VTS. Additional systems are in various stages of development to include the following areas: San Francisco, Houston-Galveston, New York and Long Island Sound, New Orleans/Baton Rouge, and Prince William Sound, Alaska. Other areas are being considered including U.S./Canada coordination for the Great Lakes and the West Coast.*

SUBPART B—PUGET SOUND VESSEL TRAFFIC

General Rules

Purpose and Applicability

SEC. 161.101 (a) This subpart prescribes rules for vessel operation in the Puget Sound vessel traffic service area (VTS Area) to prevent collisions and groundings and to protect the navigable waters of the VTS Area from environmental harm resulting from collisions and groundings.

(b) The General Rules in §§ 161.101–161.111 and the TSS Rules in §§ 161.150–161.154 and § 161.156 (b) and (c) of this subpart apply to the operation of all vessels.

(c) The Communication Rules in §§ 161.120–161.136, the Vessel Movement Reporting Rules in § 161.142, the TSS Rule in § 161.156(a), and the Rosario Strait Rules in §§ 161.170–161.174 of this subpart apply only to the operation of—

(1) Each vessel of 300 or more gross tons that is propelled by machinery;

(2) Each vessel of 100 or more gross tons that is carrying one or more passengers for hire;

(3) Each commercial vessel of 26 feet or over in length engaged in towing another vessel astern, alongside, or by pushing ahead; and

(4) Each dredge and floating plant.

Definitions

SEC. 161.103
As used in this subpart—

(a) "Vessel traffic center" (VTC) means the shore based facility that operates the Puget Sound vessel traffic system.

(b) "Vessel traffic service area" (VTS Area) means the area described in § 161.180 of this part.

(c) "Traffic separation scheme" (TSS) means the network of traffic lanes, separation zones, and precautionary areas in the VTS Area.

(d) "Traffic lane" means an area of the TSS in which all vessels ordinarily proceed in the same direction.

(e) "Separation zone" means an area of the TSS that is located between two traffic lanes to keep vessels proceeding in opposite directions a safe distance apart.

(f) "Precautionary area" means an area of the TSS at the entrance of one or more traffic lanes where vessel traffic converges from two or more directions.

(g) "Person" includes an individual, firm, corporation, association, partnership, and governmental entity.

(h) "ETA" means estimated time of arrival.

Vessel Operation in the VTS Area

SEC. 161.104 No person may cause or authorize the operation of a vessel in the VTS Area contrary to the rules in this subpart.

Laws and Regulations Not Affected

SEC. 161.105 Nothing in this subpart is intended to relieve any person from complying with—

(a) The Navigation Rules for Harbors, Rivers, and Inland Waters Generally (33 U.S.C. §§ 151–232);

(b) Vessel Bridge-to-Bridge Radiotelephone Regulations (Part 26 of this chapter);

(c) Pilot Rules for Inland Waters (Part 80 of this chapter);

(d) Puget Sound gill net fishing rule (33 CFR 206.93);

(e) The Federal Boat Safety Act of 1971 (46 U.S.C. 1451–1489); and

(f) Any other laws or regulations.

VTC Directions

SEC. 161.107 (a) During conditions of vessel congestion, adverse weather, reduced visibility, or other hazardous circumstances in the VTS Area, the VTC may issue directions specifying times when vessels may enter, move within or through, or depart from ports, harbors, or other waters in the VTS Area.

(b) The master of a vessel in the VTS Area shall comply with each direction issued to him under this section.

Authorization to Deviate from These Rules

SEC. 161.109 (a) The Commander, Thirteenth Coast Guard District may upon request issue an authorization to deviate from any rule in this subpart if he finds that the proposed operations under the authorization can be done safely. An application for an authorization must state the need for the authorization and describe the proposed operations.

(b) The VTC may, upon request, issue an authorization to deviate from any rule in this subpart for a voyage or part of a voyage on which a vessel is embarked or about to embark.

Emergencies

SEC. 161.111 In an emergency, any person may deviate from any section in this subpart to the extent necessary to avoid endangering persons, property, or the environment.

Communication Rules

Radio Listening Watch

SEC. 161.120 The master of a vessel in the VTS Area shall continuously monitor the radio frequency designated in the Puget Sound VTS Operating Manual for the sector of the VTS Area in which the vessel is operating, except when transmitting on that frequency.

Radiotelephone Equipment

SEC. 161.122 Each report required by this subpart to be made by radiotelephone must be made using a radiotelephone that is capable of operation on the navigational bridge of the vessel, or in the case of a dredge, at its main control station.

English Language

SEC. 161.124 Each report required by this subpart must be made in the English language.

Time

SEC. 161.126 Each report required by this subpart must specify time using—
(a) The zone time in effect in the VTS Area; and
(b) The 24-hour clock system.

Initial report

SEC. 161.128 At least 30 minutes before a vessel enters or begins to navigate in the VTS Area the master of the vessel shall report, or cause to be reported, the following information to the VTC:

(a) The name of the vessel.

(b) The position of the vessel.

(c) The estimated time of entering or beginning to navigate in the VTS Area.

(d) Point of entry in the VTS Area.

(e) Destination in the VTS Area.

(f) ETA of the vessel at its destination.

(g) Any condition on the vessel that may affect its navigation in the VTS Area such as fire, defective propulsion machinery, or defective steering equipment.

(h) Whether or not any dangerous cargo listed in § 124.14 of this chapter is on board the vessel.

Follow-up Report

SEC. 161.130 At least 15 minutes, but not more than 45 minutes, before a vessel enters or begins to navigate in the VTS Area, the master of the vessel shall report the following information by radiotelephone to the VTC:

(a) Name, type, length, and draft of the vessel.

(b) Any revisions to the initial report required by § 161.128 of this subpart.

(c) The speed at which the vessel will proceed in the VTS Area.

(d) Any tow that the towing vessel is unable to control or can control only with difficulty.

(e) If the vessel intends to enter the TSS, the ETA and point of entry in the TSS.

Final Report

SEC. 161.131 Whenever a vessel anchors or moors in, or departs from, the VTS Area, the master shall report, or cause to be reported, the place of anchoring, mooring, or departing to the VTC.

Radio Failure

SEC. 161.133 Whenever a vessel's radiotelephone equipment fails—

(a) Compliance with §§ 161.120 and 161.142 of this subpart is not required; and

(b) Compliance with §§ 161.128, 161.130, and 161.131 of this subpart is not required unless the reports required by those sections can be made by telephone.

Report of Emergency or Radio Failure

SEC. 161.134 Whenever the master of a vessel deviates from any section in this subpart because of an emergency or radio failure, he shall report, or cause to be reported, the deviation to the VTC as soon as possible.

Report of Impairment to the Operation of the Vessel

SEC. 161.135 The master of a vessel in the VTS Area shall report to the VTC as soon as possible.

(a) Any condition on the vessel that may impair its navigation such as fire, defective propulsion machinery, or defective steering equipment; and

(b) Any tow that the towing vessel is unable to control, or can control only with difficulty, unless this information has already been reported.

Ferry Vessels

SEC. 161.136 (a) Whenever a ferry vessel is operated in the VTS Area on a schedule and a route that crosses the TSS, both of which have been previously furnished to the VTC, compliance with §§ 161.128, 161.130, 161.131, and 161.142 of this subpart is not required.

(b) The master of a ferry vessels that enters the TSS at any place other than Rosario Strait between sunset and sunrise or during reduced visibility shall report the following information by radiotelephone to the VTC at least five minutes before entry:

(1) The name of the vessel.

(2) The direction the vessel will proceed in the TSS.

(3) The point of entering the TSS.

(4) The estimated time the vessel will operate in the TSS.

Vessel Movement Reporting Rules

Movement Reports

SEC. 161.142 (a) Whenever a vessel passes a reporting point listed in § 161.189 of this subpart, the master of the vessel shall report the following information to the VTC by radiotelephone:

(1) The name of the vessel.

(2) The reporting point.

(3) The time of passing the reporting point.

(4) The next reporting point.

(5) ETA at the next reporting point.

(6) If the vessel is at a point of entry in the TSS, any change in speed of the vessel from the speed reported under § 161.130(c) of this subpart.

(7) If the vessel is at a point of departure from the TSS, the course and the destination or intentions of the vessel.

(b) Whenever the ETA of a vessel at a reporting point changes by more than 10 minutes, the master of the vessel shall report a revised ETA to the VTC by radiotelephone.

Traffic Separation Scheme Rules

Vessel Operation in the TSS

SEC. 161.150 The master of a vessel in the TSS shall operate the vessel in accordance with the TSS rules prescribed in §§ 161.152–161.156.

Direction of Traffic

SEC. 161.152 (a) A vessel proceeding in a traffic lane shall keep the separation zone to port.

(b) A vessel in a precautionary area, except the Port Angeles precautionary area or any temporary precautionary area, shall keep the center of the precautionary area to port.

Anchoring in the TSS

SEC. 161.154 No vessel may anchor in the TSS.

Joining, Leaving, and Crossing a Traffic Lane

SEC. 161.156 (a) A vessel may join, cross, or leave a traffic lane only at a precautionary area unless the VTC has been notified of the point at which the vessel will join, cross, or leave the traffic lane.

(b) A vessel crossing a traffic lane shall, to the extent possible, maintain a course that is perpendicular to the direction of the flow of traffic in the traffic lane.

(c) A vessel joining or leaving a traffic lane shall steer a course to converge on or diverge from the direction of traffic flow in the traffic lane at as small an angle as possible.

Rosario Strait Rules

Communications in Rosario Strait

SEC. 161.170 Before a vessel meets, overtakes, or crosses ahead of any vessel in Rosario Strait, the master shall transmit the intentions of his vessel to the master of the other vessel on the frequency designated under the

Bridge-to-Bridge Radiotelephone Act for the purpose of arranging safe passage.

Report Before Entering Rosario Strait

SEC. 161.172 At least 15 minutes before a vessel enters the TSS at Rosario Strait, the master of the vessel shall report the vessel's ETA at, and point of entry in, Rosario Strait to the VTC by radiotelephone.

Entering Rosario Strait

SEC. 161.174 (a) A vessel may not enter Rosario Strait unless—

(1) The report required by § 161.172 of this subpart has been made;

(2) The radio equipment on the vessel that is used to transmit the reports required by this subpart is in operation;

(3) During periods of visibility of 2 miles or less, the radar on a vessel equipped with radar is in operation and manned; and

(4) The vessel is free of any conditions that may impair its navigation such as fire, defective propulsion machinery, or defective steering equipment.

(b) The master of a vessel shall operate the vessel in accordance with paragraph (a) of this section.

Descriptions and Geographic Coordinates

VTS Area

SEC. 161.180 The VTS Area consists of the navigable waters of the United States inshore of the boundary line of inland waters described in § 82.120 of this chapter. This area includes the waters in the Strait of Georgia, Haro Strait, and the Strait of Juan de Fuca that are east of the line of demarcation, and Rosario Strait, Bellingham Bay, Padilla Bay, Admiralty Inlet, Puget Sound, Possession Sound, Elliot Bay, Hood Canal, Commencement Bay, the Narrows west of Tacoma, Carr Inlet, Case Inlet, and navigable waters adjacent to these areas.

Separation Zones

SEC. 161.183 (a) Each separation zone is 500 yards wide and centered on a line that extends from one point to another, or through several points, described in paragraph (c) of this section.

(b) Two boundaries of each separation zone are parallel to its centerline and extend to and intersect with the boundary of a precautionary area. No part of any separation zone is contained in a precautionary area.

(c) The latitude and longitude describing the centerline of the separation zone are:

(1) Between precautionary area "S" and "SA",
    (i) 48°12′22″ N.   123°06′30″ W.
    (ii) 48°11′35″ N.   122°51′55″ W.

(2) Between precautionary area "R" and "RA",
    (i) 48°16′26″ N.   123°06′30″ W.
    (ii) 48°19′06″ N.   123°00′09″ W.

(3) Between precautionary area "RA" and "SA",
    (i) 48°18′45″ N.   122°57′30″ W.
    (ii) 48°12′40″ N.   122°51′01″ W.

(4) Between precautionary area "RA" and "RB",
    (i) 48°20′26″ N.   122°57′01″ W.
    (ii) 48°24′14″ N.   122°48′00″ W.
    (iii) 48°25′28″ N.   122°46′23″ W.

(5) Between precautionary area "RB" and "SA",
    (i) 48°25′12″ N.   122°44′40″ W.
    (ii) 48°24′10″ N.   122°44′12″ W.
    (iii) 48°12′52″ N.   122°49′06″ W.

(6) Between precautionary area "SA" and "SC",
    (i) 48°10′43″ N.   122°47′50″ W.
    (ii) 48°07′43″ N.   122°39′56″ W.
    (iii) 48°01′43″ N.   122°38′02″ W.

(7) Between precautionary area "SC" and "SF",
    (i) 48°00′36″ N.   122°37′24″ W.
    (ii) 47°57′21″ N.   122°34′12″ W.
    (iii) 47°55′24″ N.   122°30′16″ W.
    (iv) 47°53′39″ N.   122°28′21″ W.

(8) Between precautionary area "SF" and "SH",
    (i) 47°52′34″ N.   122°27′40″ W.
    (ii) 47°44′31″ N.   122°25′41″ W.
    (iii) 47°40′18″ N.   122°27′33″ W.

(9) Between precautionary area "SH" and "T",
    (i) 47°39′05″ N.   122°27′42″ W.
    (ii) 47°34′54″ N.   122°26′54″ W.

(10) Between precautionary area "T" and "TC",
    (i) 47°33′42″ N.   122°26′33″ W.
    (ii) 47°26′53″ N.   122°24′12″ W.
    (iii) 47°23′07″ N.   122°21′08″ W.
    (iv) 47°19′54″ N.   122°26′37″ W.

(11) Between precautionary area "CA" and "C",
    (i) 48°44′15″ N.   122°45′39″ W.
    (ii) 48°41′39″ N.   122°43′34″ W.

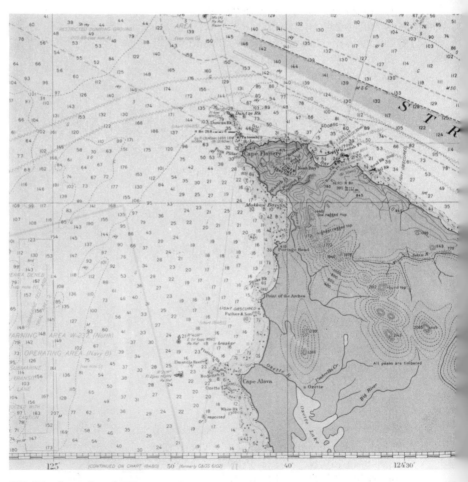

FIG. V1.   Puget Sound VTS.

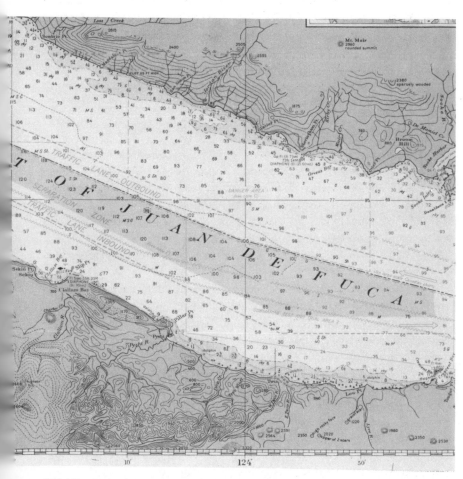

FIG. V2.   Strait of Juan de Fuca Traffic Separation Scheme.

Traffic Lanes

SEC. 161.185 (a) Except as provided in paragragh (c) of this section, each traffic lane consists of the area within two parallel boundaries that are 1000 yards apart and that extend to and intersect with the boundary of a precautionary area. One of these parallel boundaries is parallel to and 250 yards from the centerline of a separation zone.

(b) No part of any traffic lane is contained in a precautionary area.

(c) The traffic lane in Rosario Strait consists of the area enclosed by a line beginning at latitude 48°26'50" N., longitude 122°43'27" W.; thence northerly to latitude 48°36'06" N., longitude 122°44'56" W.; thence northeasterly to latitude 48°39'18" N., longitude 122°42'42" W.; thence westerly and northwesterly along the boundary of precautionary area "C" to latitude 48°39'37" N.; longitude 122°43'58" W.; thence southerly to latitude 48°38'24" N., longitude 122°44'08" W.; thence southwesterly to latitude 48°36'08" N., longitude 122°45'44" W.; thence southerly to latitude 48°-29'30" N., longitude 122°44'41" W.; thence southwesterly to latitude 48°-27'37" N., longitude 122°45'27" W.; thence northeasterly and southeasterly along the boundary of precautionary area "RB" to the point of beginning.

Precautionary Areas

SEC. 161.187 The precautionary areas consist of:

(a) *Port Angeles precautionary area.* An area enclosed by a line beginning on the shoreline at New Dungeness Spit at latitude 48°11'00"N., longitude 123°06'30" W.; thence due north to latitude 48°17'10" N., longitude 123°06'30" W.; thence southwesterly to latitude 48°10'00" N., longitude 123°27'38" W.; thence due south to the shorelines; thence along the shoreline to the point of beginning.

(b) *Precautionary area "RA".* A circular area of 2,500 yards radius centered at latitude 48°19'46" N., longitude 122°58'34" W.;

(c) *Precautionary area "RB".* A circular area of 2,500 yards radius centered at latitude 48°26'24" N., longitude 122°45'12" W.;

(d) *Precautionary area "C".* A circular area of 2,500 yards radius centered at latitude 48°40'34" N., longitude 122°42'44" W.;

(e) *Precautionary area "CA".* A circular area of 2,500 yards radius centered at latitude 48°45'19" N., longitude 122°46'26" W.;

(f) *Precautionary area "SA".* A circular area of 3,000 yards radius centered at latitude 48°11'28" N., longitude 122°49'43" W.;

(g) *Precautionary area "SC".* A circular area of 1,250 yards radius centered at latitude 48°01'06" N., longitude 122°37'54" W.;

(h) *Precautionary area "SF".* A circular area of 1,250 yards radius centered at latitude 47°53'10" N., longitude 122°27'48" W.;

(i) *Precautionary area "SH".* A circular area of 1,250 yards radius centered at latitude 47° 39'42" N., longitude 122°27'48" W.;

(j) *Precautionary area "T".* A circular area of 1,250 yards radius centered at latitude 47°34'19" N., longitude 122°26'47" W.;

(k) *Precautionary area "TC".* A circular area of 1,250 yards radius centered at latitude 47°19'30" N., longitude 122°27'19" W.

Temporary Precautionary Areas

SEC. 161.188 The Commander, Thirteenth Coast Guard District, may amend the description of the TSS in §§ 161.180–161.189 of this subpart to establish temporary precautionary areas to provide for seasonal activities such as fishing that affect the safe passage of vessels in the TSS.

Reporting Points

SEC. 161.189 The reporting points are—
(a) Buoy "R" at latitude 48°16'26" N., longitude 123°06'30"W.
(b) Buoy "S" at latitude 48°12'22" N., longitude 123°06'30" W.
(c) Buoy "SA" at latitude 48°11'28" N., longitude 122°49'43" W.
(d) Buoy "RB" at latitude 48°26'24" N., longitude 122°45'12" W.
(e) Buoy "C" at latitude 48°40'34" N., longitude 122°42'44" W.
(f) Buoy "SC" at latitude 48°01'06" N., longitude 122°37'54" W.
(g) Buoy "SH" at latitude 47°39'42" N., longitude 122°27'48" W.
(h) Buoy "TB" at latitude 47°23'07" N., longitude 122°21'08" W.
(i) The boundary of the TSS.[4]

[4] *Limited radar surveillance of the more congested traffic was installed in October 1975. Expansion of the traffic separation scheme into the Straits of Juan de Fuca as far west as Cape Flattery, in cooperation with Canada, went into effect on 1 March 1975 (see Fig. V2).*

APPENDIX W
IMCO Adopted Traffic Separation Schemes

ROUTEING SYSTEMS[1]

The Assembly

NOTING Article 16(i) of the Convention on the Inter-Governmental Maritime Consultative Organization concerning the functions of the Assembly,

RECALLING Regulation 8, Chapter V of the International Convention for the Safety of Life at Sea, 1960, and the amendment thereto adopted by Resolution A.205(VII),

RECALLING FURTHER Resolution A.228(VII) on observance of traffic separation schemes,

NOTING that the International Regulations for Preventing Collision at Sea, 1972, and, in particular Rules 1(d) and 10 thereof provide for adoption by the Organization of, and the behaviour of vessels in or near, traffic separation schemes,

RECOGNIZING that there is a need to bring the terms, definitions and general principles concerning traffic separation and routeing, as set out in Annex II to Resolution A.161(ES.IV), into harmony with the International Regulations for Preventing Collisions at Sea, 1972,

RECOGNIZING ALSO that the practice of complying with routeing measures adopted by IMCO for international use would contribute considerably to the avoidance of collisions between ships,

RECOGNIZING FURTHER that such practice would consequently reduce the risk of pollution of the marine environment and the risk of damage to marine life resulting from collisions or standings,

CONFIRMING that IMCO is recognized as the only international body for establishing and adopting routeing measures on an international level,

NOTING that the Ninth International Hydrographic Conference charged the International Hydrographic Bureau to deal with matters relating to

---

[1] *IMCO Resolution A.284(VIII), adopted 20 Nov 73.*

presentation on the charts and in sailing directions, details of routeing provisions which have been considered, approved and adopted by IMCO for international use,

HAVING CONSIDERED the Recommendations by the Maritime Safety Committee at its twenty-fifth, twenty-seventh, and twenty-eighth sessions,

RESOLVES:

(a) to adopt the general provisions pertaining to Ships' Routeing approved by the Maritime Safety Committee at its twenty-seventh and twenty-eighth sessions, the text of which appears at Annex I to this Resolution, as a substitute for the terms, definitions and general principles covering traffic separation and routeing set out in Annex II to Resolution A.161(ES.IV);

(b) to adopt the routeing measures approved by the Maritime Safety Committee at its twenty-fifth, twenty-seventh and twenty-eighth sessions, the text of which appears at Annex II to this Resolution,

REQUESTS the Maritime Safety Committee to revise and update as necessary the publication on "Ships' Routeing" to reflect the decisions taken in the foregoing part of this Resolution and to approve new routeing measures and revisions, cancellations and suspensions of routeing measures previously adopted by the Organization and to submit recommendations thereon to the Assembly for adoption,

INVITES the governments concerned to advise ships under their flag to comply with the adopted routeing measures,

URGES governments, when planning either to introduce new traffic separation schemes similar to those included in the IMCO publication on "Ships' Routeing" or to amend existing schemes in that publication, to consult the Organization in advance whenever practicable,

REQUESTS the Secretary-General to advise the International Hydrographic Bureau on details of the routeing provisions to facilitate the hydrographers' work on inclusion of this material in the appropriate nautical charts and related publications for the use of mariners,

REVOKES the following Resolutions by which the Assembly adopted terms, definitions and general principles concerning traffic separation and various traffic separation schemes and areas to be avoided: Resolutions A.90(IV), A.161(ES.IV), A.186(VI), A.226(VII) and A.227(VII).

SHIPS' ROUTEING[2]

PART I General Provisions

Adoption and Recommendation

1. IMCO is recognized as the only international body responsible for

[2] *'Ships' Routeing', Third Edition, 1973, Supplement 1975*

establishing and recommending measures on an international level concerning ships' routeing.

2. In deciding whether or not to adopt a traffic separation scheme, IMCO will consider:

(a) whether the aids to navigation proposed will enable mariners to determine their position with sufficient accuracy to navigate in the scheme in accordance with the principles regarding the use of Routeing Schemes;

(b) whether or not the scheme complies with the established Methods of Routeing.

3. Having due regard to paragraph 5, a Government shall when establishing, reviewing or adjusting a routeing system, take due account of:

(a) the rights and practices of Governments in respect of the exploitation of living and mineral resources of the high seas and of the sea-bed and subsoil underlying the high seas;

(b) the environment, traffic patterns or established routeing systems in the waters under such Government's jurisdiction;

(c) the aids to navigation already established in the area, and the effect the routeing system may have upon demands for hydrographic surveys and for improvements or adjustments in the navigation aids provided in the waters concerned.

4. IMCO shall not adopt or amend any scheme that is in the proximity of waters under a Government's jurisdiction without the agreement of that Government, where that scheme may affect:

(a) the rights and practices of such Government in respect of the exploitation of living and mineral resources of the high seas and of the sea-bed and subsoil underlying the high seas;

(b) the environment, traffic patterns or established routeing systems in the waters under such Government's jurisdiction;

(c) demands for improvements or adjustments in the navigation aids provided in the waters concerned.

5. (a) A Government proposing a routeing system, any part of which lies within international waters, should consult with IMCO, so that such system may be adopted by IMCO for international use.

(b) A Government may establish or adjust a routeing system lying partly within international waters, before consulting with IMCO, where local conditions require that early action be taken, with a view to later adoption by the Organization.

(c) A Government, when proposing or establishing a traffic separation scheme, should be guided by the following criteria, having due regard to the class of vessel for which the scheme is intended:

(i) the availability of visual aids to navigation, or

(ii) the possibility of position-fixing by the use of direction finder or radar.

6. When establishing areas to be avoided by certain ships, the necessity for creating such areas should be well established and the reasons stated. In general, these areas should be established only in places where inadequate survey or insufficient provision of aids to navigation may lead to danger of stranding, or where local knowledge is considered essential for safe passage or where there is the possibility of unacceptable damage to wildlife, which may result from a casualty. These areas shall not be regarded as prohibited areas unless specifically stated otherwise; the classes of ships which should avoid the areas should be considered in each particular case.

7. Routeing systems should be reviewed, resurveyed and adjusted as necessary, so as to maintain their effectiveness and compatibility with trade patterns, resource exploitation, changes in depth of water, and other developments.

8. Except where local conditions require that early action be taken, a routeing system adopted by IMCO should not come into force before a period of three months has elapsed since the date of adoption by the Assembly.

9. Nothing in the foregoing shall affect the rights, claims or views of any Government in regard to the limits of territorial waters.

Terminology and Symbols

1. The following terms and symbols are used . . . in connexion with matters related to ships' routeing:

(a) *Routeing*

A complex of measures concerning routes aimed at reducing the risk of casualties; it includes traffic separation schemes, two-way routes, tracks, areas to be avoided, inshore traffc zones and deep water routes.

(b) *Traffic separation scheme*

A scheme which separates traffic proceeding in opposite or nearly opposite directions by the use of a separation zone or line, traffic lanes or by other means.

(c) *Separation zone or line*

A zone or line separating traffic proceeding in one direction from traffic proceeding in another direction. A separation zone may also be used to separate a traffic lane from the adjacent inshore traffic zone.

(d) *Traffic lane*

An area within definite limits inside which one-way traffic is established.

(e) *Roundabout*

A circular area within definite limits in which traffic moves in a counter-clockwise direction around a specified point or zone.

Table 1

Detail	Presentation	Description
1. Outside limit of traffic lanes, two-way routes and inshore traffic zones		Dashed line — the symbol used for maritime limits in general
2. Outside limit of "roundabout"(1)		
3. Separation zone(2) (of any shape)		The zone shall be indicated by means of a tint light enough to reveal any hydrographic details
4. Separation line		A single tinted line
5. Centre of "roundabout" with no separation zone inside		A circle
6. Arrows indicating direction of traffic flow(3)		Open-outlined arrows so situated and shaped as to indicate general directions of traffic flow
7. Boundary of "areas to be avoided by ships of certain classes"(4) 8. Limit of sea exploration and/or exploitation regions which may be dangerous for free navigation		A line composed of a series of T-shaped signs, the cross-bar of the T being long and the down stroke short and pointing towards the area in question, within which a suitable legend may be inscribed
9. Recommended track when based on a system of fixed marks		A single or double continuous line
10. Recommended track when not based on a system of fixed marks		A single dashed line in which arrowheads are inserted at regular intervals, either singly to indicate a one-way track, or in opposing pairs to indicate a two-way track
11. Outside limit of deep water route, when depicted		A dashed line

Detail	Presentation	Description
12. Deep water route when both outside limits are depicted	DW DW	Dashed lines and the letters DW inserted at regular intervals between them. The minimum depth shall be inserted beside the abbreviation when considered critical
13. Deep water route, based on fixed marks	—DW——— DW— =DW====DW=	A double or single continuous line with the abbreviation DW inserted at regular intervals. The minimum depth shall be indicated beside the abbreviation when considered critical. When using this symbol, the direction of traffic flow shall be indicated conventionally
14. Deep water route not based on fixed marks, direction of traffic flow	--> -DW> -DW> - - < >DW< > —DW-	A single dashed line in which arrowheads are inserted at regular intervals, either singly to represent a one-way route, or in opposing pairs, to represent a two-way route. The abbreviation DW shall also be inserted at regular intervals along the symbol, and the minimum depth indicated beside the abbreviation when considered critical

Remarks

(1) The dashed line, representing outside limits of 'roundabout' should be interrupted in places where ships are recommended to enter or to leave the scheme.
(2) In places where traffic is separated by natural features (islands, marked shoals, etc.) representation of the separation zone may be omitted.
(3) Dispersion of arrows, instead of placing them in a line is felt desirable.
(4) Notes on conditions of avoidance (classes and sizes of ships, nature of cargoes carried, etc.) may be given on charts and shall always be given in Sailing Directions.

General Observations

The routeing and traffic separation symbols to be used on charts should be printed in colour, preferably magenta.

Secondary details of routeing and traffic separation, such as figures indicating directions of traffic, schemes and their details, dimensions, distances from coast, etc., should not be shown on charts unless considered critical. These are given in this IMCO publication and may be given in Sailing Directions if so decided by hydrographic offices.

(f) *Inshore traffic zone*

A designated area between the landward boundary of a traffic separation scheme and the adjacent coast intended for coastal traffic.

(g) *Two-way route*

A route in an area within definite limits inside which two-way traffic is established.

(h) *Track*

The recommended route to be followed when proceeding between pre-determined positions.

(i) *Deep water route*

A route in a designated area within definite limits which has been accurately surveyed for clearance of sea bottom and submerged obstacles to a minimum indicated depth of water.

2. The symbols in the following table are those recommended by the International Hydrographic Organization for representation of details of routeing measures on nautical charts. They are included in this publication for readers' information on what may be generally found in charts. Individual countries may, however, use on their charts symbols different from those given below.

Methods of Routeing

1. When establishing routeing systems the following are among the methods which may be used:

(a) separation of traffic by separation zones or lines;

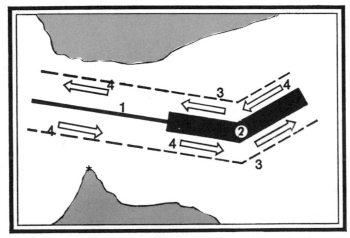

FIG. W1. Traffic separation by separation line and zone.
      1—Separation line
      2—Separation zone
      3—Outside limits of lanes
      4—Arrows indicating main traffic direction

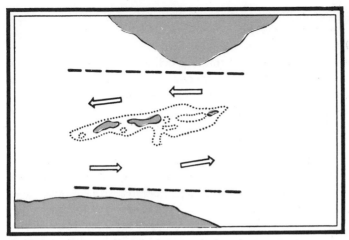

FIG. W2.   Separation of traffic by natural obstacles.

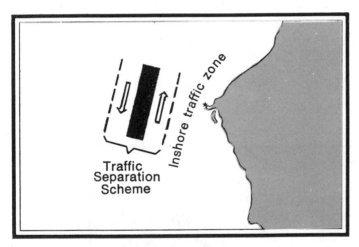

FIG. W3.   Inshore traffic zone for coastal traffic.

(b) separation of traffic by natural obstacles and geographically defined objects;

(c) separation of traffic by inshore traffic zones intended for keeping coastal traffic away from traffic separation schemes;

(d) separation of traffic by sectors at approaches to focal points;

(e) separation of traffic by roundabouts intended to facilitate navigation at focal points, where traffic separation schemes meet;

(f) routeing of traffic by deep water routes, two-way routes or tracks for ships proceeding in specific directions.

2. A description of methods (a) to (e) with drawings intended only to explain their function is given in the following:

(a) *By separation zones or lines* (Fig. 1)

In such cases, the separation of traffic is achieved by a separation zone or line between streams of traffic proceeding in opposite or nearly opposite directions. The outside limits in such a scheme are the outer boundaries of lanes intended for one-way traffic. Beyond such limits ships can navigate in any direction. A separation zone may also be used to separate a traffic lane from an inshore traffic zone.

The width and length of separation zones and traffic lanes are determined after careful examination of local conditions, traffic density, prevailing hydrographic and meteorological conditions, space available for manoeuvring, etc., and generally their length is kept to the minimum necessary. In narrow passages and restricted waters a separation line may be adopted instead of a zone, for the separation of traffic, to allow for more navigable space.

(b) *By natural obstacles and geographically defined objects* (Fig. 2)

This method is used where there is a defined area with obstacles such as islands, shoals or rocks restricting free movement and providing a natural division for opposing traffic streams.

(c) *By inshore traffic zones* (Fig. 3)

By using inshore traffic zones coastal shipping can keep clear of through

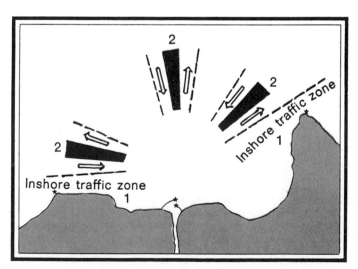

FIG. W4. Sectorial traffic separation scheme at approaches to focal point.
        1—Inshore traffic zone
        2—Separation schemes for main traffic

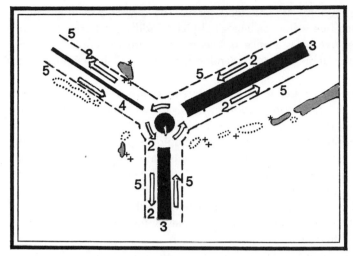

FIG. W5. A roundabout where several traffic separation schemes meet.
  1—Circular separation zone
  2—Arrows indicating traffic direction
  3—Separation zone
  4—Separation line
  5—Outside limits of lanes

traffic in the adjacent traffic separation scheme. Ships navigating in any direction may be encountered in an inshore traffic zone.

(d) *By sectors at approaches to focal points* (Fig. 4)

Such a method is used where ships converge at a point or a small area from various directions. Port approaches, sea pilot stations, positions where landfall buoys or light vessels are fixed, entrances to channels, canals, estuaries, etc., may be considered as such focal points. The number of shipping lanes, their dimensions and directions depend mainly on the type of the local traffic.

(e) *By roundabouts* (Fig. 5)

To facilitate navigation at focal points where several traffic separation schemes meet, ships should move in a counter-clockwise direction around a specified point or zone until they are able to join the appropriate lane.

General Principles of Ships' Routeing

The Use of Routeing Systems

1. The International Regulations for Preventing Collisions at Sea apply to navigation in routeing systems.

2. Routeing systems are intended for use by day and by night in all weathers, in ice-free waters or under light ice conditions where no extraordinary manoeuvres or assistance by icebreaker(s) are required.

3. Routeing systems are recommended for use by all ships unless stated otherwise.

4. A deep water route is primarily intended for use by ships which because of their draught in relation to the available depth of water in the area concerned require the use of such a route. Through traffic to which the above consideration does not apply should, if practicable, avoid following deep water routes. When using a deep water route mariners should be aware of possible changes in the indicated depth of water due to meteorological or other effects.

5. A vessel using a traffic separation scheme shall:

(i) proceed in the appropriate traffic lane in the general direction of traffic flow for that lane;

(ii) so far as practicable keep clear of a traffic separation line or separation zone;

(iii) normally join or leave a traffic lane at the termination of the lane, but when joining or leaving from the side shall do so at as small an angle to the general direction of traffic flow as practicable.

6. A vessel shall so far as practicable avoid crossing traffic lanes, but if obliged to do so shall cross as nearly as practicable at right angles to the general direction of traffic flow.

7. Inshore traffic zones shall not normally be used by through traffic which can safely use the appropriate traffic lane within the adjacent traffic separation scheme.

8. A vessel, other than a crossing vessel, shall not normally enter a separation zone or cross a separation line except:

(i) in cases of emergency to avoid immediate danger;

(ii) to engage in fishing within a separation zone.

9. A vessel navigating in areas near the terminations of traffic separation schemes shall do so with particular caution.

10. A vessel shall so far as practicable avoid anchoring in a traffic separation scheme or in areas near its terminations.

11. A vessel not using a traffic separation scheme shall avoid it by as wide a margin as is practicable.

12. The arrows printed on charts merely indicate the general direction of traffic; ships need not set their courses strictly along the arrows.

13. The signal "YG" meaning "You appear not to be complying with the traffic separation scheme" is provided in the International Code of Signals for appropriate use.

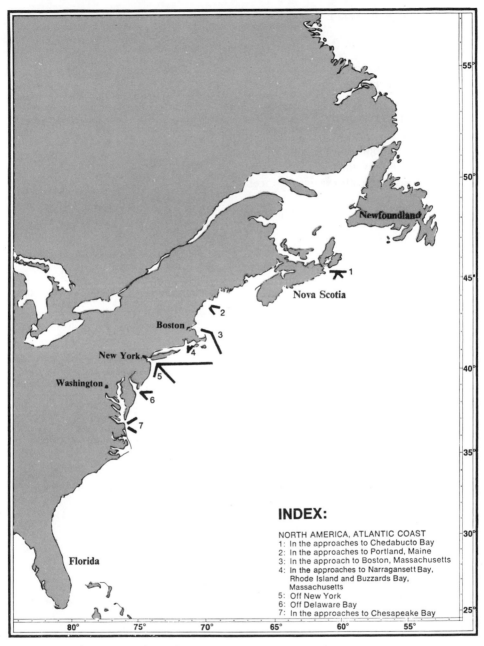

Newfoundland

1

Nova Scotia

Boston 2

3

New York 4

Washington 5

6

7

Florida

INDEX:

NORTH AMERICA, ATLANTIC COAST
1: In the approaches to Chedabucto Bay
2: In the approaches to Portland, Maine
3: In the approach to Boston, Massachusetts
4: In the approaches to Narragansett Bay,
   Rhode Island and Buzzards Bay,
   Massachusetts
5: Off New York
6: Off Delaware Bay
7: In the approaches to Chesapeake Bay

FIG. W6.   North America, Atlantic Coast

PART II Traffic Separation Schemes (Excerpts from)

Navigation in the Vicinity of the Grand Banks of Newfoundland

Attention is drawn to Regulation 8 of Chapter V of the Convention for the Safety of Life at Sea, 1960. It directs that all ships proceeding on voyages in the vicinity of the Grand Banks of Newfoundland avoid as far as practicable the fishing banks of Newfoundland north of latitude 43°N. The reasons for avoiding the area are:

(a) high concentration of fishing vessels;

(b) prevailing adverse weather conditions;

(c) seasonal existence of icebergs.

In the Approaches to Chedabucto Bay

(Reference charts: Canadian Hydrographic Service 4013 and 4335)

Description of the Traffic Separation Scheme

The traffic separation scheme for Chedabucto Bay consists of three parts. *Part I:*

(a) A separation zone bounded by a line connecting the following geographical positions:

(1)	45°24′00″N.,	60°36′42″W.
(2)	45°24′12″N.,	60°27′10″W.
(3)	45°23′42″N.,	60°28′12″W.
(4)	45°23′49″N.,	60°36′29″W.

(b) A traffic lane for westbound traffic is established between the separation zone and a line connecting the following geographical positions:

(5)	45°26′00″N.,	60°23′12″W.
(6)	45°25′26″N.,	60°41′42″W.

(c) A traffic lane for eastbound traffic is established between the separation zone and a line connecting the following geographical positions:

(7)	45°22′18″N.,	60°34′30″W.
(8)	45°22′09″N.,	60°31′36″W.

The main traffic directions are:

$$092°-267°.$$

Part II:

(a) A separation zone bounded by a line connecting the following geographical positions:

(9)	45°22′34″N.,	60°40′00″W.
(10)	45°19′53″N.,	60°36′30″W.
(11)	45°19′18″N.,	60°37′48″W.
(12)	45°22′41″N.,	60°42′10″W.

(b) A traffic lane for north-westbound traffic is established between the

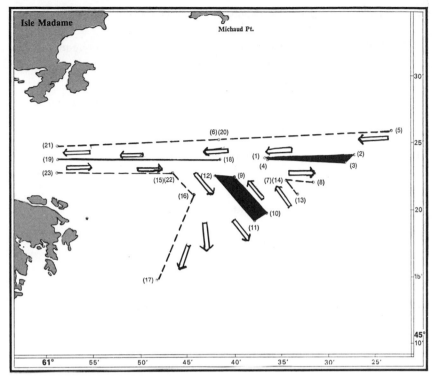

FIG. W7.   In approaches to Chedabucto Bay.

separation zone and a line connecting the following geographical positions:

           (13)   45°21′21″N.,   60°33′18″W.
           (14)   45°22′18″N.,   60°34′30″W.

The main traffic direction is 318°.

(c) A traffic lane for southbound traffic is established between the separation zone and a line connecting the following geographical positions:

           (15)   45°22′54″N.,   60°46′30″W.
           (16)   45°21′17″N.,   60°44′24″W.
           (17)   45°14′28″N.,   60°48′23″W.

The main traffic directions are:

                    138° and 202°.

Part III:

(a) A separation line connects the following geographical positions:

           (18)   45°23′54″N.,   60°41′42″W.
           (19)   45°23′54″N.,   60°58′48″W.

(b) A traffic lane for westbound traffic established between the separation line and a line connecting the following geographical positions:

     (20)   45°25′26″N.,   60°41′42″W.
     (21)   45°24′54″N.,   60°58′48″W.

(c) A traffic lane for eastbound traffic is established between the separation line and a line connecting the following geographical positions:

     (22)   45°22′54″N.,   60°46′30″W.
     (23)   45°22′54″N.,   60°58′48″W.

The main traffic directions are:

$$090°–270°.$$

In the Approaches to Portland, Maine

(Reference chart: United States National Ocean Survey C & GS 1106)

Description of the Traffic Separation Scheme

The traffic separation scheme in the approaches to Portland, Maine, consists of two parts:

Part I—Eastern approach

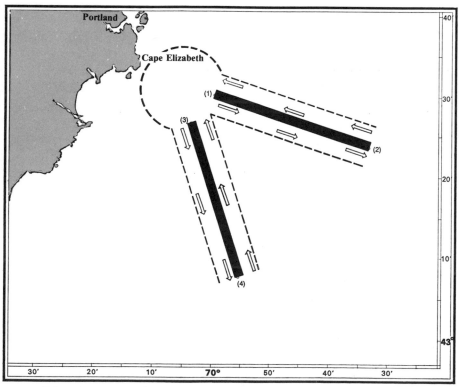

FIG. W8. In approaches to Portland, Maine.

A separation zone, one mile wide, is centred upon the following geo-graphical positions:

(1) 43°30'.2N.,   69°59'.4W.
(2) 43°24'.75N.,   69°33'.0W.

A traffic lane, two miles wide, is established on each side of the separation zone.

The main traffic directions are:

107° and 287°.

Part II—Southern approach

A separation zone, one mile wide, is centred upon the following geo-graphical positions:

(3) 43°26'.8N.,   70°03'.5W.
(4) 43°07'.8N.,   69°55'.3W.

A traffic lane, two miles wide, is established on each side of the separation zone.

The main traffic directions are:

162° and 342°.

Note:

Precautionary area

A precautionary area of radius five miles is centred upon geographical position 43°31'.5N., 70°06'.0W.

In the Approach to Boston, Massachusetts

(Reference chart: United States National Ocean Survey C & GS 1107)

Description of the Traffic Separation Scheme

A separation zone, one mile wide, is centred upon the following geo-graphical positions:

(1) 42°21'.0N.,   70°40'.7W.
(2) 42°08'.5N.,   69°53'.6W.
(3) 40°49'.5N.,   69°00'.0W.

A traffic lane, two miles wide, is established on each side of the separation zone.

The main traffic directions are:

110°—290° and
153°—333°.

Note:

Precautionary area

A precautionary area of radius five miles is centred upon geographical position 42°22'.7N., 70°48'.0W.

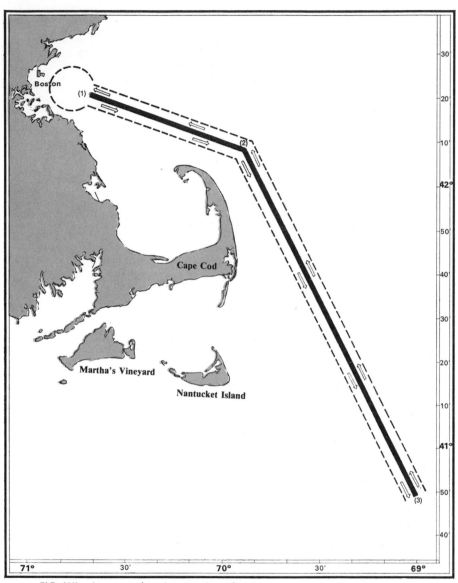

FIG. W9.   In approach to Boston, Massachusetts.

In the Approaches to Narragansett Bay, Rhode Island and Buzzards Bay, Massachusetts

(Reference charts: United States National Ocean Survey C & GS 1107, 1108 and 1210)

Description of the Traffic Separation Scheme

The traffic separation scheme in the approaches to Narrangansett Bay, Rhode Island and Buzzards Bay, Massachusetts, consists of two parts:

Part I—Narragansett Bay approach

A separation zone, two miles wide, is centred upon the following geographical positions:

(1) 41°22'.7N., 71°23'.4W.

(2) 41°11'.1N., 71°23'.4W.

A traffic lane, one mile wide, is established on each side of the separation zone.

The main traffic directions are:

000° and 180°.

Part II—Buzzards Bay approach

A separation zone, one mile wide, is centred upon the following geographical positions:

(3) 41°10'.15N., 71°19'.15W.

(4) 41°24'.9N., 71°03'.9W.

A traffic lane, one mile wide, is established on each side of the separation zone.

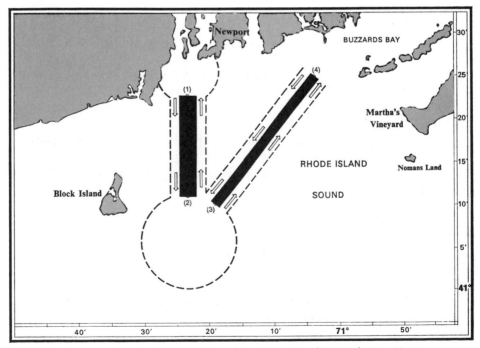

FIG. W10.   In approaches to Narragansett Bay, Rhode Island and Buzzards Bay, Massachusetts.

The main traffic directions are:

038° and 218°.

Note:

Precautionary areas

A precautionary area of radius 5.4 miles is centred upon geographical position 41°06'.0N., 71°23'.4W.

A precautionary area of radius 3.55 miles is centred upon geographical position 41°25'.6N., 71°23'.4W.

Restricted area

A restricted area, two miles wide, extending from the northern limit of the Narragansett Bay approach traffic separation zone to latitude 41°24'.7N. has been established.

The restricted area within the precautionary area will only be closed to vessel traffic by the Naval Underwater System Center during periods of daylight and optimum weather conditions for torpedo range usage. The closing of the restricted area will be indicated by the activation of a white strobe light mounted on Brenton Reef Light and controlled by a Naval vessel supporting the torpedo range activities. There would be no vessel restrictions expected during inclement weather or when the torpedo range is not in use.

Off New York

(Reference charts: British Admiralty 2755 and United States National Ocean Survey C&GS 1108)

NOTE: Under review—possible insufficient navigational marking in the eastern and southeastern approaches.

Description of the Traffic Separation Scheme

The traffic separation scheme off New York consists of three parts.

Part I—Eastern approach

(a) A separation zone bounded by a line connecting the following geographical positions:

(1)	40°28'.5N.,	69°27'.9W.
(2)	40°24'.2N.,	73°11'.5W.
(3)	40°26'.0N.,	73°40'.8W.
(4)	40°27'.0N.,	73°40'.7W.
(5)	40°27'.2N.,	73°11'.5W.
(6)	40°31'.5N.,	69°28'.1W.

(b) A traffic lane for westbound traffic is established between the separation zone and a line connecting the following geographical positions:

(7)	40°36'.5N.,	69°28'.2W.
(8)	40°32'.2N.,	73°11'.5W.
(9)	40°27'.9N.,	73°40'.6W.

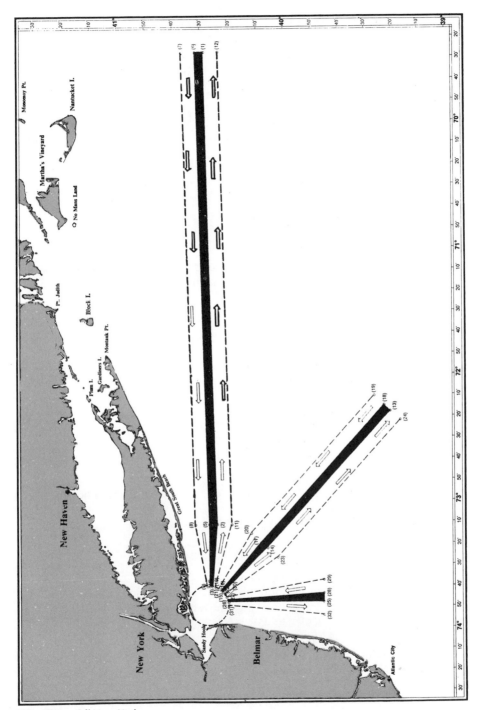

FIG. W11. Off New York.

(c) A traffic lane for eastbound traffic is established between the separation zone and a line connecting the following geographical positions:

(10)	40°25'.0N.,	73°41'.2W.
(11)	40°19'.2N.,	73°11'.5W.
(12)	40°23'.5N.,	69°27'.8W.

Part II—South-eastern approach

(a) A separation zone bounded by a line connecting the following geographical positions:

(13)	39°20'.7N.,	72°18'.0W.
(14)	40°06'.3N.,	73°22'.7W.
(15)	40°22'.4N.,	73°43'.5W.
(16)	40°23'.0N.,	73°42'.7W.
(17)	40°08'.6N.,	73°20'.1W.
(18)	39°23'.0N.,	72°15'.2W.

(b) A traffic lane for north-westbound traffic is established between the separation zone and a line connecting the following geographical positions:

(19)	39°26'.7N.,	72°10'.8W.
(20)	40°12'.2N.,	73°15'.7W.
(21)	40°24'.0N.,	73°41'.9W.

(c) A traffic lane for south-eastbound traffic is established between the separation zone and a line connecting the following geographical positions:

(22)	40°21'.7N.,	73°44'.5W.
(23)	40°02'.7N.,	73°27'.2W.
(24)	39°17'.0N.,	72°22'.4W.

Part III—Southern approach

(a) A separation zone bounded by a line connecting the following geographical positions:

(25)	39°45'.7N.,	73°48'.0W.
(26)	40°20'.5N.,	73°48'.3W.
(27)	40°20'.7N.,	73°47'.0W.
(28)	39°45'.7N.,	73°44'.0W.

(b) A traffic lane for northbound traffic is established between the separation zone and a line connecting the following geographical positions:

(29)	39°45'.7N.,	73°37'.7W.
(30)	40°21'.2N.,	73°45'.8W.

(c) A traffic lane for southbound traffic is established between the separation zone and a line connecting the following geographical positions:

(31)	40°20'.4N.,	73°49'.6W.
(32)	39°45'.7N.,	73°54'.4W.

Note:

Precautionary area

A precautionary area of radius seven miles is centred upon the Ambrose Light in geographical position 40°27'.5N., 73°49'.9W.

Off Delaware Bay

(Reference charts: British Admiralty 2563 and United States National Ocean Survey C & GS 1219)

Description of the Traffic Separation Scheme

The traffic separation scheme of Delaware Bay consists of two parts.
Part I—Eastern approach

(a) A separation zone bounded by a line connecting the following geographical positions:

(1)	38°46'.8N.,	74°34'.6W.
(2)	38°46'.8N.,	74°55'.7W.
(3)	38°47'.8N.,	74°55'.4W.
(4)	38°47'.8N.,	74°34'.6W.

(b) A traffic lane for westbound traffic is established between the separation zone and a line connecting the following geographical positions:

(5)	38°49'.8N.,	74°34'.6W.
(6)	38°48'.8N.,	74°55'.3W.

(c) A traffic lane for eastbound traffic is established between the separation zone and a line connecting the following geographical positions:

(7)	38°45'.8N.,	74°56'.1W.
(8)	38°44'.8N.,	74°34'.6W.

Part II—South-eastern approach

(a) A separation zone bounded by a line connecting the following geographical positions:

(9)	38°27'.0N.,	74°35'.6W.
(10)	38°43'.4N.,	74°58'.0W.
(11)	38°44'.2N.,	74°57'.2W.
(12)	38°27'.6N.,	74°34'.6W.

(b) A traffic lane for north-westbound traffic is established between the separation zone and a line connecting the following geographical positions:

(13)	38°29'.1N.,	74°32'.9W.
(14)	38°45'.1N.,	74°56'.6W.

(c) A traffic lane for south-eastbound traffic is established between the separation zone and a line connecting the following geographical positions:

(15)	38°42'.8N.,	74°58'.9W.
(16)	38°27'0N.,	74°39'.2W.

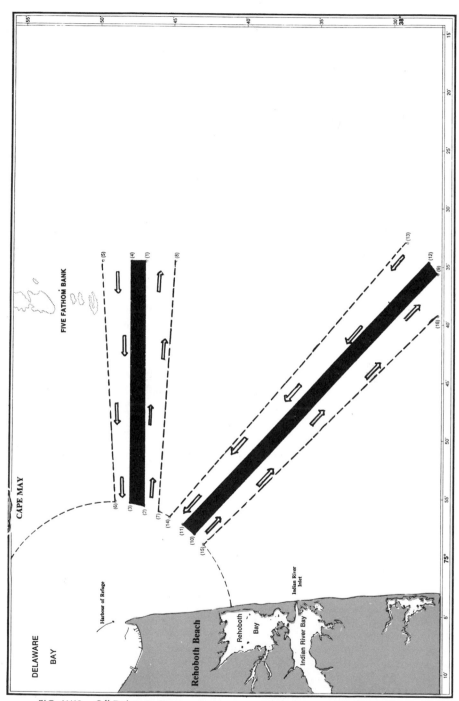

FIG. W12.   Off Delaware Bay.

Note:

Precautionary area

A precautionary area of radius eight miles is centered upon Harbour of Refuge Light in geographical position 38°48'.9N., 75°05'.6W.

In the Approaches to Chesapeake Bay

(Reference charts: British Admiralty 2843 and United States National Ocean Survey C & GS 1222)

Description of the Traffic Separation Scheme

The traffic separation scheme in the approaches to Chesapeake Bay consists of two parts.

Part I—Eastern approach

A separation line connects the following geographical positions:

        (1)   36°58'.7N.,   75°48'.7W.
        (2)   36°56'.5N.,   75°56'.3W.

A traffic lane, half a mile wide, is established on each side of the separation line.

The main traffic directions are:

           070° and
           250°.

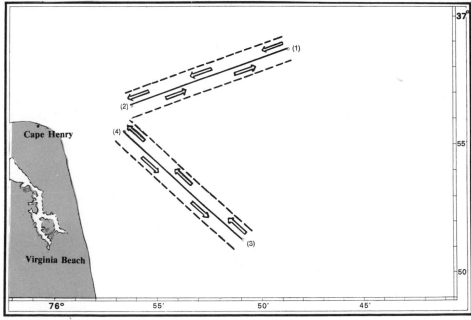

FIG. W13.   In approaches to Chesapeake Bay.

Part II—Southern approach

A separation line connects the following geographical positions:

    (3)   36°51'.3N.,   75°50'.9W.

    (4)   36°55'.5N.,   75°56'.6W.

A traffic lane, half a mile wide, is established on each side of the separation line.

The main traffic directions are:

    132° and

    312°.

Off San Francisco

(Reference chart: British Admiralty 229)

Description of the Traffic Separation Scheme

The traffic separation scheme off San Francisco consists of three parts.

Part I—Northern approach

(a) A separation zone bounded by a line connecting the following geographical positions:

    (1)   37°48'.6N.,   122°47'.5W.

    (2)   37°57'.1N.,   123°03'.5W.

    (3)   37°55'.7N.,   123°04'.6W.

    (4)   37°47'.8N.,   122°48'.2W.

(b) A traffic lane for north-westbound traffic is established between the separation zone and a line connecting the following geographical positions:

    (5)   37°49'.4N.,   122°46'.6W.

    (6)   37°58'.5N.,   123°02'.3W.

(c) A traffic lane for south-eastbound traffic is established between the separation zone and a line connecting the following geographical positions:

    (7)   37°54'.3N.,   123°05'.7W.

    (8)   37°46'.8N.,   122°48'.7W.

Part II—Southern approach

(a) A separation zone bounded by a line connecting the following geographical positions:

    (9)   37°39'.1N.,   122°40'.3W.

    (10)   37°27'.0N.,   122°36'.9W.

    (11)   37°27'.0N.,   122°34'.8W.

    (12)   37°39'.3N.,   122°39'.1W.

(b) A traffic lane for northbound traffic is established between the separation zone and a line connecting the following geographical positions:

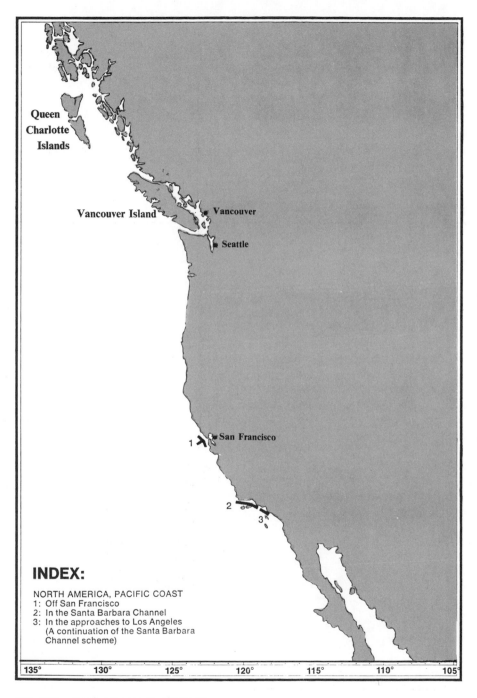

FIG. W14.   North America, Pacific Coast

(13)	37°27'.0N.,	122°32'.6W.
(14)	37°39'.7N.,	122°37'.9W.

(c) A traffic lane for southbound traffic is established between the separation zone and a line connecting the following geographical positions:

(15)	37°39'.0N.,	122°41'.6W.
(16)	37°27'.0N.,	122°39'.0W.

Part III—Main approach

(a) A separation zone bounded by a line connecting the following geographical positions:

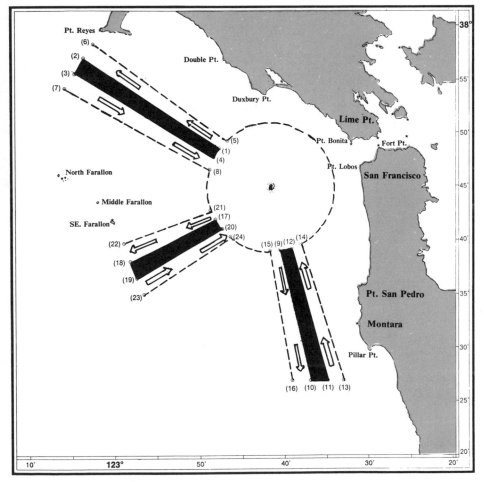

FIG. W15. Off San Francisco.

(17)	37°41'.9N.,	122°48'.0W.
(18)	37°38'.1N.,	122°58'.1W.
(19)	37°36'.5N.,	122°57'.3W.
(20)	37°41'.1N.,	122°47'.2W.

(b) A traffic lane for south-westbound traffic is established between the separation zone and a line connecting the following geographical positions:

(21)	37°42'.8N.,	122°48'.5W.
(22)	37°39'.6N.,	122°58'.8W.

(c) A traffic lane for north-eastbound traffic is established between the separation zone and a line connecting the following geographical positions:

(23)	37°35'.0N.,	122°56'.5W.
(24)	37°40'.4N.,	122°46'.3W.

Note:

Circular traffic separation zone

A circular traffic separation zone of radius half a mile is centred upon geographical position 37°45'.0N., 122°41'.5W.

Precautionary area

A precautionary area of radius six miles is centered upon geographical position 37°45'.0N., 122°41'.5W.

In the Santa Barbara Channel

(Reference charts: British Admiralty 899 and United States National Ocean Survey C & GS 5101 and 5202)

Description of the Traffic Separation Scheme

A separation zone, two miles wide, is centred upon the following geographical positions:

(1)	34°20'.1N.,	120°30'.4W.
(2)	34°04'.6N.,	119°19'.6W.
(3)	33°44'.1N.,	118°36'.3W.

A traffic lane, one mile wide, is established on each side of the separation zone.

The main traffic directions are:

105°—285° and

120°—300°.

Note:

Port Hueneme Fairway

The fairway at Port Hueneme is extended to meet the eastern edge of the northbound lane.

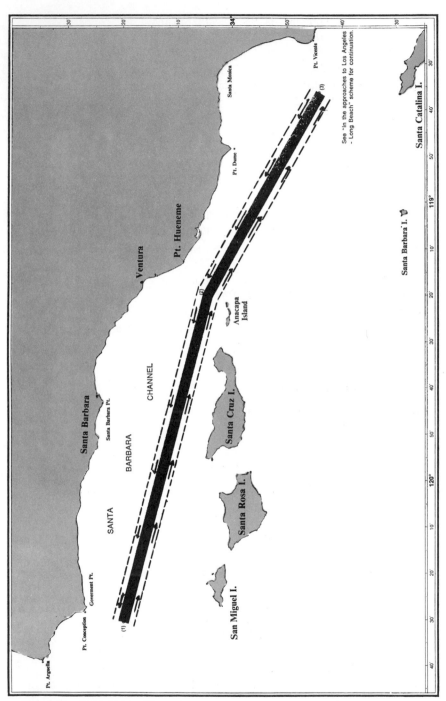

FIG. W16.   Santa Barbara Channel.

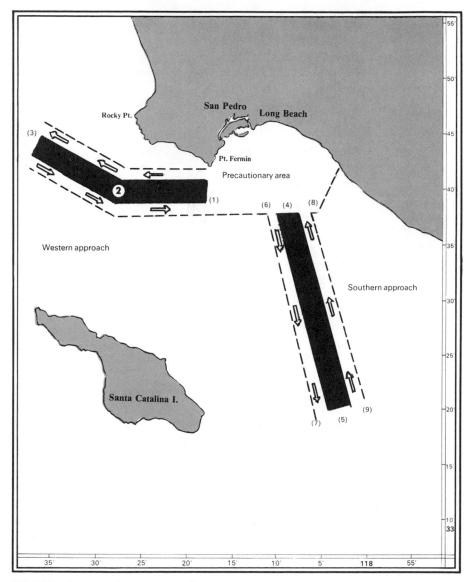

FIG. W17. In approaches to Los Angeles—Long Beach.

In the Approaches to Los Angeles—Long Beach

(A continuation of the Santa Barbara Channel scheme) (new scheme in southern approach)

(Reference charts: United States National Ocean Survey C & GS 5101, 5142, 5147, and 5148)

Description of the Traffic Separation Scheme

Part I:
Western approach
(a) A separation zone, two miles wide, is centred upon the following geographical positions:

(1)	33°39'.7N.,	118°17'.6W.
(2)	33°39'.7N.,	118°27'.3W.
(3)	33°44'.1N.,	118°36'.3W.

(b) A traffic lane, one mile wide, is established on each side of the separation zone.
(c) The main traffic directions are:

090°–270° and
120°–300°

Part II:
Southern approach
(a) A separation zone, two miles wide, is centred upon the following geographical positions:

(4)	33°37'.7N.,	118°08'.9W.
(5)	33°19'.7N.,	118°03'.4W.

(b) A traffic lane for southbound traffic is established between the separation zone and a line connecting the following geographical positions:

(6)	33°37'.7N.,	118°11'.3W.
(7)	33°19'.1N.,	118°06'.3W.

(c) A traffic lane for northbound traffic is established between the separation zone and a line connecting the following geographical positions:

(8)	33°37'.7N.,	118°06'.5W.
(9)	33°20'.3N.,	118°00'.5W.

(d) The main traffic directions are:

167° and 345°.

Precautionary area
The Los Angeles—Long Beach precautionary area consists of the water area enclosed by a line connecting Point Fermin Light at 33°42'.3N., 118° 17'.6W. to 33°37'.7N., 118°17'.6W., thence to 33°37'.7N., 118°05'.4W., thence to the shoreline at 33°41'.7N., 118°02'.8W.

IMCO Recommendations on Navigational Watchkeeping[1]

Basic Principles to Be Observed in Keeping a Navigational Watch

Introduction

1. The master of every ship is bound to ensure that the watchkeeping arrangements are adequate for maintaining a safe navigational watch. Under his general direction, the officers of the watch are responsible for navigating the ship safely during their periods of duty when they will be particularly concerned to avoid collision and stranding.

2. This Section includes the basic principles which shall at least be taken into account by all ships.

Watch Arrangements

3. The composition of the watch, including the requirement for look-out(s), shall at all times be adequate and appropriate to the prevailing circumstances and conditions.

4. When deciding the composition of the watch on the bridge the following points are among those to be taken into account:

(a) at no time shall the bridge be left unattended;

(b) the weather conditions, visibility and whether there is daylight or darkness;

(c) the proximity of navigational hazards which may make it necessary for the officer in charge to carry out additional navigational duties;

(d) the use and operational condition of navigational aids such as radar

---

[1] *IMCO Resolution A285(viii)*

or electronic position-indicating devices and any other equipment affecting the safe navigation of the ship;

(e) whether the ship is fitted with automatic steering;

(f) any additional demands on the navigational watch that may arise as a result of special operational circumstances.

Fitness for Duty

5. The watch system shall be such that the efficiency of the watch-keeping members of the crew is not impaired by fatigue. Accordingly, the duties shall be so organized that the first watch at the commencement of a voyage and the subsequent relieving watches are sufficiently rested and otherwise fit when going on duty.

Navigation

6. The intended voyage shall be planned in advance taking into consideration all pertinent information and any course laid down shall be checked.

7. On taking over the watch the ship's estimated or true position, intended track, course and speed shall be confirmed; any navigational hazard expected to be encountered during the watch shall be noted.

8. During the watch the course steered, position and speed shall be checked at sufficiently frequent intervals using any available navigational aids necessary to ensure that the ship follows the planned course.

9. The safety and navigational equipment with which the ship is provided and the manner of its operation shall be clearly understood; in addition its operational condition shall be fully taken into account.

10. Whoever is in charge of a navigational watch shall not be assigned or undertake any duties which would interfere with the safe navigation of the ship.

Look-out

11. Every ship shall at all times maintain a proper look-out by sight and hearing as well as by all available means appropriate in the prevailing circumstances and conditions so as to make a full appraisal of the situation and of the risk of collision, stranding and other hazards to navigation. Additionally, the duties of the look-out shall include the detection of ships or aircraft in distress, shipwrecked persons, wrecks and debris. In applying these principles the following shall be observed:

(a) whoever is keeping a look-out must be able to give full attention to the task and no duties shall be assigned or undertaken which would interfere with the keeping of a proper look-out;

(b) the duties of the person on look-out and helmsman are separate and the helmsman should not be considered the person on look-out while steering; except in small vessels where an unobstructed all round view is provided at the steering position and there is no impairment of night vision or other impediment to the keeping of a proper look-out;

(c) there may be circumstances in which the officer of the watch can safely be the sole look-out in daylight. However, this practice shall only be followed after the situation has been carefully assessed on each occasion and it has been established without doubt that it is safe to do so. Full account shall be taken of all relevant factors including but not limited to the state of weather, conditions of visibility, traffic density, proximity of navigational hazards and if navigating in or near a traffic separation scheme. 'Assistance must be summoned to the bridge when any change in the situation necessitates this and such assistance must be immediately available.'

Navigation with Pilot Embarked

12. Despite the duties and obligations of a pilot, his presence on board does not relieve the master or officer in charge of the watch from their duties and obligations for the safety of the ship. The master and the pilot shall exchange information regarding navigation procedures, local conditions and the ship's characteristics.

Protection of the Marine Environment

13. The master and officer in charge of the watch shall be aware of the serious effects of operational or accidental pollution of the marine environment and shall take all possible precautions to prevent such pollution particularly within the existing framework of existing international regulations.

SECTION II

Operational guidance for officers in charge of a navigational watch

Introduction

1. This Section contains operational guidance of general application for officers in charge of a navigational watch, which masters are expected to supplement as appropriate. It is essential that officers of the watch appreciate that the efficient performance of their duties is necessary in the interest of safety of life and property at sea and the avoidance of pollution of the marine environment.

General

2. The officer of the watch is the master's representative and his primary responsibility at all times is the safe navigation of the vessel. He must at all times comply with the applicable regulations for preventing collisions at sea (see also paragraphs 23 and 24).

3. The officer of the watch should keep his watch on the bridge which he should in no circumstances leave until properly relieved. It is of especial importance that at all times the officer of the watch ensures that an efficient look-out is maintained. In a vessel with a separate chart room the officer of the watch may visit this, when essential, for a short period for the necessary performance of his navigational duties, but he should previously satisfy himself that it is safe to do so and ensure that an efficient look-out is maintained.

4. There may be circumstances in which the officer of the watch can safely be the sole look-out in daylight. However, this practice shall only be followed after the situation has been carefully assessed on each occasion and it has been established without doubt that it is safe to do so. Full account shall be taken of all relevant factors including but not limited to the state of weather, conditions of visibility, traffic density, proximity of navigational hazards and if navigating in or near a traffic separation scheme.

When the officer of the watch is acting as the sole look-out he must not hesitate to summon assistance to the bridge, and when for any reason he is unable to give his undivided attention to the look-out such assistance must be immediately available.

5. The officer of the watch should bear in mind that the engines are at his disposal and he should not hesitate to use them in case of need. However, timely notice of intended variations of engine speed should be given when possible. He should also keep prominently in mind the manoeuvring capabilities of his ship including its stopping distance.

6. The officer of the watch should also bear in mind that the sound signalling apparatus is at his disposal and he should not hesitate to use it in accordance with the applicable regulations for preventing collisions at sea.

7. The officer of the watch continues to be responsible for the safe navigation of the vessel despite the presence of the master on the bridge until the master informs him specifically that he has assumed responsibility and this is mutually understood.

Taking Over the Watch

8. The officer of the watch should not hand over the watch to the relieving officer if he has any reason to believe that the latter is apparently

under any disability which would preclude him from carrying out his duties effectively. If in doubt, the officer of the watch should inform the master accordingly. The relieving officer of the watch should ensure that members of his watch are apparently fully capable of performing their duties and in particular the adjustment to night vision.

9. The relieving officer should not take over the watch until his vision is fully adjusted to the light conditions and he has personally satisfied himself regarding:

(a) standing orders and other special instructions of the master relating to the navigation of the vessel;

(b) the position, course, speed and draught of the vessel;

(c) prevailing and predicted tides, currents, weather, visibility and the effect of these factors upon course and speed;

(d) the navigational situation including but not limited to the following:

(i) the operational condition of all navigational and safety equipment being used or likely to be used during the watch;

(ii) errors of gyro and magnetic compasses;

(iii) the presence and movement of vessels in sight or known to be in the vicinity;

(iv) conditions and hazards likely to be encountered during his watch;

(v) the possible effects of heel, trim, water density and squat on underkeel clearance.

10. If at the time the officer of the watch is to be relieved a manoeuvre or other action to avoid any hazard is taking place, the relief of the officer should be deferred until such action is completed.

Periodic Check of Navigational Equipment

11. The officer of the watch should make regular checks to ensure that:

(a) the helmsman or the automatic pilot is steering the correct course;

(b) the standard compass error is established at least once a watch and when possible, after any major alteration of course. The standard and the gyro compasses should be frequently compared; repeaters should be synchronised with their master compass;

(c) the automatic pilot is tested in the manual position at least once a watch;

(d) the navigation and signal lights and other navigational equipment are functioning properly.

Automatic Pilot

12. Officers of the watch should bear in mind the need to station the helmsman and to put the steering into manual control in good time to allow any potentially hazardous situation to be dealt with in a safe man-

ner. With a vessel under automatic steering it is highly dangerous to allow a situation to develop to the point where the officer of the watch is without assistance and has to break the continuity of the look-out in order to take emergency action. The change-over from automatic to manual steering and vice versa should be made by, or under the supervision of, a responsible officer.

Electronic Navigational Aids

13. The officer of the watch should be thoroughly familiar with the use of electronic navigational aids carried, including their capabilities and limitations.

Echo-sounder

14. The echo-sounder is a valuable navigational aid and should be used whenever appropriate.

Navigational Records

15. A proper record of the movements and activities of the vessel should be kept during the watch.

Radar

16. The officer of the watch should use the radar when appropriate and whenever restricted visibility is encountered or expected and at all times in congested waters having due regard to its limitations.

17. Whenever radar is in use, the officer of the watch should select an appropriate range scale, observe the display carefully and plot effectively.

18. The officer of the watch should ensure that range scales employed are changed at sufficiently frequent intervals so that echoes are detected as early as possible and that small or poor echoes do not escape detection.

19. The officer of the watch should ensure that plotting or systematic analysis is commenced in ample time, remembering that sufficient time can be made available by reducing speed if necessary.

20. In clear weather, whenever possible, the officer of the watch should carry out radar practice.

Navigation in Coastal Waters

21. The largest scale chart on board, suitable for the area and corrected with the latest available information, should be used. Fixes should be taken at frequent intervals; whenever circumstances allow, fixing should be carried out by more than one method.

22. The officer of the watch should positively identify all relevant navigation marks.

Clear Weather

23. The officer of the watch should take frequent and accurate compass bearings of approaching vessels as a means of early detection of risk of collision; such risk may sometimes exist even when an appreciable bearing change is evident, particularly when approaching a very large vessel or a tow or when approaching a vessel at close range. He should also take early and positive action in compliance with the applicable regulations for preventing collisions at sea and subsequently check that such action is having the desired effect.

Restricted Visibility

24. When restricted visibility is encountered or suspected, the first responsibility of the officer of the watch is to comply with the relevant rules of the applicable regulations for preventing collisions at sea, with particular regard to the sounding of fog signals, proceeding at a moderate speed and he shall have the engines ready for immediate manoeuvres. In addition, he should:

(a) inform the master (see paragraph 25);

(b) post look-out(s) and helmsman and, in congested waters, revert to hand steering immediately;

(c) exhibit navigation lights;

(d) operate and use the radar.

It is important that the officer of the watch should have the manoeuvring capabilities including the 'stopping distance' of his own vessel prominently in mind.

Calling the Master

25. The officer of the watch should notify the master immediately under the following circumstances:

(a) if restricted visibility is encountered or suspected;

(b) if the traffic conditions or the movements of other vessels are causing concern;

(c) if difficulty is experienced in maintaining course;

(d) on failure to sight land, a navigation mark or to obtain soundings by the expected time;

(e) if land or a navigation mark is sighted or a change in soundings occurs unexpectedly;

(f) on the breakdown of the engines, steering gear or any essential navigational equipment;

(g) in heavy weather if in any doubt about the possibility of weather damage;

(h) in any other emergency or situation in which he is in any doubt.

Despite the requirement to notify the master immediately in the foregoing circumstances, the officer of the watch should in addition not hesitate to take immediate action for the safety of the ship, where circumstances so require.

Navigation With Pilot Embarked

26. Despite the duties and obligations of a pilot, his presence on board does not relieve the officer of the watch from his duties and obligations for the safety of the ship. He should co-operate closely with the pilot and maintain an accurate check on the vessel's positions and movements. If he is in any doubt as to the pilot's actions or intentions, he should seek clarification from the pilot and if doubt still exists he should notify the master immediately and take whatever action is necessary before the master arrives.

The Watchkeeping Personnel

27. The officer of the watch should give the watchkeeping personnel all appropriate instructions and information which will ensure the keeping of a safe watch including an appropriate look-out.

Ship at Anchor

28. If the master considers it necessary a continuous navigational watch should be maintained. In all circumstances, however, the officer of the watch should:

(a) determine and plot the ship's position on the appropriate chart as soon as practicable and at sufficiently frequent intervals check when circumstances permit, by taking bearings of fixed navigational marks or readily identifiable shore objects, whether the ship is remaining securely at anchor;

(b) ensure that an efficient look-out is maintained;

(c) ensure that inspection rounds of the vessel are made periodically;

(d) observe meteorological and tidal conditions and the state of the sea;

(e) notify the master and undertake all necessary measures if the vessel drags the anchor;

(f) ensure that the state of readiness of the main engines and other machinery is in accordance with the master's instructions;

(g) if visibility deteriorates notify the master and comply with the applicable regulations for preventing collisions at sea;

(h) ensure that the vessel exhibit
that appropriate sound signals are

(i) take measures to protect th
ship and comply with the applicable

APPENDIX Y

Conversion Table for Meters, Feet, and Fathoms

Meters	Feet	Fathoms	Meters	Feet	Fathoms	Feet	Meters	Feet	Meters	Fathoms	Meters	Fathoms	Meters
1	3.28	0.55	61	200.13	33.36	1	0.30	61	18.59	1	1.83	61	111.56
2	6.56	1.09	62	203.41	33.90	2	0.61	62	18.90	2	3.66	62	113.39
3	9.84	1.64	63	206.69	34.45	3	0.91	63	19.20	3	5.49	63	115.21
4	13.12	2.19	64	209.97	35.00	4	1.22	64	19.51	4	7.32	64	117.04
5	16.40	2.73	65	213.25	35.54	5	1.52	65	19.81	5	9.14	65	118.87
6	19.68	3.28	66	216.54	36.09	6	1.83	66	20.12	6	10.97	66	120.70
7	22.97	3.83	67	219.82	36.64	7	2.13	67	20.42	7	12.80	67	122.53
8	26.25	4.37	68	223.10	37.18	8	2.44	68	20.73	8	14.63	68	124.36
9	29.53	4.92	69	226.38	37.73	9	2.74	69	21.03	9	16.46	69	126.19
10	32.81	5.47	70	229.66	38.28	10	3.05	70	21.34	10	18.29	70	128.02
11	36.09	6.01	71	232.94	38.82	11	3.35	71	21.64	11	20.12	71	129.85
12	39.37	6.56	72	236.22	39.37	12	3.66	72	21.95	12	21.95	72	131.67
13	42.65	7.11	73	239.50	39.92	13	3.96	73	22.25	13	23.77	73	133.50
14	45.93	7.66	74	242.78	40.46	14	4.27	74	22.56	14	25.60	74	135.33
15	49.21	8.20	75	246.06	41.01	15	4.57	75	22.86	15	27.43	75	137.16
16	52.49	8.75	76	249.34	41.56	16	4.88	76	23.16	16	29.26	76	138.99
17	55.77	9.30	77	252.62	42.10	17	5.18	77	23.47	17	31.09	77	140.82
18	59.06	9.84	78	255.90	42.65	18	5.49	78	23.77	18	32.92	78	142.65
19	62.34	10.39	79	259.19	43.20	19	5.79	79	24.08	19	34.75	79	144.48
20	65.62	10.94	80	262.47	43.74	20	6.10	80	24.38	20	36.58	80	146.30
21	68.90	11.48	81	265.75	44.29	21	6.40	81	24.69	21	38.40	81	148.13
22	72.18	12.03	82	269.03	44.84	22	6.71	82	24.99	22	40.23	82	149.96
23	75.46	12.58	83	272.31	45.38	23	7.01	83	25.30	23	42.06	83	151.79
24	78.74	13.12	84	275.59	45.93	24	7.32	84	25.60	24	43.89	84	153.62
25	82.02	13.67	85	278.87	46.48	25	7.62	85	25.91	25	45.72	85	155.45
26	85.30	14.22	86	282.15	47.03	26	7.92	86	26.21	26	47.55	86	157.28
27	88.58	14.76	87	285.43	47.57	27	8.23	87	26.52	27	49.38	87	159.11
28	91.86	15.31	88	288.71	48.12	28	8.53	88	26.82	28	51.21	88	160.93
29	95.14	15.86	89	291.99	48.67	29	8.84	89	27.13	29	53.04	89	162.76
30	98.42	16.40	90	295.28	49.21	30	9.14	90	27.43	30	54.86	90	164.59
31	101.71	16.95	91	298.56	49.76	31	9.45	91	27.74	31	56.69	91	166.42
32	104.99	17.50	92	301.84	50.31	32	9.75	92	28.04	32	58.52	92	168.25
33	108.27	18.04	93	305.12	50.85	33	10.06	93	28.35	33	60.35	93	170.08
34	111.55	18.59	94	308.40	51.40	34	10.36	94	28.65	34	62.18	94	171.91
35	114.83	19.14	95	311.68	51.95	35	10.67	95	28.96	35	64.01	95	173.74
36	118.11	19.68	96	314.96	52.49	36	10.97	96	29.26	36	65.84	96	175.57
37	121.39	20.23	97	318.24	53.04	37	11.28	97	29.57	37	67.67	97	177.39
38	124.67	20.78	98	321.52	53.59	38	11.58	98	29.87	38	69.49	98	179.22
39	127.95	21.33	99	324.80	54.13	39	11.89	99	30.18	39	71.32	99	181.05
40	131.23	21.87	100	328.08	54.68	40	12.19	100	30.48	40	73.15	100	182.88
41	134.51	22.42	101	331.36	55.23	41	12.50	101	30.78	41	74.98	101	184.71
42	137.80	22.97	102	334.64	55.77	42	12.80	102	31.09	42	76.81	102	186.54
43	141.08	23.51	103	337.93	56.32	43	13.11	103	31.39	43	78.64	103	188.37
44	144.36	24.06	104	341.21	56.87	44	13.41	104	31.70	44	80.47	104	190.20
45	147.64	24.61	105	344.49	57.41	45	13.72	105	32.00	45	82.30	105	192.02
46	150.92	25.15	106	347.77	57.96	46	14.02	106	32.31	46	84.12	106	193.85
47	154.20	25.70	107	351.05	58.51	47	14.33	107	32.61	47	85.95	107	195.68
48	157.48	26.25	108	354.33	59.06	48	14.63	108	32.92	48	87.78	108	197.51
49	160.76	26.79	109	357.61	59.60	49	14.94	109	33.22	49	89.61	109	199.34
50	164.04	27.34	110	360.89	60.15	50	15.24	110	33.53	50	91.44	110	201.17
51	167.32	27.89	111	364.17	60.70	51	15.54	111	33.83	51	93.27	111	203.00
52	170.60	28.43	112	367.45	61.24	52	15.85	112	34.14	52	95.10	112	204.83
53	173.88	28.98	113	370.73	61.79	53	16.15	113	34.44	53	96.93	113	206.65
54	177.16	29.53	114	374.02	62.34	54	16.46	114	34.75	54	98.76	114	208.48
55	180.45	30.07	115	377.30	62.88	55	16.76	115	35.05	55	100.58	115	210.31
56	183.73	30.62	116	380.58	63.43	56	17.07	116	35.36	56	102.41	116	212.14
57	187.01	31.17	117	383.86	63.98	57	17.37	117	35.66	57	104.24	117	213.97
58	190.29	31.71	118	387.14	64.52	58	17.68	118	35.97	58	106.07	118	215.80
59	193.57	32.26	119	390.42	65.07	59	17.98	119	36.27	59	107.90	119	217.63
60	196.85	32.81	120	393.70	65.62	60	18.29	120	36.58	60	109.73	120	219.46

Index of Cases

Index

Failure of steering gear as cause of
collision, 440
Failure to keep lookout violation of
Rule 5 and Art. 29, 203, 411
Failure to maintain anchor watch,
anchored vessel at fault for, 396
Failure to veer chain, anchored vessel at
fault for, 397
First rule of good seamanship, 409
Fishing vessels
additional signals for vessels in close
proximity, 14, 117
day signals for, 153, 172
lights for, 115, 148
Flare-up light, 150
as danger signal, 274
Fog,
delay through stopping engines
necessary in, 365
excessive speed in, 358
LaBoyteaux's rules in, 363
law in, 344–70
Lushington's rule in, 366
moderate speed in, 223, 356
precautions when approaching, 360
requirement to slow to bare
steerageway on hearing fog signal
ahead, Int. waters, 223, 224, 362
requirement to stop engines on hearing
fog signal ahead, inland waters, 222,
337
rules in, 222–27, 344
rules in, are for safety and should be
obeyed, 365
safe speed, 203, 210, 222
special necessity of lookout in, 421
speed in, 222
sufmary of law in, 368
three short blasts when reversing if
another vessel in sight, 365
vessel colliding with vessel at anchor is
guilty of excessive speed, 359
vessel must navigate with caution in,
364
vessel must navigate with caution in, 364
Fog bank, precautions when near, 360
Fog signals, 183, 184
anchored vessels, 183, 184, 353
binding on naval vessels, 347
danger signal in inland waters, 179, 202,
352
density requiring, 346
differences in, 349–56, 369
differences in, unjustifiable, 355
four or more short blasts, inland waters,
202, 352
prescribed intervals are maximum
intervals, 199, 348
prolonged blast defined, 175
sailing vessel underway, 183, 200
scope of prolonged and two short
blasts, 183, 201, 350
small vessels, etc., 184
steam or other power-driven vessel
underway, high seas, 183, 348

steam or other power-driven vessel
underway, inland waters, 183, 348
steam or other power-driven vessel
underway without way,
International Rules, 183, 200, 349
time intervals between, 199, 348
two prolonged blasts cannot be used in
inland waters, 200, 350
vessel aground in fog, 184, 200, 355
vessel at anchor, 183, 184, 200, 353
vessel broken down, International
Rules, 183, 350, 351
vessel fishing, 183, 201
vessel towing or towed, 183, 201
vessel underway without way,
International Rules, 183, 200, 349
vessel working on cable, International
Rules, 182, 351
vessels in nest, each must sound, 354
when required, 200, 346
Four possibilities of liability in collision,
232, 430
Function of running and riding lights, 244

General characteristics of side lights, 40,
44, 249
General Prudential Rule, 25, 371
General rule for boundary lines of inland
waters, 38, 452
Give-way vessel, action by, 217, 220
Good seamanship
defined in Art. 29 and Rule 2(a), 25, 213,
389, 409
discussion, 389–409
first rule of, 409
in extremis, example, 391
rule of, requires three blasts when
backing less than full speed, 408
special right of way under, 406
summary, 409, 410
Governing rule
crossing situation, 216
meeting situation, 215
overtaking situation, 214
Great Lakes Rules, text of, 564–74
Rules 1, 2, 564
Rules 3, 565
Rules 4–7, 566
Rules 8, 9, 567
Rules 10–14, 568, 569
Rules 15–25, 569–71
Rules 26–30, 572
authority for Pilot Rules, 573
penalty and regulations, 573

Half-mile rule, inland waters, 197, 281
Half-mile rule partly valid, inland waters,
281
Head-and-head situation
discussion, 215, 286–302
summary, 302
Head-on collisions
illustrative cases, 299
usual cause of, 299
Head-on situation. See meeting situation

Helm signals, one and two blasts under
International Rules, 175, 197, 267
Helmsman, error of, vessel liable for, 527,
572
High seas, boundary lines of, 36, 450–65
History of rules, 238

IMCO, 40
IMCO Adopted Traffic Separation
Schemes, 684
IMCO Recommendations on Navigational
Watchkeeping, 715
Immaterial absence of lookout not a
fault, 416
Immediate danger is special circumstance,
372
Importance of lookouts, 209, 391, 428
Important significance of exchanging
signals in overtaking situation, 308
Improper anchor lights on barge, 258
Improper lights, anchored vessel at fault
for, 244, 395
Improper lights, vessel at fault for
aground, 260
anchored, 244, 256, 395
naval vessels, 248
side lights, 250
towing, 253, 254, 255
underway, 246, 249–53
Improper position, anchored vessel at
fault for, 256, 393
Improper steering, vessel at fault for, 407
In extremis, 377–81
In personam, action in, 234, 242
In rem, action in, 234, 242
Inevitable accident
cases rare, 431
defense of, 432
defined, 433
discussion, 430–45
due to disability of crew, 445
due to failure of steering gear, 448
due to mechanical failure, 440
due to uncharted rock, 444
due to vis major, 433
mechanical failure not excuse for if due
to negligence, 443
miscellaneous cases, 444
plea barred if action not taken
reasonably, 439
reasons for studying, 431
summary, **446**
Inland Rules, 513–27
Arts. 1, 2, 516
Arts. 3–6, 517, 518
Arts. 7–9, 518–20
Arts. 10–11, 520
Arts. 12–15, 521
Arts. 16–17, 522, 523
Art. 18, 523
Arts. 19–24, 525
Arts. 25–28, 526
Arts. 31–32, 527
authority for Pilot Rules, 514
Enacting clause, 513

Inland Rules, special rules duly made by
local authority, 240
Inland waters, boundary lines of, 450–65
International Conference of 1972, 1–16
International Regulations for Preventing
Collisions at Sea, 1972, 1, 38
International Rules, application of, 17, 238
International Rules successful in restricted
waters, 241
International Rules, summary of changes,
1–16
International Rules, text of, 478–82
Annexes I–IV, 502–11
Enacting Clause, 483
Arts. I–IX, 478–82
Rule 1, 483
Rules 2, 3, 484
Rules 4–6, 485
Rule 7, 486
Rules 8, 9, 487
Rule 10, 488
Rules 11–13, 489
Rules 14–17, 490
Rules 18, 19, 491
Rules 20, 21, 492
Rules 22, 23, 493
Rule 24, 494
Rules 25, 26, 495
Rule 27, 496
Rule 28, 497
Rules 29–32, 498
Rules 33, 34, 499
Rule 35, 500
Rules 36, 37, 501
Rule 38, 502

Jurisdiction in collision cases, 230

Keynote is caution in meeting situation,
294
"King can do no wrong" theory, 234, 347
Knight's *Seamanship*
length of anchor chain required, 435

LaBoyteaux's rules in fog, 363
Law in fog, discussion, 344–70
Lawful lights
discussion, 244–63
summary, 263
Legal effect of assent to passing,
overtaking situation, inland waters,
315–18
Legal characteristics of crossing situation,
327–31, 340
Legal characteristics of meeting situation,
291
Legal characteristics of overtaking
situation, 303
Legal personality of vessel, 231
Legal theory of crossing rules, 327–31
Length of hawsers, seagoing barges, inland
waters, 558
Liability for collision under American
admiralty law, 231, 232, 430
Light-draft vessels passing floating plant,
rule for, 550